THE LAW OF TORTS

Examples and Explanations

THE LAW OF TORTS

Examples and Explanations

Joseph W. Glannon

Professor of Law
Suffolk University Law School

Little, Brown and Company
Boston   New York   Toronto   London

Library of Congress Catalog No. 94-73112

ISBN 0-316-31599-0

ICP

Published simultaneously in Canada
by Little, Brown and Company (Canada) Limited

Printed in the United States of America

I dedicate this book to my wife, Annie.

Contents

Preface to Students

This book is based on the common sense premise that students encountering complex legal issues for the first time will appreciate a book that provides clear, straightforward introductions to these issues, together with examples that illustrate how these principles apply in typical cases.

I have good reason to believe that the premise is valid. Eight years ago I wrote a book on civil procedure, entitled *Civil Procedure: Examples and Explanations*, which uses the same approach. The book has been widely used in law schools across the country. Not only do many faculty members assign or recommend it, but many students have found their way to the book on their own or on the recommendation of other students who have found the approach helpful. Naturally, I have been moved to try my hand at a sequel.

Each chapter of the book includes a brief introduction to the topic, followed by a set of examples that apply the concepts to particular fact situations. After the examples, I have included my analysis of each example. Unlike the typical questions found in the casebooks, which are often either too hard to answer or downright unanswerable, the examples here tend to start with the basics and move on to more sophisticated variations. If you study the readings for your Torts class and the introductions in this book, you should be able to respond effectively to most of the examples. Trying your hand at them and comparing your analysis to mine should help to deepen your understanding of the issues and your ability to think critically about legal issues in general. It may also help to convince you that you are *capable* of learning the law, a type of feedback that law school seldom seems to provide.

You will also want to use the book to review the course toward the end of the year. Most casebooks contain representative cases and provocative questions and notes, but they do not explain the state of the law, or provide much context for the issues raised. Reading these chapters and reviewing the examples should help you to test your understanding of the topics covered and fill in the gaps left by your casebook.

Like every author, I hope that this book will go through many editions. If you have comments or suggestions for improvement, drop me a note at Suffolk University Law School, 41 Temple Street, Boston, MA 02114.

Acknowledgments

I wish to thank Suffolk University Law School, John E. Fenton, Dean of the Law School, and Paul R. Sugarman, the former dean of the Law School, for the support they provided while this book was being written. I also appreciate the assistance of Professors Alvan Brody, Charles Burnim, Linda Fentiman, Stephen Hicks, Stephen McJohn, and Linda Simard, all of Suffolk University Law School, who critiqued various chapters. Thanks, too, to Professor Sumner LaCroix of the University of Hawaii at Manoa, Steven P. Perlmutter of the Massachusetts bar, and Professor Richard Wright of Chicago-Kent College of Law, for reading parts of the manuscript. Also, to the legion of Suffolk University Law School students who served as my research assistants in developing the materials.

I especially want to thank Suffolk Professors Steven Eisenstat and Michael Rustad, who read parts of the manuscript and gave me invaluable moral support as well.

Little, Brown has, as usual, provided excellent editorial support, not only in editing the manuscript, but also in making suggestions and soliciting responses from faculty reviewers over the six years since I began this book. I extend my thanks to Carol McGeehan, Carolyn O'Sullivan, and Betsy Kenny for their support in developing the book, and to Tony Perriello for carefully and skillfully editing the manuscript.

Thanks, too, to my wife Annie, for her patience and support throughout.

Finally, thanks to the American Law Institute for permitting me to quote from the following works:

American Law Institute, Restatement (First) of Torts. Copyright © 1934 by the American Law Institute. Reprinted with permission.

American Law Institute, Restatement (Second) of Torts. Copyright © 1979 by the American Law Institute. Reprinted with permission.

American Law Institute, Restatement (Second) of Agency. Copyright © 1958 by the American Law Institute. Reprinted with permission.

Special Notice

For several frequently cited treatises I have used shortened forms after the initial citation to the work. These are as follows: Harper, James & Gray, The Law of Torts (2d ed. 1986), cited as Harper, James & Gray; Prosser and Keeton, The Law of Torts (5th ed. 1984), cited as Prosser & Keeton; Minzer, Nates, eds., Damages in Tort Actions (1994), cited as Minzer, Nates; Schwartz, Comparative Negligence (2d ed. 1986), cited as Schwartz; and Speiser, Recovery for Wrongful Death and Injury (3d ed. 1992), cited as Speiser.

THE LAW OF TORTS

Examples and Explanations

PART ONE

Intentional Torts

1

Fundamental Protections: The Tort of Battery

Introduction

The primitive world must have been a fairly scary place. Our ancestors had to cope not only with the awesome forces of nature, impossible to predict or control, but also with another unpredictable danger — other human beings. Doubtless, one of the primary reasons they decided to become "civilized" was to ensure physical security from each other.

Medieval England, from which our tort law evolved, sought to deter physical aggression through a criminal remedy, the "appeal of felony" for physical assaults and other invasions of personal interests. Harper, James & Gray, The Law of Torts §3.1 (2d ed. 1986). If the defendant was found guilty, she would be fined, that is, she would have to pay a sum of money or forfeit her goods to the crown. The appeal of felony helped to enforce the King's peace, but it did nothing to compensate the injured victim for her injury.

Over time, the English courts also developed civil tort remedies to compensate victims of physical aggression. This tort remedy differed according to the nature of the defendant's invasion. The tort of battery authorized damages for deliberate, unwanted touchings of the plaintiff's person. Assault would lie for placing the plaintiff in fear of an unwanted touching. False imprisonment was the remedy for unwarranted restraints on the plaintiff's freedom of movement. This chapter examines the action of battery, that most basic of tort remedies for invasion of the most basic of personal rights, the right to freedom from unwanted bodily contact.

It seems as though this ought to be a very short chapter. Even the law, with its tendency to overanalyze, can only complicate a seemingly simple matter so much. And battery seems like a simple matter. Jones hits Smith: She has invaded Smith's right to freedom from physical aggression and should be liable for any resulting injuries. All that is left to decide is how much Jones should pay.

Sometimes it is that simple, but often it is not. Jones may have bumped into Smith because Lopez pushed her, or she may have collided with Smith while jumping out of the way of an oncoming car. Perhaps she pushed Smith in order to prevent the car from hitting *her*, or while thrashing around in an epileptic seizure. Each of these cases involves an unauthorized touching of Smith, but Jones should not be required to compensate Smith for such blameless — or even helpful — invasions of Smith's physical autonomy.

Since the courts have refused to condemn all unwanted touchings, they have struggled to craft a definition of battery that limits recovery to those types of touchings the law seeks to prevent. Most courts define battery as the intentional infliction of a harmful or offensive contact with the person of the plaintiff. See Restatement (Second) of Torts §13. Under this definition the defendant must act, her act must be intentional (in the restricted sense peculiar to tort law), the act must cause a contact with the victim, and the contact must be either harmful or offensive to the victim. These requirements are discussed in detail below.

The Intent Requirement

As this definition indicates, battery protects against *intentional* invasions of the plaintiff's physical integrity. No contact is intentional if it is not the result of a voluntary act. If Lopez faints and falls on Jones, Lopez is not liable for battery, because she has not acted. It hardly seems fair to require her to pay damages to Jones for something she didn't do in any meaningful sense, that is, something that was not the result of her voluntary conduct. Similarly, if Smith pushes Lopez into Jones, Lopez has not acted, and would not be liable for battering Jones. See Restatement (Second) of Torts §2 (defining an act as an "external manifestation of the actor's will").

Even if the defendant has acted, however, in the sense of making a voluntary movement, that act may not be intentional as that term is used in the context of intentional torts. Suppose, for example, that Chu fails to look carefully in stepping off a bus, does not see Munoz coming along the street, and bumps into her. Chu's act of stepping off the bus is intentional in the sense that it was deliberate: She certainly intended to put her foot down and move off the bus, although she did not intend to bump into Munoz. To commit a battery, however, the defendant must not only intend to act; she must act *for the purpose of* inflicting a harmful or offensive contact on the plaintiff, or realize that such a contact is *substantially certain* to result.

> The word "intent" is used . . . to denote that the actor desires to cause consequences of his act, or that he believes that the consequences are substantially certain to result from it.

Restatement (Second) of Torts §8A. This definition lets Chu off the hook in the bus case, since her act was not intentional in the intentional tort sense. She did not act for the purpose of hitting Munoz, nor was she substantially certain that she would. The contact resulted instead from her failure to take proper precautions (such as looking where she was going) to avoid hitting Munoz. Chu may be liable for negligence, but she has not committed a battery.

Indeed, the purpose of the intent requirement is to confine intentional tort liability to cases in which the defendant acts with a higher level of culpability than mere carelessness: where she acts with a purpose, or with knowledge that the act will cause harmful or offensive contact to the victim. If Chu pushed Munoz to get her out of the way, she would meet this intent requirement, since she would be substantially certain that Munoz would find such a contact offensive. She would also meet the intent requirement if she pushed her to embarrass her in front of a friend — an offensive contact — or to cause her to fall in front of a car, an obviously harmful one.

The intent requirement in the Restatement is disjunctive, that is, it is met *either* by a purpose to cause the tortious contact *or* substantial certainty that such a contact will result. Suppose, for example, that Smith heaves a stone at her enemy Jones, though she thinks Jones is probably beyond her range. She is not substantially certain that she will hit Jones, but she acts with the desire to do so. This satisfies the intent requirement; if the stone hits Jones, Smith has committed battery.

Under this definition, an actor can possess tortious intent even though she bears the victim no ill will whatsoever. If Chu sees Jones walking along the street below and deliberately throws a bucket of water on her from a second story window, it is no defense that she was simply emptying the scrub bucket and did not mean to offend Jones. In intentional tort terms, she intends those contacts that she is substantially certain will occur, as well as those she desires to see happen. Indeed, a battery can be committed with the best of motives. In *Clayton v. New Dreamland Roller Skating Rink, Inc.*, 82 A.2d 458 (1951), *cert. denied*, 100 A.2d 567 (N.J. 1953), for example, the defendant's employee attempted to set the plaintiff's broken arm, against her protests. While the employees were only trying to help, they knew (because the victim told them so) that she found the contact unwelcome, and consequently met the intent requirement for battery.

Transferred Intent

Although intentional tort law requires a very specific type of intent, that standard may be met if the actor intends to commit a battery on one person and actually inflicts one on somebody else. Suppose, for example, that Chu throws a rock at Smith, hoping to hit her, but her aim is bad and she hits Lopez instead. Chu would argue that she cannot be held liable to Lopez, since she had no intent to hit her — she was aiming at Smith.

Although Chu had no tortious intent toward Lopez in this example, she *did* have tortious intent toward Smith. In such cases, courts hold that the tortious intent to hit Smith *transfers* to Lopez. Restatement (Second) of Torts §16(2). Thus, where the actor tries to batter one person and actually causes a harmful or offensive contact to another, she will be liable to the actual victim.

Obviously, transferred intent is a legal fiction created to achieve a sensible result despite lack of intent toward the person actually contacted. The rationale for the doctrine is that the tortfeasor's act is just as *culpable* when her aim is bad as when it is good; it would be unconscionable if she were exonerated just because she hit the wrong person. Under transferred intent, she will be liable whether she hits her intended victim or someone else.

The transferred intent fiction also allows recovery where the actor attempts one intentional tort but causes another. If, for example, Chu tries to hit Smith with a hammer but misses, placing Smith in fear of a harmful contact but not actually causing one, her intent to commit a battery suffices to hold her liable for assault. Conversely, if she tries to frighten Lopez by shooting near her, but the bullet hits her instead, she will be liable for battery even though she intended to commit an assault instead.

Harmful or Offensive Contact

Not all intentional contacts are unwanted or injurious. It would make little sense to allow Jones to bring a battery suit against every subway passenger who jostled her during rush hour. This kind of contact is an accepted fact of city life. Similarly, if Smith taps Jones on the shoulder to tell her that she dropped a glove, it is reasonable for Smith to expect that this touching is acceptable to Jones, as it would be to most of us.

To distinguish between such common, socially accepted contacts and actionable batteries, courts require that the defendant intend to cause a harmful or offensive contact. *Harmful* suggests broken arms, black eyes, and the like, but a great deal less will do. Section 15 of the Restatement (Second) of Torts defines *bodily harm* as "any physical impairment of the condition of another's body, or physical pain or illness." Of course, if the harm is minor, the plaintiff will recover very little, or be limited to nominal damages, but the courts will still have vindicated her right to physical autonomy.[1]

---

1. While it is true that a plaintiff can sue for even a trivial battery, the majesty of the law is tarnished somewhat by practical realities. Most lawyers take tort cases on a contingent fee basis, under which they receive a percentage of the damage award. Where there is little prospect of substantial damages, the plaintiff will probably not find a lawyer willing to take the case, unless she is willing to pay substantial hourly fees for the service. Consequently, victims seldom recover for minor batteries, even if they are clearly actionable.

Even if the contact is not harmful, it is tortious if it is offensive. If Smith chucks Jones under the chin in a demeaning manner, or spits on her, she has caused an offensive contact. Allowing a battery suit for such offensive contacts not only deters such personal invasions, it also provides Jones with a civilized alternative to retaliation. Since offensive acts are particularly likely to provoke retaliation, it is appropriate to provide a battery remedy for such contacts instead.

Of course, people don't all react the same way to every contact. If Smith goes around slapping folks on the back at the office party, Jones may find it obnoxious, but Cimino may be flattered by the attention. If the definition of offensive contact depended on the subjective reaction of each plaintiff, Smith would not know whether her conduct was tortious until she saw the reaction to it. Smith should have some way of determining whether a contact is permissible *before* she acts. To allow such advance judgments, courts use an objective definition of offensive contact. The Second Restatement, for example, defines a contact as offensive if it "offends a reasonable sense of personal dignity." Id. at §19.

Under this test, a contact is offensive if a reasonable person in the circumstances of the victim would find the particular contact offensive. An actor is not liable under this definition for a contact that is considered socially acceptable (i.e., that would not offend a "reasonable sense of personal dignity"), even though the victim turns out to be hypersensitive and is truly offended. On the other hand, if she makes a contact that the reasonable person *would* find offensive, it is not a defense that she did not mean to give offense, or that she did not realize that the victim would be offended.

What the reasonable person would find offensive varies greatly with the circumstances. Often a prior course of conduct between the parties indicates that they accept contacts that would ordinarily be considered offensive. Suppose that Burgess and Munoz routinely engage in horseplay at work, including backslapping, arm locks, bear hugs and the like. A stranger would undoubtedly find such contacts offensive, but Burgess and Munoz expect these contacts from each other. Burgess would be justified, given their previous interactions, in inferring that Munoz will not find such contacts offensive, though they would offend the "reasonable sense of personal dignity" of a new employee.

The Difference Between Contacts and Consequences

It is crucial to distinguish the intent to cause a harmful or offensive contact from the intent to cause a particular consequence which results from that contact. Suppose, for example, that Brutus decides to humiliate Cassius by tripping him as he leaves the Senate building. Unfortunately, Cassius suffers a freak fall sideways over a railing and down a flight of stairs, causing a severe concussion. While Brutus intended to trip Cassius, he certainly did not intend the resulting freak injury. He did not act with a purpose to cause this unusual train of circumstances, nor was he substantially certain that tripping Cassius would result in serious injury.

However, Brutus did commit a battery on Cassius, and is therefore liable for all of Cassius's injuries. Brutus acted with the purpose to trip Cassius, which is surely an offensive contact. He succeeded in causing that contact when Cassius tripped. At that point, the battery was complete, and the law holds Brutus liable for all the consequences of the battery. Cassius may suffer no injury at all, or more injury than Brutus expects, or less, but if the touching itself is a battery, Brutus is liable for the resulting harm, whatever its extent may be.

The language of §8A of the Restatement is a bit confusing on this point: It states that the actor must intend "the consequences" of the act. The consequence to which §8A refers is the harmful or offensive contact itself, not the injuries that result from it. Perhaps another example will help to make this important distinction clear. In *Lambertson v. United States*, 528 F.2d 441 (2d Cir.), *cert. denied*, 426 U.S. 921 (1976), an inspector ran up behind a worker in a meat packing plant, jumped on his back, and pulled a bag over his head. The worker stumbled forward, struck his face on some meat hooks, and sustained serious injuries. Evidently, the inspector in *Lambertson* acted in the spirit of horseplay; there was no suggestion that he intended the worker to hit the meat hooks or suffer serious injuries. Yet the court concluded that the inspector had battered the worker when he intentionally jumped on his back, since the reasonable person in the victim's circumstances would find that contact offensive. Since he battered the worker when he jumped on him, the inspector could be held liable for the resulting facial injuries, though he did not intend to cause them.

It is not hard to see the reason for this seemingly Draconian rule: Batteries are intentional invasions of others' rights of personal security. One purpose of intentional tort law is to deter such unauthorized contacts from the outset. Imposing the cost of all resulting injuries on the actor should serve this deterrent purpose. After all, intentional torts are eminently avoidable: Because they require a *deliberate choice* to invade another's rights, the actor need only restrain herself to avoid the invasion. Where she fails to do so, it seems appropriate to impose all resulting damages — even unintended damages — on her rather than the innocent victim.

The Contact Requirement

Even the seemingly self-evident requirement of a contact requires some explanation. Suppose Smith doesn't touch Jones at all, but pokes her with a ten foot pole or stretches a wire across the sidewalk as Jones approaches, causing her to fall. Surely the underlying policy of protecting physical autonomy supports liability in these cases. In each, Smith invades Jones's physical integrity in one way or another and intends to do so under the definition discussed above.

Although no part of her body has touched Jones in these examples, Smith has imposed an unauthorized *contact* on Jones. The defendant need not actually touch the plaintiff at all, or even be present at the time of the contact, to commit a battery. For example, setting the wire out for Jones, knowing that she will trip over it later, will satisfy the contact requirement. See Harper, James & Gray, §3.3, at 274-276. An actor is liable, regardless of whether she uses her fist, a nightstick, or an automobile to cause the contact, if it is intended to cause a harmful or offensive contact to the victim.

The contact requirement has also been extended to include objects intimately associated with the victim's body. Chu's sense of personal space can be breached as effectively if Lopez pulls her coat lapels or knocks off her hat as by a direct touching to the skin. Extending the sphere of personal autonomy to include such items protects against intrusive contacts that are very likely to be offensive, thus raising the ante in physical confrontations. Obviously, however, there are limits; if Lopez kicks the fender of Chu's vintage Ford Mustang, the contact requirement is not met.

The following examples illustrate the elements of battery. In analyzing them, assume that the Restatement definitions apply.

EXAMPLES

The Bard, Updated

1.   Romeo likes to drive his souped-up Trans Am around the high school parking lot, racing the motor, accelerating rapidly, and stopping on a dime. He arrives at school one winter morning, speeds across the parking lot, and screeches to a halt in a parking space, hoping to impress the ladies with his hot shot driving. Unfortunately, the parking lot is icy; the rear end of the car skids out of control, jumps the curb sideways, and knocks Thibault to the ground. Has Romeo battered him?

2.   When Romeo gets out of the car to apologize, Thibault yells, "What's the idea?" and gives him a push. Romeo slips on a patch of ice, hits his head on one of the mag wheels of his Trans Am, and suffers a serious concussion. Is Thibault liable for Romeo's injuries?

3.   Romeo and Juliet are an item, "going steady" as they used to say. Romeo comes up to Juliet in the school parking lot on Monday morning and gives her a hug, as he is accustomed to doing each morning. Unfortunately, Juliet is standing on a patch of ice and Romeo's embrace causes her to fall and fracture her arm. Is Romeo liable for battery?

4.   In an effort to make amends, Romeo starts to help Juliet up. Thoroughly annoyed, Juliet growls, "Don't touch me." Romeo, determined

to be gallant, helps her up anyway, despite her efforts to pull away. Is this a battery?

Introducing Judge Fudd

5.   Romeo and Thibault are bitter rivals for Juliet's favor. After gym class, Romeo leaves a bar of soap on the floor of the shower Thibault usually uses, hoping that Thibault will slip and fall. He does, suffers injury and sues Romeo for battery. At trial, Judge Fudd, a well-meaning but sometimes inartful jurist, instructs the jury as follows:

> If you find that, when the defendant acted, he did not know that his act was substantially certain to cause a harmful or offensive contact to the plaintiff, you must find for the defendant.

Which party will object to Judge Fudd's instruction, and what is wrong with it?

6.   Romeo is sitting on a wall in front of the school. He sees Thibault wandering across the lawn, with his nose in a book, toward a trench recently excavated for some utility work. Cheering silently, he watches as Thibault ambles absent-mindedly toward disaster. To his delight, Thibault walks right into the trench, suffering minor injuries and considerable humiliation. Thibault sues Romeo for battery. What result?

No Offense Intended?

7.   Romeo considers himself irresistible. He is accustomed to flirting with the girls at will. He comes up to Ophelia, a new student, on her first day in the school and, by way of introduction, gives her a hug. She sues him for battery. Is he liable?

8.   Romeo is a sprinter on the track team. At the first meet of the season, he is nosed out by Mercutio, the star of the visiting team. In a burst of good sportsmanship, he goes over to Mercutio, slaps him heartily on the back, and says "great run, Mercutio!" Mercutio, who, it turns out, is very sensitive about being touched by strangers, reacts with rage at the contact. Is Romeo liable for battery?

9.   Romeo and Mercutio meet again at the regional finals. This time Romeo ends up the victor. After the race, he turns to Mercutio on the track, punches his shoulder playfully and says, "Well, Mercutio, turnabout is fair play!" The humorless Mercutio sues him for battery. Is he liable this time?

10. Romeo races Mercutio again in the state finals, and loses. Infuriated, he takes his track shoes and hurls them into the crowded stands. They hit Polonius, causing facial lacerations. Can Polonius sue Romeo for battery?

Star-Crossed Lovers

11. Alas, poor Romeo. He still holds a candle for Juliet, and she won't even talk to him anymore. He finds her asleep at one of the carrels in the school

library. A confirmed romantic, he slips up to her and kisses her on the cheek. Malvolio, the school sneak, later tells Juliet.

    a. Upset, she heads for court. Battery?

    b. Assume Romeo had kissed the sleeping Juliet while they were still going together. However, Juliet does not find out about it until after they have broken up. Can she sue him for battery?

Some Touching Cases

12. Romeo gets the idea that Juliet is seeing Thibault. He decides to get even. Which of the following vengeful acts makes Romeo liable for battery?

    a. He confronts Thibault in the cafeteria and makes some very offensive allusions to his moral character.

    b. At the prom, he laces Thibault's lemonade with 100 proof vodka. Thibault drinks it.

    c. He laces Thibault's lemonade with vodka, but the gallant Thibault gives his drink to Juliet, who drinks it.

    d. He blows cigarette smoke in Thibault's face.

    e. He shocks Juliet by offering to show her a photo of her favorite rock group but shows her some pornographic pictures instead.

13. Regan and Goneril, two teenagers, decide to wile away the afternoon standing on a bridge over the interstate, watching the traffic. Regan takes a mirror from her pocket and starts to shine it in the eyes of on-coming drivers. Cordelia, driving under the bridge, is temporarily blinded, swerves out of control and hits the bridge. Is Regan liable for battery?[2]

EXPLANATIONS

The Bard, Updated

1.   Romeo has done a dumb thing, a clearly negligent thing, but he has not committed a battery. A battery requires an intent to cause a harmful or offensive touching. While Romeo certainly *did* cause one, he didn't intend to under the Restatement definition. He did act intentionally in the sense that he deliberately drove his car across the lot. However, while this act was voluntary, he did not act with the purpose of hitting Thibault or with knowledge that he was substantially certain to do so; he was headed in another direction entirely. Nor, the facts suggest, was he trying to frighten Thibault or another student, which might support an argument for transferred intent. He was just showing off. Thus, his act was not intentional in the limited sense in which courts use that term for defining intentional torts.

---

2. The author thanks his colleague, Professor Alvan Brody, for this interesting example.

In analyzing battery cases, always distinguish the intent to act from the intent to cause a harmful or offensive contact. The requirement of intentional conduct for a battery requires intent to cause the contact or substantial certainty that it will result, not just a deliberate act. If the latter sufficed, any driver who intentionally drove a car would commit a battery if she got into an accident, though she did not intend the contact. A joker who threw a snowball at a tree would commit a battery if he hit a pedestrian who stepped unexpectedly into the snowball's path. Such acts may be negligent, but they are not intentional in the sense of deliberately trying to cause or knowing that the act will cause the resulting contact with the plaintiff.

2.   Although Thibault is justly angry with Romeo, that does not give him a license to retaliate against him. He has intentionally inflicted a contact that Romeo will find offensive, and perhaps harmful as well, and he is liable to him for battery.

But is he liable for the unanticipated and unintended concussion? As in the Brutus example in the introduction, Thibault is fully liable for all harm resulting from the battery. Although he had no intent — as that term is used in either the Restatement or everyday life — to cause Romeo's concussion, he did intend to hit him. Since he has committed a battery, he is liable for all the resulting injuries, even unexpected ones.

This rule, that a defendant who commits an intentional tort is liable for all the resulting harm, does not apply in negligence cases. Under negligence law, liability is limited to the foreseeable consequences of the defendant's act. See Chapter 8. However, because intentional torts are deemed more culpable, the courts generally hold the defendant liable for all the ensuing consequences, foreseeable or otherwise. This rule imposes very severe damages on Thibault for what seems like a relatively innocuous act—but it didn't turn out to be innocuous, did it? The Solomons of tort law have concluded that the loss in such cases should fall on the actor rather than the victim.

3.   Given their relationship and Juliet's past acceptance of Romeo's embraces, Romeo is justified in inferring that Juliet will not find his customary hug offensive. The reasonable person in Juliet's circumstances would not be offended by a hug from her boyfriend. But surely she finds falling down and breaking her arm harmful or offensive. Even if Romeo's hug isn't a battery, isn't causing her to fall on the ice one? (Remember that the contact need not be with the defendant; it can be with the ground or anything else.)

In this case, Romeo did not act with the intent of causing a harmful or offensive contact to Juliet. He had no reason to believe she would find the contact he intended — the hug — offensive, due to their relationship. And the contact she found harmful — the fall — he had no intent to cause: He did not act with a purpose to cause Juliet to fall or with substantial certainty that she would. While Romeo may be liable for negligence, for hugging her where the footing is slippery, he is not liable for battery.

Distinguish this case from Example 2. In that case, Thibault intended a harmful contact. Thus, he committed a battery and was held liable for all the resulting harm, even though it was greater than he reasonably would have anticipated. Here, since Romeo did not intend a harmful or offensive contact, he did not commit a battery and consequently is not liable for battery even though the contact itself turned out to have harmful consequences.

4.   Poor Romeo; he was only trying to help. Maybe he even *was* helpful. But he still committed a battery.

In analyzing battery cases, it is important to distinguish between intent and motive. The motive for Romeo's act was honorable, but he still intended to cause a contact to Juliet that he knew she would find offensive. The elements of battery do not include acting from a malicious motive, nor will a virtuous motive prevent liability if those elements are present. The plaintiff has the right to decide for herself which contacts are beneficial; she need not submit to the prodding of any Romeo who wishes to be gallant. Juliet may prefer the higher risk of slipping to the touch of the klutzy and out-of-favor Romeo. That decision is hers, not his. Where Romeo substitutes his judgment for hers, he is liable for battery.

Because of the fundamental value placed on physical self-determination, it is not unusual for courts to hold defendants liable for battery, even though their motives were pure and their contacts beneficial. The classic example is *Mohr v. Williams*, 104 N.W. 12 (Minn. 1905), in which a doctor was held liable for battery when he operated on the plaintiff's left ear after the plaintiff had consented to surgery only on the right. Although the left ear was diseased, and the surgery was successful, the court concluded that the doctor had violated the patient's "right to complete immunity of his person from physical interference of others. . . ." Id. at 16.

Introducing Judge Fudd

5.   Thibault will object to the instruction, and rightly so. If Judge Fudd's instruction were correct, Romeo would not be liable. Although he hoped that Thibault would slip and fall, he could hardly be substantially certain that he would do so, since he did not know that Thibault would use that shower or that if he did, he would slip on the soap. However, the intent requirement is satisfied either by an act done with substantial certainty that the contact will result *or* by an act done with the desire to cause the contact. Restatement (Second) of Torts §8A, p.5, supra.

In the practice of law, a word can make a world of difference. Here, the word *or* indicates that either substantial certainty or a desire to cause the result will suffice to establish intent. Since Romeo acted with the desire to cause the contact, he cannot defend by arguing that it was a long shot that his plot would succeed. Judge Fudd's instruction is wrong. Thibault's lawyer should object to it and have it corrected before it leads the jury to return an erroneous verdict.

6.   If desire can make a battery, Romeo has surely committed one, since he fervently hoped Thibault would fall in, and was delighted when he did. And

we know that Romeo need not directly touch Thibault to batter him: Contact with the trench suffices to meet the contact requirement. And certainly Thibault found the contact both harmful and offensive.

But Romeo is still not liable to Thibault. He has not done anything to cause the contact. To incur liability, he must *act*; he must inflict the contact, not simply hope for it. This contact results from the acts of others, not Romeo.

No Offense Intended?

7.   Obviously, Romeo is of the opinion that no woman in her right mind would object to his attentions. However, the question is not whether Romeo finds his conduct offensive. It is not even whether Romeo thinks that Ophelia will. As the introduction points out, the question Romeo must ponder before his dalliance with Ophelia is whether the reasonable person in Ophelia's circumstances would find it offensive. The answer to that question is almost certainly "yes." Most teenagers don't like being hugged by strangers, even attractive strangers.

Even if Romeo asks the right question ("Would the reasonable person in Ophelia's position find the hug offensive?"), he is liable if he is too conceited to realize that the answer is "yes." If he could avoid liability by arguing that he *believed* she would like it, social boors would escape liability simply because they have poor judgment, even though they inflict unwanted contacts on others.

8.   Romeo has again acted with good intentions, but we saw in Example 4 that good intentions will not negate a battery if the elements of the tort are established. However, those elements are not met here, since Romeo has no reason to believe that his slap will be offensive to a reasonable person under these circumstances: Congratulatory hugs and slaps are common among athletes on such occasions.

The requirement that the contact "offen[d] a reasonable sense of personal dignity" (Restatement (Second) of Torts §19) allows actors to make contacts with others that the ordinary person will not find offensive, without fear of a suit for battery. This requirement places the burden on the party with unusual sensibilities, such as Mercutio, to inform people of his susceptibility. Until he does, they are protected if they conform to generally accepted standards of behavior.

If actors were liable to hypersensitive plaintiffs for generally accepted contacts like this, many everyday interactions would entail the risk of liability. Under that rule, Romeo could be sued for tapping a stranger on the shoulder to tell her she had dropped her umbrella, or brushing past a fellow passenger on the subway. To avoid liability, he would have to avoid all contact. The world might be a marginally safer place for the hypersensitive, but a great deal of spontaneity would be sacrificed.

9.   This example is like the last, except that here Romeo is aware before he acts that Mercutio is sensitive to physical contacts, even those generally accepted by others. The issue is whether the actor is liable for contacts that are not offensive under the Restatement's "reasonable-sense-of-personal-dignity" standard, but which the actor knows *will be* offensive to a particular hypersensitive individual.

The Restatement refuses to take a stand on this variation.

> The Institute[3] expresses no opinion as to whether the actor is liable if he inflicts upon another a contact which he knows will be offensive to another's known but abnormally acute sense of personal dignity.

Restatement (Second) of Torts §19, caveat. Despite the Restatement's caution, doesn't it seem clear that the values underlying battery support liability in this case? The purpose of battery is to protect individuals from unwanted intrusions on physical security. Where an actor knows that another *accepts* contacts that others would find offensive (for example, friends who routinely engage in rough horseplay), his actual knowledge protects him, despite the objective standard usually applied. Conversely, where he knows that another rejects contacts others would tolerate, that knowledge, not the objective standard, should govern his liability. Here Romeo knows this intrusion will be offensive to Mercutio, and he ought to avoid it, even if others would accept the contact.

10.   Romeo will doubtless argue that he had no intent, in the battery sense of the term, to hit Polonius. He did not desire to hit him, nor did he know to a substantial certainty that he would hit him — the shoes could have hit anyone.

Clearly, this is an anemic defense. As long as Romeo knew to a substantial certainty that the shoes would hit *someone*, he knew his act would cause a harmful or offensive contact to the person of another. It should not negate the tort that his act had a large number of potential victims. If that were the case, a terrorist who threw a bomb onto the mezzanine at O'Hare Airport would not be liable to the strangers he injured, since he couldn't be sure which ones would be hurt, and wished no ill will to any one of them in particular.

This is not really a case of transferred intent. It is not a situation in which he threw at a specific victim and hit another instead. Rather, it is a case in which the actor knows at the outset that he will cause a harmful or offensive

---

3. The Restatement is a summary of the accepted principles of tort law, published by the American Law Institute. It is not "the law" of any state unless expressly adopted by court or legislature, but it often reflects widely accepted principles. This is certainly true of the intentional tort sections of the Restatement, which are frequently followed in intentional tort cases from many states.

touching to someone, but does not know who the victim will be. However, as in transferred intent cases, the intent requirement should be considered met, since Romeo's culpability is just as great here as if he threw at a particular victim.

Star-Crossed Lovers

11a.   Romeo's romantic gesture would be tortious if Juliet were awake, because it is an intentional contact that he knows she would find offensive. But can it be a battery if she doesn't even know about it?

One need only contemplate examples like the lecherous dentist and the anesthetized patient to confirm that battery must lie in this case. The underlying purpose of battery, to prevent invasions of physical security, will not be fully served if such conduct escapes liability. Juliet's right to be free of unpermitted touchings is infringed just as clearly when she is asleep as it would be if she were awake.

Romeo will probably argue that she did not find it offensive, since she was not even aware of the contact at the time. The argument will not fly. The requirement of offensive contact is met if it is a contact that the reasonable person in Juliet's circumstances would reject if given the choice. If immediate awareness of the contact were essential, a surgical patient could not be battered, even if the doctor gave her a nose job instead of the contemplated appendectomy. *Mohr v. Williams*, the case in which the doctor operated on the wrong ear, clearly indicates that the unconscious patient can be battered.

b. Although Juliet may now be offended at the thought that Romeo had kissed her, she presumably would not have been at the time of the contact. The offensiveness of the contact must be judged at that time, not in retrospect. Romeo must act on his understanding of what Juliet considers offensive *when he acts*; he cannot be expected to assess his conduct against the future possibility that they may have a falling out. This is not a battery.

Some Touching Cases

12a. This is not a battery. It is offensive contact, not offensive conduct, that is required.

b. This is a case of indirect contact. Romeo did not touch Thibault but has caused him to come into contact with the alcohol because he knew that Thibault would pick it up and drink it after he laced it. This is no different from lacing his drink with poison, although the effect is less drastic. So long as the reasonable teenager at the prom would find this offensive (a debatable issue, perhaps) this is a battery.

c. Romeo's intent was to see Thibault drink the vodka, not Juliet. He did not desire nor was he substantially certain that he would cause a contact with Juliet. However, under the doctrine of transferred intent, a party who attempts a battery on one person but mistakenly contacts another is liable for battery. Since Romeo intended to batter Thibault, he is liable if he causes a harmful or offensive contact with Juliet instead.

This fiction furthers the underlying purpose of battery law, to protect victims of acts intended to cause unwelcome or harmful touchings. Romeo is just as culpable when his plot goes awry as if it hits his intended target. Under the transferred intent doctrine, liability follows in either case.

d. There is no doubt that Romeo's act here was intentional and meant to offend. The issue is whether Romeo has caused a contact with Thibault. Clearly, if he spat on Thibault, or took pebbles in his mouth and shot them at him, this would be a battery. But smoke? Why not? Smoke is a substance, the particulate products of burning. Why should it matter if the contact is with small particles propelled through the air, instead of a large rock propelled through the air? Although smoke is (arguably) less harmful, it is equally likely to offend, and was clearly meant to in this case. And isn't it equally likely to provoke a breach of the peace?

These arguments have been made by advocates of the rights of nonsmokers, who conclude that there should be a battery remedy for smoking. See A. Brody & B. Brody, The Legal Rights of Non-Smokers 75-80 (1977); O. Reynolds, Jr., Extinguishing Brushfires: Legal Limits on the Smoking of Tobacco, 53 U. Cin. L. Rev. 435, 456-458 (1984). An earlier case on point, *McCracken v. Sloan*, 252 S.E.2d 250 (N.C. App. 1979), held that smoking was not a battery, primarily on the ground that contact with smoke was not offensive; this might be considered dubious reasoning today.

Although science is challenging many of the formalistic assumptions of traditional tort law, courts will likely be reluctant to reframe battery, that most ancient of remedies, beyond traditional types of contact. If smoke is deemed a contact, how about obnoxious horn honkers, the odor of greasy french fries, or loud football spectators? It would be difficult to avoid turning such nuisances into battery cases. The law has moved in recent decades toward protection of emotional tranquility as well as physical security, but it has primarily done so through actions for invasion of privacy and infliction of emotional distress rather than by expanding the scope of battery.

e. The battery action is not a general remedy for obnoxious behavior, but a limit on physical invasions of the person. Here again there is no contact, unless the court were to stretch the contact requirement to include light waves. If it did, battery would lie in every case in which an unpleasant scene was foisted on the unwilling eye. The courts will leave the plaintiff to other remedies on these facts, such as infliction of emotional distress.

13. On first glance, this seems to be a battery, despite the last example, because the plaintiff crashed into the bridge abutment. That's a contact if there ever was one.

However, Regan did not have the necessary intent to cause that contact. She did not either desire or know to a substantial certainty that Cordelia would crash into the wall. Presumably, she merely meant to annoy drivers, not to cause a crash, and it is far from substantially certain — though clearly possible — that this brief distraction would cause Cordelia to crash.

Regan did, on the other hand, intend to flash the mirror in Cordelia's eyes: She desired to cause that result, even if she was not substantially certain that her aim would be good enough to hit such a small moving target. But, of course, there's a contact issue here, since the contact is by light rays, not particularly different from the light rays in Example 12e.

Even the seemingly objective contact requirement, it seems, involves close slippery slope judgments. If Regan had used a high powered laser which burns through steel, I have little doubt the court would find a contact. On these facts, however, the court might conclude that there was no contact, and therefore no intentional tort. If not, there surely was recklessness or gross negligence, which, of course, gives rise to tort liability as well.

2

The Action for Assault: A Tort Ahead of its Time

Introduction

Historically, tort law has been reluctant to protect mental tranquility alone. For example, courts have not allowed recovery for insult, or for disturbing the plaintiff's peace of mind through distasteful behavior or voicing unpopular opinions. True, some courts have recently begun to redress limited forms of psychic injury, such as infliction of emotional distress and invasion of privacy. But these have gained currency only in the last few decades. If the duration of the common law were an hour, this would represent only the past few minutes.

Assault, however, is an exception to this general principle. The action for assault, which has been with us virtually since the inception of the common law, does allow recovery for interference with peace of mind, even where there is no physical invasion of the victim's person or property. Unlike battery, which requires a tangible, physical invasion, assault protects one form of mental tranquility, the right to be free from fear or apprehension of unwanted contact. In this sense, assault has truly been a tort ahead of its time.

> One of the most important objects to be attained by the enactment of laws and the institutions of civilized society is, each of us shall feel secure against unlawful assaults. Without such security society loses most of its value. Peace and order and domestic happiness, inexpressibly more precious than mere forms of government, cannot be enjoyed without the sense of perfect security. We have a right to live in society without being put in fear of personal harm.

19

Beach v. Hancock, 27 N.H. 223, 229 (1853). Assault, like battery, protects this right of personal security by authorizing damages for threatened invasion of the person. However, assault is definitely not a general remedy for interference with mental tranquility: It only protects against one narrow type of mental distress, the apprehension of immediate physical aggression.

The Restatement Definition

Because assault is an ancient remedy applied in many jurisdictions, the cases vary somewhat in describing its elements. In *Cucinotti v. Ortmann*, 159 A.2d 216, 217 (Pa. 1960), for example, the court held that "an assault may be described as *an act* intended to put another person in reasonable apprehension of an immediate battery, and which succeeds in causing an apprehension of such battery." Compare *Western Union Tel. Co. v. Hill*, 150 So. 709, 710 (Ala. App.), *cert. denied*, 150 So. 711 (Ala. 1933): "To constitute an assault there must be an intentional, unlawful, offer to touch the person of another in a rude or angry manner under such circumstances as to create in the mind of the party alleging the assault a well-founded fear of an imminent battery, coupled with the apparent present ability to effectuate the attempt. . . ." Despite such differences, the essence of these definitions is quite similar. The elements of the tort are distilled in the Second Restatement definition of assault:

> (1) An actor is subject to liability to another for assault if
>   (a) he acts intending to cause a harmful or offensive contact with the person of the other or a third person, or an imminent apprehension of such a contact, and
>   (b) the other is thereby put in such imminent apprehension.

Restatement (Second) of Torts §21. Under this definition, the defendant must (1) act with intent (2) to place the victim in apprehension of a harmful or offensive contact or to make such a contact, and (3) the victim must reasonably be placed in fear of such a contact. These requirements are discussed in detail below.

The Intent Requirement

Assault, like battery, requires intentional conduct, and in the same restrictive sense. The defendant must act with the *purpose* to cause apprehension of a contact or *substantial certainty* that the apprehension will result. Restatement (Second) of Torts §8A. Thus, as in a battery case, the defendant may not avoid liability by claiming that he did not mean to place the plaintiff in fear of an unwanted touching, if he knew to a substantial certainty that fear of a touching would result. Suppose that Owens throws a shot put across the infield while Jackson is standing in the landing area. Owens cannot avoid liability for assault by arguing that he was just warming up for the decathlon. If Jackson was looking at him, he must have known that Jackson would reasonably fear being hit. Thus his act is intentional under the Restatement definition, even though he did not do it for the purpose of placing Jackson in fear.

On the other hand, many cases in which plaintiffs are placed in fear of a touching are not intentional as that term is used in intentional tort law. If Jackson loses control of her car on Main Street, and careens over the curb in Owens's direction, Owens will doubtless be placed in fear of being run down. However, Jackson has not acted with a purpose to frighten Owens, or with substantial certainty that the act will frighten him. Jackson may be liable to Owens for negligence, but she has not assaulted him.

Even if Jackson acts intentionally in the sense that she *deliberately* swerves toward the curb, she lacks intent in the intentional tort sense if she does not desire or know to a substantial certainty that she will hit Owens. For example, if Jackson suddenly realizes that her brakes have failed, and steers for the curb to stop the car, her act is intentional in the sense that it was a voluntary, deliberate act, but it would not be an assault if she did not know that Owens was there and would be placed in fear of being hit.

The Restatement definition also provides that one who attempts to batter the plaintiff but misses is liable for assault if the plaintiff is placed in apprehension of a blow. Restatement (Second) of Torts §21(1). Suppose, for example, that Rose, infuriated by Owens's bragging that he won more Olympic medals than she did, throws a shot put at him but misses. Even though Rose has tried to commit a battery, rather than an assault, she is liable to Owens for assault if he sees the shot put coming and is placed in fear of being hit. On the other hand, if Owens is looking the other way and doesn't know of her act, he is not placed in fear of a harmful touching and has no tort claim for assault.

This principle, that the intent to batter can satisfy the intent requirement for assault as well, is obviously akin to the transferred intent doctrine illustrated in Chapter 1. See Example 12(c) from Chapter 1, in which Romeo tried to batter Thibault by lacing his drink, and Juliet drank it instead. In that example Romeo was liable to Juliet for battery, though he had no intent to cause an offensive touching to her. Similarly, here, Rose is liable for assault though she meant to hit Owens, not to frighten him, since she acted with tortious intent. Her act is just as reprehensible if it causes fear of the touching rather than the touching itself. She is liable to Owens under the Restatement definition even though the blow did not hit home.

Because assault only protects against fear of a harmful or offensive contact, the plaintiff must prove that she feared the type of contact that would support a battery claim if it actually occurred. Thus, the analysis in Chapter 1 of the meaning of *harmful or offensive* is also necessary in assault cases. If a contact would not have been harmful or offensive had it been made, the threat of that contact is not an assault either. If Leonard and Spinks often slap each other on the shoulder in jest before sparring, their contacts are not offensive and do not constitute battery. Thus, if Spinks moves to slap Leonard, he does not commit an assault, since Leonard anticipates a touching, but not a harmful or offensive one.

Nothing to Fear But Apprehension Itself

Actually, the word *fear*, though it is often loosely used in the cases, is not quite accurate. The Restatement definition requires that the defendant cause "apprehension" of a harmful or offensive contact. *Apprehension* as used here means the perception or anticipation of a blow, rather than fright. Assault protects not only against the fear of an unwelcome contact, but also against the mere expectation or anticipation of one. If Dillard threatens to spit on Baxter's shoes, Baxter will anticipate, or apprehend, an unwelcome and demeaning contact, which would be a battery if it actually took place. This anticipation is sufficient for an assault claim, even though Baxter is not frightened in the usual sense of that term.

The Restatement definition also requires that the apprehended contact be *imminent*, that is, the defendant's act must cause the victim to apprehend that he is about to be touched. This imminence requirement obviously raises slippery-slope problems. Since the dawn of the socratic method, Torts professors have tortured (no pun intended) students with barely distinguishable assault hypotheticals: Dillard swings an axe at Oda from a foot away, from four feet away, through a window, from across the room, from the end of the street but he's a faster runner than Oda, and so on. The Restatement suggests that imminent

> does not mean immediate, in the sense of instantaneous contact, as where the other sees the actor's fist about to strike his nose. It means rather that there will be no significant delay. It is not necessary that one shall be within striking distance of the other, or that a weapon pointed at the other shall be in a condition for instant discharge. It is enough that one is so close to striking distance that he can reach the other almost at once, or that he can make the weapon ready for discharge in a very short interval of time.

Restatement (Second) of Torts §29 cmt. b.

This exegesis hardly eliminates all ambiguities in applying the imminence requirement. However, the fact that there will be close cases (again, no pun intended!) is hardly a fatal criticism of the requirement. Close factual issues of this sort will be decided by the jury, under careful instructions as to the meaning of assault. The jurors' practical intuition about what actions are likely to cause reasonable apprehension will lead to a just decision in most cases. On the other hand, it is clear that fear of a *future* contact will not support liability for assault. "If you try out for the Olympic team next month,

I'm going to bust your nose" is not an assault, since the threat is not of an imminent contact.

Perhaps such threats for the future *should* be assaults. They are reprehensible, and may be very unsettling indeed to aspiring athletes. Realistically, however, the law can't protect everyone from everything; it has to pick its targets. Such general, future threats suggest possible, vaguely formed (and hence, changeable) intention, perhaps even mere braggadocio. Consequently, they are likely to be less intimidating than the raised fist of an incensed assailant. In addition, future threats leave the victim time to take other steps to prevent the harm, such as going to the police or avoiding the assailant. Thus, they are less likely to provoke immediate retaliation by the victim.

The requirement that the victim anticipate an imminent battery has led many courts to hold that *mere words* alone cannot constitute an assault, because they do not sufficiently show the defendant's purpose to immediately batter the victim. For example, a defendant who growls at the victim "I'm going to wring your neck!" might be held not to commit an assault, but if he extracts a rope from his pocket and proceeds to wind it around his hands, his act provides the necessary evidence of an imminent intent to batter the plaintiff.

This problem of assault by words alone is intractable. The requirement that the defendant go beyond mere words to commit a threatening act is meant to distinguish between bluster and real aggression. Some cases have been quite strict in requiring such an act. In *Cucinotti v. Ortmann*, 159 A.2d 216 (Pa. 1960), for example, the plaintiffs alleged that the defendants confronted them and threatened that they would commit "immediate bodily harm upon the plaintiffs, and would strike the plaintiffs with blackjacks and would otherwise hit them with great force and violence." Id. at 218. The court held that the complaint did not state a claim for assault since no threatening act was alleged. The *Cucinotti* court even held that an allegation that the defendants produced the blackjacks and showed them to the plaintiffs would not state a claim for assault. Id. at 218-219.

The Second Restatement of Torts, however, suggests a more flexible approach to this problem:

> Words do not make the actor liable for assault *unless together with other acts or circumstances* they put the other in reasonable apprehension of an imminent harmful or offensive contact with his person.

Restatement (Second) of Torts §31 (emphasis added). The italicized clause suggests that circumstances may suffice to make words actionable as an assault, if they reasonably cause the victim to fear an imminent contact. Courts are likely to be realistic in assessing the defendant's intent; where the circumstances clearly indicate that he is about to strike, a very little more than words — such as a step, a rolling up of sleeves, or a drawing back of fists — will suffice to take the case to the jury. Even without that, courts may allow recovery based on the words and surrounding circumstances alone, if those circumstances are compelling enough. For example, some courts, relying on §31 of the Second Restatement, would probably allow recovery on the facts of *Cucinotti*.

The cases also frequently state that an assailant is liable for assault if he manifests the "apparent present ability" to cause an unwanted contact, even if he in fact was unable to do so. For example, if Landy brandishes a toy pistol at Oda, he may have the apparent present ability to shoot her, since it reasonably appears to Oda that the pistol is real and that Landy intends to shoot her. This is an assault, though Landy has no *actual* present ability to shoot Oda. Assault protects the plaintiff's peace of mind; thus, her reasonable apprehension gives rise to a claim even if the defendant could not in fact carry out the threat. On the other hand, if Oda knows the pistol is a toy, she will not apprehend a touching, and Landy will not be liable for assault.

Conditional Threats

Other factors may also undermine the imminence element of assault. Suppose that Oda snarls at Rudolph, "If you hadn't fouled out of the hundred-meter competition, I'd beat you to a pulp." Here, Oda's own threat defeats the assault, since her words indicate that she does not plan to carry it out. Her comment is still unpleasant and unwelcome, but it is not likely to make Rudolph anticipate immediate invasion of her physical security. Similarly, the defendant who states, "If you were not an old man, I would knock you senseless," does not assault the plaintiff, since his own words negate the intent to cause a harmful contact.

Some threats, however, will constitute assault even though they are conditional. Suppose that Oda snarls at Rudolph, "If you don't get off this track, I'll kick your tail into next week." This folksy threat is conditional, in the sense that Rudolph can avoid the threatened battery by leaving. At least in theory, she need not fear a blow, because she holds the means of avoiding it. Obviously, however, this should still be an assault. Otherwise, Rudolph could be forced to abandon her right to walk the streets (or run the track) in order to avoid battery. Bullies would be able to impose their will on others by the threat of force, yet incur no liability. One need only pose a slightly more extreme hypothetical ("If you don't go to bed with me, I'll throw you out this window") to make clear that the imposition of a condition that the assailant has no right to impose will not defeat an assault, even though the plaintiff can avoid being struck by complying with the unlawful demand.[1] See Harper, James & Gray, §3.5, at 284.

---

1. On the other hand, if the defendant *does* have a right to make a conditional threat, he is not liable for doing so. "If you don't get off my land, I will put you off," threatens physical force, but the owner has a right to use reasonable force to eject a trespasser. Restatement (Second) of Torts §77. Even if this frightens the trespasser, it is not an assault, since the statement is privileged.

Criminal Assault Distinguished

Since the early days of the common law, assault has been recognized not only as a tort, but as a crime as well. However, the crime of assault has not always been equated with the tort of assault. Historically, criminal assault has been defined as an attempt to commit a battery. See R. Perkins and R. Boyce, Criminal Law 159 (3d ed. 1982); *Pope v. State*, 79 N.Y.S.2d 466, 471 (1948), *aff'd*, 99 N.Y.S.2d 1019 (1950) (defining assault as "an unlawful offer or attempt with force or violence to do corporal hurt to another"). This definition does not specify that the victim must anticipate the blow; the mere attempt to batter suffices. Under this criminal law definition, if Haines throws a javelin at Mathias, intending to injure him, he commits a criminal assault, whether or not Mathias sees it coming. However, this would not be a civil assault if Mathias were unaware of the oncoming javelin, since he would not be placed in apprehension of a blow.

By contrast, if Owens pretended to throw the javelin at Mathias simply to frighten him, without intending to release it, this would be a civil assault, since it would doubtless place Mathias in fear of being skewered. But it would not be criminal assault under the traditional approach if Owens had no intent to throw, since he had not in fact attempted a battery. Similarly, if an assailant has no ability to cause the battery, as where Mathias threatens Owens from a distance with an empty gun, he does not commit a criminal assault under the traditional definition, but would commit the tort of assault.

In recent years, many states have amended their criminal statutes to make conduct that constitutes assault in the tort sense punishable as a criminal assault as well. A majority of states now make either act — attempted battery or placing in fear of a battery — a criminal offense. W. LaFave and A. Scott, Criminal Law §7.16, at 691 (2d ed. 1986). But the historical distinction lingers in the form of confusing statements in the cases, such as the oft-repeated statement that "every battery includes an assault." *Western Union Tel. Co. v. Hill*, 150 So. 709, 710 (Ala. App.), *cert. denied*, 150 So. 711 (Ala. 1933). That is clearly untrue in the tort context: If the defendant kicks a sleeping plaintiff, he commits the tort of battery, but not the tort of assault, since he has not placed the defendant in fear of the contact.

The following examples probe the various elements of assault. In considering them, assume that the Restatement definition applies. After the examples, there is a brief discussion of how to plead the elements of assault and battery, together with an illustrative complaint.

EXAMPLES

Fear and Trembling

1.   Hennie, an Olympic figure skater, is about to perform her final routine in the womens' individual skating event. She brings her music tape, meticulously

edited and carefully guarded over four years of preparation, into the arena and puts it on the table by the tape player. Wilson, a sports cartoonist with a sick sense of humor, puts the tape on the floor and pretends to jump up and down on it while Hennie looks on from across the ice. Hennie is appalled. Can she sue Wilson for assault?

2.   The malicious Wilson crawls into the grid above the rink and loosens a heavy Olympic banner above the rink. He drops the banner as Hennie skates under him, but it sails a bit and lands ten feet behind her. She then turns and sees the banner lying on the ice and is shocked to think how close she came to being injured.

  a. Does she have an assault claim against Wilson?

  b. Is Wilson guilty of the *crime* of assault?

3.   Wilson lets the banner go, aiming for the unsuspecting Hennie, who is concentrating on her routine. As the banner falls, she looks up, sees it coming, and skates to safety. Is this an assault?

4.   Assume that Hennie sees the banner coming, but she can't get out of the way in time. Hennie is hit, though not injured. Can she sue for assault?

5.   Button, Hennie's partner in the doubles competition, is sitting in the stands and sees the banner fall. He is terrified that she will be hit. He sues Wilson for assault. What result?

6.   Suppose that Button was warming up at the same time as Hennie. Wilson, while climbing across the grid to loosen the banner, knocks an iron clamp off of a beam. Button, alerted by a spectator, looks up in alarm and sees it coming at him, but manages to duck out of the way. Is Wilson liable to him for assault?

7.   Wilson, a fan of the Russian sprinters, approaches the U.S. track coach. He shakes his fist and snarls, "If you run Ashford on the anchor leg of the women's four-hundred-meter relay tomorrow, I'll see that you never walk again." Is this an assault?

Judge Fudd at the Olympics

8.   Hennie is practicing for her routine while the Zamboni (that big machine that grooms the ice) circles the rink. As she gracefully executes a backward glide, Wilson yells to her, "Watch it! You're going to hit the Zamboni!" Although Hennie is startled, the Zamboni is actually on the other end of the rink. Hennie sues Wilson for assault.

  a. Whether Wilson is liable for this conduct will depend on how the jury is instructed on the definition of assault. Consider the Restatement definition and the definition in the *Cucinotti* case, quoted at p.20. If you represented Hennie, which would you ask Judge Fudd to use in instructing the jury, and why?

b. If you represented Wilson, what other argument would you raise that Hennie could not meet the prima facie elements of an assault claim?

The Impossible Dream

9.   Corbett, a four-foot-nine-inch gymnast, approaches Press, a two-hundred-fifty-pound shot putter who has just beaten out the American favorite in the shot put competition. Shaking her fist at her, she growls, "Press, wipe that smile off your face or I'll wipe it off for you!" Press sues Corbett for assault. Is she liable?

10. Press, as it turns out, is a sensitive type. She is so upset by Corbett's threat that she develops a phobia about competition and goes into therapy to overcome it. She sues Corbett for a substantial sum for these consequences. Is Corbett liable for them?

The Domino Theory

11. Mathias gets in a heated exchange with Weismuller near the high jump pit. To scare him, Weismuller lunges at him. Mathias turns to run and hits Baxter, who was approaching for his last jump. Baxter falls and breaks his leg.
   a. Is Weismuller liable to Baxter, and if so, for what tort?
   b. Baxter is taken to the hospital. Lamentably, there is a fire in the hospital the next day, and Baxter is badly burned. Is Weismuller liable for Baxter's burns?

EXPLANATIONS
Fear and Trembling

1.   In this example, Hennie clearly would be traumatized by Wilson's conduct, but would not succeed in an action for assault. Assault addresses only one narrow form of emotional distress, apprehension of a contact with the person of the plaintiff. That is not what Wilson has threatened in this case. Wilson did not intend to touch Hennie, nor did she fear that he would. Since assault only protects against threatened contacts with the plaintiff herself, this is not an assault.

It surely is obnoxious behavior, though. Hennie ought to have a remedy for such conduct, even if it can't be shoe-horned into the elements of assault. If it isn't assault, it must be *something*, or else the law ought to make it something and give it a name so Hennie can recover. Traditionally, the common law did not provide a remedy for such antisocial acts — the courts did not attempt to redress all grievances, but confined themselves to the most venal. Only recently have the cases begun to develop the tort of infliction of emotional distress, which allows recovery for acts that cause severe distress, regardless of whether a physical threat was made. See also Restatement (Second) of Torts §870 (supporting liability for intentional infliction of harm that does not fit the elements of traditional intentional torts). But the assault tort, too hoary with age to learn new tricks, only applies to threats to the plaintiff herself.

2a.   When Hennie turns and sees the banner, she realizes that she might have been hit and is justifiably upset, but this is still not an assault. There is a difference between apprehending an imminent injury and realizing, after the fact, that you have narrowly escaped one. The elements of assault require that the plaintiff be placed in fear of an imminent contact. Hennie's post hoc awareness that the banner almost hit her may be equally disturbing, but it isn't an assault.

As in the last case, our instincts tell us there should be a remedy for this kind of behavior. If there is, however, it will have to be under the rubric of intentional infliction of emotional distress or some other cause of action such as "prima facie tort" (see Restatement (Second) of Torts §870), not assault. The assault cause of action is too arthritic to be stretched this far.

b.   Under the traditional criminal law approach, an attempted battery is an assault. Wilson's act would constitute criminal assault if, as the example suggests, he acted with a purpose to hit Hennie when he dropped the banner. But the *tort* of assault is not synonymous with attempted battery; it requires that the actor place the plaintiff in fear of an impending, not a past, touching.

3.   In this case, Wilson tried to hit Hennie, not frighten her. Indeed, the success of his scheme probably turned on her ignorance of the peril, since she could skate away if she knew it was on the way. Thus, Wilson may try to argue that he did not intend to cause Hennie to apprehend an imminent contact, only to make the contact itself.

The argument fails under the Restatement definition of assault. Although Wilson only tried to commit the battery itself, he is liable for assault since he acted with tortious intent and placed Hennie in apprehension of a harmful touching. Under Restatement (Second) of Torts §21, the intent requirement is met if Wilson was trying *either* to cause the contact (as he was in this case) or to cause Hennie to apprehend it, and she actually suffers such apprehension.

4.   Since the banner actually hit Hennie, this is a battery, even though she suffered no injury. Only an unwelcome touching, not resulting harm, is necessary to complete the battery. But Hennie suffered an assault as well, since she saw the banner coming and was placed in apprehension that she would be hit by it. The torts of battery and assault often occur together, though of course the elements of each must be separately satisfied.

If Hennie had not seen it coming, she would have suffered a battery but not an assault, since she would not have experienced fear of the impending contact, but only the contact itself.

5.   In this example, Button has been placed in fear that Hennie will suffer a harmful or offensive contact. This is not assault, however, because assault

protects only the intended victim, not bystanders, from threats of bodily contact. Restatement (Second) of Torts §26 cmt. a.

Since threats to physical security are considered so antisocial, and are so easily avoided by a little self-restraint, why not allow Button to recover on facts like these? Broadening the right to recover would further deter assaultive conduct, and remedy real infringements of Button's mental tranquility.

Perhaps so, but if we allow Button to recover, why not Hennie's manager — or her boyfriend, or anyone in the audience, or anyone who sees it on TV? Naturally, Button has more at stake than some of these bystanders, but each may suffer real distress from the fear that Hennie will be injured. Opening up the tort to third persons may not be worth the candle, since in most cases the truly distressed person will be the intended victim.

The nascent cause of action for intentional infliction of emotional distress has been extended to *some* plaintiffs who are not direct victims of the tortfeasor's conduct. See Restatement (Second) of Torts §46(2), which allows members of the victim's family to recover if present at the time of the defendant's conduct, and other bystanders to recover if they are both present and suffer emotional distress that results in bodily harm.

6.   Wilson has placed Button in fear of a harmful or offensive contact with the clamp, but he has not acted intentionally in the restricted intentional tort sense. He may have carelessly knocked the clamp down, but he did not do it for the purpose of hitting or frightening Button, nor was he substantially certain at the time that it would do so.

At the time of the act, however, Wilson was on his way to commit an intentional tort on Hennie by dropping the banner on her. Can Button's counsel make a transferred intent argument based on this? It seems not; transferred intent applies where a specific act is done with tortious intent and misfires. Here, the act of knocking down the clamp was not done with intent to hit or frighten anyone. To prove assault, Button must focus on this act, not Wilson's brewing plot to assault Hennie.

7.   In this example Wilson has threatened the coach with physical violence if he does not comply with Wilson's demands. Naturally, Wilson has no right to tell the U.S. track coach who to run in the relays, so the fact that he can avoid liability by doing as he is told does not prevent this from being an assault. However, it isn't an assault anyway, since Wilson has not threatened the coach with an imminent contact. A threat to do something tomorrow almost certainly is not imminent; a future threat, while reprehensible, does not satisfy the imminence requirement.

Judge Fudd at the Olympics

8a.   It would be crucial for Hennie to convince the judge to instruct the jury in terms of the Restatement definition instead of that given in the *Cucinotti* case. *Cucinotti*, if you read the definition carefully, requires that the defendant place the plaintiff in apprehension of a *battery*. Here, presumably Hennie anticipated an accidental collision with the Zamboni, not a deliberate battery by the driver. If apprehension of a battery is necessary, Wilson would not be liable.

Under the Restatement definition, however, the defendant need only cause the victim to apprehend a harmful or offensive contact, not necessarily a contact by the defendant, or one which meets the elements of battery. See Restatement (Second) of Torts §25 (victim need not be placed in fear of a touching from the actor in order to constitute assault). Under the Restatement definition, Wilson could be liable, since he caused Hennie to fear a harmful contact, though not a contact with Wilson or one which would constitute a battery at all.

There are many ways an actor can place a victim in fear of harmful or offensive touchings without threatening a battery. Consider the following:

- When passing a construction site: "Watch out, a plank is falling on your head!"
- While camping in the desert: "Don't move; there's a rattler next to your foot!"
- While riding up in a ski lift: "Jump! the cable's about to snap!"

Such obnoxious tricks can be mighty disturbing to one's mental tranquility. The drafters of the Restatement evidently concluded that inflicting such apprehension should be actionable. See Restatement (Second) of Torts §25 illus. 1 (actor liable for sounding a buzzer behind the victim in the desert, placing him in fear of a snake bite). However, there apparently are no cases either imposing or denying liability in such circumstances.

b. Wilson's counsel will doubtless argue that this is a case of mere words, without any act. Yet, as the introduction suggests, words together with circumstances can create reasonable apprehension of unwanted contact. The Second Restatement (§31, cmt. d) gives the example of a thief who stands in the dark road, holding a gun but without moving, and says "stand and deliver!" These mere words, in context, certainly incite a fear of an imminent harmful touching; the discussion in the Restatement comment clearly suggests that the thief could be sued for assault.

Similarly, here, it seems likely that Wilson's words and excited tone of voice, together with the circumstance that Hennie is skating backwards while the Zamboni is grooming the ice, would reasonably cause her to fear hitting the machine, even if Wilson does not move a muscle. Under the Restatement's approach, a court would likely uphold a finding of assault on these facts.

The Impossible Dream

9.   Perhaps your first response here is that Press would have to be dreaming to be at all intimidated by Corbett's threat. Given the disparity in their size,

the reasonable shot putter would not have feared a threat from Corbett, so that, arguably, no assault occurred.

However, while Press doubtless was not *frightened* by Corbett's threat, her conduct does cause Press to *apprehend* an unwelcome contact from her — surely Corbett has the present ability to attack Press, even if she was unlikely to cause her any substantial harm. The action for assault protects victims from the anticipation of unwelcome contacts, even where they are confident that they can adequately defend themselves. Put another way, assault turns on the acts and intent of the defendant, not on how good the victim is at self defense. The strong have a right to physical autonomy as well as the weak, and should not be placed in the position of having to defend themselves from such invasions.

10. In this example, the plaintiff reacts to the assault in an unexpected manner. Corbett's threat would be a minor annoyance to the average shot putter, but Press is a hypersensitive soul who is really upset and permanently affected by it. The example is reminiscent of Example 8 in Chapter 1, in which Mercutio is upset by a good-natured slap on the back that other athletes would casually accept.

Although it may be reminiscent of the Mercutio example, this case is different. In that example, Romeo did not commit a battery, since the reasonable person under the circumstances would not be offended by the contact. Consequently, he was not a tortfeasor at all, and was not liable even though Mercutio was actually distressed. Here, however, Corbett did commit an assault, since she threatened a contact that would be offensive to the reasonable person. Consequently, she *is* a tortfeasor, and is liable for the damages Press suffers as a result of the tort — *all* the damages she suffers, even though they exceed the damage one would anticipate from the conduct.

The difference between these two examples is important to understand. In the Mercutio example, the fact that the reasonable person would not be offended by the contact goes to the existence of liability in the first place. In the Press example, because a reasonable person would find the impending contact offensive, the threat is tortious. Since Corbett has committed a tort, she "takes the plaintiff as she finds her"; she is liable for the actual damages Press suffers, even if they are greater than the average shot putter would experience from the tortious conduct.

The Domino Theory

11a. This is another case in which a party acts with tortious intent, but the injury caused differs from the one intended. Weismuller intended to assault Mathias, but he had no intent to assault Baxter. Baxter, however, will argue that once Weismuller committed an intentional tort, he became liable for all the consequences of his tortious act. Since he intended to assault Mathias, it should not matter that he did not desire or know that Mathias would run into Baxter.

It is true that courts usually hold tortfeasors liable for all the consequences of their intentional torts. However, this case is different from the typical situation, like the last example, in which the tortfeasor's *intended* victim suffers more harm than expected. Here, Weismuller's assault on one victim leads to an independent act by the victim that causes injury to an unintended victim, Baxter. At least we should recognize that holding Weismuller liable on these facts goes beyond the usual scenario involving unanticipated consequences *to the actor's intended victim*.

It may be useful to compare this problem to the analogous principle of proximate cause in negligence law. Where the defendant's act is negligent rather than intentional, negligence law limits the consequences for which he will be held liable: He will not be liable for injury to unforeseeable plaintiffs or for unforeseeable injuries. See Chapter 8. Conversely, a defendant in a negligence action *is* liable for foreseeable injuries to foreseeable plaintiffs. It seems very likely that, had Weismuller been merely negligent here, (if, for example, he obliviously ran toward Mathias, causing him to jump back into Baxter's way) he would be liable for Baxter's injury, since it is quite foreseeable that Mathias would react as he did. *A fortiori*, it appears likely that the court would hold Weismuller liable where he acted intentionally.

If Weismuller is liable, what tort has he committed? He attempted to assault Mathias, but ended up causing a harmful touching to Baxter. Presumably, through the fiction of transferred intent, his intent transfers twice: from Mathias to Baxter and from assault to battery. He would be liable to Baxter for battery.

b. The burn injury to Baxter is entirely unforeseeable; if Weismuller had caused this injury through negligence, most courts would not hold him liable for it, based on a lack of proximate cause. See Chapter 8. Where Weismuller's act was intentional, however, the result is less clear. The Restatement (Second) of Torts takes the position that an intentional tortfeasor may be held liable for unforeseeable harm. Section 435B of the Second Restatement provides that the court, in deciding whether to allow recovery, should consider the actor's intention to cause harm, the degree of his moral wrong, and the seriousness of the harm that he intended when he acted.

While a court could hold an intentional tortfeasor liable for bizarre consequences under this standard, it seems doubtful that most courts would on these facts. Weismuller's spur-of-the-moment spat with Mathias seems relatively mild compared with the gravity and the unexpected nature of Baxter's burn injuries. Although courts often state that actors are broadly liable for the consequences of their intentional torts, this example suggests that there is an outer limit on liability for the consequences of intentional torts, just as there is on liability for negligence, despite the higher level of fault.

Pleading Claims for Assault and Battery

These two chapters have analyzed the substantive elements of assault and battery, that is, the basic facts the plaintiff must show to establish that the defendant is liable. It may be useful to see how these elements are presented to a court in a complaint for assault and battery.

The first step in seeking recovery for a tort claim is to file a complaint alleging that the defendant has committed a tort and demanding damages. A well crafted complaint should allege a *prima facie* case, that is, the basic facts establishing that defendant's conduct fits the elements of the tort for which the plaintiff seeks damages. In an assault complaint, the plaintiff must allege facts that show that the defendant intentionally placed her in fear of a harmful or offensive touching. A battery complaint must allege facts that show that the defendant intentionally caused such a harmful or offensive touching. In addition, the plaintiff should allege the harm that resulted from the assault, and the relief (usually money damages) that she seeks as compensation.

Often, a single incident will support claims for both assault and battery. Figure 2-1 is an example of such a complaint. Like most court papers, it is basically straightforward. It begins by identifying the parties (paragraphs 1 and 2) and then briefly setting forth the events that gave rise to the claim. See paragraphs 3-5. The complaint then recasts the facts in terms of legal causes of action, in individual *counts* or *claims for relief.* Paragraph 7 of Juliet's First Claim for Relief specifically alleges that Romeo's conduct satisfies the elements of an assault: an act ("threatened to strike her and shook his fist"), intent ("intentionally"), and resulting fear of a touching ("placing her in fear that he was about to strike her"). Paragraph 8 does the same for the second assault alleged. Paragraph 11 similarly alleges the elements of battery. Thus, the complaint demonstrates that the plaintiff claims she can establish the facts necessary to recover for each tort. In addition, it alleges the injuries suffered as a result of the defendant's tortious acts (paragraphs 9 and 13).

Finally, Juliet's counsel includes a demand for damages (the "wherefore" clause following paragraph 13). The damage demand here far exceeds the actual out-of-pocket costs Juliet incurred; a large part of the injury in intentional tort cases is intangible emotional harm, such as distress, pain and suffering, and humiliation resulting from the invasion. Such damages are genuine but hard to quantify; hence, plaintiffs often demand a good deal more than their out-of-pocket damages in cases involving such intangible elements as pain and suffering, emotional distress, interference with reputation, or other psychic injuries. Similarly, punitive damages, which may be awarded for intentional torts in some states to punish and deter tortious conduct, also may lead to an award of damages which far exceeds the plaintiff's economic damages from the tort.

STATE OF WEST DAKOTA

CONKLIN COUNTY, SS.   CIVIL ACTION NO. 94-7192

JANE JULIET,

      Plaintiff,

   v.   COMPLAINT FOR ASSAULT AND
                                     BATTERY

RONALD ROMEO,

      Defendant

----

1. The plaintiff is an individual residing at 332 Ruiz Circle, Arlington, West Dakota.

2. The defendant is an individual residing at 11 Rolvag Way, Arlington, West Dakota.

3. On February 6, 1994, the defendant approached the plaintiff in the main hall of Arlington High School, in Arlington, West Dakota, raised his right arm with the fist clenched, and threatened to punch her if she did not stop seeing a classmate, Michael Mercutio.

4. When the plaintiff refused to agree, the defendant deliberately grabbed her by the arm, squeezed it hard, and knocked her to the ground.

5. As a result of the defendant's acts, the plaintiff suffered a bruised arm, and abrasions on both knees requiring medical treatment. She also suffered severe pain, fear, and emotional distress.

FIRST CLAIM FOR RELIEF — ASSAULT

6. The plaintiff repeats and realleges the allegations in paragraphs one to five of the complaint.

7. The defendant committed an assault on the plaintiff when he intentionally and without her consent threatened to strike her and shook his fist, placing her in fear that he was about to strike her.

8. The defendant committed a further assault when he intentionally and without her consent reached out to grab the plaintiff's arm, placing her in fear that he was about to strike her.

Figure 2–1

9. As a result of these assaults, the plaintiff suffered fear, humiliation, and emotional distress, and was unable to attend school or engage in other usual activities for two weeks.

SECOND CLAIM FOR RELIEF — BATTERY

10. The plaintiff repeats and realleges the allegations in paragraphs one to five of the complaint.

11. The defendant committed a battery upon the plaintiff when he intentionally and without her consent grabbed her arm and threw her to the ground.

12. As a result of the defendant's acts, the plaintiff suffered extensive bruises and abrasions on both knees, extensive pain and suffering, fear, humiliation, and emotional distress.

13. As a further result of the defendant's acts, the plaintiff incurred $400 in medical expenses for treatment, and was unable to return to school or engage in other usual activities for a period of two weeks.

WHEREFORE, the plaintiff seeks the following relief:

1. Compensatory damages in the amount of $8,000.

2. Punitive damages in the amount of $10,000.

3. Interest from the date of judgment as allowed by W.D. Rev. Code §14:103.

4. Her costs of suit.

The plaintiff claims trial by jury in this action.

By her attorney

_____

Luis Mendez
84 Main Street, Suite 4
Arlington, WD 58102
(901) 225-1093

Figure 2–1 (*continued*)

3

The Far Side of the Coin: Classic Defenses to Intentional Torts

Introduction

The preceding chapters describe the formal elements a plaintiff must prove in order to recover for battery and assault. These elements, it is said, are necessary to establish a prima facie case, that is, a showing sufficient to allow a jury to conclude that the tort has been committed. However, the case is not over once the plaintiff has presented evidence to establish these prima facie elements. The defendant must be heard from, and very likely, she will offer another side to the story.

The defendant may defend by simply negating one or more of the prima facie elements of the tort. For example, she may present evidence in a battery case that she never touched the plaintiff, that she did so unintentionally, or that the touching was not one that the reasonable person would find offensive under the circumstances. In other cases, however, the defendant takes the position that, *even if* the prima facie elements of the tort are shown, she is not liable anyway, because of additional facts that allow her to avoid liability. Such additional facts are often referred to as *affirmative defenses*.

Some affirmative defenses have nothing to do with the underlying incident itself. For example, if Jones sues Smith for battery, Smith might defend on the ground that the claim is barred by the statute of limitations, the statutory period within which suit must be brought on a claim. This defense asserts that, even if Jones can prove that Smith intentionally inflicted a harmful or offensive touching on her, she is not liable, because the suit was brought too late. Or, Smith might plead that Jones had signed a release from liability (a contractual agreement not to sue on the claim, usually given for a sum of money paid in settlement). Again, this defense does not rely on a showing that no battery occurred, but rather on additional facts that demonstrate that there is no longer a right to sue for the claim.

Other affirmative defenses, however, relate more directly to the events that give rise to the claim. The classic example is self-defense. In Jones's action for battery, for example, Smith might plead that she hit Jones because she was warding off a blow from Jones. If she acted in self-defense, she was privileged to inflict the harmful or offensive touching on Jones, and will not be held liable for doing so.

Another common affirmative defense to intentional tort is consent. Courts generally hold that the victim's consent bars recovery for touchings that would otherwise constitute batteries. If Jones proves that Smith slapped her in the face, Smith might plead that she and Jones were rehearsing for a play, and that Jones consented to the slap as part of the script. If this is true, Smith's act was privileged; she will not be liable even if the slap was offensive and intentional.

A number of other privileges may also constitute defenses to battery and assault claims. Police officers enjoy a privilege to use reasonable force in the course of arrest. An actor who inflicts a harmful or offensive touching may sometimes assert the defense of *necessity*, that an otherwise tortious touching was privileged because it was done to prevent a greater harm. Teachers and parents enjoy a limited privilege to use force in disciplining children. And there are others. This chapter, however, will focus on self-defense and consent as examples of the effect of privileges on tort liability.

The Privilege to Use Force in Self-Defense

Self-preservation, they say, is the first law of nature. It is not surprising, then, that the law of torts has long recognized the privilege to use force to protect oneself from an aggressor. An actor who is privileged to use force in self-defense incurs no liability for doing so, even if she inflicts serious bodily injury or death upon her assailant.

However, self-defense is a limited privilege. It is not a general license to attack an aggressor, or to respond to unwarranted provocation, or to give blow for blow; it only authorizes the use of force to prevent an impending battery or to stop one which is in progress. Suppose, for example, that Jones slaps Smith on the face and announces, "There, now we are even." Smith has no privilege of self-defense on these facts. She does not need to use force in her own defense, because she is no longer threatened with a battery. True, she has been the *victim* of one, and may sue for it, but self-defense does not authorize a tort victim to respond to force with force. It is a privilege to forestall an impending battery, not to retaliate for prior ones.

Similarly, there is no right to attack another simply because the other may deserve it. Smith may not strike Jones because she makes derogatory statements about Smith's lineage or her politics. Nor may she invoke self-defense against threats of future harm, such as a threat to attack her at a later time. In such cases, Smith has peaceful legal remedies, and is required to resort to them rather than "taking the law into her own hands" by immediate physical force.

Even where the privilege arises, it is limited: the victim of an aggressor may only use reasonable force in self-defense. The victim is not licensed to extract an "eye for an eye," but only to use the force that she reasonably believes is necessary to avert the threatened harm. Smith may not knife Jones in the ribs to avoid a slap in the face, though she would certainly be privileged to block the blow or push Jones away. Smith may not even be privileged to use the same level of force used by the initial aggressor, if less will do to prevent the contact. Remember that the purpose of self-defense is not to remedy the wrong already inflicted; such redress should be sought through criminal prosecution or intentional tort damages. Self-defense is authorized solely to prevent a further intrusion that cannot be avoided by waiting for legal redress.

On the other hand, the victim will sometimes be privileged to use *more* force than was necessary to avert a threatened battery. The privilege to use force in self-defense turns on the victim's *reasonable belief* that force is necessary, even if, in fact, it is not. If Enemy Jones raises a knife before her, Smith has no time to conduct an investigation of Jones's motives before forestalling the blow. Smith would be privileged to strike Jones if she reasonably concluded that Jones was about to stab her, even if Jones actually intended to scratch his back with the knife. Restatement (Second) of Torts §63 cmt. i.

The limits on the privilege of self-defense reflect a policy of minimizing the use of force as a means of self-protection. Arguably, this goal would be furthered by always requiring victims to retreat — that is, to run away — before using self-defense. However, courts have refused to create a duty to retreat (even if it can be done with perfect safety) before using *nondeadly* force in self-defense. Such a duty would require the victim of threatened violence to relinquish her right to walk the streets. Our culture places a high premium on personal choice and independence; consequently, a "duty to run" has not met with public or judicial acceptance. Thus, at least where nondeadly force is threatened, the victim is privileged to stand her ground and use nondeadly force in self-defense, even if retreat is feasible. Restatement (Second) of Torts §63 cmt. m.

Deadly Force In Self-Defense

While all courts recognize a limited right to self-defense, most impose additional restrictions on the right to use deadly force, that is, force that is "intended or likely to cause death or serious bodily harm." Restatement (Second) of Torts §65(1). Under the Restatement, for example, the actor may use deadly force in self-defense only if she reasonably believes that she is threatened with deadly force "which can be prevented only by the immediate use of such [deadly] force." Id. Under this widely accepted approach, there is no right to use deadly force in response to the lesser threat of nondeadly force. If Smith raises her hand to slap Jones, Jones may not shoot her dead, or swing at her head with a hammer. Jones may use nondeadly force, or retreat, or suffer the slap and sue for battery, but she is not privileged to escalate the conflict by using deadly force.

Jones may not even be privileged to use deadly force if she is attacked with deadly force. Some jurisdictions, following the Restatement, require a victim of deadly force to retreat if it is safe to do so before using deadly force against the assailant. The Restatement offers this rationale for imposing a duty to retreat:

> the interest of society in the life and efficiency of its members and in the prevention of the serious breaches of the peace involved in bloody affrays requires one attacked with a deadly weapon, except within his own dwelling place, to retreat before using force intended or likely to inflict death or serious bodily harm upon his assailant, unless he reasonably believes that there is any chance that retreat cannot be safely made.

Restatement (Second) of Torts §65 cmt. g. A majority of jurisdictions, however, reject the Restatement approach. Instead, they hold that the victim of an assault with deadly force is privileged to stand her ground and use deadly force in self-defense, even if retreat is feasible. Prosser, Wade & Schwartz, Cases and Materials on Torts 104-105 (9th ed. 1994). Even the Restatement recognizes that one threatened with deadly force in her home need not retreat. This obviously reflects the widely shared view that one's home, if not quite a castle, ought at least to be an inviolable place of refuge. The Restatement also recognizes that the victim need not retreat unless it is clearly safe to do so. If the victim has any doubt of that (as most will), she may use deadly force in self-defense.

The "Defense" of Consent

A second common affirmative defense to intentional torts is *consent*. Tort law generally accepts the maxim, *volenti non fit injuria* ("to one who is willing, no wrong is done"). Prosser & Keeton, The Law of Torts §18 at 112 (5th ed. 1984). If the victim of a harmful or offensive touching manifests consent to the contact, the defendant is usually not liable for causing it. This is an example of the premium our society places on the individual's right to craft her own fate, to choose for herself, even to make choices most of us would consider stupid or self-destructive.[1]

Although consent avoids liability, it may not be entirely accurate to call it a defense. If an element of battery is the unwelcome nature of the contact, arguably the plaintiff's consent negates a basic element of her prima facie case. See Restatement (Second) of Torts §892(1) (consent is "willingness in fact for conduct to occur"). On this reasoning, *lack of consent* should be an element of the plaintiff's prima facie case of battery, and the plaintiff should include an allegation of lack of consent in her complaint.[2] There is considerable authority that this is so. See Prosser & Keeton, 112; Harper, James & Gray, §3.10, at. 298-299; see also Restatement (Second) of Torts §10 cmt. c (plaintiff must plead lack of consent in cases involving personal interests, such as assault and battery). But some cases treat consent, like most privileges, as an affirmative defense. See, e.g., *Sims v. Alford*, 118 So. 395 (Ala. 1928).

This somewhat scholastic pleading question is less important than understanding what constitutes consent, and when it is effective to protect the actor from liability. Largely, common sense dictates the scope of consent. Common sense tells us that a person may consent to one touching but not another. Smith's acceptance of a "kiss in the moonlight" does not authorize Torres to have intercourse with her, nor does Vega's agreement to a fist fight with Jones authorize Jones to use a shotgun if he fares poorly in the battle. Common sense also tells us that one can manifest consent to a touching without signing a contract, or even uttering a word. Smith may agree to Torres's kiss with a look or a blush — and may similarly refuse without speaking.

Naturally, difficult factual issues will often arise as to whether the victim consented to the contact. However, paradoxically, the privilege does not turn on *actual* consent. Most courts hold that the defendant is privileged to make a contact where the plaintiff's words, gestures, or conduct reasonably manifest consent to it, even if she was not actually willing to be touched. Restatement (Second) of Torts §892(2). The classic case for this proposition is *O'Brien v. Cunard S.S. Co.*, 28 N.E. 266 (Mass. 1891), in which the plaintiff received a shipboard vaccination prior to entering the United States. Although she later testified that she was unwilling to be vaccinated, she had stood in a line of two hundred women waiting to be vaccinated, had watched those in front of her receive their vaccinations, and had held up her arm to receive the shot. On these facts, the court held that the doctor was "justified in his act, whatever her unexpressed feelings may have been. In determining whether she

---

1. Another example is the negligence doctrine known as "assumption of the risk," discussed in Chapter 4.

2. Note that Juliet did include this allegation in her complaint for assault and battery. See Figure 2-1, pp.34-35, paragraphs 7 and 11.

consented, he could be guided only by her overt acts and the manifestations of her feelings." Id. at 266.

Common sense also suggests that consent that is based on a fundamental misunderstanding of the facts does not evidence true acceptance of a contact. This is illustrated by two recurring scenarios. In one, a doctor obtains a patient's consent to an examination by representing that it is for treatment purposes, but actually is seeking sexual gratification. In another, the defendant obtains the plaintiff's consent to sexual intercourse without revealing that she has a communicable venereal disease. In both cases, the plaintiff's consent is invalid, since, due to the defendant's misrepresentation, (or, in the second case, failure to reveal crucial facts relevant to the plaintiff's choice) she did not appreciate the true nature of the intended contact and thus did not meaningfully consent to it.

Where the legislature has barred conduct to protect a disadvantaged class, even the plaintiff's *actual* consent may not create a privilege. For example, it has been held that consent to intercourse by a minor under the legal age of consent does not bar the minor from suing for battery. Laws of this sort are intended "to protect a definite class of persons from their own immaturity." Harper, James & Gray §3.10, at 308. They prohibit the defendant's conduct *regardless of the minor's consent*, since the minor is deemed incapable of making a proper judgment about whether to engage in the conduct. Consequently, the defendant (the party who induces the minor to engage in the conduct) is subject to criminal prosecution even if the minor consented. To reinforce this legislative policy, courts hold that the defendant should also be barred from raising the minor's consent as an affirmative defense in a tort action based on the same conduct. See Restatement (Second) of Torts §892C(2).

Consent to Medical Treatment

Consent issues often arise in the context of medical treatment, since, traditionally, even therapeutic touchings have been viewed as batteries if the patient has not consented to them. Thus, the medical cases illustrate in one frequently recurring context the consent issues discussed more generally above.

For example, the treatment cases mirror the common sense principle that consent may include one touching but not another. In *Mohr v. Williams*, 104 N.W. 12 (Minn. 1905), *overturned on other grounds by Genzel v. Halvorson*, 80 N.W.2d 854 (Minn. 1957), a physician obtained a patient's consent to operate on her right ear, but, finding the left more seriously diseased, operated on it instead. Although the surgery was carefully done, it was held a battery, since the doctor's touching went beyond the scope of contact to which the patient had consented.

Mohr was a pretty clear case of exceeding consent, but many medical consent situations are more ambiguous. A recurring scenario is the surgeon who, after commencing surgery with the consent of the patient, encounters unexpected conditions which require extension of the procedure beyond that which the patient has approved. For example, the surgeon might find it necessary, in an operation on the intestine, to remove part of it, or, in an operation for ovarian cysts, to remove the ovary. In a heart by-pass operation, the surgeon might find it necessary to make extensive, unanticipated incisions in the legs to locate suitable arteries for the by-pass procedure.

It would be nice if surgeons could satisfy the law's sense of propriety by waking the patient in such cases to obtain consent to the extension of surgery, but that would usually be impracticable or even dangerous to the patient. Ideally, such complications should be anticipated and addressed in advance, by obtaining the patient's consent (or refusal) to various predictable scenarios the surgeon may encounter. However, this is often not possible, because there is no reason to anticipate the extension. It is common practice for physicians to seek consent from a relative of the patient in such situations. Although it is not entirely clear that such "substituted consent" is valid, patients are much less likely to challenge a decision in which their family members have concurred. Thus, this practice greatly reduces the likelihood that suit will be brought based on lack of consent.

If no relative is available, the cases support a limited privilege to extend the surgery within the area of the initial incision, unless the extension involves the destruction of a bodily function, such as the amputation of a limb or loss of reproductive function.[3] See Prosser & Keeton at 118; Harper, James & Gray, §3.10, at 306. While it is sometimes said that there is implied consent to such extensions, (see Harper, James & Gray, §3.10, at 306) this privilege is not really based upon consent — which, by definition, has not been given. It arises from the exigencies of the situation, which allow the surgeon to choose for the patient based upon what the reasonable patient would consent to if she could be consulted.

A related issue is the emergency privilege to treat an unconscious patient, for example, the victim of an auto accident or an assault who requires immediate treatment, but is unconscious due to her injuries. If no relative is able to consent, the cases recognize a privilege to render such treatment if the reasonable person would consent to it, there is no reason to believe that the particular patient would not, and delay would involve a risk of death or serious bodily harm to the patient. See Prosser & Keeton at 117.[4]

The advance of medical science has also spawned a host of difficult consent issues now analyzed under the rubric of the "right to refuse treat-

---

3. Even here, the surgeon may be privileged if delay would itself lead to death or loss of a bodily function.

4. Here again, there may be a stricter standard if the treatment involves destruction of a major bodily function, as, for example, an amputation. In such cases, the privilege may only attach if delaying treatment would risk death or very serious consequences to the health of the patient. Prosser & Keeton, §18, at 117-118.

ment" or the "right to die." Such cutting edge issues take us far afield from traditional battery law, but they do reiterate, in an extreme context, the fundamental value our society places on personal autonomy. Most courts recognize the right of a competent adult to refuse treatment, even life-saving treatment, based on common law battery principles or the constitutional right of privacy or liberty. See *Cruzan v. Missouri Dept. of Health*, 497 U.S. 261, 269-279 (1990) (reviewing cases based on consent and other theories). These cases reflect the same right to autonomy in making choices concerning one's body that underlies the traditional consent privilege in battery cases. Most of the current issues in this area involve not *whether* the individual has the right to refuse treatment, but *how* one must manifest that decision (for example, by advance health care directives or "living wills") and under what circumstances others, such as family members, may exercise a "substituted judgment" for a patient who is unable to make the decision herself.

The examples that follow explore the application of self-defense and consent to some fairly straightforward cases — and a few be-Fuddling ones as well.

EXAMPLES

The Best Defense. . . .

1.   Zilla is standing on a street corner when Kong, an old enemy, spies her. Kong advances toward her, shaking her fists and threatening to knock her down. Zilla, who is bigger, pushes at Kong with both hands as she is about to be hit, knocking Kong down. Unexpectedly, Kong falls on the stub of a metal post that had been cut off several inches above the sidewalk, and is gouged in the back. The wound requires eighteen stitches and lands Kong in the hospital for three weeks. Is Zilla liable to her?

2.   Stein insolently threatens to knock Franken's hat off and lunges toward her, reaching for the hat. To prevent Stein from knocking the hat off, Franken punches her in the stomach, causing substantial bruises to Stein. In the process, she cuts her knuckles on Stein's belt buckle.

    a. Is Franken liable to Stein, and if so, for what?

    b. Is Stein liable to Franken, and if so, for what?

Never Sound Retreat

3.   Zilla is sitting in the front seat of her car, with the door open. Kong, an old enemy, sees her from a hundred yards down the street and charges at her with a knife. Zilla steps out of the car with a baseball bat, swings hard at Kong with the bat, and hits her.

    a. Assume that the principles of the Restatement (Second) §65, requiring retreat in certain deadly force cases, apply. Who is liable, and for what?

    b. Assume that the incident takes place in a state that does not require retreat before the use of deadly force. Is Zilla liable to Kong?

    c. Assume again that Kong's attack takes place in a jurisdiction that does not require retreat, even from an attack with deadly force. Zilla jumps out of the car and swings at Kong's head with the bat, but Kong swerves as the bat approaches her, and the blow only causes a large bruise on Kong's shoulder. Is Zilla liable to her?

4.   Zilla is standing on a street corner when she sees Kong charging at her with a knife. Convinced that she can evade the knife, she confronts Kong and deftly trips her as she lunges forward. Kong falls on her face and suffers bruises and lacerations. Assume that Kong's assault takes place in a jurisdiction that has adopted the Restatement (Second) approach, requiring retreat in certain deadly force cases. Is Zilla liable?

5.   Goliath meets David, who is considerably smaller than him, on the street. Goliath objects to David's coat, which has a picture of the American flag covered over with a peace sign. He threatens to tear the flag right off the coat while it is on David's back, and moves toward him in obvious anger. David, convinced that it is his only means of self-defense, stabs Goliath with a pitchfork he is carrying.

    a. Is either party liable to the other, and if so, for what?

    b. On the same facts, assume that Goliath sees the pitchfork coming. To prevent being impaled, he hits David on the head with a two-by-four he is carrying. David suffers a concussion. Is Goliath liable for the injury to David?

    c. Assume that Galahad comes on the scene and sees David rushing at Goliath with the pitchfork. To protect Goliath, he swings at David with a crowbar, hitting him on the head and injuring him. Is Galahad liable to David?

    d. Assume that David defended himself by pushing at Goliath with his arms outstretched, in an effort to knock Goliath down. Goliath, surprised by David's aggressive response, swings at him, knocking him down. Who is liable to whom?

    e. On the facts of Example 5d, suppose that Galahad happens on the scene, sees David about to push Goliath, and hits him in the stomach. Is Galahad liable to David for battery?

Judge Fudd on the Cutting Edge of the Law

6.   Zilla is sitting on the bench at a softball game when she sees Kong bearing down on her with a knife. Unable to retreat, Zilla wards off the blow by hitting Kong with a baseball bat. On later examination, it turns out that the knife Kong was carrying was a child's toy, made of soft rubber.

Kong sues Zilla for battery. The case arises in a jurisdiction that does not require retreat before the use of deadly force. At trial, Judge Fudd instructs the jury as follows:

> You are instructed that the defendant was privileged to use that level of force reasonably necessary to defend herself from a threat of bodily harm.
>
> If you find that the defendant was attacked with nondeadly force, then the defendant was only privileged to use nondeadly force in self-defense. If you find that the defendant was attacked with nondeadly force, and that the defendant used deadly force in self-defense, then you must find for the plaintiff.
>
> If you find that the defendant was attacked with deadly force, then the defendant was privileged to use that level of force reasonably necessary for her self-defense, which may include deadly force. If you find that the defendant used more force than reasonably necessary, you must find for the plaintiff.

Who will object to the instruction, and why?

Consent or Coercion?

7.   Franken approaches Stein in the street and threatens him: "If you don't hightail it out of here I will give you two black eyes." Stein refuses to budge, and Franken socks him in the eye. Has Stein consented to the touching?

8.   Franken threatens to tweak Stein's nose. Stein growls in response: "If you do, I will break your jaw with this hammer!" Franken proceeds with his tweak, and, true to his word, Stein hits Franken in the jaw and breaks it. Does Franken have a battery claim against Stein?

Macho Consent

9.   Hulk, a wrestler, brags to his friends at a bar about how strong he is. He braces himself and invites them to "just try to push me over." Brower, with a mighty shove, pushes at Hulk with both hands. Hulk loses his balance, stumbles backwards, and falls against the footrest in front of the bar. He suffers a separated shoulder which ends his wrestling career. He sues Brower for battery. Is Brower liable?

Shooting from the Hip

10. Seaman is about to undergo surgery to remove a bony growth on his hip. As he is being prepped for the operation, Dr. Langone, the surgeon, comes in to see him. She presents Seaman with the following consent form, which Seaman signs:

1. I, _Walter Seaman_, hereby give my authorization and consent to an operation to be performed on me on _September 1_, 1994, by Dr. _Paula Langone_ for the purpose of correcting the following condition: _remove bony growth from right hip_

2. I also consent to any further procedures, during, preceding, and after the operation, which Dr. _Langone_ deems necessary or desirable in order to correct the above-specified conditions or to remedy any other unhealthy condition she may encounter during the operation.[5]

Langone proceeds with the surgery. During the surgery, she discovers — as is commonly the case — that the hip joint is badly deteriorated, and performs a total hip replacement instead.

Seaman never regains full use of the hip. Upset that Langone had decided to do the replacement operation, he sues for battery. Which of the following arguments for the defendant do you find persuasive?

a. "This procedure was authorized even without the consent form. Virtually all patients would consent in this circumstance, since there was hardly any chance of improvement in function without the hip replacement. Thus, since the reasonable person would consent, I was justified in inferring that Seaman would as well."

b. "Even if the consent form is not valid, it would be unreasonable to interrupt this complex, invasive surgery to wake the patient and ask for consent. Frankly, as an experienced surgeon, I would never do it: There is a substantial risk in the surgery itself, and the incision would have to be opened a second time, which would multiply the chances of infection and retard the patient's recovery."

c. "The patient signed the consent form, which very clearly authorizes me to go beyond the procedure contemplated. Since the hip replacement was 'necessary or desirable to correct' the patient's problem, it was authorized by the consent."

d. "I'm a surgeon, not a lawyer. I acted under the reasonable belief that the consent form provided proper authority for me to extend the surgery if it were indicated. Consent, if apparently manifested, need not actually exist at all. The actor's reasonable conclusion that consent has been given is enough."

---

5. Adapted, with changes, from a similar form in 15 Am. Jur. 2d Legal Forms, §202:161 (1993 revision).

You're the Doc

11. Seaman is about to have his hip surgery. Dr. Langone, fully aware of the need (both legal and ethical) to inform Seaman of the risks involved in the surgery, comes in to discuss these with Seaman. As she begins her spiel about possible side effects and unexpected problems that may arise, Seaman stops her. "Doctor," he says, "I'm a businessman; I know stocks and bonds. You're a doctor; you know surgery. I'm sure there are risks involved, but I trust you. Do what has to be done for me and that'll be fine with me."

    a. During the operation, Langone determines that Seaman's hip has deteriorated to the point where a full hip replacement is necessary. She proceeds to do it. Seaman, upset with the result, sues her for battery. Is his claim barred by consent?

    b. During the surgery, Langone discovers that a major artery in Seaman's thigh has deteriorated, and should be excised. She does so. Later, Seaman has pain in the leg and sues Langone for excising the artery without consent. Is the claim barred by consent?

Damned If You Do. . . .

12. Willis is in an auto accident and is brought to the hospital unconscious. Because he has sustained internal injuries, Dr. Langone concludes that good medical practice requires immediate surgery. However, Willis is unconscious. Langone therefore talks with Willis's wife, but she refuses to agree to the surgery, on the ground that she is not sure that it is necessary and that surgery "gives her the creeps." What should Langone do?

EXPLANATIONS

The Best Defense. . . .

1. This example is reminiscent of several from the first two chapters, in which more injury than intended results from the actor's intended blow. Here, Zilla intended the push, but she did not intend to impale Kong on the metal post. As in the earlier examples, Zilla's liability turns on whether she committed a tort in the first place. If she did, she is liable for the resulting harm, though greater than anticipated. If her act was not tortious, she is not liable, although serious injury resulted.

    Here, of course, whether Zilla's act is tortious turns on whether she was privileged to push Kong down in self-defense. It certainly appears that she was. She was threatened with nondeadly force, a push, and responded with appropriate nondeadly force to ward off the blow. Since she was privileged to push Kong, the touching is not a battery, and Zilla is not liable, even though serious injury resulted.

2a. When Franken acted, she was threatened with an *offensive* touching to an object intimately associated with her body, which qualifies as a battery.

Restatement (Second) of Torts §18 cmt. c. However, Franken was not threatened with a *harmful* touching. To forestall the offensive contact, she used force which was likely to be and was harmful to Stein.

Even though Franken was not threatened with harm, she was privileged to use force in self-defense. Victims have the right to protect themselves from offensive touchings as well as harmful ones. Even if the force reasonably needed to prevent the offensive touching may cause harm, it is still privileged.

The further question, however, is whether the punch in the stomach went beyond the force reasonably necessary to prevent Stein's threatened battery. If such a punch constitutes deadly force, it was excessive by definition: A tort victim is not authorized to use deadly force to avoid the infliction of nondeadly force, and Stein's threat to Franken's hat was surely nondeadly. This may present a question of fact. If Franken has a black belt in karate, her blow could perhaps have caused serious bodily harm. Absent such unlikely facts, however, a punch in the stomach is not the kind of force "intended or likely to cause death or serious bodily harm."

Even if the blow is not deadly, it may still be excessive, if it was obvious that less would suffice to save Franken's hat. This, too, may depend on the facts, such as the relative size of the parties, where the incident took place, and what other means Franken had to stop Stein. Franken is entitled to use such nondeadly force as she *reasonably believes* necessary for her own defense under the circumstances, even if later reflection suggests that something less might have done the trick. In deciding whether the force was excessive, a jury would doubtless give much deference to the fact that Franken must choose her means of defense on the spur of the moment, without time to reflect on what might be the least invasive way of deterring Stein's battery. Most likely, Franken's punch was privileged, and she would not be liable to Stein.

b. Stein is certainly liable to Franken for assault, since she placed Franken in fear of an unwanted touching when she rushed at Franken. The more difficult question is whether she is liable for the injury to Franken's hand. Her assault did cause Franken to defend herself and suffer the cut, but it is awkward to conclude that Stein, who never touched Franken, has committed a battery.

Presumably, Stein would be liable for Franken's cut as a consequential injury from her assault on Franken. Courts generally hold defendants liable for unintended consequences of their intentional torts, as well as intended consequences. Franken's injury is a consequence of Stein's assault, even though it was not the invasion Stein meant to cause, and even though it happened through Franken's deliberate, privileged act of self-defense.

Never Sound Retreat

3a. Section 65 of the Second Restatement requires a person attacked with deadly force to retreat, if she may safely do so, before responding with deadly force in self-defense. The facts here suggest that Zilla could have retreated by closing the car door and driving away. If this is true, she would not have a privilege to defend herself with a baseball bat. If her blow is not privileged, it is a battery, so Zilla would be liable to Kong for the injury she inflicts.

Kong would also be liable to Zilla. Her charge down the street with the knife is clearly an assault — Zilla's overreaction doesn't change that fact, though it makes Zilla liable as well.

b. As the introduction indicates, many states do not require retreat before the use of deadly force. Yet Zilla might be liable even in a jurisdiction which takes this view. A threat of deadly force does not automatically authorize the use of similar force in self-defense. Rather, it gives the victim a privilege to use force she reasonably believes necessary to prevent the threatened battery. That may include deadly force if such force appears necessary, but here Zilla could presumably have prevented the battery by simply closing and locking the car door. If so, she is not authorized to do more simply because Kong's attack threatens more serious harm.[6]

c. Here Zilla did not cause serious injury or death, just a bruise, due to Kong's evasive action. However, if Zilla exceeded her privilege, under the analysis in 3b, above, by using deadly force unnecessarily, her blow is a battery. Whether her blow was privileged turns on the level of force used, not the amount of injury caused. If she exceeded her privilege of self-defense by using deadly force unnecessarily, the touching is a battery and Zilla is liable for whatever injury results. Compare Example 1, in which the touching was privileged, and Zilla was therefore *not* liable even though more harm resulted than she expected.

4.   Here, Zilla chooses to stand her ground and defend herself rather than retreat. But this example is different from Example 3a, because the force Zilla uses — tripping her assailant — is probably nondeadly force. The Restatement does not impose a general duty to retreat from an assailant threatening deadly force. Rather, it requires the victim to retreat before *using deadly force herself*, if retreat is safe. If Zilla thinks she can prevent the injury by nondeadly force, she may do so. Thus, Zilla's act is probably privileged.

5a.   Goliath is liable to David for assault. He has no right to redesign David's jacket, and his move toward David reasonably puts David in fear that he is about to do so by force. But Goliath's assault does not justify David's use of deadly force in self-defense. The threat to David was of nondeadly force. Such a threat does not authorize him to use deadly force in self-defense. Thus, David is also liable to Goliath since he exceeded the scope of his privilege of self-defense.

---

6. Might a court hold that Zilla need not close the door because that would constitute "retreat"? Probably not; by closing the door, Zilla is not running away (a loss of face which many jurisdictions refuse to compel) but simply blocking the battery without directly exerting force against the aggressor.

The facts suggest that David, a smaller man than Goliath, used the only means at his disposal — his pitchfork — which would avoid the invasion of his person. However, this does not change the result: David is not authorized to use deadly force to prevent the threat of nondeadly force, even if his only alternatives are to run or submit to the battery. See Restatement (Second) of Torts §63 cmt. j. While this may be humiliating to David, the policy reason for this conclusion appears sound: It is better that David suffer temporary humiliation and be vindicated later in court, than cause a serious injury or death to Goliath to prevent a fairly minor intrusion on David's rights.

This presupposes, of course, that David does not fear anything beyond having his coat ripped. If Goliath's conduct leads David to reasonably fear serious bodily injury himself, he would be entitled to use similar force in self-defense.[7] In order to determine the scope of David's privilege, it is necessary to characterize the type of force *Goliath* has threatened — or, more accurately, the type of force David reasonably anticipates. It is often difficult to say after the fact that the victim was unreasonable in perceiving a threat of deadly force, even if the assailant really intended something less — which is a forceful argument for aggressors to think twice before striking.

b. Here, Goliath is the initial, nondeadly aggressor, and David overreacts by using deadly force to protect himself from nondeadly force. By overreacting, he becomes a batterer himself, and would be liable to Goliath for any injuries resulting from his excessive force.

If Goliath is now the victim of a battery, it follows, doesn't it, that Goliath has a privilege to use self-defense against David's battery? Yet, Goliath is the original aggressor here. Had he not provoked the fight, he would have had no need for self-defense. If Goliath is privileged to respond to the pitchfork with deadly force, he might provoke a quarrel fully expecting David to overreact, and then use his privilege to injure or kill him. It seems like poor policy to authorize Goliath to do that. On the other hand, it hardly seems sensible to require Goliath to meekly accept his fate at the hands of a pitchfork, either.

A middle ground would require Goliath, as the original aggressor, to retreat, if possible, before using deadly force against the victim-turned-aggressor. Apparently, the criminal cases have taken this approach. See Model Penal Code §3.04(2)(b)(1) and cmt.4(b) (Proposed Official Draft 1962), J. Dressler, Understanding Criminal Law §18.02[b][2][c], at 195 (1987). The Second Restatement of Torts takes the position that Goliath is privileged to use deadly force in self-defense once David converts the nondeadly quarrel into a deadly one. "One who intentionally invades or attempts to invade any of another's interests of personality, does not by

---

7. Unless he has a duty to retreat, as he might in jurisdictions following the Restatement (Second) of Torts §65.

his wrongdoing forfeit his privilege to defend himself by any means which would be privileged were he innocent of wrongdoing against any excess of force which the other uses in self-defense." Restatement (Second) of Torts §71(c) cmt. d. However, since no privilege arises under the Second Restatement to use deadly force if retreat is feasible, the Restatement position appears to echo the criminal cases. If this is true, Goliath would only be liable if he could have retreated safely before invoking the two-by-four.

c. Here Galahad, an interloper, comes on the scene, concludes that David is the aggressor, and intervenes to protect Goliath. If his interpretation were correct, there would be no doubt of his right to come to Goliath's aid. Tort law provides a privilege to defend others threatened with battery as well as to defend oneself. Restatement (Second) of Torts §76.

However, here Galahad is wrong; David is not the initial aggressor, he is acting in self-defense (but exceeding his privilege by using deadly force). Courts have taken two approaches to the situation in which an intervenor acts to protect an apparent victim of a tort (here Goliath) who was actually the initial aggressor. Some courts say that the intervenor may act on her reasonable belief that a battery is about to be committed. Under that rule, Galahad's act would be privileged, since it reasonably appeared to Galahad that David's attack was a battery. Other courts say that the intervenor steps into the shoes of the apparent victim, in this case, Goliath. Prosser & Keeton §20, at 130-131. Under this approach, Galahad would only be privileged to use deadly force to defend Goliath if Goliath were privileged to do so himself. If Goliath had no privilege of self-defense, Galahad's intervention would be battery.

Even under this second, shoe-stepping rule, Galahad's act may have been privileged. If Goliath had no chance to retreat, he was privileged to respond to David's pitchfork with deadly force, even though he was the initial aggressor. See Example 5b. If so, then Galahad shares Goliath's privilege.

d. This is like Example 5b in that Goliath, the original aggressor, responds to David's self-defensive efforts by defensive efforts of his own. Here, however, David has not exceeded his privilege: He is using a reasonable method to ward off Goliath's initial attack. Thus, David is not a batterer; consequently, Goliath is not privileged to act in self-defense; here he must either retreat or suffer David's blow. If he does more, he is liable, while David is not.

e. The outcome of this case will depend on the approach the jurisdiction takes to defense of a third person. If, under the relevant law, the intervenor is authorized to act on his reasonable perception, Galahad would be privileged, since David appeared to be the aggressor. If the law of the jurisdiction only gives Galahad a privilege to defend Goliath if Goliath would have a privilege of self-defense (the "shoe-stepping" approach), Galahad would not be privileged and would be liable for battery.

Judge Fudd on the Cutting Edge of the Law

6.   Judge Fudd's instruction is incorrect for several related reasons that would seriously prejudice Zilla's case. First, the instruction suggests she must have *actually* been attacked with deadly force in order to have a privilege to use deadly force in self-defense. This is not always true: Zilla would have the right to use deadly force if she *reasonably believed* that she was threatened with deadly force. See Restatement (Second) of Torts §65 (premising right to use deadly force on reasonable belief that assailant threatens deadly force).

Second, Judge Fudd's instruction makes her privilege turn on whether the force she used was *actually* necessary to repel Kong's attack. Because Kong's knife was harmless, Zilla did not actually have to use deadly force to avoid it. However, she may have *reasonably believed* that such force was necessary for her self-defense, if she thought the knife was real. Because an assault victim has no time to verify her perceptions of the force with which she is threatened, the law allows her to act on her reasonable belief that deadly force is necessary. Because Judge Fudd's instruction does not allow the jury to consider Zilla's state of mind in determining whether she was privileged, it is improper.

Such distinctions may appear hypertechnical, but many verdicts in tort cases are reversed for such subtle mistakes in instructing the jury. The be-Fuddled instructions throughout this book should give you useful practice in reading jury instructions critically. If you acquire this skill, sometime down the road you will be glad that you did.

Consent or Coercion?

7.   This example is reminiscent of the conditional threat example (Example 7) in Chapter 2. As in that example, the aggressor here threatens to hit the victim if she does not comply with a condition. As in those examples, the condition ("hightail it out of here") is one which the aggressor has no right to impose. In Chapter 2 we concluded that such threats are assaults. By the same logic, the aggressor commits a battery if she follows through on the threat.

Obviously, this analysis of conditional threats compels the conclusion that Stein does not consent to Franken's punch by standing his ground. Franken has no right to force Stein to choose between his freedom of movement and a punch in the eye. His refusal to comply with this impermissible condition does not constitute consent to the ensuing blow, which is an obvious battery. Nor would the reasonable person construe his act of standing his ground as a manifestation of consent. The more logical inference is that Stein simply refuses to be bullied.

8.   Here, Stein's use of deadly force is clearly excessive, since he was only threatened with nondeadly force. However, Stein warned Franken of his intent to use excessive force in self-defense if Franken touched him. Stein

then acted with knowledge of Stein's intent. Does Franken, by going forward with his battery with knowledge of Stein's intent, consent to Stein's overreaction?

Almost certainly he does not. Franken may be aware of Stein's intent, but he is hardly willing to be hit; nor would the reasonable person in Stein's position infer that Franken was willing to be hit simply because he proceeded with the quarrel in the face of a warning. Put another way, it is very doubtful that a warning that the actor intends to react with excessive force if provoked can create a consent privilege to use such force. Most courts would hold Franken liable for battery for using excessive force here, even though he had threatened to use it if Stein touched him. Cf. Restatement (Second) of Torts §85 illus. 1 (warning of spring gun to prevent trespass does not avert liability for resulting injury from its use).

Macho Consent

9.   Forgive me for belaboring the distinction between *contacts* and *consequences*. Here, Hulk, for his own macho reasons, has invited his friends to try to knock him over. He is willing that they should try, though he does not expect any of them to succeed. He has consented to the exact contact that Brower has imposed, though he did not anticipate the harmful consequence (the separated shoulder) of the contact. Since he consented to the contact, it is not tortious, and Brower is not liable despite the ensuing injury.

Shooting From the Hip

10a. This argument appears to be based on the the premise that Langone need not ask for Seaman's consent where it is obvious that the reasonable person would consent. The argument is unimpressive. The privilege of consent is based on the *individual patient's* acceptance of the contact, not on the fact that most patients would agree to it. The value our society places on personal autonomy supports the individual's right to make a choice that is different from that of the hypothetical reasonable person. This is well illustrated by the cases upholding the right of patients to refuse blood transfusions, a very widely accepted therapy that some patients refuse on religious or other grounds.

Langone's argument would change the question from whether the patient *did* consent to whether the reasonable person under the circumstances *would* consent. If that were the standard, the surgeon would not have to seek the patient's consent at all, but only to assess what the hypothetical reasonable person would do in similar circumstances. This would not be a consent privilege, but a privilege to make a substituted judgment for the patient based on whether the hypothetical "reasonable person" would consent.

b. This argument appears to invoke the privilege discussed in the introduction, to extend a surgery already in progress if the conditions encountered require it, without sewing up the patient to obtain consent. As the introduction indicates, courts have established a limited privilege to extend surgery within the area of the initial incision to remedy *unanticipated* problems revealed by the surgery. Langone's counsel will doubtless make much of the following language from one of the leading cases, *Kennedy v. Parrott*, 90 S.E.2d 754, 759 (N.C. 1956):

> In major internal operations, both the patient and the surgeon know that the exact condition of the patient cannot be finally and definitely diagnosed until after the patient is completely anesthetized and the incision has been made. In such case the consent — in the absence of proof to the contrary — will be construed as general in nature and the surgeon may extend the operation to remedy any abnormal or diseased condition in the area of the original incision whenever he, in the exercise of his sound professional judgment, determines that correct surgical procedure dictates and requires such an extension. . . .

Despite this strong language, Langone's argument may well fail. This is not a situation in which an unexpected condition first becomes apparent during surgery. The example indicates that bone deterioration requiring a full replacement is common in patients with Seaman's problem. Thus, it would be practical for Langone to discuss this foreseeable scenario in advance with the patient and obtain consent to the replacement if required. Through this procedure, the demands of good health care and the patient's autonomy can both be served. By failing to discuss this scenario with Seaman, Langone has foreclosed Seaman's opportunity to choose for himself.

This is akin to, but slightly different from the typical informed consent case, in which the patient claims that her consent was not effective because she was not informed of possible side effects of surgery which, had she been aware of them, would have caused her to refuse the treatment. Here, Seaman was not informed of a common *extension* of the surgery. But the underlying principle, that where possible the patient should be given all the relevant facts to make a rational choice, is much the same.

c. Langone is certainly right that this consent form is broad enough to encompass extension to a full hip replacement. The question, of course, is whether a court will enforce a consent clause this broad. Certainly, one can hypothesize circumstances under which the court would *not* enforce the clause. Suppose, for example, that Langone waltzed into Seaman's room an hour before the surgery was scheduled, described the surgery as routine, and indicated that Seaman just had to "complete a few forms" before they could proceed. On these facts, most courts would conclude that Seaman's signature does not manifest a meaningful consent to this unexplained extension of surgery. The privilege of consent is based on the patient's "willingness in fact" (Restatement (Second) of Torts §892(1)) that the touching occur;

cursory presentation of a form on a clipboard, in the coercive context of imminent surgery, would not fill the bill.

On the other hand, the circumstances might indicate that Seaman signed this form with a full understanding that a full replacement might be done. If Langone spent an hour with him explaining the details, possible extensions, and complications of the procedure, a court would likely conclude that his signature on the form reflected a meaningful consent to the more extensive surgery, in light of the parties' prior discussions. But it is certainly unwarranted to conclude that the consent avoids liability simply because it is broad enough on its face to encompass what Langone actually did.[8] See B. Furrow, S. Johnson, T. Jost, R. Schwartz, Liability and Quality Issues in Health Care 377-378 (1991) (summarizing study which concludes that consent forms "played an insignificant role" in the medical decisionmaking process, and were generally treated as a mere ritual confirming a decision already made).

d. This is a very interesting argument. Langone argues that, even if the consent form is not enforceable because it is too broad, was signed without adequate information, or was extracted under coercive circumstances, she *reasonably believed* that it was valid, since it clearly authorizes more extensive procedures. See Restatement (Second) of Torts §892(2) (words which are reasonably understood to manifest consent are effective as consent). Langone, after all, is a doctor, not a lawyer. She is hardly in a position to make close judgments about the enforceability of a general consent form. She presented an apparently appropriate form to Seaman, who signed it. From Langone's point of view, this reasonably looks like consent to the more extensive procedure. Cf. *O'Brien v. Cunard S.S. Co.*, 28 N.E. 266 (Mass. 1891), in which the doctor was protected by the patient's reasonable manifestation of consent.

If Seaman was adequately informed of the nature and risks of the surgery, this argument might carry the day, even if he did not fully understand what was to be done. Certainly doctors have to act; they cannot obtain court approval every time they perform surgery. However, in cases where no information is provided to the patient, or the consent is extracted under coercive circumstances, Langone's argument would negate the basic principle that consent is based on the actual willingness of the patient after being informed of the relevant facts. If the broad consent form here were simply presented

8. This case should be distinguished from "informed consent" cases. Here, the issue is whether Seaman consented to a hip replacement at all. By contrast, in informed consent cases the patient admits that she consented to the procedure performed, but claims that the doctor did not provide her with sufficient information about the risks and consequences to make a proper judgment about whether to consent. Informed consent cases are generally viewed as negligence cases — based on failure to live up to the professional standard of care in disclosing risks — while cases in which the patient claims that the procedure was not authorized at all are still frequently analyzed under battery law and the consent privilege.

to the patient without any accompanying explanation, most courts would reject Dr. Langone's "apparent consent" argument.

You're the Doc

11a. In this example the patient effectively delegates the decisionmaking to his doctor, on the ground that the doctor knows best how to treat his condition, and should use her best judgment in doing so. There is no bar to a patient making this choice, if it is deliberately made. Presumably, the autonomy to make decisions about one's body also includes the right to allow someone else to do it for you: That principle is frequently honored in various substituted consent situations, in which a patient designates a family member to make health-care decisions for him if he is incapacitated. Naturally, a court would look for signs of coercion or misunderstanding in reviewing a situation such as the one in the example, but absent such problems Seaman's delegation of the decision is probably effective.

b. This case may be different. While Seaman has apparently delegated to Langone the authority to make some decisions concerning his treatment, presumably there is a limit to her authority. Surely Langone could not give him a new nose or install a pacemaker while Seaman is anesthetized.

The scope of Seaman's consent will be construed in the context of the discussions between him and Langone, and the purpose of his treatment. The jury will have to decide, as a matter of fact, whether Langone would reasonably have understood Seaman's consent to extend beyond repair of the hip to performance of a different procedure in the same general surgical field. A major consideration will presumably be whether the artery problem was contributing to Seaman's symptoms. If it was, the inference is stronger that Seaman meant to authorize Langone to deal with it as well as the anticipated bone problem. If it was not, Dr. Langone's act might be held an unrelated procedure which she could not reasonably conclude that Seaman had authorized.

Damned If You Do. . . .

12. In the typical "emergency privilege" case, the physician is privileged to provide emergency treatment if the patient is unable to consent, if good medical practice calls for immediate treatment, and if the reasonable person would consent to it. If Willis's wife had not been available, Langone would probably have been privileged to proceed with the operation under this emergency privilege. But Willis's wife *was* available and refused to consent. What should Langone do?

Many sources suggest that the consent of a relative to medical treatment of an incompetent patient is effective and is widely relied upon in medical practice. See, e.g., Curran, Hall & Kaye, Health Care Law, Forensic Science, and Public Policy 1020 (4th ed. 1990) (noting "universal" use of spouse as substitute decisionmaker in such cases). However, in the usual case, the spouse *gives* consent, so there is no conflict between what the physician wishes to do and the spouse's choice. Consequently, the decision is not often challenged. If it were, it is not entirely clear that spousal consent would protect the defendant from liability. See *Gravis v. Physicians and Surgeons Hosp. of Alice*, 427 S.W.2d 310 (Texas 1968) (suggesting that husband does not have automatic authority to consent for wife).

Unlike the usual case, Langone and Mrs. Willis are at odds on whether to operate. If we assume that a spouse has the authority to consent to treatment of her incompetent husband, then it seems that she should also have the authority to *refuse* to consent: It hardly seems logical that the relative's decision should be honored only when she agrees with the doctor. Consequently, it appears that Langone would have to desist, since she would commit a battery if she operated without permission. This would doubtless be very difficult for the surgeon to accept, if she views immediate surgery as necessary. It is one thing for the patient himself to make treatment decisions that the physician deems unwise, but it is another to see the patient's health jeopardized by the decision of a relative with no medical expertise (and even, perhaps, with motives unrelated to the patient's health.)

Very likely Langone's lawyers would advise her on these facts that she should not go forward in face of Willis's refusal, but should go to court to seek a judicial determination of her right to proceed. While the courts usually honor a patient's right to refuse treatment, they are a good deal more likely to put aside the decision of a family member, which may not accurately reflect the patient's own views. (Here, for example, the fact that surgery gives Mrs. Willis "the creeps" should not determine whether surgery should be performed on Mr. Willis.)

Some states have enacted statutes which expressly authorize relatives to consent for an incompetent patient. See, e.g., Ark. Code Ann. §20-9-602 (Michie 1987 & Supp. 1993); Idaho Code §39-4303 (1948 & Supp. 1993); Miss. Code Ann. §41-41-3 (Supp. 1993). Interestingly, the Arkansas statute provides that the court may consent to treatment if a person authorized to consent for another has refused. See Ark. Code Ann. §20-9-604(a). Under a provision like this, the court could supersede Mrs. Willis's decision not to allow surgery. The same result would likely be reached on common law principles in a state that had no statute on point.

PART TWO

The Concept of Negligence

4

One can be negligent without being "liable for negligence."

That Odious Character: The Reasonable Person

Introduction

Surely the most common basis for tort liability is negligent conduct. This chapter is about the meaning of negligence.

Let's begin by clarifying our terminology. Courts often speak of a "claim for negligence." In this sense, negligence is a tort with four elements: (1) a duty of reasonable care, (2) breach of that duty, (3) causation, and (4) resulting damages. A plaintiff must prove all four of these elements to "recover on a claim for negligence." But courts also use the term "negligence" in a related but more limited sense, to refer to the failure to live up to the standard of due care. In this sense, "negligence" refers to the *second element* of a claim for negligence, breach of the standard of due care. To say that the defendant "was negligent" is to say that he failed to exercise reasonable care under the circumstances.

duty
breach
Cause
damages

Since courts do not always distinguish these two meanings of "negligence," students often get confused between the tort of negligence and the concept of negligence as a breach of the standard of due care. A defendant may be negligent without necessarily being "liable for negligence," (if, for example, the plaintiff does not suffer damages from the defendant's failure to exercise due care). It is important to distinguish the *tort* of negligence from the second *element* of that tort. This chapter is about the latter, the failure to live up to the standard of reasonable care.

The Standard of Reasonable Care

The basic premise of negligence law is that we generally owe our fellow citizens a duty to exercise reasonable care in the conduct of our own affairs. This duty does not require that we avoid all injury to others, but only that we avoid injuring others by carelessness in our actions. Since the duty owed is the duty to exercise reasonable care, that duty is breached (element (2) of a negligence claim) by failing to exercise reasonable care:

> Negligence is the omission to do something which a reasonable man, [sic] guided upon those considerations which ordinarily regulate the conduct of human affairs, would do, or doing something which a prudent and reasonable man [sic] would not do.

Blyth v. Proprietors of the Birmingham Waterworks, 156 Eng. Rep. 1047, 1049 (1856). See also Restatement (Second) of Torts §283 (to avoid being negligent, actor must act as "a reasonable man [sic] under like circumstances").

Who is this "excellent but odious character,"[1] the Reasonable Person? He is a model of propriety and common sense, a person of sound judgment who acts at all times with "ordinary prudence, . . . reasonable prudence, or some other blend of reason and caution." Prosser & Keeton §32, at 174.

> He is an ideal, a standard, the embodiment of all those qualities which we demand of the good citizen. . . He is one who invariably looks where he is going, and is careful to examine the immediate foreground before he executes a leap or bound; who neither stargazes nor is lost in meditation when approaching trapdoors or the margin of a dock; . . . who never mounts a moving omnibus and does not alight from any car while the train is in motion, . . . and will inform himself of the history and habits of a dog before administering a caress; . . . who never drives his ball till those in front of him have definitely vacated the putting-green; . . . who uses nothing except in moderation, and even while he flogs his child is meditating only on the golden mean.[2]

Odious indeed, the Reasonable Person is a fiction, an impossible creature who always exercises proper self-restraint and weighs appropriately not only his own interests, but those of others as well in regulating his affairs.

How the Reasonable Person Thinks

The reasonable person standard seems self-evident, even tautological: Of course we should all act reasonably to avoid injury to others. But the standard

---

1. A. P. Herbert, Misleading Cases in the Common Law 12 (7th ed. 1932).
2. Herbert, supra n.1, at 9-11.

is also desperately vague. It hardly projects the majesty of The Law to admit that every year millions of dollars in damages turn on such a homespun, common sense idea of fault. Yet, courts obviously cannot prescribe more specific rules in advance as to what is reasonable in every situation: The variety of human experience is much too great to allow such a catalogue of proper behavior. It is possible, however, to describe in a general way the factors that the reasonable person considers before acting, and how he weighs those factors.

First, in deciding whether a course of conduct is appropriate, the reasonable person considers the *foreseeable risks of injury* that that conduct will impose on the community. This does not suggest that Mr. Reasonable always avoids conduct that creates risks to others: We all accept the fact that people must act, and that most activities impose some risk on the community. But the reasonable person considers those risks in light of the *utility* of the conduct. Restatement (Second) of Torts §291. For example, lighting a fire in dry woods imposes a risk that the fire will spread. It may be reasonable to impose that risk to prevent a brush fire from spreading, but not to toast marshmallows. Similarly, rapid release of a large volume of water from behind a dam imposes a risk of downstream property damage or personal injury. That risk might be reasonable to prevent a collapse of the dam, but not to lower the water level to facilitate dredging.

The reasonable person also considers the *extent* of the risks posed by her conduct. Restatement (Second) of Torts §293. Conduct may be reasonable if it threatens minor property damage, but unreasonable if it creates a risk of serious personal injury. The dam release, for example, might be appropriate if it risks minor flooding of grazing land but not if it threatens to drown campers down river. Placing a gas tank in a particular place on a truck might be reasonable if it poses a risk of stalling the engine, but unreasonable if it could cause the tank to explode in a collision. And, since a risk is greater if it exposes many to a risk of injury than if it endangers a few, our odious paragon considers that too.

The reasonable person also considers the *likelihood* of a risk actually causing harm. It often makes sense to do a useful thing that imposes low-probability risks, but may not be if the risk is greater. Placing the gas tank in a particular place may be reasonable if it risks a one-in-a-million explosion, but not if one in a thousand will blow up. Distributing a vaccine may be a reasonable choice if an adverse reaction will happen to one patient in ten thousand, but not if one in ten will suffer it. Restatement (Second) of Torts §293(d).

Our Model of Propriety also considers whether *alternatives* to her proposed conduct would achieve the same purpose with lesser (or greater) risk. Restatement (Second) of Torts §292(c). If a live vaccine poses a risk of serious injury to one patient in ten thousand, but a dead vaccine achieves the same protection with injury to only one in a million, it may be unreasonable to use the live vaccine. On the other hand, if there is no alternative to the live vaccine, the one-in-ten-thousand risk may be reasonable, given the benefit to the other nine thousand nine hundred and ninety-nine users.

It must also be admitted that this obnoxious paragon of ours is a little bit cold-blooded: He also considers the *costs* of various courses of action in determining what is reasonable. He does not take every precaution which might reduce the risk of injury, but only those which are "worth it" in the sense that the injuries avoided outweigh the cost of the extra precaution. If it would cost fifteen dollars to add a kill switch to a fifty dollar skill saw, and the switch would prevent a hand injury to one in 20,000 users but would also substantially impede the operation of the saw, it would likely be reasonable to leave off the switch. Adding the switch would increase the costs of the machine by $300,000 for each injury avoided, ($15/saw × 20,000 saws) and reduce its efficiency for all users. The "trade-off" to avoid one hand injury doesn't seem worth it.

Similarly, if a live vaccine that risks side effects to one in 10,000 costs $1 per dose, while a dead vaccine that will only injure one patient in 100,000 costs $25, the drug manufacturer may be "reasonable" to market the live form, even though it will mean, statistically speaking, nine more injured kids per 100,000 users. This economic dimension to reasonableness analysis is hard to swallow — one of those kids might be yours — but there is little question that it exists. Otherwise we would all drive tanks instead of vulnerable automobiles.

The "Hand Formula"

While it is useful to identify the factors the reasonable person considers in contemplating action, it is more difficult to specify exactly how he weighs those factors, or what conclusion is reasonable on a given set of facts. One estimable jurist, Judge Learned Hand, endeavored to do so in the famous case of *United States v. Carroll Towing Co.*, 159 F.2d 169 (2d Cir.), *reh'g denied*, 160 F.2d 482 (2d Cir. 1947). Judge Hand postulated that the defendant's duty in controlling its barge in that case was

> a function of three variables: (1) The probability that [the barge] will break away; (2) the gravity of the resulting injury, if she does; (3) the burden of adequate precautions. Possibly it serves to bring this notion into relief to state it in algebraic terms: if the probability be called P; the injury L; and the burden B; liability depends upon whether B is less than L multiplied by P; i.e., whether B is less than PL.

Id. at 173. This celebrated "Hand formula," $B < PL$, is meant to suggest not only the factors the Reasonable Person considers, but how he balances those factors in reaching a judgment. The reasonable person, Hand postulates, takes a precaution against injury if the burden of doing so is less than the

B < PL

loss if the injury occurs multiplied by the probability that the injury will occur. To illustrate, suppose that a safety catch costs $20 per machine, that one in 100 of the machines will cause an injury without the catch, and that the likely damages from the injury if it happens are $1,000. The Hand formula suggests that the reasonable person will not attach the safety catch. It will cost $2,000 to put the guard on 100 machines, but will only prevent $1,000 in injury costs. On the other hand, if the guard cost $5 per machine, the formula would compel the conclusion that the reasonable person would add it.

The Hand formula has been applauded particularly by economic theorists, who see negligence law as a means of regulating social conduct to promote efficiency. See, e.g., R. Posner, A Theory of Negligence, 1 J. Legal Stud. 29, 32-34 (1972). But it is also very easy to criticize. What, for example, does "L" really mean in the formula? A single risk, such as a bald tire on the defendant's car, could cause a wide variety of losses, from a broken axle to a nine car collision with multiple fatalities. How is the reasonable person to apply the formula where such a range of "L"s is possible? And, of course, *valuing* even a known loss is a very speculative business. How is the defendant, in deciding whether to drive on the bald tire, to assign a value to a serious personal injury if he does not know the age, employment, susceptibility to pain, family circumstances or other characteristics of his future victim? Similarly, assigning probabilities to particular types of risks is a highly speculative business. The defendant may have a vague sense that bald tires are a bad idea, but that is a far cry from assigning a meaningful quantitative value to "P" in the Hand formula.

The formula, standing alone, also fails to consider other possibilities, such as adopting an entirely different method of achieving a given result. It may be prohibitively expensive to design an alarm system which would eliminate a small risk of a release of a poisonous gas used in a certain manufacturing process. If so, the Hand formula suggests that it is reasonable to conduct the operation without such a system. But the reasonable person would also consider other alternatives: It may be possible to change the process to eliminate the gas entirely, and ordinary prudence may dictate that course if the danger cannot otherwise be adequately reduced. In other cases where precautions to eliminate a risk are too expensive, the only reasonable choice may be to *forgo the conduct entirely*, a possibility not accounted for in Hand's calculation.[3]

Such criticisms of the Hand formula are valid, but they may miss the point. Judge Hand never viewed his formula as a mechanical solution to the

---

3. Other more global criticisms have been leveled at the formula as well. For example, the formula appears devoid of any moral content, suggesting that tort law is a purely economic calculation rather than a system to compensate victims or deter injurers. Beyond that, of course, lies the plain fact that people simply don't think in formulas, and won't be made to by judges.

complex human problem of reasonableness. Certainly he made no attempt to quantify the elements of the formula in *Carroll Towing*, and suggested elsewhere that it is in fact impossible to do so. *Moisan v. Loftus*, 178 F.2d 148, 149 (2d Cir. 1949). Rather, the formula is *suggestive* of the balancing process we all engage in every day in making choices about risk-creating conduct. In an intuitive, impressionistic way, we all balance the dangers of our conduct against its utility and (when we are acting reasonably) avoid those acts that appear unduly risky in light of the benefits they offer.

Applying the Reasonable Person Standard: The Relevance of Personal "Circumstances"

While the reasonable person is a fictitious construct, people are not. Each individual possesses unique physical and mental characteristics. How can this artificial, uniform standard of good judgment account for our individuality . . . or should it?

To some extent, the negligence standard does account for the personal characteristics of the actor. One's duty is to act as a "reasonable person under the circumstances." Some individual characteristics of the actor are considered part of "the circumstances" in determining reasonableness. For example, it is generally held that a person with a physical disability is required to act as a reasonable person *with that disability* would act. Thus, it is not negligent for Lear, a blind person, to walk the streets, though he will occasionally bump into others. The blind have to live in the same world as the rest of us, and it is reasonable for them to impose the risk of occasional sidewalk collisions (and more serious motor vehicle accidents as well) in order to do so. It might be a closer case if Lear ventured forth without a cane, but the important point is that his conduct will be judged against that of other actors in the same "circumstances," not against the population at large.

While allowance is made for physical disabilities, no allowance is made for the "circumstance" that a person lacks good judgment, is hasty, awkward, or perennially oafish. This was well settled in the torts classic, *Vaughan v. Menlove*, 132 Eng. Rep. 490 (1837), in which poor Menlove argued that he had exercised his judgment to the best of his ability, and should not be held liable just because his "best" wasn't very good. If Lear is not held to the standard of a sighted person, why should a Menlove be held to the standard of a person with good judgment? Isn't his obtuseness a "circumstance" that the law should take into account as well?

In the courts of heaven, Menlove's argument will doubtless weigh heavily, but as a legal standard his suggested test (whether he "had acted honestly and bona fide to the best of his own judgment," (id. at 493)) would obviously be a disaster. Had Menlove's test been adopted, we would not have one standard of care for negligence, but a million. We would not try the defendant's *conduct* in negligence actions, but his character and intelligence. The perennially careless would enjoy the right to endanger their neighbors with impunity. By sticking with the "reasonable person under the circumstances" test, the courts have provided instead an objective test that allows impartial application, avoids subjective judgments about individual character, and allows some measure of prediction about the consequences of conduct.

This same refusal to consider individual personality is illustrated in the treatment of the mentally ill. The traditional rule, still generally accepted, is that the mentally ill are held to the same standard as everyone else, despite the "circumstance" of their illness:

> Unless the actor is a child, his insanity or other mental deficiency does not relieve the actor from liability for conduct which does not conform to the standard of a reasonable man [sic] under like circumstances.

Restatement (Second) of Torts §283B. This is a harsh, perhaps indefensible rule. It holds a mentally ill adult to a standard that any psychology student will tell you he cannot meet. But it is at least consistent with *Menlove*, in the sense that it is based on a refusal to make the standard a subjective one, to account for individual personality in administering the negligence system. These rules send the same message to those who, due to mental illness or weak intelligence, may have trouble meeting the objective standard: "Since the law will not hold you to a lesser standard, you will have to curtail your activity or exercise particular self-restraint (or be restrained by others) in order to avoid liability."

This treatment of the mentally ill and those of weak judgment confirms that the reasonable person standard is a legal judgment, not a moral condemnation. Morally, we could hardly fault a Menlove for a judgment which was the best he could do, or a mentally ill defendant for conduct that was compelled by delusion or neurosis. But for legal purposes, we need a standard that defines "fault" in some predictable, universal way. The "reasonable-person-under-like-circumstances" test provides a neutral instrument for deciding disputes, not a value judgment about a person's character.

Given the refusal of negligence law to account for mental deficiencies, the application of the "reasonable person" standard to children may seem inconsistent. Children are *not* held to the adult standard of care, but rather the standard of a "reasonable person of like age, intelligence, and experience under like circumstances." Restatement (Second) of Torts §283A. Unlike the unitary adult standard of care, this child standard clearly *does* make allowance for their mental ability and development. The rationale is that children have to *learn* to be careful, and ought not be exposed to tort liability for conduct that is reasonable in light of their stage of development during the learning process. Adults, however, have had eighteen years to become "reasonable;" if they don't make it by that age, they probably never will.

They must then suffer the liability consequences or adopt a low-risk lifestyle to avoid causing injury to others.

The child standard does not mean that children cannot be found negligent. There is little doubt that most children of ten have developed the judgment to understand that setting a fire can burn a building, or shooting an arrow at a playmate can put out an eye. In many respects a child of sixteen is as capable of due care as an adult (in crossing streets, stacking lumber, or playing football, perhaps) and will effectively be required to meet the adult standard of care. In addition, a good many recent cases hold children who engage in certain high risk activities primarily engaged in by adults, such as driving, to the adult standard of care. Prosser & Keeton §32, at 181.

Applying the Reasonable Person Standard: The Relevance of External "Circumstances"

While the personal characteristics of the actor are sometimes relevant to determining whether she acted reasonably, the external circumstances in which she acted are always relevant. Decisions about conduct are not made in a classroom or an armchair, they are made in the hurly burly of every day events, in the factory, on the road, in the operating room. The reasonableness of the defendant's decision is always judged in relation to the unique context or "circumstances" in which she made it.

For example, a defendant may make a decision in the split second of an impending accident that he would not have made if he had the time to weigh the choices more carefully. In judging that decision, the jury should consider whether the decision was reasonable in light of the "circumstance" that the defendant had to act in a split second. The so-called "emergency doctrine" means no more than this, that in judging the reasonableness of conduct in an emergency, the "circumstance" that the defendant must act quickly is relevant.

Other circumstances are also relevant. It is relevant that the defendant acted as others customarily do in like circumstances. The fact that conduct is generally engaged in by those in a particular trade or profession at least suggests that such conduct is acceptable. For example, if a roofer is injured in a fall from the roof of a two-story building, it is relevant on the issue of his negligence that roofers ordinarily do not wear safety harnesses in reshingling two story buildings (or that they do). If most roofers consider that an acceptable risk for the extra freedom of movement or time savings involved, it may well be that they are right.

However, while relevant, evidence of custom is not dispositive. In some circumstances, custom and reasonableness may diverge dramatically. To save costs, out of inertia, tradition, or for other reasons, a practice may continue long after thoughtful analysis would compel its rejection, or a new precaution may be ignored despite its obvious benefits. Seat belts offer a good example. Aware of the proven safety advantages of seat belts, our odious paragon doubtless buckles up every time he motors forth, although a substantial majority of the population refuses to follow his pious example.[4] Similarly, if some enterprising roofer develops a new easy-snap, no-hassle safety harness, it may be that the reasonable roofer would use it. Even if it is hard to teach old roofers new tricks, they may be unreasonable to follow the older custom under changed circumstances.

Another "circumstance" that commonly colors the reasonableness of conduct is whether a statute requires a particular course of action under the circumstances. Generally speaking, the reasonable person obeys the law; thus, evidence that the defendant ignored a statutory standard will frequently suffice to establish that he was negligent. This problem, proving negligence based on violation of statute, is explored further in the next chapter.

A further relevant circumstance is whether the actor has acted as an expert in a particular field. If you have a tax accountant prepare your taxes for you, you justifiably expect a higher level of knowledge and judgment than if your bookkeeper or your neighbor does. If you entrust your yacht to a licensed merchant marine captain, she should have a higher level of skill than a beach bum. This does not mean that persons with specialized knowledge are held to a higher *standard* of care than others: Their standard, like that of others, is reasonable care under the circumstances. But their expert status is a "circumstance" which colors the meaning of reasonableness.

The facilities or resources available to the actor are also relevant to the reasonableness analysis. It may be reasonable to perform exploratory surgery in a community where less invasive methods of diagnosis are unavailable, but not in an area were they are. It may be reasonable for a general practitioner to litigate an antitrust case in northern Maine, where antitrust lawyers are hard to come by, but not in Washington, D.C., where one is lurking on every block.

Beyond these recurring types of relevant circumstances, there are the utterly miscellaneous facts of every individual case to be considered. Facts about weather, about what the parties knew, about how they observed events, about the condition and behavior of animals, vehicles, computers, or machines, about the purposes the actors hoped to achieve by their conduct and alternative ways they might have done so. Reality is infinitely diverse, and each case is unique. It is up to the parties to bring out the circumstances that conditioned the actors' choices, and argue the reasonableness of those

---

4. Ironically, courts and legislatures have gone to considerable lengths to avoid the ineluctable conclusion that it is unreasonable to drive without buckling up. See e.g., D. Westenberg, Buckle Up or Pay: The Emerging Safety Belt Defense, 20 Suffolk U.L. Rev. 867, 885, 923-943 (1986) (detailing statutes limiting use of evidence of failure to wear seat belt to prove negligence).

choices in light of the flesh and blood context in which they were made. It is exactly this multifariousness of *facts* that requires the *legal standard* of negligence to be so frustratingly general, and makes the practice of negligence law interesting.

The examples below explore the factors involved in the negligence calculus, and the process by which they are weighed.

EXAMPLES

Burdens and Benefits

1.   Costard, owner of a large estate, throws an all day party for a few hundred of his close friends. During the day, some of his guests wander through the woods and come to an abandoned quarry on the property, which has filled up with water. They opt for a dip. Trinculo is injured when he dives into the quarry and hits his head on a submerged promontory only three feet under the surface. He sues Costard for negligence.

Costard argues that he was not negligent, since, though the injury was foreseeable, filling in the quarry was prohibitively expensive. In Hand formula terms, the burden was too great given the relatively low risk of injury to a wandering entrant on the property, which is normally not open to outsiders. What is the problem with this argument?

2.   Suppose that, instead of a quarry, an abandoned well existed on the property, covered with some boards placed there a few years ago and now beginning to rot. Trinculo, wandering the grounds, does not see the well, which is covered with autumn leaves. He falls through, is injured and sues Costard for negligence. Is he likely to prove negligence?

3.   The town of Stratford is given a piece of vacant land adjacent to a quiet residential street. Since there is considerable demand for recreational space, and little open space in town, they build a baseball field on the parcel. The edge of the field is thirty feet from the road. In the course of a game, Feste hits a high foul ball, which is caught by the wind and angles into the street. Glendower, driving by, suddenly sees the ball coming, instinctively swerves away from it, and is injured when his car turns into a ditch. He sues the town for negligence in locating the field where it did. Do you think the jury will find the town negligent?

4.   Moth is hit by Feste while crossing Main Street. Discovery reveals that Feste was driving to the video store to rent an X-rated movie. The store was only three blocks from his home. There is no evidence that Feste was driving carelessly at the time of the accident.

     a. Moth sues him for negligence, arguing that the utility of choosing to drive to rent a dirty movie is so low that it does not justify the risk imposed by driving. How should the court respond to this argument?

b. Moth argues that Feste was negligent for failing to choose a less dangerous alternative — walking — since the trip was so short. How should the court respond to this argument?

Fudd and Foreseeability

5. Falstaff, anxious to get to a pub, passes a driver on a curve, and collides with Bottom coming the other way. Sued for negligence, Falstaff argues that he was not negligent, because the road was little traveled, and it was very unlikely that a car would come around the curve at the time he was in the wrong lane. Judge Fudd instructs the jury as follows:

> If you find that it was more probable than not that a car would be traveling in the opposite lane and collide with the defendant's car, then you should find that the defendant violated the standard of reasonable care in passing as he did.

What is wrong with Fudd's instruction? Can you write a more accurate one?

A Duty of Much Care

6. Gobbo, a gas station attendant, has just started a cigarette break when Mariana drives up for gas. He goes out to fill her gas tank with the cigarette in his mouth. Annoyed by a persistent bee, he takes a swipe at it and knocks the cigarette out of his mouth. It falls near the nozzle of the hose, causing an explosion that injures both him and Mariana. She sues him for negligence.

At trial, her counsel asks the judge to instruct the jury that Gobbo, in dispensing the gas, owed her a duty of extreme care, due to the explosive nature of gasoline. Should the judge give the instruction?

An Almost Perfect Record

7. Dr. Quince operates on Peasblossom to remove a bony growth from her lower spine. During surgery, he accidentally contacts her spinal cord, causing partial paralysis of her left leg. Peasblossom sues him for negligence.

At trial Quince seeks to establish that he exercised due care in surgery by offering evidence that he has an almost perfect record as a back surgeon. He has performed over three hundred and seventy similar surgeries, and only twice come into contact with the spinal cord. His counsel argues that this proves that he is a careful surgeon.

a. Does this evidence establish that Quince complied with the standard of reasonable care?

b. How is the jury to know what due care requires in this case?

Menlove in Reverse

8.   Dogberry has been skiing since he was four, has participated in several skiing competitions, and is generally acknowledged to be a first class skier. One morning, he is executing a turn on a moderate ski run, loses control, and slides backwards into Portia, breaking Portia's ankle. She sues him for negligence. At trial, Portia argues that the jury should be instructed that Dogberry must exercise the level of care that would be exercised by "the reasonable expert skier under the same circumstances." Should the instruction be given?

9.   Assume that Dogberry, due to his skiing experience, is aware that executing a certain type of turn in spring skiing conditions poses a serious risk of losing control. Assume also that the average (or, more precisely, the reasonable) skier would not know this. Dogberry attempts the maneuver, loses control and injures Portia. Is he liable for the injury?

10.   Overdone, a tenant in Abhorsen's apartment building, hears a mouse at night and buys mouse poison to solve the problem. She leaves a box of it open on top of an electric heat vent. Unbeknownst to her, the stuff will ignite if exposed to moderate heat over a period of time, and does, causing a fire. Abhorsen sues her for damage to the building. Should she be found negligent?

An Elementary Example

11.   Falstaff heads home after drinking nine beers at the local pub. Much the worse for wear, he is proceeding along at twenty-eight miles per hour, just below the speed limit, within his lane of traffic, when a pickup truck, going the other way, makes a sharp stop in the opposite lane. Moth, a boy of five, is leaning over the side of the bed of the pickup and is thrown out immediately in front of Falstaff's left front wheel. Falstaff runs him down and is sued for negligence. Leaving aside possible contributory negligence of Moth, would Falstaff be liable?

EXPLANATIONS

Burdens and Benefits

1.   Costard has tried to take charge of the negligence analysis here by looking at one possible means of addressing the risk and applying the Hand formula with only that in mind. The argument might hold water (so to speak) if filling in the quarry were the only possible means of dealing with the risk. But other, less burdensome "B"s exist here. Costard could have fenced the quarry, or posted signs warning of the danger of rocks beneath the surface. The burden of taking these alternative precautions is much lower, and the balance of risk against cost of prevention is a great deal closer on these facts.

This is not to say that Trinculo will necessarily win, but that it is important for his counsel not to let Costard frame the negligence issue only in terms of a prohibitively expensive precaution, since other means of prevention are possible.

2. In this case, Costard's negligence is clear because the burden of prevention is so low. Even filling in the well would likely be an appropriate precaution to eliminate the risk of serious injury from falling in. But much less would prevent most accidents. Building a fence around the well or capping it with a solid concrete cover would eliminate the risk at a clearly acceptable cost. Surely our Paragon of Propriety, the reasonable person, would have done so.

3. Stray foul balls like Feste's are certainly foreseeable; indeed, even an accident like Glendower's is foreseeable. But foreseeable risk is not the end of the analysis. The reasonable man eschews unreasonable risks, but not all risks. If the risk here was low enough, in relation to the utility of the activity, it is not negligent for the town to impose it.

Here, that may well be the case. The facts suggest that there was little open land and a need for recreational facilities in the town. The town sited the field with a substantial margin beside the road. Certainly, a few fouls will still reach the road, but, since it is a quiet street, most will not hit a car. Those that do will not usually cause much damage. In view of the value of the field to the citizenry, the lack of alternative sites, the relatively low risk of accidents, and the minimal damage likely if an accident does take place, the town's choice is probably reasonable.

One lesson of this example is that plaintiffs do not always win negligence suits just because an accident actually happens. The test is not whether injury was caused, or even whether injury was foreseeable, but whether the defendant's conduct was reasonable in view of *all* the circumstances, including the possibility of injury, the utility of the conduct, the alternatives available, and others.

The example also illustrates that the peculiar circumstances of every individual case really do matter. This case might come out differently if there were more alternatives to the site, if the space outside the foul line were only ten feet, or if the road was a busy high-speed freeway. *Facts* are ever so important to negligence cases, because each fact colors the "circumstances" against which the defendant's conduct must be judged.

4a. In this example, Moth cannot prove that Feste was negligent in the *manner* in which he drove — the example indicates that he drove with due care. Instead, she argues that the Hand formula compels the conclusion that it was negligent for Feste to drive *at all*. The Hand formula requires the court to balance the utility of the defendant's conduct against the risks it imposes; here (Moth argues) the utility of Feste's errand was so low that it did not justify even the relatively low risk of careful driving. Moth asks the court to weigh the value to Feste of *this particular automobile trip* against the risk it will impose on the community, instead of weighing the general value of driving against its general risks.

If Moth's argument were accepted, it would require courts to determine the value of the actor's purpose in each case. One need only imagine a few hypotheticals to illustrate the interesting questions which could result: Is it unreasonable to impose the risks of driving to see one's illicit lover? to buy drugs? to have a few beers? to gamble? to make a baby stop crying?[5] This inquiry would not only complicate the trial, but would also raise very thorny problems in ascertaining the value of the conduct. If the court used a subjective standard for value — what the trip was worth to Feste — it would be very hard to ascertain the true value. Doubtless Feste will testify that it had great value to him. On the other hand, it would be very difficult to define some "objective" standard for valuing Feste's trip: The value of human activity seems inherently subjective to the actor.

Clearly, the law is not going to delve into these matters. Instead, the risk/utility balancing takes place at a more generalized level: whether the activity of driving in itself is socially useful enough to justify the attendant risks of non-negligent injury. If the answer to this question is "yes" (as it clearly is) the defendant will not be held liable for *choosing to drive*, though he still may be for driving carelessly. See Restatement (Second) of Torts §291 cmt. e:

> The law attaches utility to general types or classes of acts as appropriate to the advancement of certain interests rather than to the purpose for which a particular act is done. . . . Thus, the law regards the free use of the highway for travel as of sufficient utility to outweigh the risk of carefully conducted traffic, and does not ordinarily concern itself with the good, bad, or indifferent purpose of a particular journey.

Under strict economic analysis, there is a good argument for Moth's position. In a friction-free economic world, it would make sense to balance the *actual* utility of *this* trip against the actual risk imposed. However, given the difficulties of valuing the conduct and the large investment necessary in adjudicating such issues, it is unrealistic to do so. Judge Posner, in noting the courts' refusal to individualize the assessment, simply states that "such a judgment is too difficult for a court to make in an ordinary tort case." R. Posner, Economic Analysis of Law 176 (4th ed. 1992).

On the other hand, courts *do* consider the actor's purposes in determining whether it was reasonable to impose a risk *beyond* those ordinarily incident to the activity. For example, if Feste hit Moth while speeding, it would be relevant that he was driving an injured friend to the hospital. The factfinder would be free to conclude that Feste's departure from the usual standard was justified by the increased utility of his purpose.

---

5. With some babies, it works like a charm. Unfortunately, the effect wears off when you stop the car.

b. This argument will also fail. It is true that the calculus of reasonableness includes consideration of the alternative ways of accomplishing the desired objective. But again, the court will only consider other methods of transportation in determining whether driving in general is reasonable conduct; it will not particularize the analysis by looking at alternatives to this particular trip. Since the risks imposed by driving per se are acceptable in light of its utility, driving is considered reasonable conduct. Since it is not unreasonable to drive, Moth will only prevail if she shows that Feste was negligent in the *way* he drove.[6]

Fudd and Foreseeability

5.   Fudd has grievously confused the burden of proof with the standard of care. His instruction suggests that Falstaff was negligent only if the accident was "more probable than not." In fact, Falstaff's act may have been negligent even if an accident was very unlikely.

In a civil case, the plaintiff must convince the jury that it is more probable than not that each of the elements of the claim are true. Here, most juries would conclude that it was more probable than not that Falstaff *was negligent*, even though the probability that his conduct would cause an accident was quite low. As the Hand formula suggests, a risk does not have to be *likely* to happen before the reasonable person avoids it. The reasonable person avoids even small risks if the resulting injuries, if they occur, are likely to be great. Since the damages from a head-on collision with an on-coming car are likely to be grievous, the reasonable driver in Falstaff's circumstances would not take that risk, even if it was a very small risk. In Hand formula terms, while P is low, L is very great, and B, the burden of avoiding the risk, is very low: Falstaff need only wait for a clear stretch of road before passing.

Opinions in negligence cases often state that conduct was negligent because injury was the "natural and probable consequence" of the defendant's act. This is promiscuous language; "probable" here really means *foreseeable*. A risk may be foreseeable, and worth avoiding, even though the chances are a great deal less than 50 percent that it will actually come to pass.

---

6. Here again, economic analysis suggests that actors *should* be encouraged to consider not only whether the risks imposed by an activity are generally acceptable, but also whether the balance of risks favors an alternative means of achieving the desired result in the particular instance.

One way to encourage such individualized consideration of alternatives would be to impose strict liability for driving. If drivers were liable even for non-negligent auto accidents, they might choose to walk two blocks to the video store, though they would still choose to drive for longer trips. See Posner, Economic Analysis of Law 175-176 (4th ed 1992) (discussing how strict liability may reduce accident costs by inducing individuals to modify activity levels).

The Honorable Fudd would be better advised to instruct the jury along these lines:

> If you find that the defendant passed on the curve without being able to tell whether a car was coming the other way, and that the risk of a collision was sufficiently foreseeable and the likely resulting injury sufficiently serious that a reasonable person in the defendant's circumstances would not have acted as he did, then you should find that the defendant breached the standard of due care.

This instruction requires the jury to engage in the same balancing process that the Reasonable Person does, to weigh risks and advantages to determine what Falstaff *should have done* and then to compare that to what he actually did. In effect, the jury first decides what the standard means in the context of the facts (what is "reasonable" under *these* circumstances) and then decides whether the defendant acted that way or not.[7]

A Duty of Much Care

6.   The judge should refuse the instruction. Negligence law holds defendants to a duty of reasonable care under the circumstances, not different duties depending on the degree of risk of each activity. The jury should be instructed that Gobbo owed Mariana a duty of reasonable care under the circumstances.

However, the circumstances here involve a high risk of injury. Reasonable care in the dispensing of gasoline undoubtedly requires a greater *amount* of care than dispensing ice cream sodas. But this is not a different *standard* of care, it is just what the reasonable person would do under *these* circumstances. It would be perfectly appropriate for the judge to instruct the jury as follows:

> If you find that dispensing of gasoline involves a high risk of explosion, and that the reasonable person in the defendant's circumstances would have known or should have known of that risk, then the defendant was required to exercise a high level of care commensurate with the high risk involved in that activity.

This instruction may be only subtly different from the one Gobbo's counsel requested, but it is different in an important respect: It states that the reasonable person, acting under the usual due care standard, exercises a higher

---

7. Frankly, the answer here seems so clear that the judge ought to direct a verdict in the plaintiff's favor on the ground that, as a matter of law, it is negligent to pass on a curve without being able to see the on-coming traffic. If Fudd took this course, he would instruct the jury as follows:

> If you find that the defendant, at the time he passed the car in front of him, was unable to see whether traffic was coming the other way due to a curve in the road, then you must find that the defendant was negligent.

This instruction leaves the jury to determine whether in fact Falstaff did pass without being able to see, but establishes as a matter of law that he was negligent if he did. By contrast, the instruction in the text leaves the jury the option of finding that he passed on the curve but was not negligent in doing so.

amount of care if the circumstances involve high risk. The requested instruction wrongly suggests that a different *standard* of care applies.

Very likely, the jury won't catch the subtle distinction between these two instructions: They will just pick up on the fact that the defendant was required to be very careful. But getting the instruction right is still important, especially to Mariana. If the inaccurate one is given, her verdict may be reversed on appeal. The correct instruction will communicate much the same message to the jury, but without the risk of reversal for legal error.

An Almost Perfect Record

7a.   In baseball, .300 is a good batting average, and Quince is batting nearly a thousand. This tends to show that Quince is a careful doctor. If I were choosing a doctor, such information would make me more likely to choose Quince.

But this case is not about whether Quince is a careful doctor: It is about whether he exercised due care *on this occasion*. We are not testing his general virtue or his career accomplishments, we are testing his conduct in one particular operation. It is no answer to Peasblossom that Quince was careful in all those *other* cases; she couldn't care less about those. She claims — and is entitled to — the exercise of reasonable care in the performance of *her* operation.

On the other hand, how can we hold Quince to a standard of perfection? We all make mistakes, and Quince makes fewer than most (if, indeed, those two cases were mistakes, which is unclear from the facts). How can we condemn him if the knife slips once?

Well, we aren't condemning him. A finding of negligence is not a moral judgment passed upon a person, or a finding of incompetence, but a post hoc evaluation of a single event against an abstract standard set up by the law. Since that is all that we are doing, evidence of Quince's batting average, that he usually meets the standard of care in his operations, is beside the point, just as evidence that he had made mistakes on other patients would not establish that he was careless in Peasblossom's operation. See Fed. R. Evid. 404 (evidence of character generally inadmissible "for the purpose of proving action in conformity therewith on a particular occasion").[8]

b.   The average jury is made up of a cross-section of individuals with varying educational backgrounds, professions, experiences, and values. Very likely, few, if any, know anything about lower lumbar surgery. They are in

---

8. This evidence might even be offered by Peasblossom to *establish* Dr. Quince's negligence. She would argue that his excellent record of avoiding injury in other operations tends to prove that injury of this type is avoidable, so that where it occurs it is likely to result from negligence. Such evidence is certainly not conclusive — a side effect may be rare but unavoidable — but it at least seems relevant to the question of whether the injury resulted from inevitable accident or negligence.

no position, based on their general knowledge, to say what reasonable care requires in such operations.

Thus, the parties will have to educate the jury not only about what the defendant did, but also about what the standard of reasonable care required under the circumstances in which he did it. Each side will offer expert evidence (doubtless from lumbar surgeons in Peasblossom's case) as to the proper way to perform surgery of this type. The jury will have to find for themselves, on the conflicting testimony of these experts, what the reasonable surgeon does in such cases. Having determined that, they will then have to decide whether Quince failed to meet that standard.

In many cases, the jury's life experience suffices to allow them to determine what reasonable care means without the testimony of experts. Jurors can pass judgment on the reasonableness of driving a car, operating simple machinery, controlling children in a classroom, crossing the street, or climbing a ladder based on their general knowledge. But a great many cases require expert evidence in order for the jury to determine the standard of reasonable care. The proper way to reinforce a bridge, to pilot an ocean vessel, to analyze a financial statement, to ride a race horse, to land a 747, or to treat a drug overdose, to name a few examples, are beyond the common experience of jurors. In such cases, trial must include an expensive "battle of the experts" on what reasonable care demands in those circumstances.

Menlove In Reverse

8.   Portia can make a pretty good argument for holding Dogberry to the standard of care of an expert: He is a highly experienced skier who is probably capable of better control than your basic weekender on the slopes. Why should he be held to a lesser standard of care than he is able to meet?

There is some force to the argument, but there are also problems with it. First, it tends (like Menlove's argument) to destroy the uniformity of the standard of care. If the argument were accepted, the jury would have to ascertain in each case just how good the defendant was at what he did before deciding what standard to apply to him. Should the jury "grade" the defendant as "expert," "very good," "good," or "average" before determining what standard he must meet? Suppose he is a sub-par skier? Ratcheting the standard of performance *up* for the able seems to imply lowering it for the less able as well, yet *Menlove* certainly indicates that the court will not do that. If the goal is a single objective standard, it appears to make sense to stick to the reasonable-person-under-the-circumstances test for Dogberry, at least where he is engaging in ordinary maneuvers engaged in by skiers with a wide range of abilities.

It would be different if Dogberry were *acting as an expert* at the time of the injury. For example, if Dogberry were a member of the ski patrol in the course of a rescue, he would be acting as an expert and should be held to that standard. But in this example Dogberry is just skiing, like every one else on the slopes, and should be held to the same standard of care as the reasonable skier under the circumstances. Similarly, a trucker driving his car to the movies may be an "expert" driver, but will be held to the general reasonable person standard for ordinary driving. See *Fredericks v. Castora*, 360 A.2d 696, 698 (Pa. Super. 1976) ("to vary the standard according to the driver's experience would render the application of any reasonably uniform standard impossible").

The result here is not entirely clear, however. Some authorities suggest that Dogberry should be held to the standard of an expert in this example. See Restatement (Second) of Torts §299, cmt. f; see also Harper, James & Gray, §16.6, at 415-21. As a practical matter, of course, if the evidence shows that Dogberry is highly experienced, the jury is likely to demand more of him anyway, whether or not they are instructed to do so.

9.   Here, Dogberry knows something about "the circumstances" that the ordinary skier would not. You or I might not be negligent for executing the same maneuver, because we would not recognize the risk. But Dogberry *does* recognize it, and goes ahead anyway.

While it may be inappropriate to hold Dogberry to a higher *standard of care* due to his superior skiing experience, it is appropriate to require him to exercise reasonable care under the circumstances, *including* the circumstance that he knows of the danger involved. Dogberry will not be allowed to ignore facts he knows, just because someone else wouldn't know them. Similarly, a driver with superior vision is not entitled to ignore a vehicle she sees because a person with average vision wouldn't see it. The question to ask is, would a reasonable person *who knew what Dogberry did* have made the decision he did. If not, he is liable. Restatement (Second) of Torts §289(b).

The distinction between this example and the last is subtle, perhaps too subtle. But it does appear clear, as a matter of public policy, that we should not allow parties who know of dangers to disregard them simply because others might not know of the same danger. Otherwise a doctor would not be negligent for sending her child to school with a highly contagious disease, simply because a lay person would not recognize the symptoms.

10. To an actor with all the relevant information, Overdone's act would clearly be negligent. The reasonable person takes considerable precautions to avoid even a small risk of fire, since it threatens both serious personal injury and extensive property damage. And in Hand formula terms, the burden here is minimal; she need only place the poison away from the heat vent to prevent the loss.

But Overdone doesn't have all the relevant information; she doesn't know the poison can ignite under prolonged heat. Is her ignorance a defense? The standard of care is that of a reasonable person under the circumstances. Since her circumstances are that she does not know of the risk, it seems that she is not unreasonable in failing to guard against it.

If the risk is an unusual one that the ordinary person would not appreciate, this is probably the answer. Omniscience is not required of the reasonable person, any more than perfect (as opposed to reasonable) judgment is. However, there are limits to this. Actors will not be heard to say that they don't know basic facts about the world which the reasonable person *would* know. The reasonable person will be held to understand a good deal about the environment in which he moves about and creates risks, such as "the law of gravity, the fact that fire burns and water will drown, that inflammable objects will catch fire, that a loose board will tip when it is trod on, the ordinary features of the weather to which he is accustomed, and similar phenomena of nature." Prosser & Keeton, §32, at 183 (footnotes omitted). And, as Example 9 indicates, where the actor *does* know a fact, he will be required to act reasonably in light of that knowledge, even though the "reasonable person" might not know it.

An Elementary Example

11. This chapter began by drawing the distinction between negligent conduct and liability on a negligence claim. We end with the same distinction. Falstaff was clearly negligent here in the sense that he breached the standard of due care by driving drunk. He failed to act as a reasonable person under the circumstances would. That satisfies Element #2 of the cause of action for negligence.

But the *tort* of negligence has three other elements, and one of those is causation. Here, the facts suggest that Falstaff was not negligent in the way he handled the car, even though he was drunk. He was in his lane, driving below the speed limit. Because Moth fell right in front of the car, there was nothing he could have done to avoid hitting him; even if he had been sober, the accident would have happened the same way. Liability for negligence turns not just on *being* negligent, but upon negligent conduct *causing* injury.

But Falstaff's negligence did cause the harm, didn't it? He was negligent to be on the road *at all* while drunk, and his driving caused the accident. This argument proves too much. On this theory, Falstaff would be liable to Moth if he had bald tires, worn windshield wipers, or a loud muffler, and had the same accident, even though none of these conditions contributed in any way to the injury.

In order for a negligent act to be considered a cause of the plaintiff's injury, the risk that makes the conduct negligent must lead to the harm. Driving while drunk is negligent because it impairs the ability to control the car: It is only where this impairment contributes to the occurrence of the accident that the negligence becomes a "cause" of resulting harm. Falstaff would be liable if Moth fell far enough in front of the car that an unimpaired driver could have braked in time, but Falstaff failed to brake because of his inebriation. On those facts his negligence would have affected the outcome, and the causation requirement — Element #3 — would be established. See generally Chapter 7 on Actual Causation.

5

Borrowing Standards of Care: Violation of Statute as Negligence

Introduction

As the previous chapter indicates, the plaintiff in a negligence case must prove four elements, duty, breach, causation, and damages, in order to recover in a negligence case. To establish the second element, breach of the duty of care, or negligence, the plaintiff must show that the defendant failed to act with reasonable care, to behave as the ordinary prudent person would under like circumstances.

This reasonable person standard has been criticized as too vague to provide any meaningful guidance to the jury in evaluating the defendant's conduct. Juries are supposed to find facts, not to establish the rules of law that determine whether the defendant is liable. Arguably, the negligence standard is so broad that it licenses the jury to find as they please, without constraining them by meaningful legal rules.

On the other hand, how can the rule be any more specific? The variety of human experience, the range of circumstances that may cause injury, is so great that it would be impossible for courts to formulate specific rules in advance to govern liability for all careless conduct. Since it is impossible to "particularize" the negligence standard, the jury is usually instructed under the reasonable person standard. The jurors are left to use their common sense, experience, and, where appropriate, expert testimony, to pass judgment on the defendant's conduct under this very general standard.

While courts cannot elaborate specific negligence rules to define how parties should behave in all circumstances, *legislatures* routinely enact statutes establishing standards of care for common situations. This chapter addresses the role that such statutes play in proving the second element of a claim for negligence, that a party breached the standard of care or "was negligent."

Legislative Standards of Conduct

Legislatures very commonly enact statutes that establish standards of care for private conduct. Many such statutes govern that ubiquitous, highly practical, but potentially lethal instrumentality, the automobile. Here are some hypothetical, but typical, examples:

> No person shall make a turn onto or off of a public way without signaling his or her intention to turn, either by hand or by an electrical signal device. West Dakota Ann. Laws Title V, §12.

> No person shall drive a motor vehicle without a muffler or other suitable device to control excessive noise. West Dakota Ann. Laws. Title V, §212.

> No person shall drive an unlighted vehicle upon any public highway during the period from one-half hour after sunset until one-half hour before sunrise. West Dakota Ann. Laws Title V, §94A.

> No person shall leave a vehicle on the main-traveled portion of any highway without posting adequate warning lights thereon. West Dakota Ann. Laws Title V, §99.

> The driver of a vehicle on any public highway, traveling in any direction, shall stop before reaching any bus marked "school bus" and exhibiting flashing red lights. Said driver shall not proceed until the bus resumes motion or the lights are no longer flashing. West Dakota Ann. Laws Title V, §74.

Many statutes establish standards of care in other areas as well:

> No person shall enter upon or be employed upon the premises of an active construction site without wearing a construction helmet. West Dakota Ann. Laws Title IX, §111.

> No person shall leave a refrigerator, freezer, or similar appliance in any unsecured area accessible to children, whether for disposal or otherwise, without detaching the door from said appliance. West Dakota Ann. Laws Title XXIX, §51.

> Every owner or lessor of property used for rental purposes shall maintain every outside stair and porch in sound condition and good repair. West Dakota Ann. Laws Title XVII, §19.

> No person shall operate any mobile piece of heavy construction equipment unless said equipment is equipped with a beeper which sounds at all times while such equipment is operating in reverse. West Dakota Ann. Laws Title XXIII, §123.

Statutes like these are intended to promote safety by establishing standards of conduct for particular situations. They are legislative commands which, if applicable, every citizen is bound to obey. Usually, such safety statutes establish a small criminal penalty for violations of the standard, but do not say anything about whether violation of the statutory standard establishes negligence in a civil action for damages. Not surprisingly, however, persons injured due to a violation of such a statute usually claim that the defendant was negligent for failing to comply with the statutory standard of care.

Suppose, for example, that Bourjailly drives past a stopped school bus with flashing lights and hits Hellman, a child alighting from the bus. If the school bus statute above applies, Hellman will argue that Bourjailly should be found negligent because he violated the statute. Or suppose that Updike is injured by a falling object on a construction site, and sues the contractor. If the helmet statute quoted above applies, and if Updike was not wearing one, the defendant would argue that Updike's violation of the statute proves, in and of itself, that he failed to live up to the standard of due care.

Arguments for and Against the Negligence Per Se Rule

There are some good arguments that a violation of a statute should be treated as negligence per se, that is, negligence in itself. Where the legislature has decreed that certain precautions must be taken, or that certain acts should not be done, a person who violates the statute has ignored the standard of care established by the legislature. Arguably, reasonable people don't do that.

In addition, if the jury is allowed to assess the defendant's conduct under a general reasonable care standard, despite his violation of a statutory standard of care, the jury is being allowed to disregard the command of the legislature. Suppose, for example, that the jury finds that Updike was not negligent in failing to wear a helmet. Doesn't this ignore the legislature, the voice of the people, which has barred such conduct? Shouldn't the standard of conduct enforced by the courts be the same as that established by the legislature, so that court decisions in negligence suits will reinforce rather than contradict the policy of the legislature?

There is much logic to these arguments, but the negligence per se cases vividly illustrate Justice Holmes's famous maxim, "The life of the law has not been logic: it has been experience." O. W. Holmes, Jr., The Common Law 1 (Little, Brown 1881). Automatic adoption of general legislative standards has proved too rigid. While it may be generally true that the reasonable person obeys the law, it is not always true. In unusual circumstances, it may be reasonable to disregard the statute, as where a driver swerves across the center line to avoid a child in the street, or stops in a no stopping zone to attend to a seriously ill passenger. In other cases, it may be impossible to obey the law, despite the best will in the world, as where blizzard conditions overwhelm efforts to keep a street clear. Imposing liability in cases like these, simply on the ground that the defendant violated the statute, would look more like strict liability than liability based on fault.

Another argument against automatic adoption of the legislative standard is that most statutes that establish standards of care say nothing about what role the legislative standard should play in a tort action for damages. Since the legislature has not provided that violation of the statutory standard of care automatically establishes negligence, it is fair to infer that courts have some discretion to "borrow" that standard selectively.

Last, it is doubtful that the legislature intended blind adherence to statutory standards regardless of the circumstances. Legislators tend to be practical people, and practical people recognize that there are circumstances in which the ordinary rules do not pertain. If asked, no legislator who voted for a statute requiring drivers to keep to the right would testify that she intended them to run down small children in order to fulfill the statutory command, or to smash into a stalled oil delivery truck.

Common Approaches To Borrowing Statutory Standards

Some early cases appear to hold that violation of a statutory standard of care always constitutes negligence per se. Under this approach, if the defendant violated the statute, the jury would be required to find her negligent, without regard to any excuse she might offer. One of the classic cases, *Martin v. Herzog*, 126 N.E. 814 (N.Y. 1920), might be read to stand for this position,[1] and early cases from other jurisdictions appear to agree. See, e.g., *Decker v. Roberts*, 3 A.2d 855 (Conn. 1939); *O'Bannon v. Schultz*, 169 A. 601 (Conn. 1933); cf. *Zeni v. Anderson*, 243 N.W.2d 270, 281 (Mich. 1976) (noting that the negligence per se rule bars evidence of excuse). Under this approach, the only way the defendant could avoid liability would be to show that the statute did not apply under the circumstances (see, e.g., *Tedla v. Ellman*, 19 N.E.2d 987 (N.Y. 1939)), or that the violation, while admittedly negligence, did not cause the plaintiff's injury.

However, as Holmes's maxim portends, increased experience with the negligence per se doctrine has led virtually all courts to soften this Draconian stance. Most courts have adopted one of the following approaches, which allow the jury to consider the violation of a statutory standard of care in determining negligence, but avoid making it automatically determinative.

---

1. However, even *Martin*, despite its strong language, intimated that the violation in that case established negligence per se because it was "wholly unexcused." 126 N.E. at 815.

A. Negligence Per Se with "Excuse"

The most common formula is to hold that an unexcused violation of a relevant statute is negligence per se, but that the party who violated the statute may offer evidence of an excuse or justification for violating it. Suppose, for example, that Hellman tries to prove that Bourjailly was negligent by showing that he passed the stopped school bus in violation of the statute. Suppose further that Bourjailly produced no explanation for the violation. On these facts, the jury would be instructed that, if they find that Bourjailly violated the statute, they must find that he was negligent. If, however, Bourjailly produced evidence of a sufficient reason for violating the statute, the jury would be free to conclude that the violation was "excused," and would not, in and of itself, establish negligence.

The Restatement (Second) of Torts adopts this approach to the problem. Section 288A provides that an excused violation of a statute is not negligence per se, and recognizes the following excuses:

a. incapacity (for example, the actor is a minor unable to comply with the usual standard of care)
b. lack of knowledge of the need to comply (for example, where a driver's tail light goes out while he is driving and before he has the opportunity to discover it)
c. inability to comply (for example, where a blizzard makes it impossible to comply with a statute requiring a railroad to keep its fences clear of snow)
d. emergency (as where a driver swerves across the center line to avoid a child in the street)
e. compliance poses greater risk than violation (as where a pedestrian walks with her back to the traffic due to unusually heavy traffic going the other way)

These listed excuses are not exclusive; Bourjailly would be free to offer some other reason for the violation as well. Restatement (Second) of Torts §288A cmt. a.

Under the Restatement approach, Bourjailly would be deemed negligent if he violated the statute and offered no evidence of an acceptable excuse. However, if he did present evidence of an excuse, the plaintiff's effort to prove negligence simply by proving a violation of the statute would fail. The jury would be instructed to determine whether Bourjailly acted reasonably under all the circumstances, including his violation of the statute, the reasons offered for noncompliance, and others. That sounds a good deal like a general reasonableness inquiry.

B. "Presumption" of Negligence

Some jurisdictions hold that proof of a statutory violation creates a "presumption" that the violator was negligent. The violator is still free, however, to rebut the presumption by showing that the reasonable person would have acted as he did. It is not clear that there is much difference between this approach and the Restatement approach. Under each, the plaintiff may use evidence of a statutory violation to establish negligence. Under each, the defendant may offer evidence of a good reason for her conduct. If she does not offer such evidence, the violation of the statute establishes her negligence. If she does, the jury is left to assess her conduct under a reasonable person standard.

One difference between the presumption and Restatement approaches is that there is no specific list of valid excuses under the presumption approach. The defendant is free to offer any competent evidence of an appropriate reason for violating the statute. This may not be much of a difference, however, since the list of excuses is not exclusive under the Restatement. However, some jurisdictions appear to treat the five listed exceptions in the Restatement as exclusive. See, e.g., *Murray v. O & A Express, Inc.*, 630 S.W.2d 633, 636 & n.4 (Tex. 1982) (defendant must produce evidence of one of the five excuses recognized in the Restatement to avoid negligence per se). This approach would be more restrictive than the open-ended proof of excuse allowed under the presumption approach.

Under both the Restatement and the presumption approaches, most courts hold that the burden of proof remains on the plaintiff.[2] The plaintiff can prove negligence by proving violation of a relevant safety statute, if the defendant does not offer evidence of an adequate reason for the violation. If evidence of an excuse *is* offered, the burden remains on the plaintiff to convince the jury that, in light of the violation and the reasons offered, the defendant did not behave as a reasonable person would under the circumstances. See, e.g., *Moughon v. Wolf*, 576 S.W.2d 603, 604-605 (Tex. 1978) (where plaintiff proves statutory violation and defendant offers evidence of excuse, plaintiff bears the burden to convince the jury that defendant's conduct was negligent under the reasonable person standard).

C. Evidence of Negligence

The third common approach is to treat violation of a statutory standard of care as evidence of negligence. Under this approach, evidence that the defendant violated a statute is admissible at trial. The jury may consider it along with all the other evidence that the defendant did or did not exercise ordinary

---

2. A few states appear to shift the burden of proof to the defendant to prove due care, once a violation of statute has been shown. See, e.g., *Resser v. Boise-Cascade Corp.*, 587 P.2d 80, 84 (Or. 1978) (once violation is shown, burden shifts to violator to prove that he nevertheless acted reasonably). It is not always clear, however, whether these courts mean that the burden to produce evidence of excuse shifts to the defendant, or the actual burden of proof.

care. They may be persuaded (on that evidence alone, or along with other evidence) that the defendant was negligent. But they are not compelled to find him negligent, *even in the absence of rebutting evidence from the defendant.*

This is meaningfully different from the per se and presumption approaches. Under those approaches, if no excuse is offered, the judge should instruct the jury that, if they find that the defendant violated the statute, they must find that the defendant was negligent. Under the evidence-of-negligence approach, proof of an unexcused violation would support a finding of negligence by the jury, but they would still be free to find that the defendant was not negligent, *even if no excuse were offered.* It is certainly conceivable that a jury would refuse to find negligence despite the violation: For example, a jury might well find that driving 57 m.p.h. on a clear dry day on a rural interstate highway is not negligence, even if the speed limit were 55 and the defendant had no excuse. Under the evidence-of-negligence approach, the jury would be free to reach that conclusion. Under the presumption or per se approaches, however, this violation would establish negligence unless an excuse were offered.[3]

The Requirement of Relevance

As the foregoing section indicates, evidence of the violation of a statutory standard of care is usually admissible, and can be conclusive, on the negligence question. However, such evidence may not be used to establish breach of the duty of care unless the statute establishes a *relevant* standard of care. If Bourjailly causes an accident by turning into the path of Perelman's oncoming car, common sense tells us that it is irrelevant that he violated a statute requiring him to curb his dog, or even one requiring working windshield wipers (assuming the weather was dry at the time of the accident). Allowing evidence of these violations might prove that Bourjailly was a generally negligent person, but would not show that his negligence caused this particular accident.

Courts frequently state that a statute is only relevant in establishing negligence if it is meant to protect persons like the plaintiff from the type of harm which actually occurred. The dog curbing statute was not aimed at preventing intersection collisions, but the turn signal statute quoted at p.82 clearly was enacted to protect other drivers from collisions with turning vehicles, exactly the type of accident which resulted from Bourjailly's failure

---

3. It is sometimes said in the cases that violation of a relevant statute establishes "*prima facie* evidence of negligence." This sounds very much like the "evidence of negligence" approach, but most courts that use this phrase actually appear to apply the presumption of negligence approach. See, e.g., *Zeni*, 243 N.W.2d at 276, 283, in which the court appears to use the presumption and prima facie evidence language interchangeably.

to comply with the statute. This statute establishes a relevant standard of care, because it was meant to protect drivers like Perelman from the type of harm — turning accidents — which resulted in this case. Prosser & Keeton, §36, at 222-26.

This requirement is nicely illustrated by one of the classic cases on the point. In *Gorris v. Scott*, 9 L.R.-Ex. 125 (1874), the plaintiff's sheep were washed overboard while being transported by sea. The plaintiff tried to establish the carrier's negligence by proving that it had violated a regulation requiring that animals on shipboard must be kept in pens of a certain size. Had the defendant complied with the statute, the plaintiff argued, the sheep would not have been washed overboard.

The court refused to find negligence on the basis of the violation. The regulation, the court concluded, was not meant to protect animals from being washed overboard, but rather to prevent the spread of disease by preventing overcrowding. Since it was not aimed at preventing the type of harm that occurred, it did not establish a standard of care relevant to the circumstances, and could not be used to establish the shipper's negligence.

Another case which nicely illustrates the point is *Kansas, Okla. & Gulf Ry. Co. v. Keirsey*, 266 P.2d 617 (Okla. 1954), in which the plaintiff's cow entered a railroad right of way and ate itself to death. The plaintiff claimed that the railroad was negligent per se, because it had violated a statute which required it to maintain fences to prevent animals from straying onto the right of way. The court refused to find negligence based on the violation, however, since the statute was aimed at protecting farm animals from being hit by trains, not from eating too much grass.

Courts will also refuse to treat violation of a statute as negligence if the statute was not intended to protect the class of persons to which the plaintiff belongs. See Restatement (Second) of Torts §286(a). For example, a statute requiring elevator shafts in a factory to be guarded might be intended to protect workers but not a delivery person or a police officer who enters to apprehend a suspect. If the court finds that the standard was not meant to protect such entrants, it will not allow consideration of the statute, since it does not establish a relevant standard of care.

Similarly, a building code might be intended to protect building occupants, not workers involved in the construction of the building. If so, the court would likely refuse to apply the building code standards to determine negligence in an action by a worker injured during construction, since the legislature was thinking about a different group with a different set of expectations and different opportunities to protect themselves. Thus, the statute is not relevant on the question of proper precautions during construction. Another nice example is a firefighter injured fighting a fire in a building that lacks sprinklers required by statute. The court might well refuse to allow the firefighter to establish negligence based on the lack of sprinklers, since the statute was meant to protect occupants, not emergency personnel.

If the defendant successfully argues that the statute was not aimed at the type of harm the plaintiff suffered, or at protecting persons in the plaintiff's situation, violation of the statute is irrelevant to the case. It will not be given per se effect or even be admitted in evidence. That does not mean that the plaintiff must lose the case. All it means is that she cannot prove the second element of her claim — breach of the standard of care — by proving a violation of the statute: She must shoulder the usual burden to show negligence under the reasonable person standard discussed in the previous chapter.

The Persuasive Force of the Negligence Per Se Argument

It is easy to see why the negligence per se argument is attractive to lawyers. If Hellman can prove that Bourjailly was negligent just by showing that he violated the school bus statute, it substantially eases her burden of proof. It is a lot easier to prove that he didn't stop for the bus than to prove that his conduct was careless under the vague ordinary-prudence-under-the-circumstances standard. In addition, proving that Bourjailly violated the statute brands him as a "lawbreaker" in the eyes of the jury, which can't do his case a lot of good. Thus, using the violation to establish negligence has great tactical value for Hellman. Similarly, if the contractor in the second example can prove that Updike was negligent simply by showing that he wasn't wearing a helmet, its defense looks a good deal stronger than it would under a general negligence standard.

The use of statutory standards to prove negligence also reduces the likelihood that the jury will decide the case on grounds unrelated to the merits. A jury sympathetic to the injured Updike in the helmet case might be tempted to ignore his negligence and find for him anyway. It will be harder for them to do that if they are instructed that they *must* find him negligent if they find that he did not wear a helmet. Indeed, if it were undisputed that Updike had no helmet on, the court might take the negligence issue from the jury entirely, on the ground that the undisputed and unexcused violation of the statute establishes his negligence as a matter of law.[4]

All this appears complex, but is pretty much a matter of common sense in actual operation. Perhaps the following examples will help.

EXAMPLES

Some Relevant Questions

1.   A good place to start in any negligence per se situation is to ask whether the statute was intended to protect the plaintiff from the type of harm which

---

4. Even if instructed that the violation constitutes negligence, the jury in a comparative negligence jurisdiction would still have to determine the plaintiff's percentage of negligence.

she actually suffered. In which of the following cases do you think the court would find the statutory standard relevant to the plaintiff's claim?

   a. Porter, the town dog officer, quarantines a dog who had bitten a child. The officer allows the owner to take the dog after a week, in violation of a quarantine statute that requires him to hold the dog for fourteen days. The next day, the dog runs in front of Jones's car. Jones swerves to avoid the dog and is injured.

   b. Oliver, a seven-year-old child, finds an abandoned refrigerator in a vacant lot, crawls in to hide, and suffocates. In an action for his death, the estate tries to prove the owner's negligence by showing violation of the statute quoted on p.82, requiring removal of doors from appliances left in places accessible to children.

   c. Welty hits Capote broadside when she is driving down Main Street and fails to see Capote pulling out into the street at an intersection. Capote alleges that Welty was negligent because she violated the statute quoted above at p.82, requiring a working muffler on all motor vehicles.

   d. Porter, pulling out of a parking lot, hits Austin, who is riding her bicycle down the sidewalk. Porter argues that Austin was negligent for riding on the sidewalk, in violation of a statute that provides that "No person shall ride a bicycle on a sidewalk in a business district."

   e. Welty is driving east on Main Street when a school bus coming in the other direction stops. Since she can see that the only child around is already stepping into the bus, Welty drives on. As she passes the bus, she hits Capote's car coming out of a side street. Capote claims that Welty's negligence is established by her violation of the statute quoted on p.82, requiring traffic to stop when school buses do. How should the court rule?

   f. Austin, riding her bicycle down the street, approaches a truck parked in a loading zone. To clear the truck, she steers further into the street, and is hit by a passing motorist. She alleges that Porter, the owner of the truck, was negligent for violating a statute that limits parking in the loading zone to one-half hour during morning hours. Porter's truck had been there for nearly two hours.

2. After reading about the various ways in which the defendant may excuse a statutory violation, it may seem that the negligence per se doctrine is a toothless tiger. The plaintiff can use it to suggest negligence, but the defendant can rebut it, so it all comes down to general reasonableness anyway. Here are a few cases that illustrate that the doctrine can make a big difference in a negligence case. In each case, ask yourself why the per se negligence doctrine will make an important difference in the outcome.

   a. Salinger is driving east on a rural West Dakota highway when Ginsberg comes toward him from around a curve, driving astride the center line of the road. Their cars collide and Ginsberg is killed. Salinger sues Ginsberg's estate for negligence. To prove that Ginsberg failed to exercise due care, he testifies that Ginsberg violated a statute that requires vehicles to keep to the right of the center line.

b. Salinger is injured when Ginsberg's car turns in front of him while he is driving down Maple Street. He seeks to establish Ginsberg's negligence by proving that Ginsberg failed to signal his turn, as required by the statute quoted above on p.82. Ginsberg claims that he did signal before turning.

c. Perelman hits Woolf, a construction worker, while backing up a large bulldozer. Perelman was watching carefully, but the beeper on the bulldozer was broken, and had been for five days. The statute on p.82, requiring a beeper on heavy construction equipment, applies.

Statutory Enlightenment

3.   Cheever owns a three-unit apartment building in Oakley, West Dakota. He fails to replace a burnt out light bulb in the upstairs hall, and O'Connor trips and falls down the stairs. She sues him for negligence, and offers to prove his negligence by showing that he violated West Dakota Stat. Ann. Title XVI, §31, which requires landlords to maintain adequate lighting in all common areas of their buildings.

a. Does the statute establish a standard of care relevant to the case?

b. Assume that Cheever defends by offering evidence that the light was not out; thus, he does not offer any reason for failing to replace the bulb. Assuming that West Dakota applies the negligence per se doctrine, should the judge direct a verdict for O'Connor on the negligence issue?

c. Assume again that Cheever claims the light was on, and that West Dakota applies the negligence per se doctrine. How should the judge instruct the jury on the negligence issue?

d. If there were no statute establishing a relevant standard of care in this case, how would the judge instruct the jury on the negligence issue?

e. Assume now that West Dakota takes the position that violation of a relevant statute is admissible evidence of negligence rather than negligence per se. If O'Connor claims that Cheever violated the statute, how should the judge instruct the jury on the issue?

4.   Assume again that O'Connor relies on the violation of the lighting statute to prove Cheever's negligence. Cheever testifies that he was aware of the burnt out bulb, but had asked Porter, another tenant, to replace it and Porter had told him that he would do it right away.

a. Assume that West Dakota applies the negligence per se with excuse approach, but that, like some states, it recognizes only the five excuses listed in the Restatement (Second) of Torts §288A (see p.85). How will the negligence issue be resolved?

b. Assume that the Restatement (Second) of Torts §288A is applied. How would the negligence issue be resolved?

c. Assume that West Dakota applied the "presumption of negligence" approach. How would the negligence issue be resolved?

5. One more variation on Cheever's woes. Assume that his building is in a high crime area. Calisher, accosted on the street by a robber, runs into his building to escape. Because the light is out, she stumbles over a child's tricycle and is injured. In a negligence action, can she rely on his violation of the lighting statute to establish negligence?

Judge Fudd Rules Again

6. Calisher runs a small, low-budget theater in the round. Wharton, a patron, is injured when her seat collapses during a performance, evidently because a bolt sheared off underneath it. In her negligence action against Calisher, she introduces evidence that Calisher had violated West Dakota Ann. Laws Title XIX, §21A, which requires that theater owners have their premises inspected and certified annually by the city building inspector.

a. Assume that West Dakota follows the evidence of negligence approach. Judge Fudd instructs the jury, in part, as follows:

> If you find that West Dakota Ann. Laws Title XIX, §21A is intended to protect a class of persons including the plaintiff from the danger of injuries such as that suffered by her, and that the defendant violated that statute, then you are instructed that the violation is evidence, along with all the other evidence in the case, that you may consider in determining whether the defendant was negligent.

Can you spot a fundamental flaw in Judge Fudd's instruction?

b. Assuming that the statute establishes a relevant standard of care, what other basic problem do you see in Wharton's case?

The Goose and the Gander

7. A West Dakota statute requires a fence at least four feet high around private pools. Beverly has such a pool, with a four foot fence. Allen, a child of seven, climbs over the fence, jumps into the pool, and drowns. Allen's parents sue Beverly for negligence in failing to prevent children from entering the pool area.

a. What will Beverly argue in his defense?

b. How should the court rule on the defense?

EXPLANATIONS

Some Relevant Questions

1a. Clearly, this statute is aimed at protecting people from being bitten by diseased dogs, not at preventing dogs from running into the street, which could happen no matter when the dog is released. Since the statute is not meant to protect against the *type of harm* suffered by Jones, the court will not allow her to prove Porter's negligence by showing this violation.

b. This statute was clearly aimed at exactly the risk that caused the harm here: A child getting caught in the appliance when the door closes on her. In the absence of an excuse, the violation of this statute would establish negligence in a per se or a presumption jurisdiction.

c. In order to invoke the muffler statute to prove Welty's negligence, Capote will have to demonstrate that it was aimed, at least in part, at preventing the type of accident that took place here. At first glance, the statute appears aimed at preventing excessive noise from passing cars. But it is entirely plausible that it was also aimed at assuring that drivers could *listen* for traffic hazards as well as see them. A statute may be aimed at preventing a variety of evils. So long as one purpose of the statute is to avert the type of injury suffered by the plaintiff, the violation should be considered relevant to the negligence issue.

Of course, Welty's violation of the muffler statute would only establish liability if it *caused* the accident. Her noisy muffler would be irrelevant unless her inability to hear contributed to the accident. The evidence might show, however, that Capote had blown his horn to warn Welty, but that she was unable to hear due to the muffler noise. If so, Welty's violation of the muffler statute would be a cause of the accident.

d. This example is based on an Oregon case, *Reynolds v. Tyler*, 670 P.2d 223 (Or. App. 1983). In *Reynolds*, the court concluded that the ordinance in issue was aimed at protecting pedestrians from being hit by bicycles, not to protect cyclists from cars pulling out into the street. Consequently, it rejected the argument that the plaintiff's violation could be used to establish her contributory negligence.

Often there is little legislative history to assist in determining what risks the legislature was trying to prevent by the passage of a statute. The court must infer the statute's purposes primarily from the provisions of the statute itself. Thus, courts exercise a good deal of judgment in determining whom the statute was meant to protect, and from what hazards. Many courts, I suspect, would be more liberal than the *Reynolds* court on both of these questions. It seems plausible that the legislature had in view a variety of hazards posed by bicycles on the sidewalk, including the risk of collisions with entering vehicles, which would not anticipate fast moving vehicles on the sidewalk. It also seems plausible that the ordinance was meant to prevent injury to cyclists as well as to others.

In *Reynolds*, the provision at issue was a local ordinance rather than a state statute. Some courts have refused to give per se effect to ordinances or administrative regulations, even if they apply the doctrine to statutes promulgated by the legislature itself. Harper, James & Gray, §17.6, at 642. Such enactments are promulgated by bodies with fewer resources to investigate, and do not represent as broad-based a judgment about proper conduct as a vote of the state legislature. Other cases, however, give per se effect to ordinances and regulations as well.

e. This statute was obviously aimed at protecting school children from injury, not other drivers. On that rationale, the Supreme Court of Rhode Island held on similar facts that violation of the statute could not be used to establish negligence. *Paquin v. Tillinghast*, 517 A.2d 246 (R.I. 1986).

However, the fact that the statute would not conclusively establish Welty's negligence does not mean that it is irrelevant in this case. It may be, for example, that Capote pulled out because he expected Welty to stop for the bus, as the statute required her to do. If so, Capote could prove those facts in order to show that Welty was negligent for failing to do what the reasonable person would do under the circumstances. But this is quite different from equating negligence with violation of the statute, as the per se approach does. Rather, the statute would be introduced here to prove that, in light of the normal expectations of drivers, Welty was negligent under the usual reasonable person standard.

f. This statute is aimed at assuring access to adequate parking for deliveries, not at preventing the type of accident Austin has suffered here. Austin does not claim the truck was too far out into the street, but only that it was *there*. She could just as well have suffered the same accident if the truck had only been there ten minutes. Indeed, if Porter had left on time, another truck would likely have been there anyway. This statute is irrelevant to the case; Porter's violation of it should not be considered by the jury on the negligence question. See *Capolungo v. Bondi*, 224 Cal. Rptr. 326 (Cal. App. 1st Dist. 1986).

2a. Under either the per se or presumption approaches, Salinger's evidence of the violation will, if the jury believes it, establish Ginsberg's negligence, unless evidence of an adequate excuse is offered. Here, Ginsberg is not around to offer exculpatory evidence. He may have had a good reason for the violation, but if the proof is not offered, the presumption governs. The doctrine is very powerful in cases like this, where the violator is unable to offer the countervailing evidence that would rebut the presumption.

b. Here, instead of trying to prove a good reason for violating the statute, the defendant claims that he did not violate it. It is a little hard for the defendant to play both sides of the street (no pun intended) in these cases. Usually, she will have to either try to explain a violation or deny that it took place. If she stakes her case on the factual contention that she did not violate the statute, and the jury finds that she did, that finding will determine the negligence issue: Under either the negligence per se or presumption approach, the violation establishes negligence, in the absence of any evidence of an acceptable excuse.

c. Here, the defendant violated the statute, which was clearly intended to prevent the type of accident which took place, and just has no acceptable excuse. In a per se or presumption jurisdiction, the evidence that the beeper was not working will establish Perelman's negligence. The fact that he looked carefully will not avert a required finding of negligence, because the jury is not free to make a general finding on the negligence issue: If it finds that the statute was violated, and Perelman has no excuse, it must find that he breached the duty of due care.

This will doubtless be the situation in many negligence per se cases: The defendant simply has no excuse for the violation of the statute. In such cases, the statutory negligence doctrine provides a powerful weapon for the plaintiff, since it establishes the most ambiguous element which she must prove to recover: breach of the duty of due care.

Statutory Enlightenment

3a. The lighting requirement in the statute is clearly aimed at protecting tenants like O'Connor from the type of harm — injury while trying to negotiate the stairs in the dark — that she has suffered. Thus, it establishes a standard of care relevant to the case, and it is appropriate to consider that standard in resolving the negligence issue.

b. The judge should not direct the verdict, even if the negligence per se doctrine applies. The violation of the lighting statute only establishes Cheever's negligence if the light *was* out. Whether it was out is a factual issue the jury must decide. Thus, the jury still has an important role to play, even in a negligence per se jurisdiction. But their task will be much more circumscribed than it would be under a general reasonable care standard, since they need only decide whether Cheever violated the statute. If he did, and offers no excuse, his negligence is established under the negligence per se doctrine.[5]

c. The judge should instruct the jury along the following lines:

> Under West Dakota law, the violation of a statute intended to protect against the type of harm suffered by the plaintiff establishes negligence. If you find in this case that the defendant violated West Dakota Ann. Laws Title XVI, §31, by failing to provide adequate lighting in the hallway of the building, then you must find that the defendant was negligent.

Note that the judge would not instruct the jury on the effect of an excuse for the violation, since Cheever has not offered such evidence. He has staked his case on the position that he did not violate the statute.

---

5. In addition, of course, the jury in a comparative negligence jurisdiction will have to assign a percentage of fault to Cheever's negligence, if they find that he did violate the statute.

d. If there were no statute relevant to the case, the judge would instruct the jury to consider whether Cheever was negligent under the usual reasonable person standard:

> Negligence is the failure to use that degree of care that an ordinary prudent person would use under the circumstances. If you find that the defendant exercised the degree of care that an ordinary prudent person would exercise in maintaining the common areas of the building, then you should find that he was not negligent. If you find that the defendant failed to exercise the degree of care that an ordinary prudent person would exercise in maintaining the common areas of the building, you should find that he was negligent.

It is not hard to see why O'Connor would prefer to see the jury given the instruction in Example 3c. That instruction narrows the issue from the general "throw-it-to-the-jury" due care standard to a very specific fact question, and requires the jury, if it finds the light was out, to find for O'Connor on the critical issue of negligence (assuming no evidence of excuse is offered). Thus, the adoption of the statutory standard of care substantially eases her burden of proof. It also brands Cheever as a "wrongdoer," which may color the way the jury looks at other issues in the case.

e. The judge should give the jury a general negligence instruction, such as the instruction in Example 3d. She should then add a further instruction along these lines:

> If you find that the defendant violated West Dakota Ann. Laws, Tit. XVI, §31, requiring adequate lighting in the common areas of apartment buildings, you may consider that violation together with all the other evidence in the case in determining whether the defendant failed to exercise reasonable care under the circumstances.

This instruction would leave it to the jury to consider the statutory duty along with all the evidence in deciding whether Cheever was negligent. The jury could conclude, under the ordinary reasonable person standard, that he was negligent. On the other hand, the jury would also be free to conclude otherwise, even if it finds that the light was out. This more flexible rule gives a good deal more latitude to Cheever to persuade the jury that he acted reasonably under all the circumstances, even if he violated the statute.

4a. On these facts, the trial judge should probably direct a verdict for O'Connor on the question of negligence. Cheever has admitted that he did not comply with the statute, so the only question is whether he has an adequate excuse for noncompliance. Relying on his tenant's assurance does not appear to meet any of the five categories of permissible excuses in §288A: Cheever is not a minor; he is not unable to replace the bulb; he was aware of the need to do so; no emergency intervened, and compliance did not pose any risk. Thus, if these are the only permissible excuses, Cheever has none, and his negligence is established by his admission that he violated the statute.

b. The Restatement allows the violator to prove one of the five listed categories of excuses, but also allows proof of others not listed. Restatement (Second) of Torts §288A cmt. a. Under the Restatement, presumably the jury would have to decide whether Cheever's reliance on his tenant was an adequate excuse for the violation. Thus, the case would go to the jury if the Restatement applied, but not in a state that regarded the five categories as exclusive.

c. In a presumption state, proof of the violation establishes negligence, unless the violator offers evidence of an excuse. Here, Cheever has offered evidence of an excuse. Unless the offered excuse were patently insufficient, it would be for the jury to evaluate the adequacy of that excuse. Thus, as under the Restatement, the case would go to the jury.

5. To be relevant, a statute must not only protect against the harm suffered by the plaintiff, but must also be intended to protect a class of persons to which the plaintiff belongs. Certainly, the lighting statute was meant to prevent stumbling over obstacles in the dark, but it is questionable whether it was meant to protect *Calisher* from such risks. It was doubtless aimed at protecting tenants, and probably guests as well . . . maybe even meter readers. But it hardly seems that it was meant to protect passersby who enter unexpectedly to avoid a robbery. Thus, arguably, Calisher cannot use the statute to show a standard of care relevant *to her*. But cf. *Nixon v. Mr. Property Mgmt. Co.*, 690 S.W.2d 546 (Tex. 1985) (building owner may be held liable for failing to secure vacant apartment to which plaintiff was abducted and raped).

Judge Fudd Rules Again

6a. The problem here is that the jury is not the proper body to decide whether the standard of care established in the statute is relevant . . . Judge Fudd is. The jury is there to try the case, not the statute. The question of whether the statute establishes a relevant standard of care is an issue of law that the court should decide prior to trial. The parties will brief and argue the issue and the judge will make a legal determination as to whether the statute was meant to protect parties in the plaintiff's position from the type of harm suffered. If the judge concludes that the statute establishes a standard that is relevant to the case, evidence that it was violated will be admitted; otherwise, the jury will hear nothing about it.

b. Wharton may be able to convince the jury that the inspection statute was meant to prevent injuries by identifying safety problems on the premises. But she will still have a hard time establishing that the violation of the inspection statute *caused* her injury. It appears extremely unlikely that an inspection would have revealed that a bolt in the chair was about to shear off. Presumably, most of the bolt is not even visible, and it may be impossible to spot this type of metal fatigue from a visual inspection anyway. It is doubtful that the inspector would get down and look underneath the chairs anyway;

probably she would check for major risks such as blocked aisles, inadequate emergency lighting, or broken sprinklers. Thus, Calisher will argue that, even if the required inspection had been done, the bolt problem would not have been detected. If this is so, the violation is not an actual cause of Wharton's injury.

That does not mean that Wharton must lose: It simply means that she must fall back on the general negligence standard to establish Calisher's negligence. She might well prove that Calisher was negligent in other ways. Perhaps she continued to use the seats beyond their useful life or after other similar accidents. Perhaps she was notified of this type of risk by the manufacturer, but failed to repair the seats. Maybe she replaced the bolt herself with one too small for the task. Any of these might show that Calisher was negligent under the usual reasonable person standard.

The Goose and the Gander

7a. Of course, Beverly will argue that "what is sauce for the goose is sauce for the gander": If failure to comply with a statute constitutes negligence, *compliance* with a statute ought to constitute due care. Here, the statute required a four foot fence. That, Beverly will argue, is the measure of due care, and he should be found "careful per se" for complying with the statute.

b. The argument has an immediate appeal to it but has been generally rejected. Standards of care imposed by the legislature are often minimum standards, intended to avoid the most dangerous practices but not to immunize persons who do the minimum from liability where more precaution is appropriate. It may be that it is unreasonable to ignore the minimum standards set by the legislature, but it does not follow that the reasonable person takes *only* those minimum precautions. See Restatement (Second) of Torts §288C (compliance with statutory standard "does not prevent a finding of negligence where a reasonable man would take additional precautions"). For example, a four foot fence around a pool may suffice in some areas, but in others where many children live a reasonable person might conclude that a four foot fence is insufficient to prevent them from entering.

Speed limits provide another good example of this point. In setting a limit, the legislature may have concluded that it is dangerous to exceed a particular speed, but that does not imply that it is always reasonable to travel at that speed. In fog, snow, or heavy traffic, a much slower speed may be called for and a rule that compliance with the posted limit absolves the defendant would be inappropriate.

6

A Phrase In Latin: Res Ipsa Loquitur

Introduction

The last chapter considered the use of statutory standards of care to prove that the defendant breached the duty of due care or "was negligent." This chapter considers another means of proving negligence, through circumstantial evidence and particularly through the mystic doctrine of res ipsa loquitur.

Sometimes proving negligence is straightforward. Suppose that Cisneros goes to the neighborhood garage to have the wheels of his Maserati balanced. After driving away, the right front wheel falls off. Cisneros gets out and looks around, but is only able to find three of the lug nuts that hold the wheel on. He returns to the station, where another customer tells him that he saw the mechanic leave the other lug nuts off. Negligence? No problem: What happened is clear from direct evidence, the testimony of the other customer, and a jury would almost certainly conclude that the mechanic was negligent in failing to replace all the lug nuts.

Would that all negligence cases were so easy. If they were, few negligence cases would be tried, because cases in which liability is clear almost always settle before trial. The cases that reach the trial stage are likely to present substantial disputes of fact, in which proof of essential elements — particularly negligence — is more problematic.

The Difference Between Direct and Circumstantial Evidence

In the Maserati example, Cisneros produces compelling evidence of the mechanic's negligence, direct testimony from a witness who observed the negligent act. However, negligence need not always be proved by direct evidence. In many cases, plaintiffs will have to rely on "circumstantial" evidence, that is, evidence of facts from which a jury could *infer* that the defendant was negligent. Cisneros might, for example, return to the garage and find two Maserati lug nuts sitting next to the wheel balancing apparatus. This might suffice to allow a jury to infer negligence on the part of the mechanic. The argument runs like this: If the wheel fell off shortly after Cisneros drove away, and if two Maserati lug nuts were sitting at the garage, and if Cisneros could only find three at the scene, it is likely that the mechanic only refastened three. Common experience tells us that leaving some of the lug nuts off creates an unreasonable risk that the wheel will come loose. Therefore, it appears probable that the mechanic was negligent in failing to secure the wheel.

Cisneros might have to rely on even less compelling circumstantial evidence to establish negligence. He might only be able to prove that the wheel fell off shortly after he left the garage, and that he was unable to locate all the lug nuts at the scene of the accident. This does not directly show that the mechanic failed to refasten them, but it again suggests (though less forcefully than the last scenario) that the likely explanation of the accident is the failure to refasten all the lug nuts. A jury could still reasonably infer from the facts Cisneros *has* proved that the accident more probably than not happened because the lug nuts were not refastened or were improperly fastened. Thus, proof of the circumstances allows an inference of further facts which would establish the mechanic's negligence.

Circumstantial evidence is commonly used in proving all sorts of tort cases. The plaintiff offers evidence of a pile of freshly cut maple logs in the defendant's backyard to establish that the defendant cut down his maple trees. Scratches or paint scrapings on the defendant's fender are offered to establish that it was his car that hit the plaintiff's. Evidence of large, unexplained deposits in defendant's bank account is offered to establish that he converted the plaintiff's funds. In each case, evidence of one fact is offered because it tends to establish another.

The "banana peel cases" offer a classic example of the use of circumstantial evidence to establish negligence. The plaintiff slips on a banana peel on the supermarket floor, and sues for his injuries. To establish negligence, he must show that the banana peel was there long enough that store employees should have seen and removed it. It would be ideal to introduce direct evidence, say, three customers who saw it on the floor over the course of several hours before the accident. Such direct evidence isn't likely to be available, however. If three customers had seen it, one would likely have told someone about it, or picked it up. (Similarly, in the Maserati case, if another customer had seen the lug nuts left off, he would likely have said something to the mechanic and averted the accident.)

Absent such direct evidence, banana peel plaintiffs usually offer circumstantial evidence to prove that the banana peel was on the floor long enough to be noticed. They will testify that the banana peel was black, or gritty, or trampled flat. From such facts, a jury could reason as follows: Most people don't hold onto old banana peels; they throw them away immediately after eating the banana. Therefore, if a black and gritty banana peel was on the floor, it was probably on the floor long enough to *turn* black and gritty. Common experience suggests that this takes an hour or so, and that's long enough that an employee should have found it and picked it up. Similarly, if the banana peel had been trampled, the jury could infer that it had been stepped on repeatedly over a period of time. Such evidence does not exactly provide an airtight case, but it will often be the best that the plaintiff can do, and may well convince a jury that it is "more probable than not" that the defendant was negligent.

From Circumstantial Evidence to Res Ipsa Loquitur

If circumstantial evidence is one step away from direct testimony, the classic doctrine of res ipsa loquitur is a further step beyond the traditional use of circumstantial evidence. The doctrine originated in the famous case of *Byrne v. Boadle*, 159 Eng. Rep. 299 (1863), in which the unfortunate plaintiff was hit on the head by a flour barrel which fell from the defendant's second story window. While there was no evidence of what caused the flour barrel to fall on Byrne's boodle, the court allowed him to recover. "Res ipsa loquitur," the court opined, "the thing speaks for itself."

Dean Prosser offers the following whimsical response to this tautological logic: "*res ipsa loquitur, sed quid in infernos dicet?*" ("The thing speaks for itself, but what the hell did it say?") Prosser, Wade, and Schwartz, 233. Well, the *Byrne* judges took it to say that flour barrels don't just fall out of windows on their own; that when they do fall, the most likely reason is the negligence of the person in control of the premises. Thus, even though the plaintiff cannot offer direct or circumstantial evidence of exactly what caused the barrel to fall, he should be allowed to reach the jury on the issue of negligence by proving the circumstances of the accident itself, because they bespeak negligence even without a more specific showing of the chain of events.

There is nothing particularly mystical or sophisticated about this idea. As Lord Shaw quipped: "If that phrase had not been in Latin, no one would have called it a principle." *Ballard v. North British R. Co.*, 1923 Sess. Cas. 43 (1923). Res ipsa is not really a separate principle, but rather a special form of circumstantial evidence. The underlying rationale of res ipsa loquitur, as of circumstantial evidence in general, is that facts can sometimes be inferred from other facts. In a case like Cisneros's tire problem, the circumstantial evidence allows the jury to infer *a particular negligent act*, failure to replace the lug nuts. In res ipsa loquitur cases, the circumstantial evidence allows the jury, based on evidence about the accident itself, to infer that it must have resulted from *some negligent act* by the defendant.

Here are some examples of cases in which the plaintiff might use res ipsa loquitur to establish negligence.

- A railway company hires a contractor to install a temporary boarding platform for trains, and it collapses under Feinstein shortly after it is put into use. Even if the collapse makes it impossible to produce evidence of the exact cause, a jury might well infer that negligent construction caused the collapse.
- A brick falls from a roof where a chimney is being repaired and hits the plaintiff. Here again, the plaintiff may not be able to demonstrate what caused the brick to fall; indeed, the workers may not be able to either. Again, however, a jury might fairly infer that the brick probably fell due to some negligent act by the workers.
- An elevator stops abruptly between floors, throwing the plaintiff to the floor.

In each of these cases, there is no showing of exactly how the accident happened, but the fact that it happened at all suggests that someone was probably negligent.

A Critique and a Defense

We saw in Chapter 4 that the plaintiff must prove all the elements of a negligence claim in order to hold the defendant liable. Arguably, courts that apply res ipsa loquitur play fast and loose with the negligence element of the claim, since they allow the jury to find for the plaintiff without proving any specific negligent act. In the platform case, for example, if the plaintiff merely offers evidence that the platform fell shortly after it was constructed, he has not "proved" any particular negligent act by the contractor. Similarly, in the brick case, evidence that the brick fell while the defendant's employees were working on the roof does not prove what negligent act (if any) caused it to fall. The jury cannot determine exactly what caused the brick to fall on the basis of such general evidence. How then, are they to know that there was negligence involved at all?

Well, they don't *know* that negligence was involved, of course. On the other hand, they don't *know* what caused the accident in the Maserati example, either; they simply make a reasonable estimate of the probabilities based on what they do know. Similarly, in res ipsa loquitur cases, the jury may not be able to reconstruct the sequence of events, but they may be able to make an educated inference that, whatever it was, it probably involved the defendant's failure to exercise due care in some respect. The inference may not be infallible, it may not be satisfying to the ruthlessly syllogistic mind, but it is accepted by the legal system as sufficient to satisfy the "more probable than not" standard of proof in negligence cases. Courts, as practical institutions, must face the fact that irrefutable proof is seldom available in practical affairs, that the system is imperfect by its nature and must settle for a reasonable balance of the probabilities.

Consider the alternative. The judicial system could send Byrne away empty handed, explaining the result to him thus:

> Sorry, Byrne, about your busted boodle. But we aren't willing to make Boadle pay you unless you show that he did something wrong. You haven't met your burden of proof, because you haven't shown us what Boadle did that was negligent. Unless you produce such evidence, you are not entitled to recover.

This reasoning sounds pretty good, but it doesn't comport with most people's sense of elementary fairness. Most people *would* make the inference that Boadle or his employees must have slipped up for that barrel to get loose. Similarly, most people would infer that the platform collapse was caused by faulty construction, or that the brick fell because of negligence. The res ipsa loquitur doctrine allows juries to make the same inference of negligence that most of us would make from our common experience.

The "Foundation Facts" In a Res Ipsa Case

Not every plaintiff can get to the jury by intoning the magic Latin, however. For the res ipsa doctrine to apply, the circumstances must support an inference of negligence:

> There must be reasonable evidence of negligence. But where the thing is shewn to be under the management of the defendant or his servants, and the accident is such as in the ordinary course of things does not happen if those who have the management use proper care, it affords reasonable evidence, in the absence of explanation by the defendants, that the accident arose from want of care.

Scott v. London & St. Katherine Docks Co., 159 Eng. Rep. 665, 667 (1865). This early statement of the doctrine remains essentially intact. Most courts hold that the plaintiff can make a case for the jury under res ipsa loquitur by showing that (1) he was injured by an accident that would not normally happen without negligence and (2) that the negligence is more likely than not attributable to the defendant, rather than to the plaintiff or a third party.

A. The Requirement that the Accident Ordinarily Would Not Happen Without Negligence

The first "foundation fact" is that the accident is of a type that ordinarily does not happen without negligence. Many accidents would not support an inference that negligence was involved. It is doubtful that a court would allow the jury to infer negligence from the fact that the plaintiff trips going down the defendant's stairs, or that the defendant's car skids into plaintiff on a rainy day. There are common explanations for such occurrences which do not involve negligence. But many other accidents, by their very nature, do support an inference of negligence. For example, most courts would probably conclude that the following accidents would not have occurred without negligence:

- a patient awakens from a podiatry procedure with teeth missing
- an airplane disappears without a trace in good weather
- a chunk of glass or a tack is found in a can of spinach
- oil spills from a tank truck on the highway

In each of these cases, common knowledge suggests that this is probably not an "accident" in the pure sense of the word; that someone's careless conduct is the likely explanation. That is not to say that negligence is the *only conceivable* explanation for the accident. It is always possible to hypothesize other causes — for example, terrorism in the airplane case, or an undiscoverable defect in the tank truck case. But the plaintiff's burden of proof in a negligence case is not to eliminate all possible alternative causes of his injury. His burden is to show that the *more probable* cause was negligence. In the example cases just given, a jury might reasonably conclude that it was.

B. The Requirement that the Negligence, If Any, Is Attributable to the Defendant

The second "foundation fact" in a res ipsa case is that the negligence is attributable to the defendant. It is not enough to show that someone's negligence probably caused the harm. The evidence must point to the defendant as the negligent party. Often this is obvious, as where a load of cement drops from the defendant's crane, or a scaffold just erected by the defendant falls. In these examples, the defendant is in control of the source of the accident and responsible for its safe operation. If an accident bespeaks negligence in these cases, it very likely bespeaks the defendant's negligence.

This attribution requirement is more difficult, however, where a product causes injury after leaving the defendant's hands. A frequent example is the explosion of a bottle of soda or beer in the hands of a consumer. Many courts have concluded that beverages bottled under pressure should not explode unless someone was negligent in filling or handling the bottle. Thus, the probably-would-not-happen-without-negligence element is met. But in these cases the bottle may have been handled by the distributor, the retailer, and the consumer after it left the bottler's hands. Thus, it is harder to show that the negligence, if there was any, was the bottler's.

The cases often state that this attribution requirement is not met in a res ipsa loquitur case unless the instrumentality that caused the harm was "under the defendant's control" at the time of the accident. This formula is clearly too narrow. For example, in the glass-in-the-spinach case, the canner was clearly not in "control" of the can when the plaintiff ate the spinach and was cut by the glass. Yet it is highly likely that the glass got in the can when the spinach was canned. Thus, a jury could reasonably infer that the negligence, if any, is attributable to the canner. Similarly, the collapsing railroad platform may not be in the "control" of the contractor who built it at the time of the collapse, but it is very likely that the negligence took place at the time of construction and is therefore attributable to the contractor. Although this "control" language is often found in the cases, most courts have not taken it so literally as to preclude use of res ipsa in such obviously appropriate cases.[1]

The formulation of the res ipsa loquitur doctrine in the Second Restatement of Torts nicely avoids the misleading "control" language:

> (1) It may be inferred that harm suffered by the plaintiff is caused by negligence of the defendant when
> (a) the event is of a kind which ordinarily does not occur in the absence of negligence;
> (b) other responsible causes, including the conduct of the plaintiff and third persons, are sufficiently eliminated by the evidence. . . .

Restatement (Second) of Torts §328 D. Under this statement of the doctrine, the plaintiff may invoke res ipsa loquitur even if the defendant did not have exclusive control of the source of the harm, so long as the plaintiff can demonstrate that the negligence was likely that of the defendant rather than himself or other parties.

Courts often state as a third requirement of the res ipsa doctrine that the plaintiff must show that the accident was not attributable to his own conduct. This is not really a separate requirement, however, but rather another way of emphasizing that the plaintiff must be able to establish not just that the accident results from negligence, but that it results from *the defendant's* negligence. In the exploding bottle cases, for example, if the plaintiff sues the bottler, he must eliminate his own conduct as well as the retailer's, in order to show that the explosion is attributable to some negligence of the bottler.

---

1. But see *Kilgore v. Shepard Co.*, 158 A. 720 (R.I. 1932), in which the plaintiff was injured when she sat down in a chair at the defendant's store and it collapsed under her. Although the cause of the collapse was very likely negligent maintenance of the chair, the court refused to apply res ipsa loquitur. Taking the control element too literally, the court concluded that the foundation elements of res ipsa were not established, since the plaintiff, not the defendant, was in control of the chair at the time of the accident.

The Effect of the Doctrine at Trial

Even if a case is tried, a judge has the power to refuse to submit it to the jury if there is no credible evidence in support of one or more of the elements of the plaintiff's claim. Frequently, the defendant will argue that the judge should take the case from the jury (by "directing a verdict" for the defendant[2]) since the plaintiff has not produced proof of a specific negligent act by the defendant. The crucial impact of res ipsa loquitur is that it allows the plaintiff's case to go to the jury even though he has not proved a specific act of negligence. Since juries tend to be plaintiff-oriented, plaintiffs are very keen to avoid directed verdicts and reach the jury. Not surprisingly, the res ipsa doctrine is very popular with the plaintiff's bar.

If the plaintiff establishes the "foundation facts" discussed in the preceding section, and the judge allows the case to go to the jury, they will then decide whether the accident was more probably than not the result of the defendant's negligence. They are free to infer that his negligence caused the accident, but they are also free to conclude, based on the evidence presented, that the defendant's negligence is *not* the more likely explanation. The doctrine, in other words, permits the jury to infer negligence, but it does not require them to. There is loose language in some of the cases suggesting that res ipsa loquitur shifts the burden of proof to the defendant, or creates a presumption of negligence which requires a finding of negligence if not rebutted. Most courts hold, however, that the doctrine merely provides evidence sufficient to support an inference that the defendant was negligent, but does not compel a finding for the plaintiff even where there is no rebuttal evidence. See Restatement (Second) of Torts §328D(3) & cmt. m.

Instructing the Jury on Res Ipsa Loquitur

Logically, it would seem unnecessary to confuse the jury by giving them specific instructions about res ipsa loquitur. It should suffice to tell them that the plaintiff must prove the defendant's negligence by the preponderance of the evidence, and that they are free to infer negligence or not, as they choose, from the evidence presented. The risk of resting on such general instructions, however, is that the jury will take a more technical view of the plaintiff's burden than the courts do, and find for the defendant simply because the plaintiff has not shown the exact cause of the accident. Thus, courts usually give specific instructions detailing the "foundation facts" for res ipsa loquitur and the effect of finding those foundation facts. Here is an example adapted (not quite *verbatim*) from a Minnesota case:

---

2. For a discussion of directed verdict practice, see J. Glannon, Civil Procedure: Examples and Explanations 309-312 (2d. ed. 1992)

> When an accident is such that it would not ordinarily have happened
> unless someone was negligent, and if the thing which caused the acci-
> dent is shown to have been under the exclusive control of the defen-
> dant at the time that the negligent act, if any, must have happened,
> then you are permitted to infer from the mere fact that the accident
> happened and the circumstances surrounding it that the defendant
> was negligent.

See *Bossons v. Hertz Corp.*, 176 N.W.2d 882, 886 (1970). Note how this
instruction tracks the elements of the doctrine. It tells the jury that they *may*
conclude that the defendant was negligent, *if* they find that it was the type
of accident that does not ordinarily happen without negligence, and that the
thing which caused it was under the defendant's control at the time of the
negligence. (This instruction, like many currently in use, does include the
dubious "exclusive control" language, which has raised problems when taken
too literally. However, it focuses on control at the time of the likely negligence
rather than at the time of the accident.)

The Defendant's Case

The res ipsa doctrine may warm the hearts of plaintiff's counsel, but it places
the defendant in a very difficult position. How is he to refute the plaintiff's
proof of negligence, where plaintiff hasn't proved any specific negligent act?
Certainly, the most comforting way to rebut a res ipsa loquitur case is to
prove the actual cause of the accident. For example, proof that the station
platform collapsed because the transit authority was tunneling underneath it
will completely undermine (excuse the pun) the res ipsa inference.

Short of that, the defendant can attack each of the foundation facts
necessary to support res ipsa loquitur. He may probe the attribution requirement by showing that other persons mishandled the product which caused
the injury after it left his hands (for example, the retailer in the exploding
beverage case). He may undermine the required showing that the type of
accident does not ordinarily happen without negligence, by showing other
common, non-negligent causes of this type of accident. A chain is only as
strong as its weakest link; if the jury is not convinced that each of the foundation facts is established, it should refuse to infer the ultimate fact of negligence.
If the defendant's proof on either of these points is strong enough, the judge
may even direct a verdict for him, on the ground that the jury could not
reasonably conclude that the proper foundation for the res ipsa doctrine has
been established.

Where the defendant does *not* have evidence of the exact cause of the
accident, he may try to refute the res ipsa inference by proving that he
generally exercised due care. In the case of the glass in the spinach, for
example, the canner might produce evidence of the careful quality control
measures it takes to avoid objects getting into the cans. The airline in the
lost plane example might produce evidence of its careful training, mainte-

nance, and inspection procedures. This does not conclusively eliminate negligence as the cause, but it could influence the jury's thinking about the probabilities. On the other hand, this can backfire: The more careful the defendant's procedures, the less likely that an accident would happen if they had in fact followed those procedures. Thus, such proof could lead the jury to conclude that, had the procedures been followed, there would not have been an accident at all. For a fine example of this, see G. Fricke, The Use of Expert Evidence in Res Ipsa Loquitur Cases, 5 Vill. L. Rev. 59, 70-72 (1959), quoting cross-examination of a defendant's expert, which very effectively showed that the accident could not have happened unless the usual precautions were not taken.

The cases often suggest that the plaintiff should be able to rely on res ipsa loquitur because the defendant has better access to evidence of the cause of the accident than the plaintiff does. It is certainly true that the doctrine creates a strong incentive for the defendant to produce evidence within its control, at least if it is exculpatory. However, most courts do not restrict the doctrine to cases in which the defendant has better access to proof. See Restatement (Second) of Torts §328D cmt. k; Prosser & Keeton, §39, at 254-255. Often, the defendant has no better chance of explaining the accident than the plaintiff does. In the disappearing plane case, or the glass-in-the-spinach case, for example, the airline or the canner may have no idea what caused the accident, or any way of finding out. Yet the likely explanation of the accident may still be negligence. In such cases, the defendant should not be able to avoid res ipsa simply by showing that it knows no more about the accident than the plaintiff does.

The following examples should help you to understand the types of cases in which the res ipsa doctrine applies, and how this mystic doctrine assists the plaintiff in getting to the jury in those cases.

EXAMPLES

Victims of Circumstance

1.   In which of the following cases do you think plaintiff could reach the jury by invoking res ipsa loquitur?

    a.   Lindsey's front tire blows out while he is driving down Sunset Boulevard. He sues Firewall Tire, the manufacturer of the tire.

    b.   Daley visits a local shoe store. While sitting in a chair trying on shoes, he bumps a set of shelves behind him, and a display rack on top of the shelves falls on his head, injuring him. He sues the store for negligence.

    c.   Young, a three-year-old toddler, comes home from day care. Throughout the evening, he complains of a sore arm. His parents finally take him to the emergency room, where an x-ray reveals that his arm is broken. The parents sue the day care center for negligence.

d. Brown, a five-month-old baby, comes home from day care. Throughout the evening she shows obvious discomfort on her left side. Her parents take her to the emergency room, where x-rays reveal that her left arm is broken. The parents sue the day care center for negligence.

e. Flynn is walking past a high rise hotel when a wine glass falls on his head from one of the balconies above. He sues the hotel for negligence.

Possibly Probable Negligence

2. Consider again Example 1c above, in which Young, a three-year-old toddler, came home from day care with a broken arm. Suppose that the only evidence before the court is the evidence of Young's injury. Suppose further that the judge recognizes that there is a good deal of uncertainty about the more likely cause of the accident. He believes that negligence of the day care center may have been involved, but doubts that it was the *more likely* cause. Perhaps he views negligence as a 40 percent likelihood, and an accident resulting from the toddler's general exuberance a 60 percent likelihood. Should the judge direct a verdict for the day care center, or allow the case to go to the jury?

Firming Up the Foundation

3. Alioto makes up a yummy salad for lunch. He throws in some lettuce, a tomato, a can of artichokes, some mushrooms, and some sliced turkey. Then he pours Newton's Own Natural Russian Salad Dressing over the top. While enjoying the salad, Alioto bites into a piece of glass and breaks a tooth. He sues Newton's.

a. Which of the foundation facts poses a problem here?

b. How might Alioto strengthen the argument for applying res ipsa loquitur to the case?

4. Ulner undergoes leg surgery by Dr. Eastwood to correct an arterial problem in his thigh. After the operation, he notices that he has decreased sensation along the left side of the leg, which gets worse over the ensuing weeks. He sues Eastwood for negligence.

a. What foundation fact raises problems in applying res ipsa loquitur to this case?

b. In addition to the basic facts described above, Ulner presents a medical expert, who testifies that reduced sensation does not ordinarily occur as a result of the type of surgery Ulner had, if ordinary care was exercised. Should Ulner's case go to the jury on a res ipsa loquitur theory?

c. Assume that Ulner's expert testifies that nerve damage of the type he suffered would not happen unless the surgeon was negligent. Dr.

Eastwood then offers an expert who testifies that such loss of sensation may result from a number of causes, including the underlying medical problem, poor post surgical nursing care, unavoidable surgical abrasion of the nerve, or negligence. Given the contradictory expert testimony as to the likelihood of negligence, should the judge allow the case to go to the jury on a res ipsa theory?

d. Suppose that after Ulner's expert testifies, Dr. Eastwood takes the stand. He testifies that the surgery was unremarkable, that he followed standard procedure, and that he definitely did not touch, cut, or pinch any of the surrounding nerves. At the close of his evidence he moves for a directed verdict. How should the judge rule?

e. Assume instead that Dr. Eastwood takes the stand and testifies that during the surgery an artery in Ulner's leg began to hemorrhage, due to an unanticipated weakness in the artery wall. To prevent a life-threatening loss of blood, Eastwood was forced to clamp off the artery, which was directly in contact with the major nerve in the left side of the leg. This procedure risks damage to the nerve, but is unavoidable where such surgical complications arise. This evidence is confirmed by the surgical notes and by the assisting physician. After offering this evidence (which is not contradicted by the plaintiff), Dr. Eastwood moves for a directed verdict. Should it be granted?

Not for Attribution

5. Should the court apply res ipsa loquitur in the following cases?
   a. Feinstein rents a dry cleaning shop from Bradley. The shop is destroyed by fire in the middle of the night. Investigation indicates that the fire began near or along the wall between the office and the cleaning area, but there is no explanation as to the cause. Bradley sues Feinstein for negligently burning the shop.
   b. Bradley, a guest at the Fontainbleau hotel, leaves his suite for dinner. A half hour later there is a fire in the room. The evidence indicates that the fire started in a sofa in the sitting room of the suite. The hotel sues Bradley for negligence.
   c. Smith is driving down a rural two-lane highway on a clear, dry day. Her car goes off the road and into a gully. Both Smith and her passenger, Jones, are killed in the crash. Jones's estate sues Smith's estate for wrongful death.

6. Young is hit by a piece of wood which falls from the open third floor of a construction site. At the time, Koch and Alioto, two employees of the Wagner Construction Company, the framing sub-contractor, were the only workers on that floor.

a. Unable to discover exactly what caused the board to fall, Young sues Koch and Alioto. Can he invoke res ipsa?

b. Young has an easy alternative here; what is it?

Fudd Ipsa Loquitur

7. Assume that Judge Fudd tries the case described in example 5b, in which the hotel fire started in a couch in the defendant's room. Judge Fudd, after brushing up on his res ipsa learning, gives the following instruction to the jury:

> If you find that the fire in this case was not likely to have happened in the absence of negligence, and that the instrumentality which caused the harm was under the control of the defendant at the time of the likely negligence, then these facts give rise to an inference of negligence on the part of the defendant.

What is the problem with the Honorable Fudd's instruction?

8. Farmer Jones decides to take a break from the spring plowing. He turns off the ignition and gets off his new tractor. Suddenly, the tractor unaccountably starts up with Jones standing next to it. Jones, perhaps ill-advisedly, jumps for the driver's seat to stop it, is thrown off and injured. He sues International Tractor Company, alleging negligence in causing his injuries. At trial, he proves the above facts, and argues that he should get to the jury based on res ipsa loquitur.

The defendant asks Judge Fudd to give the following jury instruction:

> No inference of negligence by the defendant is permitted, unless the plaintiff has shown that the injury-causing occurrence was not due to any contribution or voluntary activity on the plaintiff's part.

Should Judge Fudd give the instruction? Assume that the jurisdiction applies comparative negligence.

EXPLANATIONS

Victims of Circumstance

1a. As the introduction states, res ipsa loquitur only applies where the nature of the accident indicates that it would not ordinarily happen without negligence. Most courts would probably hold that a tire blowout does not satisfy this requirement. Tires can blow out from a number of causes, including over- or underinflation, glass or other sharp objects in the road, excessive wear, a Chicago-sized pot hole, and probably others as well. Of course, it could result from a defect in the tire, but given all the other potential causes, this accident is probably not the type that "ordinarily does not happen without negligence."

b. Res ipsa loquitur would probably not apply in this case, because there is no need for it. Here, the parties are able to present direct evidence of all the relevant facts about the accident. The store personnel can testify about where the display rack was located and how it was supported. Daley can testify about how hard he hit the shelves and how close they were to the chair. Thus, the jury will have direct evidence upon which to determine whether the store was negligent, without resort to any general inference of some unspecified negligence, as they must do in a true res ipsa situation. See *Shutt v. Kaufman's, Inc.*, 438 P.2d 501 (Colo. 1968), which refused to apply res ipsa loquitur on similar facts.

c. Surely any parent can testify to the fact that many toddlers are more enthusiastic than careful. They try new things, fall down a lot, bump into things. It seems quite credible that an active three-year-old would fall off a swing, trip, or get hit hard enough to break an arm, even if the day care personnel were exercising due care in supervising him. Thus, it is at least doubtful that a jury could infer negligence of the day care center from the mere fact of this accident. See, e.g., *Ward v. Mount Calvary Lutheran Church*, 1994 WL 124872 (Ariz. App. 1994), which refused to apply res ipsa on similar facts.

d. Although three-year-olds get around very well and consequently take some pretty hard knocks, a five-month-old can hardly navigate at all. It seems improbable that Younger could manage to break her arm all by herself; it is much more likely that someone dropped her, or left her unattended on a changing table. This case seems a much stronger candidate for application of res ipsa loquitur.

e. This accident is not likely to happen without someone's negligence. The problem is in attributing the negligence to the hotel owner. It is quite likely that a guest, rather than an employee, knocked the glass off a balcony railing. While hotels have a duty to exercise due care in controlling the conduct of guests, the hotel cannot have guards in every room to interdict every careless act of its guests. Thus, res ipsa will probably fail here because it is impossible to show that the negligence, if there was any, was attributable to the defendant.

Possibly Probable Negligence

2.   This example raises a tough but important question. Here, it is a debatable proposition whether the accident was more probably the result of negligence or pure accident. The judge puts the probabilities at 40 percent negligence/60 percent pure accident, but recognizes that others (in particular, the jury) might disagree. Should he let the jury decide, or direct a verdict for the defendant on the ground that one of the foundation facts (that the accident "ordinarily would not have happened without negligence") has not been established?

Presumably, if the jury could reasonably conclude that the accident "ordinarily would not happen without negligence," they should be allowed to decide. They are the factfinders, so presumably they decide the *foundation facts* as well as the ultimate issue of negligence. If they agree with the judge that negligence is not the more probable explanation, they should find for the defendant. But if they conclude that the accident does bespeak negligence (and that the negligence is likely attributable to the defendant) they would be entitled, under res ipsa, to make an inference that the defendant was negligent.

Put another way, the judge's role is not to make findings himself that the foundation facts are established, but rather to determine whether the jury reasonably could conclude that those facts are proved. If there is evidence from which the jury could find that the plaintiff has established the foundation facts, they must be given the opportunity to do so, and (if they do) to decide whether to make the further inference that the defendant was negligent.

Firming Up the Foundation

3a.   It seems very likely that glass would not have ended up in Alioto's salad unless someone was negligent. The problem in the case, of course, is to decide whose negligence it was. The glass could have come from the mushrooms, the lettuce, the artichokes, perhaps even the sliced turkey, as well as from the salad dressing. It may also have fallen into the salad from a shelf or the kitchen counter. Thus, the circumstances do not of themselves demonstrate that the negligence is attributable to the defendant.

b. Alioto may be able to shore up his res ipsa foundation against Newton's by eliminating the other possible sources of the glass. He may be able to testify that he washed the lettuce, drained, washed, and cut up the artichokes, rubbed each mushroom before cutting it into the salad, and sliced the turkey on a clean cutting board. He may also be able to testify that he washed the counter before making the salad. Depending on the particulars, such testimony could lead the jury to eliminate the other items in Alioto's lunch as the source of the glass, leaving Newton's the likely culprit.

It is quite common for plaintiffs to offer testimony to eliminate the negligence of others, including themselves, so as to satisfy the requirement that the negligence be attributable to the defendant. In an exploding bottle case, for example, the plaintiff will try to show careful handling by the retailer and himself, in order to prove that the negligence was likely that of the bottler. In a disappearing airplane case, the plaintiff will offer testimony that the weather was clear to bolster the inference that negligence, not weather, caused the plane to crash.

4a.   If there was negligence at all in this case, it was very likely attributable to Dr. Eastwood. However, it is not at all clear that this side effect results from negligence. It is very doubtful that a jury could conclude, from their general knowledge, that decreased sensation after thigh surgery bespeaks negligence of the surgeon. Thus, the jury is not in a position, based on the mere fact of the injury, to determine that the foundation for the res ipsa inference is established.

b. Ulner's expert testifies that nerve damage does not usually result when the type of surgery Ulner had is carefully performed. However, it does not follow, just because this side effect doesn't usually occur, that when it occurs it probably results from negligence. There are many side effects of surgery that occasionally happen despite the exercise of due care. Surely, negligence should not be inferred just because such side effects are rare. For example, surgical patients rarely get infections from careful surgery, but this does not mean that, if a patient does get infected, the surgeon was probably negligent. In a small percentage of cases, it just happens anyway, despite all reasonable precautions.

Many courts state that res ipsa applies to "the type of injury that ordinarily would not occur if reasonable care had been used." *Wick v. Henderson*, 485 N.W.2d 645, 649 (Iowa 1992). However, this language is misleading. It is one thing to say that the type of accident does not ordinarily happen when the actor is careful. It is another to say that, *when the accident does occur*, it is more likely than not that negligence was the cause. Tire blowouts do not ordinarily happen if car owners are careful, but it does not follow that when tires *do* blow out, it is probably the result of negligence. People do not ordinarily fall down on the sidewalk, but when they do, it does not follow that negligence is the likely cause.

A better statement of this requirement is that the accident "would not ordinarily happen without negligence." (Note that Ulner's expert did not testify to that.) Res ipsa requires that the accident not only be unusual, but that it be unlikely to happen unless someone failed to exercise due care. If Ulner's expert testified that nerve damage does not occur in this type of surgery *unless the surgeon was careless*, his testimony would provide an evidentiary basis for the jury to conclude that his injury probably resulted from negligence. On that testimony, Ulner would be allowed to reach the jury on a res ipsa theory.

c. Here, Ulner's expert has provided testimony that would support the first "foundation fact." However, Dr. Eastwood has offered expert testimony that contradicts that testimony. Presumably, it is for the jury, as the factfinders, to resolve this conflict in the evidence. If they believe Ulner's expert, they may conclude that injuries of this type most likely result from negligence, and be in a position to make the further inference that this one in fact *did* result from Dr. Eastwood's negligence. Compare Example 2. If they are convinced by Eastwood's expert, they will conclude that negligence is not the most likely explanation, and find for the defendant.

d. Eastwood's motion should be denied. Ulner's evidence suggests that this type of outcome likely results from negligence of the surgeon. Eastwood then testifies that he did not make the type of mistake which would likely explain Ulner's complications. If the jury believes Eastwood's testimony, they will presumably refuse to make the inference permitted by the res ipsa loquitur doctrine.

They are free to do that, but they are also free to disbelieve Eastwood's testimony and make the res ipsa inference based on the evidence that such results usually do result from negligence of the surgeon, and the further fact that the injury did in fact occur. On this state of the evidence, the case is for the jury.

e. The res ipsa loquitur doctrine allows a jury to conclude that an unexplained accident more than likely happened due to negligence. But here, the defendant has offered an uncontradicted, fully corroborated explanation that the injury occurred without negligence. Unless there is some basis to conclude that the witnesses are lying, this accident is no longer unexplained, and there is no need for the jury to estimate the probabilities concerning an unexplained occurrence. Thus, res ipsa would no longer have a role, and the judge would likely direct a verdict for the defendant.

If there were some basis in the evidence for the jury to disbelieve Eastwood's testimony concerning the ruptured artery, they would be entitled to do so. If they did disbelieve it, they would be free to infer other causes, and could do so if the proper res ipsa foundation had been laid.

Not For Attribution

5a. Most courts would probably refuse to allow this case to go to the jury on the basis of res ipsa. Ordinary experience suggests that there are a number of possible causes for this fire which do not involve negligence of the tenant, including electrical problems, a customer's smoldering cigarette, vandalism, or mechanical problems. The fire may be attributable to the operator's negligence: She could have spilled cleaning fluids, left oily rags near the wall or left a pressing machine on. But it seems doubtful, where the fire occurs overnight and cannot be directly tied to the cleaning machines, that it can reasonably be inferred that one of these is the more likely cause.

b. Although this is another fire case, it is a much better candidate for application of res ipsa loquitur. Here, the evidence indicates that the fire started in a sofa, not a usual place for fires absent someone's negligence. In addition, it started shortly after Bradley left the room, which supports the inference that, if negligence led to the fire, it was his. Cf. *Olswanger v. Funk*, 470 S.W.2d 13 (Tenn. App. 1970).

In this case, further evidence may strengthen the inference of Bradley's negligence. If he locked the room, for example, this tends to eliminate vandalism as an alternative explanation. If Bradley is a smoker, that would greatly strengthen the inference that he had caused the fire.

c. Since there is no evidence of the cause of this crash, Jones's estate will only be able to reach the jury on a res ipsa loquitur theory. If there was negligence, it was probably Smith's, but can it be said that this accident probably would not have happened without negligence?

The likely causes of an accident of this sort are weather, negligence of the driver (or another driver), and mechanical defect. The evidence eliminates weather as a cause, so that leaves negligence and mechanical failure as possible causes. A mechanical failure might result from negligent maintenance by Smith — in which case it would still support an inference of her negligence — or from an unknowable defect, which would not be culpable.

I suppose the judge (and the jury if the case gets to them) must make an intuitive judgment as to whether, when cars go off the road in good weather, and there is no evidence that another car was involved, negligence of the driver is the most likely explanation. What would you think? Whatever you think, it still seems like a very unscientific way to decide cases, doesn't it, based on intuitive guesses about probable causes of accidents most of us do not experience and know little about.

Wouldn't it make sense for Jones's estate to introduce statistical information (or expert testimony) concerning the causes of such accidents? At least one study has shown that human error is a great deal more likely to cause motor vehicle accidents than mechanical failure. See D. Seidelson, Res Ipsa Loquitur — The Big Umbrella, 25 Duq. L. Rev. 387, 413-414 (1987) (citing Florida study showing that "human factors" caused over 50 percent of accidents while "vehicular" factors caused less than 8 percent). Such evidence is extremely persuasive on whether negligence can be inferred in this case. Resourceful parties should seek out such evidence to help establish the foundation facts in res ipsa cases.[3]

6a. This case resembles *Byrne v. Boadle*, the flour barrel case that gave rise to the res ipsa doctrine. As in *Byrne*, it seems fairly clear that a jury could find, based on their own experience, that this accident would not ordinarily happen without negligence. Someone must have left the board too near the edge of the building, or dropped it in the course of the work, or *something*.

The problem is with the other foundation requirement, attributing the negligence to a particular defendant. Granted, it is probably attributable to *one of the defendants*, but it is not clear which one. Even where the plaintiff relies on the general inference of negligence permitted by res ipsa, it must be an inference of a particular person's negligence, not just someone's. Otherwise, Young could simply sue all possibly negligent parties and argue that one of them must have been negligent.[4] On these facts, most courts would refuse to send the case to the jury on a res ipsa theory.

---

3. On the other hand, the fact that the cause was "human error" does not necessarily mean *Smith's* human error in this case. It could have been another driver who forced Smith off the road.

4. *Ybarra v. Spangard*, 154 P.2d 687 (Cal. 1944), appears to hold that the plaintiff can do just that. However, *Ybarra* has not been generally accepted outside of the unique context (surgery on the unconscious patient) in which it arose. Even in that context, it may be a dubious proposition that the defendants should bear a burden of explanation which they probably cannot meet. See D. Seidelson, Res Ipsa Loquitur — The Big Umbrella, 25 Duq. L. Rev. 387, 446-450 (1987).

b. Young can rely on res ipsa loquitur in this case if he sues Wagner Construction Company. The accident is of a type that ordinarily would not happen without negligence. Wagner, as an employer, is liable for the negligence of any of its employees in the course of the work. See Chapter 18. Thus, it is liable regardless of which employee caused the board to fall. Even though Young could not invoke res ipsa against Koch or Alioto, he could show that the negligence must be attributable to someone for whom Wagner is responsible.

Fudd Ipsa Loquitur

7. Fudd's instruction tells the jury that, if they find the foundation facts established, "these facts give rise to an inference of negligence on the part of the defendant." This suggests to the jury that they *should* make the inference that Bradley was negligent if they find the foundation established. On the contrary, res ipsa permits, but does not require a jury to infer negligence where the foundation facts are shown. The instruction would be much improved if the Honorable Fudd told the jury that, if they find the foundation facts are established, they *may* but are not required to infer that the defendant was negligent.

One may well wonder if such subtle distinctions in a complex verbal instruction have any real meaning for a jury. If the jury understands the res ipsa instruction at all, they may well understand it as Judge Fudd mistakenly phrased it, to mean that they should find for the plaintiff if they find the foundation facts established. Jury instructions play an ironic role in the trial of cases. When they are correct, it is not clear that the jury understands them or pays them undue attention. But when they are wrong, the losing party is very likely to appeal on the ground that the jury was given the wrong rules for decision. Thus, it may be more important not to get the instructions wrong than it is to get them right.

8. You will very frequently see language of this sort in the statement of the res ipsa loquitur requirements. See, e.g., *Stillman v. Norfolk & W. Ry. Co.*, 811 F.2d 834, 837 (4th Cir. 1987). The rationale is apparently that, if the plaintiff contributed to the accident, the inference that the negligence leading to it was the defendant's is undermined. In addition, res ipsa dates from the era of contributory negligence, when any negligence by the plaintiff barred recovery even if the defendant was negligent.

In this case, however, Jones should be able to invoke res ipsa loquitur even if he was a partial cause of his injury. Although Jones may have been negligent *after* the tractor started, for jumping on board, there is nothing to suggest that he contributed in any way to causing it to start. Thus, his conduct does not undermine the inference that any negligence that led to the tractor starting up was International's. Brand new tractors should not roar into life on their own. When they do, a jury could reasonably infer that the manufacturer was negligent. The fact that Jones reacted negligently to the risk should not bar him from using res ipsa to establish the initial negligence of International. If Jones reacted negligently to the situation, and thus contributed to his own injury, this can be accounted for under comparative negligence by reducing his recovery.

Thus, in instructing the jury, Judge Fudd should separate the issue of International's negligence in causing the initial problem from Jones's negligence in reacting to it. He should instruct the jury that they could infer negligence of International based on res ipsa loquitur, and further instruct them on comparative negligence to account for Jones's subsequent conduct. See, e.g., *Giles v. City of New Haven*, 636 A.2d 1335 (Conn. 1994) (allowing plaintiff to invoke res ipsa in a similar situation under comparative negligence).

PART THREE

The Causation Enigma

7

Reconstructing History: Determining Cause In Fact

Introduction

As previous chapters have indicated, the common law has developed a consistent set of elements — duty, breach, causation, and damages — which plaintiffs must prove in order to recover in a negligence action. This chapter addresses the very difficult — and fascinating — problem of proving the third element, causation.

No writer could venture into the mysteries of causation without profound trepidation. In a philosophical sense, the causes of any event may be traced back to the dawn of time, and the consequences of the most trivial act ripple forth in all directions to irrevocably change the world. Every cause has its own causes, and every consequence, consequences.

This is fancy language and causation is a profound problem. We could think about it for centuries, and perhaps at the end be little closer to understanding it. Yet one of the majesties of the law is that it must answer the unanswerable: It must decide, *today*, between plaintiff and defendant, and lacks the luxury of indefinite speculation. Consequently, judges must settle for some working approaches to thorny problems like causation, approaches which are no doubt imperfect, perhaps not even fully intellectually consistent, always subject to refinement and eventual change.

Although causation is a complex problem, fundamental fairness obviously requires that a defendant be held liable only for injuries he actually caused. If Jones, an electrician, wires Smith's house, and leaves exposed wires in the wall, which cause a spark and burn down the house, Smith's loss is a direct result of Jones's negligence. It would not have happened if Jones had been careful, and it did happen because Jones wasn't careful. It seems fair to shift the loss from the blameless Smith to the careless Jones. However, if the house burns down because Smith's toddler starts the fire, Jones did not cause the harm and should not pay, even if he was negligent in wiring the house.

To assure that liability will only be imposed where the plaintiff's loss is fairly attributable to the defendant's conduct, courts have developed two causation requirements, causation *in fact* and *proximate*, or legal, causation. Cause in fact, the subject of this chapter, requires that, as a factual matter, the defendant's act contributed to producing the plaintiff's injury. Proximate causation, considered in the next chapter, deals with limits on liability for remote or unexpected consequences of tortious conduct.

It is often quite clear from the events themselves that the defendant's negligence was the cause in fact of an injury. Suppose, for example, that Wright drops a sheet of plywood from a building onto Sullivan's car, obscuring her ability to see the road, and she crashes into a parked car. There is little doubt that Wright's negligence "caused" the accident. Sullivan will doubtless testify that she swerved off the road *because* the plywood obscured her view. The accident would not have occurred otherwise. Similarly, if Darrow, a lawyer, draws a will for a client and fails to include one of the intended beneficiaries, it is clear that this omission is the cause in fact of the beneficiary's inability to take under the will. Common sense tells us that the problem happened because the beneficiary was left out, and would not have happened if she had been included. We would all accept that Darrow's mistake "caused" the beneficiary's damages, and so would any court.

In other cases, we could all agree, philosophers included, that the defendant's negligence did not cause the plaintiff's injury. Suppose that Pei's truck hits Gaudi on Maple Street. Investigation shows that the truck was carefully driven and in good working order, except that the windshield wipers were broken. However, the weather was dry at the time. No court will hold Pei liable for the accident because of the broken wipers. The wipers weren't needed; the accident would have happened the same way if they had been working. Even though Pei was negligent, his negligence was irrelevant "negligence in the air," unconnected to Gaudi's injury.

Reconstructing History: Cause in Fact as a Problem of Proof

In many cases, the act that caused the injury is clear, but the plaintiff faces a difficult causation problem in identifying the actor who did that act. Suppose in the plywood example that three subcontractors were working on the floor from which it fell. Although the falling plywood clearly caused Sullivan's injury, Sullivan will have the very practical causation problem of proving who dropped it. Or, suppose that Fleming is injured when a crowbar she is using snaps in half, sending a splinter of steel into her eye. Here again, the mechanism which caused the harm is clear, but Fleming faces a formidable problem in proving who made the crowbar, since crowbars look pretty much alike and may not carry any identifying marks.

The causation issue in these who-done-it cases may not be *conceptually* difficult, but poses difficult practical problems in identifying the proper defendant. If we had an omniscient observer (we'll call him Solomon) and a time machine, we could send him back to re-view the relevant events and solve these identification problems. Without Solomon, however, plaintiffs must do the best they can to tie the act to the defendant, and often lose cases because they cannot establish that the defendant committed that act.

A different set of proof problems arises in cases in which the defendant committed a negligent act, but it is unclear whether the act produced the resulting harm. Suppose that Schwartz lives near Ace Corporation's toxic waste landfill and contracts leukemia. Although she may believe that she contracted the disease from drinking well water contaminated by chemicals from the landfill, she faces a formidable problem in establishing that this caused her disease. First, she must establish that the chemicals are capable of causing leukemia. If she establishes this, she must further prove that exposure to the chemicals actually *did* cause hers. Since leukemia often occurs without such exposure, there must be other causes of the disease as well. Even if she shows that the chemicals *can* cause leukemia, Schwartz will have a difficult time establishing that they, rather than one of the other possible causes, *did* cause hers.

This problem is also illustrated by the Agent Orange cases, in which veterans of the Vietnam War alleged that they contracted various diseases from contact with dioxin used as a defoliant in Vietnam. The plaintiffs in those cases faced two major hurdles in proving that dioxin caused their diseases. *First*, it was not clear that dioxin was capable of causing the diseases they suffered. *Second*, it was clear that other agents could cause these diseases, because they were found in patients who had *not* been exposed to dioxin. Thus, even if they proved that dioxin *could* cause these diseases, they would still have to show that it, rather than other possible agents, *did cause* their individual illnesses.

If our Solomonic time traveler were omniscient, or if science had reached the point of fully understanding disease processes, this proof problem would go away. However, because our scientific knowledge is imperfect (indeed, downright rudimentary in many areas of toxic exposure), these what-done-it causation problems are often very difficult. Often plaintiffs cannot link their disease to the toxic exposure. Indeed, the Agent Orange plaintiffs failed to prove causation at the first level, that dioxin had the capacity to cause the diseases they suffered. See *In Re "Agent Orange" Prod. Liab. Litig.*, 611 F. Supp. 1223, 1258-1263 (E.D.N.Y. 1985).

Rewriting History: Hypothetical Alternatives in Determining Cause in Fact

In another set of negligence cases, it is clear that the defendant acted negligently, but it is still unclear whether that act was a *cause in fact* of the plaintiff's injury. Suppose, for example, that a motorcyclist is killed when he pulls out in front of a bus that is going seven miles over the speed limit. Or suppose that the plaintiff suffers chest pains and his doctor fails to diagnose it as a heart attack and provide suitable emergency treatment. Last, suppose that a landlord fails to provide a fire escape, and the tenant dies in a fire.

In each of these cases, we know that the defendant was negligent, but we don't know whether things would have come out differently if the defendant had not been negligent. If the bus had been driving at the speed limit, could it have stopped before hitting the cyclist? If the doctor had provided timely treatment, would the patient have survived? If there had been a fire escape, would the tenant have reached it and escaped the fire? The defendant should not be held liable in such cases if the harm would have taken place regardless of the negligence. However, to determine whether the defendant's negligence affected the outcome, the jury must not only decide what actually happened, but must also speculate about a hypothetical alternative version of events: what would have happened if the defendant had not been negligent.

Courts generally hold that cause in fact is established if the plaintiff would not have suffered the harm *but for* the defendant's negligence. But-for causation is not present in the broken wiper case, for example, because the accident would have taken place just the same if the wipers were working. By contrast, but for the worker dropping the plywood in the second example, that accident would not have occurred. Thus, the negligence in the plywood case was a but-for cause of that accident.[1]

In the last set of examples, however, applying the but-for test is problematic, because it is difficult to determine how history would have unfolded without the defendant's negligence. In such cases, the but-for test

> challenges the imagination of the trier to probe into a purely fanciful and unknowable state of affairs. He is invited to make an estimate concerning facts that concededly never existed. The very uncertainty as to what *might* have happened opens the door wide for conjecture.

Malone, Ruminations on Cause in Fact, 9 Stan. L. Rev. 60, 67 (1956).

---

1. A fancy way of saying the same thing is that the defendant's negligence must be the *sine qua non* of the accident. "Sine qua non" is defined as that "without which it is not; an indispensable requisite." Ballentine's Law Dictionary 1182 (3rd ed. 1969).

Our omniscient observer cannot help us with this problem. Even his perfect perception and understanding of historical events could not resolve the question of what *would have happened* if history had been different. Yet the defendant's argument in these cases has much force: "I should not be held liable, even if I was negligent, unless my negligence contributed to the outcome." Even if the but-for inquiry involves a speculative comparison between actual events and hypothetical alternatives, it still seems necessary to make that comparison, to distinguish consequences that would have happened anyway from those that were truly brought about, in whole or in part, by the defendant's negligent conduct.

Although this type of counterfactual inquiry is inherently speculative to some degree, the parties can reduce the uncertainties involved by presenting evidence to help the jury compare what actually happened with what might have been. For example, evidence in the fire escape case that the decedent died at the window certainly strengthens the inference that he would have used an available fire escape. In the motorcycle example, the distance between the bus and the cycle when the cyclist pulled into the street will be critical in determining whether the excessive speed of the bus made a difference. In the heart attack example, medical experts may establish that the plaintiff would have recovered with prompt treatment, or, conversely, that death was inevitable even with immediate care. Although we can never achieve Solomonic certainty about these cases, the jury can usually make a reasoned judgment as to whether the negligence contributed to the outcome.

The Problem of Multiple Causation

Accidents very frequently result from a number of causes. Suppose, for example, that the Edison Company negligently attaches a transformer to a light pole, and Gaudi negligently backs into the pole and knocks the loose transformer down on a child waiting for the school bus. It may well be that the transformer would not have fallen, even though Gaudi hit the pole, if it had been tightly secured. Similarly, the transformer might not have fallen, even though it was loose, if Gaudi had not negligently hit the pole.

If this is so, *both* negligent acts would be but-for causes of the accident. Each contributed to the accident; if either defendant had used due care, the accident would not have happened, even assuming the negligence of the other. In such cases, the courts hold both defendants liable for the resulting injury. Put another way, it is no defense for one defendant that someone else's negligence also contributed to the accident: There is no requirement that the defendant's act be the *sole* cause of the injury, only that it be *a* cause. Edison cannot avoid liability because the transformer would not have fallen if Gaudi hadn't hit it. Although the loose transformer was not the sole cause of the accident, it was a but-for cause that combined with the negligence of the driver to lead to the injury.

This point is important enough to merit another illustration. Suppose Olmstead, a mason, is building a chimney on top of a townhouse while pedestrians are using the sidewalk below. Richardson, the general contractor, was required to place a protective scaffold with a roof over the sidewalk to protect pedestrians from falling objects during construction, but failed to do so. Olmstead drops a brick and it injures Wren walking by on the sidewalk. On these facts, the negligent acts of both Richardson and Olmstead are but-for causes of the harm. The accident would not have happened if Olmstead had not dropped the brick. It also would not have happened (even if Olmstead dropped the brick) if Richardson had put up the scaffold.

This logic applies both to successive negligent acts, as in the Edison example, and to negligent acts that take place simultaneously. Suppose that Sullivan is driving down the street without looking carefully, and that Pei runs a stop sign coming out of a side street. They collide and one of the cars careens into a pedestrian. The jury might find that the accident would not have happened if Pei had stopped for the stop sign or (even assuming Pei's negligence) if Sullivan had been keeping a proper lookout. On this reasoning, both drivers' negligence would be necessary antecedents to the accident, and both would be liable.

The Substantial-Factor Test

But-for analysis has been the traditional basis for analyzing actual causation in negligence cases.[2] Cause in fact will virtually always be established if the but-for test is met. Harper, James & Gray, §20.2 at 91-92. On the other hand, it is not invariably true that courts will refuse to find cause in fact if the but-for requirement is *not* met. In several unusual categories of cases, courts have abandoned the "but for" test because it leads to unsatisfactory results.

One situation in which the but-for rule falters is the case in which two defendants act negligently, and either's act would suffice to cause the plaintiff's injury. Suppose, for example, that two motorcyclists roar past the plaintiff's horse and wagon, scaring the horse and injuring the plaintiff. See *Corey v. Havener*, 182 Mass. 250 (1902). The plaintiff will not be able to establish cause in fact under the but-for approach: Each cyclist can argue that his act was not *necessary* to cause the harm, since the noise of the other cycle was *sufficient* to do so.

The court wrestled with this dilemma in *Anderson v. Minneapolis, St. Paul & S. St. Marie R.R. Co.*, 179 N.W. 45 (Minn. 1920), in which two

---

2. For a sophisticated discussion of "but for" causation, and a suggested alternative (but basically consistent) test, see R. Wright, Causation, Responsibility, Risk, Probability, Naked Statistics and Proof: Pruning the Bramble Bush by Clarifying the Concepts, 73 Iowa L. Rev. 1001, 1018-1023 (1988).

fires merged into one and burned the plaintiff's property. Only one of the fires was due to the defendant's negligence. It was impossible to say that "but for" the defendant's fire, the plaintiff's barn would still stand, because the other fire would likely have caused the damage anyway. Yet the defendant's culpable act clearly contributed, and it seemed "fair" to hold him liable for it.

In *Anderson*, the court resolved this dilemma by applying a different, less stringent test of causation, which required the jury to find that the act of the defendant was "a material or substantial element" in producing the damage. 179 N.W. at 46. Under that test, the defendant was held liable even though the property would probably have been burned by the other fire anyway. This substantial factor test clearly leaves more leeway to the jury in assigning causal responsibility for the harm. Unlike the "but for" test, the "substantial factor" test is a matter of degree, and it is left to the jury to make an intuitive judgment both as to what degree of causation is "substantial" and whether the defendant's negligence reaches that level. See Robertson, Powers & Anderson, Cases and Materials on Torts 158-159 (substantial-factor test "incorporates no particular mental operation but appeals forthrightly to instinct"); see also, for a more jaundiced view, B. Black and D. Hollander, Unravelling Causation: Back to the Basics, 3 J. Envtl. L. 1, 10 (1993) (substantial-factor test allows jury "to do essentially what it pleases").[3]

It is also important to understand that the "substantial factor" test is an *alternative* to the but-for test, not an additional requirement. *Anderson* illustrates the point: Although but-for causation could not be proved, the defendant was held liable under the substantial-factor approach.

In the situation illustrated by *Anderson*, the substantial-factor test has gained wide acceptance. See Restatement (Second) of Torts, §431(a). Indeed, some courts hold that the jury should be instructed under the substantial-factor test in all cases. See, e.g, *Mitchell v. Gonzales*, 819 P.2d 872, 878-879 (Cal. 1991). However, even if the court uses a substantial-factor instruction, the defendant should still not be held liable (except in *Anderson*-type multiple-sufficient-cause cases) if the harm would have occurred even if she had not been negligent. See Restatement (Second) of Torts, §432(1) (an actor's negligence is not a substantial factor in causing harm if the harm would have been sustained even if the actor had not been negligent);[4] see also Prosser &

---

3. Because the "substantial factor" test requires the factfinder to make a judgment about how much causal contribution is "enough," it arguably melds the actual causation inquiry with proximate cause analysis. See R. Wright, Causation in Tort Law, 73 Cal. L. Rev. 1735, 1782-1783 (1985) ("[T]he question of limiting liability due to the *extent* of contribution, rather than to the absence of *any* contribution, is clearly a proximate-cause issue of policy or principle, rather than an issue of actual causation (contribution to the injury)").

4. For a review of the debate about the relation between the two tests, see Wright, 73 Cal. L. Rev. at 1781-1784.

Keeton 267-268 (in almost all situations, defendant's conduct will not be a substantial factor if the harm would have occurred without it).

The examples immediately below illustrate basic problems in determining cause in fact. After these examples, several sophisticated variations on these cause in fact problems are discussed. (The explanations begin on p.137.)

EXAMPLES

Railroad Roulette

1.   Malone, who owns an appliance store in Moline, Illinois, orders ten television sets from a California wholesaler. They are packed in a box car and shipped by rail. One carrier hauls the boxcar from Sacramento to Denver, a second from Denver to Cedar Rapids, and a third from Cedar Rapids to Moline. Upon arrival, it is discovered that the sets, which were placed near the doors of the box car, have been ruined due to water damage. Evidently at some point during the journey someone left the doors open, allowing rain to get in and soak the merchandise. Malone wishes to sue to recover the value of the sets. Which type of causation problem does he have?

Causation and Consequence

2.   Gray, a cabinet maker, is driving his delivery truck on the interstate when it suffers a freak blowout and jackknives to a halt across the three lanes of traffic. Harper, who is tuning the radio dial instead of looking where his car is going, plows into the truck and smashes the front end. James, who is combing his hair in the little mirror on the visor, crashes his car into the back of Gray's truck and spills three expensive cabinets from the truck onto the pavement. Gray sues them both. Who is liable for what?

A Distinction with a Difference

3.   Gray's truck suffers a blowout on the interstate. Harper, tuning the radio, doesn't see it until too late and applies his brakes hard, swerving into the next lane. James, who is working on his hair again, hits Harper, sending Harper's car careening into Gray's truck, causing personal injuries to Gray. Who is liable to Gray?

Nature and Negligence

4.   Corbusier, driving down a country road, comes around a curve and encounters a deep puddle due to recent heavy rains. He tries to stop, but his brakes have been so poorly maintained that he cannot control the car. The car swerves to the left and hits Saarinen driving in the opposite direction, causing serious injuries. Is Corbusier liable under the but-for test?

Revisionist History

5. Haines, a student, is raped in a college dormitory. Investigation determines that the assailant, Grady, had been admitted to the dorm to visit another student. Haines sues the college, alleging that it was negligent in failing to hire enough security officers to assure adequate security.

    a. What is the nature of Haines's problem in proving causation in this case?

    b. What will the college argue on the causation issue?

    c. What will the plaintiff's counterargument be?

    d. If you represented the plaintiff, would you prefer that the jury be instructed under the but-for or substantial-factor test for causation?

6. Smith applies to Jones, the Chief of Police, for a permit to carry a handgun. A statute requires the Chief to check with the state Department of Public Safety to determine whether an applicant has a criminal record before issuing the permit, and to refuse the permit if the applicant has a record. Jones fails to do so and issues the permit. Three days later, Smith shoots Doe on the street with the gun. Doe sues the Chief for negligence.

    a. Assume that Smith had no criminal record. Is causation in fact established?

    b. Assume that Chief Jones fails to check, and issues the permit to Smith even though he has a criminal record. Can the plaintiff prove causation in fact?

Pestiferous Problems

7. Smith and Jones, two farmers, both sell tomatoes that have been sprayed with Icthar, a banned pesticide, to a local market. The market puts the tomatoes out together in a bin. Wren buys one and gets sick from the pesticide.

    a. If Wren sues the farmers, what type of causation problem will he face?

    b. How does the problem compare to the problem in *Anderson v. Minneapolis, St. Paul & St. Marie R.R. Co.*?

    c. Can this problem be solved by use of the substantial-factor test?

Cause-in-Fact Conundrums: Four Variations on Basic Cause-in-Fact Problems

The discussion to this point has introduced several analytical issues in determining cause in fact. This section discusses four difficult cause in fact problems which illustrate, in sophisticated contexts, the same basic types of cause in fact problems already discussed.

A. Causation in DES Cases

The first problem is proving causation in DES cases. DES is a drug which was widely prescribed for several decades to prevent miscarriage, but which has subsequently been shown to cause various medical problems in the daughters of women who took it during pregnancy. Because DES was marketed in chemically identical form by over two hundred companies, a plaintiff injured by DES exposure faces a very difficult cause in fact problem: Even if all companies were negligent for marketing the drug, only one of them — the manufacturer which manufactured the DES pills her mother took — caused her injuries.

This is an enormously difficult proof problem, but there is nothing *conceptually* hard about it. The chemical which injured the plaintiff is known. The problem is simply a matter of "who done it." Solomon could solve this problem easily enough, by just going back and watching the relevant events and jotting down the name of the drug on the bottle.

Sometimes the plaintiff can solve it too. She may be able to identify the manufacturer if her mother recalls the shape, color, or brand of DES she took.[5] In many cases, however, the evidence will show that the mother took DES, but not which manufacturer's pill it was. In such cases, the plaintiff will be unable to establish that a particular manufacturer caused her injury. If she is held to the usual burden to prove causation, she must lose.

While this result appears inexorable under traditional tort theory, the California Supreme Court in *Sindell v. Abbott Lab.*, 607 P.2d 924, *cert. denied*, 449 U.S. 912 (1980) found it unacceptable. To avoid this outcome, the court fashioned the "market share" theory, which allows the plaintiff to sue a number of manufacturers and hold them each liable (assuming negligence, of course) for part of the plaintiff's damages. Under the *Sindell* approach, each manufacturer's share of the liability is determined by the proportional share of DES it sold in the relevant market area.

Sindell does not "solve" the cause in fact problem, it redesigns it. Instead of asking who caused the particular plaintiff's damages, it asks who contributed to the creation of a general risk of injury, and distributes the damages among those risk creators in proportion to the risk each created. It is entirely clear under *Sindell* that defendants will be held liable to a plaintiff *even though they did not cause her any harm*. If Sindell sues six manufacturers, but her mother only took one brand of DES, five of them will be held partially liable without having caused the injuries for which she sues.

---

5. The plaintiff hit a snag with this approach in *Krist v. Eli Lilly & Co.*, 897 F.2d 293 (7th Cir. 1990). Her mother testified repeatedly, under the defendant's examination, that the DES she had taken was a "little red pill." The defendant then introduced evidence that it had indeed sold DES in a little red pill, but that it had done so only *after* the mother's pregnancy.

On the other hand, if all DES daughters sued all manufacturers under the market share approach, the manufacturers would, theoretically, pay in proper proportion to the injuries they caused. A manufacturer who made ten percent of the DES sold would be held liable for ten percent of each plaintiff's injuries. Since it actually caused *all* the injuries suffered by ten percent of DES daughters, this should work out, in the aggregate, about right. Of course, all plaintiffs will not sue all defendants for their DES injuries, nor have all states (or even a majority) adopted the market share theory. Consequently, while in theory there is logic to the market share approach, its effect is rather haphazard in practice.

Market share liability looks more like a legislative solution to the causation problem than a judicial one, but complex problems of modern life have forced courts to fashion such nontraditional remedies in a variety of contexts. While it is easy to criticize the California court's approach, the alternative — leaving plaintiffs without a remedy for negligent conduct — isn't very satisfying either. In lawsuits, unlike philosophy classes, courts have to decide. Refusal to refashion traditional doctrine in cases like *Sindell* usually means that the plaintiff loses.[6]

B. Causation in Multiple Exposure Cases

A somewhat different problem is posed by cases of multiple exposure to a dangerous substance such as asbestos. Suppose, for example, that Corbusier worked as a pipe insulator in a shipyard for 30 years and was exposed over the years to asbestos fibers sold by six companies. Eventually, he contracts asbestosis, a disease of the lungs which has been definitively linked to breathing asbestos fibers.

As in the DES cases, (but unlike the Agent Orange case) this case does not involve ambiguity in the mechanism of harm: It is clear that Corbusier got the disease from asbestos exposure. The problem here is also a who-done-it problem, but of a different sort. Here *all* the defendants exposed the plaintiff to the injury causing agent.

If it were clear that *cumulative* exposure to all the asbestos was necessary to cause Corbusier's disease, the but-for test would dispose of this problem. The plaintiff could argue that, but for the negligence of each defendant, he would not have gotten asbestosis. Each would be liable under traditional causation principles.

In most cases, however, the evidence will *not* show that each defendant's product was essential to causing the disease. The plaintiff's expert will testify that breathing asbestos causes asbestosis and that the more you breathe, the

---

6. Other courts have recognized that unfortunate consequence but still refused to adopt market share liability. See, e.g., *Smith v. Eli Lilly & Co.*, 560 N.E.2d 324 (Ill. 1990).

greater the chances of contracting the disease, but that a fairly brief exposure can suffice. She will be unable to state in Corbusier's case how much was necessary, though she will state with certainty that asbestos exposure caused the harm. On these facts, each defendant can argue that but-for causation is not established because, even if its product had not been at the site, Corbusier would have contracted asbestosis from the other defendants' products anyway.

In this type of case, most courts have invoked the substantial-factor test for cause in fact. The jury is left to consider, based on the evidence of each defendant's contribution to the risk, whether its product was a substantial factor in causing Corbusier's disease. If the exposure to Company #6's product was minimal, the jury may conclude it did not meaningfully contribute to the harm. But if Company #6's product was there on a consistent basis and its asbestos particles were more than a minimal percentage of the exposure, they would be free to conclude that it had "caused" Corbusier's disease, even though he might have contracted it from the other manufacturers' products anyway.

Use of the "substantial factor" test in such cases remains inherently subjective and gives the jury wide latitude. On the other hand, allowing the jury to make this judgment is probably more satisfactory than denying liability simply because the other manufacturers' asbestos might have sufficed to cause the disease anyway.

C. Toxic Exposure Cases

A third thorny cause in fact problem arises in cases like the Agent Orange case, which involve exposure to toxic chemicals. Science has been able to establish that persons who have been exposed to toxic substances are more likely to contract certain diseases, but it is not clear how such evidence should be used in establishing causation in tort cases. Suppose, for example, that epidemiological studies demonstrate that individuals exposed to quasimega-methane are more likely to contract liver cancer. The studies might show, perhaps, that there are 60 cases of liver cancer per 100,000 among the general population, but 80 cases per 100,000 among those exposed to quasimega-methane. Suppose further that Wren was exposed to quasimegamethane and that he subsequently contracts liver cancer.

There are two problems with using this evidence to prove that quasimega-methane caused Wren's cancer. First, although liver cancer is *correlated with* exposure to quasimegamethane, this does not necessarily prove that quasimeg-amethane has the capacity to *cause* liver cancer. Here is a nice example to prove the point: Although production of pig iron in the United States and the birth rate in Great Britain follow the same linear increase, it is relatively clear that the one did not cause the other! See B. Black & D. Lilienfeld, Epidemiologic Proof in Toxic Tort Litigation, 52 Fordham L. Rev. 732, 755 (1984) (citing G. Snedocor & W. Cochran, Statistical Methods, 189 (6th ed. 1967)). Similarly, exposure to quasimegamethane could be correlated to liver cancer for many reasons, even though it did not cause the cancer. Perhaps the lives of factory workers are more stressful for economic reasons, so that they smoke more. Or perhaps they had poorer nutrition as children, and this increases their rate of liver cancer.

If studies are carefully done to correct for such extraneous factors, it may be reasonable to infer that quasimegamethane *can* cause liver cancer.[7] Doubtless, epidemiologists would accept strong correlations based on careful studies as proof of causal capacity. However, even assuming that to be established, there remains the further question whether quasimegamethane caused *Wren's* cancer. The statistics given clearly show that people get liver cancer *without* being exposed to quasimegamethane. Indeed, of the 80 cancer victims in the group exposed to the toxin, presumably 60 contracted cancer from natural causes: There is no reason to believe that the rate of cancer from background causes would be lower in the exposed group. Thus, even if quasimegamethane *can* cause liver cancer, this does not show that it *did* cause Wren's.

Unlike the first two situations, in which the mechanism of harm was clear but the identity of the proper defendant was problematic, the mechanism of harm here is itself uncertain both on the general level ("can quasimegamethane cause liver cancer?") and on the particular level ("did quasimegamethane, rather than one of the other possible causes, cause Wren's cancer?"). This is a what-done-it problem, and a very difficult one indeed.

Sometimes the plaintiff in these cases can provide evidence to link her disease to a particular toxic agent. The medical evidence may establish that the agent can cause the disease, and that it runs a different course in patients who contract it from that agent, or that these patients have unique symptoms that support an inference that the agent induced it. The plaintiff might show that the disease appears after an unusual latency period if it is caused by the defendant's chemical, and that hers did as well, or that the diseased cells actually look or act a little differently if they are caused by the chemical. Evidence of this sort allows the jury to infer that *this plaintiff* contracted the disease from the exposure instead of other known causes for which the defendant is not responsible.

In other cases, however, the plaintiff is only able to show that she was exposed to a toxic chemical and that persons exposed to it contract the disease at an increased rate. In such cases, most courts would refuse to allow a jury to find the defendant liable. Even if statistical evidence establishes a general causal relationship between the chemical and the disease, this does not establish that *this* plaintiff contracted the disease from the exposure. See, e.g., S.

---

7. In the Agent Orange cases, the plaintiffs were unable to surmount even the first hurdle, proving that Agent Orange had the capacity to cause their illnesses.

Gold, Causation in Toxic Torts: Burdens of Proof, Standards of Persuasion, and Statistical Evidence, 96 Yale L.J. 376, 379-380 (1986). Most courts require some "particularistic evidence" that the individual plaintiff's disease was caused by the chemical rather than background causes not attributable to the defendant.

The refusal to allow plaintiffs to prove individual causation on the basis of statistical correlation is frustrating to plaintiffs, especially if the correlation between the chemical and the disease is strong. If studies show that quasimega-methane increases liver cancer rates by 40 percent (and extraneous reasons for the correlation are properly factored out), it is possible to say that 40 percent of exposed plaintiffs got the disease from that exposure. If each of those plaintiffs loses her case for lack of particularized proof that her cancer was caused by the chemical, the manufacturer will avoid compensating for many injuries it has caused. Dangerous conduct will be inadequately deterred, and plaintiffs injured by that conduct uncompensated.

Some commentators have suggested a *Sindell*-type approach to this problem, based on risk creation. Under this approach, the manufacturer would be liable to each liver cancer victim who had been exposed to the chemical for 40 percent of her damages. See, e.g., D. Rosenberg, The Causal Connection in Mass Exposure Cases: A "Public Law" Vision of the Tort System, 97 Harv. L. Rev. 851, 859 (1984) (advocating proportional liability in toxic exposure cases). Under this approach, the manufacturer would pay the "right" amount in damages, since it can be said, on a class-wide basis, that it caused 40 percent of the cases. However, 60 percent of the plaintiffs (those who contracted cancer from other causes) would be overcompensated and the 40 percent who were actually injured by the toxic chemical would be seriously undercompensated.[8]

D. Loss-of-a-Chance Cases

Another difficult cause-in-fact problem is illustrated by medical malpractice cases in which the defendant's negligence has reduced a plaintiff's chances of survival or cure. In *Herskovits v. Group Health Coop.*, 664 P.2d 474 (Wash. 1983), for example, the decedent died of lung cancer. The evidence indicated that he had a 39 percent chance of surviving with prompt diagnosis of his cancer, but that the defendant's negligent delay in diagnosing it reduced his survival chance to 25 percent. The suit was for wrongful death.

---

8. Even if courts were willing to adopt such an approach, many plaintiffs would still go uncompensated. Science has not yet established reliable correlations between exposure to many toxic chemicals and resulting diseases. There are simply too many toxins to study, and credible epidemiological studies are long-term, expensive endeavors. In other cases, researchers can establish a correlation but are unable to quantify the increase in risk with any precision.

Naturally, the defendant in cases like this will argue that he did not "cause" the harm. It is impossible to say that Herskovits would have lived but for the delay in diagnosis since, even if his cancer had been promptly diagnosed, chances were better than even (61/39) that he would have died.

This loss-of-a-chance causation problem is a variant of the revisionist history dilemma. The factfinder must compare what did happen to what would have happened if the defendant had not been negligent. Here, statistics suggest that the outcome *might* have been different absent the defendant's negligence, but probably would not have been. Yet the plaintiff takes little solace from these cold statistics: She still feels she has lost something very valuable, a significant chance that her husband would still be with her.

The lead opinion in *Herskovits* held that the causation issue should go to the jury under a substantial-factor instruction. This is not a very satisfactory solution to a vexing problem: It simply licenses the jury to find for the plaintiff on intuitive grounds, despite the likelihood that the negligence did not change the outcome.

There is an obvious relationship between this loss-of-a-chance problem and the toxic chemicals problem just discussed. There the epidemiological evidence established an increased risk of harm, but could not show whether the chemical had injured the individual plaintiff. Here, the statistical survival evidence establishes that the defendant's negligence decreased the plaintiff's chance of survival, but cannot resolve the issue of whether he would have survived otherwise. Here, as there, some scholars have suggested a proportional approach to the problem: If a defendant reduced the decedent's chance of survival by 15 percent, she should be held liable for 15 percent of the wrongful death damages. See J. King, Causation, Valuation, and Chance in Personal Injury Torts Involving Preexisting Conditions and Future Consequences, 90 Yale L.J. 1353, 1363-1364 (1981). However, this solution, (advocated by the concurring justices in *Herskovits*), is subject to the same objection: It overcompensates in every case in which the decedent would have died anyway, and undercompensates in every case in which the delayed diagnosis caused the death.

These four problems are illustrative of some tough cause-in-fact issues facing courts today. Each is, in a sense, insoluble, if to solve it means to determine the exact cause of the plaintiff's harm. In each situation, however, courts have to decide. Some have fashioned novel approaches, such as market share or valuation of the lost chance, in order to further the interests of compensation and deterrence. Other courts have adhered to more traditional analysis, which often means concluding that causation has not been proved. For present purposes, it is more important to recognize the nature of the issues these cases pose than to seek definitive answers. The remaining examples illustrate some of these problems and should help you to distinguish the issues they raise.

EXAMPLES

Identity Crisis

8.   Waltz, a five-year-old child, is diagnosed with learning disabilities and discovered to have high lead levels in his blood. It is very likely that he ingested the lead from the apartment he has lived in since birth, which has been painted with leaded paint many times over the years. Although it is impossible to identify the manufacturer of each coat of paint, only six companies made the white lead that went into leaded paint during the half century that leaded paint was used in the United States. Waltz sues these manufacturers for his injuries. What type of causation problem does Waltz face in recovering for his injuries?

9.   Suppose that Waltz lives in an apartment that contains lead paint. He has lived there for 18 months when it is discovered that he suffers from lead poisoning. Before that, he lived in another apartment for a year, another for the year before that, and another up to the age of one. All are tested and found to contain lead paint.

Instead of suing the lead manufacturers, Waltz sues Blair, his current landlord, for negligently exposing him to lead paint. What type of causation problem does he face, and how might it be resolved by a court?

Judge Fudd Takes His Chances

10.   Henry, an industrial worker, was exposed to pseudomonomethane, an industrial chemical, over a period of seven years. After being retired for ten years, he develops leukemia. Henry sues the company that supplied the pseudomonomethane he worked with.

At trial the plaintiff relies on an epidemiological study to prove causation. The study shows that among the general population 200 individuals per 100,000 will develop leukemia. However, workers exposed to pseudomonomethane develop the disease at a rate of 450 per 100,000. Nothing in the course or symptoms of the disease allows experts to distinguish leukemia caused by pseudomonomethane from leukemia caused by other agents.

At the close of the evidence, the defendant moves for a directed verdict, arguing that Henry has failed to prove causation. Judge Fudd denies the motion, and the plaintiff wins at trial. Should Judge Fudd have granted the directed verdict motion?

11.   Mesa went to Dr. Dee in November with symptoms that should have led Dee to suspect cancer. Dee did not diagnose the cancer then, but did the following May. The evidence indicates that Mesa had a 55 percent chance of being cured if he had been diagnosed promptly, but only a 41 percent chance due to the delay in diagnosis. Mesa dies of cancer and his survivors sue Dee for wrongful death. Judge Fudd instructs the jury as follows:

If you find that the defendant negligently failed to diagnose the plaintiff's condition in a timely manner, and that plaintiff probably would have survived if he had, you should find that the defendant's negligence was a cause of the plaintiff's death.

What is troubling about Judge Fudd's instruction?

EXPLANATIONS

Railroad Roulette

1. Malone's causation problem is a basic "who-done-it" proof problem. The mechanism that caused the harm was very probably rain coming in through the doors — but any one of the carriers could have left them open, or perhaps more than one. To recover, Malone must prove which carrier caused the harm.

This identification problem can be formidable, but it is not necessarily insuperable. Malone might be able to show that it only rained at one place along the route while the goods were in transit, which would support a conclusion that the carrier hauling the goods at that point was responsible. But absent such a lucky chance, he will have a hard time proving which carrier caused the damage. This proof problem actually led courts to create a presumption that the damage was caused by the last carrier to haul the goods. See Harper, James & Gray, §19.7 n.17. This presumption, which shifts the burden to the defendant to prove that an earlier carrier caused the damage, may be warranted by the fact that each carrier may inspect the goods upon receipt.

Causation and Consequences

2. Although the two collisions took place almost simultaneously, the defendants here acted separately and caused distinct losses. Each defendant should be held liable only for the damage attributable to his negligence. Harper should be liable for the front end damages and James for the broken furniture.

A Distinction with a Difference

3. In this example the negligence of both Harper and James contributed to causing the accident which led to Gray's injuries. Both are but-for causes of the accident. But for Harper's sharp stop, which sent him into James's lane, James would not have hit him. But for James's failure to watch the road, he would have avoided hitting Harper and knocking his car into Gray's truck. Here, unlike the last example, they have both contributed to causing a single, indivisible injury to Gray, and each is liable for the entire injury.

Nature and Negligence

4.   This accident is caused by both Corbusier's negligent maintenance of his car and the puddle that created the dangerous condition in the road. Although only one of these causes is due to negligence, that negligence is still a but-for cause of the harm. The accident would not have happened if Corbusier had not been negligent. True, it would not have happened, *even if Corbusier was negligent*, if the puddle had not been there, but that does not exonerate him. It is not a defense for him that other circumstances (whether natural or negligent) also contributed to the accident, if his negligence was one of those causes.

Corbusier might argue that he should not be liable even if he did cause the accident, because the puddle was unforeseeable. This is a *proximate cause* argument, not a cause-in-fact argument. However, it is dubious on the facts, given the heavy rains referred to in the example.

Revisionist History

5a.   The causation problem here is to determine whether the defendant's negligence affected the result, that is, whether the plaintiff would have been assaulted if the college had provided adequate security. It requires the fact-finder to compare what did happen to what *would have happened* absent the defendant's negligence.

b. The college will argue that it should not be held liable, even if security was inadequate, because any inadequacy in security did not cause the rape. It will argue that having more security officers would not have affected the outcome, because the student did not slip into the dorm illegally; he was admitted through the ordinary procedures.

There is certainly force to this argument. Grady did not break into the dorm, he entered openly for a legitimate reason. Consequently, inadequate security did not affect Grady's ability to get into the dorm. Even if there had been additional officers available, they would not have barred his entry and prevented the rape.

c. Haines will argue that, even if the inadequate security did not "cause" Grady's entry, it still caused the rape because, had Grady known that the campus was well patrolled, he would have feared being caught and therefore not have attempted the crime. This illustrates the speculative role of the jury in this type of case. Unlike the earlier examples, in which the jury need only reconstruct what happened, in this example they must try to get into Grady's mind and decide what he would have done under different circumstances.

d. Under the but-for test, the jury could only find causation if it concluded that Grady would not have committed the rape if security had been better. The "substantial factor" test, however, would allow the jury to find for the plaintiff on the causation issue if they concluded that inadequate security was a substantial factor in causing the rape. This is clearly less demanding than the but-for standard. The substantial-factor instruction is less clear-cut, and thus leaves the jury more leeway to conclude that inadequate security contributed in a meaningful way to Grady's act, without resolving the harder question of whether Grady would have acted the same way if security had been stronger.

6a. This is another case that requires the jury to compare what actually happened to what would have happened if the defendant had not been negligent. Here, Jones's negligence in failing to check Smith's criminal record was not a but-for cause of Doe's injury. Had he checked, he would have discovered that Smith had no record; consequently, he would have issued the permit anyway. Thus, Doe cannot show that, but for Jones's failure to check the record, Smith would not have obtained the gun permit and shot Doe. Although that failure was negligent, it was not causal negligence.

   b. The argument for causation is a great deal stronger in this case. If Jones had checked, he would have discovered that Smith had a record and refused the permit. But for his failure to check, the permit would not have been issued.

   However, Smith might have carried the gun without the permit and shot Doe anyway. Perhaps the evidence would even show that he would have. But the evidence might also lead the jury to conclude that Smith would not have carried a gun without a permit, and that Doe would therefore not have been shot. The plaintiff need not show that Smith could not possibly have shot Doe without the permit; she need only convince the jury that it is more probable than not that she would not have been injured but for the defendant's negligence. Though there is certainly a measure of speculation involved, one can imagine facts on which the jury could reasonably reach that conclusion here.

Pestiferous Problems

7a. These facts are analogous to the famous case of *Summers v. Tice*, 199 P.2d 1 (Cal. 1948), in which two hunters fired at a bird and the shot from one of the guns injured the plaintiff. Here, as in *Summers*, we know what caused the harm, eating the tomato laced with pesticide, but we need to know whose tomato it was. It is a proof problem that Solomon could solve for us if he went back and watched the events carefully enough. But we don't have a Solomon and we don't have any way of determining which farmer's tomato Wren ate.

   b. In *Anderson*, there were two causes of the harm, either of which was sufficient to produce it. Each defendant could argue that its negligence was not a but-for cause of the harm, because the negligence of the other would have caused it anyway. However, each was clearly a sufficient cause of the fire. Here, by contrast, there was only one cause of the harm: Wren only ate one tomato, supplied by one of the farmers but not by the other. The problem — probably an insuperable one, as a practical matter — is to identify which defendant's tomato was the but-for cause of his illness.

c.   Using a substantial-factor test for causation does not resolve this problem. Even under this test, there was only one substantial factor that caused the injury. The basic problem of tracing the tomato remains.

In *Summers*, the court resolved this dilemma by shifting the burden of proof to the defendants, since they were both negligent. This does not solve the identification problem; it simply places the risk of nonidentification on the defendants. Since they are no more able to solve it than the plaintiff, they will both be held liable, and will end up splitting the loss under contribution principles if both are solvent. This resolution of the dilemma may lack intellectual elegance, but it does provide a kind of rough and ready justice that courts must often settle for in real disputes.

Identity Crisis

8.   This case poses a who-done-it problem akin to the DES cases. Even if Waltz can show that all six manufacturers were negligent for selling white lead for use in paint over the years, he faces a difficult problem in determining which manufacturer made the white lead that went into the paint he ingested. If there is no way to distinguish the lead of one manufacturer from that of another, he will be unable to identify the proper defendant.

Doubtless, Waltz will urge the court to adopt a market share approach to this case, by analogy to *Sindell*. If all the lead makers were negligent, and contributed to the risk of lead paint poisoning, he will argue, they should share in the damages according to their shares of the white lead market.

In *Santiago v. Sherwin Williams Co.*, 3 F.3d 546 (1st Cir. 1993), the court refused to apply the market share approach to this scenario. The court noted that, unlike the DES context, the plaintiff here could have been injured by paint sold at any time during the fifty-year period. Thus, it would be impossible to establish a meaningful market share, other than the average market share for each manufacturer over the entire 50 years. In addition, the court predicted (applying Massachusetts law under the *Erie* doctrine) that the Massachusetts courts would be reluctant to endorse a theory which held defendants liable for harm they did not cause — which the market share theory clearly does.

But Waltz's case is different from the DES cases in an important respect. In those cases the plaintiff almost always took the drug of a single manufacturer. Here, however, it is possible — indeed probable — that the plaintiff was injured by *cumulative* exposure to lead manufactured by several of the manufacturers. The apartment had been painted many times, probably with different brands of paint containing lead from different lead manufacturers. Perhaps Waltz would do better to argue for liability under a substantial-factor test, on the ground that the jury could find that all the manufacturers had contributed to the harm. However, the argument for this solution is weaker than in the asbestos cases, because some manufacturers may not have contributed *any* of the lead in Waltz's apartment.

Waltz might also argue that the burden of proof should shift to the defendants, analogous to *Summers v. Tice*. The *Sindell* court refused to do that where there were several hundred defendants, but a court might be more receptive where there were only six. The California court did so in *Ybarra v. Spangard*, 154 P.2d 687 (1944), where the defendants were sued for causing injury to an unconscious patient during surgery. However, in *Ybarra* there was at least an argument that the defendants acted jointly in treating the patient, and were in a better position than he was to identify the cause of the injury.

9.   In this case, as in the asbestos cases, the plaintiff was exposed to a similar risk by the negligence of a number of defendants. It is a little different, since in the asbestos cases the plaintiff is often exposed to different manufacturers' products simultaneously, while here the exposure is successive. But the proof problem is similar, to establish that Blair's lead paint caused, at least in part, Waltz's lead poisoning.

The effect of lead paint exposure is cumulative — exposure to some lead can cause minimal impairment, and the greater the exposure, the greater the impairment. Thus, Blair may have contributed to Waltz's injuries even if he ingested lead in the other apartments as well. In this situation, the court is likely to use the same approach as in the asbestos cases, that is, to instruct the jury to determine whether the lead paint in Blair's apartment was a substantial factor that contributed to Waltz's damages. The jury will consider the evidence about the length of time in each apartment, Waltz's age during each exposure, the severity of his poisoning, the condition of the paint, the extent to which Waltz was supervised by adults, and so on, in determining whether the exposure in Blair's apartment substantially contributed to his problem. The jury might very well find that it did, since Waltz lived there for a year and a half, at an age when he was quite mobile and active, and hold Blair liable for all the damages Waltz suffered.[9] On the other hand, the evidence might show that by the time he moved to Blair's apartment he had learned not to eat paint, and never did.

The case would be a great deal harder if Waltz sued the owner of the apartment he lived in for the first year of his life. Infants are much less mobile than toddlers; for the first few months they can't even pick up paint chips. In addition, parents tend to watch infants more closely. A jury might conclude

---

9. Blair might argue that he has caused a separable portion of Waltz's injuries, and should only pay for that part of the poisoning caused by exposure in his apartment. Perhaps, for example, the damages could be apportioned based on the time Waltz spent in each apartment. If they cannot be rationally apportioned, the defendants will be held liable for the entire loss. See Prosser & Keeton 346-352.

on such evidence that it is likely that the later exposures caused the problem, and that the first landlord's negligence did not contribute materially to Waltz's condition. On the other hand, a smaller child will be affected by a smaller amount of lead, so that might influence the jury's judgment as well. The more evidence of this sort the parties provide, the more accurate the jury's cause-in-fact determination will be under the substantial factor standard.

Judge Fudd Takes His Chances

10. This example poses the difficult, increasingly common problem of increased risk. Here, the jury must make two causal inferences to find for Henry. *First*, it must conclude that pseudomonomethane has the capacity to cause leukemia. The epidemiological study shows that it is correlated with increased leukemia rates, but remember, so is pig iron and pregnancy (see p.132).

Second, assuming that the studies are rigorous enough to establish that pseudomonomethane *can* cause leukemia, they still do not show that it caused Henry's particular disease. Certainly, exposure to pseudomonomethane increased Henry's risk of contracting leukemia. Indeed, if the study is valid, it shows that his exposure *more than doubled* his chances of getting it. If a hundred workers exposed to pseudomonomethane contract leukemia, it is a fair inference if the studies are valid that more than half of them got it from the exposure. In a statistical sense, it is "more probable than not" that Henry got it from the exposure.

Courts, however, are reluctant to allow a jury to find causation based on purely statistical correlations. It is frequently said that evidence of statistical correlation, even at the level in this example, cannot suffice in itself to establish causation in a negligence action, since it does not prove anything about the cause of *the particular plaintiff's* injury. Ordinarily, there must be testimony about the plaintiff's disease that provides a basis for the jury to infer that *his* disease results from the exposure. In a jurisdiction that takes this approach, Judge Fudd's refusal to grant the directed verdict motion would be reversed on appeal.

Despite this frequently stated proposition, the cases are mixed on the impact of such statistical proof. Perhaps some courts would allow recovery where the plaintiff proves that exposure more than doubled the risk. See, e.g., *DeLuca v. Merrell Dow Pharmaceuticals, Inc.*, 911 F.2d 941, 958-959 (3rd Cir. 1990) (suggesting that doubling of the "relative risk" might satisfy the more-probable-than-not standard under New Jersey law). Usually, however, the plaintiff will offer increased risk evidence *along with* the testimony of an expert, who will testify that the exposure actually caused the particular plaintiff's disease. The crux of the problem then becomes whether the plaintiff's expert has any individualized basis for that conclusion, rather than relying on the same statistics that courts consider insufficient standing alone.

11. This case, like *Herskovits*, requires the court to solve a very difficult what-might-have-been problem. We do not know whether, but for the late diagnosis, Mesa would be alive today. The evidence indicates that the defendant's negligence reduced his chance of recovery by 14 percent — just as in *Herskovits*. Here, however, unlike in *Herskovits*, Mesa's chances of recovery were greater than fifty/fifty if diagnosed in time (55 percent probability) but less than fifty/fifty due to late diagnosis. The jury could find that in a purely statistical sense, it is more probable than not that Mesa would be alive without the negligent conduct. Judge Fudd's instruction, which states the usual more-probable-than-not standard of proof, authorizes them to do that.

Some courts would likely approve Judge Fudd's instruction, yet this result is problematic. *First*, the defendant has only caused the loss of a 14 percent chance of survival, yet he is held liable for the death itself. If the reduction were from 45 percent to 31 percent, many courts would refuse to hold him liable, on the theory that the plaintiff would likely have died anyway. It seems at least quizzical that the result should change just because the percentages hover around the 50 percent mark.

Second, the proof here, as in the toxic exposure/increased risk cases, is purely statistical. Most courts would refuse to allow a plaintiff to recover in those cases by showing that exposure to an agent increased the risk of a disease by 15 percent. Compare Example 10. The loss-of-a-chance cases present the mirror image of the increased risk problem, and courts ought to reach consistent results in the two types of cases. Some courts have recognized this, and allowed the plaintiff to recover partial damages based on the percentage of decreased chance, even if, as here, the initial chance of recovery exceeded 50 percent. See, e.g., *DeBurkarte v. Louvar*, 393 N.W.2d 131 (Iowa 1986).

8

Drawing a Line Somewhere: Proximate Cause

Introduction

One of the nice things about the inch is that virtually everyone who has anything to do with one agrees about what it is. While it is a purely human construct, an *idea*, we have achieved such a wide consensus about its meaning that we can use the term effectively without wasting energy arguing about its definition. This is probably true for the vast majority of concepts we manipulate through language. If it weren't, language wouldn't communicate much and people would rebel and vote in a new one.

Unfortunately, proximate cause is the exception that proves the rule (please excuse the pun). A great deal of confusion persists about what the term "proximate cause" is meant to convey. Students find this very frustrating: Justifiably, you would like some answers, some solid ground on which to base an understanding of a difficult concept. Frankly, so would I; I have done my homework on this problem, read a lot of heady articles, sorted through the cases, but if I ever thought I could *settle* this problem, in my own mind or in yours, I was wrong.

On the other hand, there is no need to be lachrymose about it either. If exact definition eludes us (as it does, of course, for other useful concepts, like "negligence" or "justice") we can still achieve a working knowledge of the problem sufficient for most purposes. This chapter seeks such a working knowledge of "proximate cause."

The Crux of the Problem

Despite differences in approach to proximate cause, all courts agree that the crux of the problem is that defendants cannot be held liable for every consequence of their conduct, even if that conduct is negligent. Here are a few examples in which courts would likely balk at imposing liability:[1]

- Defendant store owner leaves a box lid on the sidewalk. Plaintiff stumbles over it, skins her knee, and stops to get first aid. Consequently, she misses her train and gets a later one. She is injured when that train crashes into another at a crossing.
- Defendant, a restaurant owner, leaves a box of rat poison on a shelf, near the stove, that is used to store food. Although the owner had no reason to expect it, the poison explodes due to heat from the stove, injuring a customer.
- Defendant drives negligently, and collides with plaintiff, causing him injuries. Plaintiff is taken to the hospital, and injured three days later when the hospital burns.
- Defendant leaves his car unlocked, with the keys in the ignition. A terrorist steals the car, loads it with explosives, and sets off an explosion at a foreign embassy, injuring a passerby.
- Defendant, a firearms dealer, sells a revolver to a twelve-year-old boy. The boy takes it home and is injured when he drops it on his foot.

In each of these cases, the defendant was negligent, yet most courts, perhaps all, would deny recovery, on the ground that the plaintiff's injury is too unusual, too far removed from the type of harm to be anticipated from the defendant's negligence to warrant imposing liability.

It is important to emphasize at the outset that this is not based on a lack of *actual* causation. If the only issue were cause-in-fact, the defendant would likely pay in all of the examples, since her conduct was a necessary antecedent of the plaintiff's harm in each. If the store owner had not left out the box lid, the pedestrian would have gotten the earlier train and would not have been injured in the crash; if the restaurant owner had not placed the poison on the shelf, it would not have exploded, and so on.[2] Indeed, unless actual causation is found, there is no need to consider issues of proximate cause at all. If the defendant was not a cause-in-fact of the harm, the court will dismiss the case without reaching the complex policy question of whether

---

1. Many of the examples in this chapter are drawn from cases discussed in Judge Robert Keeton's helpful book, Legal Cause in the Law of Torts (1963).

2. But-for causation is arguable in the keys-in-the-car example. Defendant would argue that, had the terrorist not stolen his car, he would have stolen someone else's. He might also argue that the terrorist could just as well have stolen his car if he had locked it and taken the keys.

liability should follow. For this reason, courts often describe the proximate cause problem as one of "legal cause," to emphasize that the issue is whether liability should be imposed, not whether the defendant's act was a cause-in-fact of the plaintiff's harm. "An actual cause question asks, 'What happened?'; a legal cause question asks, 'What shall be done about it?'" C. Morris, On the Teaching of Legal Cause, 39 Colum. L. Rev. 1087, 1089 (1939).

Certainly, courts must impose some further limit on liability, apart from the cause-in-fact requirement. Otherwise it is too easy to come up with absurd hypotheticals. Reynolds, not looking where he is going, bumps Carpenter on the sidewalk, knocking her down. Carpenter then walks to the corner and meets Dias, an old boyfriend, crossing the other way. They have dinner, end up at Dias's apartment, and Carpenter contracts a venereal disease. Reynolds's negligence is a necessary historical antecedent of the harm; had he not delayed Carpenter, she would not have spotted Dias, and so on. Yet no system could countenance holding Reynolds liable for Carpenter's disease. As a matter of policy, the relation between the negligence and the injury is too tenuous, the consequence too out of proportion to the fault, to make Reynolds pay:

> In a philosophical sense the causes of any accident or event go back to the birth of the parties and the discovery of America; but any attempt to impose responsibility upon such a basis would result in infinite liability, and would "set society on edge and fill the courts with endless litigation."

W. Prosser, Proximate Cause in California, 38 Cal. L. Rev. 369, 375 (1950) (quoting from *North v. Johnson*, 59 N.W. 1012, 1012 (1894) (Mitchell, J., dissenting)). Thus, all courts agree that a line must be drawn, *somewhere*, to limit liability for the consequences of a negligent act. The problem, of course, is how to define that limit.

Some Proximate Cause Formulas

Courts have labored for over a century to articulate such a definition, to draw a defensible line between consequences of negligence that are actionable and others too remote to support liability. Perhaps it is a mistake to try; proximate cause decisions, even within a single jurisdiction, often appear inconsistent or hard to predict based on previous precedents. It may be like pornography, of which Justice Stewart said that perhaps he could not define it, but "I know it when I see it." *Jacobellis v. Ohio*, 378 U.S. 184, 197 (1964) (Stewart, J., concurring). Most courts, however, have attempted to define the limits of proximate or "legal" cause. Here are some of the verbal formulas they have offered to reconcile their decisions:

A. Direct Cause

Some courts have held that the defendant is liable if his conduct is the *direct cause* of the plaintiff's injury, as opposed to a *remote* cause. The most famous case taking this approach is *In Re Polemis and Furness, Withy & Co.*, 3 K.B. 560 (1921). In *Polemis*, a workman dropped a board into the hold of the plaintiff's ship, which caused a spark and ignited petrol vapors in the hold, thereby destroying the ship. Although the explosion was deemed unforeseeable, the court held that the defendant was liable, since the negligent act of its employee was the "direct cause" of the harm. Although the English court questioned *Polemis* in *Overseas Tankship (U.K.) Ltd. v. Morts Dock & Engg. Co., Ltd. (The Wagon Mound)*, A.C. 388 (1961), the direct cause approach sometimes appears in American cases.

This approach has a number of problems. First, of course, is determining what "direct" means. "Direct" is just a word rather than a method of analysis; it does not in itself help judges or juries to draw the line between direct and remote causes.

Another problem with the direct-cause test is that it is "not responsive to the decisions either as a test of inclusion or exclusion." W. Seavey, Mr. Justice Cardozo and the Law of Torts, 52 Harv. L. Rev. 372, 389 (1939). In other words, it simply does not explain the results in real cases. It is often more restrictive than the cases: Since "directness" suggests the lack of a later cause after the defendant's negligence, it tends to limit liability where subsequent conduct also contributes to the accident. Yet courts often conclude that the defendant should be liable despite intervening forces. Suppose, for example, that the boy in the revolver case discharged the revolver, injuring a playmate. Although this act intervenes after the negligent sale, so that the sale might be considered an indirect or remote cause of the injury, most courts would impose liability on the seller for this foreseeable injury.

The direct-cause test may also be too inclusive: The act of the restaurant owner in leaving the rat poison near the stove appears to be a direct cause of the explosion in that case, yet many courts would be uncomfortable imposing liability for that unexpected consequence of the owner's negligence. Similarly, the negligent acts in *Polemis* and *Palsgraf* led rather directly to the injuries in those cases, yet most courts would deny recovery for these unforeseeable consequences. See Harper, James & Gray, §20.6 at 174-176.

One virtue of the direct cause test is that it emphasizes that events after the defendant's negligent act may weaken the case for holding her liable. Courts often hold that a subsequent, unexpected occurrence "supersedes" the defendant's negligence, even though that negligence was a but-for cause of the plaintiff's injury. In the terrorist case, for example, most courts would conclude that the terrorist's act was so unusual, so unexpected, that it supersedes the negligence of the driver in leaving the keys in the car. Similarly, if Reynolds negligently injured Carpenter, he would probably not be held liable if Carpenter were attacked in the hospital by a deranged patient who escaped from another ward.

B. Natural and Probable Consequences

Courts very frequently say that the defendant is only liable for the "natural and probable consequences of his act." This formulation of proximate cause is also frustratingly ambiguous, and often deceptive. What makes the explosion of rat poison, for example, "unnatural"? It followed inexorably from a set of conditions according to laws of nature. Nor is there anything "unnatural" about the dropping of the gun on the boy's foot. "Natural" is apparently intended to mean "usual," or "predictable," but it is just as likely to confuse as to inform a jury in a proximate cause instruction.

The term "probable" is also less than rigorous, if not misleading. It suggests that the result must be *likely* to occur as a result of the defendant's act. But many acts are culpable even though they pose a relatively small risk of injury. If Smith throws a flower pot out a third story window without looking, there may be only a ten percent chance that someone will be hit. But this conduct is clearly negligent, because it poses an unreasonable risk of injury to passersby. No court in the country would deny liability in such a case on proximate cause grounds. "[F]oreseeability is not to be measured by what is more probable than not, but includes whatever is likely enough in the setting of modern life that a reasonably thoughtful person would take account of it in guiding practical conduct." Harper, James & Gray, §18.2, at 657-659.

This "natural and probable" test is frequently used in instructing juries on proximate cause. See, e.g., *Lanzet v. Greenberg*, 594 A.2d 1309, 1321 (N.J. 1991) (proximate cause is a "cause which naturally and probably led to and might have been expected to produce the occurrence complained of"). Perhaps this language conveys the general notion that the defendant should not be held liable for freakish or bizarre results of his negligence, but it does so quite imprecisely, and really restates the problem rather than offering guidance in solving it.

C. Substantial Factor

Some courts have held that the defendant is liable if his conduct was a substantial factor in bringing about the harm suffered by the plaintiff. This formulation has several problems. *First*, it is too vague to give judges or juries any meaningful guidance in assessing liability in future cases. Would it support liability in the revolver case or not? How about the burning hospital case? It merely suggests that the defendant's conduct must be important, more than de minimis, or not overwhelmed by other causes. "[I]t begs the question while dissembling ability to point to the answer." C. Morris, On the Teaching of Legal Cause, 39 Colum. L. Rev. 1087, 1101 (1939). Although some courts purport to use a substantial-factor test (see Harper, James & Gray,

§20.6, at 184, n.55), most of these decisions invoke some version of foresee-ability to determine whether the defendant's conduct was a substantial factor. See, e.g., *Doe v. Manheimer*, 563 A.2d 699, 704 (Conn. 1989) (substantial factor "reflects the inquiry fundamental to all proximate cause questions," whether injury was of the general nature foreseeable from the defendant's neg-ligence).

Second, the substantial-factor formula has also been used as an alternative to the but-for test in determining cause-in-fact. See Chapter 7. Most commen-tators agree that it is useful there, particularly in cases where the but-for test does not work. As a test for cause-in-fact, it relaxes to some extent the strictures of but-for analysis, but when used as a proximate cause test it is intended to *limit* liability. Even apart from its inherent vagueness, it is confus-ing to use the same formula for both actual and proximate cause analysis. See *Mitchell v. Gonzales*, 819 P.2d 872, 884 (Cal. 1991) (Kennard, J., dissenting) (noting the confusion generated by adopting a substantial-factor test for cause-in-fact without a separate definition of proximate cause).[3]

Last, this test simply seems to point to the *wrong* answer in some situa-tions. For example, placing the rat poison next to the stove was undoubtedly a substantial factor in causing the explosion in that case, yet liability seems unwarranted, since the defendant had no reason to anticipate the harm that took place.

D. Foreseeability

A great many proximate cause cases have turned on whether the plaintiff's injury was a foreseeable consequence of the defendant's conduct. The princi-pal virtue of this approach to the problem is that it ties the scope of liability to the scope of the defendant's fault: Since negligence consists of failing to guard against foreseeable injuries, it seems consistent to impose liability on the defendant only for those injuries he should have foreseen. There is no reason to expect an explosion from rat poison. Nor are injuries in a train wreck a foreseeable consequence of leaving a box lid on the sidewalk. The defendant escapes liability because he could not have foreseen the injury that occurred, and was therefore not required to guard against it.

The disadvantage of a foreseeability test is that it is too elastic to provide a sure guide to decision in close cases. Foreseeability, like "directness," is in the eye of the beholder; in those ambiguous cases where clarity is most needed, it fails to draw a predictable line. How, for example, should the following cases be decided under foreseeability analysis?

---

3. The First Restatement of Torts appeared to adopt a substantial-factor test for proximate cause, but was later clarified to confine the substantial-factor test to cause-in-fact problems. See Harper, James & Gray, §20.6 at 180-182 & n.45.

a. A dredger, though warned of a gas main in the area, negligently breaks it while dredging. A factory a mile away, supplied with gas through the main, suffers damage to its equipment and products due to the sudden loss of power.

b. Honore is driving along a rural road when he is passed by a tractor trailer. The truck cuts back into the right hand lane quickly, risking a collision. Hart, a passenger in the car, fears a collision and grabs the wheel. As a result, the car swerves into a ditch, injuring Honore.

c. A rural electric company erects a pole carrying high voltage wires. A support cable running down to the ground is allowed to come in contact with a barbed wire fence. There is a twenty-eight inch gap between the cable and the electric wires. Two chicken hawks, locked in aerial combat, bridge the gap between the electric wire and the cable, causing current to jump down the cable to the fence and start a fire which burns plaintiff's barn.

d. A train approaching a station hits a pedestrian at a crossing. The pedestrian is thrown 50 feet against the plaintiff standing on the platform, injuring him.

(These cases are discussed in detail in Example 10.)

E. The Scope of the Risk

An approach to proximate cause that appears to be gaining favor looks to the nature of the unreasonable risk created by the defendant. Under the risk approach, the court considers what the risks were that made the defendant's conduct negligent in the first place, and whether it was one of these risks that caused the plaintiff's harm. See Restatement (Second) of Torts §281, cmt. e. In the terrorist example, the reasonable person would realize that leaving the keys in the car created a risk that children would be injured tampering with the car, that a thief would take it and drive negligently, or that vandals would damage it. But it hardly seems that the reasonable person should foresee a terrorist using the car to dynamite an embassy. Under the "risk" approach, the defendant would not be liable, since the risk that caused the harm was not the risk that made the act negligent at the time it was done.

Similarly, the seller in the revolver case was negligent because he disregarded the risk that the boy might fire it carelessly, not for disregarding the risk that the boy might drop it on his foot. Likewise, careless driving is negligent because it creates an unreasonable risk of injury from a collision, not from a fire in the hospital three days later.

Of all the approaches to proximate cause, this may be the most helpful in providing some analytical basis for consistent decisionmaking. Like foreseeability, it relates the scope of liability to the faulty aspect of the defendant's conduct. And it refers the decisionmaker to something other than an intuitive guess in rendering judgment; the judge or jury can ask what unreasonable risks the defendant was bound to anticipate at the time she acted, and compare those risks to the injury which actually occurred.

Varieties of Foreseeability: Wagon Mound and Palsgraf

The two most famous proximate cause cases, *Overseas Tankship (U.K.) Ltd. v. Morts Dock & Engg. Co., Ltd. (The Wagon Mound)*, 1 All E.R. 404 (1961), and *Palsgraf v. Long Island R.*, 162 N.E. 99 (N.Y. 1928), exemplify two aspects of the proximate cause problem.

In *Palsgraf*, the defendant's conductors were negligent in assisting the rushing passenger onto a moving train, causing him to drop a package. Although there was no reason for the conductors to suspect it, the package contained firecrackers, which exploded, overturning some scales a distance away. The scales fell and injured the reluctantly famous Mrs. Palsgraf.

Although the railroad's employees were evidently negligent in *Palsgraf*, the railroad argued that their negligence only posed a foreseeable risk of injury to the passenger or his package, not to Mrs. Palsgraf. Justice Cardozo, writing for the majority, held that the duty to avoid injuring others extends only to those risks the actor should anticipate from her negligent act. Here, the unreasonable risk created by the conductors' conduct was that the passenger or his package would be injured, not Mrs. Palsgraf. Since the conductors would not have anticipated injury to her from their conduct, they owed no duty to avoid the injury. Since she was an "unforeseeable plaintiff" to whom no unreasonable risk was to be anticipated, Mrs. Palsgraf was denied recovery.[4]

In *Wagon Mound*, the defendant's oil fouled the waters around the plaintiff's dock, where welding was in progress. Because of its high ignition point, the oil was unlikely to burn, but it did, through a strange concatenation of circumstances found in the case to be unforeseeable.[5] Other injury to the dock, however, *was* foreseeable, and in fact took place: the fouling of the docks by the oil. The dock owner argued that, since the defendant could foresee *some* injury to the dock, it was liable for *all* injury which actually resulted.

The Privy Council held that the plaintiff could only recover for the injuries that the defendant should have anticipated at the time it released the

---

4. Another way to look at this is to say that there is no doctrine of "transferred negligence" analogous to that of transferred intent in intentional tort cases. See G. Williams, The Risk Principle, 77 Law Q. Rev. 179, 185-190 (1961).

5. Indeed, it required nearly 100 experiments to reconstruct a means by which it could have burned. A. Goodhart, The Brief Life of the Direct Consequences Rule in English Tort Law, 53 Va. L. Rev. 857, 866 (1967).

oil into the water. It would be liable for fouling the slips of the plaintiff's dock, a foreseeable consequence of releasing the oil, but not for the unforeseeable fire which destroyed the dock itself.

Palsgraf and *Wagon Mound* both apply a scope-of-the-risk approach to proximate cause. They both restrict liability to injuries that the defendant should have foreseen when he acted. This scope-of-the-risk approach closely resembles the analysis courts use in deciding whether a statutory standard of care will be adopted in a negligence case. In that context, the court asks whether the plaintiff was a member of the class the statute was intended to protect, and whether the statute was meant to protect against the hazard which actually injured the plaintiff. See Chapter 5. Similarly, under the risk rule, the court asks whether the defendant could have foreseen injury to the particular plaintiff from her carelessness (see *Palsgraf*) and whether she could have foreseen the type of injury that the plaintiff actually suffered (see *Wagon Mound*).

Some Guideposts in the Wilderness

While many courts pay homage to one or another of the proximate cause formulas, these formulas "are insincere volunteers when a court is wrestling to reach a result; they look useful, but their spurious usefulness fades with attempts to put them to work." C. Morris, 39 Colum. L. Rev. at 1099.[6] It may be, as Leon Green has suggested, that no formula can be devised which will resolve proximate cause questions, so that the results in hard cases must always turn on the good judgment of judges and juries. L. Green, The Causal Relation in Negligence Law, 60 Mich. L. Rev. 543, 568 (1962). Yet the cases do yield some fairly firm principles that at least help to frame the problem.

First, and most fundamentally, if the plaintiff's injury is truly beyond the type of harm to be expected from the defendant's conduct, the plaintiff will virtually always go uncompensated. A basic sense of justice demands that liability should not extend to consequences radically different from those to be anticipated from an act, and courts — whatever language they use — will find a way to reach that result. In the venereal disease hypo, for example, the court may dub Carpenter's disease too remote, unforeseeable, or beyond the risk that made the conduct negligent, but one way or another, it will reason to a judgment for the defendant.

Conversely, it is worth noting that most tort cases pose no legal cause problem because the harm suffered is exactly the type to be expected. In the run-of-the-mill motor vehicle case, for example, there is no question that a collision is the type of harm to be anticipated, and that, if the other elements

---

6. Personally, I would exclude the risk rule from this condemnation. I find the scope-of-the-risk analysis helpful in deciding whether liability should attach in many cases, though it cannot mechanistically compel a conclusion in all.

are proved, the defendant must pay. Like *Erie* problems in civil procedure, the close cases are excruciatingly hard, but the great majority of the cases are not hard at all.

Second, where a particular type of injury to the plaintiff is foreseeable, the defendant is liable for the injury sustained, even though it is more serious than might have been anticipated. If, for example, Goodhart knocks Gregory down, causing small lacerations, he is liable if Gregory contracts an infection and becomes seriously ill, or if he is a hemophiliac and dies from loss of blood. If Goodhart injures Bohlen in an auto accident, disabling him for six months, he must pay the value of Bohlen's lost wages, whether he is a day laborer or the CEO of a Fortune 500 company. It is said that the defendant "takes the plaintiff as he finds her." The fact that she is more susceptible to injury than the average person, has a "thin skull," so to speak, is not a defense to liability. If Goodhart could foresee personal injury to Bohlen, he is liable for the actual injury caused, not some hypothetical average ordinarily to be expected from the act.

Third, the cases distinguish unforeseeable consequences of a negligent act from consequences that are foreseeable but take place in an unusual manner. This "foreseeable-injury-in-an-unforeseeable-manner" principle is nicely illustrated by *United Novelty Co. v. Daniels*, 42 So. 2d 395 (Miss. 1949). In *Daniels*, the defendant allowed its employee to clean some machines with gasoline in a small room heated by a heater with an open flame. A rat, drenched with gas, ran from under one of the machines over to the heater, caught fire, and ran for refuge back to the machine, causing an explosion which killed the employee. The court concluded that, while the manner in which the accident took place was unusual, an explosion was exactly the type of accident to be anticipated from using a volatile, flammable liquid in a small room with an open flame. The defendant was held liable.

There is something to this distinction. The exact sequence of events in every accident is unique, but in most the general nature of the damage threatened was foreseeable. Distinguish from the rat case, for example, the terrorist bombing hypo at the beginning of the chapter. In the rat case, the general nature of the accident threatened by the conduct actually took place. In terms of the risk rule, the risk of an explosion of the vapors, causing personal injury to the employee, was the very risk that made the defendant's conduct negligent. But in the terrorist case, the general nature of the risk to be expected from leaving the keys in the car was far afield from that which injured the passerby at the embassy.

The trick, of course, is in making the distinction: In many cases the line between unforeseeable consequences and unforeseeable manner is fine one, if indeed a defensible line can be drawn at all. Consider, for example, *Doughty v. Turner Mfg. Co.*, 1 Q.B. 518 (1964). In *Doughty*, the plaintiff was standing next to a vat of molten liquid when the cover of the vat was negligently knocked into it. Nothing happened at first, but several minutes later there was an explosion within the vat, caused by a chemical reaction of the lid with the liquid. The plaintiff argued that the defendant's employees negligently created a risk that he would be splashed by the liquid, and that, indeed, he *was* injured by such splashing (when the explosion threw the liquid out of the vat) though in an unusual manner. The court, however, held that he was injured by a different risk, the risk of an unforeseeable chemical reaction causing explosion, not physical splashing from the dropping of the cover. I think the case was rightly decided, but it turns on a nice distinction indeed.

Fourth, it is very important to recognize that courts often use proximate cause language to limit liability *even for clearly foreseeable harm*. For example, most courts hold that consequential economic losses suffered by third parties as a result of the defendant's negligence are not actionable. Suppose, for example, that Goodhart negligently causes a fire that shuts down a factory for three months. It is obviously foreseeable that a fire would cause such a shutdown, and that, if it does, the employees would suffer lost wages. Yet most courts would deny recovery for the lost wages since the burden of liability for such secondary consequences is too great. (Imagine, for example, the potential liability if Goodhart had burned down a bridge, interrupting the business affairs of an entire town.) See generally Harper, James & Gray, §25.18A.

Although courts in such cases frequently state that the defendant's conduct was "not the proximate cause" of the secondary losses, it is clear that liability is denied because of the burden such losses would impose, *not* because secondary economic losses are unforeseeable. The use of proximate cause analysis in cases like these is unfortunate, but widespread.

New York's early rule limiting recovery for damages by fire provides another example of a court choosing, for policy reasons, to limit recovery for foreseeable harm. In *Ryan v. New York Central R.R. Co.*, 35 N.Y. 210 (1866), the New York court restricted liability for fire damage to the first adjacent property burned. The *Ryan* court dubbed the burning of further properties "not the immediate but the remote result of the negligence of the defendants." 35 N.Y. at 212. This conclusory proximate cause analysis, to borrow Dean Prosser's language in a related context, is "moonshine and vapor."[7] Anyone but a Menlove could foresee that a fire would burn beyond the next lot. The true rationale for the rule was the crushing burden such liability would impose, and the general availability of fire insurance as an alternative source of protection:

> To sustain such a claim as the present, and to follow the same to its legitimate consequences, would subject to a liability against which no prudence could guard, and to meet which no private fortune would be adequate. . . To hold that the owner must not only meet his own

---

7. W. Prosser, Proximate Cause in California, 38 Cal. L. Rev. 369, 376 (1950).

loss by fire, but that he must guarantee the security of his neighbors on both sides, and to an unlimited extent, would be to create a liability which would be the destruction of all civilized society.

35 N.Y. at 216.[8]

Unfortunately, courts often mask these policy limitations in proximate cause language. Early liquor liability cases refused to hold bar keeps liable for serving intoxicated patrons who caused motor vehicle accidents, on the ground that the drunk driving, not the service of liquor, was the proximate cause of the injury. Yet few acts are more foreseeable than a drunk driving home from a roadside bar. The real thrust of these cases (since repudiated in many jurisdictions) was a policy decision to place the liability on the more blameworthy of two negligent parties. One of the great challenges for the tort lawyer is to cut through promiscuous foreseeability references to determine whether some other policy is in fact driving the decisions.[9]

The law of torts would be tidier if the courts would use *duty* analysis when they deny recovery for foreseeable harm for other policy reasons, and use *proximate cause* analysis in cases involving unforeseeable harm. Frequently, courts do use duty analysis to limit liability for foreseeable harm. (See pp. 181-182.) But many other cases that deny recovery for policy reasons — as in the fire and drunk driving cases just discussed — have used proximate cause language instead.

Last, a *caveat*: Many, many decisions that use the term "proximate cause" have nothing to do with the problem addressed in this chapter. Courts have an unfortunate tendency to use this phrase when they really mean cause-in-fact. This will probably not matter in a jury instruction, since the jury usually hasn't a notion that "proximate cause" means anything *but* actual cause, but it tends to confuse those of us who have an inkling of the difference.

Judge and Jury

Although the issue of proximate cause is often put before the jury, it is doubtful that juries consider proximate cause at all in most cases. *First*, if the

---

8. Most states have rejected the rigid limits of the *Ryan* rule. New York has modified it as well. See Prosser, Wade & Schwartz, Cases & Materials on Torts, 292 (9th ed. 1994).

9. A few states even hold that foreseeability is only relevant to the negligence element, and view legal cause as *solely* a question of policy. Once negligence is found, these courts conclude, the defendant is ordinarily liable, even for unforeseeable injury. "[U]nder the methodology of this court, it is not necessary that either the person harmed or the type of harm that would result be foreseeable. The act or omission in the face of foreseeable harm was negligence." *A.E. Investment Corp. v. Link Builders, Inc.*, 214 N.W.2d 764, 767 (Wis. 1974). However, these courts, like Judge Andrews in *Palsgraf*, will still refuse to impose liability for public policy reasons. 214 N.W.2d at 770. Since one such reason noted by the Wisconsin courts is the "highly extraordinary" nature of the resulting harm (*Rolph v. EBI Companies*, 464 N.W.2d 667, 673 (Wis. 1991), it is not clear that this approach differs greatly from that of other courts.

injury is sufficiently bizarre, the court will probably direct a verdict for the defendant, so that the jury never considers the case. Many courts would direct a verdict, for example, in the examples given on p.146. *Second*, it is very doubtful that the jury understands the proximate cause issue when it is submitted to them. Here, for example, is a typical proximate cause instruction:

> Proximate cause means that cause which, in a natural and continuous sequence, unbroken by any effective intervening cause, produces an event, and without which cause such event would not have occurred.

It is very doubtful that a jury, hearing this instruction, will have any idea of the complexities discussed in this chapter. At best, it may convey some hazy sense that truly weird outcomes are not actionable, but even that is questionable. More likely the jury will infer, as one judge concluded based on a statistical study of proximate cause instructions, that "proximate cause [is] just a fancy way of saying causation." C. Mikell, Jury Instructions and Proximate Cause: An Uncertain Trumpet in Georgia, 27 Ga. St. Bar J. 60, 63 (1990). Proximate cause is "a term which few lawyers would voluntarily attempt to define, and which must inevitably be beyond the comprehension of the ordinary citizen. The effect [of submitting the issue to the jury] is to leave the decision to nothing more than the good sense of the jury." W. Prosser, Proximate Cause in California, 38 Cal. L. Rev. 369, 420 (1950).

Thus the practical impact of the doctrine is that it prevents some plaintiffs from reaching the jury at all due to directed verdicts based on lack of proximate cause, or leads to reversal on appeal because, as a matter of law, the defendant's act was not a proximate cause of her harm. If the plaintiff surmounts these hurdles, the proximate cause issue probably drops out of most cases entirely.

The following examples illustrate the basic issues involved in proximate cause cases. In analyzing them, assume that the court adopts a scope-of-the-risk approach to the proximate cause issues, unless otherwise noted.

EXAMPLES

Revisionist History

1. Bingham is running for a Long Island Railroad train that is about to pull out of the station. He is carrying a small package wrapped in brown paper. Two conductors, seeing the train start to leave, reach out to help Bingham onto the train, and one clumsily knocks the package onto the tracks. Alas, the package contains an antique music box which Bingham had just had valued at $5,000. The music box is demolished upon landing.
    a. Is the railroad liable under a foreseeability approach?
    b. Is the railroad liable under a scope-of-the-risk approach?

2. Bingham is running for a Long Island Railroad train that is about to pull out of the station. He is carrying a small package wrapped in brown

paper. Two conductors, seeing the train start to leave, reach out to help Bingham onto the train, and one clumsily knocks the package onto the tracks. Alas, the package contains fireworks, which explode upon impact. A certain Mrs. Falsgraf, running to the same train immediately behind Bingham, is injured by the explosion.

    a. Is the railroad liable for her injuries?

    b. Assume, on the facts of Example 2a, that Mrs. Falsgraf sued Bingham. Would Bingham be liable for her injuries?

    c. Assume, on the facts of *Palsgraf*, that Mrs. Palsgraf had sued the passenger. Would the court have denied recovery on proximate cause grounds?

3.   A Gregory Railroad train negligently collides with a car at an intersection. The car is thrown into a switch, throwing the switch and turning the train onto a side track, where it collides with some standing boxcars. Beale, a passenger, is injured when he is thrown from his seat due to the collision. Will lack of proximate cause bar recovery for Beale's injuries?

Scoping Out the Risks

4.   On March 16, 1994, the Gregory Railroad Company accepts electric motors from Pollack for shipment. Because Pollack needed the motors as components for a finished product, he required, and the railroad agreed, to make delivery of the goods within ten days. Through the negligence of the railroad, shipment of the goods is delayed for five days. On March 30, while in transit on board a Gregory freight train, the goods are damaged in a flood. Is the railroad liable under the "risk rule"?

5.   On October 15, 1994, the Gregory Railroad accepts a shipment of apples to deliver for Pollack. Because the weather is cool and frost could spoil the apples, Pollack requires that the apples be delivered within four days. Gregory delays, and the apples are spoiled by freezing on October 23. Is the railroad liable?

Causes, Remote and Proximate

6.   Icarus Airlines negligently fails to fill all the fuel tanks on a passenger plane. Consequently, the plane is forced to land on a Pacific Island. Morris, a passenger, is injured when a volcano on the island erupts while they are refueling. Is the airline's negligence a proximate cause of Morris's injury?

7.   Apex Alarm Company installs a security system in Smith's home. The alarm is designed to sound at the Apex office if the system is activated by an intruder. The Apex employee on duty then calls the police department, which ideally apprehends the culprit.

    On a balmy June evening, a burglar breaks a window at Smith's home. This should activate the alarm system, but due to negligent rewiring at the

Apex office, it fails to go off. The burglar makes off with Smith's valuables, and Smith sues Apex. Apex moves for summary judgment on the ground that the burglar's intentional criminal act supersedes its negligence in wiring the alarm improperly. Assuming these facts are established on the motion, how should the court rule?

8. Morris buys a table saw from Harper Power Tools, a tool manufacturer, in Idaho in 1986. Subsequently, he moves to Alabama and sells the saw in Alabama to a neighbor, Dias. The saw has a guard over the blade which is bulky and makes certain kinds of cuts difficult. Eventually, Dias gets tired of the guard and removes it, which is easily done. In 1993, he allows his fifteen-year-old boy to use the saw. Dias Jr. cuts his hand while pushing a small piece of wood through the saw, and sues Harper for negligence in designing the guard. Harper argues that its negligence was not a proximate cause of the accident. Should the argument prevail?

Judge Fudd Does the Foreseeable

9. The Bentham Construction Company excavates a deep foundation for an office building in downtown St. Louis, immediately adjacent to a main street. Beale, a Bentham crane operator, sets down a load of iron beams in the street, on the edge of the excavation, but his touch is off and the load lands heavily, causing the wall of the excavation to collapse. The landslide breaks a large water main under the street, flooding the foundation and delaying the construction. Bentham's employees were not aware that the water main was there.

The owner sues for the delay caused by the flooding. Judge Fudd instructs the jury, in part, as follows:

> If you find that the defendant's employees were unaware that the water main was under the street, then you must find that any negligence of Bentham's employees in causing the collapse was not the proximate cause of the plaintiff's damages.

What is wrong with Judge Fudd's instruction?

Fore-Guessability

10. If the court applies a foreseeability analysis, how should it resolve the four cases given on p.151?

EXPLANATIONS
Revisionist History

1a. A court that applies a foreseeability approach to this problem will have to decide *what* must be foreseeable in order to resolve the case. The railroad will argue that the conductors would never foresee that the passenger was carrying a $5,000 music box. Bingham, on the other hand, will argue that they could foresee that their negligence would damage the package, whatever it was, and that they need not foresee exactly what was in the package.

Bingham is likely to have the better of the argument here, based on the reasoning of the "thin skull" cases. It should not be a defense for the railroad that the conductors did not know the contents of the package. They could foresee that Bingham would be carrying a package, that it might fall if they were not careful, and that the contents — whatever they were — might be damaged if it fell. See C. Morris, Proximate Cause in Minnesota, 34 Minn. L. Rev. 185, 192 (1950) (defendant may be liable though she did not foresee the details of the accident). Where damage of the general type sustained was foreseeable, courts usually hold defendants liable for the damage *actually* caused, even if that is greater than one might ordinarily expect.

b. Whether the railroad is liable under the scope-of-the-risk rule also depends on how broadly you define the risk. Arguably, the presence of an expensive antique was not a risk that the conductors would have foreseen, and therefore they were not negligent for failing to foresee it. But most courts would define the risk more generally. They would conclude that the risk that makes the conductor's act negligent is the risk that either the passenger or his belongings would fall and be injured. Where one of those risks comes to fruition, the defendant is liable, because it is a risk that she should have anticipated and averted. The fact that the package contained a valuable antique goes to the *extent* of the risk rather than its nature. The nature of the unreasonable risk was damage to personal property from falling, and that was the risk that led to the harm.

2a.   There are some obvious differences here from the facts of *Palsgraf*. Here, because Mrs. Falsgraf is next to Bingham, personal injury to her is foreseeable: The package could fall on her foot and injure her, or the conductor or the passenger could hit her, causing her to fall to the platform or even under the train. Falsgraf will argue that, on these facts, the conductors could foresee a risk of personal injury to her. Consequently, she is a foreseeable plaintiff and should recover for her injuries.

However, the court will probably not accept this argument. True, the conductors could foresee personal injury of one sort to Mrs. Falsgraf — from falling or being hit by the package — but could not foresee injury of the sort that actually occurred — explosion. Most courts would conclude that the injury she suffered arose from a different risk than those the railroad could anticipate, and would therefore deny recovery. See, e.g., the *Doughty* case, described above at p.154-155.

Example 1 illustrates that the proximate cause analysis must avoid defining the foreseeable risk too *specifically*. This example shows that the court may also go awry if it defines the risk too *generally*. If the defendant need only foresee "personal injury" of some sort, the plaintiff who tripped over the box lid, missed her train and was injured when the later train crashed could recover: The box lid left on the sidewalk created a risk of personal injury, she suffered personal injury, ergo liability. The same reasoning would support liability in the revolver case: Selling the revolver to the boy created a risk of personal injury and he suffered personal injury, so the seller should pay.[10] Yet this analysis would be too broad in both of these cases. The court must focus on the *particular* risks to be anticipated from the defendant's act. At the same time, as Example 1 illustrates, it must avoid getting bogged down in the idiosyncratic "details" of the accident.

b. Mrs. Falsgraf's case against Bingham is distinguishable from her case against the railroad. Since Bingham *knows* that the package contains dynamite, he is aware of the risk of explosion. Most courts would conclude that he is negligent for bringing fireworks into a crowded place, precisely because they might be detonated by some kind of incident such as the scenario here. Since the risk of an explosion is one of the risks that makes his conduct negligent, most courts would hold him liable to those injured when an explosion actually takes place.

c. In the *Palsgraf* case, Mrs. Palsgraf was not directly injured by the blast, but by a set of scales some distance from the explosion, which were knocked over on her foot. Yet it does not seem unusual that a bystander, even at some distance, should be injured by flying debris if an explosion takes place. The details are unique — as they always are — but the general nature of the accident is within the scope of the risk to be anticipated.

Suppose you went up to the Reasonable Person and asked her whether she would anticipate that, if a package of explosives exploded in a public place, a bystander might be injured by an object dislodged by the blast. Doubtless, our odious character would view this as foreseeable, even if she could not tell you that the object would be a set of scales. Since this is a foreseeable risk of carrying explosives in a train station, the passenger would likely be held liable to Mrs. Palsgraf.

3.   The result in this example turns on whether the court characterizes Beale's injury as unforeseeable or as a foreseeable injury which takes place in an unforeseeable manner. In the early case from which it is drawn, *Engle v. Director Gen. of RR.*, 133 N.E. 138 (Ind. App. 1921), the court denied recovery on the following reasoning:

> That an automobile should suddenly appear upon a railroad track and be struck by an approaching train is not a matter of unusual oc-

---

10. In fact, that case is the converse of this one, isn't it? In the revolver case, the defendant created an unreasonable risk of personal injury through explosion by selling to the boy, who suffered personal injury through dropping the gun. The conductors created risks of injury through dropping the package, but the injury resulted instead from a different risk, explosion.

currence, and is one that might reasonably be anticipated; but that such a collision should result in the automobile being thrown against a switch stand in such a manner as to open the switch is a possibility so remote as to be beyond the realm of events reasonably to be anticipated. This being true, the independent agency so intervening must be treated as the sole proximate cause of the injuries. . . .

133 N.E. at 140. However, this court may have gotten too caught up in the "details" of the accident. While the particular sequence of events was certainly bizarre, the general nature of the harm — injury to the passenger when a collision throws him from his seat — is entirely foreseeable from a crossing accident. (Compare the burning rat case, discussed at p.154.) Many modern courts, I suspect, would look to the general nature of the risk threatened by the engineer's negligence, and hold the railroad liable on these facts.

Scoping Out the Risks

4.   This is a recurring fact pattern that has spawned contradictory holdings in the cases. But the result under the risk rule seems clear. The risk that made the railroad's delay negligent was the risk that Pollack would suffer commercial delays, not the risk that, if the motors were shipped later rather than sooner, they would be damaged in transit by a flood. That risk is presumably the same whether they are in transit from March 16 to March 26, or March 21 to March 31, for all we know from the facts. Thus, the risk of flood was not a risk that made it negligent to delay the shipment. Under the risk rule, the railroad should not be held liable.

5.   This example contrasts nicely with the last. Here, the railroad agreed that the apples would be shipped immediately, and was presumably aware, or should have been, that delay posed a risk that the apples would be spoiled by cold weather. Thus, one of the risks that made the delay negligent here was the risk of freezing as the weather got colder, and it was exactly this risk that caused the damage. Consequently, the railroad would likely be held liable for the resulting damage. See *Fox v. Boston and Maine RR. Co.*, 19 N.E. 222 (Mass. 1889).

Causes, Remote and Proximate

6.   In this example, borrowed from Prosser, Wade & Schwartz 319, virtually any court would conclude that the airline's negligence was not the proximate cause of Beale's injury. Injury from an erupting volcano is not a foreseeable consequence of failing to fill all the fuel tanks. Under the risk approach, leaving the fuel out creates an unreasonable risk that the plane would have to ditch in the water or make an emergency landing, but not that the plane would land on an island at the time of a volcanic eruption. Under either approach, the court will deny recovery to Beale for this bizarre occurrence.

Many courts would phrase this in terms of "superseding" cause; that is, they would hold that the eruption of a volcano near the airport where the plane was forced down was such an unexpected later event that it supersedes the negligence of the airline. But labeling the eruption a "superseding cause" is more a conclusion than a helpful method of analysis. The court must still separate superseding causes from others which do not cut off liability. Most courts do so on the basis of the extraordinary or unforeseeable nature of the subsequent events.

7.   In this example, Apex was negligent in rewiring the system, but a later, deliberate criminal act of a third person leads to the plaintiff's injury. The issue is whether this act supersedes the negligence of Apex, so as to cut off its liability for the theft.

Subsequent intentional acts may cut off liability in some cases. A nice example is the owner who allowed a child trespasser into its building, only to have the boy usher a visitor into an unguarded elevator shaft. See *Cole v. German S. & L. Soc.*, 124 F. 113 (8th Cir. 1903). No one, not even a law professor, would anticipate such a twisted sense of humor. But other intentional acts are entirely foreseeable. Here, Apex was hired to avert the very type of act which caused Smith's loss. It hardly seems appropriate to take his money to protect him from theft, and then when they fail to do so, to deny that such theft was foreseeable!

The Restatement's treatment of this issue reflects the risk rule approach to proximate cause:

> If the likelihood that a third person may act in a particular manner is the hazard or one of the hazards which makes the actor negligent, such an act whether innocent, negligent, intentionally tortious, or criminal does not prevent the actor from being liable for harm caused thereby.

Restatement (Second) of Torts §449. Here, illegal entry by a burglar is clearly one of the hazards that makes it negligent to wire the system improperly. Apex's motion for summary judgment should be denied.

8.   Presumably, Harper's argument is based on the long chain of consequences between its negligence in designing the safety guard and the plaintiff's injury. The accident is remote from Harper's negligence in several senses. It takes place seven years and half a continent away from the point of the negligent act. It is also, arguably, remote in the sense that it would not have caused the accident (we will assume) without several conscious intervening acts by others: the resale to Dias Sr., his decision to remove the guard, and his decision to allow his son to use the saw.

Despite these factors, many courts would hold that this sequence of events was foreseeable. The very reason for designing a better guard (or one that cannot be easily removed) is to prevent the user from taking the guard off and exposing himself and other users to unreasonable risk of injury. While Dias Sr. may be negligent for removing the guard, his act is not unforeseeable.

Nor is it unforeseeable that the saw would be resold, or that the buyer would allow a member of the family to use it. Thus, while the injury is removed in time and space from the negligent act, the sequence of events is entirely predictable, and the risk that caused the injury is exactly the risk that made the seller negligent in designing the guard.

Judge Fudd Does the Foreseeable

9.   Judge Fudd's instruction requires the jury to find for the defendant if they find that its employees did not know that the water main was there. Presumably, his reasoning is that, if its employees were unaware of the water main, they had no reason to foresee the risk of water damage.

This is seriously Fuddled reasoning. If actual knowledge were required, the Menlove who threw the flower pot out the third story window without looking would not be liable if it hit a pedestrian. The important question is what Beale, the employee who dropped the beams, could *foresee* as a consequence of his negligence, not what he knew would happen. Surely he could foresee that underground utilities *might* be under the street and that, if they were, they might rupture if the excavation collapsed. Since this was one of the risks that made his act negligent, he should be liable, even if he was not sure what utilities actually ran under the street.

Fore-Guessability

10a. In the case from which this example is drawn, the court held that, while injury to persons or property from the escaping gas would be foreseeable, injury to the plaintiff's business was not.

> [T]he damage arising from the loss of natural gas supply, in turn causing the shut down of electric turbines, in turn causing a loss of electric power vital to the aluminum reduction process, with the ultimate result being substantial damage to equipment and product-in-process, goes beyond the pale of general harm which reasonably might have been anticipated by negligent dredgers.

Consolidated Aluminum Corp. v. C.F. Bean Corp., 833 F.2d 65, 68 (5th Cir. 1987), *cert. denied*, 486 U.S. 1055 (1988). With all due respect, this conclusion is dubious. It seems eminently foreseeable that the interruption of gas service will cause many commercial losses to nearby businesses.[11] Couldn't the court have, with stronger justification, written as follows:

---

11. In fact, such secondary economic losses are so foreseeable, and are claimed so frequently in tort cases, that courts have developed a doctrine, the "economic loss doctrine," to address them. As a general matter, such economic losses to third parties are not recoverable. See Harper, James & Gray, §25.18A.

> It is hardly unforeseeable that severing a major gas supply line (of which the defendant had been informed) will interrupt the flow of energy to a nearby manufacturer dependent upon that supply line, causing injury from the sudden disruption of complex manufacturing sequences and loss of products in process.

This case is an example of a court misusing foreseeability analysis to limit liability for other reasons. As stated in the introduction, courts often limit liability for clearly foreseeable harm, for other policy reasons. Doubtless, the court here denied liability because of the extreme burden that liability for secondary economic losses would impose in a case like this: If the dredger were liable to this plaintiff, it would be liable to all those who suffered from the interruption in service. It is certainly understandable that courts will refuse to impose overwhelming liability for secondary consequences of negligence. But it does little for clarity of analysis to mask this policy conclusion in the guise of foreseeability.

b. The question here is whether the subsequent act of Hart in grabbing the wheel is so unexpected that it supersedes the truck driver's negligence. It hardly seems that it is. Even if Hart was negligent, it is probably foreseeable that he will react instinctively to the emergency created by the defendant.

In some situations, proximate cause issues are simplified by well established lines of precedent. This example is a case in point. Most courts hold that subsequent negligence — of a third party or of the plaintiff — is foreseeable, so that the initial tortfeasor remains liable. Similarly, where a tortfeasor injures the plaintiff, and the initial injuries are aggravated by negligent medical treatment, the first tortfeasor is generally held liable, on the theory that the subsequent negligence is foreseeable.

Another area in which precedent simplifies the proximate cause issue is liability to rescuers. Courts generally hold rescuers foreseeable, so that a party who negligently placed the initial victim in peril is liable to the rescuer as well if she is injured trying to rescue the victim.

c. Believe it or not, this was held foreseeable in *Chase v. Washington Water Power Co.*, 111 P.2d 872 (Idaho 1941). Interestingly, the court analyzed foreseeability after the fact, that is, it asked whether, looking back at the events, they seemed so highly extraordinary that the defendant should escape liability:

> While, from an anticipatory point of view, the exact manner in which these hawks interfered with the wires upon this occasion may seem unusual or extraordinary, viewed in retrospect it cannot be said to have been unforeseeable.

111 P.2d at 875. This approach, assessing foreseeability after the fact, was suggested by Judge Andrews in his *Palsgraf* dissent. 162 N.E. at 104-105. It has even been approved in the Second Restatement:

> s. 435(2). The actor's conduct may be held not to be a legal cause of harm to another where after the event and looking back from the

harm to the actor's negligent conduct, it appears to the court highly extraordinary that it should have brought about the harm.

Frankly, I have never understood this hindsight type of foresight. If the rationale for a foreseeability test is that liability extends to consequences defendants ought to anticipate, the test should focus on what the defendant could anticipate when he acted, not the Monday-morning-quarterback approach of §435(2). Second, nothing is truly extraordinary when it has actually happened. Even bizarre accidents look fore-ordained once the sequence of events that caused them is fully known. This hindsight approach is relatively rare in the cases. Indeed, one of the dissents in *Chase* takes the majority to task for using it. 111 P.2d at 876-878.

Aside from the question of the court's retrospective approach to foreseeability, there is also a sense in the *Chase* opinion that policy factors influenced the court's supposedly neutral finding on the question of foreseeability. The opinion repeatedly emphasizes that electric companies must exercise the "highest degree of care" (111 P.2d at 874). Technically this is irrelevant to the analysis of proximate cause, but the court may have stretched its causation analysis based on an intuitive judgment that a dangerous enterprise such as high voltage distribution of electricity should generally pay the costs of the risks it creates.

It is not surprising that courts will interpret an elastic concept like foreseeability in light of other values. For example, whether it is foreseeable that a rescuer will intervene to help an accident victim may be debatable, but the desire to encourage rescue inclines courts in such cases to conclude that rescue is foreseeable.

d. This injury was held unforeseeable in *Wood v. Pennsylvania R. Co.*, 35 A. 699 (Pa. 1896): "The injury, at most, was remotely possible, as distinguished from the natural and probable consequences of the neglect to give warning." 35 A. at 701. (Note the misleading reference to "possible" injuries, though it is clear that defendants are bound to anticipate many accidents which are merely "possible.")

This decision also seems questionable. This case could fairly be regarded as one in which a foreseeable injury takes place in an unforeseeable manner. It certainly seems foreseeable that a speeding train approaching without warning would collide with persons or vehicles at the intersection, and that such a collision would throw debris a distance of 50 feet. Nor would it seem unforeseeable that passengers would be waiting on a platform located that distance from the crossing. The unusual feature is that it was the victim's body that was thrown against the plaintiff instead of debris from a car, for instance. Consider this redraft of the *Wood* opinion:

> If the plaintiff's evidence is believed, the defendant's engineer ran through a crossing at high speed without giving the slightest warning of his approach. It is hardly beyond the realm of reasonable anticipation that such negligence could cause a collision at the crossing, that

the momentum of such a collision, if it occurred, would throw debris a considerable distance or that passengers waiting at the nearby platform might be hit by such flying objects. While the fact that the object in this case was the body of a pedestrian is unusual, the defendant need not anticipate the exact manner in which the accident takes place in order to be held liable [citing hundreds of cases].

Sounds pretty convincing, doesn't it?

PART FOUR

*The Duty
Element*

9

The Elusive Element of Duty: Two Principles in Search of an Exception

Introduction

It is hornbook law that the plaintiff in a negligence case must prove four elements in order to recover: duty, breach, causation, and damages. Even if the defendant was negligent, and that negligence caused injury to the plaintiff, the defendant will not be liable unless he also owed the plaintiff a duty of care. This chapter addresses the elusive element of duty.

It hardly seems that this should be a problem: Don't we all owe a duty to *everyone* not to injure them by our own negligence? Such a universal duty of care would simplify negligence law considerably: It would effectively eliminate the duty element from the plaintiff's burden of proof, since a duty of care would always exist. Although such a broad rule is tempting, courts have not been willing to impose a universal duty of due care. Instead, they have often refused to hold defendants liable, even though they have caused clearly foreseeable harm to the plaintiff. Here, for example, are some situations in which many courts would deny recovery even though harm was to be anticipated from the defendant's conduct:

a. Adler visits city hall to pay a traffic ticket. While walking up the stairs, he sees a pen lying on the edge of one of the stair treads. He fails to pick it up, and Skinner falls on it, breaking a leg.

b. Federal Safety Insurance Company provides fire insurance for industry. To reduce claims, Federal inspects the premises of the companies it insures for fire hazards before issuing a policy. Federal Safety inspects Rainbow Paint Company's factory, but neglects to enter a small room in which oily rags have been left in a pile. A week later, Skinner, an employee at the plant, is burned in a fire started by those rags. He sues Federal for failing to prevent the fire by seeing that the rags were removed.

c. Reik is driving down a rural highway and witnesses an accident in which White drives into a tree. Unwilling to get involved, she drives on. White is not found for an hour, and his injuries are aggravated by the delay in receiving treatment.

d. Dr. Rogers treats Jung for an infectious form of hepatitis. He is aware that Jung is a professional dancer, and warns him that the disease can be transmitted through contact. However, he makes no effort to warn other dancers who may have contact with Jung. Klein, a member of Jung's dance troupe, contracts hepatitis from Jung.

In each of these examples, the actor was (we will assume) negligent, and that negligence caused the plaintiff's damages. Yet many courts would refuse to allow recovery in these cases, on the ground that the actor did not owe a duty of care to the plaintiff.

Why Courts Impose Duties, or Refuse to Impose Them

Tort duties are not like chemistry's Periodic Table of Elements. Nature's elements (they tell me) have a physical existence quite apart from anything we might think about them. Chemists have identified them, but (with perhaps a few high-tech exceptions) they have not created them. Tort duties, on the other hand, do not exist in nature; they are *made up* by judges because they conclude that a duty *ought* to exist under the circumstances. "[L]egal duties are not discoverable facts of nature, but merely conclusory expressions that, in cases of a particular type, liability should be imposed for damage done." *Tarasoff v. Regents of the Univ. of California*, 551 P.2d 334, 342, (Cal. 1976). "[I]t should be recognized that 'duty' is not sacrosanct in itself, but is only an expression of the sum total of those considerations of policy which lead the law to say that the plaintiff is entitled to protection." Prosser & Keeton at 358. If a court concludes that society will be better off if store owners exercise due care to assist injured customers, it will create such a duty; if a court concludes that bystanders should not be legally bound to render aid in an emergency, it will refuse to create a duty to intervene, and so on.

This fundamental fact of tort life is not something to be embarrassed about: Determining the legal rights and obligations of the parties is the most fundamental task of judging. "The scope or extent of duty in any case can only be resolved by the learning, experience, good sense and judgment of the judge — the molding of law in response to the needs of the environment." L. Green, Duties, Risks, Causation Doctrines, 41 Tex. L. Rev. 42, 45 (1962). On the other hand, it is not particularly satisfying to students simply to tell them that the duty issue is difficult and judges have to decide it. Understandably, students want more guidance about such an important issue.

Though the duty issue is complex, some guidance is possible. To begin with, we can identify major factors that judges consider in deciding whether to impose a duty in a given case. These factors include the judge's sense of morality, the foreseeability and extent of the likely harm from the defendant's conduct, the burden that the new duty will impose on the defendant, alternative ways of protecting the plaintiff's interest, the increased safety likely to result from imposing the duty, the chilling effect the duty may have on defendants' conduct, administrative problems for the courts in enforcing the duty, problems of proof, and others.

Certainly, the foreseeability of harm weighs heavily in favor of imposing a duty on the actor, since it makes basic good sense that a defendant "should" avoid foreseeable injuries to others. For example, it is highly foreseeable that a mental patient who threatens to kill a relative will do so if released from custody, or that a parent will suffer traumatic shock if a negligent driver hits his child. Where resulting harm is so likely to follow, the argument is persuasive that the court should impose a duty of care to prevent it.

The moral argument is also strong in many duty cases. Most people would believe that it is "right" for an employer to go to the aid of an injured worker, or a doctor to take steps to assure that an HIV infected patient does not engage in unsafe sexual practices. This argument is particularly persuasive if the defendant is uniquely positioned to prevent harm. The psychiatrist who releases a patient who has threatened a relative, for example, may be the only one in a position to warn the relative. The police officer who stops a drunk driver is uniquely placed to prevent that driver from causing an accident.

Other factors, however, weigh against imposing a duty of care, even if harm is foreseeable and avoidable. Courts hesitate to create duties that impose excessive burdens on actors. A court might, for example, refuse to impose a duty on school officials to supervise school children at bus stops. Such a duty would impose an onerous burden on operations, and can be fulfilled as well, if not better, by parents. Similarly, many courts have refused to impose a duty of care on municipalities to properly inspect private property. Here too, the burden on municipalities would be exceedingly broad, and the risk can be averted by owners. Similarly, a recent case refused to hold that a hospital has a duty to warn all patients of the risks of medications, on the ground that the duty would be too broad, and that it can be better fulfilled by the patient's doctor. *Kirk v. Michael Reese Hosp. & Medical Ctr.*, 513 N.E.2d 387, 396-397 (Ill. 1987), *cert. denied*, 485 U.S. 905 (1988).

Administrative problems of enforcing the duty may also influence the court's judgment. For many years, courts denied liability for infliction of emotional distress on the ground that the risk of fraudulent claims and excessive litigation was too great. Similarly, they rejected claims for injury to fetuses partly on the ground that it would be extremely difficult to prove that the defendant's conduct was the cause of the injury.

In other cases, the chilling effect of imposing the duty has counseled hesitation. In *Eiseman v. State*, 511 N.E.2d 1128 (N.Y. 1987), the court refused to hold that a college had a duty to control the acts of a parolee admitted to a college enrichment program. The court was unwilling to create a duty that would force colleges to place discriminatory restrictions on the very persons the program was meant to assist in reintegrating into society. Similarly, some courts have refused to impose a duty on theater operators to prevent violence by viewers of violent movies, to avoid chilling activity protected by the First Amendment. See, e.g., *Yakubowicz v. Paramount Pictures Corp.*, 536 N.E.2d 1067, 1071-1072 (Mass. 1989).

Policies established by the legislature will also influence the court's duty analysis. Courts that have imposed a tort duty on the police to arrest drunk drivers have noted the firm legislative policy of controlling drunk driving. See *Irwin v. Ware*, 467 N.E.2d 1292, 1302 (Mass. 1984). Similarly, the *Tarasoff* court, in concluding that the psychiatrist had a duty to warn, rejected the argument that it would impair doctor/patient confidentiality in part because a statute rejected the privilege in situations involving danger to third persons. 551 P.2d at 346-347.

Other policy considerations may also be relevant to the duty analysis, depending on the facts of each case. In most, no single factor will be determinative; the judge will balance many to reach a conclusion. As an advocate, you may not always be able to predict that conclusion, but you can learn to identify factors relevant to the duty analysis, and to formulate arguments for or against imposing a duty based on those factors.

In many common situations, decades of precedent have defined fairly clearly the extent to which the courts will recognize a duty of care. The remainder of this introduction addresses common situations in which courts impose such a duty — or refuse to. However, it is important to remember that the duties described are not immutable truths; they are pragmatic policy judgments that may be reconsidered by future judges as society and public attitudes evolve.

First Principles: Torts and the Couch Potato

I find it useful to analyze tort duties in terms of two basic principles, each liberally qualified with exceptions. The first principle is that courts generally refuse to impose liability for doing nothing. If Adler, a couch potato, spends all of his time on the sofa watching TV, he is in an excellent position to avoid tort liability. Indeed, as a Torts professor, I would advise you to do just that. People get into tort suits in the weirdest of ways, but they have little to fear from being inert.

This long held view of the common law, that there is no liability for the failure to act, is illustrated by the hypothetical of the callous bystander who watches a blind man walk into a busy street and fails to call out a warning. Our moral sense is repulsed by the illustration, yet in most states the bystander still has no *legal* duty to act to protect another, and therefore is not liable for failing to do so. Similarly, a sunbather who watches a child going under the waves has no duty to dive in the water, throw her a life ring, or even notify a nearby lifeguard:

> The fact that the actor realizes or should realize that action on his part is necessary for another's aid or protection does not of itself impose upon him a duty to take such action.

Restatement (Second) of Torts §314. According to the Restatement,

> The origin of the rule lay in the early common law distinction between action and inaction, or "misfeasance" and "non-feasance." In the early law one who injured another by a positive affirmative act was held liable without any great regard even for his fault. But the courts were far too much occupied with the more flagrant forms of misbehavior to be greatly concerned with one who merely did nothing, even though another might suffer serious harm because of his omission to act. Hence, liability for nonfeasance was slow to receive any recognition in the law.

Restatement (Second) of Torts §314 cmt. c.

Although torts scholars usually cite this no-duty-to-act principle with embarrassment, there are some substantial policy arguments to support it. The defendant whose act (misfeasance) endangers the plaintiff has "created a new risk of harm to the plaintiff, while by 'nonfeasance' he has at least made [the plaintiff's] situation no worse, and has merely failed to benefit him by interfering in his affairs." Prosser & Keeton at 373. Other defenders of the principle emphasize the infringement on individual liberty posed by coercing services from unwilling bystanders,[1] and the difficulty of defining the duty if it is to be imposed. For example, how great an effort would the

---

1. Consider the case posed by Professor Epstein in his defense of the rule:

> X as a representative of a private charity asks you for $10 in order to save the life of some starving child in a country ravaged by war. There are other donors available but the number of needy children exceeds that number. The money means "nothing" to you. Are you under an obligation to give the $10?

R. Epstein, A Theory of Strict Liability, 2 J. Legal Studies 151, 198-199 (1973).

defendant have to make? Would a bystander have to dive in after the child if he could not swim? *Which* bystanders would have the duty — a whole beachful? Would bystanders be required to subordinate important interests of their own to effectuate rescue (for example, postpone visiting a seriously ill relative to assist at an accident scene)?

These objections are probably not insurmountable; most European countries impose a limited duty to aid, as does the state of Vermont. See Vt. Stat. Ann. tit. 12 §519 (1993). Yet most American courts have not rejected the no-duty-to-act rule outright. Instead they have nibbled away at it by carving out exceptions (discussed below at pp.177-180).

Second First Principles: Risk Creation as a Source of Duty

The second broad duty principle complements the first: Those who do act, who choose to engage in activities that create a risk of injury to others, *do* have a duty to exercise care to avoid injuring others. If Bruner drives his car negligently and hits Gilligan, he has set loose a dangerous force that creates a risk to others. If Freud is reroofing his garage and drops his hammer on a pedestrian, that also creates a new risk of harm. If Chef Adler bakes a quiche with spoiled ingredients, causing food poisoning, he too has set in motion a new force capable of causing harm. These defendants, unlike the bystander in the nonfeasance cases, have "created new risks" by their activities which have caused injury.

Far and away the largest proportion of negligence cases — perhaps 90 percent — involve situations like these, in which defendants have let loose dangerous forces that have caused injury. In these cases, the defendant's choice to engage in risk-creating conduct for his own benefit imposes the reciprocal duty to exercise due care toward those who may foreseeably be injured by that conduct. The law tolerates, indeed, encourages, activity, including activities that impose risks of injury on others. But it has long recognized that those who unleash such forces owe a duty to others to keep that risk to a reasonable level.

In most cases, risk creation is the obvious basis of the duty to exercise due care. Duty is probably the least frequently contested element of a negligence claim, because most negligence cases arise from active conduct, and it is clear that the actor owed a duty to exercise due care toward those who might foreseeably be injured by it. For example, the duty issue is seldom raised in highway accident cases, since we all understand that we owe a duty of due care to others in driving a car. Similarly, it is clear that a utility company that erects a telephone pole owes a duty of care to anyone who might foreseeably be injured if it falls.

In analyzing duty issues, it is important to keep in mind these two divergent first principles — on the one hand, the bystander who has not created any risk and who declines to get involved, and, on the other, the actor whose conduct creates a risk of injury. However, these two paradigms do not, unfortunately, resolve all the cases. For various policy reasons, courts have spawned exceptions to both principles. As discussed below, a person who has done nothing may sometimes be held liable for failing to act. And, at times, a person who has created a risk will *not* be held liable, even though her risk-creating activity leads to foreseeable injury.

Exceptions to the No-Duty Rule: Duties of Affirmative Action

Let's look first at some exceptions to the no-duty-to-act rule. Courts have not hesitated to create "affirmative duties" to act for the protection of another where some policy justifies departing from the no-duty rule. Where such a duty of affirmative action is found, the actor may not defend on the basis that "I just didn't want to get involved": The law imposes a duty to get involved.

A. Duty Based on a Special Relationship to the Victim

Courts often impose a duty to aid based on a preexisting relationship between the defendant and the person who needs assistance. See Restatement (Second) of Torts §§314A, 314B. Here are some typical examples in which courts have imposed a duty to act for the protection of another due to a "special relationship" to the plaintiff:

- A train conductor sees a passenger being assaulted by another, but fails to come to the victim's aid.
- A factory owner fails to assist an employee who is trapped in an elevator in the course of his employment.
- School officials note that a child is feverish but fail to seek medical care for the child.
- A prison inmate complains repeatedly to a guard of stomach pains, but the guard fails to take any steps to get him medical help.

In each of these situations, the defendant is not the source of the injury-producing conduct. The school officials, for example, did not cause the child's fever, nor did the train conductor assault the passenger. However, because of the defendant's relationship to the victim in these cases, the courts impose a duty on the defendant to take affirmative steps to minimize or avert the harm. In the factory example, the duty is based on the fact that the employer is uniquely situated to mitigate the harm and that the employee is acting for the benefit of the employer. The duty in the school case is based on the fact that school officials take charge of children with knowledge of their need for protection. The duty to prisoners is premised on taking charge of the prisoner and depriving him of the ability to act for his own protection. See Restatement (Second) of Torts §320 cmt. b.

B. Duty Based on a Special Relationship to the Perpetrator

A second category of special relationship exceptions to the no-duty rule involves situations in which courts impose a duty to control one person to prevent him from injuring others. Examples include the duty of a parent to control a child in certain circumstances (Restatement (Second) of Torts §316) and the duty of an employer to control an employee. Restatement (Second) of Torts §317. The Restatement imposes a similar duty on one who takes charge of another with "dangerous propensities":

> One who takes charge of a third person whom he knows or should know to be likely to cause bodily harm to others if not controlled is under a duty to exercise reasonable care to control the third person to prevent him from doing such harm.

Restatement (Second) of Torts §319. This exception, which applies primarily to those in charge of mental patients or prisoners, reflects the courts' conclusion that the defendant accepts a duty of care by taking charge of a person who poses a risk of injury. The employer's duty to control an employee is presumably based on the benefit the employer derives from the activities of the employee. In addition, as noted above, the defendant in those situations is often uniquely positioned to prevent the harm.

Perhaps the most famous affirmative duty case, *Tarasoff v. Regents of the Univ. of California*, 551 P.2d 334 (1976), was decided on the basis of this special relationship principle. The *Tarasoff* court concluded that the psychiatrist's relationship to a dangerous patient gave rise to a duty to warn the patient's intended victim that the patient had threatened to kill her. This particular application of the special relationship approach has been controversial. Because of the burden this duty imposes on defendants, some courts have refused to extend it beyond situations involving a threat to a particular victim. See *Leonard v. Iowa*, 491 N.W.2d 508, 512 (Ia. 1992) (holding psychiatrist owes no duty to members of general public for discharging patients).

C. Duty Based on Innocent Creation of the Risk

Another set of exceptions to the no-duty rule involves situations in which the defendant, without negligence, creates the risk that causes injury to the plaintiff. See Restatement (Second) of Torts §321, which provides:

(1) If the actor does an act, and subsequently realizes or should realize that it has created an unreasonable risk of causing physical harm to another, he is under a duty to exercise reasonable care to prevent the risk from taking effect.

The Restatement gives the example of a driver whose truck suddenly becomes disabled on the road and fails to warn on-coming traffic. Restatement (Second) of Torts §321 illus. 3. Under §321, the driver, though not negligent, is the author of the risk, and owes an affirmative duty to warn other drivers of the danger. Similarly, under Restatement (Second) of Torts §322, an actor who has injured another, even without negligence, has an affirmative duty to render assistance to prevent further harm to the injured party. For example, if Freud hits Adler, a pedestrian, with his car and knocks him into the street, §322 requires Freud to take reasonable steps to protect Adler from further injury.

These exceptions to the no-duty rule are presumably based on the risk creation rationale. Even though Freud was not negligent, he has, by his risk-creating conduct for his own purposes, placed Adler in a position of danger. To require him to go to Adler's aid "is simply requiring [a person] to minimize the consequences of risks which society gives him a privilege to create." F. James, Jr., Note, Scope of Duty in Negligence Cases, 47 Nw. U. L. Rev. 778, 804 (1953).

D. The Gratuitous Services Exception

Another widely recognized exception to the no-duty-to-act principle arises where the defendant, though under no initial duty to do so, goes to the aid of another:

> One who, being under no duty to do so, takes charge of another who is helpless adequately to aid or protect himself is subject to liability to the other for any bodily harm caused to him by
> (a) the failure of the actor to exercise reasonable care to secure the safety of the other while within the actor's charge, or
> (b) the actor's discontinuing his aid or protection, if by so doing he leaves the other in a worse position than when the actor took charge of him.

Restatement (Second) of Torts §324. This exception is illustrated by the bystander who sees a pedestrian hit by a car, and goes to the pedestrian's assistance, but negligently causes further injury to her by handling her roughly or using clearly inappropriate first aid techniques.

Ironically, this exception to the no-duty principle imposes the risk of tort liability on the bystander who makes the worthy choice to render assistance. Once Smith decides to "get involved," he assumes a duty of care, although, had he simply stood by or walked away, he would have incurred no liability. See Restatement (Second) of Torts §314. Presumably, the rationale is that the actor, while virtuous, is still a risk creator in rendering assistance, and should not be licensed to mishandle the victim with impunity.

E. Duties Assumed by Contract

Most negligence cases involving contracts arise from negligent performance of the obligations created by the contract, rather than the failure to act. Suppose, for example, that Ellis agrees to build a bridge over a stream on Rogers's property, does it poorly, and Rogers falls through. Ellis had no duty to undertake the project, but when he does, his conduct poses a foreseeable risk of injury to Rogers and others. As a risk creator, he could be held liable for negligence even absent the contract — if he built the bridge out of the goodness of his heart. He is no better off because he has done so pursuant to an agreement with Rogers. A duty of care arises from the risk-creating conduct itself, apart from the agreement to undertake it.[2] See Harper, James & Gray, §18.6, at 726-727.

In some contract cases, however, risk creation does not resolve the duty issue. Suppose, for example, that Rogers's building is damaged by fire, and he hires Ellis to board up the open windows. If Ellis fails to appear, and vandals enter and further damage the building, Rogers may wish to sue Ellis in tort, to recover the full damage to the building. However, Ellis has not created any new risk; he has simply failed to perform his contractual obligation to avert one. This area — imposing tort liability for nonperformance of a contract — is a hazy one, as to which it would be dangerous to overgeneralize. But it is fair to say that in some circumstances at least, a party who has assumed a duty to act by contract may be liable in tort to persons suffering foreseeable injury from his failure to act as agreed. See, e.g., *Parent v. Stone & Webster Engg. Corp.*, 556 N.E.2d 1009, 1012 (Mass. 1990); Prosser & Keeton, §93, at 669-670.

Exceptions to the Risk Creation Rule: Duty as a Limiting Factor in Negligence Cases

This introduction began by describing two "first principles": First, that there is no general duty to act for the benefit of another, and second, that those who choose to act owe a duty to others to use due care in such conduct. Then, we explored some exceptions to the no-duty principle, situations in which courts have imposed a duty on one person to act for the benefit of another. Now, let's consider some exceptions to the second "first principle,"

---

2. One consequence of this analysis is that Ellis may be liable to third parties — a visitor who falls through — as well as to his contracting partner.

that persons who choose to engage in risk-creating activity owe a duty of care to others who might foreseeably be injured by that activity.

One school of thought argues that there should be *no* exception to this second "first principle": Those who engage in risk-creating activities should be liable for all injuries foreseeably caused by their negligence. The argument traces its roots to the following statement in *Heaven v. Pender*, 1881-85 All E.R. Rep. 35, 39 (1883).

> [W]henever one person is by circumstances placed in such a position with regard to another that any one of ordinary sense who did think would at once recognise that, if he did not use ordinary care and skill in his own conduct with regard to those circumstances, he would cause danger of injury to the person or property of the other, a duty arises to use ordinary care and skill to avoid such danger.

Despite the intuitive appeal of this statement, no court accepts it without qualification. Liability for all foreseeable injury from negligent conduct would impose too heavy a burden on defendants in some situations. Sometimes, the extent of this burden leads courts to restrict liability for foreseeable harm by holding that the defendant "owed no duty" to the plaintiff.

Many casebooks illustrate the point with two classic limited duty problems, duties to the unborn and duties to avoid inflicting emotional distress. In each of these areas, courts have drawn the circle of duty considerably more narrowly than the limits of foreseeable harm. For example, many early cases held that a defendant who injured a fetus (for example, by negligently hitting the mother with a car), was not liable, because there was "no duty to the unborn." See, e.g., *Magnolia Coca Cola Bottling Co. v. Jordan*, 78 S.W.2d 944, 945-950 (Tex. 1937), overruled, *Leal v. C. C. Pitts Sand & Gravel Inc.*, 419 S.W.2d 820, 822 (Tex. 1967). In these cases, there was no doubt that the defendant's risk-creating conduct had caused the injury. Nor was there doubt that the injury was foreseeable. The early cases denied liability for policy reasons, including the difficulties of proving the cause of prenatal injury, reluctance to treat fetuses as "persons" in the absence of statutory authority, and the risk of fraudulent claims.

More recently, many courts have recognized a duty of care to the unborn in at least some circumstances. This is not because the defendant's conduct is any different or the plaintiff's injury any more foreseeable. Late twentieth-century courts, for various reasons of policy, are simply more willing to impose a duty in such cases. Doubtless two reasons for the shift are the improved ability to trace the source of fetal injury and the wide availability of insurance for such claims.

Similarly, early cases refused to allow recovery for infliction of emotional distress unless the plaintiff suffered a physical impact. For example, recovery was denied where the plaintiff, narrowly missed by a speeding car, suffered serious fright and a resulting heart attack. Here again, it was often clear that the defendant had created the risk and that the risk had caused foreseeable injury to the plaintiff. The courts simply drew the circle of liability more narrowly than the circle of foreseeable risk, out of fear of fraudulent claims and greatly increased litigation. Recent cases have broadened this duty as well, but liability for negligent infliction remains considerably narrower in most states than the all-foreseeable-risks principle argued for in *Heaven v. Pender*. See Chapter 10, which analyzes in detail claims for negligent infliction of emotional distress.

Courts have similarly limited the duty of care in many other types of cases, based on policy considerations unique to each situation. Some examples include liability for serving alcohol to intoxicated patrons, liability of lawyers to beneficiaries for negligent drafting of a will, liability of accountants to parties (other than their clients) who rely on their opinions, liability for secondary economic losses and the liability of landowners for injury to entrants on their land. In these and other situations, courts often refuse, for policy reasons, to impose liability even though the defendant has caused foreseeable harm to others.

The Relation of Duty to Proximate Cause

Much confusion exists, for almost anyone who has thought about it, as to the distinction between the duty element in negligence cases and proximate cause limitations on liability. It may help, however, to distinguish two types of limitations that courts place on liability: First, limiting liability to the foreseeable consequences of the defendant's negligent act, and second, denying liability for consequences that *are* foreseeable, for the types of policy reasons discussed immediately above.

Courts very frequently use the concept of *proximate cause* to limit liability to the foreseeable consequences of a negligent act. Consider, for example, the hypothetical in which the defendant leaves the ignition key in his car, and it is stolen by a terrorist and used to bomb an embassy. The defendant may well owe a duty not to leave his car open to theft, particularly in an area where teenagers congregate. Yet the result here is so idiosyncratic, so beyond the scope of harm to be expected, that most courts would refuse to hold the defendant liable for the bombing damages. The rationale here is that liability should be limited to the circle of foreseeability, the consequences that the defendant could reasonably anticipate at the time he acted.

By contrast, courts often use the *duty* concept to deny liability for consequences that *are* foreseeable, as in the early emotional distress and fetal injury cases. These courts refused to impose liability for policy reasons, and found the duty concept a proper tool for limiting recovery much more narrowly than foreseeability analysis would.

Unfortunately, this distinction between duty and proximate cause analysis is not consistently honored in the cases. The issue in *Palsgraf*, for example, was foreseeability, yet Justice Cardozo used duty analysis to reject Mrs. Palsgraf's claim, while Justice Andrews's dissent concluded that she was owed a duty and analyzed the case in proximate cause terms. In other cases courts use proximate cause language in placing policy limits on liability for clearly foreseeable harm. For example, earlier cases held that a barkeep who served liquor to an intoxicated patron was not "the proximate cause" of her drunk driving, though nothing could be more foreseeable than a drunk driver causing an accident.

When they make me the King of Torts, my first decree shall be that courts must always use proximate cause analysis to bar liability for unforeseeable harm, and duty analysis to impose policy limits on liability for harm which *is* foreseeable. But in our motley kingdom as it stands today, we have to live with the fact that the two concepts are sometimes used interchangeably. Even if the courts' duty and proximate cause analysis is not always consistent, however, it will still be helpful to keep in mind the above distinction between refusing to impose liability for unforeseeable consequences (the classic proximate cause situation), and refusing, for policy reasons, to impose liability for ones that are foreseeable (the classic duty limitation).

EXAMPLES

Matters of Principle

1.   Consider the four example cases described on p.172. Which of these should be analyzed under the no-duty principle (and its exceptions) and which under the risk creation principle (and its exceptions)?

2.   On a breezy morning after a storm, Ellis leaves his house to walk to the train station. As he passes the house of his neighbor, Klein, he notices a tree limb in the road opposite her driveway. Pressed for time, he continues on his way to catch his train. Klein is injured when her car hits the limb as she backs out of the driveway. She sues Ellis for failing to warn her of the danger. Ellis moves to dismiss Ellis's complaint, on the ground that, as a matter of law, he had no duty to Klein under the circumstances.

   a. Should this case be analyzed under the no-duty principle (and its exceptions) or the risk creation principle (and its exceptions)?
   b. Will the motion be granted?

3.   Muller, while tearing down an old shed with a friend, Ehrlich, negligently knocks out a post which supports the upper floor. The floor falls on Ehrlich, who suffers a concussion. She is taken to the hospital and kept for observation overnight. During the night, the hospital wing catches fire, and she is burned. She sues Muller for her injuries.

   a. Is this a risk creation case or a no-duty case?
   b. How should the court rule if Muller moves to dismiss the claim for the burns?

The Priest and the Levite

4.   Dr. Rogers, a doctor in general practice, is driving to work one morning on a quiet country road. He witnesses a single-car accident in which the driver, Jung, hits a tree, opens the driver's side door and falls to the ground. Anticipating a busy morning at the office, he drives on. Jung suffers permanent injuries which would have been considerably less severe if he had received prompt treatment. He brings a negligence action against Rogers.

    a. Did Dr. Rogers cause any injury to Jung?

    b. Will the court dismiss the case for lack of duty?

    c. How do you think the court would rule if Rogers recognized Jung as a patient he had treated for ulcers, yet still failed to stop?

5.   Assume, on the facts above, that Dr. Rogers *did* stop to help Jung. In an effort to make him more comfortable, he moves Jung over onto the grass. However, because Jung's leg was broken, the move caused serious additional damage to Jung's leg. Jung sues Rogers for negligence. Rogers moves to dismiss on the basis that he owed no duty of care to Jung. How will the court rule on the motion?

6.   Suppose, on the facts of Example 4, that Klein happens by and sees Jung lying unconscious on the ground. She moves Jung off the road and then, realizing that Jung is severely injured, she becomes upset and drives away. Jung suffers serious injuries from loss of blood, which could have been avoided had Klein remained with him and bound up his wound. Would Klein be liable to Jung under §324 of the Second Restatement (quoted above at p.179-180?

7.   While Skinner is driving down a West Dakota street a mudflap from a truck blows onto his windshield. Skinner instinctively ducks, and his car swerves onto the sidewalk, pinning Klein, a pedestrian, against a building. Skinner gets out and tries to extract Klein by lifting her leg. Instead, the car rolls farther forward, aggravating Klein's injury. Klein sues Skinner for negligently causing the increased injury.

    Skinner moves to dismiss based on West Dakota's Good Samaritan statute, which provides in part that "A person who renders emergency care at or near the scene of an emergency, gratuitously and in good faith, is not liable for any civil damages as a result of any act or omission by the person rendering the emergency care, unless the person is grossly negligent." How should the court rule on Skinner's motion?

Crushed Hopes

8.   Bettelheim is injured when his car collides with a Corvette owned by Klein but driven by Couch, a friend of Klein's. Bettelheim threatens to sue Couch for negligence, but Couch maintains that the accident happened because the car's brakes suddenly failed and suggests that Bettelheim sue Hotrod Coupes, which had just repaired the brakes, instead.

After the accident, however, Klein sells the car for junk, and it is crushed and recycled. When Bettelheim consults a lawyer, he is advised that without the car, it is extremely unlikely that he will be able to prove that the breaks were defective. Bettelheim now sues Klein for preventing him from recovering for his injuries by negligently destroying crucial evidence in his case.

    a. Should this case be analyzed under the no-duty-to-act principle or under the risk creation principle?

    b. Will Bettelheim survive a motion to dismiss for lack of duty?

Her Spouse's Keeper

9.   Antell, an alcoholic, injures Freud while driving drunk. Freud learns that Antell had been drinking at home all day before the accident. Antell's wife had threatened to take away his car keys (usually left hanging on a hook in the kitchen when not in use) but had failed to do so. Freud sues Mrs. Antell for negligence, and she moves to dismiss.

    a. Should this case be analyzed under the no-duty principle (and its exceptions) or the risk creation principle (and its exceptions)?

    b. How should the court rule on the motion?

10.   Bettelheim, a bar owner, is working behind the bar when a distraught citizen runs in to call the police to stop a robbery out on the street. Bettelheim refuses to allow him to use the phone. Couch, the victim of the robbery, is then stabbed by his assailant and sues Bettelheim for his injuries.

    a. Which of our two principles should we start from in analyzing this case?

    b. Should Bettelheim be held liable?

Judge Fudd Does His Duty

11.   Jack, a convicted murderer, escapes while being transported to court by Freud, a prison guard, and attacks White on the street while trying to steal his car. White sues Freud for his injuries. Judge Fudd instructs the jury in part as follows:

> If you find that the defendant had charge of Jack at the time of the incident, and that Jack was likely to cause harm to others if not controlled, then you may find that the defendant owed a duty to the plaintiff to prevent the attack by Jack on the plaintiff.

Can you spot two fundamental problems with Judge Fudd's instruction?

EXPLANATIONS

Matters of Principle

1a.   This is a clear no-duty situation. Adler did not create the risk by dropping the pen on the stairs. He is a mere bystander who notes a situation of danger and fails to alleviate it. As in the hard-hearted example in the Restatement, Adler is under no duty to act for Skinner's protection.

b. This example is tricky, because it is hard to decide whether Federal has failed to act or engaged in risk-creating conduct. Arguably, Federal Safety simply did nothing; it did not create the fire hazard itself, but simply failed to warn the employer to abate the risk. But this is like saying that the driver who fails to put on his brakes to avoid an accident is guilty of nonfeasance. Hardly. The driver has engaged in risk-creating conduct, driving, and has done so negligently. Similarly, Federal's affirmative conduct in doing the safety inspection in a negligent manner has created a risk that the employer will rely on the inspection and assume that the premises are safe. If the employer here had hired Couch, a private inspector, to do the inspection, and Couch had failed to report the problem, she would be hard put to argue that she owed the employer no duty because she had done nothing!

If, then, Federal Safety has created a risk, it may be liable under our second principle, for creating a foreseeable risk by its conduct; certainly the fire and Skinner's injury were foreseeable if the condition was not abated. However, many courts would conclude that liability should not extend to the limits of foreseeability in this situation. Federal Safety has no relation to Skinner and has never offered him any assurance of safety. It has not even undertaken to make periodic inspections for Rainbow; it has only conducted a one-time inspection for its own purposes. As a policy matter, creating a duty to Skinner (remember, that is what the court does, *create* the duty) would discourage insurers from conducting such inspections. By inspecting, they would run the risk of incurring broad liability for a faulty inspection, while they would incur no liability for staying away.

The result might be different if Federal conducted a periodic inspection program for Rainbow Paint, which therefore did not develop an inspection program of its own. On these facts, Skinner could argue that Federal had *assumed a duty* to Rainbow and to him by undertaking the inspection program. See *Hill v. United States Fidelity & Guar. Co.*, 428 F.2d 112, 120 (5th Cir. 1970), *cert. denied*, 400 U.S. 1008 (1971) (concluding that duty existed under Florida law where insurer conducted periodic inspections); Restatement (Second) of Torts §324A (liability may be based on voluntary assumption of a duty or reliance by others on voluntary performance of services).

c. This is another bystander case. Reik has not created any risk that led to White's injury. She merely sees a person in need of assistance and chooses not to render it. Most courts would dispose of this on the general not-your-sister's-keeper basis that there is no duty to aid or rescue another.

d. Certainly, Dr. Rogers has assumed a duty of care to Jung by accepting him as a patient and beginning to treat him. If he failed to warn *Jung* of a risk associated with his disease, he would be negligent in the risk-creating activity of medical treatment, which would be actionable. But most courts would analyze *Klein's* claim under the no-duty principle and its exceptions. Rogers has not created the risk that threatens injury to Klein, nor has he induced any reliance on Klein's part by treating Jung. Rather, Rogers has perceived a danger to third persons, which he has failed to take steps to avert, like Adler in the first case.

Klein would doubtless argue that the court should make an exception to the no-duty rule since, by treating Jung, Rogers has assumed a duty to others who might be placed at risk by his medical condition. She would likely draw an analogy to the duty of the psychiatrist in *Tarasoff* to warn of the risk his patient posed. Some courts have imposed such a duty where a patient infects a family member. *Cf. Shepard v. Redford Community Hosp.*, 390 N.W.2d 239, 241, *appeal denied*, 430 N.W.2d 458 (1988) (hospital had "special relationship" to decedent who died of meningitis due to failure to diagnose and treat mother's meningitis); see also the annotation at 3 A.L.R.5th 370 (1992). However, it is questionable whether courts would impose a duty on doctors to warn others who might foreseeably come in contact with Jung. *Cf. Gammill v. United States*, 727 F.2d 950, 954 (10th Cir. 1984) (doctor owed no duty to warn friends of patient who contracted hepatitis while babysitting for patient's children). Such a duty could be very burdensome and ill defined. For example, to whom would the duty run? Casual dance partners? Significant others? Members of Jung's dance troupe only? The duty would also raise delicate confidentiality problems.

2a. This case should be analyzed under the first principle that there is no general duty to act for the protection or aid of another. Ellis has not created a risk to Klein; Mother Nature is responsible for that. The question is whether, for one reason or another, the court will impose a duty on Ellis to take affirmative steps to protect Klein from a risk he did not create.

b. As the introduction suggests, the general rule is that Ellis is not his neighbor's keeper. He is under no legal duty to aid another simply because she may need it, because it would be easy or morally appropriate, or because the risk to the other person is great. Archaic though the rule may seem, it is alive and well. The court will grant Ellis's motion, on the ground that he owed no duty to Klein, unless she can establish some basis for an exception to the no-duty principle.

The facts here do not suggest a basis for such an exception. Ellis has not created the hazard, so the most likely basis for avoiding the effect of the general rule is to argue that a special relationship between him and Klein supports a duty to aid her. The only source of such a relationship in this case is the fact that Ellis and Klein are neighbors. But in a society that puts a premium on individualism, it is very doubtful that a court would transform neighborliness into a legally enforceable duty. Becoming a neighbor is not like taking charge of a pupil or running a train service. People hardly expect that they have assumed any degree of care for their neighbors, whom they may like, loath, or ignore as the case may be.[3]

While imposing such a duty might lead to a marginal decrease in injuries, it would also create potentially intrusive relationships between abutters who may have no interest in anything but being left alone. Can't you just imagine the busybody next door coming over weekly with a list of dangerous conditions you should abate immediately, for your own good? Those dead limbs should come off your trees; that big flower pot on the railing could fall; you need a safer lid on your well; you ought to trim those bushes at the end of your driveway, and so on. It's enough to make the no-duty rule look halfway respectable!

3a. This case is clearly based on Muller's risk-creating conduct. Muller's active conduct in demolishing the shed has created a risk of injury to Ehrlich, and she has suffered injury from that risk.

b. This example illustrates the distinction between existence of a duty and the *extent* of liability in a situation where a duty clearly exists. Any court would conclude that Muller owed Ehrlich a duty of care in working on the shed, and that he is liable for her concussion. He engaged in risk-creating conduct, and Ehrlich's injury results from it. It was foreseeable that, if the floor collapsed, the collapse would cause personal injury, and it did.

However, many courts would refuse to hold Muller liable for Ehrlich's burns, since the risk that she would be burned in a fire at the hospital was unforeseeable. To me, this is best explained in proximate cause terms, as a refusal to hold a defendant liable for bizarre consequences. Yet many courts would conclude, following Cardozo's approach in *Palsgraf*, that Muller "owed no duty" to Ehrlich to prevent this type of harm, since being burned in a hospital fire was not one of the foreseeable risks of knocking out the porch post.

Whichever formula the court uses, the crux of the matter here is that courts are unwilling to extend liability for risk-creating conduct beyond the circle of foreseeable risk. They sometimes draw the liability limit *short* of foreseeability (see, e.g., Example 1b), but very seldom impose liability *beyond* its bounds.

The Priest and the Levite

4a. Rogers certainly did not cause Jung's injury from running into the tree, but he may be a but-for cause of the aggravation of the injury. If Jung's injuries would have been less severe with prompt treatment, Rogers's failure to stop is a but-for cause of the aggravation. Certainly if Rogers owed a duty

---

3. For a provocative feminist critique of the no-duty rule, clearly rejecting the result in examples like this, see L. Bender, A Lawyer's Primer on Feminist Theory and Tort, 38 J. of Legal Ed. 3, 33-36 (1988).

to Jung (for example, if Jung were a student in his charge), a court would have no problem concluding that he had caused the aggravated injuries by his failure to aid.

b. This is also a nonfeasance case, in the sense that the defendant Rogers has not created the risk to Jung or done anything to cause his initial injury. The question is whether a court will impose a duty on Rogers, due to his awareness of Jung's need for assistance or his ability to render it.

Most courts would conclude that this falls squarely under the no-duty principle, that a bystander owes no duty to aid another unless the bystander has placed the victim in peril or has a previous relationship with the victim that supports a finding of duty. Since Rogers, as a doctor, is obviously in a superior position to help Jung, there is a strong moral argument that he should stop. The cases, however, do not find a duty to aid based on the fact that the defendant would be good at it.

If duties are based on public policy, why shouldn't the court jettison the special relationship theory and impose a duty on Rogers frankly based on common sense? Courts can create whatever duties they wish; the special relationship concept is simply a rationale for the court's decision to do so. Imposing a duty on doctors to assist accident victims should lead to an overall increase in societal welfare, since more victims would get timely professional assistance — so why not go for it?

Maybe courts should. Maybe they will some day. But most courts remain unwilling to press strangers into service by creating such a duty. Instead, many states have sought to encourage bystanders to assist by passing statutes that limit their liability for injuries they may cause while rendering aid. Typically, such "good samaritan" laws immunize those who assist in an emergency from liability for negligence, though not for grossly negligent or reckless conduct. See e.g., Alaska Stat. §09.65.090 (1993); Kan. Stat. Ann. §65-2891 (1993) (health care providers only).

c. In this example Rogers is still guilty of nonfeasance, so the issue is whether the court would find that his prior treatment of Jung imposes a duty on Rogers to succor him on the roadside. If Rogers were Jung's banker, no court would conclude that he had assumed a duty to aid Jung under these circumstances by taking care of his money. But Rogers is Jung's doctor. Shouldn't that support a duty to help him?

Probably not. It hardly seems that either Rogers or Jung would expect that Rogers had accepted such a duty by his unrelated prior treatment of Jung. Suppose Rogers had treated Jung six years ago? Or suppose Rogers were an allergist; would *that* impose a duty to treat Jung's leg at the accident scene? Or suppose Jung was not physically injured at all, but trapped in his car? On balance, it seems difficult to impose or define a legal duty based on this limited prior relationship.

5. This case is squarely addressed by §324 of the Second Restatement, quoted at pp.179-180. Once Dr. Rogers decides to intervene, the Re-

statement takes the position that he must exercise due care in assisting Jung. This view is understandable: Rogers is now a risk creator, an actor whose negligent conduct may foreseeably injure Jung. It hardly seems appropriate that he should be immune from liability no matter how badly he bungles the rescue. On the other hand, as Prosser so eloquently puts it:

> The result of all this is that the Good Samaritan who tries to help may find himself mulcted in damages, while the priest and the Levite who pass by on the other side go on their cheerful way rejoicing.

Prosser & Keeton at 378. Good Samaritan statutes provide a middle ground in such cases, by limiting the rescuer's liability to grossly negligent or reckless conduct.

6.   In this case Klein, a bystander with no duty to aid Jung, elects to come to his aid. The Restatement takes the view that Klein's laudable decision to act gives rise to at least a minimal duty of care to Jung, though she owed him none before. On the other hand, Klein's duty should presumably be limited: Her admirable conduct should not obligate her to pay Jung's hospital bills or take him home and tend to him until he recovers.

Section 324 of the Restatement tries to walk this line, by imposing only a limited duty on the rescuer. Klein probably has no liability under subsection (b): She has not left Jung in any worse position than he was before. But hasn't she run afoul of subsection (a), by failing to "exercise reasonable care to secure the safety of [Jung] while within [her] charge"?

It is not clear whether Klein is liable under §324(a) or not. While Klein had Jung in her charge, she improved his circumstances by taking him out of the road. But she did not "secure his safety," since she did not bind up his wound. Comment g to §324 states that the bystander's choice to intervene "does not require him to continue his services until the recipient of them gets all of the benefit which the actor is capable of bestowing." But it also states that the actor must "act with reasonable consideration for the other's safety."

The drafters probably intended to require Klein to use reasonable care for the victim's safety *while she chooses to continue her aid*, but to leave her free to discontinue her services at any time. This conclusion follows from the basic assumption that the victim's need for services does not create a duty to render them. The opposite reading, that §324 imposes a duty on the rescuer to continue aid until the victim is "safe," would create a positive duty to continue aiding the victim for an uncertain period. Section 324(b), which only holds the rescuer liable for making the victim's situation worse while in her charge, suggests that the drafters did not intend to impose such a duty of continuing care.

7.   The court should deny the motion. The purpose of Good Samaritan laws is to encourage bystanders who are not obligated to render assistance to do so anyway, by giving them a measure of protection from liability. Such statutes are not intended to grant immunity to persons who *already have a*

duty to render assistance. Skinner's risk-creating conduct (driving) caused the original injury to Klein. Under the Second Restatement, he has a duty to come to her aid, whether or not he was negligent in causing the accident. Restatement (Second) Torts §322. Thus, he was not "gratuitously" assisting Klein, but fulfilling a duty to assist her under the circumstances. The court would probably conclude that he is not protected by the Good Samaritan statute. See, e.g., *James v. Rowe*, 674 F. Supp. 332 (D. Kan. 1987).

Crushed Hopes

8a. Bettelheim's claim against Klein is not for the original accident, but for negligently disposing of the evidence by having her Corvette crushed. This was active conduct that created a risk to Bettelheim, the risk that he would be unable to prove his case for lack of the crucial evidence. This is best analyzed as risk-creating conduct under our second "first principle."

b. This is a hot topic in tort law, the evolving tort of "spoliation of evidence." Some courts have recognized a duty to preserve evidence, emphasizing the foreseeability of the harm from the loss of the evidence. See, e.g., *County of Solano v. Delancy*, 264 Cal. Rptr. 721, 729-730 (Cal. Ct. App. 1st Dist. 1989). Other courts, however, have refused to impose a duty to preserve evidence, on the ground that it would place an undue burden on the defendant to anticipate future litigation and that there is no relationship to the plaintiff that would impose a duty. See, e.g., *Koplin v. Rosel Well Perforators, Inc.*, 734 P.2d 1177, 1179 (Kan. 1987).

The example illustrates again the tension in the law between foreseeability and duty analysis. Certainly injury to Bettelheim is foreseeable if the evidence he needs is destroyed. At the same time, creating a duty to preserve evidence entails problems. Here, for example, it interferes with Klein's ability to dispose of her property, and makes her the unwilling custodian of useless property for an undetermined period of time, for the benefit of someone she may not know and has never agreed to assist. It is not surprising that courts have come down on both sides of this issue, since the duty conclusion requires a close balancing of competing values.

Her Spouse's Keeper

9a. This case should be analyzed under the no-duty principle and its exceptions. This is not a case in which Mrs. Antell has created the risk that injured Freud. The direct risk-creating conduct was her husband's — the supremely antisocial act of driving while intoxicated. If she is liable for it, it will have to be based on some affirmative duty to avert that risk.

b. This motion should be granted unless some exception to the no-duty principle applies. Naturally, the special relationship exceptions spring to mind as a promising source of such a duty; what relation is "special" if not marriage?

Marriage is indeed sacred, but it is not an automatic source of vicarious liability for the torts of one's spouse, nor have courts concluded that tying the knot gives rise to a duty to control an errant spouse. Even though it would have been easy and socially beneficial for her to palm the keys, most courts would conclude that Mrs. Antell is not liable to Freud for failing to do so.

Plaintiffs in cases like this will have a better chance of recovering under the risk creation principle. Suppose, for example, that Mrs. Antell had provided her husband with keys to her car and he was driving that car at the time of the accident, or she had insisted that he drive to the store for more disks for her laptop. On these facts, she would have participated in the creation of a foreseeable risk, and could be held liable for doing so.

10a. The analysis here must begin with the no-duty principle. White was not injured by any risk created by Bettelheim. The threat is from his assailant, and Bettelheim is asked to act to prevent the harm by helping to summon aid.

b. It is hard to fashion an argument for liability in this case based on the recognized exceptions to the no-duty principle. Bettelheim has no relation to either the perpetrator of the accident or to Couch. The owner of a bar, a place of public accommodation, might owe a duty to Couch if he were injured in the bar, or if he were a patron, but he was not. While the conduct appears gratuitously obnoxious, it does not appear actionable.

The California Court of Appeal, however, ruled otherwise in *Soldano v. O'Daniels*, 190 Cal. Rptr. 310 (Cal. Ct. App. 5th Dist. 1983). The *Soldano* court recognized the prevalence of the no-duty rule embodied in §314 of the Second Restatement, and admitted that it would be "stretching the concept beyond recognition" (190 Cal. Rptr. at 314) to find any special relationship between the barkeep and the injured plaintiff. It then openly rejected the no-duty rule based on an analysis of various policies California cases have considered in determining duty issues.[4]

The *Soldano* case may portend the abandonment of the no-duty principle, long tort law's ugly duckling. However, reaction to the case does not suggest any rush to bury the rule. See, e.g., *Clarke v. Hoek*, 219 Cal. Rptr. 845, 852 (Cal. Ct. App. 1st Dist. 1985) (suggesting more limited reading of *Soldano* and that California Supreme Court has reaffirmed the no-duty rule since).

---

4. "These factors include: 'the foreseeability of harm to the plaintiff, the degree of certainty that the plaintiff suffered injury, the closeness of the connection between the defendant's conduct and injury suffered, the moral blame attached to the defendant's conduct, the policy of preventing future harm, the extent of the burden to the defendant and consequences to the community of imposing a duty to exercise care with resulting liability for breach, and the availability, cost, and prevalence of insurance for the risk involved.'" 190 Cal. Rptr. at 315 (quoting *Rowland v. Christian*, 443 P.2d 561, 564 (Cal. 1968).

Indeed, the ALR annotation on *Soldano* may win the prize for the shortest annotation ever: Ten years after *Soldano* was decided, it included only *one* case — *Soldano* itself! See 37 A.L.R.4th 1196 (1985 & Supp. 1993). If this is the wave of the future, it is still a long way from shore.

Judge Fudd Does His Duty

11. The first problem with Fudd's instruction is that it tells the jury to decide whether Freud owed a duty to White or not ("[Y]ou may find that the defendant owed a duty. . . ."). Unlike the other elements of a negligence claim, duty is a question of law. It is up to courts to define enforceable legal duties, not juries. If Judge Fudd's language were proper, the jury would be left to create the substantive law of torts in each case, by determining the extent of the defendant's duty anew in every trial. Consequently, there would not be one standard for liability, but a different one for each case. *Au contraire*, the judge should instruct the jury as to the duty owed in each case. If none is owed under the circumstances, the case should never go to the jury at all.

The second problem with the instruction is equally basic: Fudd's language implies that Freud had a duty to *prevent* the attack. This would be a duty indeed, a duty of absolute protection of White no matter what the circumstances. The law seldom imposes such a stringent burden, although it does at times impose greater or lesser duties than the duty of due care.[5] In this situation, as in most, the Restatement states the duty as a duty to *exercise reasonable care* to prevent injury from the dangerous person. Restatement (Second) of Torts §319.

---

5. See the introduction to Chapter 11, at p.218.

10

Vicarious Displeasure: Claims for Indirect Infliction of Emotional Distress and Loss of Consortium

Introduction

Hamlet hit the nail on the head when he complained of the "thousand natural shocks that flesh is heir to."[1] Even in a "civilized" society such as ours, life is fraught with stresses, anxieties, fears, and sorrows. Many are indeed natural shocks, the inevitable concomitants of unfolding human experience from birth to death (and let's not forget adolescence either). Much emotional distress, however, is inflicted upon us by other people as well, either deliberately or carelessly.

We live in a culture that attempts a legal response to most problems, probably too many problems, so it should not prove surprising that courts have been asked to fashion a remedy for emotional distress as well. This chapter considers the approaches courts have taken to one of tort law's most

---

1. W. Shakespeare, Hamlet, act 3, sc. 1.

intractable problems, claims for indirect infliction of emotional distress. It then contrasts such claims with another type of claim for emotional injuries, loss of consortium.

Claims for indirect infliction of emotional distress (frequently referred to as "bystander" claims) are based on emotional trauma suffered by one person who witnesses or learns of an injury to another. Here are some examples:

- A worker at a construction site sees a co-worker crushed under a dump truck.
- A father, watching from the living room window, sees his child hit by a car which careens over the curb and onto the front lawn.
- A wife suffers emotional distress from watching her husband's health decline due to medical malpractice.
- A parent learns by telephone that his son has just suffered a serious injury in a fire negligently caused by the defendant.
- The wife of a comatose patient visits him at the hospital and discovers that he has just been severely bitten by rats.

In each of these cases, the person who suffers direct physical injury from the defendant's negligence obviously has a claim for those injuries. However, those who witnessed or soon learned of the injury may also seek damages for emotional distress resulting from the traumatic experience of either witnessing that injury or learning of it. Such claims are referred to as claims for "indirect infliction" of emotional distress because they are asserted by bystanders who suffer emotional injury indirectly from witnessing physical injury to another.

The distress in such cases is often both foreseeable and severe. Thus, the plaintiff will frequently be able to establish that the defendant's negligence was an actual and proximate cause of his emotional damages. Consequently, courts which have sought to limit liability for indirect infliction of emotional distress have usually used duty analysis to do so. Many courts have held that defendants owe no *duty* to avoid inflicting emotional distress on bystanders, or only owe such a duty in very limited circumstances. That is why this chapter, which seems to deal primarily with a type of damages, appears in the duty section of the book.

It is not hard to see why courts are reluctant to impose a duty to avoid indirect infliction of emotional distress. Several important factors relevant to duty analysis suggest caution in creating such a duty. *First*, the very foreseeability of such distress argues for restraint. For every victim who suffers negligent physical injury, a number of bystanders may suffer emotional distress:

> It would be an entirely unreasonable burden on all human activity if the defendant who has endangered one person were to be compelled to pay for the lacerated feelings of every other person disturbed by

reason of it, including every bystander shocked at an accident, and every distant relative of the person injured, as well as all his friends.

Prosser and Keeton, §54, at 366.

Second, courts are reluctant to impose a duty to persons who have no relationship to the defendant. While the defendant usually has some relationship to or awareness of the direct victim of his negligence — the child hit by the car, the patient diagnosed, the worker actually hit by the dump truck — he usually has had no contact with bystanders who suffer indirect emotional distress. He may not know who they are, where they are, or how many of them there are.

Third, judges are justifiably concerned about the impact that creating a duty will have on the administration of justice. Recognition of indirect infliction claims could clog the courts with suits over trivial unpleasantries better dealt with by "a certain toughening of the mental hide." C. Magruder, Mental and Emotional Disturbance in the Law of Torts, 49 Harv. L. Rev. 1033, 1035 (1936). In addition, courts have feared the specter of fraudulent claims. It is easy enough for a plaintiff to carry on about how distressed he was by the defendant's conduct, and even to believe it after a while. It is difficult to verify such claims, or to attribute the plaintiff's distress to the defendant's conduct, as opposed to the thousand natural shocks that take their toll on us all.

Thus, for many years courts severely limited indirect infliction claims, lest such claims open a Pandora's box of woes for both courts and defendants. However, the compelling nature of the suffering inflicted on indirect victims has led to a gradual recognition of some claims for indirect infliction of emotional distress. How can a court refuse recovery to a father who watches a driver negligently run down his child and suffers a heart attack on the spot? Many courts, unable to turn such sympathetic plaintiffs away, have created a duty to avoid inflicting emotional distress, at least in limited circumstances.

Once a court opens this box a crack, however, it is very hard to close it on other equally sympathetic indirect victims. The history of the law in this area has been a constant struggle to define some limiting principle that will allow recovery for deserving victims without throwing the courts open to a flood of litigants upset over something that the defendant did to someone else. (Other useful metaphors for the jurisprudence in this area might be a series of defense lines by a retreating army, or successive walls of sandbags holding back a flooding Mississippi.) Indirect infliction claims are a useful study, because they vividly illustrate the difficulty of establishing satisfactory limits to a duty once it has been recognized. The effort of courts to limit indirect infliction claims has led to tortured line-drawing, evasive distinctions, and some of the least intellectually defensible doctrine in the annals of tort law.

The Historical Approach to Emotional Distress Claims

Courts have long awarded emotional distress damages in negligence cases if the defendant causes direct physical injury to the plaintiff. For example, if Marat's car knocks DuBarry down, DuBarry may recover for any physical injury sustained and for any emotional distress from the accident as well. Restatement (Second) of Torts §456; Prosser & Keeton, §54, at 362-363. This would include pain and suffering resulting from the physical injury, emotional distress resulting from disfigurement or physical impairment (such as a facial scar or a limp), and any other demonstrable emotional damages.

This principle, that recovery for emotional distress was proper if the plaintiff also suffered physical injury, became known as the "impact rule." Emotional distress damages were often described as "parasitic": They could be added on if the plaintiff suffered a traditional physical contact from the defendant's negligence, but could not sustain an action on their own. If Marat's car narrowly missed DuBarry, he could not recover, even if he was badly frightened by the near miss, since he suffered no "impact."

The impact rule was tort law's first effort to keep the flood of emotional distress claims at bay. While it defined a limit, many courts found it an intellectually indefensible one. The plaintiff was allowed full recovery for emotional distress if the defendant barely touched him, but denied recovery if the defendant inflicted the same degree of distress (or much more) but just missed hitting the plaintiff. Even if the emotional distress *led* to a physical illness (for example, if DuBarry suffered a heart attack from fear of being hit by Marat's car), recovery was barred if there was no physical impact upon which to piggyback the distress damages. The obvious artificiality of this rule invited courts to evade it by literal application. In *Porter v. Delaware, L. & W. R.R.*, 63 A. 860 (1906), for example, the court found the impact requirement satisfied where the plaintiff got dust in her eyes, and therefore allowed full recovery for emotional distress from the accident.

Although the impact rule was no "hymn to intellectual beauty,"[2] it did address some of the policy concerns relevant to duty. It alleviated fears of fraudulent claims, perjured (or at least, exaggerated) testimony and excessive damages based on jury sympathy. It premised liability on an objective fact that could be proved or disproved, and, in a rough sort of way, (alright, a *very* rough sort of way) filtered out frivolous claims while allowing the most serious ones to proceed. Some courts still apply the rule, at least in some

---

2. "[A]s law is an instrument of governance rather than a hymn to intellectual beauty, some consideration must be given to practicalities." *Newman-Green, Inc. v. Alfonzo-Larrain R.*, 854 F.2d 916, 925 (7th Cir. 1988), *rev'd on other grounds*, 490 U.S. 826 (1989).

types of cases. See, e.g., *Deutsch v. Shein*, 597 S.W.2d 141 (Ky. 1980); see generally Comment, Negligent Infliction of Mental Distress: A Jurisdictional Survey of Existing Limitation Devices and Proposal Based on An Analysis of Objective versus Subjective Indices of Distress, 33 Vill. L. Rev. 781, 792 (1988).

The "Zone-of-Danger Rule"

The impact rule bars recovery in most indirect infliction cases, because these claims are generally asserted by bystanders who were not directly involved in the accident. Some courts, unwilling to turn all bystander plaintiffs away, have adopted alternative tests to define the duty in indirect infliction cases. Some allow a bystander to recover for emotional distress if he was in the "zone of danger," that is, if he was close enough to the defendant's negligent conduct to be placed at risk of physical injury, even though he was not actually touched. Under the zone-of-danger rule a mother walking next to a child hit by a negligent driver would recover for emotional distress due to witnessing injury to her child, since she might have been hit herself.

The rationale for the zone-of-danger approach is that the defendant owes these bystanders a duty of care because they are within the area of the risk created by his conduct, and hence injury to them is foreseeable. This rationale derives from Justice Cardozo's proximate cause analysis in *Palsgraf v. Long Island R.R. Co.*, 162 N.E. 99 (N.Y. 1928). Since injury to the bystander is foreseeable, the argument goes, the defendant has a duty to avoid injury — either physical or emotional — to him.

The zone-of-danger rule compensates a limited class of indirect victims, a class that is reasonably likely to be seriously affected by the accident. However, like other limiting principles in this area, it is easier to criticize than to justify. The father who watches from the house as his wife and child cross the street will suffer just as much distress if the child is hit as the mother will. In addition, his presence is foreseeable, though he is not within the zone of risk of physical injury. Yet, because he is out of range of the car, he is barred from recovery under the zone-of-danger rule, no matter how manifest his distress may be. The line drawn is basically arbitrary. In the words of the leading decision on emotional distress, it suffers from "hopeless artificiality." *Dillon v. Legg*, 441 P.2d 912, 915 (Cal. 1968).

Limited Foreseeability: The Dillon Rule

The arbitrariness of the zone-of-danger rule has led other courts to seek a more flexible approach to indirect infliction claims. Many states have found such an approach in the California Supreme Court's decision in *Dillon v. Legg*. In *Dillon*, a mother suffered emotional distress from seeing her daughter fatally injured by a car while crossing the street. The *Dillon* court held that defendants have a duty to avoid infliction of emotional distress that is reasonably foreseeable, including infliction of such distress on indirect victims. However, the court established three factors to be considered in determining whether such distress was foreseeable:

> 1) whether plaintiff was located near the scene of the accident as contrasted with one who was a distance away from it; 2) whether the shock resulted from a direct emotional impact upon the plaintiff from the sensory and contemporaneous observance of the accident, as contrasted with learning of the accident from others after its occurrence; 3) whether plaintiff and the victim were closely related, as contrasted with an absence of any relationship or the presence of only a distant relationship.

441 P.2d at 920.

Although *Dillon* purports to establish a foreseeability standard based on the above factors, the *Dillon* rule, like the impact and zone-of-danger rules, also bars recovery to many bystanders whose distress is foreseeable. For example, the first factor implies that a close relative would be barred if she was not present at the scene of the accident, though it is virtually inevitable that close relatives will suffer severe distress when a family member is injured. The second factor implies that a plaintiff who is summoned to the scene after the accident cannot recover, though the potential for severe distress is still great. And the third factor suggests that a stranger, friend or co-worker would not recover, though it is surely foreseeable that anyone could suffer traumatic distress from witnessing massive injury to another.

Requiring Further Corroboration: Resulting Physical Injury

Some courts that apply the zone-of-danger or *Dillon* approaches to indirect infliction claims *also* require that the plaintiff suffer some physical symptoms *as a result of* the emotional distress caused by the defendant's conduct. This "resulting-physical-injury" requirement is intended to provide additional corroboration that the plaintiff's claim is genuine. *See Payton v. Abbott Labs.*, 437 N.E.2d 171, 180 (Mass. 1982) (resulting-physical-injury rule "will serve to limit frivolous suits and those in which only bad manners or mere hurt feelings are involved, and will provide a reasonable safeguard against false claims"). California initially suggested that resulting physical injury must be shown along with the *Dillon* factors, but abandoned this additional requirement in 1983. See *Hedlund v. Superior Court*, 669 P.2d 41, 47 n.8 (1983). Other courts have adopted the *Dillon* guidelines for indirect infliction cases without requiring resulting physical injury. See, e.g., *Paugh v. Hanks*, 451 N.E.2d 759 (Ohio 1983).

It is important to distinguish the resulting-physical-injury approach from the impact rule. The impact rule allows a plaintiff who sustains a direct physical impact (from the defendant's car, for example) to recover for emotional distress. The resulting-physical-injury rule, on the other hand, allows the plaintiff who is missed by the car, but frightened by the near miss, to recover for emotional distress *if* the emotional distress itself leads to some form of physical injury, such as a heart attack.

Some courts have imposed other corroborative requirements along with one of the above approaches. Some require the plaintiff to prove "serious resulting distress" in order to recover. *Culbert v. Sampson's Supermarkets Inc.*, 444 A.2d 433 (Me. 1982). Others require expert testimony to establish the existence of the distress. *Kinard v. Augusta Sash & Door Co.*, 336 S.E.2d 465, 467 (S.C. 1985). Some cases have refused recovery, even if the distress is genuine, unless the *direct* victim of the accident suffers serious injury. *Portee v. Jaffee*, 417 A.2d 521, 527-528 (N.J. 1980).

A Distinction with a Difference: Distress Distinguished from Distress

An injury to one person is likely to cause a variety of emotional reactions in others. A bystander who witnesses traumatic injury to a family member may suffer acute emotional shock from the unexpected, wrenching experience of witnessing serious physical injury to a loved one. She may also experience feelings of grief, loss, sympathy or sadness due to the fact that the immediate victim has been injured or killed.

Although the general term "emotional distress" (or "mental anguish") is often applied to both of these types of injuries, they are meaningfully different. The shock of witnessing the accident is sudden and traumatic, aggravated by the very fact that it is unanticipated, so that one can make no emotional preparation to sustain it. Consider, for example, the gruesome facts of *LeJeune v. Rayne Branch Hosp.*, 556 So. 2d 559 (La. 1990), in which the wife of a comatose patient came into his room shortly after he had been bitten all over by rats. There is a fundamental difference between the impact that kind of horror scene engenders and the grief or sadness one experiences from knowing that a loved one has suffered an injury and must cope with its consequences.

It is the first type of emotional distress — the trauma of witnessing a horrific event or injury — which gives rise to a claim for indirect infliction of emotional distress. This cause of action does *not* compensate for general feelings of grief, loss, or empathy for an injured person. See, e.g., *Frame v. Kothari*, 560 A.2d 675, 678 (N.J. 1989) (claim applies to "the observation of shocking events that do not occur in the daily lives of most people," such as "bleeding, traumatic injury and cries of pain"); *Thing v. La Chusa*, 771 P.2d 814, 828 (Cal. 1989) ("the impact of personally observing the injury-producing event . . . distinguishes the plaintiff's resulting emotional distress from the emotion felt when one learns of the injury or death of a loved one from another, or observes pain and suffering but not the traumatic cause of the injury"). While watching a loved one suffer is surely one of life's most gut-wrenching experiences, it is one of the "natural shocks" that we all must bear when a loved one suffers. Most courts do not allow emotional distress claims for such general grief and suffering of third parties.

Because indirect infliction claims are based on the sudden shock of witnessing injury, factors like those cited in *Dillon*, which emphasize proximity to the traumatic events themselves, make sense as limiting factors. Proximity to the accident, actually witnessing it, and being closely related to the victim, all tend to increase the traumatic impact of witnessing serious injury. By contrast, liability has usually been denied where relatives learn of an injury, or even observe an injured family member after the fact. Similarly, where relatives of a direct victim suffer emotional distress, but the victim has not suffered a traumatic accident, recovery is usually denied. In *Frame*, for example, the direct victim was allegedly injured due to medical malpractice by the defendants. Although relatives witnessed his suffering, they did not witness a sudden traumatic injury to him. Their claims for indirect infliction of emotional distress were denied. See *Frame*, 560 A.2d at 680 (a misdiagnosis "normally does not create the kind of horrifying scene that is a prerequisite to recovery").

Another Distinction, and Another Difference: Loss of Consortium

When one person suffers physical injury due to a defendant's negligence, relatives of the victim will also suffer a third type of emotional damage, "loss of consortium." This term refers to the impairment of a relative's opportunity to relate to the party directly injured by the defendant. The classic loss of consortium claim is brought by the spouse of a person whose physical injury prevents him or her from enjoying the usual satisfactions of the marital relationship. If, for example, Josephine is seriously injured due to Robespier-re's negligence, her injury may interfere drastically with her ability to relate to her spouse. The injury may interfere with recreational activities the couple shared, the division of labor within the household, the sexual society they shared, and the comfort, affection, advice, and moral support that ideally flow from marriage. These associational losses, the "constellation of companionship, dependence, reliance, affection, sharing and aid" (*Hopson v. St. Mary's Hosp.*, 408 A.2d 260, 261 (Conn. 1979) (quoting *Brawn v. Kistleman*, 98 N.E. 631 (1912)) which derive from the marital relationship, are generally referred to as "loss of consortium" or "loss of society."

Like indirect infliction, loss of consortium compensates an emotional loss to one party due to a direct injury to another. But the two claims compensate very different losses (and may frequently be brought together). Loss of consortium does not stem from a sudden traumatic experience, but from the impairment over a period of time — perhaps years or decades — of the opportunity to relate to the injured spouse. While a large component of the loss is emotional, it is not a claim for shock or trauma from witnessing the injury. Indeed, it is entirely immaterial to a consortium claim whether the consortium plaintiff witnessed the accident.

Loss of consortium also differs subtly from grief and sadness. Loss of consortium compensates for the inability to relate to the direct victim, not for general feelings of sadness or empathy for him. While grief and sadness tend to fade over time, the impairment of the relationship may persist as long as the injury does. In theory, a jury should consider only the interference with the relationship in determining consortium damages, not the general grief a spouse feels due to injury to his partner. Obviously, however, it is easier for lawyers to draw conceptual distinctions between these types of emotional losses than it is for juries to separate them in reaching a damage award.

The Evolution of Loss of Consortium Claims

The history of consortium claims has not been the common law's finest hour. Under early doctrine the wife owed her husband services. Where injury to the wife impaired her ability to render them, the husband had a cause of action against the tortfeasor for that impairment. The wife, however, had no corresponding claim, since at common law the husband had no duty to render services to her. Prosser & Keeton, §125, at 931.

Gradually, the concept of "services" was broadened to encompass not only loss of services, but also emotional losses, including affection, comfort, companionship, and sexual society. Despite the obvious reciprocity of these emotional blessings of marriage, the claim remained limited to the husband until 1950, when the court in *Hitaffer v. Argonne Co., Inc.*, 183 F.2d 811, 813-819 (D.C. Cir. 1950) rejected the common law analysis and granted consortium recovery to the wife as well. Most courts quickly followed suit in granting equal consortium rights, though a few ironically equalized them by eliminating the husband's right rather than extending it to wives. Prosser & Keeton, §125, at 932. In most states today both spouses have a right to full recovery for loss of consortium due to injury to the other.

While spousal consortium claims are well established, there is no consensus on the right of parents or children to claim consortium losses. Historically, the common law accorded a father the right to his children's services, and authorized a claim for the loss of those services where the child was injured. Prosser & Keeton at 934. But no claim existed for interference with the emotional relationship with a child. Since the broadening of spousal consortium rights, some states have approved parental claims for loss of "filial consortium" when a child is injured, but most have rejected such claims. Some states have also recognized claims for loss of consortium in the reverse situation, for children whose parents have been injured. But many have rejected those claims as well, choosing to restrict consortium recovery to spouses only. See *Guenther v. Stollberg*, 495 N.W.2d 286 (Neb. 1993) (reviewing the decisions going both ways).

If judges were writing on a blank slate, most would probably find a small child's relationship to a parent at least as worthy of protection as the spousal relationship. It is difficult to imagine a more serious loss than the support, advice, comfort, and education that a parent provides over a child's younger years. However, unlike spousal consortium claims, which have been recognized in a limited way for many years, there was no historical precedent for consortium claims for loss of a parent. Approving such claims would represent a new burden on defendants (and insurers). That burden would often be substantial, since parents often have several children, while only the most adventurous have multiple spouses. Thus many courts have refused to create a duty to avoid loss of parental society, even though the logical case for doing so may be stronger than for spousal consortium. For the same reason, courts have not extended the consortium cause of action to other close relatives such as siblings.

The examples that follow are intended to help you distinguish the types of claims discussed in this chapter and to understand the varying standards courts have applied to them.

EXAMPLES

Unnatural Shocks

1. Marat is shaken up but not injured when the car she is riding in, driven by her husband De Sade, collides with a car negligently driven by Robespierre. De Sade suffers gruesome injuries and is in severe pain. Marat brings suit against Robespierre for the distress she suffers from seeing her husband seriously injured in the accident.

    a. Would Marat recover in a state that applies the impact rule?

    b. Would she recover in a state that applies the zone-of-danger rule?

    c. Would she recover in a state that applies the *Dillon* approach?

2. Assume that Marat was driving to work with a friend, Blanc, instead of her husband when the accident took place. She suffers severe emotional distress from witnessing serious injury to Blanc.

    a. Would she recover under zone-of-danger rule?

    b. Would she recover under the *Dillon* approach?

    c. Would she recover under the impact rule?

3. Cardet, an elementary school student, falls asleep on the school bus on Friday afternoon. The driver completes his route, returns the bus to the parking area, and locks it, without noticing the student. She is not found for almost two days, driving her parents to distraction. Under which rules for indirect infliction would her parents recover for their distress?

Hard Cases Make Sad Law

4. As indicated in the introduction, efforts by courts to establish defensible limits on a defendant's duty to avoid indirect infliction of emotional distress have led to arbitrary decisions and seemingly indefensible distinctions. The following examples illustrate some typical problem cases under the various rules. Consider how each should be resolved under the applicable standard.

   a. Roget is walking with his daughter on the sidewalk when a car careens off the road from behind them and hits the girl. Roget sues for his emotional distress from seeing her seriously injured. May he recover under the zone-of-danger rule?

   b. Carnot is visiting his wife in the hospital when she has cardiac arrest. Two nurses rush to the bedside to attempt to revive her. His wife is clearly in great pain, although she survives. Later, Carnot learns that the nurses negligently used a type of resuscitation technique that is dangerous for a patient with her illness, thereby greatly exacerbating her pain. He sues for his distress at witnessing the episode. What result if the zone-of-danger rule applies? What result if the *Dillon* standards apply?

   c. Cordet hears a crash and comes running out as a small child, evidently her son, is hit by a car, flies through the air and lands on a lawn across the street. She suffers a cerebral hemorrhage and dies. Her estate sues for indirect infliction. However, it turns out that the child is not her son. How should this case be decided under the *Dillon* approach to indirect infliction?

   d. Cordet hears a screech of brakes while weeding the flower beds and turns to see a car careening off the street right at her son. Terrified, she faints. As it turns out, the car missed little Johnny, but she suffers severe traumatic neurosis from the incident and sues the driver. What result under *Dillon*?

   e. Carnot hears shouts and sirens from his neighbor's yard, and races over in time to see his son lying beside his neighbor's pool, very close to death from drowning. He collapses in distress and later sues the neighbor (who had left the pool gate open) for negligent infliction. What result if the *Dillon* approach applies?

   f. Danton witnesses an accident in which his wife is seriously injured when hit by Roget's car. As a result of the incident, he experiences anxiety, sleeplessness, and loose bowel for several months. He sues Roget for indirect infliction of emotional distress. What result in a jurisdiction that applies the *Dillon* factors, but also requires resulting physical injury?

g. Consider the example given at the beginning of the chapter, in which a parent learns by phone that her son has just been badly burned in a fire negligently started by the defendant. What result under *Dillon*?

Consortium Compared

5.   DeFarge's adult daughter Belle is seriously injured in an auto accident while driving with DeFarge. Belle is hospitalized for three months, and is left with a permanently disfigured left leg. Which of the following claims will support recovery, and under what theories (i.e., indirect infliction or loss of consortium)?

a. DeFarge claims damages for the loss of Belle's company during the time she is hospitalized.

b. DeFarge is knocked unconscious from the accident. She wakes up in the hospital and suffers severe distress when told of the extent of her daughter's injuries.

c. DeFarge claims damages due to the fact that Belle is withdrawn, quiet, and unwilling to go out in public due to humiliation at her disfigurement.

d. DeFarge claims damages for Belle's inability to play tennis with her due to her disability.

e. DeFarge claims damages for the depression she suffers as a result of watching Belle trying to cope with the disability caused by the accident.

f. As a result of her injuries, Belle is unable to work, and consequently unable to contribute to the rent of the apartment she shares with her mother. DeFarge claims damages for these lost payments.

g. Marlene, Belle's twin sister, was also in the car at the time of the accident. She is slightly injured, but is extremely upset from seeing Belle seriously injured at the scene. She claims damages for indirect infliction of emotional distress and for loss of consortium due to Belle's inability to participate in many activities they previously enjoyed together.

Judge Fudd's Dilemma

6.   Consider again the facts of Example 3, in which Cardet is unintentionally locked in the school bus overnight. Assume that Cardet, the student, sues for her own emotional distress in a jurisdiction that follows *Dillon*. The defendant asks Judge Fudd to instruct the jury that Cardet can recover if she establishes that the three *Dillon* factors are met. Should he do so?

An Elementary Example

7.   DuBarry is driving down Rue Street when she has a sudden heart attack. Her car careens off the street and hits Louis, who is seriously hurt. Antoinette, his wife, witnesses the accident and sues for indirect infliction. Will she recover if the jurisdiction applies the *Dillon* approach to indirect infliction claims?

EXPLANATIONS

Unnatural Shocks

1a.   Although Marat was not injured, she did sustain an impact from the accident. Under the impact rule, a plaintiff who suffered a physical impact to her person was allowed to recover for emotional distress as well as physical injury. But this example goes a step beyond the usual case, since the plaintiff who suffered an impact seeks recovery for distress caused by injury to another person.

The impact rule is based on the premise that physical contact corroborates the likelihood of actual emotional distress. That premise seems justified where the distress is "parasitic" to the impact itself, that is, where it is suffered due to the accident and the injury. But it is more attenuated to conclude that Marat has suffered genuine distress due to injury to her husband simply because she also sustained an impact in the accident. The rule seems a poor fit for indirect infliction cases.

However, some courts have allowed recovery for indirect infliction of emotional distress under these circumstances. In *Binns v. Fredendall*, 513 N.E.2d 278 (Ohio 1987), for example, the court allowed recovery to a passenger who suffered emotional distress due to injuries to the driver. The court noted the difficult proof problem of separating her distress from the accident itself (which is compensable along with her own injuries under the impact rule) from the additional distress from injury to the driver. The court also suggested that, since impact is basically a corroborative factor, once it is satisfied the door is open to all emotional damages from the accident, not just those directly flowing from the impact to her. For another case with a full discussion of this twist on the impact rule see *Pieters v. B-Right Trucking, Inc.*, 669 F. Supp. 1463 (N.D. Ind. 1987) (also allowing recovery for distress due to injury to another).

b.   Marat was in the zone of danger in this case, that is, she was herself at risk of physical injury from the defendant's conduct. Thus, she can recover for her emotional distress from injury to her husband under the zone-of-danger approach. Courts that apply the zone-of-danger rule reason that defendants can foresee injury to persons who are in danger of physical injury from their negligence. Thus, the defendant owes such persons a duty of care and is liable to them even if they only suffer emotional distress.

However, some states that follow the zone-of-danger approach *also* require that the indirect infliction plaintiff suffer physical injury as a result of the emotional distress. See, e.g., *Rickey v. Chicago Transit Auth.*, 457 N.E.2d 1, 4-5 (Ill. 1983). Marat would not recover in such a state since she did not suffer physical injury from her distress. The *impact* she suffered in the accident would not satisfy this requirement; the physical injury must be caused by the *distress*, not by the accident itself.

c. The *Dillon* approach would probably also support recovery on these facts. Marat satisfies all three of the *Dillon* requirements for "foreseeability." She was present at the time of the accident, witnessed it, and is a close relative of DeSade. Robespierre might argue that Marat did not witness the accident unless she was actually looking at her husband at the time of the collision, but it is doubtful that the court would be that rigid about the requirement that the plaintiff observe the accident. Presumably, realizing that the accident was taking place would suffice. See *Bliss v. Allentown Pub. Library*, 497 F. Supp. 487, 488-489 (E.D. Pa. 1980) (rejecting the argument that the plaintiff should be denied recovery because she was looking in the other direction at the moment the accident occurred).

Although the basic *Dillon* factors would support recovery on these facts, some courts have imposed the additional requirement that the plaintiff's emotional distress result in physical injury as well. See, e.g., *Champion v. Gray*, 478 So. 2d 17 (Fla. 1985). In a state that takes this view, Marat would have to demonstrate resulting physical injury from her emotional distress in order to recover.

2a. The zone-of-danger analysis is no different here than in Example 1. However, the driver here is not a member of the plaintiff's family; does the zone-of-danger approach still apply?

Nothing in the zone-of-danger test itself suggests that it only allows recovery to members of the direct victim's family. Nor does the logic of the test, which is based on the fact that the defendant could foresee injury to those near the victim. However, it is very doubtful that recovery would be allowed to non-family members. Even though distress is clearly foreseeable in a case like this, allowing recovery would greatly expand the scope of liability. It is likely that the balance of burdens and benefits (the "practical politics" of tort law Justice Andrews notes in his *Palsgraf* dissent[3]) is likely to weigh against extending a duty to unrelated bystanders. See Minzer, Nates, et al., Damages in Tort Actions, (Matthew Bender 1989) §5.25[2] (most courts have rejected bystander claims by non-family members under all theories). Similarly, the construction worker who witnesses a co-worker's injury — or,

---

3. *Palsgraf v. Long Island R.R. Co.*, 162 N.E. 99, 103 (N.Y. 1928).

a fortiori, a stranger — will likely be denied recovery, even if she was nearly hit herself.

b. Two of the factors established in *Dillon* are clearly met here: Marat witnessed the accident and was at the scene. However, it is not clear that the third factor, closeness to the injured party, is met, since the plaintiff and the driver were friends, not relatives. Thus, the example poses two issues under the *Dillon* approach. *First*, is each of the factors a *prerequisite* to recovery, or only a consideration in making a case by case assessment of the foreseeability of serious emotional distress? And *second*, is friendship a close enough relationship to satisfy the third *Dillon* factor?

The *Dillon* court did not hold that all three criteria must be satisfied to allow recovery. Rather, it suggested that they were relevant "factors" in the foreseeability analysis. 441 P.2d at 921. However, the California Supreme Court subsequently held that each of the *Dillon* factors must be satisfied to support recovery for indirect infliction. *Thing v. La Chusa*, 771 P.2d 814, 829-830 (Cal. 1989). In other words, *Thing* converts the *Dillon* factors from relevant considerations to absolute prerequisites to recovery. The court in *Thing* acknowledged that it was "arbitrary" to require each factor, but concluded that "drawing arbitrary lines is unavoidable if we are to limit liability and establish meaningful rules for application by litigants and lower courts." 771 P.2d at 828.

While the California court now requires all three factors to be present, other courts continue to view the *Dillon* factors as relevant rather than essential. See, e.g., *Paugh v. Hanks*, 451 N.E.2d 759, 766 (Ohio 1983). Marat would obviously have a better chance of recovery in a state that views the factors as guidelines rather than absolute prerequisites to recovery.

If a "close relationship" is required, will friendship satisfy it? Virtually all of the cases involve recovery for family members, and it seems very doubtful that the courts will go beyond the family sphere in allowing recovery. Several California cases have refused to do so. See *Kately v. Wilkinson*, 195 Cal. Rptr. 902, 905-907 (Cal. App. 1983) (emotional distress recovery denied under *Dillon* analysis for witnessing injury to close friend, but allowed on product liability theory); *Eldon v. Sheldon*, 758 P.2d 582 (Cal. 1988) (refusing to allow indirect infliction claim resulting from injury to cohabiting lover of accident victim); but see *Dunphy v. Gregor*, 642 A.2d 372 (N.J. 1994) (allowing recovery to unmarried cohabitant fiancee of victim); *Paugh v. Hanks*, 451 N.E.2d at 766-767 (blood relationship not necessarily required).

c. Example 1a indicates that some courts have allowed recovery for distress due to injury to another person under the impact rule. However, it is likely that many courts would refuse to extend indirect infliction claims to cases in which the direct victim is not a close relative, for the same policy reasons already discussed.

3.   Although it is hard to imagine a scenario more likely to inflict emotional distress than this, Cardet's parents are unlikely to recover under any of the common approaches to indirect infliction claims. They have not suffered an impact. They are not within a zone of physical danger. And the *Dillon* factors are not satisfied, since they have not witnessed traumatic injury to their child.

Cases like this have repeatedly defeated the efforts of courts to develop a consistent set of precedents on recovery for emotional distress. After the court establishes a purportedly clear rule such as zone-of-danger or *Dillon*, a case like this comes along, which cries out for relief but doesn't fit the rule. Very frequently, the court then writes a confusing decision that blurs the lines but comes out "right."

For example, some California courts have allowed recovery in indirect infliction cases that don't meet the *Dillon* standards if the defendant owed a "direct" duty to the bystander. See, e.g., *Huggins v. Longs Drug Stores California*, 14 Cal. Rptr. 77 (Cal. App. 5th Dist. 1992) (concluding that parents who administered improper dose of medication to infant could recover for distress resulting from injury to infant, despite failure to meet *Dillon* test, since pharmacist owed them direct duty to provide proper dosage).[4] Some cases have purported to use a straight foreseeability standard in hard cases, which certainly would favor recovery here, but would lead to a dramatic increase in such claims, and difficult issues as to the limits of foreseeability. See, e.g., *Masaki v. General Motors Corp.*, 780 P.2d 566, 575-576 (Ha. 1989) (recovery allowed based on foreseeability though parents did not witness the accident); compare *Kelley v. Kokua Sales and Supply*, 532 P.2d 673 (Ha. 1975) (recovery denied where decedent in California died of a heart attack upon being informed of his relatives' death in Hawaii).

Hard Cases Make Sad Law

4a. In this example Roget is in the zone of danger but does not know it since the car approached from behind. Must he be *aware* of the risk to himself in order to recover for distress at the injury to his daughter? The logic of the zone-of-danger test would not seem to require this; the rationale is that the defendant can foresee injury to Roget because he is close to the accident, so it is not unreasonable to hold the defendant liable if Roget suffers emotional distress rather than physical injury.

This seems like the right answer, and many courts would probably so hold. However, some zone-of-danger cases suggest that the bystander plaintiff must *both* be in the zone *and* fear for his own safety before he can recover for distress at injury to another. See, e.g., *Rickey v. Chicago Transit Auth.*,

---

4. This dubious holding was overruled by the California Supreme Court. 862 P.2d 148 (1993). But many other equally dubious holdings in hard emotional distress cases have not been.

457 N.E.2d 1 (Ill. 1983), in which the court held that the bystander must fear for his own safety and suffer resulting physical injury from the emotional distress.

b. A court that sticks by the zone-of-danger rule will provide no relief on these facts. Carnot is simply not in any physical danger. His distress at witnessing his wife's suffering is foreseeable and doubtless severe, but this arbitrary line cuts him out.

It is unclear whether Carnot would recover if the *Dillon* standards applied. Carnot suffered emotional distress from witnessing his wife's medical crisis, but at the time he was not aware that it resulted from negligence on the part of the nurses. Must he be aware that the injury is being caused by negligence, if he satisfies all the *Dillon* criteria? Logically, such awareness seems unnecessary. The gravamen of the indirect infliction claim is traumatic distress caused by the defendant. This comes from witnessing the injury, whether the bystander realizes that it results from negligence or not. This logic was followed in *Mobaldi v. Board of Regents*, 127 Cal. Rptr. 720, 727-728 (Cal. App. 2nd Dist 1976), which allowed recovery on analogous facts.

Indeed, it seems unnecessary that the indirect infliction victim witness the defendant's negligent act at all. The mother who sees a car hit her child suffers the same degree of distress whether it resulted from the driver's negligence or that of a mechanic who failed to properly repair the brakes. Yet it is not clear that recovery will be allowed in cases of antecedent negligence. Typically, there are cases going both ways. See *Love v. Cramer*, 606 A.2d 1175, 1178 n.4 (Pa. Super. 1992) *appeal denied, Cramer v. Love*, 621 A.2d 580 (indicating that Pennsylvania law requires bystander to witness the negligent act); compare *Kearney v. Philips Indus., Inc.*, 708 F. Supp. 479 (D. Conn. 1987) (allowing recovery where bystander only witnessed resulting injury, not the negligent act that caused it).

c. This change in the facts challenges the line drawn in *Dillon*. In *Dillon* the direct victim actually was the bystander's child; here, Cordet mistakenly thought he was. The impact on Cordet could still be traumatic; indeed, in the case upon which this example is based (*Barnes v. Geiger*, 446 N.E.2d 78 (Mass. 1983)) the bystander really did suffer a cerebral hemorrhage and die. If the defendant's duty to bystanders were based solely on foreseeability, it seems clear that this plaintiff would recover. But in this area, as in others, public policy frequently requires that the limits of the defendant's duty be drawn well short of foreseeability. Although the Massachusetts courts use an approach much like *Dillon*, *Barnes* denied recovery, emphasizing the practical need to limit liability:

> Daily life is too full of momentary perturbation. Injury to a child and the protracted anguish placed upon the witnessing parent is, on the scale of human experience, tangible and predictable. Distress based on mistake as to the circumstances is ephemeral and will vary with the disposition of a person to imagine that the worst has happened.

> We are unwilling to expand the circle of liability . . . to such an additional dimension, because to do so expands unreasonably the class of persons to whom a tortfeasor may be liable.

Id. at 81. Whenever courts draw a line like this, ivory tower academics (who don't have to decide the case) will argue that the line is arbitrary. Such caviling is easy; of course the line is arbitrary. Still, it must be drawn.

d. Here again, foreseeability and practical politics suggest different results. It is obviously foreseeable that a mother would be traumatized by seeing her child nearly killed by a car. Yet allowing recovery would again expand the ambit of liability substantially. The *Barnes* court would deny recovery on these facts: "Whether the mistake be as to the identity of the victim . . . or the gravity of the injury, the anxiety, perforce, is transitory, and 'a fleeting instance of fear or excitement' . . . does not present a set of circumstances against which a tortfeasor can fairly be asked to defend." 446 N.E.2d at 81. Some courts have required that the direct victim suffer serious injury if bystanders are to claim for indirect infliction (see, e.g., *Portee v. Jaffee*, 417 A.2d 521, 527-528 (N.J. 1980)), but others have not. See *Paugh v. Hanks*, 451 N.E.2d at 767 (direct victim need not suffer actual physical harm).

e. This example tests the limits of the *Dillon* requirement that the indirect victim witness the injury. Many cases have turned on whether the relative must be on the scene, see or hear the accident, arrive immediately, or simply see the injured victim in pain. Recovery has usually been denied where relatives learn of an accident later, but this case is closer, since Carnot arrives in the immediate aftermath of the accident.

The introduction to this chapter distinguished between grief at injury to another and the trauma of witnessing a shocking event. Here, the parent has suddenly come upon the child in a desperate condition immediately after being pulled from the pool, amid frantic efforts to revive him. This is a sudden, terrible shock. It does no violence to the *Dillon* requirement of witnessing the injury to hold it met here. The court so held in *Nazaroff v. Superior Court*, 145 Cal. Rptr. 657 (Cal. App. 1st Dist. 1978), but *Nazaroff* was overruled in *Thing v. La Chusa*, 771 P.2d at 830. But again, other cases in which the timing is a little different (but the distress still obviously genuine) have come out differently. See, e.g., *Brooks v. Decker*, 516 A.2d 1380 (Pa. 1986), in which the court denied recovery to a father who arrived on the scene, saw the ambulance arrive, saw his son's bicycle on the ground, and accompanied his injured son to the hospital. Compare *Ferriter v. Daniel O'Connell's Sons, Inc.*, 413 N.E.2d 690 (Mass. 1980) (allowing recovery where plaintiffs rushed to hospital and saw seriously injured direct victim).

f. Danton satisfies the three basic *Dillon* factors, but must also show that he has suffered "physical injury" as a result of the distress from witnessing the accident. In most cases there is no dramatic physical injury such as a heart attack or cerebral hemorrhage. Yet, if the courts require one, plaintiffs will try to come up with something. Many tedious, unsatisfactory cases consider whether headaches, upset stomach, loose bowels, depression, social withdrawal, insomnia, perspiration, muscle tension, loss of appetite, and other general complaints satisfy the "resulting physical injury" standard.

Because such symptoms are subjective and hard to disprove, the resulting-physical-injury requirement has failed miserably as a bright line test to corroborate distress. In the same way that skeptical courts turned the impact requirement into a token, they have eviscerated the "resulting physical injury" requirement by finding such vague complaints sufficient. See *Sullivan v. Boston Gas Co.*, 605 N.E.2d 805 (Mass. 1993), (discussing range of symptoms that satisfy the requirement, and approving virtually any evidence that corroborates plaintiff's claim of distress). As with the other requirements, however, some courts have taken a tougher line. See, e.g., *Muchow v. Lindblad*, 435 N.W.2d 918, 921-922 (N.D. 1989) (loss of sleep and weight insufficient).

g. This case will fail under the *Dillon* standard, since the parent was not on the scene and did not witness the accident. See, e.g., *Harmon v. Grande Tire Co.*, 821 F.2d 252 (5th Cir. 1987). Perhaps this result makes sense, if recovery is to be limited to the trauma of witnessing the injury itself, as opposed to the sudden grief of learning that a loved one has been injured. Yet this parent *has* suffered a traumatic experience, which is foreseeable and attributable to the defendant's conduct. The nice distinctions made by the indirect infliction rules will make little sense to this plaintiff in light of the emotional suffering the defendant has inflicted upon him.

Consortium Compared

5a. This is a proper element of a loss of consortium claim. DeFarge does not seek damages for the shock of witnessing injury to Belle, but for the interference with her ability to associate with Belle while she is hospitalized *after* the accident. Although DeFarge witnessed the accident in this case, her right to sue for loss of consortium does not require this; she suffers the consortium loss whether she saw the accident that led to it or not.

However, this claim is for loss of "filial consortium," that is, for interference with the relationship to a child. As the introduction states, courts are divided on whether parents may recover for loss of consortium with a child. A majority have refused to allow such claims.

b. This is a claim for distress at the thought that Belle has suffered serious injury. In one sense, it looks like an indirect infliction case, since DeFarge is distressed due to the injury of another. But it is not based on sudden shock at the scene of the accident itself, but the distress and grief of learning that her daughter has been injured. She would experience the same grief if she had not been with her at the time of the accident, and learned of it at home. This does not meet any of the usual tests for indirect infliction of emotional distress.

Arguably, this is like Example 1a, in which a passenger who suffered impact in an accident sought emotional distress damages from witnessing the injuries to the driver. However, in that example the plaintiff saw the injuries immediately at the scene. Here, DeFarge passed out so she did not perceive the injury to Belle.

c. The example here is ambiguous. Does DeFarge seek damages for *Belle's* emotional reaction of withdrawal from social activities, or for the loss of her own (DeFarge's) opportunity to engage in such activities with Belle? If the claim is for Belle's social withdrawal itself, this is an element of Belle's negligence claim, not DeFarge's. Plaintiffs who suffer physical injury are always entitled to prove their full damages, including emotional damages like Belle's, that result from or accompany physical injury. Chapter 12, p.245.

If DeFarge seeks damages for loss of the opportunity to engage in social activities with Belle as they did previously, or to relate to her due to her emotional withdrawal, this would be a proper element of a loss of consortium claim in states that recognize filial consortium. Note again that the injury claimed is the on-going impairment of DeFarge's relationship with Belle after the accident, not the trauma of witnessing the accident itself.

d. This chapter considers consortium claims together with indirect infliction claims because both are injuries to one person as a result of a separate injury to another. But consortium claims are substantially broader than infliction of emotional distress claims, since loss of consortium compensates a variety of losses due to impairment of the relationship to an accident victim, including interference with social and recreational aspects of the relationship. The loss of the opportunity to play tennis with Belle is a loss the jury may consider in valuing DeFarge's consortium claim.

e. This is not an indirect infliction claim — at least, not in the sense in which the courts have recognized them. It stems from DeFarge's sadness at seeing her daughter cope with a disability, not from witnessing the injury that gave rise to it. Nor is it, strictly speaking, within the ambit of a loss of consortium claim. It is not a claim for Belle's inability to do things with DeFarge, or to relate to her emotionally and socially. It is a form of grief distinct from either of the claims addressed in this chapter.

As previously noted, the distinction between DeFarge's depression from watching Belle struggle with disability and the emotional impairment of their relationship may be too subtle for most juries. Their award for emotional damages is likely to be a general one, based on their overall impression of the impact Belle's injury has had on DeFarge.

f. This is obviously not a claim for emotional distress, nor is it properly recoverable on a loss of consortium claim. Even if DeFarge loses rent due to Belle's injury, she may not sue the negligent driver for it. Belle will recover directly for her lost future wages in her negligence action against the other driver. If DeFarge could recover for the contributions Belle would have made to the rent from her future wages, the defendant would be made to pay the same loss twice.

It is not unusual for third parties to suffer substantial secondary losses as a result of an injury. If Belle is an indispensable executive, for example, her company may suffer serious economic losses from her absence. Generally speaking, however, courts have refused to allow recovery for these types of derivative losses to others. See generally, Harper, James & Gray, §25.18A, at 619-623.

g. Marlene has a better claim than DeFarge for indirect infliction of emotional distress, since she was in the car and saw Belle's injuries at the scene. This would probably state a claim for indirect infliction under the impact rule (see Example 1a) and the zone-of-danger rule. It would also probably satisfy the *Dillon* factors, since siblings have generally been considered close enough relatives to recover under *Dillon*.

However, Marlene will almost certainly not recover for loss of consortium, since most courts have denied consortium recovery to siblings. Once again, this has nothing to do with foreseeability; impairment of Marlene's relationship to her sister is highly likely when Belle is seriously injured. It is another example of the practical need to keep liability within manageable limits.

It is not surprising that most courts have extended indirect infliction claims to siblings but barred their claims for loss of consortium. Cases in which siblings witness traumatic injury to accident victims are unusual. But many seriously injured accident victims will have siblings who suffer loss of consortium. Thus, allowing sibling recovery for indirect infliction does not expand liability substantially, while allowing sibling recovery for loss of consortium clearly would.

Judge Fudd's Dilemma

6. It would make no sense to apply the *Dillon* factors to this case, since Cardet did not suffer distress from witnessing injury to another; she suffers *direct* infliction, that is, emotional distress from fear for *herself*, the immediate victim of the negligent conduct.

Plaintiffs may suffer direct infliction of emotional distress in many ways. Here are a few examples:

- The plaintiff suffers serious fright when a ski lift operator fails to secure her seat belt before she is carried up the mountain on an open chair lift and she nearly falls.
- The defendant negligently repairs an elevator, and the plaintiff, who is trapped inside for four hours, suffers extreme anxiety.
- The defendant misdiagnoses the plaintiff, telling her she has cancer when in fact she has a minor digestive disorder.
- The defendant's airplane loses an engine and dives suddenly. The passengers are terrified by the prospect of a crash, though the plane pulls out of the dive and lands safely.

In these cases, the plaintiff suffers emotional distress due to fear of injury to herself; they are not "bystander" cases.

Although Fudd should *not* instruct the jury under *Dillon*, which established standards for indirect infliction, it is more difficult to state how he *should* instruct them. The standards applicable to direct infliction are even less clear than those for indirect infliction. Few courts have even taken consistent note of the distinction, or addressed whether the distinction should lead to different standards for liability. Consequently, it is difficult to summarize the state of the law on direct infliction claims, other than to say that it is exquisitely unclear. Some courts have applied the impact or zone-of-danger rules; some appear to require resulting physical injury; some appear to require only foreseeability of distress.

An Elementary Example

7.   This example is deceptively simple. The *Dillon* factors are clearly met, since Antoinette is closely related to the direct victim, witnesses the accident and is close at hand. However, satisfying the *Dillon* factors merely proves that DuBarry owed Antoinette a duty to avoid negligently inflicting emotional distress upon her. It does not show that she breached that duty of care, and the facts here suggest that she didn't. She did not drive negligently, but was overtaken by a sudden illness that prevented her from controlling her car at all. See, e.g., *Cohen v. Petty*, 65 F.2d 820 (D.C. Cir. 1933) (no liability where driver fainted from sudden illness).

Students often get so caught up in the special standards for allowing indirect infliction claims that they forget that those standards only address the issue of whether a duty of care is owed. These are still claims for negligence, and that means that all four elements of a negligence claim must be proved to recover. In other words, the special standards for indirect infliction claims are not a separate set of elements which support recovery in themselves, but rather prerequisites to establishing one of the usual elements of a negligence claim, duty. If they are met, the plaintiff must still shoulder the burden of proof on the other three as well. Here, DuBarry will fail to establish that old stand-by, Element #2, breach of the duty of due care.

11

Caveat Actor: Strict Liability for Abnormally Dangerous Activities

Introduction

Many students come to law school with the lay person's misconception that an actor who causes injury to another is *always* liable for that injury. However, in cases governed by negligence law, this is not the case. Recovering in an action for negligence requires proof that the defendant breached the duty of due care. Since many accidents result from unexpected circumstances, unknowable mechanical defects, weather conditions or other non-negligent causes, injured parties are often unable to recover, even though it is clear that the actor caused their injuries.

In *Cohen v. Petty*, 65 F.2d 820 (Ct. App. D.C. 1933), for example, the plaintiff was denied recovery where the defendant suffered a sudden fainting spell, lost control of his car and injured the plaintiff. The plaintiff lost in *Cohen* because the defendant did not owe her an absolute duty to avoid injuring her, but only a duty to *exercise reasonable care* to prevent injuries from his driving. Where injury results despite the exercise of reasonable care, that duty has not been breached, and the injured party cannot recover under a negligence standard.

However, the negligence standard is not the only possible basis for imposing tort liability. In some situations tort law imposes either more demanding or lesser duties of care on actors. For example, many courts hold that common carriers owe their passengers "the highest degree of care," clearly a more stringent standard than negligence. See Prosser & Keeton at 208-209. In other situations, courts hold that a defendant owes a lesser duty than the exercise of reasonable care. For example, many courts hold that a landowner only owes a trespasser a limited duty to warn and to avoid wanton injury. D. Dobbs, Torts and Compensation, 320 (2d ed. 1993).

This chapter deals with situations in which the law imposes a very heavy duty on actors, a duty to avoid injury to the plaintiff entirely or pay for any resulting injuries. Where such a duty exists, the defendant is liable regardless of the care with which she conducts the activity. The liability flows not from carelessness, but from the very choice to conduct the activity at all. Such "strict liability" is not premised on fault in the conventional sense of the term, but on the policy choice to place accident losses from the activity on the actor rather than on its victims. The defendant, it is said, "acts at her peril" in conducting such activities. No matter how much care she takes to avoid injuries to others, she will be held "strictly liable" if such injuries result.

Some History

Although strict liability is often thought of as a controversial recent development in the law of torts, all early common law causes of action were apparently "strict." Liability was imposed simply for injuring another, regardless of fault. C. Peck, Negligence and Liability Without Fault in Tort Law, 46 Wash. L. Rev. 225, 225-226 (1971). In the last 150 years, however, fault has come to the fore in the law of torts. Today, most common tort claims require either intentional conduct or negligence.

Despite that predominance, strict liability has continued to apply in some areas. For example, keepers of wild animals have long been held strictly liable for injuries caused by them. If Springsteen keeps a boa constrictor in his apartment and Boa escapes through a heating duct and injures Neville, Springsteen is liable, even if he took every precaution to prevent Boa's escape:

> A possessor of a wild animal is subject to liability to another for harm done by the animal to the other, his person, land or chattels, although the possessor has exercised the utmost care to confine the animal, or otherwise prevent it from doing harm.

Restatement (Second) of Torts §507(1). Under §507(1), Springsteen's duty is not just a duty of extreme care, it is a duty to prevent the injury entirely or pay the resulting damages. If the injury results, precautions are no defense.

The rationale for imposing strict liability for keeping wild animals is easy enough to see. Keeping a wild animal in a community is an uncommon, unnecessary, and highly dangerous activity. Given the low utility, inappropriate location, and high risk of such activity, it might be appropriate to ban it entirely; doubtless many communities do. If such conduct is tolerated, strict liability makes good sense for several reasons. *First,* those who are tempted to keep a tiger or two will hopefully give serious thought to the risk of liability. Some may decide to forgo the questionable pleasures of tiger keeping rather than risk the broad liability it may entail. *Second,* those who simply can't do without a tiger will at least take all possible precautions to restrain them, in order to avoid liability. *Last,* under strict liability the tiger's victims will at least be compensated for injuries resulting from an arguably frivolous or even antisocial choice by the owner.

There is an obvious analogy between this arcane doctrine of strict liability for wild animals and the broader strict liability doctrine that traces to *Rylands v. Fletcher,* 1 Ex. 265 (1866), *aff'd,* 3 H.L. 330 (1868). The defendant in *Rylands* had introduced a dangerous force — a large body of water — onto his land, which escaped unexpectedly and injured his neighbor's property. There was no evidence that the defendant had been negligent in containing the hazard, but the court held that the keeping of this metaphorical tiger supported strict liability for the resulting damage:

> We think that the true rule of law is that the person who, for his own purposes, brings on his land, and collects and keeps there any thing likely to do mischief if it escapes, must keep it in at his peril, and if he does not do so, he is prima facie answerable for all the damage which is the natural consequence of its escape.

Fletcher v. Rylands, (1861-1873) All E.R. 7. (Blackburn, J., Exchequer Chamber opinion). Unfortunately, the decision in *Rylands* was not clearly premised on the very sensible policy underlying the wild animal cases. Although neither nuisance nor trespass directly applied,[1] the rationale of *Rylands* appeared to limit such liability to activities on land of the defendant that injure land of an abutter. In addition, Lord Cairns, in the House of Lords opinion, appeared to narrow Blackburn's rationale still further. He suggested that strict liability only applied to "non-natural" uses of land, (*Rylands v. Fletcher* at 339), evidently referring to unusual activities that are out of place in the area where the defendant chooses to conduct them.

Regardless of these doctrinal complexities, the underlying spirit of *Rylands* is to impose strict liability on those who (like tiger keepers) impose grave and truly unusual risks on the community. In the century since *Rylands,*

---

1. Trespass did not lie, because the injury was not direct. Neither did nuisance, because the injury resulted from a single incident, rather than a continuing interference with the plaintiff's use and enjoyment of his property. See Prosser & Keeton at 545.

the doctrine of strict liability for abnormally dangerous activities has shed much of the doctrinal baggage of its origins in *Rylands*, and come to focus increasingly on this factor. *Rylands* contained the kernel of an idea that has grown to much greater proportions since.

If an activity poses such high risk, one might ask why it is not simply banned entirely. Life is risky enough without people blowing off dynamite, spraying the unsuspecting with pesticides, and terrorizing them with tigers. Legislatures often *do* ban dangerous activities under particular circumstances or in particular places. But many activities that pose unusual risk are also unusually productive: Try clearing the way for a road with a pick and shovel sometime, and you will gain a renewed appreciation for the social value of dynamite. Strict liability allows such socially useful activities, but requires them to bear the accident costs associated with them.

The Current Doctrine

Today, many jurisdictions accept the principle that actors should be held liable without fault for injuries resulting from activities that pose an unusually high risk of injury. The Restatement formulation of the doctrine, which is widely followed, is as follows:

> One who carries on an abnormally dangerous activity is subject to liability for harm to the person, land or chattels of another resulting from the activity, although he has exercised the utmost care to prevent the harm.

Restatement (Second) of Torts, §519(1). The rationale offered in the Restatement is heavily reminiscent of the policy underlying the wild animal cases:

> The liability arises out of the abnormal danger of the activity itself, and the risk that it creates, of harm to those in the vicinity. It is founded upon a policy of the law that imposes upon anyone who for his own purposes creates an abnormal risk of harm to his neighbors, the responsibility of relieving against that harm when it does in fact occur. The defendant's enterprise, in other words, is required to pay its way by compensating for the harm it causes, because of its special, abnormal and dangerous character.

Restatement (Second) of Torts, §519 cmt. d.

Although only hinted at in the Restatement, current economic concepts of cost avoidance and loss spreading also support strict liability for high risk activities. Strict liability encourages those who conduct high risk enterprises to avoid costs in two ways. *First*, the threat of liability will encourage actors to forgo these risky activities entirely. Because it makes the actor pay for all injuries associated with the activity, strict liability encourages her to consider alternative ways of achieving the same goal: Perhaps the same cellar can be dug with a backhoe instead of blasting. Thus, imposing strict liability may lead to less high risk activity and fewer accident losses from it. R. Posner, Economic Analysis of Law 177-178 (4th ed. 1992).

Second, because actors who conduct abnormally dangerous activities must compensate even for blameless injuries, strict liability encourages them to reduce the cost of accidents by taking extra precautions. Thus, the threat of liability will make high risk activities safer, though it cannot make them completely safe.[2]

Third, economic analysts (and, increasingly, courts) argue that losses should be placed on the party who can most easily *spread the costs* of the enterprise by adding the cost of compensation for accidents resulting from the activity to the price of the product. This policy also supports strict liability for abnormally dangerous activities. A blasting company, for example, can spread the cost of blasting accidents (including non-negligent accidents) by purchasing liability insurance to pay the damages. It will redistribute this cost to consumers of its service by raising the price of its product. *Chavez v. Southern Pacific Transp. Co.*, 413 F. Supp. 1203, 1209 (E.D. Cal. 1976). By contrast, if the cost of a blasting injury falls on the victim, she will have no means of reducing its impact by spreading the loss to others.

Of course, the increased cost of blasting due to strict liability may lead to a reduction in the amount of blasting done, but if so, this is because the price, adjusted to include the accident costs it imposes, *reflects the true cost of the activity*. Generally, economists consider such "internalization" of the costs of an enterprise (requiring it to "pay its way") a good thing, rather than imposing the injury costs of the enterprise on accident victims who derive no benefit from it. Under a negligence regime, unlike strict liability, the costs of *non-negligent* accidents are externalized to their victims, since those victims cannot recover these costs from the defendant.

Defining Abnormally Dangerous Activity

The toughest issue for the courts has been determining which activities should be subject to strict liability. The First Restatement of Torts confined strict liability to "ultrahazardous activities." Restatement of Torts, §519. The Second Restatement, however, applies strict liability to "abnormally dangerous"

---

2. Economic analysts may dispute this, on the ground that the rational economic actor takes the same level of precautions under strict liability or negligence: That is, she will take precautions to the point where the expense of the precautions outweighs the projected liability for the activity. See R. Posner, Tort Law: Cases and Economic Analysis 4-5. My intuition tells me, however, that if *I* kept a tiger, and knew I had to pay for any resulting injuries, I would keep it *very* carefully indeed, regardless of what the economic literature says about the efficient level of precautions.

activities, which appear to encompass a somewhat broader range of activities. Restatement (Second) of Torts, §519. Section 520 of the Second Restatement sets forth six factors that courts should consider in deciding whether to impose strict liability:

> In determining whether an activity is abnormally dangerous [and hence, subject to strict liability], the following factors are to be considered:
>
>   (a) existence of a high degree of risk of some harm to the person, land or chattels of others;
>   (b) likelihood that the harm that results from it will be great;
>   (c) inability to eliminate the risk by the exercise of reasonable care;
>   (d) extent to which the activity is not a matter of common usage;
>   (e) inappropriateness of the activity to the place where it is carried on; and
>   (f) extent to which its value to the community is outweighed by its dangerous attributes.

Like so many other current legal tests, these "factors" do not provide a mechanical means of deciding whether strict liability applies:

> [A]ll [of the factors are] to be considered, and are all of importance. Any one of them is not necessarily sufficient of itself in a particular case, and ordinarily several of them will be required for strict liability. On the other hand, it is not necessary that each of them be present, especially if others weigh heavily.

Restatement (Second) of Torts §520 cmt. f.

Factors (a), (b), and (c) in section 520 are closely related. All three emphasize that strict liability should apply to activities that pose unusual risks to the community. Most human activities pose some risk of injury, but strict liability is reserved for those that pose a high risk of injury (factor (a)), that threaten particularly serious or widespread injury (factor (b)), and from which the risk cannot easily be reduced (factor (c)). These, in other words, are activities that, whatever their social usefulness, are particularly dangerous, and cannot be made completely safe despite the exercise of due care.

Cases in which courts have applied strict liability illustrate the types of risks referred to in subsections (a) to (c) of §520. Strict liability has been applied to blasting, large artificial ponds for retention of mining wastes, crop dusting, fumigation, storage of large quantities of gasoline, rockets, experimental aircraft, and use of radioactive materials. Each of these activities involves forces or substances capable of causing extensive damage if not properly controlled. Each usually goes forward without mishap, but can misfire badly without negligence. The risk of such activities may differ only in degree from other activities, but the extra risk has been enough to convince courts to apply strict liability to them.

Abnormal Danger: the Effect of "Common Usage"

Where the unusual risk emphasized in the first three subsections is *not* present, strict liability will probably not apply. However, even if the first three factors *are* met, strict liability will not necessarily apply under the Second Restatement formula. Section 520 contains three more factors that the court must consider, suggesting that strict liability will sometimes not apply even if the activity involves unusual risk.

For example, subsection (d) of §520 requires the court to consider whether the activity is a "matter of common usage." A classic example is driving. Doubtless, more people are injured in a week by the automobile than are injured in a decade by blasting. Yet, because it is so common (and so useful), courts have not applied strict liability to driving. Recovery for motor vehicle accidents still requires a showing of negligence, and many innocent victims who cannot make that showing go uncompensated.

If an activity poses unusual risk to others, why should the plaintiff be put off with the explanation that the danger is a common one? One reason is historical: This "common usage" factor traces to Lord Cairns's requirement in *Rylands* that the injury result from a "non-natural" use. Whatever His Lordship actually meant by this,[3] many courts have concluded that strict liability only applies if the defendant's use of his property is unusual or extraordinary as well as dangerous. See Prosser & Keeton, §78, at 546; Harper, James, & Gray, §14.4, at 201. This suggests that an activity might give rise to strict liability in an area where it is common, but not in another where it is rare. Some cases bear this out: One court refused to impose strict liability for drilling an oil well in rural Oklahoma, (*Sinclair Prairie Oil Co. v. Stell*, 124 P.2d 255 (Okla. 1942)) but another held a defendant strictly liable for drilling one in downtown Los Angeles. See *Green v. General Petroleum Co.*, 270 P. 952 (Cal. 1928) (relying primarily on trespass theory).

Another rationale for the "common usage" factor is that activities that are common, such as driving or building excavation, often involve creation of *reciprocal* risks between actor and victim. The plaintiff who is hit by a car at one time probably travels by car herself at other times, and thus imposes a similar risk of injury on others. By contrast, those who conduct unusual activities such as fumigation or blasting impose hazards on the community

---

3. The phrase is enigmatic at best; virtually any human economic activity is "non-natural" by definition. Most courts have read the phrase to refer to an unusual or inappropriate use. Prosser & Keeton at 545-546. But Lord Cairns may have meant only that the defendant had introduced a force onto his property (there, an accumulation of water) which did not occur there by operation of nature. See F.H. Newark, Non-Natural User and *Rylands v. Fletcher*, 24 Modern L. Rev. 557 (1961).

that are generally not imposed on them by similar activities of others. See G. Fletcher, Fairness and Utility in Tort Theory, 85 Harv. L. Rev. 537, 543-548 (1972). It is not surprising that courts impose strict liability on actors who impose a risk on the community disproportionate to the general risks they are exposed to themselves.[4]

Abnormal Danger: "Inappropriateness" of the Activity

Under the Second Restatement factors, the "inappropriateness of the activity to the place where it is carried on" is also relevant in determining whether to impose strict liability. Restatement (Second) of Torts §520(e). This factor will weigh heavily in favor of strict liability if an activity is carried on in an inappropriate place: For example, a company that processes volatile chemicals will more likely be held strictly liable if its factory is located in a densely populated area than in sparsely populated countryside.

However, it is unlikely that courts will *reject* strict liability for high risk activity simply because the defendant chose an *appropriate* locale for the activity. For example, it is entirely appropriate to blast for a new road in the location where the road is to go; indeed, there is no other appropriate locale. But most courts impose strict liability for blasting anyway. Similarly, it is "appropriate" to store mining wastes in retaining pools near the mine, but the court is unlikely to be persuaded that strict liability is unwarranted simply because it is stored there. See, e.g., *Cities Service Co. v. State*, 312 So. 2d 799, 803-804 (Fla. Dist. Ct. App. 1975) (imposing strict liability on similar facts, despite argument that location was appropriate).[5] Thus, the fact that the activity could have been carried on elsewhere with less risk to the community will strengthen the case for liability, but choosing an appropriate site will probably not, by itself, preclude application of strict liability. See Prosser &

---

4. This rationale may help to explain the difference in the common law's treatment of wild and domestic animals. Keeping a wild animal involves an unusual danger seldom matched by similar activity of one's neighbors. Large dogs, on the other hand, are a common risk. A great many more people are bitten by dogs than by tigers but under the common law they were required to prove negligence in order to recover.

It also illuminates the Second Restatement's treatment of ground damage from aircraft, which obviously impose a nonreciprocal risk on persons and property on the ground. The Restatement would hold aviation operators strictly liable for ground damage caused by aircraft, but not for damage to those (including passengers) who actually take part in the aviation activity. Restatement (Second) of Torts §520A. This provision has not, however, met with general acceptance by the courts. See, e.g., *Crosby v. Cox Air Co.*, 746 P.2d 1198 (Wash. 1987).

5. Perhaps the *Cities Service* court was influenced by the fact that the pool was in an appropriate place while it *stayed* there, but if the dam burst, it threatened communities a considerable distance away.

Keeton at 555 (doubting that appropriate location should preclude strict liability for unusually dangerous activities).

In some cases, however, the fact that the activity is located in an appropriate area, *together with other factors*, may tip the balance away from strict liability. In *Turner v. Big Lake Oil Co.*, 96 S.W.2d 221 (Tex. 1936), for example, the Texas court refused to impose strict liability for impounding salt water in rural areas as part of an oil drilling operation. In rejecting strict liability, the court emphasized the rural nature of the area, the need for such facilities due to the lack of rainfall, the common usage of retaining ponds associated with oil drilling, and the great importance of the oil industry to the state. *Turner* at 165-166.

Abnormal Danger: Importance of the Activity to the Community

The most controversial factor in the §520 calculus is the last, "the extent to which its value to the community is outweighed by its dangerous attributes." This suggests that a particularly important local industry may escape strict liability, even though it imposes great risk on the community. It also suggests that an actor would be strictly liable for the same activity in a location where there are many industries (and any one is therefore expendable) but not in another where the community depends heavily on the activity.

This factor was apparently included to avoid burdening locally important but economically fragile industries with the extra expense associated with strict liability. It has been criticized by many (including the later editors of Prosser's own treatise — see Prosser & Keeton at 555), as reintroducing a "Hand formula" negligence analysis into strict liability doctrine. See *Koos v. Roth*, 652 P.2d 1255, 1261-1262 (Or. 1982) (refusing to consider value to the community in determining liability standard).[6] Despite this factor, strict liability has frequently been imposed on economically productive, even critical industries such as railroads. This factor may be most important where the activity has *little* value to the community. For example, a court might be more willing to impose strict liability for stunt flying, which has marginal social value, than on some other type of aviation activity that has an important economic impact on the community.

The Two Restatements Contrasted

It is interesting to compare the treatment of strict liability in the Second Restatement, published in 1977, with the analogous provisions of the First

---

6. Evidently Dean Prosser himself viewed the requirement as marginal, and included it largely for political reasons. See *Koos* at 1262 n.5 (quoting Prosser's remarks from proceedings of the American Law Institute).

Restatement, published in 1934. Section 519 of the First Restatement applied strict liability only to "ultrahazardous" activities. Section 519 of the Second Restatement applies to "abnormally dangerous activities," a broader term that would appear to encompass less extreme risks. In addition, §520 of the First Restatement requires a higher level of risk than the Second; it defines an activity as ultrahazardous if it

> (a) necessarily involves a risk of serious harm to the person, land or chattels of others which cannot be eliminated by the exercise of the utmost care, and
> (b) is not a matter of common usage.

Under subsection (a) of the First Restatement, the activity must pose a risk of serious injury despite the "utmost care." Section 520(c) of the Second Restatement, by contrast, refers to activities that cannot be made safe by "reasonable care." See also Restatement (Second) of Torts §520 cmt. h (not necessary "that the risk be one that no conceivable precautions or care could eliminate").

The First Restatement also appears to give the court less flexibility in determining whether strict liability should be imposed. Under the First Restatement, that decision turns solely on the extent of the risk and whether it is a matter of common usage. Neither the "appropriateness" of the activity to the location where it is carried on nor its value to the community is considered. By contrast, these factors in the Second Restatement allow the court to consider the social value of an enterprise and its location in deciding whether to impose strict liability.

While some commentators prefer the stricter standard of the First Restatement (see, e.g., Prosser & Keeton at 555-556), the Second Restatement approach has been widely cited, and has been adopted by a number of jurisdictions. Whatever their differences, the essence of the two provisions is similar: They impose the accident costs of particularly dangerous activities on those who conduct them, regardless of their care in doing so.

Abnormally dangerous activities are not the only example of strict liability in American tort law. The most common is strict products liability, which holds a manufacturer or seller strictly liable for injuries resulting from the sale of defective products. Strict products liability is based on different rationales than strict liability for abnormally dangerous activities and requires proof of different elements. This burgeoning area of tort law is a topic for another day, if not another course.

The following examples illustrate the application and the limit of strict liability for the conduct of abnormally dangerous activities. In analyzing them, assume that the principles of the Second Restatement apply unless otherwise indicated.

EXAMPLES

Clearing the Air

1. Franklin Pest Control Company is called in to fumigate an apartment house. The process calls for spraying the premises with Vikane, a toxic chemical which kills bugs. Unfortunately, Vikane is also toxic to people.

Prior to spraying the building, Ciccone, an employee of Franklin, carefully investigates to be sure that the chemical fumes can not spread through the party wall into the adjacent apartment building. She is assured that the party wall is an impenetrable fire wall, and her own inspection confirms this. Unfortunately, a crack, almost impossible to find, exists in the wall. The chemical fumes spread through the wall and overcome Prince in the next building.

Prince sues Franklin for his injuries. The company argues that it took all reasonable precautions and had no reason to suspect that the fumes could travel into Prince's building. Assume that the court concludes that fumigation is a strict liability activity, and agrees that the company's conduct was reasonable. Is Franklin liable to Prince?

A Dull Fthudd

2. Franklin Company's tank truck delivers Vikane to an apartment building for use in the fumigation. The driver carefully backs up to the loading dock, checking his mirrors and beeping as he goes. Unfortunately, Jackson, a child, runs impulsively behind the truck and is hit. Jackson sues Franklin Co. for his injuries. At trial, Judge Fudd instructs the jury as follows:

> I instruct you that the process of fumigation with Vikane is a strict liability activity. If you find that the plaintiff's injury took place in the course of the defendant's fumigation activities, then the defendant may be found liable without proof of negligence.

a. By instructing the jury that strict liability applies to the activity of fumigation, Judge Fudd has decided that question as a matter of law. Was that proper?

b. Who will object to Fudd's instruction, and why is it improper?

3. On the facts of Example 1, Prince sues Ciccone, the employee who sprayed the Vikane, for his injuries. Should the court apply a negligence or strict liability standard in determining liability?

Driving to Endanger

4. Neville is driving a Petrosur Oil Company tank truck containing gasoline south on Interstate 591 when Dean, driving a pick-up truck, cuts in front of him. Neville swerves to the right to avoid a collision and tips over. The tank car ruptures, and the gasoline explodes and injures Hendrix, who was

driving north in the opposite roadway. Hendrix sues Petrosur for damages, and claims that Petrosur is strictly liable for his injuries.

    a. Would strict liability apply under the holding of *Rylands v. Fletcher* (see p.219)?

    b. If the Second Restatement applied, would Neville be barred from relying on strict liability because the activity did not take place on the land of the defendant?

    c. Under both the First and Second Restatement, it is relevant whether the activity is a "matter of common usage." Is transportation of gasoline a matter of common usage?

    d. Would strict liability apply under the Second Restatement?

5. Based on the facts in Example 4, Petrosur claims that it is not liable, even if gasoline hauling is a strict liability activity, since the accident resulted from the negligence of Dean. How should the court rule?

6. Assume that after the truck fell over, but before the gasoline exploded, a state trooper was stationed in the road waving down vehicles before they reached the scene. Hendrix, in a hurry and thinking there was just an ordinary accident, ignores the trooper, proceeds up the road and is injured when a spark from his car ignites the gasoline vapors from the overturned truck. Petrosur claims that liability should be reduced or denied due to Hendrix's contributory negligence. How should the court rule?

7. Baez Construction Company is engaged in the construction of a sky-scraper in a small but growing city. A worker drops a plank from the seventh floor and injures a passing pedestrian. Is Baez strictly liable?

Crying Over Spilled Pseudomonomethane

8. Ronstadt Plastics Company has a major plant in a suburban area near Nashville. As part of its process for manufacturing certain plastic toys, Ronstadt keeps a large tank of pseudomonomethane on its property. Pseudomonomethane is not explosive, caustic, or flammable. It is easy to work with and essential to Ronstadt's manufacturing process. However, it has been identified as a very potent carcinogen if ingested.

    While one of Ronstadt's delivery trucks is arriving at the plant, it loses its brakes (non-negligently, we will assume), and careens off the road and into the tank. The tank is knocked over, and pseudomonomethane spills on the surrounding earth. The chemical migrates underground and enters the city's water supply, requiring the closing of its wells. The city sues for damages, and argues that Ronstadt is strictly liable for the damage to its water supply. How should the court rule?

Cause for Concern

9. Guthrie Hospital uses hydromegasulfate, a highly explosive chemical, in several sophisticated medical applications. Because the chemical is so explo-

sive, Guthrie stores it in a heavy gauge tank on its grounds, two hundred feet behind the hospital.

One morning, the cashier at the hospital is held up at gun point. He alerts the police, who respond and chase the culprit out the back door. An officer fires a warning shot, which unfortunately hits the tank on a ricochet. The tank explodes, injuring Dean, who was emptying trash into a nearby dumpster. Assuming that the storage of hydromegasulfate is a strict liability activity, is Guthrie strictly liable for Dean's injury?

10. One of the most famous strict liability cases is *Foster v. Preston Mill Co.*, 268 P.2d 645 (Wash. 1954). In *Foster*, the plaintiff ran a mink farm. Mink, it seems, are of "exceedingly nervous disposition." *Foster*, 268 P.2d at 648. When the defendant conducted blasting operations to build a road several miles from the plaintiff's farm, many of the mother mink were so upset by the noise that they killed their young. The farmer sued, but the defendant was not held liable. Why not?

EXPLANATIONS

Clearing the Air

1. Franklin can hardly be faulted here for the way in which it conducted its operation. Ciccone investigated carefully, and only proceeded after she was satisfied that it was safe to do so. If liability turned on a showing of negligence, Prince would not recover.

However, liability does *not* turn on a showing of negligence, since strict liability applies. Prince may recover by showing that his injury was caused by the defendant's conduct of the activity, no matter how carefully it was done. Franklin is liable, since its use of the toxic chemical caused his injuries.

The defendant's plea, "but we didn't do anything wrong!" has considerable appeal, but it does not carry the day in a strict liability case. (If it did, it wouldn't be very strict, would it?) The basis of strict liability is not fault, but the choice to engage in the activity in the first place. Because of the nature of that activity, courts place the damages flowing from that choice on the actor, rather than those who suffer injury, even blameless injury, from it. See *Old Island Fumigation, Inc. v. Barbee*, 604 So. 2d 1246, 1247-1248 (Fla. Dist. Ct. App. 1992) (imposing liability on similar facts "regardless of the level of care exercised in carrying out th[e] activity.")

A Dull Fthudd

2a. Judge Fudd may be on the dull side at times, but he has quite properly decided the applicable liability standard as a matter of law. The decision to impose strict liability is a policy decision as to the nature of the duty owed in the conduct of the activity. This is a question of law for the court, just as the existence of a duty of care is an issue of law in a negligence case. If the jury were allowed to decide whether fumigation is a strict liability activity, they would not only be applying the rules of law, but *making* them as well. This is the court's job. Restatement (Second) of Torts §520 cmt. l.

Of course, the judge's decision whether or not to apply strict liability will require Judge Fudd to take evidence and weigh the facts under the six-part analysis in §520. Fudd will have to consider how toxic Vikane is, how quickly it spreads, whether it is easily detected, alternative means of fumigation, the value to the community of the activity, and other factors. Although facts must be considered (just as they must be, for example, in deciding whether a duty is owed to avoid emotional distress to a bystander in a negligence case), it is the court which must balance the Restatement factors in deciding whether strict liability is appropriate.

b. Franklin, the defendant, will object to the instruction, because it suggests that it is strictly liable for any injury that takes place in the course of fumigation. It makes sense, though, doesn't it, to confine strict liability to the types of risks that make the activity abnormally dangerous. Although Jackson was injured while Franklin was in the general course of its fumigation activities, he was not injured by the peculiar risk that makes fumigation "abnormally dangerous." His injury arose from related, ordinary activity incident to fumigation. Delivering Vikane by truck is no more likely to cause this kind of accident than delivering topsoil or lumber or collecting garbage by truck. Fumigation is not a strict liability activity because of the risk of truck accidents, but rather due to the risk of Vikane poisoning, which has nothing to do with this case.

The Second Restatement explicitly bars strict liability for such collateral injuries:

> §519(2). This strict liability is limited to the kind of harm, the possibility of which makes the activity abnormally dangerous.

This provision would also bar strict liability if a Franklin employee poked a resident in the eye with the chemical applicator, or an employee of a blasting company dropped a box of dynamite caps on the foot of a passerby.

3. The question here is whether an employee who conducts abnormally dangerous activity is strictly liable for resulting injuries, as well as the enterprise for which she works. The Second Restatement is ambiguous on the point: It makes "one who carries on an abnormally dangerous activity" strictly liable. Restatement (Second) of Torts §519.

Certainly, Ciccone participated in the creation of the unusual, nonreciprocal risk that injured Prince. But so did the secretary who made the appointment for the fumigation, the driver who delivered Vikane to the apartment building, and the workers who dug Rylands' reservoir. If individual negligence is not required, it is hard to know which individuals who participated in some manner in creating the risk would be subject to strict liability.

In addition, the rationale for strict liability suggests that it is the *enterprise* undertaking the activity that should be strictly liable, not employees who carry out the operation. The owner or corporation makes the decision to conduct the abnormally dangerous activity and derives profit from doing so. It is in a position to decide how much fumigation it will undertake, whether alternative safer products should be used, the precautions that will be taken, and how to insure the risk or spread the risk of loss through the price of the service. Strict liability is meant to place the loss on those who make such decisions about the activity. See Restatement (Second) of Torts §519 cmt. d (stating that "the defendant's enterprise" should be required to pay its own way through strict liability). Although there is little authority on the point, it appears that Franklin, not Ciccone, should be held strictly liable for Prince's injury.

Driving to Endanger

4a. Petrosur would not be liable under *Rylands,* since the accident did not arise from conduct of an activity on the defendant's property that caused injury on surrounding property. *Rylands* dealt only with dangerous activities on the land of one person, which "escaped" and caused injury on the land of another. Indeed, the later English cases rather rigidly confined *Rylands* to this situation. In *Read v. J. Lyons & Co.*, 1947 A.C. 156 (1947), for example, the court held that *Rylands* did not apply to a case in which a government inspector was injured on the premises of the defendant's munitions plant, since there was no "escape" from the defendant's property!

b. Although *Rylands* tied strict liability to land use, there is nothing in the Second Restatement that suggests such a limitation. Section 519 imposes strict liability if the activity is abnormally dangerous and causes harm to the *person, land, or chattels* of another. Clearly, these prerequisites can be met in many situations that do not arise directly from land use by either the actor or the injured party. Comment e to §520 specifically states that it does not limit strict liability to activity on the defendant's property. Thus, strict liability could apply in Hendrix's case even though the accident did not arise from an abnormally dangerous use of real property.

c. Most people would say, based on common sense, that hauling gasoline on an interstate highway *is* a matter of common usage. It happens every day, all over the country. It would be hard to take a trip of any length on an interstate without seeing several gasoline trucks along the way.

However, this phrase may refer not to how visible the activity is, but to the number of people who engage in the activity. See, e.g., Restatement (Second) of Torts §520 cmt. i, (noting that use of explosives, while frequent, is "carried on by only a comparatively small number of persons . . ."). If this is the test, gasoline hauling looks a lot less "common." It is a highly specialized activity performed by a relatively small number of entities. Similarly, tens of thousands of buildings may be fumigated every year; in this sense fumigation is "common." (A quick look at the Boston Yellow Pages indicates that there are about 150 fumigation companies in the Boston area alone.) But it is still a specialized activity carried on by a small number of experts in the field, rather than an every day activity that ordinary people undertake. In this sense it imposes an unusual, non-reciprocal risk and may be found not a matter of "common usage." *Luthringer v. Moore*, 190 P.2d 1, 8 (Cal. 1948).

d. Obviously, there is no mechanical way to answer this question. Whether strict liability applies to Hendrix's case will depend on a balancing of the six factors in §520, and different courts might balance them differently. Under the first three factors an activity is "abnormally dangerous" if it poses a high risk of serious harm that cannot be eliminated by reasonable care. Gasoline transportation is likely to satisfy these factors. Although it does not usually cause injury, the stuff is highly flammable; when it does explode, resulting injuries are likely to be severe indeed. The risk can certainly be kept down by reasonable care, but explosions still happen, as this one did.

The fourth factor in §520 requires the court to consider whether the activity involved is a matter of common usage. Under the Second Restatement common usage is only a *factor to be considered*, along with the others, in determining whether strict liability should apply. Compare §520(b) of the First Restatement (activity must not be a matter of common usage). If the other factors weigh heavily in favor of strict liability, Petrosur could be held strictly liable even if gasoline hauling is deemed "common." However, most courts would probably view gasoline hauling as a specialized, unusual activity under this factor anyway. See Example 3c above.

The last two factors in the Second Restatement analysis do not support strict liability. Gasoline transportation is appropriate to an interstate highway, which is probably the safest place to haul it; and the availability of gasoline is obviously of great value to the community.

In *Siegler v. Kuhlman*, 502 P.2d 1181 (Wash. 1972), *cert. denied*, 411 U.S. 983 (1973) the court applied strict liability to the transportation of gasoline. While the court adopted the provisions of the Second Restatement, its opinion concentrated almost exclusively on the extreme risk that gasoline hauling poses. This suggests that in some cases, the risk factors are alone sufficient to support strict liability, even if the other factors weigh against it. For example, the *Siegler* court was unimpressed by the argument that major highways are an "appropriate" place for gasoline hauling:

> That gasoline cannot be practicably transported except upon the public highways does not decrease the abnormally high risk arising from its transportation.

502 P.2d at 1187. Despite the balancing required under the Second Restatement, *Siegler* and some other courts appear to take the commonsensical

position that, if an activity is not just dangerous, but damned dangerous, the enterprise ought to pay regardless of its common use or social value. See also *Koos v. Roth*, 652 P.2d 1255, 1261-1262 (Or. 1982) (emphasizing importance of the extraordinary danger of the activity and questioning the relevance of the last three Second Restatement factors).

5.   In Example 1, the defendant argued that it should not be held liable, since it conducted the activity with reasonable care. Petrosur's defense here goes a bit further. It argues that, not only was it *not* negligent, but that someone else *was*. The accident was caused by Dean's negligent driving. Since there is a faulty cause of the accident, Petrosur argues, the party at fault should bear the liability.

This defense is unlikely to prevail. The accident was caused not only by the negligence of Dean, but also by the unusual risk that gasoline hauling imposes on the community. If Dean had hit an ordinary car, he might have caused injury to an occupant of that vehicle, but not an explosion that would injure Hendrix many feet away. The accident results in part from the peculiar risk Petrosur has imposed on the community. It is not unreasonable to apply strict liability even though the accident was *also* caused by a third party's negligence. See Restatement (Second) of Torts §522(a). But see *Seigler* at 1188 (Rosellini, J., concurring) (majority should not be read to apply strict liability where third party's negligence causes accident).

Looked at another way, one of the risks of hauling gasoline around the countryside is that the hauler may encounter a negligent driver, leading to an accident that triggers a dangerous explosion. As long as drivers remain human, that risk is impossible to eliminate. Under strict liability, the actor who chooses to engage in the activity that poses this risk is liable for any resulting injuries.[7]

6.   Most courts have held that the plaintiff's contributory negligence is not a defense to a strict liability claim. Harper, James & Gray, §14.5. "The reason is the policy of the law that places the full responsibility for preventing the harm resulting from abnormally dangerous activities upon the person who has subjected others to the abnormal risk." Restatement (Second) of Torts §524. Other authorities suggest that, since strict liability is not based on negligence, plaintiff's negligence should not be relevant either. Posner suggests that, under economic analysis, contributory negligence is not recognized as a defense because only the enterprise, not the plaintiff, is in a position to control or reduce the risk. Posner, Economic Analysis of Law 178 (4th ed. 1992). Last, it has been questioned how, assuming comparative negligence applies, one is to compare negligent conduct with the defendant's non-negligent conduct of an abnormally dangerous activity.

---

7. Of course, Dean will be liable as well. The fact that Petrosur is strictly liable does not affect Hendrix's right to sue Dean for negligence.

None of these explanations seems entirely satisfying. The rule "involves the seemingly illogical position that the fault of the plaintiff will relieve the defendant of liability when he (the defendant) is negligent, but not when he is innocent." Prosser & Keeton at 565. In this case, Hendrix could have avoided injury entirely by use of due care, even though the injury stemmed from a strict liability activity. In terms of accident prevention, it would make sense to give him an incentive to do so. On the other hand, Hendrix's negligence is presumably just as foreseeable as Dean's. The defendant conducting the high risk activity can anticipate that either may unleash the unusual hazard that activity imposes. Thus, it may be defensible to impose the loss on the activity which poses extreme risk anyway.

Courts have been less sympathetic to the plaintiff who *deliberately* exposes himself to the risk posed by a strict liability activity. (That is probably not the case here, because Hendrix, while ignoring the trooper farther up the road, did not fully comprehend the danger ahead.) Most courts hold a plaintiff barred from recovery in a strict liability case if she "knowingly and unreasonably subject[s] [her]self to the risk of harm from the [abnormally dangerous] activity." Restatement (Second) of Torts §524(2). This is very closely akin to the defense of assumption of the risk in negligence cases. See Chapter 20.

7. The construction of high rise buildings certainly imposes risks on the community, including the risk of objects falling from high above the street. Although this building may be unusually high for the area, the court will probably not impose strict liability. The risk of falling objects is a common one, as is construction activity in general. Many engage in it in the community, and many are subject to it. In addition, although such activity may cause serious harm, it does not pose the extreme risk of an explosion or a dam collapse, which may injure many or wipe out an entire community. Last, most of the risks of ordinary construction work can be reduced to a minimum by precautions in the course of the work.

Other arguably dangerous but very common activities have similarly been shielded from strict liability. For example, courts have not generally applied strict liability to distribution of water, electricity, or natural gas. See, e.g., *New Meadows Holding Co. v. Washington Water Power Co.*, 687 P.2d 212, 217 (Wash. 1984) (natural gas transmission).

Crying over Spilled Pseudomonomethane

8. In this case, pseudomonomethane carries the potential for very widespread harm if it gets into the water supply. However, unlike volatile agents like nitroglycerine or gasoline, it has no unusual tendency to cause an accident. The example suggests that the likelihood of an accident taking place from storing pseudomonomethane is no higher than from storing molasses, water, or anything else. Thus, factor (a) of §520 does not appear to apply.

Nor is there is any indication that the risk of damage from storing pseudomonomethane is irreducible. Restatement (Second) of Torts §520(c). Careful handling will not *absolutely eliminate* the risk of a spill, but it seems unlikely that subsection (c) means that, since there are few activities from which the risk of harm can be completely eliminated. Presumably, it applies where, despite due care, there remains an unusual risk of an accident that simply cannot be eliminated. This is true of the activities in the earlier examples — fumigation with poisonous gas, transportation of gasoline, storage of explosive chemicals — but it is not true of storing pseudomonomethane, which is not explosive, volatile, or flammable. This chemical is very nasty *if* it escapes (see §520, subsection (b)), but it is no more likely to escape than many other relatively innocuous substances.

In *Indiana Harbor Belt R.R. Co. v. American Cyanamid Co.*, 916 F.2d 1174 (7th Cir. 1990), the court, in overruling a district court decision imposing strict liability for spill of a highly toxic chemical during shipment, relied heavily on factor (c). The court (speaking through Judge Posner, a leading advocate of economic analysis of tort doctrine), emphasized that courts make defendants strictly liable to encourage them to relocate activities, to substitute other, less hazardous ways of accomplishing the task, or to reduce the extent of the activity. 916 F.2d at 1177. Where the risk can be substantially controlled by due care, Posner concludes, such extreme measures are not called for, and strict liability should not be imposed. 916 F.2d at 1179.

It seems likely that other courts, however, would impose strict liability even though a toxic chemical is not unusually likely to escape. In *Rylands*, the court spoke of a thing "likely to do mischief if it escapes" without suggesting that the force had to be one that is especially likely to escape. Some courts appear to focus primarily on the extent of the threat *if the chemical does escape*. See, e.g., *State, Department of Envtl. Protection v. Ventron*, 468 A.2d 150, 157 (N.J. 1983); Harper, James & Gray, §14.5, at 224; see also Restatement (Second) of Torts §520 cmt. (g):

> If the potential harm is sufficiently great, however, as in the case of a nuclear explosion, the likelihood that it will take place may be comparatively slight and yet the activity be regarded as abnormally dangerous.

The rationale for imposing strict liability supports placing the pollution loss from an accident like this on the operator, who creates and uses chemicals that pose a risk of widespread injury, is able to take steps to reduce the risk or substitute safer alternatives, and can insure against the risk it imposes on the community. As an example, legislatures have begun to impose strict liability for the costs of cleaning up toxic discharges. See, e.g., N.J. Stat. Ann. §58:10-23.11g(c) (West 1992 & Supp. 1994). Such statutes reflect the same policy underlying common law strict liability, that the risks associated with unusually hazardous activities should be borne by the industries that generate them.

Cause for Concern

9.   In this case, the plaintiff's injury results from the hazardous activity, but the intervening act that causes the explosion is unforeseeable. Were this a negligence case, most courts would conclude that the storage of the chemical was not the proximate cause of the resulting harm. So the example poses the issue of whether proximate cause limitations applicable to negligence cases apply to strict liability claims as well.

The Second Restatement would allow recovery in strict liability cases even if an unexpected act intervened:

> The reason for imposing strict liability upon those who carry on abnormally dangerous activities is that they have for their own purposes created a risk that is not a usual incident of the ordinary life of the community. If the risk ripens into injury, it is immaterial that the harm occurs through the unexpectable action of a human being, an animal or a force of nature.

Restatement (Second) of Torts §522 cmt. a. This reasoning makes sense. In this case, the hospital chose, for its own purposes, to impose the explosion risk on the community. The premise of strict liability is that it is fair to impose the unavoidable losses from such high risk activities on the actor rather than the victim.

A good many cases, however, reject the Restatement view, and deny recovery where the accident results from unforeseeable events, natural disasters or intentional acts of third persons, even though the risk that makes the activity abnormally dangerous causes the injury. See *Smith v. Board of County Commissioners*, 146 N.W.2d 702, 704 (Mich. 1966), *aff'd*, 161 N.W.2d 561 (1968) (excessive rainfall); *Klein v. Pyrodyne Corp.*, 810 P.2d 917, 925 (Wash. 1991) (unforeseeable acts of third persons); see generally Prosser & Keeton at 563-564.

Such holdings illustrate the firm grip that the fault concept holds on the judicial mind. Negligence law limits liability to foreseeable accidents because the defendant is not negligent in failing to foresee the unforeseeable. But the basis for strict liability is unusual risk, not fault. The defendant is held liable for introducing a risk into the community that poses extreme danger if it miscarries, regardless of why it miscarries. Since the source of liability is creating the risk itself, imposing foreseeability limitations seems an unwarranted "judicial retreat from the logic of strict liability." J. Fleming, The Law of Torts 319 (7th ed. 1987). See also Harper, James & Gray, §14.5, at 225-232 (arguing persuasively against foreseeability limitations on strict liability).

10.   Arguably, the defendant's conduct in this case was not the proximate cause of the plaintiff's harm. Blasting would foreseeably cause concussion damages, or hurl rocks on neighboring property, but it seems well beyond anticipation that it would cause the damages in this case. However, this in itself might not suffice to prevent recovery. *First*, as Example 9 explains, the

Restatement view is that strict liability should not be limited to foreseeable harm. See Restatement (Second) of Torts §522 (actor liable even if harm is caused by "unexpectable . . . action of an animal. . ."). *Second,* (though I didn't say so in the example) in *Foster* the plaintiff had *told* the defendant that his blasting was causing the mink to kill their young, and only sought damages for those killed after giving notice. 268 P.2d at 646-647. Thus, it is hard to argue that the harm was unforeseeable.

The better ground for denying strict liability in this case is that the type of harm caused was not the type that made defendant's conduct abnormally dangerous. Blasting creates a serious, irreducible risk of concussion, throwing of debris, and vibration of structures, not the scaring of mink. Under the Restatement (and the reasoning of *Foster*), strict liability is limited to the type of harm that makes the conduct abnormally dangerous. See Restatement (Second) of Torts §519(2); *Foster,* 268 P.2d at 647. Thus, the court refused to apply a strict liability standard to the case.[8]

Note the analogy here to negligence per se doctrine. That doctrine allows a party to use violation of a statute to establish negligence only if the statute is aimed at preventing the particular type of harm that arises in the case before the court. See Chapter 5, p.87-89. Similarly, courts limit strict liability to the type of harm that makes the activity abnormally dangerous.

---

8. Even if the court refused to impose strict liability, wouldn't the defendant be liable on a negligence theory, since it was on notice of the risk? The testimony showed that to suspend blasting operations until the whelping season was over would have cost the defendant a full year of logging and required it to shut down its mill. In light of this, and the unusual sensitivity of the mink, the plaintiff evidently declined to proceed on a negligence theory.

PART FIVE

Damages for Personal Injury

12

Personal Injury Damages: The Elements of Compensation

Introduction

Plaintiffs bring lawsuits for a variety of reasons, but when the cause of action is in tort, the reason is almost always to obtain monetary compensation for the injury.

We might well pause for a moment to ask whether this makes sense. If Krutch runs down Gray, breaking Gray's leg, why should the legal system respond by ordering Krutch to pay money to Gray? Aren't there other responses that would make more sense? Perhaps the court should order Krutch to perform services for Gray, take a driving course, or publicly acknowledge responsibility. Or maybe the court should provide social services to Gray, or retraining, or visits from neighbors, or who knows what.

Such responses to personal injury might be more creative than the impersonal transfer of dollars from the defendant (or his insurer) to the plaintiff. But the fact is that the usual balm the law provides to personal injury plaintiffs is money. Such payments are called "compensatory damages," and it is sometimes said that they are intended to "repair[] plaintiff's injury or . . . mak[e] him whole as nearly as that may be done by an award of money." Harper, James & Gray, §25.1, at 493.

Clearly this goal is an idle dream in many cases: No amount of money could possibly compensate an active, healthy adult who is rendered paraplegic in an auto accident, a child disfigured by severe burns, or a patient brain-damaged by excessive anesthesia. These plaintiffs can never be put back in their pre-injury position, and none of us would incur their injuries for any sum. However, while money damages for such injuries may seem an inadequate response to such injuries, they do help. A paraplegic with a two million dollar trust fund is a lot better off than he would be with no money and no earning power, and a remedy that provides the trust fund is, if imperfect, still a good deal better than nothing. And so tort law endeavors to provide the injured plaintiff a sum of money adequate to *compensate* him, though certainly not to *restore* him to his pre-injury position.[1]

The Single Recovery Rule

Perhaps the most fundamental point to grasp about tort damages is that the plaintiff must seek compensation for all his losses from the tort in a single trial. That is, he must prove both past damages and any future losses he is likely to experience from the injury — such as future medical expenses, lost wages, or medical complications — at the time of trial. The rationale for the rule is not hard to discern. Without it, cases would have to be reopened every time the plaintiff incurred further losses due to an injury, to allow recovery for those additional losses. There is simply no way the judicial system could entertain such repeated claims; it is hard enough to provide even a single hearing for the numbers of cases that confront the courts today.

While this "single recovery rule" makes administrative sense, it places the plaintiff in a difficult, at times untenable position. As the sage has noted, "the art of prediction is very unpredictable . . . particularly when it pertains to the future."[2] It is often very difficult to anticipate whether the plaintiff will need future operations, have his work life expectancy shortened, or incur a further disability due to his injury. Under the single recovery rule, however, the plaintiff must make just such predictions about events that may lie far in the future.

Even if such future problems *may* arise, they may not be sufficiently likely to support a damage award under the single recovery rule. Most courts hold that the plaintiff can recover for future consequences of an injury if he proves that they are "reasonably probable," (Minzer, Nates, eds., Damages

---

1. Two other types of damages, nominal damages and punitive damages, are not addressed in this chapter. Nominal damages may sometimes be granted if the plaintiff proves the elements of a tort but has suffered no actual damages. Punitive damages are sometimes awarded in tort cases to punish the defendant for particularly egregious conduct, and to deter such conduct in the future. Punitive damages may be awarded in addition to compensatory damages.

2. This bon mot, like so many others, has been attributed to Yogi Berra, but I don't have an official citation.

in Tort Actions §9.55[1] (1994)) but an award may not be based on "mere conjecture or speculation." Id. If the plaintiff might need future surgery, but probably will not, most courts would not allow him to recover damages for it. If, then, he actually does require the surgery, he will be barred by the single recovery rule from bringing a second suit for the losses associated with that surgery. Similarly, if the plaintiff cannot prove that injury will prevent him from working, he will not receive damages for future lost earning capacity. If in fact he is unable to return to work, that loss will go uncompensated.

Of course, this can work both ways: The plaintiff might prove that he is likely to require future surgery, and recover damages for it, but then do better than expected and not require surgery. If so, he will have received damages for a loss he ultimately did not incur, but will not have to return the damages recovered for that future risk.

The Elements of Compensatory Damages

The three usual components of compensatory damages are medical and related expenses, lost earnings and earning capacity, and pain and suffering. Let's examine each of these in a little more detail.

A. Medical Expenses

The plaintiff is entitled to compensation for all medical costs of diagnosing and treating the injuries resulting from the tort, such as doctor and hospital bills, medicines and special therapeutic equipment, rehabilitation therapy, travel for medical treatment and on-going nursing care. These services are incurred to cope with the consequences of the accident, and their cost should be shifted to the tortfeasor who caused the injury rather than borne by the victim.

Past medical expenses are often fairly easy to calculate. The plaintiff can submit medical and hospital bills and offer expert testimony to prove the reasonable value of these losses. But even such tangible economic losses as medical costs become extremely difficult to calculate if they will extend for a significant period into the future. Under the single injury rule, the plaintiff must offer proof of what his future medical expenses will be, years or decades before they occur, and the jury must attach dollar sums to these future expenses based on the evidence before them.

For example, if the jury concluded that the plaintiff would probably require future surgery to relieve muscle problems related to a burn injury, they would have to determine the proper sum to compensate him for the medical expenses of that operation, even though it might occur twenty years down the road. They would also have to value the associated pain, any resulting loss of earnings, the costs of rehabilitation, and so forth. Needless to say, any sum the jury awards for such future contingencies would be charitably viewed as a rough approximation. Measuring such damages may not be "a leap in the dark, but it is certainly a leap into the deep dusk of twilight." D. Dobbs, Law of Remedies, Practitioner Treatise Series, vol. 2, §8.1(1), at 361 (2nd ed. 1993).

B. Lost Earnings and Earning Capacity

The second component of compensatory damages is lost earnings and earning capacity. Lost earnings refers to *past* income losses due to the injury, that is, lost earnings between the time of injury and the time of trial. Clearly, if the plaintiff was out of work for ten weeks because of the injury, the tortfeasor should compensate him for the wages lost as a result. Lost earning *capacity* refers to loss of *future* earning potential. If the injury will prevent the plaintiff from going back to work for a period of time, it has affected his ability to continue to earn money in the future. Under the single recovery rule, he must be compensated at trial for this future loss.

Lost earnings, like past medical expenses, can usually be calculated fairly accurately, based on the plaintiff's earnings record for the period immediately prior to the accident, evidence of his likely advancement had he not been injured, and evidence concerning changes in the salary structure of his employer up to the time of trial. But future earning capacity is seldom so easily assessed. First, the jury will have to determine how long the plaintiff would have worked if he had not been injured. This may depend on the type of work he did, his life expectancy, state of health *prior to* the injury, and level of interest in his work. Other factors that might have led him to retire early must also be considered, such as a spouse's retirement, an unrelated medical condition which could cause him to move to a different climate, or an anticipated inheritance.

Second, the jury will have to determine what type of work the plaintiff would have done if he had not been injured. For plaintiffs with a long-established work history, this may be clear, but in other cases it is not. Maybe the plaintiff was working as a secretary for a year to pay off some loans, but planning to enter business school the year after. Maybe he graduated magna cum laude from Berkeley, but was working as a truck driver for a while as a lark. Maybe he was earning $150,000 as a partner in a law firm, but hated his work passionately and would not have lasted another six months. (Imagine the difficulty defense counsel would have proving that crucial but subjective fact.) To compound the problem, suppose that he was not working at all when injured, but likely would have returned to the work force at some point. Or consider the case of a plaintiff five years old at the time of the injury, with no work history, educational history, or other basis for estimating his future income potential.

Even if it is reasonably clear what work the plaintiff would have undertaken, the jury will have to decide what his salary would have been during those years. Ideally, this projection would include such factors as prior advancement in his job, the projected future fortunes of his employer, the general state of the sector of the economy in which he worked, the prospects that he would have been promoted or moved to a more lucrative position with another employer, possible alternative employment he may be able to find after his injury, and doubtless many others unique to each plaintiff's circumstances.

In addition, if the plaintiff is really to be fully compensated for future lost earnings, the jury should consider fringe benefits, such as health insurance, a company car, educational credits, bonuses, and stock options. And how about retirement? If the defendant's tortious conduct has deprived the plaintiff of the opportunity to build a retirement fund partially funded by the company, this benefit should also be calculated. Here again, in assessing such damages, the jury is called upon to make judgments that would intimidate the most experienced actuary.

C. Pain and Suffering

The third component of damages, "pain and suffering," can cover a lot of ground. It certainly includes physical pain from the impact of an accident, but it also includes on-going pain from a wound, or long term discomfort from a permanent condition such as a limp or weakened back. It also includes the pain of medical procedures (such as surgery, grafting, or physical therapy) to treat the injuries.

Beyond these obvious connotations, the phrase also includes many other types of mental suffering from the consequences of the injury, such as the humiliation, anguish, or embarrassment suffered from living with permanent disfigurement, the frustration of dealing with disability caused by the injury, the fright associated with a traumatic accident, fear of a recurrence of the accident, or depression induced by the injury and its consequences. Thus, "pain and suffering" is a catch-all term that can encompass almost any kind of subjective reaction to the accident or its consequences. "[T]he unitary concept of 'pain and suffering' has served as a convenient label under which a plaintiff may recover not only for physical pain but for fright, nervousness, grief, anxiety, worry, mortification, shock, humiliation, indignity, embarrassment, apprehension, terror or ordeal." *Capelouto v. Kaiser Found. Hosp.*, 500 P.2d 880, 883 (Cal. 1972).

Loss of Enjoyment of Life

In addition to the unpleasant sensations and emotions usually associated with the concept of pain and suffering, tort victims also frequently suffer loss of the opportunity to engage in many of life's pleasurable activities. If his leg is maimed in the accident with Gray, Krutch will doubtless suffer the physical pain and mental anguish generally associated with such injuries. But he may also lose the ability to play tennis, to take walks in the woods, to carry his son to school, to dance, or to enjoy many of life's other common, pleasurable experiences. These functional impairments go beyond the usual connotations of "pain and suffering," but are also common consequences of serious injuries.

Such impairments are often profound — perhaps the most profound — consequences of physical injury. Imagine, for example, that Krutch's most cherished activity is playing the violin, and that he suffers a hand injury that prevents him from doing so. Or suppose that the accident destroys his sense of sight or taste. Certainly, these are grievous losses above and beyond the sensation of physical pain or fear immediately stemming from the injury.

Many courts describe these losses, aptly enough, as "loss of enjoyment of life."[3] Most courts recognize that such losses are compensable, but the cases are split over whether damages for loss of enjoyment are analytically a type of "pain and suffering" or a separate element of compensatory damages. Some courts treat loss of enjoyment as a form of pain and suffering: The mental suffering that comes from the plaintiff's realization that he can no longer engage fully in life's pleasures. Courts that take this approach will refuse to give the jury a separate instruction on "loss of enjoyment" damages, on the ground that it duplicates the pain and suffering instruction and invites the jury to compensate the plaintiff twice for the same losses. See *McDougald v. Garber*, 536 N.E.2d 372, 375-377 (N.Y. 1989).

Other courts, particularly in recent years, have recognized loss of enjoyment as a distinct category of compensable damages. See, e.g., *Thompson v. National R.R. Passenger Corp.*, 621 F.2d 814, 824 (6th Cir.), *cert. denied,* 449 U.S. 1035 (1980), in which the court concluded that "pain and suffering compensates the victim for the physical and mental discomfort caused by the injury; and loss of enjoyment of life compensates the victim for the limitations on the person's life created by the injury." Courts that take this view allow the trial judge to instruct the jury separately about them.[4] Plaintiffs' counsel naturally prefer such a separate instruction, since it emphasizes the distinct nature of loss of enjoyment damages and invites the jury to consider them apart from a general pain and suffering award.

It is probably not of great consequence whether loss of enjoyment is characterized as part of pain and suffering or as a separate component of compensatory damages. The important thing is that everyone — the lawyers,

---

3. Another term currently in vogue is "hedonic" damages. This concept is related to loss of enjoyment damages, but is more often invoked in wrongful death cases. It endeavors to measure the general value of living itself, rather than focusing on loss of the enjoyment of particular activities. See D. Dobbs, Law of Remedies, Practitioner Treatise Series, vol. 2, §8.3(5), at 443-444. (2d ed. 1993).

4. For a good review of the cases see P. Hermes, Loss of Enjoyment of Life — Duplication of Damages versus Full Compensation, 63 N. Dak. L. Rev. 561 (1987).

the judge, and the jury — understands that, whatever called, such restrictions on the plaintiff's pre-accident opportunities are proper elements in the assessment of damages. Plaintiff's counsel may introduce evidence of all the ways in which the plaintiff's injury has impaired his ability to engage in activities he previously enjoyed. Where such evidence is offered, the judge should explain to the jury that they are entitled to compensate the plaintiff for these losses, in addition to the physical pain and emotional distress traditionally associated with "pain and suffering."

The Elusive Concept of "Disability"

Although all states recognize the three basic categories of damages discussed above, some courts may use different terms, such as "disability" or "permanent impairment" in discussing compensatory damages. These terms often overlap with several concepts already discussed, particularly loss of enjoyment and lost earning capacity.

In its strictest sense, "disability" or "permanent impairment" refers to the injured party's *condition*, not to the losses suffered as a result of that condition:

> Disability and permanent injury refer to states of ill health which preclude an injured person from carrying on normal activities of life in the manner which would have been possible had the injury in question not occurred.

Minzer, Nates, §4.12[3]. While this definition sounds similar to loss of enjoyment, it is more accurate to view loss of enjoyment as the *consequence* that flows from the plaintiff's disabled condition. For example, the loss of a leg is an impairment or disability. The loss of the opportunity to engage in activities as a result of that disability — running marathons, hiking, or whatever — constitutes a consequential loss of enjoyment for which damages may be awarded. D. Dobbs, Law of Remedies §8.1(1) (2d ed. 1993).

However, many courts use the terms "disability" and "permanent impairment" loosely as the equivalent of "loss of enjoyment of life." These courts will instruct the jury that they may assess damages for the plaintiff's "disability," but will obviously not instruct separately on loss of enjoyment damages: It would allow double counting to instruct the jury to award damages for both disability and loss of enjoyment. See Note, Loss of Enjoyment of Life — Duplication of Damages versus Full Compensation, 63 N. Dak. L. Rev. 561, 579 (1987).

There is also frequent confusion between "disability" and lost earning capacity. Here again, the *condition* of being disabled leads to the *consequence* of lost earning capacity. If the jury is instructed to award damages for lost earning capacity, the instructions should make clear that they should not award the same losses under a separate "disability" instruction, even though the earnings loss stems from the disability. On the other hand, it is quite possible to have disability without loss of earning capacity: If Krutch is a computer programmer who loses a leg in an accident, for example, he might return to work in a few weeks with little or no loss of salary. Yet clearly he has suffered a permanent, serious disability — in the sense of interference with enjoyment of life — which should be compensated.[5]

Economic v. Noneconomic Damages

The elements of damages discussed above are often grouped into *economic* and *noneconomic* damages. Lost earnings, lost earning capacity, and medical and other out-of-pocket expenses are considered *economic* or *tangible* damages, since they are actual dollar losses that can be calculated. By contrast, pain and suffering and loss of enjoyment are *noneconomic* or *intangible* damages which the jury has no mathematical or accounting basis for valuing. They must simply pick a number based on their sense of the severity of the loss the plaintiff has suffered. Consider, for example, the following fairly typical instruction on pain and suffering damages:

> In assessing damages, if you have occasion to do so, the law allows you to award to plaintiff a sum that will reasonably compensate him for any past physical pain, as well as pain that is reasonably certain to be suffered in the future as a result of the defendant's wrongdoing.
>
> There are no objective guidelines by which you can measure the money equivalent of this element of injury; the only real measuring stick, if it can be so described, is your collective enlightened conscience. You should consider the evidence bearing on the nature of the injuries, the certainty of future pain, the severity and the likely duration thereof.
>
> In this difficult task of putting a money figure on an aspect of injury that does not readily lend itself to an evaluation in terms of money, you should try to be as objective, calm and dispassionate as the situation will permit, and not to be unduly swayed by considerations of sympathy.

G. Douthewaite, Jury Instructions on Damages in Tort Actions 274 (1988).

The distinction between economic and noneconomic damages has become increasingly important in recent years. A good many legislatures, reacting to large increases in insurance costs during the nineteen eighties, have

---

5. A few courts hold that permanent disability is compensable as a per se loss, apart from any loss of enjoyment, pain and suffering, or lost earning capacity that results from it. See *Thompson v. National R.R. Passenger Corp.*, 621 F.2d 814, 824 (1980). The *Thompson* court reasoned that "permanent impairment" compensates the plaintiff "for the fact of being permanently injured whether or not it causes any pain or inconvenience" while loss of enjoyment compensates for "the limitations on the person's life created by the injury." Id. But this appears to be an isolated view. See Dobbs, Law of Remedies, Practitioner Treatise Series at §8.1(1) n.6.

enacted caps on noneconomic damages such as pain and suffering and loss of consortium. For example, Idaho Code §6-1603 (1994) provides:

> (1) In no action seeking damages for personal injury, including death, shall a judgment for noneconomic damages be entered for a claimant exceeding the maximum amount of four hundred thousand dollars ($400,000).[6]

Other states have enacted caps on noneconomic damages in particular types of cases, such as medical malpractice:

> (a) In any action for injury against a health care provider based on professional negligence, the injured plaintiff shall be entitled to recover noneconomic losses to compensate for pain, suffering, inconvenience, physical impairment, disfigurement and other nonpecuniary damage.
> (b) In no action shall the amount of damages for noneconomic losses exceed two hundred fifty thousand dollars. ($250,000).

Cal. Civ. Code Ann. §3333.2. (1994). Needless to say, statutes of this type do not warm the hearts of the plaintiffs' bar, since they reduce plaintiffs' recoveries and counsel's contingent fees. They represent a legislative compromise between the ideal of full compensation and the reality of limited resources. The debate about such compromises has been heated, and continues to be.

While the terminology courts use in analyzing compensatory damages may vary, the fundamental inquiry does not. The jury must assess the plaintiff's situation after the injury compared to his situation before. They must consider what he suffers now but didn't before, and what he has lost in terms of life's opportunities, both economic and personal, as a result of the injury. From this comparison they are to distill a sum of money damages to "compensate" him for all losses he has suffered or will suffer in the future from the injury. The examples below explore these damage issues in the context of particular cases.

EXAMPLES

The Art of Prediction

1.   Mendel, a 25 year-old truck driver, is injured in a traffic accident and rendered permanently paraplegic. He sues the other driver. If you represented Mendel, for what types of future medical and therapeutic expenses would you seek compensation?

2.   Assume that Mendel only suffers a concussion in the accident. He has minimal medical expenses, but testifies that he has developed tinnitus, or ringing in the ears, as a result of the impact. Tinnitus is a recognized medical

---

6. Section 6-1603 provides for annual adjustments to the $400,000 figure to reflect general changes in wage levels.

condition, but it is very hard to corroborate its existence by medical tests. Mendel testifies that the ringing is always there, that it is a constant irritant, that it has made him irritable and difficult with his family. He continues to work as a construction worker, but the condition interferes with his ability to concentrate on many leisure activities, such as card playing or reading. It also makes it very difficult for him to get to sleep, so that he is always tired.

Assume that liability is clear, and that medical costs and lost earnings are negligible. The defendant's insurer offers $35,000 to settle Mendel's claim. If you represented Mendel, would you take it?

3.   Audubon, a 42 year-old naturalist, is seriously injured in an accident involving his car and Darwin's. The evidence at trial indicates that Audubon is totally disabled. Due to his injury, his life expectancy has been shortened from 31 years to 20 years, and his work life expectancy from 25 years to zero. Stated another way, before the accident Audubon could have expected, based on statistical tables, to live to the age of 73, and work to the age of 67. However, due to his injuries he will now likely live only to the age of 62, and will not return to work. The evidence also indicates that he will continue to endure pain, embarrassment, and other psychic injuries from the accident until his death.

    a. If Darwin is found liable, for what time period should the jury assess damages for Audubon's lost earning capacity?

    b. Assuming that Audubon will continue to experience pain and mental anguish from the accident as long as he lives, for what period should the jury assess damages for pain and suffering?

    c. Should the jury award damages to Audubon for the shortening of his life span?

    d. For what period should the jury award damages for loss of enjoyment of life?

    e. Suppose, as sometimes happens, that Audubon really liked his job, but due to attention deficits and memory problems, is unable after the accident to engage in it, even as a hobby. Naturally, he is entitled to an award for lost earning capacity as a result of this, but, if you represented Audubon, what argument would you make to increase the damage award beyond this?

The Single Be-Fuddlement Rule

4.   Muir, a shipyard worker, contracts asbestosis, a respiratory disease caused by exposure to asbestos. He sues General Yards, the shipyard, for negligently failing to warn him of the danger of working with asbestos. At trial, he produces evidence of the pain and suffering he suffers from the disease, his medical expenses, and his impaired earning capacity. He also offers expert testimony that 20 percent of those who contract asbestosis later go on to develop cancer as well, and of the likely medical effects of this type of cancer.

Counsel for General Yards objects to all evidence relating to the cancer risk. What is the basis of the evidentiary objection and how should Judge Fudd rule on it?

Unpredictable Predictions

5.   Beebe is a college graduate with a degree in economics. She is also a mother of three. She worked as an administrative assistant at a college until her first child was born. Now, she has three children and does not work outside the home. She is injured in an auto accident and permanently disabled. If she sues the other driver, should she recover for lost earning capacity?

6.   Pinchot is injured in an auto accident at age 47. She is married to a highly paid corporate executive. She worked as a buyer for a department store for several years before she was married (now 23 years ago), and since her marriage has raised two children, who are now grown up and independent. At the time of the accident, she was not working and had no intention of ever going back to work. She is now permanently disabled. Can she recover for lost earning capacity?

7.   Thoreau, a 12 year-old child, is thrown from an off-road vehicle and sustains serious injuries. As a result, he is left with a limp and permanent weakness in his right arm and leg. Thoreau had never worked prior to the injury.

   a. In an action against the manufacturer of the vehicle, can Thoreau recover for loss of earning capacity?

   b. Assume (though it is unlikely on these facts) that the jury found that Thoreau would be unable to work at all due to the injury. What evidence would be relevant to ascertaining the value of his lost earning capacity?

   c. Assume that the jury concludes that Thoreau would have earned $900,000 as a laborer over his work life expectancy, had he not been injured, and that, due to his injury, he will not be able to do any kind of heavy work. Should they award him that sum as damages for lost earning capacity?

Missing Elements

8.   Agassiz, a retired botanist, is hit by a concrete block which falls from the fifth floor of an apartment house. He is rendered permanently unconscious by the blow, and is maintained in a comatose state by various invasive procedures such as breathing and feeding tubes. Prior to the accident, Agassiz lived on his pension and social security, which he continues to receive. The medical bills for his treatment are truly impressive; luckily, they are covered by Medicare and his supplemental health insurance.

   a. Should Agassiz recover for pain and suffering?

    b. Should he recover for loss of enjoyment of life?

    c. Should Agassiz recover for the medical expenses for treatment of his injury?

    d. Should he recover for lost earning capacity?

A Loss By Any Other Name

9.   Does the cap in the California statute quoted at p.249 limit damages for disability or loss of enjoyment of life?

EXPLANATIONS

The Art of Prediction

1.   You are probably not an expert in the medical treatment of paraplegia — though you might become one if you represented Mendel. But it is not hard to imagine the wide variety of medical problems that may result from paraplegia, and are likely to continue or worsen throughout the patient's life. Mendel, at 25, has a very long life expectancy, even if it is diminished somewhat by the injury. Over the years, he will likely require operations to cope with the consequences of his immobility, including, perhaps, plastic surgery to deal with sores on his body. He will need long-term physical therapy to preserve as much mobility as possible. He will need vocational training and counseling, sexual counseling, home care, special equipment, and home modifications to accommodate his condition. He will likely be hospitalized from time to time for more intensive care. He will need continuous medical monitoring and prescription medications, and may develop a variety of diseases that must be treated as well. He is likely to require psychotherapy as well to assist in adjusting to his disability. For a fuller discussion of the medical consequences of paraplegia, see Minzer, Nates, §126.

    Naturally, Mendel himself knows little or nothing of all this, and probably does not want to think about it. His counsel must develop the proof based on Mendel's past treatment, current condition, and expert medical and actuarial testimony. Counsel must learn a great deal about the day-to-day problems of her client's condition, including such unglamorous realities as bowel and bladder control, bed sores, and muscle atrophy. Medical specialists will testify about the likely course of treatment his condition will require over the years, the probable prognosis for his long-term health, likely complications and corrective surgery, and the types of on-going nursing and therapeutic services and medicines he will need. An accountant or economist may also testify as to the likely costs of such care, extrapolating out years or decades into the future, depending on the plaintiff's life expectancy.[7]

---

7. These experts will command substantial fees for their assistance in trial preparation and for their testimony. In the ordinary case, the fee will be advanced by plaintiff's counsel as part of the costs of suit. Ultimately the plaintiff will have to repay her counsel for these expenses (ranging perhaps into five figures) out of the judgment the defendant pays.

The defendant will likely present opposing experts on these issues, who reach substantially different conclusions concerning the required treatment and its projected cost. Ironically, the members of the jury, probably unschooled in either medical care or accounting, will then have to assign a sum to this element of damages based on their assessment of the evidence.

2.   This is typical of the type of judgment attorneys must make all the time about the value of cases. Actually, it is simpler than most: Since negligence is admitted, Mendel's counsel does not have to consider the risk that he will be unable to establish that crucial element. In addition, since earnings and medical costs are negligible, the only real issue is the value of the intangible damages for tinnitus.

Of course, Mendel's counsel does have to consider whether the jury will believe his client. Since the symptoms cannot be corroborated by objective measures, Mendel's testimony will be critical. If the jury concludes that he is making up the injury, they may find against him even though the defendant admits negligence: You have to prove all four elements to recover for negligence, including damages.

If we assume that Mendel is credible, and that the testimony of family and co-workers corroborates his story, the question then becomes what the injury is "worth." As the introduction states, there is no objective measure for such intangible damages, so it becomes very difficult to predict the number a jury will attach to it. Any settlement will be based on educated guesses of counsel as to what would happen if they went to trial. As an indication of how uncertain the damages may be, I gave these facts to my Torts class, and asked the students to decide, individually, what they would award if they were on the jury. The figures ranged from twenty thousand dollars to over half a million dollars.[8]

If Mendel's counsel concludes that the jury would award $50,000 for this, he might still settle for $35,000. He has to consider the costs of trial and the risk that the jury will disbelieve his client. On balance, it might be a reasonable choice to accept. Obviously, if counsel expects a considerably higher verdict at trial — as the figures from my class suggest he might — he should hesitate to accept the insurer's offer.

3a.   The goal of tort damages is to "place the victim in the same position he would have been in if he had not been injured." If Audubon had not been injured, he would have had income up until the age of 67. Due to the accident, all of those earnings are lost. Most courts would hold that Audubon

---

8. A fair number of students reached their awards by calculating a sum for each minute, hour or day that Mendel must live with the problem. One student gave two cents per minute; another allotted $10,000 per year; a third, a dollar an hour. The resulting awards were in the $300,000 to $500,000 range given Mendel's life expectancy.

can recover for lost earning capacity based on his *pre-accident* work expectancy, even though he is not now able to work, and will (statistically speaking) die eight years before he would have retired.

Arguably, calculating the future wages for the entire period overcompensates Audubon somewhat. If he had not been injured, he would likely have had his income for his full work life expectancy but would also have expended a large part of that on his living expenses. For the period from age 62 to 67, however, Audubon will not incur those expenses, due to his premature death (again, statistically speaking). It would be more accurate to require the jury to deduct the living expenses for that period from the earnings. Sounds a bit cold-blooded, though, doesn't it? Darwin's counsel may hesitate to raise the argument, since it sounds like he is trying to take advantage of the fact that the accident has shortened Audubon's life expectancy.

b. Damages for lost earnings are intended to compensate for the loss of future income. Pain and suffering, by contrast, compensates the victim for having to endure physical and psychic pain, humiliation, and anguish caused by the injury. The award should be based on the period during which he will actually experience pain and suffering. In Audubon's case, he will have to endure these (again, statistically speaking) for 20 more years. Pain and suffering damages should be awarded for his 20 year post-accident life expectancy, not based on his pre-accident life expectancy.

c. This is a very interesting issue. It is hard to deny that the loss of 11 years of life is grievous. It seems that Audubon ought to be compensated for that. On the other hand, if Audubon had been killed in the accident, he would have received no compensation for his lost years: Wrongful death actions compensate the *survivors* for their losses, not the decedent for his. See Chapter 14. But then, one of the rationales for the rule in death cases is that you cannot compensate the dead. Audubon is still alive. If we award him damages for his lost years, he can at least live out the years he has left a bit more pleasurably.

The courts are split on whether loss of life expectancy is a proper element of damages. English courts have allowed limited recovery for reduced life expectancy, but most American courts have denied it. See Minzer, Nates, §8.39. Some recent cases have recognized this as compensable, however, and there may be a trend in this direction. See e.g., *Morrison v. Stallworth*, 326 S.E.2d 387, 393 (N.C. App. 1985).

Even courts that deny recovery for lost life expectancy per se will often allow the jury to consider, as a part of pain and suffering, the mental anguish the plaintiff suffers from the *realization* that he will likely die before his time. In addition, since Audubon's lost earning capacity is assessed on the basis of his pre-accident life expectancy, this element of his "lost years" will be considered in assessing damages.

d. This is another interesting question. Loss of enjoyment damages compensate the plaintiff for her inability to participate in activities that she enjoyed prior to the accident. The types of losses included are legion, from walks in the park to playing softball with the kids to sky diving to bocci to sitting on the front porch and watching the world go by. Had the accident not taken place, Audubon would have engaged in whatever activities he fancied for as long as he was able, in many cases up to the end of his life. Due to the accident, he can no longer do so. The loss of enjoyment damages should be assessed with regard to his pre-accident life expectancy, not his reduced expectancy after the accident.

If a court accepts this view and allows damages for loss of enjoyment based on Audubon's pre-accident life expectancy, this recovery will also partially substitute for a separate award for the lost years themselves. Naturally, a large part of the value of Audubon's lost 11 years is the enjoyment of the activities and sensations of life during that period. If the jury can compensate for this loss, they are effectively invited to compensate for the lost years themselves. There may be a technical distinction — they are not supposed to give an award for the loss of life per se — but it is one which is likely to elude most juries.

A court which allows recovery for shortened life expectancy obviously should take care to avoid double counting of the plaintiff's damages. If the jury is instructed to consider loss of enjoyment for this period, as well as loss of life expectancy, they may well compensate Audubon twice for the same loss.

e. Audubon's accident has deprived him not only of the income from his work, but also of the pleasure he derives from it. Some people really like what they do. Some (mostly law professors) might do it for nothing, they like it so much. If Audubon is one of those, he has lost more than his salary due to his injury, he has lost a fundamental part of his life, from which he derives a great deal of satisfaction and sense of self. Replacing the salary is important, but hardly compensates him for all he has lost from the inability to pursue his profession. His counsel should argue that the jury should also award him loss of enjoyment damages for the destruction of his ability to engage in it. See Minzer, Nates at §8.01, p.8-20 (suggesting that plaintiff's counsel should make this argument, but avoid laying it on too thick).

The Single Be-Fuddlement Rule

4. Doubtless, General Yards has objected to the evidence because it only indicates a 20 percent chance that Muir will develop cancer. Most courts hold that plaintiffs are entitled to recover for future injuries that are "reasonably probable," but 20 percent does not meet this standard. If Muir's evidence is insufficient to prove that cancer is a probable consequence, the jury should not hear it.

Obviously, Muir is in a very difficult position here. If he sues for his asbestosis damages, he will not recover any cancer damages in that action, and under the single recovery rule, he will be barred from bringing a second suit if he develops cancer later. Some courts have reached this conclusion under the single recovery rule. See, e.g., *Gideon v. Johns-Manville Sales Corp.*, 761 F.2d 1129, 1136-1137 (5th Cir. 1983) (under Texas law, plaintiff must recover for present harm and all future consequences that will probably develop in the future). If Judge Fudd presides in such a jurisdiction, he should deny admission of the cancer evidence and Muir would recover nothing for this risk.[9]

Other courts, however, have recognized an exception to the single recovery rule, on the ground that cancer is a separate disease giving rise to a separate cause of action. See, e.g., *Mauro v. Raymark Indus., Inc.*, 561 A.2d 257, 262-263 (N.J. 1989). These courts would allow Muir to sue again if he contracts cancer in the future. If the Honorable Fudd presided in a state that takes this view, he would *still* deny admission of the cancer evidence in the initial action, but Muir would be able to recover for cancer in a later suit if he develops it.

This latter approach relieves the plaintiff from the difficulties of proof posed by the single recovery rule, but it has several serious implications. First, it will multiply litigation, since plaintiffs who have already sued for asbestosis will be entitled to sue again. In addition, this approach seriously erodes the single recovery rule, since plaintiffs will make the same argument in other types of cases where further complications of an injury arise that were not compensated in the original suit.

There is a third possibility in such cases. The court could award damages to the plaintiff in the initial action for her *increased risk* of developing cancer. For example, if the risk is 20 percent, the jury could determine the damages that the plaintiff will incur if cancer develops, and award her 20 percent of that. See Chapter 7, p. 132-134, for a discussion of the difficult causation issues posed by such increased risk claims.

Unpredictable Predictions

5.   Although she was not working outside the home prior to the accident, Beebe certainly should receive damages for lost earning capacity. The fact that she was not working at the time does not mean that she would not have worked later. The odds are very good that a woman in her position would return to the work force when her children were older, if only to help with

---

9.   Even in such a jurisdiction, Muir may be able to recover for the present fear that he will contract cancer in the future. Some courts have viewed this as a separate form of mental distress which, if reasonable, is compensable. See generally D. Dobbs, Law of Remedies, Practitioner Treatise Series §8.1(4), at 392-393.

the staggering cost of college. Beebe's capacity to do so has been destroyed, and she is entitled to compensation for that. Estimating her lost earning capacity, of course, will be difficult, since she has little in the way of a track record on which to predict her earning potential. The jury will simply have to do their best based on testimony about her background, interests, and opportunities, and economic testimony concerning wage trends for the kind of work she would likely have undertaken in later years.

6.   At first blush, it appears that Pinchot should not receive damages for lost earning capacity: Arguably, awarding damages for lost earning capacity would compensate her for a loss she will not actually incur, since she had no intention to seek employment outside the home.

Despite this possibility, the trend of the cases is to allow the jury to consider lost earning capacity notwithstanding the plaintiff's admission that she had no intention to enter the work force. The cases reason that the plaintiff has been deprived of the *option* to work by the accident. While Pinchot may not currently intend to put that capacity to work, her circumstances might change in the future, so that she is required to work. If so, she will not be able to do so and will have suffered a serious loss from the impairment of her earning capacity. See *Florida Greyhound Lines, Inc. v. Jones*, 60 So. 2d 396, 398 (Fla. 1952). Under the "single recovery rule" the court cannot wait to see if this possibility materializes: Pinchot must be compensated now for all her future losses. "The theory is that the injury has deprived the plaintiff of a capacity he would have been entitled to enjoy even though he may never have profited from it." *Hunt v. Bd. of Supervisors of La. State Univ.*, 522 So. 2d 1144, 1151 (La. App. 1988).

Although Pinchot's lost earning capacity is generally viewed as a proper element of damages, it is less clear how the jury is to value it. They could simply multiply her earning potential times years of work life expectancy, as they might in the case of a plaintiff who was working at the time of the accident. However, this seems too high, given her admitted intention not to work at all. Apparently, the jury should assign a figure to the *per se* loss of the ability to work, based on the severity of Pinchot's disability, their judgment of the likelihood that she would return to work, and the nature of work she would likely have taken up had she ever decided to do so. This is a pretty chancy business, if not downright fanciful in some cases, but the tort system is a human contrivance, not a scientific calculation.

7a. Surely Thoreau should not be denied recovery for loss of earning capacity simply because he has no earnings history. It would make no sense to refuse recovery to a child plaintiff who is injured before starting to work, and therefore loses *all* his potential earnings, while an adult who only lost part of his would be fully compensated for that loss. The jury should be (and is) entitled to compensate Thoreau for his lost future earning capacity, even though it is exclusively a *future* loss and he has no earnings history.

While it is clear that Thoreau has a right to recover for lost earning capacity, it is less clear whether he has actually lost earning capacity, and, if so, how much. His partial disability would certainly interfere with his earning capacity if he were likely to become a manual laborer, but the interference might be minimal if he becomes a computer programer or a stock broker. At the time of trial, Thoreau had no earnings history, no profession, probably no special skills or interests upon which to base a prediction of what work he would have chosen absent the injury. Thus, it will be very difficult for the jury to determine whether he has lost earning capacity. Yet they must decide, and might well conclude that an injury of this magnitude is likely to reduce his earning power. If they do, they may award damages, in some roughly appropriate amount, to compensate for the loss.

b. In arriving at a figure, the jury must decide what Thoreau was likely to have earned if he had not been injured, which turns on the kind of work he would have chosen. To predict this, the jury may consider such factors as Thoreau's character, his health and physical skills, his record in school, his IQ, his background (including his parents' occupations and education), the likelihood that he would have finished high school and gone on to college, and his interests, as well as government statistics about earnings for different occupations and education levels. On the basis of such factors, the jury must determine Thoreau's pre-accident earning capacity. The result will of course be a gross approximation, but on balance preferable to denying compensation for a very serious economic loss.

Ironically, Thoreau's award may be higher if the evidence shows that he was academically deficient or less intelligent. If he shows strong intellectual ability, he may have lost little earning capacity, since he can still perform the work he would likely have chosen if he had not been injured. By contrast, a plaintiff with weaker academic skills would more likely make his living through some form of manual labor. A disabling injury would have a greater impact on his earning capacity and lead to a greater award.

Issues like future earning capacity often present very delicate problems of proof for defense counsel. Consider the issue of lost earning capacity for a 14 year-old boy killed by a police officer in the course of arrest. The jury has just heard the tearful testimony of the boy's mother about how diligent he was and how he hoped to grow up to be a fire fighter. Now, counsel for the officer must present proof that the decedent had a long history of juvenile delinquency, truancy, failure at school, and general bad character, and that his most likely future was one of crime and incarceration. This evidence is clearly relevant to the issue of lost earning capacity, but it requires considerable skill to place it before the jury without alienating them.

c. The jury's calculation of Thoreau's loss begins rather than ends with the determination of what he would have earned. Thoreau's lost earning capacity cannot be measured solely by what he could have earned *before* the injury. The jury must make a separate assessment of what he can earn *after* the injury. While Thoreau won't be able to do heavy manual labor, he may still be able to perform many other kinds of work. If he can work, his award for lost earning capacity should be based on the difference between his earning potential before and after the injury. Thus, the jury should consider what type of work Thoreau will be able to do despite his disability, and determine the amount he is likely to earn from that work. They should then subtract that amount from the $900,000 he would have earned to determine the damages for lost earning capacity.

Once the jury has determined an amount for lost earning capacity, they will have to reduce this figure to present value. Since Thoreau will receive the award today to compensate for losses over a number of years, the amount must be reduced to account for the interest Thoreau can earn on the award over the years. This present value concept is considered in the next chapter.

Missing Elements

8a. Agassiz has suffered a very serious injury, but a number of the usual elements of compensatory damages will not apply to his case. The facts suggest that he was rendered unconscious immediately by the blow. If so, he has not suffered any conscious pain and suffering. Most courts hold that a plaintiff must be conscious to recover for pain and suffering, since pain and suffering compensates subjective discomfort resulting from the injury, and unconscious patients do not experience these symptoms. See D. Dobbs, Law of Remedies, Practitioner Treatise Series §8.1(4), at 388.

This basic fact of damages doctrine has led to strained, sometimes unseemly efforts by plaintiffs' counsel to prove that the victim was conscious, if only for a second, since such proof opens the door for the jury to award damages for this highly subjective element.

b. Agassiz has lost the ability to enjoy virtually all of life's pleasures. If that isn't loss of enjoyment, what is? Interestingly, the cases are divided on the question of whether a comatose patient can recover for loss of enjoyment. A leading New York case denies recovery, on the ground that the unconscious patient cannot benefit in any way from an award for loss of enjoyment, and consequently such an award would serve no compensatory purpose:

> Simply put, an award of money damages in such circumstances has no meaning or utility to the injured person. An award for the loss of enjoyment of life "cannot provide [such a victim] with any consolation or ease any burden resting on him . . . He cannot spend it upon necessities or pleasures. He cannot experience the pleasure of giving it away."

McDougald v. Garber, 536 N.E.2d 372, 375 (1989) (quoting *Flannery v. United States*, 718 F.2d 108, 111 (4th Cir. 1983), *cert. denied*, 467 U.S. 1226 (1984).

This holding has been controversial. For one thing, there can be no doubt that the plaintiff has suffered a grievous loss: Basically, he has lost *all* of life's enjoyment, whether he is aware of it or not. Had the plaintiff been totally disabled, but remained aware of it, he would have received full compensation for loss of enjoyment. It hardly seems appropriate that an even more seriously injured plaintiff should receive nothing. In addition, tort victims sometimes do obtain recoveries that they cannot enjoy, as where the estate of a decedent recovers damages in a survival action for predeath pain and suffering.

Other courts have allowed loss of enjoyment damages to comatose plaintiffs, on the theory that the loss of life's pleasures is an objective loss suffered by the plaintiff, whether or not he subjectively comprehends or experiences it. See, e.g., *Flannery v. United States*, 297 S.E.2d 433, 438-439 (W. Va. 1982); See generally Minzer, Nates at §8.40.

c. This fairly simple question requires a complex answer. There is in the law of damages a quizzical doctrine called the "collateral source" rule, which holds the defendant responsible for losses to the plaintiff even though those losses are actually paid by a collateral source. For example, if a plaintiff incurs $5,000 in medical bills, but her health insurer pays most of it, she is still entitled, under the collateral source rule, to collect the full $5,000 from the defendant. Similarly, if plaintiff loses $30,000 in wages, but is compensated by his disability insurance policy for the loss, the defendant must still pay $30,000 for the loss.

This bewildering rule is often justified on the ground that the defendant should not obtain a windfall from the plaintiff's foresight in obtaining (and paying for) insurance protection against these losses. See generally D. Dobbs, Law of Remedies §8.6(3), at 494-498. Whether or not this rationale is convincing, the rule has been applied to many types of collateral source payments, including medicare, private insurance, continuation of wages by the plaintiff's employer, unemployment compensation, worker's compensation, and others. See generally Minzer, Nates at §17.00 ff.

Although the collateral source rule has been very widely applied, it has also been widely criticized, since it compensates plaintiffs for losses that they do not actually incur. Many recent statutes have limited the rule in an effort to control insurance costs, at least for certain types of cases or certain types of collateral benefits. See, e.g., Arizona Rev. Stat. §12-713 (1993) (allowing jury to consider payments from collateral sources in assessing personal injury damages); Mich. Laws Ann. §600.6303 (1994) (requiring reduction of damages for collateral payments, adjusted for premiums plaintiff paid to obtain collateral source protection). If Agassiz's case were governed by the Michigan statute, he would recover very little despite the very substantial expense of his medical care.

d. Although lost earnings and earning capacity are basic elements of tort damages, Agassiz will presumably not recover anything for this category of damages. Agassiz has not lost his pension or social security income: They are still paid to him after his injury, just as they were before. If he has not suffered a loss of these items due to the accident, the defendant need not compensate for them.

Even if the collateral source rule applies in Agassiz's jurisdiction, Agassiz will still have no claim for these lost benefits. The collateral source rule bars the defendant from taking advantage of the fact that plaintiff's loss from the injury has been compensated by a third party. But Agassiz is entitled to be paid these amounts regardless of his state of health, and will continue to be paid them despite the injury. Thus he hasn't lost these benefits; the collateral source rule is irrelevant to this element of his damages.

In the final analysis, Agassiz's case is troubling. He has suffered catastrophic injury, yet most of the big ticket elements of compensation — pain and suffering, loss of enjoyment, and lost earnings — will hardly figure at all in his damages. Depending on the status of the collateral source rule, he may not even be compensated for medical costs.

A Loss By Any Other Name

9.   The California statute illustrates the variability and the ambiguity in the terms courts use to describe elements of intangible damages. The statute does not mention either disability or loss of enjoyment of life, yet the legislature probably meant the cap to apply to these types of intangible losses as well as all others. "Inconvenience" very likely encompasses the same losses as "loss of enjoyment," that is, the impairment of the plaintiff's ability to function as she did before the injury. And, presumably, the terms "disfigurement" and "physical impairment" would encompass any intangible losses included within the term "disability."

The ambiguities surrounding these terms can pose problems in applying the statute. "Physical impairment," for example, is strictly speaking a condition, which will give rise to both economic damages (lost earnings) and noneconomic damages such as lost enjoyment, embarrassment, depression, and others. Similarly, "inconvenience" could connote, for example, interference with performance of household services, a clearly economic loss, as well as the intangible damages associated with the reduced ability to function due to an injury. To properly apply this statute, the court will have to be very careful to assure, through proper instructions, that the jury separates the economic and noneconomic components of such losses in order to properly apply the statutory cap on noneconomic damages.

13

Astrological Calculations: Valuing Future Damages

Introduction

I dedicate this chapter to Rick, my old backpacking partner. Rick is an astronomer, and accustomed to working with large numbers. Sometimes, while our legs were getting a workout in the White Mountains, I would give his brain a little exercise as well. For example, while winter hiking once, I asked, "Rick, how many snowflakes do you think there are in New Hampshire today?" Here's how Rick came up with the answer:

Rick: Well, how big is New Hampshire?

Me: Oh, I don't know, about 60 miles by 150.

Rick: O.K., that's about 9,000 square miles. A mile is about 5,300 feet, so a square mile would have 5,300 times 5,300 square feet, which is roughly 28 million square feet. Multiply that by 9,000, and you get about 250 billion.

Now, how deep do you think the snow is in New Hampshire these days?

Me: Gee, Rick, it varies quite a bit. We didn't see much down south, but there's as much as three feet in parts of the mountains.

Rick: Well, the mountains cover only about a quarter of the state. How does a foot sound for an average?

Me: I'd say that's about right.

Rick: Alright then, if there are 250 billion square feet of surface area in the state, we're talking the same number of cubic feet of snow. Now, how many snowflakes do you think there might be in a cubic inch?

Me: That's hard to say, Rick . . . maybe a thousand?

Rick: I would have said 400, so we'll split the difference. That's 700 to the cubic inch, and there are about 1,700 cubic inches to the foot, so that's ah, 1.2 million snowflakes to the cubic foot. We'll round that off to a million. Multiply that times 250 billion, and you get 250 to the 16th power, or 250 quadrillion. So there you are, there are 250 quadrillion snowflakes in New Hampshire.

Me: Gee, Rick, that's a lot of snowflakes.

Rick was a good mathematician, and there was nothing wrong with his calculations. The problem, of course, lay in our *assumptions*, which were flagrantly, even joyously approximate.[1]

As the last chapter indicates, the same is often true in assessing future damages for such items as medical expenses and lost earning capacity. In projecting future wages, for example, the jury must often make assumptions, based on little relevant information, about the plaintiff's expected work life, the nature of his future employment, his prospects for advancement, future increases in productivity in his occupation, and others. Consequently, in assigning a dollar value to the loss, the jury will often have to reach a sum certain by multiplying uncertainties.

This chapter deals with some of the actuarial problems in assigning a sum to be paid today to compensate for damages to be suffered in the future. Although these appear to be largely accounting problems susceptible of mathematical solutions, they turn out, like Rick's snow calculations, to be based on some frequently dubious assumptions. The purpose of the chapter is to illustrate those assumptions, and the basic approaches lawyers use in valuing future damages. While the chapter is full of numbers, have no fear; it is the underlying legal principles, not the particular numbers, which you should understand.

Astronomical Hypotheticals

Two simple examples will illustrate the problems of assessing future damages. In the first, Kepler, an 83 year-old black man, retired from the banking business, is severely injured in an automobile accident, and the jury determines that he will need medical care for the rest of his life. In the second,

---

1. On another trip, I noted the striking fact that the forest floor was covered with fallen trees, but we never saw a tree fall while hiking. We figured out how long we would have to walk to see a tree fall, but I don't remember the numbers.

Hubble, a 57 year-old white woman who worked part-time in a machine shop, is disabled in an accident while working with a metal press. The jury concludes that she will not need future medical care, but that she will never work again.

In both cases, it is obvious that the jury will have to begin by determining the period over which the plaintiff's loss will be suffered. In Kepler's case, that will be his life expectancy; in Hubble's, her work-life expectancy. Life and work-life expectancy tables provide a starting point for making these determinations. These tables, compiled by insurers or government agencies, provide statistical averages of the number of years a person of a given age will live or work. Here is an excerpt from a life expectancy table:

Table 13-1:[2] Life Tables

Age	Black Both Sexes	Male	Female
77	9.1	7.8	9.9
78	8.6	7.4	9.4
79	8.2	7.1	8.9
80	7.8	6.8	8.4
81	7.4	6.4	7.9
82	7.1	6.2	7.5
83	6.7	5.9	7.2
84	6.5	5.7	6.8
85	6.3	5.5	6.6

Based on the table, Kepler, if he were the hypothetical average black male of age 83, could expect to live 5.9 more years.[3] Of course, no one is truly "average"; each of us is a unique individual. Kepler, for example, has permanent injuries from the accident that may shorten his life span considerably. It would be superficial to assume that he will live 5.9 years, and unduly rigid for courts to require juries to use the average figure. Thus, while such tables are admissible, the parties are free to introduce evidence that the plaintiff has a longer or shorter life expectancy. But the tables provide a good starting point, especially in cases, such as the wrongful death of an infant, in which there is little evidence other than such tables from which to predict life expectancy.

Similar tables are available to estimate the future work-life expectancy of Hubble:

---

2. Excerpt from National Center for Health Statistics, Vital Statistics of the United States, 1988; Vol. II, Part A, Section 6. p.11. Washington: Public Health Service 1991.

3. Some issues have been raised as to the propriety of life expectancy and work-life expectancy tables which categorize on the basis of sex or race. See D. Dobbs, Law of Remedies, Practitioner Treatise Series §8.5(2), at 464-467. These tables are used for illustration purposes only.

Table 13-2:[4]
For Women By Race 1979-1980 (White women)

| | Expectation of active life by labor force status | | |
Age	Total	Currently Active	Currently Inactive
55	5.3	7.3	2.9
56	4.7	6.8	2.5
57	4.3	6.3	2.2
58	3.8	5.9	1.9
59	3.4	5.4	1.7
60	3.0	5.1	1.5
61	2.6	4.7	1.3
62	2.3	4.4	1.2

After the accident, of course, Hubble has *no* work-life expectancy; that is the whole point of her damage action. However, in estimating her wage loss, a table of this sort provides a starting point for estimating how long she *would have worked* if she had not been injured. As a 57 year-old woman, the table indicates that Hubble (who was "active" in the labor force before her injury) had a work-life expectancy of 6.3 years. However, as with life expectancy, the parties are free to argue that her actual work-life expectancy is higher or lower, and the jury may so find. In Hubble's case, the table may be pretty accurate, since she is close to the end of her work life. But it requires many snowflake assumptions to apply such tables to a disabled child, for example.

Let's assume for the sake of argument that the jury finds Kepler's life expectancy to be four years (less than average due to his injury) and Hubble's work-life expectancy to be six, just about the average for her age. We can roughly calculate each plaintiff's loss by multiplying the estimated yearly loss (fraught, of course, with its own flaky assumptions) by the number of years it will be suffered. If Kepler will need $25,000 a year in medical treatment, the loss is roughly $100,000; if Hubble made $10,000 per year, she should receive $60,000.

Accelerating the Future: The Concept of Present Value

A moment's thought, however, suggests that these awards overcompensate both plaintiffs. The jury awards a sum today (that is, the day of the verdict) to compensate the plaintiff for losses she will suffer next year, or three years from now, or 33 years from now. Kepler will not need $100,000 this year, nor would Hubble earn $60,000 this year if she had not been injured. In

---

4. Excerpt from U.S. Bureau of Labor Statistics, Bull. 2254, Worklife Estimates: Effects of Race and Education 19 (February 1986).

each case the loss is spread over a period of future years, though the award is made at the beginning of the period.

The problem is that a dollar in the hand is worth two in the bush, or, put in more rigorous terms, the value of a dollar received today is greater than the value of a dollar that *will be received* in five years. Suppose, for example, that Hubble receives $10,000 in 1994, to compensate her for $10,000 in wages that she will lose in 1999. She can invest that $10,000 for the intervening five years, so that she will have a considerably larger sum in 1999 than the $10,000 that will be lost in that year. We all probably went to law school to avoid numbers, but it is important to understand this at least in a general way. Here's a simple illustration of the point, based on the assumption that Hubble will earn interest at eight percent on her award:

Table 13-3

Jan 1994	Receives $10,000
Jan 1995	Has $10,000 + $800 interest = $10,800
Jan 1996	Has $10,800 + $864 interest = $11,664
Jan 1997	Has $11,664 + $933 interest = $12,597
Jan 1998	Has $12,597 + $1,008 interest = $13,605
Jan 1999	Has $13,605 + $1,088 interest = $14,693

As Table 13-3 indicates, the difference is very substantial, almost half again the $10,000 that the jury expects Hubble to lose in 1999. Clearly, the time value of money must be taken into account in awarding such future damages. This is done by a process known as "discounting the award to present value," that is, reducing the $10,000 future loss to a figure, which, if invested conservatively for the five years, will yield $10,000 in the year of the expected loss. If the jury concluded, for example, that Hubble would lose $14,693 in wages in 1999, and that safe investments for the five-year period would earn eight percent, they should award $10,000 to compensate for that future loss. As Table 13-3 shows, if she receives $10,000 in 1994 it will grow to $14,693 in 1999 if eight percent interest rates are assumed.

Once again, actuarial charts, called "present value tables," are available to calculate the present value of a dollar to be received in the future at various interest rates. Here is an example of a chart for calculating present value.

Table 13-4[5]

Years Until Sum is Due	Present Value of $1 at				
	2.00%	4.00%	6.00%	8.00%	10.00%
1	.98039	.96154	.94340	.92592	.90909
2	.96116	.92456	.89000	.85734	.82645
3	.94232	.88900	.83962	.79383	.75131
4	.92384	.85480	.79209	.73503	.68301
5	.90573	.82193	.74726	.68058	.62092
6	.88797	.79032	.70496	.63016	.56447

---

5. Figures based on a similar chart in Minzer, Nates at §108.32.

This table makes it easy to calculate the sum needed today to yield a dollar in a future year at a given interest rate. For example, if the jury, deliberating in 1994, wants to compensate Hubble for a one dollar loss three years from now, and they conclude that the interest rate will be four percent during that period, they should award her $.88900. If they wish to compensate her for a one dollar loss in 1999, and they find that interest rates will average eight percent, they should award her $.68058, or 68-and-a-fraction cents. If they want to compensate her for a $10,000 loss in 1999, they should give her (10,000 × .68058), or $6805.80. If Hubble receives that amount in January 1994, and invests her award wisely (a flaky assumption in itself), here's what should happen to it:

Table 13-5

Jan 1994	Receives $6805.80
Jan 1995	Has $6805.80 plus $544.46 ($7350.26)
Jan 1996	Has $7350.26 plus $588.02 ($7938.28)
Jan 1997	Has $7938.28 plus $635.06 ($8573.34)
Jan 1998	Has $8573.34 plus $685.87 ($9259.21)
Jan 1999	Has $9259.21 plus $740.74 ($9999.95)

As this table shows, the $6805.80 "present value" figure is simply $10,000 (minus a few cents for rounding off), projected backwards to account for the interest Hubble will earn on it over the following five years.[6]

As a practical matter, litigators often hire economists to assist them with such calculations if the damages are large. These experts will give detailed testimony at trial to assist the jury in discounting future losses to present value. But it is worth a little brain strain to try to understand what is going on with calculations like these. Try your hand at the following present value calculations based on our example plaintiffs. (The explanations begin on p.275.)

EXAMPLES

Back to the Future

1.   The jury in the Hubble case, deliberating on January 1, 1994, concludes that she will lose $6,000 per year in wages due to the disability and that she would have worked for six more years if she hadn't been injured. If the jury finds that Hubble can safely expect to earn interest at six percent on her award, how much should they award for the lost earnings? (Use Table 13-4 and assume that each year's wages are received at the end of the year in which they are earned.)

---

6. This calculation is itself oversimplified: it assumes interest compounded yearly, while it may be compounded more frequently on many investments.

2. Kepler seeks recovery for the future costs of physical therapy required due to his injury. The jury finds that he will spend $2,000 per year on physical therapy for the next two years. They further find that interest rates will be ten percent for 1994, the first year, but go down to eight percent for the second year, 1995. How much should they award for the cost of the physical therapy?

Speculating Precisely: Adjustment for Future Inflation

It may seem a bit snowflaky to have the jury make speculative assessments of future earnings or expenses and then massage those numbers through adjustments like present value. Such fine-tuning suggests a level of precision inconsistent with the astrological assumptions underlying projections of future losses — sort of like tiptoeing on quicksand. Yet recent cases have required considerably more precision in adjusting the jury's speculative figures. For example, the courts increasingly hold that damages for future losses should also be adjusted to take account of inflation.

Suppose, for example, that Hubble will lose $10,000 in wages in 1994 and that inflation is running at four percent. The jury may well find that Hubble would have received cost of living increases to keep her salary at the same level in terms of real buying power. Thus, her wages for the six future years would actually be as follows:

Table 13-6

Wages for 1994	$10,000
Wages for 1995	$10,000 + $400 = $10,400
Wages for 1996	$10,400 + $416 = $10,816
Wages for 1997	$10,816 + $433 = $11,249
Wages for 1998	$11,249 + $450 = $11,699
Wages for 1999	$11,699 + $468 = $12,167

If inflation is to be considered in assessing Hubble's wage loss, it appears that the jury should first calculate the inflation-adjusted wages for each future year and *then* discount the adjusted sums to present value. Clearly, this will yield a higher figure than calculating present value without considering inflation. For example, based on Table 13-4, the present value of Hubble's 1999 wage loss, assuming a six percent interest rate, is .74726 × $10,000, or $7472.60 if the future wage is not adjusted for inflation. If inflation is considered, however, the present value will be .74726 × $12,167, or $9091.91. Accounting for inflation thus provides a considerably larger award in present dollars.

Traditionally, courts ignored inflation in calculating future losses, on the ground that it was too speculative to consider. However, the high inflation rates of the 1970s caused many courts to reconsider this somewhat unrealistic approach. The purpose of compensatory damages, after all, is to put the plaintiff in the position she would have been in if she had not been injured. If she had not been injured, her wages would doubtless have risen due to future inflation. Thus, most courts now allow the jury to take inflation into account in calculating damages, using one of several approaches. For example, the jury may be instructed to do what I have done above in Table 13-6, that is, increase each future year's wages to account for inflation, and then discount the inflation-adjusted figures to present value. See *Jones & Laughlin Steel Corp. v. Pfeifer*, 462 U.S. 523, 543-544 (1983).

Another way to account for inflation is the "total offset" method, which assumes that the rate of inflation and the rate at which the award will earn interest will be roughly equal over the future years. See, e.g., *Beaulieu v. Elliott*, 434 P.2d 665, 671-672 (Alaska 1967). On this assumption, the increase for inflation and the decrease for discounting to present value cancel each other out. Thus, the jury is simply instructed to calculate the award without increasing the future wage figures to reflect inflation *or* reducing the award to present value. This approach has the considerable virtue of simplicity, since the jury need not get into the complexities of projecting inflation and interest rates or discounting to present value.

A third method is to calculate present value by a discount rate based on the anticipated difference between inflation and interest rates. As a historical matter, interest rates tend to run between one percent and three percent above inflation; thus, the "real" earning power of money is one to three percent. Courts that use the "real interest rate" approach reason that discounting future losses by a figure in this range automatically accounts for both interest earned and inflation. For example, assume that the jury finds that inflation will run at five percent and interest rates at eight percent for the period of the future loss. Instead of increasing the wage figures by five percent to account for inflation and then decreasing them by eight percent to present value, this approach accounts for both effects in one step, by calculating the loss in present dollars and decreasing it by three percent, the differential between the inflation rate and the interest rate.

The following example illustrates the application of these methods of accounting for inflation.

Inflated Expectations

3. Assume that Hubble will lose $10,000 (in 1994 dollars) in wages for the five years from 1995 to 1999. Assume also that the jury finds that inflation will run at four percent, and that interest rates will average six percent.
    a. How much should the jury award Hubble for this loss under the total offset method?
    b. How much should the jury award if it adjusts the award for inflation and then reduces it to present value? (Use the figures in Table 13-6 to save some calculations.)

    c. How much should the jury award under the "real interest rate" approach?

4. Assume that Kepler will require $4,000 (in 1994 dollars) worth of physical therapy in each year from 1995 to 1999.

    a. Should the jury also take account of inflation in calculating this award?

    b. Assume that inflation is running at four percent and interest rates are six percent. If you represented Kepler, what argument would you make that the court should use a higher inflation rate in calculating the award for physical therapy?

Speculating More Precisely: The Effect of Taxes

Perhaps this brief excursion into the astrology of predicting future damages[7] has already convinced you to strike personal injury law from your list of possible specialties. But recent cases require still further refinements of future damage calculations. Most notably, some courts now require juries to factor the effects of taxes into their calculations.

Traditionally, courts have not instructed juries to take account of taxes in calculating personal injury awards, even for such elements as wages, which would have been subject to tax if they were earned in the regular course. One reason for this reluctance is the complexity of taking taxes into account. As one court opined, "The average accident trial should not be converted into a graduate seminar on economic forecasting." *Doca v. Marina Mercante Nicaraguensea S.A.*, 634 F.2d 30, 39 (2nd Cir. 1980), *cert. denied*, 451 U.S. 971 (1981). Considering the effect of taxes introduces many additional variables, such as future tax rates, exemptions, and deductions. For many years, courts concluded that this additional complexity, even if conceptually justified, was too flaky to get into.

There are actually two aspects to the tax problem. First, there is the question of the taxation of *the judgment itself*, the dollar sum the plaintiff receives from the defendant if she wins the lawsuit. Under the Internal Revenue Code, tort awards "received . . . on account of personal injuries or

---

7. As a former English major, I felt it wise to have an economist read this chapter. He was not taken with my astrology metaphor:

> As a thin-skinned economist, I object to comparing economic forecasting with astrology. Your basic point, with which I strongly agree, is that the forecasts are bound to have large errors sometimes, as no one can perfectly forecast the future. But the presence of large errors in forecasts for a particular individual does not mean either that the individual forecasts are random, or that they do not predict well for the population of individuals over long periods of time. Astrology? This comparison makes it seem as if the forecast for an individual contains no information about the individual's future earnings. I don't think that's correct.

Well, maybe I do overstate the case a bit. Certainly, I would be a lot more comfortable with these types of figures if they were forecasting the *average* future earnings of a large population than the *actual* earnings of Hubble.

sickness" are not taxable income. 26 U.S.C. §104(a)(2) (1988). Thus, the plaintiff will receive the full amount awarded, even if part or all of the award is for future wages that clearly would have been subject to tax if they had been earned in the normal course. Suppose, for example, that Hubble is awarded $47,000 for lost future wages. As a result of §104(a)(2), she will not be required to report any part of that sum as income for tax purposes. She will pocket the entire sum — less the considerable expenses and legal fees incurred to achieve the recovery.

Traditionally, courts have refused to inform the jury that the award is not taxed, even if a party asked the court to do so. Courts reasoned that the tax consequences of the judgment were none of the jury's business; their task was simply to calculate the amount of the loss.[8] Here again, however, some recent cases have rejected the earlier approach and approved instructions that the award is not taxable, to help the jury understand the consequences of the calculations they are making. See, e.g., *Norfolk & Western Ry. Co. v. Liepelt*, 444 U.S. 490, 496-497, *reh'g. denied*, 445 U.S. 972 (1980).

An Interim Question

5.   Which party, plaintiff or defendant, is likely to request an instruction to the jury that their award will not be subject to taxes?

———————————

The second aspect of the tax issue is whether the jury, in calculating the future wages the plaintiff would have received, should consider the fact that the plaintiff, had she earned the wages in due course, would have actually received only her *net* wages after taxes. Defendants have argued that using gross earnings to estimate future wage losses overcompensates the plaintiff, since she would have received substantially less because of the taxes due on those wages. For example, if Hubble would have earned $10,000 per year in the five remaining years of her work life expectancy, she might have paid something like $1,500 of each year's income in taxes. Thus, her net pay would only have been about $8,500 in each of those years. If the goal of compensatory damages is to "put the plaintiff in the position she would have been in but for the injury," it seems like the $8,500 figure should be used.

The argument certainly appears sound, since we all know that taxes take a considerable bite out of our gross pay. However, as with inflation

———————————

8. Here is Justice Blackmun's reason for opposing the instruction: "The required instruction . . . does not affect the determination of liability or the measure of damages. It does nothing more than call a basically irrelevant factor to the jury's attention, and then directs the jury to forget that matter." *Norfolk & Western Ry. Co. v. Liepelt*, 444 U.S. 490, 502 (1980) (Blackmun, J., dissenting). See also *Rego Co. v. McKown-Katy*, 801 P.2d 536, 539 (Colo. 1990) ("it is beyond the court's province to caution the jurors against every erroneous belief they may hold").

adjustments, factoring income taxes into the equation complicates the jury's task considerably, and moves us further into the realm of snowflake speculation. Here are a few of the factors which must be considered in predicting future taxes:

- Future tax rates. The top rate for federal income taxes was 31 percent in the late eighties, but more than twice that at the beginning of the decade. What tax rate should the jury choose for future years?
- Deductions. Will the plaintiff have children, marry (or divorce), have large medical expense deductions due to his injuries or other illnesses?
- Gross income. Since federal tax rates are progressive, a couple's tax rate will depend on both spouses' income. Should the jury hear evidence on the plaintiff's *spouse's* future income, in order to ascertain the rate of tax on their joint income for future years?
- Other taxes. Should social security, medicare, and other taxes be considered? How about state taxes? If so, should evidence be allowed as to whether the plaintiff will move to another state with a higher state tax, or with none?
- Other income sources. Should the jury hear evidence of the plaintiff's (or his spouse's) prospects of a large inheritance, which would raise his tax bracket in future years? Should it predict the future value of his stock portfolio for the same purpose?

Obviously, these and other factors could vastly complicate the trial of damages, without necessarily resulting in a more precise conclusion as to the proper damage figure. Thus, many courts concluded, and a fair number still do, that future taxes are "too speculative" to consider in valuing future wages. See the annotation, Propriety of Taking Income Tax into Consideration in Fixing Damages in Personal Injury or Death Actions, 16 A.L.R.4th 589 (1982), §8. Other recent cases, however, have allowed consideration of the tax impact, especially since the Supreme Court approved this practice in *Liepelt*. These courts recognize the uncertainties inherent in predicting taxes, but point out that many *other* factors are speculative too, so why should one more be ignored! It is not surprising that, having once tiptoed into these actuarial quicksands, it is hard for courts to refuse to consider factors, like taxes, which clearly do affect the plaintiff's actual loss.

The argument for considering the effect of taxes is especially strong in assessing damages for *past* lost wages. If the trial takes place five or six years after the injury, the jury will have to calculate the lost wages for the period between injury and trial, as well as for future years. The factors affecting the plaintiff's tax liability for this past period are relatively easy to ascertain, and thus the argument for considering taxes is strong. If taxes are deducted for past wages, however, it weakens the argument for ignoring taxes on future income.

EXAMPLES

Taxing the Patience of the Jury

6.   Assume that Hubble's case is tried in a jurisdiction that allows the jury to consider the effect of taxes on future lost earnings. If Hubble will lose $10,000 (in current dollars) in wages for the next five years, how should the jury calculate her lost future income, after taxes, for the five years? Assume that the jury finds that Hubble would have paid an average of 30 percent in taxes during those years, that inflation will run at four percent, and that interest rates will be six percent. Assume further that

  a. The jurisdiction does not allow inflation adjustments.
  b. Now, assume that the jurisdiction allows adjustments for present value and inflation, using the total offset method.
  c. Instead, assume that the jurisdiction calculates future damages with an inflation adjustment and then reduces them to present value.
  d. Finally, assume that the jurisdiction uses the "real interest rate" method.

7.   If you represented Hubble, how would you argue that reducing the future wages to account for taxes only partially accounts for the effect of taxes, and leads to an unfairly low award?

8.   Assume that the court concludes that all three of the issues addressed in this chapter, present value, inflation, and the effect of taxes, should be considered in determining future damages. Can you formulate a workable instruction to inform the jury how it should go about awarding a sum to compensate for future wages, taking each of these factors into account?

Judge Fudd Befuddled

9.   Kepler introduces evidence at trial that his injury causes constant, severe pain and suffering, which will continue as long as he lives. At the close of the trial, defense counsel asks Judge Fudd to give the following instruction to the jury:

> If you find that the plaintiff will suffer pain and suffering in the future, you may award him a sum to compensate for that pain and suffering. In the event that your verdict includes an amount for future pain and suffering, that sum should be discounted to present value in the same manner applicable to future wage losses.

How should the Honorable Fudd rule on the motion?

EXPLANATIONS

Back to the Future

1.   Table 13-4 provides the discount rate for calculating the loss. For example, to provide Hubble a dollar at the end of the first year, assuming a 6 percent

interest rate, the jury should give her $.94340. To give her $6,000 of them at the end of that year, it should give her (6,000 × $.94340), or $5,660.40. If she puts this out at interest for the year, it will make .06 × $5,660.40, or $339.62. Added to the $5,660.40 award, this equals $6,000.02, with a little splashover for rounding off. Here is how the figures work out when each future year's loss is discounted for the appropriate number of years:

For 1994:	(6,000 × $.94340)	=	$5,660.40
For 1995:	(6,000 × $.89000)	=	$5,340.00
For 1996:	(6,000 × $.83962)	=	$5,037.72
For 1997:	(6,000 × $.79209)	=	$4,752.54
For 1998:	(6,000 × $.74726)	=	$4,483.56
For 1999:	(6,000 × $.70496)	=	$4,229.76
		Total:	$29,503.98

Note several things about this process. First, the present value of the future loss has to be calculated separately for each year's loss, because a different discount rate applies depending on how far in the future the earnings would have been received.

Second, the present value of a $6,000 loss is less for each successive year. This stands to reason: The present value of $6,000 to be received in five years is less than the present value of $6,000 due in one year, because the plaintiff has four extra years to invest the money received before it must replace the future loss.

Tables are also available to simplify this calculation. These tables give you the present value of an *income stream* for a given number of years. Here's an excerpt from such a table:

Table 13-7: Present Value of $1 Per Year for Specified Number of Years

# of Years	3.00%	4.00%	5.00%	6.00%
1	.97	.96	.95	.94
2	1.91	1.89	1.86	1.83
3	2.83	2.78	2.72	2.67
4	3.72	3.63	3.57	3.47
5	4.58	4.45	4.33	4.21
6	5.42	5.24	5.08	4.92

This table allows the jury to calculate how much to give the plaintiff to provide an income stream of $1 for a period of years at a given interest rate.[9] Instead of going through each step as I have done above, you can calculate the future income in a single step using a factor from the table. To give Hubble a dollar a year for three years at a 3.00 percent interest rate, give her $2.83 today. To give her a dollar a year for six years assuming a 6.00 percent interest rate, give her $4.92. To give her $6,000 per year for six years at the

---

9. There are also formulae for calculating the present value of an income stream. One such formula is discussed in Minzer, Nates at §108.12.

6.00 percent rate, give her 6,000 × $4.92, which equals $29,520, very close to the figure I calculated above using my Neanderthal math skills. (The difference likely results from the fact that the 4.92 figure is rounded off.)
2.   This example involves future medical costs, not wage loss, but the principle is the same. The jury should determine an amount to award today that a prudent investor may use to yield the needed amount in the year in which the expense will be incurred. The only difference here is that the jury has concluded that interest rates will vary. This makes the calculation a little more complex. The sum needed to yield the first $2,000, for the 1994 therapy expenses, can be calculated from the discount table. Since Kepler will need $2,000 at the end of the first year, and the interest rate during that year will be ten percent, simply discount $2000 for one year using the discount factor under the ten percent column (.90909). The result is $2,000 × .90909, or $1818.18. If the jury gives Kepler this amount, and he earns the ten percent rate, he will have $2,000 at the end of the year to pay for his first year of therapy.

The second year's figure can't be calculated in a single step, because the interest rate is different in the second year. Here's my common sense approach to calculating the award for the 1996 therapy cost. At the end of 1995, Kepler will need an amount that, earning interest at eight percent, will grow to $2,000 a year later, at the end of 1996. That amount is $2,000 discounted for one year at eight percent, (2,000 × .92592), or $1,851.84. To get the present value of the $1851.84 he will need at the end of 1995, discount $1851.84 by the ten percent factor in the table (since Kepler will earn interest at this rate during the first year). This yields (1,851.84 × .90909) or $1,683.49. Just to confirm that this works, let's work it forward:

Jan. 1994:	Receives $1,683.49
Jan. 1995:	Has $1683.49 + (.10 × 1683.49) =
	$1683.49 + 168.35 = 1851.84
Jan 1996:	Has $1851.84 + (.08 × 1851.84) =
	$1851.84 + $148.15 = $1999.99

So the jury should award Kepler $1,818.18 for the first year's therapy and $1,683.49 for the second year, a total of $3,501.67 for the two years' expenses.[10]

Hurrah! After a frustrating half-hour with the calculator, I managed to make this very simple example come out right. But imagine 12 ordinary citizens from all walks of life trying to do it for a 25 year period with five different interest rates! Naturally, they will have the good sense not to do that: They will make a rough judgment of the average rate of interest over the entire period and apply the discount table to calculate the approximate

---

10. Even this calculation, of course, is approximate: It assumes that Jones will need $2,000 at the *end* of each period, rather than dispersing it gradually over the year, as is more likely.

future loss. That is all that we can expect them to do, and we'll be lucky if they manage that.

Inflated Expectations

3a. Under the total offset approach, the jury would determine Hubble's wage loss in current dollars for the five years and add the figures together to reach the award. If they determined that Hubble's wages would not increase due to merit raises or promotions, they would simply award $50,000, five times her current yearly wage.

Even using the offset approach, the figures for the future years may vary. The jury might find that Hubble would receive raises *above* inflation, due to the quality of her work, experience, or productivity increases in the industry. And, of course, if she were promoted to a higher paying position, they would award higher sums for the years in the new job. But in either case, they can ignore the confusing inflation and present value adjustments and focus on "real" increases in her compensation.

While the total offset method is simple, its simplicity may be at too great a cost. Since history teaches that interest rates typically outpace inflation, isn't the method automatically inaccurate? Not necessarily; history also teaches that worker productivity tends to rise over time, and that such increases will push up wages over and above inflationary increases. In fact, such productivity increases may well average roughly two percent per year. J. Jensen, The Offset Method of Determining Economic Loss, Trial Magazine, Dec. 1983, at 86. If this factor is added to the four percent inflation adjustment in the example, it would bring it up to six, which roughly equals the interest or discount rate. So the total offset method may be accurate enough in most cases.[11]

b. Under this approach, the jury calculates the inflation-adjusted wages for the future years, and then discounts each sum to present value. Table 13-6 indicates that Hubble's wages for the years 1995-1999 would be $10,400, $10,816, $11,249, $11,699 and $12,167, assuming four percent inflation. Each of these figures must be discounted separately, since each will be received at a different time. Here are the calculations, using the six percent discount column from Table 13-4:

For 1995:	$10,400 × .94340	=	$9811.36
For 1996:	$10,816 × .89000	=	$9626.24
For 1997:	$11,249 × .83962	=	$9444.89
For 1998:	$11,699 × .79209	=	$9266.66
For 1999:	$12,167 × .74726	=	$9091.91
		Total:	$47,241.06

---

11. Obviously, however, if the rationale for the method is that productivity increases balance the "real interest rate," the jury should be instructed not to make any separate adjustment for worker productivity increases in determining the plaintiff's future wages.

Note that these figures do not account for such factors as merit raises, promotions, or productivity increases within the industry. But there is nothing to prevent the jury from *further* fine-tuning the analysis by adjusting the future wages for these as well. If they do, the predicted future wage, increased for inflation and the other factors, would then be discounted to present value.

c. Under the "real interest rate" method, the jury calculates the future wages in terms of current dollars, and uses a discount rate based on the difference between inflation and interest rates. In our case, that difference is two percent. The jury would award Hubble's current wage figure, $10,000, for each of the five years, (again, assuming they did not find that she would receive promotions, merit raises, or productivity increases). This figure would be discounted using the two percent column on the present value table (Table 13-4). Again, this must be done separately for each year (unless you use a table like Table 13-7, which does it for you). Here are my results:

For 1995:	$10,000 × .98039	=	$9803.90
For 1996:	$10,000 × .96116	=	$9611.60
For 1997:	$10,000 × .94232	=	$9423.20
For 1998:	$10,000 × .92384	=	$9238.40
For 1999:	$10,000 × .90573	=	$9057.30
		Total:	$47,134.40

The present value under this approach is quite close to the result under the second approach.

The real interest rate approach has more to recommend it than just simplicity. Under this approach, the jury *need not forecast the actual rates of inflation and interest for any future period*: All they have to do is predict the average differential between the two over the period in question. Particularly in recent decades, both inflation and interest rates have varied widely, making it hard to predict them accurately. (What jury, for example, at the end of the high interest rate period of the late 1970s, would have predicted the very low rates of the early 1990s?) But the relationship between inflation and interest rates has remained more stable. Thus, the real interest rate method may provide a shortcut to a fairly reliable inflation adjustment. It will be especially helpful if the parties can agree on a rate before trial, and stipulate that the judge can make the present value calculations using raw figures reached by the jury, thus avoiding the necessity of explaining this whole problem to the jury.

4a. Inflation will affect the actual dollars Kepler will need to pay his future therapy bills, just as it affects the actual dollars Hubble would have received had she continued to work. In a jurisdiction that considers inflation in calculating future wages, it would be hard to justify ignoring it in calculating future expenses as well.

b. Kepler's counsel should argue that the general four percent inflation rate is not the relevant figure for estimating Kepler's future medical expenses: The jury should consider the rate of inflation for *medical care* instead. It is a matter of common knowledge that those expenses have risen at a far higher rate than expenses in general in recent decades. To fairly compensate Kepler, this more specific inflation rate should be used. See, e.g., *Muenstermann by Muenstermann v. United States*, 787 F. Supp. 499, 524-525 (D. Md. 1992), in which the inflation rate applicable to medical expenses was considered separately.

On the other hand, evidence might show (I really don't know whether it would or not) that much of the inflation increase in the medical area comes from new, expensive equipment and state-of-the-art diagnostic and operative procedures irrelevant to Kepler's treatment. It may be that inflation for *physical therapy* has been much more restrained. If the plaintiff is allowed to produce evidence of rates for medical care, the defendant may justifiably argue for an even more specific focus on the exact type of care Kepler will need. Certainly, this will fine tune the analysis, but it will also increase the complexity of the evidence, the expense to the parties for experts, and the burden on the courts. It is understandable that courts may resist such fine-tuning.

An Interim Question

5. The instruction is virtually always requested by defendants. They reason that, if the jury is not told that the plaintiff gets the full award, the jurors may assume that it will be taxed to the plaintiff when received. If they do, they may calculate the damages and then *increase* the amount to make sure that the plaintiff gets the amount they intended *after taxes*.

For example, if the jury concludes that Hubble has lost $47,000 in future wages, and they anticipate that she will pay about 30 percent of the award to the government, they might increase their award to assure that she will get $47,000 after taxes. Thus, they might award her $67,142 on the theory that, if she receives this much and pays 30 percent of it in taxes, she would actually end up with $47,000. If the jury did this, Hubble would end up with an extra $20,000 (paid, of course, by the defendant) since the award is not taxed as income. To avoid this scenario, the defendant would like the jury to understand during their deliberations that the plaintiff will receive the whole award free of tax.

Taxing the Patience of the Jury

6a. If inflation is not considered, the jury would presumably determine the percentage of the plaintiff's future earnings that would go to taxes, and reduce each future year's income by that percentage. If they concluded that Hubble would pay 30 percent in taxes, they would award her $7,000 for each year, and discount each year's projected income using the 6 percent figures in the present value table.[12] Here are the figures:

---

12. The same result can be reached by calculating present value without considering taxes, and then reducing that figure by 30 percent.

Wages for 1995	$7,000 × .94340	=	$6,603.80
Wages for 1996	$7,000 × .89000	=	$6,230.00
Wages for 1997	$7,000 × .83962	=	$5,877.34
Wages for 1998	$7,000 × .79209	=	$5,544.63
Wages for 1999	$7,000 × .74726	=	$5,230.82
		Total:	$29,486.59

b. Under the total offset method, the future damages for each year would be reduced to $7,000 to account for taxes, but these numbers would not be adjusted for inflation or discounted to present value. Hubble would receive $35,000 (5 × $7,000) for her future lost wages.

c. Presumably the jury would calculate the future wages for each year, with an upward adjustment for inflation, and then reduce each figure for taxes. The inflation-adjusted wages would be the same as those in Example 3, but they would be reduced by 30 percent for taxes before discounting at six percent:

Tax adjustment:

For 1995:	$10,400	× .7	=	$7,280.00
For 1996:	$10,816	× .7	=	$7,571.20
For 1997:	$11,249	× .7	=	$7,874.30
For 1998:	$11,699	× .7	=	$8,189.30
For 1999:	$12,167	× .7	=	$8,516.90

Discounting:

For 1995:	$7,280.00 × .94340	=	$6,867.95
For 1996:	$7,571.20 × .89000	=	$6,738.37
For 1997:	$7,874.30 × .83962	=	$6,611.42
For 1998:	$8,189.30 × .79209	=	$6,486.66
For 1999:	$8,516.90 × .74726	=	$6,364.34
		Total:	$33,068.74

d. It is not clear how the jury should make the calculation under the real market interest rate method. They will not actually calculate the future, inflation-adjusted wages, so they cannot make the tax adjustment the way we did just above in Example 6c. I suppose they would reduce the *unadjusted* future wage losses for taxes, as we did in Example 6a, and then discount the reduced wage figures using the two percent column in Table 13-4. That approach again yields a figure close to the market interest rate approach:

Wages for 1995	$7,000 × .98039	=	$6,862.73
Wages for 1996	$7,000 × .96116	=	$6,728.12
Wages for 1997	$7,000 × .94232	=	$6,596.24
Wages for 1998	$7,000 × .92384	=	$6,466.88
Wages for 1999	$7,000 × .90573	=	$6,340.11
		Total:	$32,994.08

Not surprisingly, the award under each of these approaches is substantially below the awards in Example 3, which ignored the effect of taxes on the same future lost wages.

7. The calculations above do not consider the fact that Hubble will pay taxes on *the income* from the award she receives. This is different from a tax on the award itself. To take a simple example, consider Table 13-5, on p.268 above. As that table shows, to provide Hubble with $10,000 in 1999, the jury should give her $6,805.80 in 1994 (assuming an eight percent interest rate). Under §104(a)(2) of the Internal Revenue Code, Hubble will not pay any tax on the $6805.80 when she receives it. However, she *will* pay taxes on the interest she subsequently earns on that sum. Because this is true, her $6805.80 will not actually grow to $10,000 in 1999; it will be substantially less. Here is a simplified illustration of the point, assuming that Hubble pays 30 percent in taxes on the yearly interest income from her award:

Table 13-8

Jan 1994	Receives $6,805.80		
Jan 1995	Has $6,805.80 + (.70 × $544.46)		
	= $6,805.80 + $381.12	=	$7,186.92
Jan 1996	Has $7,186.92 + (.70 × $574.95)		
	= $7,186.92 + 402.47	=	$7,589.09
Jan 1997	Has $7,589.09 + (.70 × $607.13)		
	= $7,589.09 + 424.99	=	$8,014.08
Jan 1998	Has $8,014.08 + (.70 × $641.13)		
	= $8,014.08 + $448.79	=	$8,462.87
Jan 1999	Has $8,462.87 + (.70 × 677.03)		
	= $8,462.87 + 473.92	=	$8936.62

As Table 13-8 shows, Hubble would actually have over $1000 less than the projected $10,000 in 1999. It may be fair enough to disregard this point if taxes on her future earnings are not considered, but once the jury is required to adjust the award *downward* for taxes on the future earnings, they should in fairness be required to adjust the award *upward* as well to compensate for the taxes she will pay on the interest on her award.[13]

Remarkably, in cases of long-term future losses, the taxes on the interest income from the award may actually exceed the taxes that would have been payable on the future wages themselves, so that the plaintiff does *better* if

---

13. One method of accounting for taxes on the interest income is to reduce the discount rate by the same percentage as the future wages. See P. Bradford, Measuring Tort Damages for Loss of Earnings Without Deducting Income Taxes: A Wisconsin Rule Which Lost Its Rationale, 70 Marquette L. Rev. 210, 234 n.91 (1987). For example, if the discount rate is six percent, and the tax rate used in calculating the future wages is 30 percent, reduce the six percent by 30 percent (.06 × .70 = .042 or 4.2 percent). Use the 4.2 percent figure instead of six percent in discounting to present value.

the jury is instructed to consider taxes in assessing the lost wages. S. LaCroix and H. Miller, Jr., Lost Earnings Calculations and Tort Law: Reflections on the *Pfeifer* Decision, 8 U. Haw. L. Rev. 31, 44-45 (1986). This will only be true, however, if the jury considers both the taxes that would have been paid on the future wages and the taxes paid on interest income on the award.

8.   Here is an instruction summarizing the necessary calculations that the court quoted with approval in *J.F.P. Offshore, Inc. v. Diamond*, 600 So. 2d 1002, 1005 (Ala. 1992):

> If you should find that the Plaintiff has proved a loss of future earnings, any amount you award for that loss must be reduced to present value. This must be done in order to take into account the fact that the award will be paid now, and the Plaintiff will have the use of that money now and in the near future, even though the total loss will not be sustained until later in the future.
>
> In order to make a reasonable adjustment for the present use of money representing a lump-sum payment of anticipated future loss, you must apply what is called a below-market discount rate.
>
> In making that calculation you should first determine the net, after-tax income the Plaintiff would have received during the remainder of his working life, including any increases he would have received as a result of any factors other than inflation. This future income stream must then be discounted or reduced by applying a below-market discount rate which represents the estimated market interest rate the award could be expected to earn over the period of the loss (adjusted for the effect of any income tax on the interest so earned), and then reduced by the estimated rate of future price inflation.

If you read this instruction carefully, in light of the discussion in the chapter, you will see that it mandates (1) reduction to present value, (2) consideration of taxes which would have been paid on future wages, (3) consideration of the taxes to be paid on interest on the award, and (4) use of the real interest rate approach to present value calculations. While all that is in the instruction, I wouldn't bet the ranch that the instruction is sufficient to *educate* a jury as to how to cope with the complexities addressed in this chapter. Perhaps the testimony of the parties' experts will help, but even this is doubtful; they will be more interested in their "bottom line" figures than explaining to the jury how they were reached.

Judge Fudd Befuddled

9.   The defendant may have a point here. If the jury makes an award for future pain and suffering, that award will be for future damages. Shouldn't those damages be discounted to account for the time value of money, just as damages for future lost wages or medical expenses are?

While the argument has logical appeal, most courts conclude that the jury awards a general figure for the various intangible losses grouped under the rubric of "pain and suffering," rather than calculating discrete amounts for future intangible losses on a year-by-year basis. L. de Jong, Comment, 19 Rutgers L. J. 1119, 1123 (1988). Thus, it would be inappropriate to make actuarial adjustments to it similar to those for economic losses. In effect, most courts acknowledge that the number is so approximate that it would be specious to use that number as the basis for inflation or present value adjustments. Consequently, in assessing pain and suffering, they generally refuse to wade into the quicksands we have explored in this chapter.

14

Compensating Somebody: Wrongful Death and Survival Actions

Introduction

We think of "the olden days" as full of dangers, and thank our stars that we live in a "civilized" era. But no one can emerge from the course in Torts without a sobering sense of how dangerous industrialized society is. A few generations back, the major risks were natural ones: disease, natural disasters, and unruly fellow creatures. Today, these have been surpassed by human contrivances, especially that very mixed blessing, the internal combustion engine.

Too often, the machines we make cause catastrophic injury and untimely death. This chapter addresses two distinct but related types of claims arising from such deaths. First is the *wrongful death* claim, which is a claim for damages for tortiously causing the death of another. Second is the *survival* claim, which is an action brought by the representative of the estate of a deceased person (called in legal parlance a "decedent") for injuries suffered by the decedent before her death.

Although these actions both arise because of the death of the tort victim, they are quite different. Wrongful death statutes usually allow damages for the losses suffered by surviving relatives, such as the loss of economic support or society of the decedent. The survival action, by contrast, allows the estate of a decedent to enforce a tort claim for damages suffered by the decedent *before* death, which she could have enforced personally had she lived.

Suppose, for example, that Mozart and Haydn are listening to a symphony at the local concert hall when a chandelier, negligently installed by Handel, falls from the ceiling. Mozart is killed instantly. Haydn suffers serious injuries, is hospitalized for seven months, and finally dies of his injuries. At common law, the estates of these decedents would have had no remedies for their injuries, regardless of whether they were negligently inflicted. Under modern tort law, however, Mozart's death would give rise to a claim for wrongful death. Haydn's would support both a survival claim for his predeath losses (such as pain and suffering, medical expenses, and lost wages) and a wrongful death claim, since he ultimately died of his injuries.

The Action for Wrongful Death

Let's first consider the claim arising from Mozart's death. Mozart died instantly; his estate has no claim for predeath pain and suffering, hospital bills, or disability caused by the accident. The sole injury to be recompensed is the death itself. The issue raised is whether Mozart's estate or his surviving relatives have any claim against Handel for negligently causing his death.

Under the English common law, the answer for five or six centuries was "no." Lord Ellenborough put it clearly in *Baker v. Bolton*: "In a civil court, the death of a human being could not be complained of as an injury." 170 Eng. Rep. 1033 (1808). If the rule was clear, the reasons for it were less so. The scholars suggest that it was rooted in the early English "felony-merger doctrine," which barred civil suits to recover damages for acts that constituted a felony. Felonies were punishable by death and forfeiture of the felon's property to the crown. Since causing the death of another, either intentionally or negligently, was a felony, there would be no defendant left to sue for wrongful death, and no property from which to collect a judgment. See *Moragne v. States Marine Lines, Inc.*, 398 U.S. 375, 382 (1970). So there was no point to such a claim.

Other reasons for the common law position were grounded in policy rather than history. Some cases argued that allowing claims for wrongful death would lead to "runaway" damages from sympathetic juries, or that it is somehow immoral to put a price on human life. Last, the cases noted the obvious impossibility of compensating the decedent for the loss of life. S. Speiser, Recovery for Wrongful Death and Injury §1.4 (3d ed. 1992).

Whatever the rationale for the common law rule, the result was that "it was cheaper for the defendant to kill a person than to scratch him." Prosser & Keeton at 942. Prosser's treatise notes the wry suggestion that this rule explains "why passengers in Pullman car berths rode with their heads to the front" and that "the fire axes in railroad coaches were provided to enable the conductor to deal efficiently with those [sic] were merely injured." Prosser &

Keeton at 942, n.24. Such speculations make the point well enough: It is manifestly indefensible to allow recovery for personal injury, but bar recovery entirely where the victim suffers the ultimate injury, death.

Although it is easy to criticize the early common law rule, American courts initially followed it without question. In the American states, as in England, it has been the legislatures, not the courts, which have established the right to recover for wrongful death. England reversed course in 1846, when Lord Campbell's Act authorized a cause of action for wrongful death. Since that time, all American states have enacted statutes (often referred to as "Lord Campbell's Acts") that authorize recovery for wrongful death.

The Statutory Right to Sue

Because actions for wrongful death are based on statutes, they differ from state to state. However, many still track quite closely the language of Lord Campbell's Act. The North Dakota statute, for example, provides:

> Whenever the death of a person shall be caused by a wrongful act, neglect or default, and the act, neglect or default is such as would have entitled the party injured, if death had not ensued, to maintain an action and recover damages in respect thereof, then and in every such case the person who, or the corporation . . . or company which, would have been liable if death had not ensued, shall be liable to an action for damages, notwithstanding the death of the person injured . . . although the death shall have been caused under such circumstances as amount in law to felony.

N.D. Cent. Code. §32-21-01.[1] Statutes like this allow recovery for wrongful death if the decedent would have had a cause of action herself had she been injured instead of killed. Thus, an "action for wrongful death" is not a separate tort in itself, it is an action for a recognized tort — usually an intentional tort or negligence — in which the victim is killed rather than injured. In a wrongful death claim based on negligence, for example, the plaintiff must prove the same elements as in a personal injury negligence claim: duty, breach, causation, and damages. Harper, James & Gray, §24.3, at 465. The proof of the first three elements will be the same as in an injury case. The major difference between a wrongful death case and other negligence cases involves the last element, damages.

---

1. The North Dakota statute, in language taken verbatim from Lord Campbell's Act, makes the tortfeasor liable "although the death shall have been caused under such circumstances as amount in law to felony." Although the felony merger doctrine never applied in the American states, this irrelevant clause repudiating the doctrine was copied into many American wrongful death statutes. Therein lies a lesson in the realities — and the shortcomings — of legislative drafting.

Wrongful Death Damages:
Who Gets Compensated?

Damages in personal injury cases compensate the injured person herself for the losses resulting from the accident, such as a broken arm, a period of lost wages, or pain and suffering. Wrongful death statutes, however, do *not* compensate the decedent herself; it is obviously impossible to compensate the decedent for anything. The best the law can do is to compensate survivors who were close to the decedent for the losses *they* suffer as a result of the decedent's death. Thus, most wrongful death statutes authorize damages for the economic or emotional losses to the survivors of the decedent, not the loss suffered by the decedent herself.

Assessing the damages to the survivors raises two thorny questions: Which survivors, and for what losses? As to the first question, most wrongful death statutes limit the recovery to the losses suffered by close relatives as a result of the decedent's death. For example, the Virginia statute provided — until quite recently[2] — that the recovery is for the benefit of

> (i) the surviving spouse, children of the deceased and children of any deceased child of the deceased or (ii) if there be none such, then to the parents, brothers and sisters of the deceased . . . or (iii) if the decedent has left both surviving spouse and parent or parents, but no child or grandchild, the award shall be distributed to the surviving spouse and such parent or parents.

Va. Code §8.01-53 (1950). South Carolina's statute is a little different:

> Every such action shall be for the benefit of the wife or husband and child or children of the person whose death shall have been so caused, and, if there be no such wife, husband, child or children, then for the benefit of the parent or parents, and if there be none such, then for the benefit of the heirs at law of the person whose death shall have been so caused. . . .

S.C. Code §15-51-20 (1976).

Provisions of this type authorize damages to general classes of relatives likely to be closest to the decedent. If there are none in the closest class, the next group is considered, and so on. Like all efforts to deal generally with human relationships, these legislative classifications may miss the mark in particular cases. Mozart might be survived by a live-in lover to whom he was very close, and a son who had ignored him for 30 years. Under the Virginia statute, the son's losses would be the measure of damages. Or, Mozart might leave no close relatives. Surely, the gravity of his death is just as profound in such a case, but under the South Carolina statute the only loss to be compen-

---

2. The statute was amended in 1992. This is the pre-1992 version, used for illustration purposes. The current version is discussed in the analysis of Example 2.

sated in such a case would be the losses of remote heirs, who perhaps never saw or cared about Mozart and will consequently be unable to prove substantial damages. However, in most cases the beneficiaries named in the statutes — husbands and wives, children, parents and siblings — are the ones likely to suffer most from the death of the decedent.

Under many wrongful death statutes, the beneficiaries do not bring suit themselves. The executor or administrator of the estate is empowered to bring the action, but the damages are measured by the losses to the statutory beneficiaries and are distributed by the executor or administrator to them. Many statutes provide that the recovery does not become part of the decedent's estate. See, e.g., Code of Ala. Tit. 6-5-410(c) (1975 & Supp. 1993); R.I. G.L. 10-7-10 (1957 & Supp. 1993). The major consequence of this is that the recovery does not go to pay the decedent's creditors. Even if the victim dies in debt, the wrongful death damages will go to the survivors the action is meant to compensate, rather than to pay the decedent's debts.

More on Damages: What Losses Are Compensated?

The second thorny question is what losses of the survivors are compensable under wrongful death statutes. The death of a loved one entails many losses. Some are concrete and quantifiable, such as loss of financial support or household services rendered by the decedent. Others are intangible, such as the loss of companionship, sexual consortium, advice, and emotional support, the same types of losses which are compensated as "loss of consortium" when the victim survives. See Chapter 10. In addition to these long-term losses from the death of the decedent, the survivors also suffer tangible immediate losses (funeral and burial expenses) and intangible immediate losses (the grief and mental anguish of learning of the death).

Historically, many wrongful death statutes have limited damages to the "pecuniary losses" resulting to the specified survivors, that is, direct financial contributions or services the decedent would have rendered to the survivors. The New Jersey wrongful death statute, for example, provides that the jury may give damages for "the pecuniary injuries resulting from such death, together with the hospital, medical and funeral expenses incurred for the deceased. . . ." N.J. Stats. §2A:31-5 (1987). The reason for this limitation is historical: Although Lord Campbell's Act provided that the jury should award the statutory beneficiaries "such damages as they may think proportioned to the injury," the Act was early held to authorize only pecuniary damages. *Blake v. Midland Ry. Co.*, 118 Eng. Rep. 35 (1852). Many of the American statutes either explicitly incorporated the "pecuniary loss" measure of damages (as the New Jersey statute does) or were initially interpreted to authorize only such damages. Under such statutes, damages for intangible losses such as loss of the society, sexual relationship, or advice and counsel of the decedent are theoretically barred.

Unless the decedent leaves a dependent spouse or children, the "pecuniary loss" standard, strictly construed to include only economic contributions the decedent would have made to the beneficiaries, is highly restrictive. In many cases, actual pecuniary losses in the nature of lost financial contributions from the decedent will be impossible to prove. If Mozart is survived by his parents only, who are financially secure, there would likely be no compensable damages under a strict "pecuniary loss" standard, and hence no recovery other than funeral and burial expenses. The same may be true if he is survived by adult children or siblings who are financially independent.[3] And, of course, the standard — if literally applied — provides no recovery for the primary loss the survivors suffer: the loss of the opportunity to be with, learn from, and receive solace and emotional support from the decedent.

The inadequacy of the pecuniary loss standard is most glaring when the decedent is a young child. In such cases, the emotional loss to the parents is frightful, yet there is seldom evidence or likelihood of actual financial loss to the survivors. Such compelling cases have led many courts to evade the strictures of the pecuniary loss standard by tortured interpretation. In *Green v. Bittner*, 424 A.2d 210 (N.J. 1980), for example, the New Jersey Supreme Court allowed recovery under a "pecuniary loss" standard for the pecuniary value of the companionship and advice a daughter would have provided to her parents as they grew older. See also *Clymer v. Webster*, 596 A.2d 905, 914 (Vt. 1991) (loss of comfort and companionship of adult child "is a real, direct and personal loss that can be measured in pecuniary terms.") See generally, A. Lehrbaum-Weiss, Note, Bullard v. Barnes — Parental Recovery for Lost Society and Companionship of a Minor Child Under the Illinois Wrongful Death Act, 34 DePaul L. Rev. 803 (1985).

Clearly, cases like *Green* and *Clymer* have stretched the concept of pecuniary loss far beyond its ordinary meaning, in order to allow substantial damages in cases in which the survivors suffer little financial loss but great emotional loss as a result of the death. This parallels the modern trend to allow recovery for loss of consortium in injury cases, at least to the spouse of the direct victim, and sometimes to her children or parents. It hardly makes sense to allow consortium recovery for *impairment* of these relationships when the direct victim is injured, but to deny recovery for similar losses (by strict

---

3. Some states interpret their wrongful death statutes to allow recovery for loss of inheritance. See Minzer, Nates §22.20-22.22. This would allow some recovery for pecuniary loss even if the decedent was making no contributions to the statutory beneficiaries before he died. Presumably, the plaintiff would still have to show that the beneficiary would have inherited the decedent's estate, *and* that he or she was in the class of beneficiaries eligible to take under the wrongful death statute.

interpretation of the term "pecuniary loss") when the relationship is completely *destroyed* because the direct victim is killed.

Some legislatures have responded to this incongruity by amending their statutes to provide that the term "pecuniary loss" *includes* such elements as loss of companionship or mental anguish. See, e.g., Ark. Stats. 16-62-102(f) (1987) (including spouse's loss of services and companionship as pecuniary loss). Others have simply amended their wrongful death statutes to authorize recovery for intangible damages *as well as* more typical pecuniary losses such as financial contributions and services by the decedent. The Kansas statute, for example, provides in part:

> (a) Damages may be recovered for, but are not limited to:
>   (1) Mental anguish, suffering or bereavement;
>   (2) loss of society, companionship, comfort or protection;
>   (3) loss of marital care, attention, advice or counsel;
>   (4) loss of filial care or attention;
>   (5) loss of parental care, training, guidance or
>   education; and
>   (6) reasonable funeral expenses for the deceased.

Kan. St. Ann. §60-1904 (1993). This statute clearly allows recovery for many types of intangible emotional losses due to the loss of the decedent. It even allows damages for grief itself, which is usually barred in actions for loss of consortium (see Chapter 10) and is barred under many wrongful death statutes as well. However, a separate section of the Kansas statute tempers the liberality of this damages provision by limiting the nonpecuniary damages to $100,000. Kan. St. Ann §60-1903(a) (1993). Other statutes, however, authorize unlimited damages for pecuniary and consortium damages alike. The Hawaii statute, for example, provides that:

> such damages may be given as under the circumstances shall be deemed fair and just compensation, with reference to the pecuniary injury and loss of love and affection, including (1) loss of society, companionship, comfort, consortium, or protection, (2) loss of marital care, attention, advice or counsel, (3) loss of filial care or attention, or (4) loss of parental care, training, guidance or education, suffered as a result of the death. . . .

Haw. Rev. Stat. §663-3 (1988). Some also authorize punitive damages for wilful or grossly negligent conduct. See, e.g., Tex. Civ. Proc. §71.009 (1986).

An Alternative Approach

A few states take a different approach to wrongful death damages, focusing on the loss to the decedent's *estate* from his premature death. See e.g., N.H. Rev. Stat. Ann. §556.12 (1974), which allows the jury to consider (as to damages caused by the death itself) "the reasonable expenses occasioned to his estate by the injury, the probable duration of his life but for the injury, and his capacity to earn money during his probable working life." Under statutes of this type, damages are frequently measured by calculating the decedent's future earnings, subtracting the amount the decedent would have spent on living expenses, and reducing the net figure to "present value." (See Chapter 13 for a discussion of present value.) The rationale for this measure is that the decedent's net earnings would have gone either to support her family while she was alive or into her estate and been distributed to her heirs or legatees after death.

The loss-to-the-estate rule provides a purely economic measure of damages, and shares some of the problems of the strict pecuniary loss rule. The loss-to-the-estate formula might not support any damages for the death of a retired person who lives on her current income. Similarly, there would be no loss to the estate of even a young person whose earnings did not exceed her living expenses. See F. McChesney, Problems in Calculating and Awarding Compensatory Damages For Wrongful Death Under the Federal Tort Claims Act, 36 Emory L.J. 149, 162-164 (1987) (concluding that persons with incomes below $20,000 in 1980-1981 dollars are unable to save at all). It seems likely that in many cases where strict application of the loss-to-the-estate standard or pecuniary loss standard would lead to no recovery, juries have ignored such instructions on the measure of damages and assessed a reasonable figure according to their own sense of justice.

Damages for Loss of Life Itself

In one sense, Lord Ellenborough's pronouncement that "the death of a human being could not be complained of as an injury" remains true. Although the loss of life itself is perhaps the most grievous loss imaginable, most wrongful death statutes do not authorize damages for the years of living that the decedent would have enjoyed but for the wrongful death. Some of the economic value of these lost years is compensated, under either the loss-to-survivors approach or the loss-to-the-estate approach, since damages are awarded for lost earnings that would have gone to the decedent's survivors. However, the most basic loss of the *experience* of living, the opportunity to enjoy life in all its richness, is not.

As stated earlier, the loss of life itself was viewed as beyond compensation, since the decedent obviously cannot benefit from any compensation awarded; any award for these lost years would simply be a windfall to her survivors. In addition, courts and legislatures have doubtless feared that, if juries were allowed to award damages for the decedent's lost years, verdicts would be too speculative and difficult to control. Thus, wrongful death statutes have focused on the damages to the survivors or the estate as both more certain and more obviously compensatory.

This problem of the "lost years" also arises when a tort victim suffers an injury that reduces her life expectancy. Plaintiffs have argued that they should recover damages for the years of life they are likely to lose as a result of the injury, that is, the difference between their pre-injury and post-injury life expectancy. Most American courts have refused to allow damages for the shortening of life itself. See Minzer, Nates §8.39. The English rule, however, is apparently to the contrary (see *Flint v. Lovell*, 1 Kings Bench 354 (1935), suggesting that it is possible to measure damages for the lost years) and a few American cases have allowed such damages. One state, Connecticut, now appears to interpret its wrongful death statute to allow the jury to consider the decedent's loss of the enjoyment of those years in assessing wrongful death damages. See Speiser, §3.2, at 27 n.41 (reviewing Connecticut cases).

Survival Statutes: Preserving Claims for Pre-Death Damages

So much for the erstwhile Mozart; now let's consider Haydn's case. He also died as a result of Handel's negligent act. Consequently his estate or survivors will have a cause of action for wrongful death. But he suffered other injuries as well from Handel's negligence: He lingered for seven months, suffered pain and suffering, and was out of work and unable to enjoy his usual activities. Had he recovered at the end of those seven months, instead of dying, he would have had a right to sue for these losses. Shouldn't his estate be able to sue for these pre-death damages, even though he died?

The common law took a hard line on these cases as well. Tort cases were classified as "personal" actions, and under the common law personal actions could only be prosecuted by the injured person herself. Speiser, §14.1.[4] Haydn could sue for his injuries while alive, but no one else could do it for him. If he died before bringing suit, the estate had no right to pursue the claim. If he brought suit but died before the suit went to judgment, most courts held that the action "abated" and could not be prosecuted further. 1 Am. Jur. 2d Abatement, Survival, and Revival, §43. The principle applied to the defendant as well. A tort action had to be brought against her personally; if she died before suit was brought, the plaintiff could not sue her estate.

This hoary common law principle, like the bar on recovery for wrongful death itself, has been supplanted by statute. Most states now have "survival"

---

4. Like so many issues, the common law dealt with this one by throwing a little legal Latin at it: "actio personalis moritur cum persona," translated, "a personal action dies with the person." Speiser at §14.1, p.2 n.1.

statutes, which provide that causes of action "survive" rather than abating at the death of either the tortfeasor or the injured party. Note that it is the *claim itself* that survives, not the plaintiff or defendant: The very point of a survival statute is that the party need not survive for suit to be brought. Typically, where the injured party dies, the statute authorizes the decedent's executor or administrator to bring suit (or continue one already in progress) to recover for the decedent's injuries. While the statutes vary, the Maine survival provision is simple and representative:

> No personal action or cause of action shall be lost by the death of either party, but the same shall survive for and against the executor or administrator of the deceased.

Me. Probate Code Tit. 18-A §3-817(a) (1981). Under a provision such as this, Haydn's estate could still recover for Haydn's predeath injuries, whether or not suit had been brought before Haydn died. If Haydn had not brought suit before his death, the executor or administrator of his estate could file suit. If Haydn had sued but died before the case was decided, his executor or administrator would be substituted as the plaintiff and continue the litigation.

The rationale for allowing causes of action to survive where the tort victim dies is not far to seek. Although a survival action, like a wrongful death action, cannot compensate the decedent, the recovery usually goes into the decedent's estate and passes to her heirs. Though the decedent takes no direct benefit from the action, she may at least take solace before death in the knowledge that *somebody* will be compensated for the tort, and that those somebodies will be of her choosing. In addition, there is an obvious anomaly between allowing recovery if a tort suit goes to judgment a day before the victim dies, but not if judgment is entered the day after.

The rationale for allowing survival of actions where the tortfeasor dies is also evident. The plaintiff is as much in need of compensation whether the defendant lives or dies. If the defendant leaves substantial assets, it seems reasonable that they should go to compensate the victim. In addition, in many cases the decedent's insurer is effectively the defendant, since it will defend the action and pay any damages awarded. It seems inappropriate that the insurer should get a windfall and the injured person go uncompensated if the negligent person fortuitously dies before recovery is awarded.

Although often associated with wrongful death statutes, survival statutes do not apply only in cases where the defendant's negligence causes death. Under a statute like Maine's, Haydn's damage claim survives whether he dies of the injuries suffered in the accident or of unrelated causes. Similarly, his claim would survive if Handel died from the accident or any other cause. Handel's administrator or executor would simply be substituted as the defendant in the action.

The following examples illustrate the operation of wrongful death and survival statutes. For an example of a complaint asserting both survival and wrongful death claims, see Chapter 15, p.321.

EXAMPLES
Laws of Relativity

1.   Purcell is run down and killed instantly. He is survived by his parents, whom he has not seen for 30 years, and a disabled sister, for whom he is the sole source of support.
> a. Who would be entitled to damages under the Virginia statute quoted at p.288?
> b. Who would be entitled to damages under the South Carolina statute quoted at p.288?

2.   Assume that Purcell is survived by an adult son, his disabled sister, and his elderly parents, with whom he has a close relationship. Who would be entitled to damages for his death under the version of the Virginia statute quoted at p.288?

3.   Assume the same facts given in Example 2, but that the case arose under the Hawaii statute, which authorizes damages for both pecuniary and intangible damages "suffered as a result of the death of the person by the surviving spouse, children, father, mother, and by any person wholly or partly dependent upon the deceased person." Haw. Stats. §663-3. Who will recover, and how will the damages for each beneficiary be ascertained?

4.   What will be the result under the South Carolina statute if Purcell dies without leaving any close relatives?

5.   Brahms, a highly successful musician, dies leaving an adult daughter with a large income, a seven-year-old son, a wife who does not work outside the home, and an elderly mother whom he frequently helps out financially. What damages could each recover if the Virginia beneficiary provision quoted at p.288 applied and
> a. the measure of damages was limited to pecuniary loss, strictly construed?
> b. the applicable measure of damage was the same as the Kansas statute quoted at p.291?
> c. the "loss to the estate" measure of damages applied?

"The Lawsuit was a Success but The Plaintiff Died"

6.   Verdi and Vivaldi are seriously injured when Strauss drops a tuba from a scaffold above the stage. Verdi survives for a year in constant pain and is unable to work. He then dies of his injuries. Vivaldi suffers a broken arm, is out of work for three months, and suffers permanent reduction of function in the arm.

    a. What causes of action would Verdi and Vivaldi have against Strauss at common law?

    b. If the Maine survival statute quoted at p.294 applied, what damages could Verdi's estate recover in the survival action?

    c. If Verdi's executor sought damages under the survival statute, could he also sue for wrongful death?

7.   Assume that Verdi suffers a broken hip from the accident and is laid up in bed. Six months later, he dies of throat cancer, without having brought any suit against Strauss. What actions may his executor or administrator bring against Strauss, if any?

Consorting With Confusion

8.   On the facts in Example 7, could Jane Verdi, his widow, bring an action against Strauss for loss of consortium under the survival statute?

9.   Assume that Verdi dies instantly when the tuba falls on him, leaving his widow, Jane, who is appointed administratrix of his estate. Six months later, before suit is brought against him, Strauss dies.

    a. What statute is implicated here, the wrongful death statute or the survival statute?

    b. Assume that Verdi dies instantly, and that Jane is appointed administratrix of his estate. Assume further that the applicable wrongful death statute only authorizes recovery for pecuniary loss and is strictly construed to encompass solely economic losses. Her complaint includes a count for wrongful death, and a second count for loss of consortium with her husband. What is the problem here?

    c. Assume that Jane, still hoping to recover for consortium losses due to her husband's death, adds a third count in her complaint, asserting a "claim for negligence" and asking for consortium damages on that claim. What is the problem with this count?

Double Indemnity?

10. Mendelssohn is seriously injured when Brahms inadvertently knocks him off the stage while conducting. While incapacitated, he sues Strauss and recovers $130,000 in damages for his lost wages, medical bills, and pain and suffering. Ten months later, he dies of his injuries.

    a. Was Mendelsssohn's suit a survival action?

    b. May his executor bring suit for wrongful death?

Judge Fudd on an Off Day

11. Mendelssohn dies immediately from his fall, and his estate sues Brahms for wrongful death. Brahms pleads as a defense that Mendelssohn was contributorily negligent for standing behind Brahms at the edge of the stage during

the crescendo. Assume that contributory negligence is a complete defense to a negligence action in the relevant jurisdiction. Assume also that the language of the applicable wrongful death statute is the same as the North Dakota wrongful death provision quoted on p.287. At trial, the Honorable Fudd instructs the jury as follows:

> If you find by a preponderance of the evidence that the decedent was contributorily negligent, and that his negligence was a proximate cause of the accident which led to his death, then you must find for the defendant.

Is Fudd's instruction proper?

EXPLANATIONS

Laws of Relativity

1a. The Virginia statute allows recovery to siblings and parents if the decedent does not leave a spouse, child, or grandchild. That is true here, so both the sister and the parents are eligible to receive damages for the death. However, it appears unlikely that the parents will be able to prove substantial damages, since they have been cut off from Purcell for many years. Thus, if the damages are assessed to the sister and parents according to their actual losses, she will receive a substantial award and they will receive little or nothing.

b. Under the South Carolina statute, the action is "for the benefit of the parent or parents" if there is no spouse or child. Thus, it appears that only they would be entitled to damages, while the sister, who suffered compelling losses, would not be entitled to recover.

2. In this example, Purcell is survived by a number of close relatives, all of whom may have suffered compensable losses, at least if the measure of damages includes consortium losses such as companionship, advice, and comfort. However, the version of the statute quoted on p.288 apparently limits the recovery to the son. He falls within the class of beneficiaries in clause (1) of the statute, and the statute apparently denies recovery to parents and siblings if there are clause (1) beneficiaries. See *Carroll v. Sneed*, 179 S.E.2d 620, 623 (Va. 1971) (suggesting that presence of a child precludes any recovery to parents under the Virginia statute).

Obviously, specifying classes of beneficiaries in this way can lead to pretty unsatisfactory results. Although it is likely in this case that the heaviest losses, both pecuniary and emotional, were suffered by the elderly parents and dependent sister, they would obtain no compensation, while the lesser losses of the son will be the sole measure of damages. One wonders if courts haven't found some way around such results, despite apparently clear statutory language. See Prosser & Keeton at 947 and accompanying notes (suggesting that some cases have winked at the statutory limits, but others have not.)

In 1992, the Virginia legislature amended its wrongful death statute to address this problem. The current version allows recovery for "any other relative who is primarily dependent on the decedent for support or services and is also a member of the same household as the decedent," even if there is a beneficiary in the primary class. Va. Code. §8.01-53, as amended by 1992 Va. Acts c. 74.[5] This provision would only help Purcell's sister, however, if she actually lived with him. Nor would it change the result as to Purcell's parents.

3.   The Hawaii statute avoids the problem illustrated in example 2, because it authorizes damages for close relatives who suffer loss from the decedent's death without setting priorities that exclude other beneficiaries. Thus, Purcell's son, parents, and sister would be entitled to recover. Presumably, their awards would depend on the actual pecuniary and consortium losses each proves at trial. If, for example, the son is estranged from the decedent, the jury would likely award him minimal damages, while the dependent sister's damages would presumably be very substantial.

This statute obviously provides greater flexibility in assessing wrongful death damages among the beneficiaries, but it is also quite open ended, leading to greater exposure. If the victim is Bach, who has 14 children, a close relationship to his parents, and several live-in siblings, the defendant may be hit with a very substantial verdict.

4.   The last clause of the South Carolina statute provides that, if there be no statutory beneficiaries, the recovery will go to those who inherit the decedent's estate. Thus, if Purcell leaves no close relatives, the wrongful death recovery will go into his estate and be distributed to his heirs, probably collateral relatives such as cousins, nieces and nephews, and aunts and uncles.

However, the damages assessed will still have to be based on actual damages suffered by these collateral relatives. The more distant these survivors are, the more difficult it will be for them to prove substantial damages — either economic or emotional — as a result of Purcell's death.

5a.   Under the Virginia beneficiaries provision, the wife and children would recover, but presumably the mother would not, since she is not in the first

---

5. The somewhat opaque current version of the beneficiary provision reads as follows:

> The damages awarded pursuant to §8.01-52 shall be distributed as specified under §8.01-54 to (i) the surviving spouse, children of the deceased and children of any deceased child of the deceased or (ii) if there be none such, then to the parents, brothers and sisters of the deceased, and to any other relative who is primarily dependent on the decedent for support or services and is also a member of the same household as the decedent or (iii) if the decedent has left both surviving spouse and parent or parents, but no child or grandchild, the award shall be distributed to the surviving spouse and such parent or parents or (iv) if there are survivors under clause (i) or clause (iii), the award shall be distributed to those beneficiaries and to any other relative who is primarily dependent on the decedent for support or services and is also a member of the same household as the decedent.

Va. Code §801-53 (1950 & Supp. 1994) (as amended by 1992 Va. Acts c.74).

class of beneficiaries.[6] Under a strict pecuniary loss standard, the wife and children would recover damages for the lost financial contributions and household services Brahms would have rendered to them. As to the adult daughter, this is likely to be small, but it will clearly be substantial as to the wife and son, who were entirely dependent on Brahms for support.

It should include, for example, the cost of maintaining the son for 12 years at home, and quite likely four more years of college. If the evidence supports it, the damages might also include four more years in medical school or seven studying mathematical linguistics in graduate school. There might also be proof that Brahms would have made monetary gifts to his children over the years, for tax reasons or maybe even out of the goodness of his heart. (Some people still think that a sufficient reason, regardless of the accounting consequences.) The wife's damages might include the cost of her support for the balance of her life expectancy, and perhaps the loss of the inheritance she would have received had Brahms accumulated a substantial estate and predeceased her. Funeral and burial expenses would also be recoverable under a pecuniary loss standard.

b. If the Kansas damages provision applied, the beneficiaries would recover fully for the pecuniary losses discussed above, and up to $100,000 dollars for grief, mental anguish, and consortium losses of the wife, daughter, and son.

An interesting question is how the $100,000 allowed for consortium damages under the Kansas statute would be allocated, if the intangible damages exceed that amount. Presumably, the options would be proportional to the actual damages, or pro rata (equal shares). Suppose, for example, that the jury came back with $300,000 in consortium losses for the wife, $200,000 for the son, and $100,000 for the daughter. Under a proportional approach to distributing the $100,000 recovery, the mother would get $50,000 ($300,000/600,000ths), the son $33,333 (200,000/600,000ths), and the daughter $16,667 (100,000/600,000ths). Under a pro rata approach, each would get $33,333.33.

In a jurisdiction that authorized unlimited recovery for consortium losses, the eligible beneficiaries would all be entitled to full recovery for the loss of society, care, counsel, and guidance that they suffered due to Brahms's death, in addition to proven pecuniary loss. However, if the Virginia provision limiting beneficiaries applied, the mother would not recover anything for economic or consortium losses, since she is not within the first tier of beneficiaries.

c. Under the loss-to-the-estate theory, the damages are often calculated by determining how much the decedent would have earned, subtracting how

---

6. The amended version of the statute (see n.5) would not allow the mother to recover either, unless she lived with Brahms.

much he would have spent on his own maintenance, and then discounting the net figure to present value. This figure represents the excess income the decedent could have contributed to his survivors or left to them in his estate. Obviously, this measure provides nothing for consortium losses, and will probably not support any recovery at all if the decedent had little income.

Under some statutes, the loss to the estate is measured by the probable financial accumulation that would have gone into the decedent's estate had he lived a normal life span. Speiser, §3.2. This differs from the net earnings approach, because it asks what the decedent would have *saved* and passed to his heirs in his estate. Ironically, under this theory, the recovery would be smaller where the decedent leaves more dependent survivors. A single woman with a large income and no dependent relatives would presumably have accumulated a large estate. Ironically, if the same woman had six dependent children, strict application of this future accumulation damage measure might yield no recovery, on the theory that all of her income would have gone for the support of her family and she would have accumulated little in her estate.

The analysis here must go one step further, however, because the example asks how much *each* beneficiary would receive. In a jurisdiction that uses the loss-to-the-estate measure of damages, the *estate* will recover the decedent's lost net income or future accumulations. But how will the recovery then be distributed to the actual beneficiaries? Here, for example, it is clear that the minor son has suffered a greater loss than the adult daughter. At least some loss-to-the-estate statutes provide that the proceeds of the wrongful death recovery shall be distributed as general assets of the estate. See, e.g., N.H. Rev. Stat. Ann. §556:14 (1974) (damages "shall become a part of the decedent's estate and be distributed in accordance with the applicable provisions of law"). Very likely, the statute of distribution would call for equal distribution to the two children in this case despite the difference in the losses they suffered as a result of the decedent's death.

"The Lawsuit Was A Success But The Plaintiff Died"

6a. This example illustrates the anomalous effects of the common law abatement rule. Under that rule Vivaldi would recover in full for his injuries, since he is personally able to bring this "personal" cause of action. At common law, however, Verdi's claim abated at his death unless he obtained judgment against Strauss before he died. His estate had no right to sue for his predeath losses, such as the pain and suffering, lost wages, and disability he experienced during the year before he died. Nor did Verdi's estate have a cause of action for wrongful death, since the common law barred wrongful death claims as well.

b. In Maine, as in virtually all states today, Verdi's claim would survive his death and could be enforced by the representative of his estate. But remember that the survival action is for Verdi's *predeath* losses from the tort.

It is not a claim for wrongful death, it is for the losses Verdi suffered before death that he could have recovered himself had he lived. Thus, his executor or administrator could recover for his predeath pain and suffering, lost wages, medical bills, and other compensable damages suffered during the year that he lingered.

c. Absolutely. The right to sue under the survival statute for losses suffered by the victim before death does not bar the right to sue for wrongful death. The two actions address distinct injuries, and often benefit different parties. The survival action compensates Verdi's estate for damages he suffered before death that he could have recovered himself if he had lived. The wrongful death action (in most jurisdictions) compensates the survivors for their losses as a result of the death.

7.   In this case, Verdi had a claim against Strauss for his injuries in the accident, but he died of an unrelated cause before bringing suit to enforce it. Under a survival statute the right survives to his estate, regardless of the cause of his death. The rationale for survival statutes is that the tortfeasor should compensate the victim's estate for the losses he caused to the victim before the victim died, even though the victim dies before suing for those predeath injuries herself. This rationale applies equally, whether the victim dies of injuries inflicted by the tortfeasor or from an unrelated cause. Thus, Verdi's estate may recover under the survival statute for the medical expenses, lost wages, and pain and suffering resulting from his broken hip, although that injury did not cause his death.

However, Verdi's executor or administrator would not have a wrongful death claim in this example. Verdi died of cancer, not a broken hip. Under basic negligence law, Strauss cannot be held liable for damages he didn't cause.

Consorting With Confusion

8.   Verdi's widow has a claim against Strauss for loss of consortium, but the survival statute has nothing to do with it. Survival statutes allow a decedent's estate to bring a claim the decedent could have brought before death. The consortium claim is a claim for Jane's own consortium losses as a result of Verdi's injury, suffered during the period when he was incapacitated. She is still alive and may bring the consortium claim in her own name against Strauss.

Her consortium claim will be limited to the impairment of her relationship with Verdi during the six months he was incapacitated by the accident. The relationship was then cut off entirely by his death from an unrelated cause. Obviously, too, it is limited to the interference caused by the hip injury, not by Verdi's other health problems, though it may be very difficult indeed to distinguish the impairment resulting from each.

9a. Both are. First, the survival statute authorizes suit against the estate of Strauss for negligently causing Verdi's death. Unlike Examples 6 and 7, in which the victim died before enforcing his claim, here it is the tortfeasor who escapes the rigors of litigation by dying before suit is brought against him. Under survival statutes death is no escape for either party: The claim survives if the tortfeasor dies or if the victim does. See, e.g., the Maine statute, p.294. If Verdi had recovered instead of dying, he would have invoked the survival statute to sue Strauss's estate. Since Verdi also died, his estate will do so instead.

The wrongful death statute is also implicated in this example, because it authorizes Jane, as administratrix of Verdi's estate, to recover damages from Strauss for causing Verdi's death. The suit will be an action for wrongful death, authorized to be brought against Strauss's estate under the survival statute. It will be entitled *Jane Verdi, Administratrix v. Estate of Strauss.*

b. In this case, the applicable wrongful death statute only authorizes recovery for the actual economic losses Jane suffers as a result of Verdi's death (because the "pecuniary loss" provision is strictly construed). It makes no provision for the consortium losses she sustains as a result of the destruction of her relationship to her husband. So Mrs. V. has simply asserted a separate count in her complaint for loss of consortium as well.

This creative effort to circumvent the limits of the wrongful death statute will fail. Because Verdi died instantly, Jane's loss of consortium claim is for the loss of his company, companionship, advice, support, and society *after* death. It is, in other words, a claim for damages resulting from the death. But these damages are *not* allowed under the applicable wrongful death statute, which has been construed to limit recovery to "pecuniary loss" in the strict sense. Since the right to recover for wrongful death is created by statute, the court will confine recovery to that allowed by the statute itself, and dismiss Jane's second claim.

There is certainly a strong policy argument for Jane's position, however. If Verdi survived, she would have been entitled to recover for the impairment of her relationship with him while he was incapacitated, under a count for "loss of consortium." See Chapter 10. Why shouldn't she have the same right when the relationship is completely cut off by his death? Does it make sense to retain the pecuniary loss measure of damages for wrongful death where much broader compensation is provided for consortium losses when the direct victim is merely injured?

This argument has led many states to amend their wrongful death statutes to authorize broad consortium damages in wrongful death cases. For example, under the Kansas provision, Verdi's widow could recover damages for loss of society, companionship, advice, counsel, and so forth, the same elements compensated under loss of consortium where the direct victim is merely injured.

c. The problem here is that the claim for negligence is really no different from the claim for wrongful death. A wrongful death claim must be based on a recognized tort that the decedent could have asserted had he survived.

Here, that claim would be negligence, for carelessly dropping the tuba on Verdi. The wrongful death action is simply a negligence action in which the damage resulting from the defendant's negligent act is death. To sue separately for negligence is simply to state the same thing another way.

A slightly different route to the same conclusion is based on the fact that there was no right to recover for wrongful death at common law. The right is a creature of statute, and recovery is limited to the terms of the statute. Thus, Verdi's wife has a claim under the wrongful death statute, but no separate right to assert a common law negligence claim against Strauss for causing Verdi's death. Thus, her third count does not state a claim for which relief can be granted.

Double Indemnity?

10a. No, it was a suit by a live plaintiff against a live defendant. The term "survival" refers to the continuing right to bring an action after the death of a party; it does not apply where the plaintiff brings suit and recovers a judgment before dying, as Mendelssohn did here.

b. As example 6c illustrates, the right to sue for wrongful death and for predeath losses under a survival statute are distinct. Both may ordinarily be brought after the decedent's death, where the decedent lives for a period of time and then dies of his injuries. However, the difference here is that the decedent brought suit and recovered for his injuries before death. How does that affect the right to sue for wrongful death?

There is an argument that the wrongful death claim should be barred. Under ordinary principles of res judicata, once a defendant has been sued on a claim, he can't be sued again for the same claim. See Glannon, Civil Procedure: Examples and Explanations 351-353 (2nd ed. 1992) (discussing obstinacy of surly myrmidons). Here Mendelssohn has sued, recovered, and been paid for the injuries he suffered, so presumably Brahms should be protected from a further action after Mendelssohn dies.

The contrary argument is that the losses compensated in a wrongful death suit are, at least in part, different from those Mendelssohn recovered in his suit. Mendelssohn recovered for his pain and suffering, lost wages, and medical bills, but his survivors suffer distinct losses as a result of his death that are compensable under many wrongful death statutes, including financial contributions they would have received from Mendelssohn and consortium losses. Why should they lose the right to claim for these losses because Mendelssohn recovered directly for others?

This issue has generated a good deal of controversy. Some cases, particularly earlier ones, held that, if the victim brought suit and recovered before death, no wrongful death action could be brought. See Speiser, §5.20 (citing a good many cases). Other courts, however, have allowed a wrongful death action, on the rationale that it compensates distinct losses to different persons — the survivors — and that the claim does not accrue until the injured victim dies. *Sea-Land Serv., Inc. v. Gaudet*, 414 U.S. 573, 579-583 (1974).

If a separate action is allowed, care must be taken to avoid duplicative damages. For example, if Mendelssohn was disabled by the accident, he probably recovered a substantial sum for future lost wages in his initial suit. That money would go into his estate after he died and pass to his survivors. If they could then recover a separate award under the wrongful death statute for lost financial contributions Mendelssohn would have made to them, the defendant would be made to pay the same losses twice — the contributions Mendelssohn would have made to his survivors would almost certainly have come from his future lost wages. See *Sea-Land Serv.*, 414 U.S. at 591-593. This problem of duplicative recovery can be dealt with by careful instructions to the jury or by barring evidence in the wrongful death action of lost future wages recovered by the decedent before death. See Restatement (Second) of Judgments, §46(2)(b) (if wrongful death action allowed despite prior recovery by decedent, the prior recovery bars damages in the wrongful death action for "such elements of loss as could have been recovered by the decedent in his action.")

Judge Fudd On An Off Day

11. Fudd is only "off" here because he's right on. The North Dakota statute, like many wrongful death acts, authorizes wrongful death recovery for claims that "would have entitled the party injured, if death had not ensued, to maintain an action and recover damages in respect thereof. . . ." If Mendelssohn had lived and brought suit, he would not have been entitled to "recover damages in respect thereof," since his contributory negligence would have been a complete defense (the example assumes). Consequently, the wrongful death suit is barred as well.[7]

An argument can (as always) be made to the contrary. The wrongful death recovery is for the benefit of the survivors. If *they* have not been negligent, arguably their recovery should not be reduced. But most courts have considered themselves bound by statutory language like North Dakota's, or by the obvious fact that the decedent's conduct would have barred recovery if he had survived.

An interesting variant on this issue is the situation where a beneficiary is negligent. Suppose, for example, that the decedent's father was the statutory beneficiary but was driving negligently at the time of the accident and was a cause of the accident that caused the son's death. Most cases under the

---

7. In a comparative negligence jurisdiction, the decedent's negligence will reduce recovery in a wrongful death case, just as it would have if the decedent had survived. Prosser & Keeton at 955.

loss-to-the-survivors type of wrongful death statute bar (or reduce, under comparative negligence) recovery by the negligent beneficiary. See Speiser, §5.7 at p.15. However, in jurisdictions that measure damages by the loss to the estate, the father might recover despite his negligence. Under that approach, the *estate* is the beneficiary; it is to be compensated for the decedent's pecuniary losses, and who actually inherits the assets in the estate may be viewed as an irrelevant fortuity. See *In Re Estate of Infant Fontaine*, 519 A.2d 227 (N.H. 1986) (concluding that the mother's negligence was irrelevant in action for wrongful death of her fetus, even though she was a beneficiary of the child's estate).

PART SIX

*Interlude:
Analyzing a
Personal
Injury Case*

15

Some Legal Anatomy: Thinking Like a Tort Lawyer

Introduction

If you had chosen medical school, your course in human anatomy would probably have been broken down into topics, like the brain, the circulatory system, the digestive system, the skeletal system, and so on. But bodies don't operate that way, they function as a unified system in which all elements interact to form a living organism.

Similarly, while most of the chapters in this book, like the Torts course itself, focus on particular elements or types of tort claims, cases do not arrive in lawyers' offices in such neat categories. Accidents present complex, miscellaneous, unorganized facts that lawyers must reconceptualize in terms of the theoretical framework of tort law. The challenge of a torts practice is to fit these unorganized real world facts into the recognized elements and defenses of a negligence claim. This chapter provides a brief opportunity to look at tort claims the way a practitioner does, to reason from raw data to legally supportable claims for damages.

To begin with, remember that the plaintiff must prove all the basic elements of a negligence claim in order to recover. If Bernhart is injured in a boating accident, the fact that she is seriously injured and needs compensation is not enough to support recovery. She must also prove that the pilot of the other boat was negligent, and that her negligence caused the accident. If Terry sells stock at a serious loss after an inaccurate financial statement is published by the corporation's accountants, she will still not recover if the court concludes that the accountants owed her no duty, or that the drop in value of the stock was not caused by the accountants' negligence. A torts chain is only as strong as its weakest link; you have to examine the whole chain to give a realistic assessment of the chances of recovery.

In addition, while we often speak broadly of a "claim for negligence," many types of negligence claims require more specific analysis. A plaintiff cannot recover for infliction of emotional distress, for example, simply by showing that the defendant's negligent conduct caused her distress. Courts have imposed additional requirements to limit emotional distress claims, such as physical contact, the *Dillon* standards, or presence in the "zone of danger." See, generally, Chapter 10. Similarly, plaintiffs seeking recovery for loss of consortium must show more than negligence, causation, and damages: Courts generally conclude that a defendant only owes a duty to avoid loss of consortium if a close relationship exists between the plaintiff and the direct victim. See Chapter 10, pp.203-204. Similarly, in wrongful death cases, only certain parties are allowed to recover. See Chapter 14. Counsel must analyze such cases with a view to these constraints on recovery for negligence.

Third, counsel must consider carefully what damages are recoverable in a negligence case. The fact that a defendant is liable does not necessarily mean that she is liable for every loss the plaintiff has suffered. This may be true because the law limits the types of damages recoverable (as in wrongful death cases), because the defendant did not cause all the plaintiff's damages (as in some multiple tortfeasor situations), or because, as a matter of policy, the law refuses to shift the loss for certain damages, under a proximate cause or duty analysis.

Without further ado, let's explore some of these limitations on negligence recovery based on the facts of this relatively simple accident case:

> Isadora Dunton was a famous opera star. On March 1, 1994, she and her husband Booth were pulling out of their driveway on to Main Street in the town of Elkton, West Dakota. Burton came speeding around a curve and hit their car broadside. Isadora, who was three months pregnant at the time, was severely injured. John, son of Isadora and Booth, was playing basketball in the driveway, about 25 feet from the point of the accident, heard the collision, and ran to the scene immediately. Isadora suffered the loss of one eye and multiple internal injuries, and was hospitalized in serious condition. The baby suffered fetal distress and cardiac arrhythmia from the trauma of the accident, and was stillborn a week later. Four months later, on July 1, Isadora died as a result of her injuries.
>
> Booth suffered minor facial lacerations. John was extremely upset by the accident, became withdrawn, suffered a severe decline in his high school grades, and more or less "dropped out" after the accident. Lydia, a married daughter of Isadora, was also seriously affected by the accident. She became tense, impatient with her husband, cried a lot, and had difficulty sleeping. She also became difficult to work with and was skipped over for promotion. She also missed her mother.

Garrick was Isadora's costar in many important productions and a close personal friend. He was extremely upset by her injury, suffered a nervous breakdown, and never quite fully recovered. Unable to find a comparable costar, his career was limited thereafter to minor supporting roles.

Burton, the other driver, was also seriously injured. He died a year later of unrelated causes.

The following examples consider the elements, special requirements and limitations on relief for the different types of claims that may be asserted based on the Dunton accident. In analyzing the claims, focus on the claims that the plaintiffs should raise, even if some claims may be vulnerable to challenge by the defendant. Assume that West Dakota has a survival statute, a wrongful death statute that authorizes pecuniary and emotional damages for survivors, and that it recognizes spousal consortium but has not decided whether children can recover for loss of parental consortium.

EXAMPLES

Setting the Stage

1. Assume that Isadora did not initiate suit before her death. Booth, the administrator of her estate, comes to you after her death, to inquire about potential claims for damages as a result of her physical injuries.
    a. What would you advise Booth about the effect of Isadora's death on the right to recover for her injuries?
    b. What would you advise Booth about the effect of Burton's death on Isadora's claims?

Act One

2. Booth retains you to bring an action against Burton for damages for Isadora's injuries. Which of the following elements of damages would you claim in a survival action for predeath losses suffered by Isadora?
    a. pain and suffering
    b. lost earning capacity
    c. loss of enjoyment of life
    d. medical bills
    e. loss of consortium with members of her family
    f. infliction of emotional distress
3. Assume that Booth also wishes to assert a wrongful death claim resulting from Isadora's death. Which of the following elements of damages would you seek in the wrongful death claim?
    a. pain and suffering
    b. lost earning capacity
    c. loss of enjoyment of life
    d. loss of consortium suffered by Isadora

  e. loss of consortium suffered by Booth and other family members due to Isadora's death

Act Two

4.   Booth also inquires as to claims he may assert on behalf of the deceased child Isadora was carrying at the time of the accident. What would you advise him as to the prospects of recovery for the child's death, and the elements of damages?

5.   Booth also inquires as to the claims he may assert on his own behalf as a result of the accident.

  a. What would you advise Booth as to the elements of damages for his own physical injuries?
  b. What would you advise Booth as to his right to assert claims for loss of consortium?
  c. What would you advise Booth concerning other claims he might have?

6.   Booth brings John with him. John is also interested in asserting claims against Burton's estate. What claims may he have, and what problems do you anticipate in recovering on them?

7.   A week after your interview with Booth and John, Lydia comes in to inquire about possible claims against Burton. What claims may she have, and what problems do you anticipate in recovering on them?

Supporting Actors

8.   Next to come in is Garrick, Isadora's costar in the opera. What would you advise him as to his rights against Burton arising from the accident?

Putting the Show on the Road

9.   Draft a complaint seeking relief on behalf of Isadora's estate, Booth, John, and Lydia. Assume that the West Dakota law allows both survival and wrongful death claims and recognizes fetal wrongful death claims, but has not yet addressed claims for loss of consortium on behalf of parents or children. Assume also that it is unclear what the standards are in West Dakota to state an adequate claim for negligent infliction of emotional distress.

EXPLANATIONS

Setting the Stage

1a.   The right to recover for Isadora's injuries depends on the applicable survival and wrongful death statutes, which vary from state to state. Thus, you might advise Booth, as lawyers frequently do, that you don't know whether suit can be brought, but will find out. However, if you were an experienced West Dakota practitioner, you would probably be familiar with the local law on these issues.

As Chapter 14 explains, virtually all states have modified the common law doctrine denying recovery for wrongful death. Here, for example, West Dakota has a wrongful death statute, which authorizes recovery of pecuniary and consortium damages suffered by Isadora's survivors as a result of her death and a survival statute which authorizes Booth, as Isadora's executor, to recover for predeath losses Isadora suffered as a result of the accident. (In some states, these two related issues — recovery for the predeath injuries and for wrongful death — are addressed in a single "wrongful death statute.")

b. The question here is whether Isadora's claims "survive" the death of Burton, the tortfeasor. Most states now provide by statute that tort claims survive the tortfeasor's death and may be brought against the tortfeasor's estate. This is true regardless of the cause of the tortfeasor's death. Thus, it makes no difference here that Burton died of causes unrelated to the accident.

Act One

2a. Most survival statutes allow recovery by the estate of a deceased tort victim for losses suffered by the decedent prior to death. Under these survival statutes, the estate recovers any damages the plaintiff sustained from the date of the accident until her death, and which she could have recovered herself if she had survived.

Had Isadora survived and filed suit herself, she could have recovered for pain and suffering. Thus, the physical pain and emotional anguish she sustained during this four month period as a result of her injuries should be proper elements of damages in the survival action.

Of course, any recovery under the survival claim will not compensate Isadora for having suffered it; she is beyond compensation in any worldly sense. Consequently, a few states view recovery for pain and suffering as a "windfall to the heirs" (see Prosser & Keeton at 943) and bar recovery for pain and suffering in survival actions. See, e.g., Ariz. Rev. Stat. Ann. §14-3110 (1975). Most states, however, allow recovery for the decedent's predeath pain and suffering: If these damages are not allowed in the survival action, the *defendant* will get a windfall due to the victim's death. Although these damages cannot benefit her, at least her survivors, through her estate, can receive the benefit of the recovery.

b. Lost earning capacity generally refers to the tort victim's loss of the ability to earn money in the future, that is, after the trial. See Chapter 12, p.244. Under most survival statutes, this is not a proper element of a survival claim, which only encompasses losses suffered prior to death. Minzer, Nates §21.03. Only her *predeath* lost earnings, for the four months from the accident until her death, would be properly sought under the survival claim. Her future earning capacity will be taken into account in assessing the damages for wrongful death. See Example 3b.

Here again, there are statutory variations. In a few states, lost earning capacity *is* allocated to the survival claim. See, e.g., *Wetzel v. McDonnell Douglas Corp.*, 491 F. Supp. 1288 (E.D. Pa. 1980). In a state with a statute of this type, the court must be very careful to assure that these same damages are not assessed again under the wrongful death claim.

c. All states recognize that an injured plaintiff's loss of the ability to enjoy normal activities and pleasures of living is a compensable element of damages in tort actions. As Chapter 12 indicates, some states view this as included in pain and suffering, while others treat "loss of enjoyment of life" as a distinct element of damages. Presumably Isadora's estate would recover for her enjoyment of life during the four months she survived, since this is a loss she suffered prior to death, for which she could have recovered herself had she lived. However, as with her earnings, she cannot recover for *future* loss of enjoyment in a survival action.

As noted above, a few states specifically bar claims for pain and suffering in survival actions. If the Dunton case arose in one of these states, counsel for Burton's estate would doubtless argue that the exclusion for pain and suffering damages also bars recovery for the related loss of enjoyment damages.

d. Under most survival statutes, medical expenses incurred prior to death would be included in the survival claim. These are losses suffered by the decedent prior to death as a result of the defendant's negligence. Had she lived, she would have been able to sue for them herself. The estate steps into her shoes for purposes of enforcing this predeath claim.

e. This is a tricky question. Isadora does not have a claim for loss of consortium as a result of her *own* injuries. Consortium claims are claims by family members of an injured person, alleging that the injury has impaired the injured person's ability to interact with those family members. Booth, John, and Lydia may have consortium claims based on the impairment of Isadora's ability to relate to them as a result of her injury, but Isadora will not. Her claim for impairment of her ability to relate to others caused by her injuries is a "loss of enjoyment" claim, which is part of the survival claim for her predeath damages. See Example 2c.

However, Isadora may have loss of consortium claims due to the injury to *other victims* of the accident, such as Booth. His injury may have impaired his ability to relate to Isadora. In fact, Booth's injury may have prevented him from providing emotional and practical support to Isadora at the very time she needed it most.

Any loss of consortium claim Isadora has as a result of the injuries to Booth would be part of the survival action, and would be limited to the four months she lived after the accident. Even though Booth's injuries might have continued to impair his ability to relate to Isadora had she lived, recovery for any loss after her death is governed by the wrongful death statute, which compensates the survivors' losses, not the decedent's.

f. Emotional distress is a slippery term that covers a lot of ground. It includes, for example, the anxiety and depression Isadora suffered due to her own injuries, fear of the impending collision, or anguish due to the fear of dying. These damages are part of the "pain and suffering" endured by Isadora prior to death. In states that allow recovery for pain and suffering in survival actions, her estate could recover for these damages, suffered over the four-month period prior to her death.

"Emotional distress" also encompasses the traumatic distress Isadora suffers from witnessing physical injury to *others*, such as Booth. This distress, suffered at the time of the accident, is also a predeath injury; if it is compensable at all, it will be under the survival statute. Whether Isadora will recover for this type of emotional distress depends on the applicable law governing indirect infliction claims. Isadora's estate would state a claim for indirect infliction if West Dakota applied the zone-of-danger rule, since she was in the zone of danger from the defendant's negligence (and in fact suffered injury herself from it). Because Isadora suffered an impact from the accident, she might also recover for indirect infliction of emotional distress under the "impact rule" as well. See Chapter 10, Example 1a. She would also have a claim for the trauma of witnessing injury to Booth if West Dakota follows *Dillon*, since she witnessed the accident and is closely related to Booth.

3a. Neither Isadora's estate nor her survivors would have a claim for future pain and suffering because Isadora, due to her death, will not experience any. Had she lived and sued, she might well have had such a claim, since she would have faced the prospect of continued suffering. (As Example 2a indicates, the claim for her predeath pain and suffering would be part of the survival claim in most states.)

b. Under most wrongful death statutes, the decedent's survivors may recover for pecuniary support they would have received from the decedent. See generally Chapter 14, pp.289-290. This recovery will not exactly equal Isadora's lost earning capacity; it only includes that part of her future earnings that would have gone to support the survivors. Certainly John would have a substantial claim, since he was still at home and dependent on his parents for support. Booth might also recover such damages under the wrongful death statute. Because Isadora was very successful, her income doubtless contributed substantially to the family's lifestyle. The loss of this income is a pecuniary loss to Booth, even if he is still able to support himself in the food-and-shelter sense of the term without it.

Lydia, however, will have a harder time making out a claim for pecuniary losses due to Isadora's death, since she was financially independent. However, if she could prove that Isadora made gifts to her from time to time (as wealthy, tax-conscious parents are known to do) she might claim that she has also suffered pecuniary losses compensable under the wrongful death statute.[1]

c. If Isadora had lived but been disabled, either temporarily or permanently, she would have had a claim for future loss of enjoyment of life caused by any impairment she sustained as a result of the accident. For example, if she survived the accident but lost an eye, this would interfere with Isadora's enjoyment of life as long as she lived. However, since she died as a result of the accident, there will be no claim for loss of enjoyment of life for any period after her death. Recovery for any damages due to her death is governed by the wrongful death statute, which compensates survivors for their losses due to the decedent's death, not the decedent for hers. See Chapter 14, p.288. While there is surely no greater loss of enjoyment than the loss of life itself, this is a loss to Isadora, not her survivors.

d. Any claim for loss of consortium suffered by Isadora would be based on injuries to *other* family members that impaired their ability to relate to her. For example, she would have a claim for loss of consortium with Booth from the date of the accident until her death, which would be asserted by her estate under the survival statute. See Example 2e. However, her estate has no claim for Isadora's loss of consortium with Booth for the period after her death, even if Booth remains incapacitated. Damages for any period after her death are governed entirely by the wrongful death statute, which only compensates the survivors' losses due to Isadora's death.[2]

e. Under many wrongful death statutes, immediate survivors of the decedent are entitled to compensation for consortium-type damages — their loss of the comfort, companionship, advice, society, and counsel of the decedent — for the period after the decedent's death. See, e.g., Kan. Stat. Ann. §60-1904 (1983 & Supp. 1993), quoted at Chapter 14, p.291, supra. Since the West Dakota wrongful death statute authorizes recovery for these emotional damages, Booth and Isadora's children will recover for this loss for the future years they otherwise would have enjoyed their relationship with Isadora.

Act Two

4.   For many years, the courts barred claims for injury or death of a fetus, on the theory that no *duty* was owed to an unborn child. Prosser & Keeton,

---

1. In a few jurisdictions, the measure of damages in the wrongful death action is the net lost future earnings that would have gone into the decedent's estate. See Chapter 14, p.291. Under this approach, the court would calculate Isadora's future earnings, and reduce them by the amount she would have spent for her own support had she lived.

2. Of course, theory and practice may diverge, to the plaintiff's benefit. Juries may either misunderstand or ignore their instructions regarding these subtle distinctions, and assess the damages with a general view to the losses of all involved, including Isadora.

§55, at 367. More recently, many states have allowed such claims, but others have held that the term "person" in their wrongful death statutes does not apply to a fetus, and passed the buck to the legislature to change the rule. See, e.g., *Witty v. American Gen. Capital Distrib., Inc.*, 727 S.W.2d 503 (Tex. 1987). Thus, whether there is a claim for the unborn child's death will turn on how the court interprets West Dakota's wrongful death statute.

If the wrongful death statute allows recovery for causing the death of a fetus, the damages would depend on the terms of the wrongful death statute. Many such statutes authorize damages for both pecuniary and consortium losses to closely related survivors such as parents and siblings. Naturally, assessing the monetary contributions this child would have made to her parents in the future, or the quality of the relationship that would have developed between the child and her family, is a surreal process. Certainly, the losses could be great, since the relationship is destroyed from the outset and all monetary contributions the child might have made are lost. If this claim is allowed, it will introduce a very emotional and uncertain element into the trial that will doubtless have great settlement value from the plaintiffs' point of view.

Are there any other claims you might assert on behalf of the deceased child? The facts indicate that Isadora miscarried a week after the accident, and that during that period the baby suffered fetal distress and cardiac arrhythmia. This suggests that the baby, though in utero, suffered pain and suffering prior to the miscarriage. Advancing medical knowledge suggests that fetuses have a good deal more awareness than previously thought. As plaintiff's counsel in this case, you might draw on this advancing medical knowledge to argue for a new type of claim for "fetal pain and suffering."

Presumably, such claims would be asserted under a survival statute, as an injury suffered by the child prior to death. It is highly doubtful that a state that rejects fetal wrongful death claims would recognize a claim for its predeath pain and suffering, but the argument might be accepted in a jurisdiction that allows fetal wrongful death claims.

Issues like fetal suffering prior to death are grim to contemplate. As plaintiff's counsel, however, it is your job to contemplate them, and to seek compensation for such losses if they may be allowable. It is through such constant probing of the boundaries by creative plaintiff's counsel that tort law grows.

5a. You would advise Booth that he is entitled to sue for his medical bills, pain and suffering, and lost wages, and for property damage to the car if he owned it. However, you would also advise him that these damages are not likely to be great, since he suffered minor injuries. Clearly, the substantial claims available to Booth are for his intangible damages — his emotional distress and loss of consortium claims arising from the serious injuries sustained by other family members.

b. Pardon me for being repetitious, but recall again that Booth's loss of consortium claims will be based on the injuries to other family members that impair their ability to relate to Booth. For example, Booth would certainly have a loss of consortium claim resulting from the injury to Isadora, his wife, since her serious injuries impaired her ability to relate to Booth as they had before. However, this consortium claim will be limited to the four-month period prior to her death. The loss of Isadora's consortium suffered by Booth *as a result of* her death is part of the wrongful death claim discussed earlier. Since the West Dakota wrongful death statute authorizes damages for loss of the relationship with the decedent, Booth will recover damages for this post-death loss. But he will do so under the wrongful death statute, and will have no separate "loss of consortium" claim for this period. If he were allowed to sue for post-death "loss of consortium," and for the same losses under the wrongful death statute, he would recover twice for the same loss.

Booth has also lost the ability to relate to his unborn child due to the child's death. However, this claim is also a claim for post-death loss of consortium, and will be compensable, if at all, under the wrongful death statute. See Example 4.

It is also possible that Booth has a claim for loss of consortium with his son John, due to John's injuries. A few jurisdictions allow a parent to recover for loss of consortium with an injured child, though most do not. See Chapter 10, pp.203-204. The facts suggest that John has suffered emotional injuries from witnessing the accident, and that these emotional injuries have affected his ability to relate to others. However, allowing Booth to assert a consortium claim as a result of this injury to John involves piling one claim for indirect injury (Booth's consortium claim for interference with his relationship to John) onto another indirect injury claim (John's indirect infliction of emotional distress claim due to witnessing injury to Isadora and Booth). The results could be fairly absurd if courts allowed such add-ons to the third and fourth power.

c. Booth will likely have a claim for indirect infliction of emotional distress. He witnessed traumatic, serious injury to Isadora and was himself injured in the same accident. As explained in Example 2f, a plaintiff who has suffered an impact may be able to recover for emotional distress, including indirect emotional distress from observing injury to a family member. Or, if West Dakota followed the zone of danger rule Booth would recover for indirect infliction of emotional distress, since he was within the zone of danger created by Burton's negligence. If the *Dillon* factors applied, he would also recover, since he was present and witnessed injury to his wife.

6.   John suffered no direct impact or physical injury in the accident. However, he did rush to the scene immediately and witness the traumatic impact of the accident on members of his family. Whether he can recover for this depends on West Dakota's law on indirect infliction of emotional distress.

Courts following the impact rule would deny recovery. Under the zone-of-danger approach, John's claim would turn on whether John was close enough to the collision to be endangered by it (how about flying debris?). Under the *Dillon* approach, John will state a claim if the court concludes that he "witnessed" injury to close family members by hearing the crash, even though he did not see it. (See Chapter 10, Example 1c for a discussion of this issue.)

Some jurisdictions also require resulting physical symptoms in order to recover for indirect infliction. The facts indicate that John became withdrawn and his grades went down. Although it would be hard to characterize these as physical symptoms, some courts might find such dubious "physical injuries" sufficient. See Chapter 10, Example 4f.

John may also have a claim for loss of consortium with Isadora for the four-month period prior to her death. Clearly her injuries impaired her ability to relate to John. Many jurisdictions do not allow children to sue for loss of consortium with their parents, but some do. The result will turn on how West Dakota decides this issue. However, John's claim for loss of the relationship with Isadora for the period after her death is compensable, if at all, under the wrongful death claim.

7.   Lydia suffered no physical injuries, but apparently did experience a great deal of emotional distress. However, it is highly doubtful that she can recover on an indirect infliction claim. Most jurisdictions limit indirect infliction claims to those who are in the zone of danger or witness the accident or its immediate aftermath.

Lydia might seek recovery for loss of consortium. Like John's claim, the result will depend on whether West Dakota allows children to recover for loss of consortium due to injury to their parents. If such claims are recognized in West Dakota, Lydia's recovery on this claim will be limited to the four months during which Isadora survived. Her claims for loss of consortium with Isadora for the period after her death, like John's, will be governed by the wrongful death statute. Even states that deny loss of consortium claims for an *injured* parent may allow the children to recover for consortium losses under their wrongful death statutes if the parent is killed.

Even if the wrongful death statute allows damages for consortium losses, the court will probably not allow the jury to award consortium losses for such extended consequences as Lydia's missed promotion. Loss of consortium is meant to compensate for the interference with the relationship with the directly injured party, not for collateral economic consequences of that interference. The defense would doubtless argue that such attenuated consequences were not "proximately caused" by Burton's negligence.

Supporting Actors

8.   Garrick has suffered very serious injury due to the negligence of Burton, but it is very unlikely that he will recover damages from Burton's estate.

Certainly, Garrick has no indirect infliction claim, since he is not related to Isadora, did not witness traumatic injury to anyone, suffered no impact, and was not in the zone of danger. Nor does he have a loss of consortium claim: Such claims are limited to family members, not operatic partners.

But doesn't he have a just plain "negligence" claim? Burton had a duty to drive carefully, he didn't, and his negligence caused injury to Isadora and consequent damages to Garrick. This is true, but most courts would hold that Burton's *duty* to drive with due care was owed to other drivers, perhaps to family members, but not to others who suffer secondary emotional or economic losses as a result of the accident. Other courts might reach the same result by holding that Burton's negligence was not the "legal cause" or "proximate cause" of the consequential injuries suffered by Garrick. Even if Garrick's injuries are foreseeable, the court must draw the line on secondary damages at some point, as a matter of policy. Whether on duty or proximate cause grounds, virtually all courts would reject Garrick's claim.

Putting the Show on the Road

9.   The complaint below is an example of the type of complaint that might be filed in the *Dunton* case. In reading the complaint, consider how the various claims for relief have been drafted to allege the elements necessary to support the claims. After the complaint are some notes on the reasoning underlying it.

STATE OF WEST DAKOTA

SUPERIOR COURT   CIVIL ACTION NO. 95-1341
CHEYENNE COUNTY

BOOTH DUNTON, Individually
  and as the Administrator
  of the estates of
  ISADORA DUNTON and BABY
  DUNTON, JOHN DUNTON, and
  LYDIA DUNTON,
                                       COMPLAINT AND
        PLAINTIFFS   DEMAND FOR JURY TRIAL

    v.

ELIZABETH BURTON,
  executrix of the
  estate of ROBERT BURTON,

        DEFENDANT

PARTIES

1. Isadora Dunton is an individual, formerly
residing at 43 Keane Drive, Elkton, West Dakota,
who died on July 1, 1994, of injuries suffered in
the motor vehicle accident which is the subject of
this action.

2. Baby Dunton is the child of Isadora and Booth
Dunton, who died in utero on March 8, 1994 of
injuries suffered in the motor vehicle accident
which is the subject of this action.

3. The plaintiff Booth Dunton is an individual
residing at 43 Keane Drive, Elkton, West Dakota. He
is the widower and duly appointed administrator of
the estates of Isadora Dunton and Baby Dunton.

4. The plaintiff John Dunton is the minor son of
Isadora and Booth Dunton. He resides at 43 Keane
Drive, Elkton, West Dakota.

5. The plaintiff Lydia Dunton is the daughter of
Isadora and Booth Dunton. She resides at 1138
Lankton Boulevard, Elkton, West Dakota.

6. The decedent Robert J. Burton is an individual,
formerly residing at 12 Lake Street, Burns, West
Dakota, who died on February 15, 1995.

7. The defendant Elizabeth Burton is the daughter and duly appointed executrix of the estate of Robert J. Burton.

FACTS

8. On March 1, 1994, the decedents Isadora Dunton and Baby Dunton were passengers in a 1992 red Toyota Camry station wagon, driven by the plaintiff, Booth Dunton.

9. At approximately 11:05 a.m., Booth Dunton started the car in the family driveway at 43 Keane Drive, Elkton, West Dakota, and began to back out of the driveway onto Keane Drive, in order to proceed in an easterly direction on Keane Drive. At the time he exited the driveway, Booth Dunton looked in both directions for traffic on Keane Drive. There were no cars visible in either direction.

10. As the car backed into Keane Drive, a blue Ford Taurus, driven by the decedent Robert J. Burton, came around the corner, traveling east at an excessive speed and without keeping a proper lookout, in violation of West Dakota St. Ann. Tit. 32, §§90 and 93.

11. As a result of his negligent driving, the decedent Robert J. Burton was unable to stop his vehicle or avoid colliding with the plaintiffs' vehicle backing out of the driveway at 43 Keane Drive.

12. As a direct and proximate result of the negligence of the decedent, Robert J. Burton, his vehicle collided violently with the Dunton vehicle, demolishing the Dunton vehicle and causing serious personal injuries to Isadora Dunton, Booth Dunton, and Baby Dunton.

13. As a direct and proximate result of the accident, the decedent Isadora Dunton suffered multiple internal traumas and extensive damage to her left eye, causing permanent blindness. She was taken to Elkton General Hospital, where she remained in the intensive care unit until her death on July 1, 1994 from injuries suffered in the accident.

14. As a direct and proximate result of the accident, the decedent Baby Dunton suffered traumatic injuries, resulting in fetal distress and cardiac arrhythmia. On March 8, 1994, Isadora Dunton miscarried, causing the death of Baby Dunton.

15. As a direct and proximate result of the accident, Booth Dunton suffered multiple lacerations requiring medical treatment, experienced pain and suffering, extreme emotional distress and temporary disability, and lost wages in excess of $2000.

16. At the time of the accident, the plaintiff John Dunton was standing in the driveway at 43 Keane Drive, in the immediate vicinity of the collision. He witnessed the accident, rushed to aid the injured members of his family and observed his mother and father covered in blood and suffering from extreme shock and pain.

17. As a result of the accident and the injuries suffered by her parents, the plaintiff Lydia Dunton has suffered serious emotional distress, inability to sleep, difficulties at work, and other damages.

18. At all times relevant to the events in this action, the plaintiffs and their decedents were in the exercise of due care.

FIRST CLAIM FOR RELIEF:
WRONGFUL DEATH OF ISADORA DUNTON

19. The plaintiff repeats and realleges the allegations in paragraphs 1 to 18 of the complaint.

20. As a result of the collision proximately caused by the decedent Robert Burton's negligence, Isadora Dunton suffered extensive personal injuries which led to her death on July 1, 1994, at the age of forty-three.

21. As a result of the death of Isadora Dunton negligently caused by the decedent Robert Burton, her husband Booth Dunton and her children John and Lydia Dunton have been deprived of both the financial support and the comfort, companionship, advice, society, and counsel they would have received from Isadora Dunton had she lived.

Wherefore, the plaintiff Booth Dunton, in his capacity as administrator of the estate of Isadora Dunton, seeks damages under the West Dakota Wrongful Death Statute, West Dakota St. Ann. Tit. 12 §143, on behalf of Booth Dunton, John Dunton, and Lydia Dunton, for the loss of financial support, comfort, companionship, advice, society, and counsel of the decedent Isadora Dunton, and for funeral and burial expenses, together with interest and costs of suit.

SECOND CLAIM FOR RELIEF: SURVIVAL CLAIM FOR PREDEATH DAMAGES OF ISADORA DUNTON

22. The plaintiff repeats and realleges the allegations in paragraphs 1 to 18 of the complaint.

23. As a result of the collision proximately caused by the decedent Robert Burton's negligence, Isadora Dunton suffered extensive personal injuries, emotional distress, pain and suffering for a period of four months prior to her death, suffered loss of the normal pleasures and enjoyment of life over the four month period, lost substantial earnings from her work as a soloist with the West Dakota Civic Opera, and incurred great medical and other expenses for her care, all of which she would have been entitled to recover in an action against the defendant had she survived.

Wherefore, the plaintiff Booth Dunton, in his capacity as administrator of the estate of Isadora Dunton, seeks damages under the West Dakota survival statute, St. Ann. Tit. 12 §147, on behalf of the estate of Isadora Dunton, for her lost earnings, medical expenses, pain and suffering, and loss of enjoyment of life from March 1, 1994 until her death on July 1, 1994, together with interest and costs of suit.

THIRD CLAIM FOR RELIEF: WRONGFUL DEATH OF BABY DUNTON

24. The plaintiff repeats and realleges the allegations in paragraphs 1 to 18 of the complaint.

25. At the time of the accident, the decedent Isadora Dunton was pregnant with a baby girl, the decedent Baby Dunton.

26. As a result of the collision proximately caused by the decedent Robert Burton's negligence, Isadora Dunton suffered extensive personal injuries which led to the death and miscarriage of her child, Baby Dunton, on March 8, 1994.

27. As a result of the death of Baby Dunton negligently caused by the decedent Robert Burton, the plaintiffs Booth Dunton, Lydia Dunton and John Dunton have been deprived of both the financial support and the comfort, companionship, advice, society, and counsel they would have received from Baby Dunton had she lived.

Wherefore, the plaintiff Booth Dunton, in his capacity as administrator of the estate of Baby Dunton, claims damages under the West Dakota Wrongful Death Statute, West Dakota St. Ann. Tit. 12 §143, on behalf of Booth Dunton, John Dunton, and Lydia Dunton, for the loss of financial support, comfort, companionship, advice, society, and counsel of the decedent Baby Dunton, as well as for funeral and burial expenses, together with interest and costs of suit.

FOURTH CLAIM FOR RELIEF:
SURVIVAL CLAIM FOR PREDEATH DAMAGES OF BABY DUNTON

28. The plaintiff repeats and realleges the allegations in paragraphs 1 to 18 of the complaint.

29. As a result of the collision proximately caused by the decedent Robert Burton's negligence, Isadora Dunton suffered extensive personal injuries which caused the child Baby Dunton to suffer cardiac arrhythmia and extreme fetal distress from the date of the accident until her death, injuries for which she could have recovered herself had she lived.

Wherefore, the plaintiff Booth Dunton, in his capacity as administrator of the estate of Baby Dunton, claims damages under the West Dakota survival statute, St. Ann. Tit. 12 §147, on behalf of the estate of Baby Dunton, for the pain and suffering she experienced from March 1, 1994 until her death on March 8, 1994, together with interest and costs of suit.

FIFTH CLAIM FOR RELIEF:
BOOTH DUNTON'S CLAIM FOR PERSONAL INJURIES

30. The plaintiff repeats and realleges the allegations in paragraphs 1 to 18 of the complaint.

31. As a result of the collision proximately caused by the decedent Robert Burton's negligence, Booth Dunton suffered facial lacerations, incurred lost wages and medical bills, experienced pain and suffering, and was temporarily disabled.

    Wherefore, the plaintiff Booth Dunton, suing in his individual capacity, seeks damages from the defendant for pain and suffering, medical expenses, lost wages, and loss of the enjoyment of life suffered as a result of his injuries, together with interest and costs of suit.

SIXTH CLAIM FOR RELIEF:
BOOTH DUNTON'S CLAIM FOR LOSS OF CONSORTIUM
WITH ISADORA DUNTON

32. The plaintiff repeats and realleges the allegations in paragraphs 1 to 18 of the complaint.

33. As a result of the collision proximately caused by the decedent Robert Burton's negligence, Isadora Dunton suffered extensive personal injuries which led to her death on July 1, 1994.

34. As a result of the serious personal injuries suffered by Isadora Dunton, the plaintiff Booth Dunton suffered the loss of his wife's comfort, companionship, advice, society, and counsel from the date of the accident until her death on July 1, 1994.

    Wherefore, the plaintiff Booth Dunton claims damages from the defendant for loss of consortium with his wife, Isadora Dunton.

SEVENTH CLAIM FOR RELIEF:
SURVIVAL CLAIM FOR ISADORA DUNTON'S
LOSS OF CONSORTIUM WITH BOOTH DUNTON

35. The plaintiff repeats and realleges the allegations in paragraphs 1 to 18 of the complaint.

36. As a result of the collision proximately caused by the decedent Robert Burton's negligence, Booth Dunton suffered extensive personal injuries which interfered with his ability to relate to Isadora Dunton.

37. As a result of the serious personal injuries suffered by Booth Dunton, Isadora Dunton suffered the loss of her husband's comfort, companionship, advice, society, and counsel from the date of the accident until her death on July 1, 1994.

Wherefore, the plaintiff Booth Dunton, as administrator of the estate of Isadora Dunton, claims damages from the defendant for her loss of consortium with Booth Dunton.

EIGHTH CLAIM FOR RELIEF:
JOHN AND LYDIA DUNTON'S CLAIMS FOR
LOSS OF CONSORTIUM WITH ISADORA DUNTON

38. The plaintiffs repeat and reallege the allegations in paragraphs 1 to 18 of the complaint.

39. As a result of the collision proximately caused by the decedent's negligence, Isadora Dunton suffered extensive personal injuries which led to her death on July 1, 1994.

40. As a result of the serious personal injuries suffered by Isadora Dunton, her children Lydia Dunton and John Dunton suffered the loss of their mother's comfort, companionship, advice, society, and counsel from the date of the accident until her death on July 1, 1994.

Wherefore, the plaintiffs Lydia and John Dunton claim damages from the defendant for loss of consortium with their mother, Isadora Dunton.

NINTH CLAIM FOR RELIEF:
JOHN AND LYDIA DUNTON'S CLAIMS FOR
LOSS OF CONSORTIUM WITH BOOTH DUNTON

41. The plaintiffs repeat and reallege the allegations in paragraphs 1 to 18 of the complaint.

42. As a result of the collision proximately caused by the decedent's negligence, Booth Dunton suffered personal injuries which interfered with his ability to relate to the plaintiffs John and Lydia Dunton.

43. As a result, the plaintiffs John and Lydia Dunton have suffered loss of the comfort, companionship, advice, society, and counsel of their father.

   Wherefore, the plaintiffs Lydia and John Dunton claim damages from the defendant for loss of consortium with their father, Booth Dunton.

TENTH CLAIM FOR RELIEF:
BOOTH DUNTON'S CLAIMS FOR
NEGLIGENT INFLICTION OF EMOTIONAL DISTRESS

44. The plaintiff repeats and realleges the allegations in paragraphs 1 to 18 of the complaint.

45. As a result of the collision proximately caused by the decedent's negligence, Isadora Dunton suffered extensive personal injuries which led to her death on July 1, 1994. Booth Dunton was also present and sustained personal injuries in the accident.

46. Immediately after the collision, Booth observed his wife in extreme pain, shock and distress from the injuries suffered in the accident.

47. As a result of the terrifying experience of observing the accident and its aftermath, Booth Dunton suffered immediate emotional trauma and permanent psychic damage, as well as direct physical injury.

   Wherefore, the plaintiff Booth Dunton claims damages from the defendant for negligent infliction of emotional distress.

ELEVENTH CLAIM FOR RELIEF:
JOHN DUNTON'S CLAIMS FOR
NEGLIGENT INFLICTION OF EMOTIONAL DISTRESS

48. The plaintiff repeats and realleges the allegations in paragraphs 1 to 18 of the complaint.

49. As a result of the collision proximately caused by the decedent's negligence, Isadora Dunton suffered extensive personal injuries which led to her death on July 1, 1994.

50. At the time of the accident, John Dunton was standing in the immediate vicinity of the collision, and immediately became aware that his parents had been involved in a serious accident.

51. Immediately after the collision, John Dunton rushed to the scene and observed his mother and father in extreme pain, shock and distress from the injuries suffered in the accident.

52. As a result of the terrifying experience of observing the accident and its aftermath, John Dunton suffered both immediate emotional trauma and long term psychological damage. Since the accident, he has become withdrawn and uncommunicative, has received low grades, lost touch with his friends, and shows other signs of post traumatic stress syndrome.

Wherefore, the plaintiff John Dunton claims damages from the defendant for negligent infliction of emotional distress.

The plaintiffs claim trial by jury on all issues in this action.

Allison Barrymore

Allison Barrymore
Attorney for Plaintiffs
132 Hayes Boulevard
Elkton, West Dakota 11111
(419) 832-1239

Comments on the Dunton Complaint

Barrymore, the Duntons' counsel, has put a lot of thought into drafting this complaint based on the facts of the Dunton accident. Doubtless, there are problems with some of the claims, either because it is not clear that they are legally sufficient, or because of difficulties of proof. Barrymore's job at this stage is to determine which claims may be legally and factually supportable, not to determine which will actually prevail at trial.

The comments below reflect some of the analysis which went into drafting this negligence complaint.

1.   Barrymore has broken down the various claims both by parties and by the particular types of claims. As the Introduction suggests, she has taken these miscellaneous facts and reconceptualized them in terms of legally recognized claims for tort damages. For example, the First Claim for Relief seeks damages for wrongful death of Isadora, and the Second for the predeath damages to Isadora. Even though these claims are both based on injuries to the same person and are both asserted by the same plaintiff, it facilitates an understanding of the claims to set them forth separately because negligence law analyzes the claims differently.

2.   Barrymore has included some claims in the complaint even though it is unclear whether they are legally sufficient. For example, the Second Claim for Relief seeks damages for Isadora's loss of enjoyment of life for the period from the accident until her death. It may be unclear under West Dakota law whether such damages can be recovered in the survival action. As long as the estate *may* be entitled to such damages, the estate may properly assert them; nothing requires them to confine their claims to those which are absolutely certain to be recognized as legally valid. See Fed. R. Civ. P. 11(b)(2) (authorizing assertion of claims which are supported by existing law or a nonfrivolous argument for extension or changes in existing law).

Similarly, the Eighth Claim for Relief alleges loss of consortium claims on behalf of John and Lydia, though it is unclear whether West Dakota law will recognize claims for loss of parental consortium. Barrymore has also included the frontier theory of a survival claim on behalf of Baby Dunton, though this one is a very long shot indeed. If such claims were clearly not viable, it would be improper to assert them, but where there may be a right to recover on these claims, Barrymore is entitled to present them and let the court decide whether they are legally cognizable.

Although Barrymore may have given considerable thought and research to these various unresolved issues, the complaint holds no hint of the doubts she may entertain about the strengths of these claims. Defendant's counsel will have to assess their viability and challenge those which she concludes are legally unsound.

3.   Other parts of the complaint reveal how the Duntons' counsel crafted the allegations to reflect the substantive requirements of each theory of relief.

For example, the Tenth Claim for Relief, seeking recovery for negligent infliction of emotional distress upon John, alleges that John immediately arrived on the accident scene and viewed his injured relatives in a sorry state. Paragraph 51. Barrymore may anticipate that West Dakota will adopt the *Dillon* approach to indirect infliction claims, which focuses on the immediacy of the event, the nearness of the bystander to the accident, and the closeness of the relationship of the bystander to the injured victims.

The allegations in Paragraph 50 lay the groundwork for an indirect infliction claim under the zone-of-danger rule as well. Barrymore has alleged that John was in the "immediate vicinity" of the accident. It is not at all clear that he *was* in the zone of danger: The facts indicate that he was 25 feet from the collision. But it is not clear that this is too far away either, so the allegation leaves the door open to litigate the issue. Similarly, she has alleged symptoms that John suffered as a result of his emotional distress which might suffice to establish "resulting physical injuries"[3] if West Dakota law turns out to require this.

Similarly, in Booth's count for negligent infliction of emotional distress, Barrymore realleges that Booth was a direct victim of the accident. See par. 45. Should West Dakota stick with the requirement of impact to support an emotional distress claim, this allegation will lay the groundwork for an argument that he can sue for *indirect* infliction because he suffered an impact. See Chapter 10, Example 1a.

Barrymore's complaint does not specifically allege that any one of these standards for recovery applies. It is not necessary to allege the exact legal standard in the complaint, but it is important to allege facts that demonstrate that the legal standard — whichever one the court ultimately applies — can be met.

4. Barrymore has given thought to other problems of proof as well. For example, she has alleged that Burton's driving violated several West Dakota statutes. Presumably, she has included these allegations to lay the groundwork for an instruction to the jury that Burton was "negligent per se" for violating these statutes. See Chapter 5.

5. The damage allegations in the various claims also reflect Barrymore's analysis of the substantive law. For example, the wrongful death claims seek damages for the financial support and consortium losses of the survivors, presumably echoing the language of the West Dakota wrongful death statute. See the "wherefore" clauses in the First and Third Claims for Relief. The survival claims, by contrast, seek damages for losses suffered prior to death. Note also that Barrymore has been careful to assert the various claims on behalf of the proper plaintiffs. The survival and wrongful death claims are

---

3. Although this seems like a stretch, some courts have construed "physical injuries" very broadly. See Chapter 10, Example 4f.

asserted by Booth as administrator of the estates of Isadora and Baby Dunton, while the other claims are asserted on behalf of the individuals named in each claim.

6.   Some issues considered by counsel have not made their way into the complaint at all. There is no claim at all for Booth's loss of consortium with John due to John's emotional distress claim. (See the discussion of this claim in Example 5b.) Counsel may have concluded that this is too long a shot, and that including it would detract from the overall credibility of the complaint. (A similar conclusion might have been warranted with regard to the Fourth Claim for Relief, the survival claim on behalf of Baby Dunton.)

7.   The Seventh Claim for Relief, for Isadora's loss of consortium with Booth, is technically part of the survival claim asserted in the Second Claim for Relief. However, Barrymore has pulled out this allegation and set it forth in a separate count. Analytically, this claim is distinct, because it is based not on Isadora's own injuries, but on her derivative injuries due to the injury to Booth. It facilitates clarity to assert it as a separate claim, even though it, like the other damages sought in the second count of the complaint, is authorized by the survival statute.

8.   Naturally, the questionable claims in Barrymore's complaint will not go unnoticed. Burton's counsel will challenge the legal sufficiency of some claims, such as the claim for prenatal pain and suffering and the claims for loss of parental consortium.

She will also probe, through discovery, the plaintiffs' ability to prove their allegations. For example, there will be difficult problems in proving the claims for Isadora's loss of consortium with Booth (Seventh Claim for Relief), since she is unavailable to testify. Similarly, the damages for the wrongful death of Baby Dunton will be very difficult to establish.

Burton's counsel will also challenge the plaintiffs' ability to prove causation on some claims. Even if John is entitled to recover for infliction of emotional distress, for example, he will have to establish that his withdrawal and poor performance in school were caused by the injury to Isadora, rather than other causes — plenty of teenagers suffer such symptoms for other reasons. Similarly, even if Lydia were entitled to consortium damages, she would have to show that her problems stem from her mother's death rather than other causes.

PART SEVEN

Liability of Multiple Defendants

16

Joint and Several Liability: The Classic Rules

Introduction

Our analysis so far has focused on the elements of intentional torts and negligence claims. For the sake of simplicity, the analysis has assumed that the plaintiff was suing a single defendant. However, in many cases an injured party has viable tort claims against a number of defendants. This chapter addresses the common law rules governing the liability of such "joint tortfeasors."

The traditional rules of liability of joint tortfeasors followed from the basic rules of causation. Quite sensibly, the courts refused to hold defendants liable for injuries they did not cause, even if they did cause some other damage. Suppose, for example, that Farmer Jones and Farmer Smith both decided to burn the stubble off their fields on a windy day, and both fires got away. If Farmer Jones's fire burned two acres on the west side of Doe's property, and Smith's burned five acres on the east side, it stands to reason that Jones would pay for the two-acre fire but not for the five-acre fire caused by Smith. Jones's negligence caused the two-acre fire, but (assuming that Jones and Smith acted independently) was not a but-for cause of the other fire and Jones was not liable for it. The same was true for Smith, who was liable for the five-acre fire but not the two-acre blaze. In such cases, where the damages could rationally be apportioned separately to the tortfeasors, the courts would do so. Restatement (Second) of Torts §881.

The converse proposition also held true. Where two parties were negligent, and the negligence of each was a cause of a single harm to the plaintiff, both were liable. Suppose that Fermi was a passenger in Joule's car, which collided with a truck driven by Edison, and that Fermi suffered a broken collar bone. If both drivers were negligent, and the negligence of each contributed to the accident, Fermi would have claims against them both for the injury. Each defendant was a but-for cause of a single, indivisible injury to Fermi. Unlike the two farmers example, there was no rational way to apportion the loss between the defendants, so the courts held both liable for the entire resulting damages. Restatement (Second) of Torts §879.

Here is another example to drive home the point. Watt, a worker on a construction site, negligently leaves an excavation unguarded, and Planck, an oblivious jogger, bumps Curie and knocks her into it, breaking her legs. Here again, Curie would have negligence claims against both Watt and Planck for her injuries. Since the negligence of each defendant contributed to causing the harm, and there was no way to ascribe a separable part of the injury to each tortfeasor, each was held liable for the entire harm.

Joint Tortfeasors Distinguished from Joint Conduct

At common law, joint liability also applied to the very different situation in which two defendants agreed to engage in tortious conduct that caused injury to the plaintiff. Suppose that Kelvin and Curie went looking for Marconi to beat him up, and Curie found him first and broke his jaw. On these facts, both Kelvin and Curie were liable to Marconi for the injuries inflicted by Curie, since they "acted in concert" to injure Marconi. Even though Kelvin never came on the scene, he encouraged and participated in a common scheme to injure Marconi and was held liable, in much the same way that conspirators are criminally responsible for the acts of other conspirators. See Restatement (Second) of Torts §876; Prosser & Keeton at 323. Similarly, if Ford and Hudson decided to race their cars on the highway, they were both liable to Lenoir if one of their cars hit him, since they jointly engaged in the negligent conduct that led to Lenoir's injury.

However, truly joint conduct such as this is relatively rare. It is much more common for the independent conduct of two actors to combine to injure the plaintiff, as in the Fermi example. In that case, Edison and Joule did not act together, probably did not know each other, may not even have known of the other's presence. However, their independent acts have contributed to cause a single injury. Such multiple causation may involve simultaneous independent acts of negligence, as in the Joule/Edison example, or successive ones, like Planck bumping Curie into the excavation left unguarded earlier in the day. See generally Chapter 7, pp.125-126, discussing cases involving more than one but-for cause of an injury.

The traditional common law rule was — and still is in many states today — that each tortfeasor in such cases was liable for all the plaintiff's injuries, since his negligence was a but-for cause of the plaintiff's injury. Courts generally refer to the defendants in such cases as "joint tortfeasors." This is clearly loose language, though universally used. Joule and Edison did not do anything "jointly," in the sense that Kelvin and Curie did in the battery example, since they acted separately, without agreement. It is the resulting *injury* that is joint, not the actions of the defendants. The phrase "joint tortfeasors" simply means that the defendants both contributed to a single, indivisible injury to the plaintiff and are each fully liable for that injury.

It is often said that joint tortfeasors are "jointly and severally liable" for the injury. This means that each is liable for the full amount of the plaintiff's damages, and may be sued for those damages either singly or along with the other tortfeasors. If the plaintiff prevails in an action against joint tortfeasors, she is entitled to a judgment against each for her full damages. For example, if the jury found for Fermi against both Joule and Edison, and found Fermi's damages to be $27,000, the court would enter judgment against both Joule and Edison for $27,000. Fermi would obtain a judgment like that in Figure 16-1. Alternatively, had he sued Edison alone he would have gotten a judgment against him for the full $27,000.

Satisfaction of Judgments

Under the judgment in Figure 16-1, Fermi would be entitled to collect his $27,000 from either Edison or Joule. Of course, he could not get $27,000 from each of them, for a total of $54,000. The plaintiff was entitled to one full "satisfaction" of his damages from joint tortfeasors, but no more. Thus, if Joule paid Fermi $27,000, the judgment was deemed satisfied, and Fermi could not collect any additional amount from Edison. Similarly, if he obtained a judgment against Edison and Edison paid, he could not collect from Joule for the same injuries. Prosser & Keeton at 331.

Suppose, however, that Fermi sued Edison alone and obtained a judgment for $27,000, but Edison was unable to satisfy the judgment. Early cases held that once Fermi obtained a judgment against one tortfeasor, the judgment extinguished his claim against all the tortfeasors, so that he could not sue Joule separately if Edison failed to pay. However, the courts later came around to the position that, as long as Fermi's judgment had not been *satisfied*, he was entitled sue Joule for the same injury, and try to collect from him instead. Or, if Edison had a $10,000 insurance policy, and paid that much, Fermi could seek a separate judgment against Joule and collect the remaining $17,000 from him.

Suppose that Joule was a close friend of Fermi's (or his boss) and Fermi, understandably reluctant to sue Joule, sued Edison only. At common law if

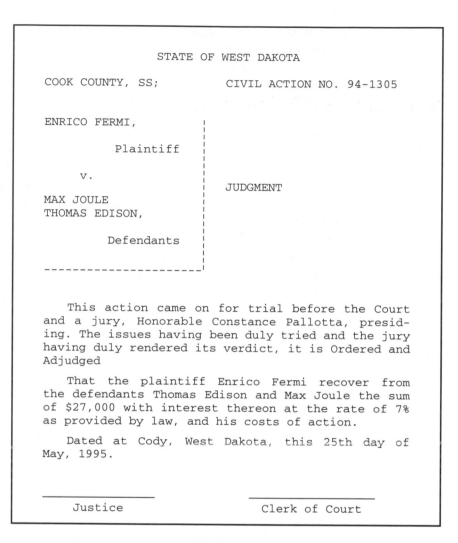

STATE OF WEST DAKOTA

COOK COUNTY, SS;   CIVIL ACTION NO. 94-1305

ENRICO FERMI,

      Plaintiff

    v.
                    JUDGMENT

MAX JOULE
THOMAS EDISON,

     Defendants

    This action came on for trial before the Court and a jury, Honorable Constance Pallotta, presiding. The issues having been duly tried and the jury having duly rendered its verdict, it is Ordered and Adjudged

    That the plaintiff Enrico Fermi recover from the defendants Thomas Edison and Max Joule the sum of $27,000 with interest thereon at the rate of 7% as provided by law, and his costs of action.

    Dated at Cody, West Dakota, this 25th day of May, 1995.

    _____

        Justice   Clerk of Court

Figure 16-1

a joint tortfeasor like Edison were found liable and paid the judgment, he had no right to force other tortfeasors to "contribute" to the judgment. Edison was liable for the damages, was justly made to pay them, and had no complaint if Joule got off without paying. The courts refused to adjust the loss as between the wrongdoers, just as it refused (under the doctrine of contributory negligence) to adjust a loss between a negligent plaintiff and a negligent defendant. This classic no-contribution rule is no longer the law in most states,[1] but it was for many years. See Chapter 17, which analyzes

---

1. Many states still refuse to allow an intentional tortfeasor to recover contribution, however.

the basic principles of contribution among joint tortfeasors, and Chapter 22, which illustrates some of the current variations.

Settlement and Release of Claims

Other problems arose if Fermi settled his claim against one tortfeasor and then sued the other. Suppose, for example, that Fermi settled with Joule, agreeing to release his tort claim against Joule for $13,000. When the plaintiff settled with a tortfeasor, he would ordinarily give that defendant a "release" in exchange for payment of the settlement amount. The release would waive all of the plaintiff's claims against that defendant arising out of a particular accident or dispute. Figure 16-2 is a simple example of a release.

RELEASE AND SETTLEMENT OF CLAIM

    In consideration of thirteen thousand dollars ($13,000), receipt of which is hereby acknowledged, I, Enrico Fermi, of Saginaw, West Dakota, on behalf of myself and my heirs, legal representatives and assigns, hereby release Max Joule of Johnstown, West Dakota, or his heirs or representatives, from all liability, claims, demands, rights or causes of action incident to property damage and personal injury sustained by me in an automobile accident that occurred on May 4, 1994 at Johnstown, West Dakota, involving an automobile driven by Max Joule. This release covers all claims which I had, now have or may have in the future against Max Joule, his heirs or representatives arising out of the May 4, 1994 accident.

    By executing this instrument, I do not waive any claim or claims that I may now or hereafter have against any person, firm or corporation other than Max Joule, the releasee named herein. I understand that Max Joule does not, by making the payment set forth above, admit any liability or responsibility for the above-described accident or the consequences thereof.

    In witness whereof, I have executed this release at Saginaw, West Dakota, on July 29, 1995.

Signature _____

Figure 16-2

A Practical Question

1.   If Joule, as a joint tortfeasor, is fully liable for the entire injury to Fermi, and the likely damages are close to $30,000, why would Fermi let him off the hook for $13,000?

———————————

At common law, giving one tortfeasor a release was a tricky business, because the courts held that a release to one tortfeasor released the plaintiff's claims against *all* joint tortfeasors. If Fermi gave a release to Joule, he was deemed to have released Edison, Watt, and any other possible defendants as well, regardless of the amount Joule paid for the release. Historically, there were several reasons for the rule. First, the plaintiff was considered to have a single cause of action for her injuries, even though each defendant was fully liable on that cause of action. *Cooper v. Robert Hall Clothes, Inc.*, 390 N.E.2d 155, 157 (Ind. 1979); Prosser & Keeton at 332. By giving a release to any tortfeasor, Fermi relinquished the cause of action itself. Thus, he was barred from bringing a subsequent suit on that cause of action against another tortfeasor.

A second, less formalistic rationale for the common law rule that a release barred suit against other tortfeasors was the concern that the plaintiff would settle successively with each tortfeasor and collect more than the value of her claim. Since each tortfeasor was liable for the full amount of the plaintiff's damages, a plaintiff could divide and conquer by extracting substantial settlements from each. Fermi, for example, might settle with Joule for $18,000 and with Edison for $18,000. Both might have the incentive to accept the settlement, since it is $9,000 less than the (assumed) $27,000 value of the claim. If they both settled, Fermi would be overcompensated by $9,000 ($36,000 − $27,000). The rule that a release barred suit against the other tortfeasors prevented this: Once Fermi gave a release to Joule, Edison would have no incentive to settle, since the release barred suit against Edison as well as Joule.

The release rule applied even if the plaintiff tried to limit the release to the settling tortfeasor. Thus, the second paragraph of Fermi's release in Figure 16-2, which states that it does not affect his claims against any other joint tortfeasor, was given no effect. Under the common law view, Fermi was trying to have his cake and eat it too, that is, to continue to prosecute a cause of action that had been surrendered by the release.

Another Practical Question

2.   Did the common law release rule encourage or discourage settlements?
This early rule that a release of one tortfeasor released them all was later abandoned, for several reasons. First, the formalistic view that the claims against Joule and Edison constitute a single, indivisible cause of

action is no longer accepted. In recent decades, courts have recognized that, even if Fermi's *damages* are indivisible, he has independent claims for those damages against each tortfeasor. Consequently, it is no longer logical to infer that he abandons claims against one tortfeasor by settling with the other.

Second, the release rule prevented settlements with individual tortfeasors who were willing to pay a part of the plaintiff's damages, but not to pay enough to induce the plaintiff to release her entire claim. This led to creative efforts by lawyers to find a way of settling with one party without relinquishing the right to sue other tortfeasors. The most common device for evading the common law release rule was the "covenant not to sue," by which the plaintiff covenanted (agreed) not to sue the defendant on the claim. In theory, she had not surrendered her claim, but merely promised that she would not bring a law suit to enforce it against the settling defendant.[2] This was fighting formalism with formalism. The actual effect of the covenant not to sue was the same as the release: Plaintiff gave up her claim against the defendant in exchange for a money payment. But, since it did not technically "release" the claim, plaintiffs argued that they were still entitled to sue other joint tortfeasors on the claim.

Because the release rule was an obstacle to sensible settlement of tort claims, some courts sanctioned its evasion through the covenant not to sue. In these states, the common law rule that a release barred any further suit against other tortfeasors became a dead letter. Counsel who understood the difference simply used the covenant not to sue instead of a release, thus achieving settlement with one tortfeasor without waiving the right to sue others. Defendants went along with the practice, because they also benefitted from such settlements: They could settle legitimate claims without having to pay more than their fair share of the plaintiff's damages. Thus a kernel of common sense was rescued from a shell of outdated legal doctrine.

Other courts, rather than endorsing evasion of the release rule through the covenant not to sue, have overruled it outright. In these jurisdictions, a release or covenant not to sue given to one tortfeasor does not release other parties, unless the release so stipulates. See Restatement (Second) of Torts §885. Under this approach, the release in Figure 16-2 would preserve Fermi's right to sue Edison, since it not only shows no intent to release Edison, but affirmatively states that it does not. See generally Harper, James & Gray, §10.1, at 32-37.

---

2. For example a covenant not to sue might provide that the plaintiff "covenants with Max Joule, of Saginaw, West Dakota, his heirs, legal representatives and assigns, to never institute any suit or action at law or in equity against Max Joule by reason of any claim I now have or may hereafter acquire relating to an accident that occurred on May 4, 1988 at Johnstown, West Dakota. . ."

Some of this common law of joint and several liability has now been replaced or modified by statute in various ways. See especially Chapter 22, which analyzes some elegant variations on these basic principles. But many states retain the common law rules, at least in part. In addition, a knowledge of this common law background is important for understanding current principles of joint liability and contribution.

If you have studied recent developments in contribution, comparative negligence, and several liability, put them aside for the moment. Analyze the examples below based solely on the "classic rules" of joint and several liability addressed in this introduction.

EXAMPLES

Joint Sheepfeasors

3.   Farmer Jones's prize field of Kentucky blue grass is eaten clean when Herder's and Shepherd's sheep escape from their pens. Investigation reveals that both Shepherd and Herder were negligent and that 30 of Shepherd's sheep got into Jones's field and ten of Herder's got in. Are Shepherd and Herder jointly and severally liable to Jones?

4.   In the Edison/Joule example, Edison and Joule caused Fermi $27,000 in damages between them. Without regard to history, one sensible and seemingly fair solution would be to split the damages, that is, to hold Edison liable for $13,500 and Joule for the same.
   a. Why would this solution appear illogical to a traditional common law judge?
   b. Suppose that a bill came before the legislature to introduce this approach to the liability of multiple tortfeasors. Who would oppose it, plaintiffs or defendants?

5.   Whiting and Hahn, two employees of an electrical contractor, are working together to install wiring in Pringle's house. They agree that Whiting will stop in the basement to cut off the power to an exposed junction box on the wall, but Whiting forgets to do it. An hour later, Shattuck, a plasterer, negligently swings his ladder into the junction box, causing a short circuit and resulting fire. Pringle's house sustains $50,000 in damages.
   a. Which of the three are liable for the damage?
   b. How much is each liable for?
   c. Assume that Pringle settled with Whiting for $40,000, and gave her a release. She then sues Shattuck for her injuries. In a jurisdiction that applied the strict common law release rule, what would the court do?
   d. What would the court do if Pringle gave Whiting a covenant not to sue, in a jurisdiction that allowed evasion of the common law release rule through a covenant not to sue?

Dissatisfaction of Judgments

6. Erg sues Kelvin for negligence in causing a fire and recovers a judgment for $16,000. Kelvin, who is bankrupt, does not pay. Can Erg now sue Volt, whose negligence also caused the fire, to recover for the fire damage?

7. Suppose that Erg settles his claim against Kelvin for damages arising from the fire, for $7000, the amount of Kelvin's insurance coverage. Now he sues Volt for the same injuries.

   a. If he gets a judgment against Volt for $16,000, how much will Volt have to pay?

   b. Suppose that Volt only has $5,000, and pays that. Can Erg sue Planck, another tortfeasor who allegedly caused the fire?

   c. Assume that Erg sued Volt, after settling with Kelvin for $7,000, and the jury determined that Erg's damages were $4,500. What would Volt have to pay?

   d. Assume that Erg settled with Kelvin for $4,000, and in a subsequent action against Volt the jury determined his damages to be $16,000. How much must Volt pay to Erg? How much must Kelvin pay to Volt?

Joint *and* Several Liability

8. Bethune is driving a backhoe during the construction of a storm drain. She negligently backs up without looking or sounding her beeper and hits Maltby, a passing pedestrian, breaking her leg and knocking her over next to the excavation. DeWolfe, a construction worker down in the pit, negligently throws a large stone up out of the excavation without looking. The stone hits Maltby on the head, causing a severe concussion. She sues them both for her injuries.

   a. Are they jointly and severally liable to Maltby?

   b. Suppose that Bethune settles with Maltby for $20,000, and Maltby then sues DeWolfe and recovers a judgment for $30,000. How much should DeWolfe pay?

Bewitched, Bewildered, and Befuddled

9. Assume that Fermi suffered a serious back injury in his accident with Joule and Edison. The undisputed evidence shows that he was out of work for six months, suffered $26,000 in lost wages, paid $21,000 in medical bills, and sustained serious pain and suffering, as well as some permanent disability.

   At trial, Judge Fudd instructs the jury as follows:

If you find that the defendants were both negligent, and that the negligence of each defendant was a cause of the plaintiff's injuries, then you must find the defendants liable for the full amount of damages suffered by the plaintiff.

The jury comes back with the verdict in Figure 16-3. Fermi's attorney is amazed that the jury could have only awarded $50,000 in damages, which allows a mere $3,000 over the proven economic losses to compensate Fermi for pain and suffering and disability. Something, she suspects, has gone amiss in the jury's deliberations.

STATE OF WEST DAKOTA

COOK COUNTY, SS;   CIVIL ACTION NO. 94-1305

ENRICO FERMI,

      Plaintiff

    v.
                        VERDICT

MAX JOULE
THOMAS EDISON,

      Defendants

We the Jury, find for the plaintiff against defendant Joule for $_____50,000_____ . (Strike out if inapplicable)

We find for the plaintiff against the defendant Edison for $_____50,000_____ . (Strike out if inapplicable)

~~We find for the defendants.~~ (Strike out if inapplicable)

Benjamin Franklin
_____
Jury Foreperson

Figure 16-3

a. What do you think the jury did, and what ambiguity in Judge Fudd's instruction led them to do it?

b. How should the plaintiff have avoided the problem?

EXPLANATIONS

A Practical Question

1.   There are many reasons why a plaintiff might settle a claim against one tortfeasor for less than the full value of her damages. She might have doubts about her ability to prove that the particular party is liable, and therefore settle for less than the full value of her claim to account for the risk that she would lose entirely at trial. (The reasonable risk-averse client would obviously prefer $13,000 in hand to a 25 percent chance of collecting $27,000.) The plaintiff might know that the party is unable to pay more than the insurance coverage available, so there is little point in obtaining an unenforceable judgment for more. She might not want to try the case against a particular party, due to jury sympathy or an anticipated aggressive defense by that party. It might also cost more to pursue the case against that defendant than she gives up by settling, perhaps due to the need for expensive expert testimony to prove negligence by that defendant.

In addition, tort claims often involve intangible damages such as pain and suffering or disfigurement. In such cases, neither party knows what value the jury will place on the plaintiff's injuries. Thus even a plaintiff who expects to win at trial may settle for less than the apparent full value of the claim, to avoid the risk that a jury will return a meager verdict.

Thus, a settlement against Joule for $13,000 may make good sense for Fermi, even if he believes that a jury would give him a $27,000 verdict. It makes particularly good sense if Fermi *retains his right to sue Edison*, since he may still collect the balance of his damages from him. The $13,000 he collects from Joule would be credited against the later judgment, but he would still be made whole despite his settlement with one of the tortfeasors.

Another Practical Question

2.   The common law release rule discouraged settlements, because a release barred the plaintiff from suing any other party on the same claim. Thus, a plaintiff would only settle with one of several tortfeasors if the amount offered came close to the amount she would likely recover if she tried the case against all three. In other words, the settlement against one had to be good enough to induce the plaintiff to abandon her claims against everyone; she couldn't settle with one tortfeasor for part of her damages with the hope of recovering more from someone else. Since the common law rule forced the plaintiff to set a high price on settlement, individual defendants in a multidefendant case would be less likely to ante up the amount necessary to settle the case.

Joint Sheepfeasors

3.   As the Introduction states, defendants were held jointly and severally liable for the plaintiff's damages if the damages could not rationally be apportioned among them, if they were "indivisible." Here, it is doubtless impossible to determine which sheep ate which blades of grass, but there is a basis for a rough apportionment of the damages based on the number of sheep of each defendant that joined the repast. Assuming a sheep is a sheep when it comes to appetite, it is a fair inference that Shepherd's sheep ate about three-quarters of the grass, and Herder's ate the other quarter. Most courts would apportion the damages between Shepherd and Herder on that basis, rather than holding them jointly and severally liable. Restatement (Second) of Torts §433A cmt. d.

While courts will endeavor to make such apportionment, even where it requires some approximation, it is worth reiterating that in most cases that is simply not possible. Where two negligent acts combine to cause a broken back, a fatal heart attack, or a fire that burns the plaintiff's barn, it is simply not possible to ascribe part of the injury to one defendant's negligence and part to the other's. In this large class of cases, joint and several liability has been the classic rule because apportionment is not a feasible alternative.

4a.   Logically, there is no reason why the multiple tortfeasor problem could not be dealt with by dividing the plaintiff's damages in this way. If there were two tortfeasors, each would be liable for half the damages; if there were seven, each would be liable for a seventh, and so on.

However, this pragmatic solution was antithetical to the conceptual approach of the common law, which viewed both Edison and Joule as having caused *all* of Fermi's damages, not half. But for Edison's negligent driving, no accident would have taken place, and Fermi would have suffered no injury. Because of Edison's negligence (helped along, admittedly, by Joule's as well), he suffered $27,000 in damages. The same was true of Joule. Because both defendants had caused the full harm, courts refused to divide the damages in half.[3]

b. Plaintiffs would resist this Solomonic solution fiercely. Under the traditional rules of joint and several liability, both Edison and Joule were fully liable. If Edison were insolvent, Joule would still have to pay the full damages under the classic rules. By contrast, if the rule were changed so that each was "severally" liable for half the damages, Fermi would collect $13,500 from Joule and nothing from Edison. Thus, Fermi would be the loser if Edison were unable to pay. Under joint and several liability, however, *Joule*

---

3. On the other hand, once courts accepted the concept of contribution between joint tortfeasors, essentially the same division ultimately resulted, if one tortfeasor paid the full judgment and sued the other for contribution.

takes the risk of Edison's insolvency, and the plaintiff has twice the chance of being fully compensated for his injuries.

5a. In this case, Whiting was negligent in failing to cut off the power, and Shattuck was negligent in swinging the ladder into the junction box. Their independent acts together caused the fire. Thus, they are joint tortfeasors in the sense that their separate negligent acts concurred to cause indivisible harm to Pringle. Both are liable to her.

What of Hahn, who was working with Whiting? The facts do not indicate that she was negligent, since she was not responsible for cutting off the power. (We will leave aside the possibility that Hahn was supposed to check the box, or some other unspecified basis for implicating her.) Nor is she liable for Whiting's negligence simply because she was working on the same job with her. That would be a tough rule indeed, making employees liable for the torts of any co-worker.

It is true that she and Whiting agreed that Whiting would turn off the power. But agreeing to split up the work in a particular way is quite different from agreeing to engage in tortious conduct. This is not a "joint tort" situation, like the concerted action example in which two drivers engage in a drag race. There, two actors consciously engaged in negligent conduct together, which they knew created unreasonable risks to others. Here, while Hahn and Whiting were both engaged in the construction work, Hahn did not agree to engage in any negligent course of conduct with Whiting. Thus, Hahn is not liable for the negligence of Whiting.

b. Under traditional causation analysis, both Whiting and Shattuck were causes of the fire, since the negligence of each was a but-for cause leading to it. Thus, each caused the plaintiff's entire loss, and was held liable for that entire loss. As joint tortfeasors, Whiting and Shattuck would each be liable for $50,000.

c. Under the strict common law release rule, a party who gave a release of her claim to any tortfeasor surrendered her right to sue all possible defendants on that claim. Thus, Pringle would be barred from bringing any further suit on the same claim against Whiting or Shattuck. If this rule applied, Pringle's suit would be dismissed.

d. In a jurisdiction that held that a covenant not to sue did not waive any rights against other tortfeasors, Pringle would still be entitled to bring suit against Shattuck. However, if she recovered $50,000, the $40,000 already paid by Whiting in settlement of the claim against her would be credited against the judgment. Shattuck would only have to pay $10,000.

Dissatisfaction of Judgments

6.   Under the earlier cases, the answer to this question was "no." A judgment was treated like a release; that is, getting a judgment on a tort cause of action was deemed to extinguish the underlying cause of action, leaving the

judgment instead. But that rule later gave way to the more recent common law rule stated in the introduction, that a judgment against one tortfeasor did not bar suit against another, unless the first judgment was satisfied. Thus, Erg could still sue Volt and get a second *judgment* for her damages, but could not *collect* more than her actual assessed damages.

7a. Because no plaintiff was entitled to more than one full satisfaction of his damages, Volt would get a credit against the $16,000 judgment for the $7,000 Erg has received in settlement from Kelvin. Thus, he would have to pay $9,000 to Erg.

b. At this point, Erg has received $7,000 in settlement from Kelvin and $5,000 from Volt under the judgment. He is still short $4,000. Since he has not yet received full satisfaction of his damages, he can still bring suit against Planck to recover for the remaining $4,000.

c. In this example, Erg settled with Kelvin for more than the jury ultimately determines Erg's damages to be. Volt would get a credit for the settlement, and that would more than cover the judgment amount. Volt would pay nothing. On the other hand, Kelvin would not get anything back either. A deal is a deal; he bought his peace, and he cannot later claim that he paid too much for it.

d. Here again, Volt gets a credit for the settlement amount. He will be liable to Erg for $12,000 (the $16,000 judgment minus the $4,000 paid by Kelvin in settlement). He will have paid more than half of the damages, but at common law this did not give him any right of contribution from Kelvin. As stated previously, the common law had no trouble requiring Volt to pay the *full $16,000* in damages he had caused. Thus, courts were not troubled if, on facts like these, he paid some lesser amount but still more than his "share." But this classic rule of the common law has been changed in most states in recent years. (See generally Chapter 17 on contribution).

Joint *and* Several Liability

8a. In this example, Bethune and DeWolfe are joint tortfeasors as to part of Maltby's injuries, but not as to all of them. The negligence of both Bethune and DeWolfe caused the concussion. Maltby would not have been hit by the stone if Bethune had not knocked her into harm's way, or if DeWolfe had not negligently thrown the stone out of the pit. It is a case of successive negligent acts that together cause the harm. So long as DeWolfe's subsequent negligence is foreseeable, it does not insulate Bethune from liability. As to Maltby's concussion, Bethune and DeWolfe are joint tortfeasors.

However, DeWolfe is not a joint tortfeasor with Bethune in causing Maltby's broken leg. DeWolfe's negligence had no part in causing the broken leg, which happened before DeWolfe entered the picture. Thus, Bethune would be solely liable for this injury, but both would be liable for Maltby's concussion damages.

b. This is a difficult problem. The settlement does not indicate whether the $20,000 in settlement was paid for the broken leg, for the concussion, or for both. How is the court to determine the proper credit to give DeWolfe toward the joint liability for the concussion?

Well, I don't know. Since the payment was made to settle all claims Maltby had against Bethune, at least some of the settlement should be allocated to the concussion damages. But how much? I suppose there are several possibilities:

- The court could assume that half the settlement amount was for the leg and half for the concussion, and therefore credit half against the judgment for the concussion damages. This would be the easiest solution to administer — DeWolfe would get a $10,000 credit. But it could be wildly inaccurate if Maltby's damages from the broken leg were limited, and he was severely disabled from the concussion.
- The court could determine the reasonable amount of damages attributable to the broken leg, assume that this separate liability was fully compensated by the settlement, and give DeWolfe a credit for anything above that. (If the reasonable value of the broken leg were $12,000, for example, DeWolfe would get a credit of $8,000 against the concussion damages.) But this would be crazy, wouldn't it? First, it requires the court to determine the damages for the leg, an issue that the parties had settled. Courts have enough to do trying cases that *aren't* settled, without resuscitating ones that are. Second, it assumes that Bethune paid full value for the leg, but Maltby probably meant to settle for a part of the damages from each injury.
- The court could determine the reasonable value of the broken leg, and give DeWolfe a proportional credit. For example, if the leg damages were $10,000, and the concussion damages (as determined by the verdict against DeWolfe) were $30,000, the court could assume that three quarters of the settlement was for the concussion, and give DeWolfe a credit of $15,000 against the judgment. Like the second solution, however, this requires findings of fact on the plaintiff's broken leg damages, an issue that Bethune and Maltby had tried to resolve by the settlement.[4]

Bewitched, Bewildered, and Befuddled

9a. It is very likely that the ambiguity in Judge Fudd's instruction led the jury to render a verdict that does not convey their intended meaning. The jury in this case probably found Fermi's damages to be $100,000 (a more likely figure given the extent of his intangible injuries), and thought it was

---

4. I sent my research assistant off to find an answer to this, but he never did. If you find one, let me know.

rendering a verdict that would require *each* defendant to pay $50,000, for a total of $100,000.

Unfortunately, under principles of joint and several liability, the jury's verdict slip only makes Joule and Edison liable for a *total* of $50,000. Fermi can collect that amount from either, or part from each, but cannot receive more than a total of $50,000. (Compare the judgment in Figure 16-1.) Judge Fudd's instruction was open to this misinterpretation, since it required the jury to find "the defendants" liable for the plaintiff's full damages, not *each* defendant liable for the plaintiff's full damages.

The verdict slip in Figure 16-3 compounded the judge's error. The verdict slip simply indicates which defendants are found liable, and how much each is liable for; it does not clearly state the plaintiff's total damages or that the jury must find each defendant liable for the plaintiff's full damages.

b. The plaintiff could have avoided this problem by pointing out the ambiguity in the judge's instruction before he gave it. Counsel for all parties will be given a chance to review proposed jury instructions before the judge instructs the jury, so that they may object to instructions that wrongly state the applicable law. If plaintiff's counsel had realized the problem, she could have asked Judge Fudd to revise the instruction along the following lines:

> If you find that both defendants were negligent, and that the negligence of each defendant was a cause of the plaintiff's injuries, then you must find each defendant liable for the full damages suffered by the plaintiff.

The distinction between this instruction and Judge Fudd's is not very great, but the difference in the effect of the two is dramatic. If the jury understood the instruction, and it actually intended the plaintiff to recover $100,000, this instruction would clearly require them to return a verdict for $100,000, not $50,000, against each defendant.

A cogent criticism of jury trial is that juries often do not understand the subtleties of their instructions. Their verdict must be based on instructions on complicated principles that they are given once, often orally. To put the matter in perspective, consider whether you, after brief treatment of joint and several liability in your torts class, would feel prepared to go into a jury room and apply these rules accurately to an actual case.

Fermi's lawyer could also have reduced the risk of jury misunderstanding by asking the court to use a special verdict form like that in Figure 16-4, which requires the jury to make specific factual findings on negligence and damages. Under this verdict, the jury does not have to fully understand the governing liability rules. So long as it answers the factual questions accurately, the court can enter an appropriate judgment under joint and several liability principles. If the jury had rendered the verdict in Figure 16-4, the judge would have clearly understood that the jury intended Fermi to recover $100,000, and would have entered judgment against each defendant for that amount.

STATE OF WEST DAKOTA

COOK COUNTY, SS;   CIVIL ACTION NO. 94-1305

ENRICO FERMI,

           Plaintiff

      v.
                                 VERDICT
MAX JOULE
THOMAS EDISON,

           Defendants

- -

1. Do you find that the defendant Max Joule was negligent?

           Yes___✔___   No_____

2. Do you find that the defendant Thomas Edison was
   negligent?

           Yes___✔___   No_____

3. If the defendant Max Joule was negligent, was
   his negligence a proximate cause of the plaintiff's damages?

           Yes___✔___   No_____

4. If the defendant Thomas Edison was negligent,
   was his negligence a proximate cause of the
   plaintiff's damages?

           Yes___✔___   No_____

5. If you find that either defendant was negligent,
   and that his negligence was a proximate cause of
   the accident, what amount do you find will fairly
   and reasonably compensate the plaintiff for the
   injuries caused by the accident?

           $___*100,000*___

                    S. Isaac Newton
           _____
                    Jury Foreperson

Figure 16-4

17

Honor Among Thieves: Basic Principles of Contribution

Introduction

The last chapter explored the common law rules governing the liability of multiple tortfeasors who cause a common injury. As that discussion indicates, courts generally hold that each tortfeasor who contributed to an indivisible injury is fully liable to the plaintiff for his damages. This basic rule, which protects the plaintiff's ability to collect as long as one tortfeasor is able to pay, remains true in many (though not all) jurisdictions today.

However, the rule of joint and several liability can lead to unfair results. Suppose that Nash negligently left his bicycle in the road, and Benchley, not looking where he was going, drove into it, lost control of the car, and injured Twain. Under the common law, Twain could sue either Nash or Benchley for his injuries. The plaintiff was in control, and could choose to impose the full loss on either of the joint tortfeasors. If Benchley was his brother-in-law, Twain could keep peace in the family by suing Nash instead. If he sued Nash and recovered, Nash would have to pay Twain's full damages, and Benchley would pay nothing, even if he also caused the accident.

Of course, in many cases the plaintiff took the prudent course of suing all possible defendants, since he might only prove that one was negligent, or that the negligence of one had caused the injury. But even if Twain sued both Nash and Benchley in our example, and recovered judgment against both, he could still choose to *collect* the judgment from either one. So he could still target Nash and let Benchley off the hook entirely if Nash was able to pay.

If Nash did pay, he had no right to force Benchley to "contribute," that is, to reimburse him for part of the damages he had paid to Twain. The common law, with its somewhat moralistic view of these matters, had no problem with the fact that Nash ended up paying the entire judgment. Nash was a wrongdoer, had caused Twain's injuries, and could fairly be made to pay. Justice was done between the plaintiff and the defendant, and that was that. Nash would not be heard to complain that Benchley had gotten off scot free, so long as Nash had actually caused the damages he was forced to pay.[1]

Although the common law rule denying contribution from joint tortfeasors was widely applied for many years, it was also widely criticized. Prosser sums up the attack with his usual incisiveness:

> There is an obvious lack of sense and justice in a rule which permits the entire burden of a loss, for which two defendants were equally, unintentionally responsible, to be shouldered onto one alone, according to the accident of a successful levy of execution, the existence of liability insurance, the plaintiff's whim or spite, or the plaintiff's collusion with the other wrongdoer, while the latter goes scot free.

Prosser & Keeton at 337-338. Most critics of the no-contribution rule accepted the basic proposition that each defendant should be fully liable to the *plaintiff*. However, they argued that a defendant who paid the plaintiff's damages should be able to redistribute the loss by making the other tortfeasors contribute to the payment of the common liability.

Most states have provided for contribution among joint tortfeasors either by statute or judicial decision. Contribution provisions now vary considerably; some of the more elegant variations are explored in Chapter 22. This chapter introduces the basic principles of contribution, using the Uniform Contribution Among Tortfeasors Act, a model contribution statute drawn up in 1955,[2] as an example. The relevant sections of the Uniform Act, which has been

---

1. The common law view is summed up in *Fidelity and Casualty Co. of New York v. Chapman*, 120 P.2d 223, 225 (Ore. 1941):

> [N]o man can make his own misconduct the ground for action in his favor. . . . [I]t is against public policy for courts to pause in the administration of justice to determine the degree of culpability between wrongdoers. The law, under such circumstances, leaves the parties where it finds them.

2. Unif. Contribution Among Tortfeasors Act, 12 U.L.A. 7 (1982). An earlier version of the Uniform Contribution Among Tortfeasors Act was promulgated in 1939. It was superseded by the 1955 Act.

followed in a good many states in drafting their contribution statutes, are set forth on p.362 below.

The Right to Contribution

The Uniform Act starts out by creating the right to contribution among joint tortfeasors:

> 1 (a) Except as otherwise provided in this Act, where two or more persons become jointly or severally liable in tort for the same injury to person or property or for the same wrongful death, there is a right of contribution among them even though judgment has not been recovered against all or any of them.
>
> (b) The right of contribution exists only in favor of a tortfeasor who has paid more than his pro rata share of the common liability, and his total recovery is limited to the amount paid by him in excess of his pro rata share. No tortfeasor is compelled to make contribution beyond his pro rata share of the entire liability. . . .

These provisions of the Uniform Act allow a tortfeasor who has paid more than his "pro rata" share of the plaintiff's damages to recover contribution from other tortfeasors who are liable for the same injury.[3] Suppose, for example, that Twain recovered a judgment of $20,000 against Nash for his injuries in the auto accident, and Nash paid the judgment. Section 1(a) of the Uniform Act authorizes Nash to recover contribution from Benchley, if Benchley was "jointly or severally liable in tort for the same injury. . . ." Thus, to establish his right to contribution, Nash would have to show that Benchley was also liable to Twain for his injuries in the accident.

Section 1(b) determines *how much* Nash can seek from Benchley. It authorizes Nash to seek contribution for amounts above his (Nash's) "pro rata" share. In this context, "pro rata" means equal. If there are three tortfeasors, the pro rata share of each is one-third; if there are five, it is one-fifth, and so on. Since there are two tortfeasors in the example, Nash's pro rata share is one-half. Thus, if he paid the $20,000, he could recover one-half the judgment, or $10,000, from Benchley. If there were four tortfeasors, the pro rata shares of each would be $5,000. On those facts, if Nash paid the $20,000 to Twain he would only be entitled to $5,000 from Benchley, since §1(b) limits each tortfeasor's liability for contribution to his pro rata share. Nash would have to go after the other two tortfeasors for their shares to obtain full contribution. If all three paid their shares to Nash, Nash would

---

3. The Uniform Act, like most contribution statutes, bars contribution claims by an intentional tortfeasor. See §1(c), quoted at p.362. The discussion in this chapter assumes that all claims are based on negligence.

collect $15,000 in contribution and end up paying $5,000 of the judgment, his own pro rata share.

Enforcing the Right to Contribution

Suppose that Twain had sued Nash alone and recovered his $20,000 judgment. As indicated above, Nash could not simply demand $10,000 from Benchley. Under §1(a), Benchley is only liable for contribution if he is a joint tortfeasor. Thus, before he could recover contribution from Benchley, Nash would have to prove that Benchley was *also liable to Twain* for the damages Nash had already paid.

The simplest way for Nash to do this would be to bring Benchley into the original suit when Twain sued him. Most states allow a defendant in Nash's position to "implead" a joint tortfeasor for contribution, that is, to make him a party to the original suit. See, e.g., Okla. Code of Civ. Pro. tit. 12 §2014 (1993) (allowing defendant to implead a person who may be liable to him for all or part of plaintiff's claim against him); Va. Sup. Ct Rules, Rule 3:10 (1994) (same). If Nash impleaded Benchley, the court would determine in a single trial whether Benchley and Nash were liable for Twain's injury. If both were found liable and Nash then paid the judgment (remember, he is still fully liable to *Twain* based on the principle of joint and several liability), he would make a motion in the original suit for contribution from Benchley. Section 3(b) of the Uniform Act expressly authorizes such orders for contribution in the original suit.

Suppose, however, that Twain sued Nash only, and Nash did not (or could not)[4] implead Benchley. If Nash were found liable, and paid the judgment, he could then bring a separate action for contribution against Benchley. This is a new lawsuit. Nash is the plaintiff, Benchley is the defendant, and the claim is for recovery of Benchley's pro rata share of the judgment which Nash has paid. Section 3 of the Uniform Act authorizes such separate suits for contribution, (see §3(a)) and establishes limitations periods for them (§3(c), (d)). Figure 17-1 is a simple example of a complaint for contribution.

Like all pleadings, Nash's complaint is basically commonsensical. Since Benchley was not a defendant in the original action, it has never been determined that he is in fact liable for Twain's injuries. Thus, to obtain contribution Nash must allege and prove that Benchley is liable to Twain for the accident due to his negligence. See par. 8, 9. He also alleges each of the further requirements for contribution established in the statute: That he (Nash) has been sued by the injured plaintiff and held liable for the same injury (par. 3-6), that he has paid more than his pro rata share (par. 7, 10), and that he is entitled to pro rata contribution under the statute (par. 10). The relief de-

---

4. Nash might not be able to implead Benchley, for example, if the court in which Twain brought suit lacked personal jurisdiction over Benchley.

STATE OF WEST DAKOTA
SUPERIOR COURT

GALLATIN COUNTY, SS: CIVIL ACTION NO. 95-0129

OGDEN NASH,

     Plaintiff

     v.   COMPLAINT   FOR   CONTRIBU-
                                TION

ROBERT BENCHLEY,

     Defendant
----

1. The plaintiff Ogden Nash is an individual residing at 14 Stow Street, Sutter, West Dakota.

2. The defendant Robert Benchley is an individual
residing at 2116 Twelfth Street, Bridger, West
Dakota.

3. On March 11, 1993, Mark Twain commenced a civil
action, captioned *Twain v. Nash*, Civil Action No.
93-219, against Ogden Nash in the Superior Court
for Glacier County, West Dakota.

4. The claim in *Twain v. Nash* arose out of an accident which took place on Maple Street in the town
of Sutter, West Dakota, on June 7, 1992. Twain was
injured in that accident after a collision between
a bicycle owned by Ogden Nash and a car driven by
Robert Benchley caused the Benchley car to swerve
into him.

5. The plaintiff in *Twain v. Nash* alleged that his
injuries resulted from the negligence of Nash in
leaving his bicycle in the road.

6. On November 7, 1994, the court entered judgment
against Ogden Nash in *Twain v. Nash*, in the amount
of $20,000 plus interest and costs.

7. On December 15, 1994, Nash, the contribution
plaintiff in this action, satisfied the judgment in
Twain v. Nash by paying $20,279 to the plaintiff in
that action, including $63 in post-judgment inter-
est and $216 in costs.

8. At the time of the accident which gave rise to the judgment in *Twain v. Nash*, the contribution defendant, Benchley, was also negligent in failing to keep a proper lookout. As a result of his negligence, he drove into the bicycle, swerved and ran into Twain. Such negligence was a proximate cause of the accident.

9. As a result of his negligence, the contribution defendant Benchley is a joint tortfeasor fully liable for the injuries sustained by Twain.

10. Plaintiff in this action has satisfied the judgment in *Twain v. Nash* in full. Thus, he has paid more than his pro rata share of the common liability and is entitled to contribution from Benchley under the provisions of West Dak. Stat. Tit. VII, §1(a) and (b), in the amount of one-half of the judgment.

11. The plaintiff in this action has demanded payment from Benchley of his pro rata share of the judgment, but he has refused to pay.

WHEREFORE, the plaintiff demands judgment against the defendant in this action in the amount of $10,139.50, plus costs of suit.

By his attorney
Angela Wu
42 River Street
Sutter, West Dakota   68534
(123) 335-8895

Figure 17-1

manded in the last paragraph of the complaint is, of course, Benchley's pro rata share of the judgment.

Effect of Settlement on the Right to Contribution

It is not unusual for the plaintiff to settle with one tortfeasor and proceed to trial against others.[5] Suppose that Twain settles with Nash for $2,000, releasing his claim against Nash only, and then recovers a judgment against Benchley for $20,000. What is the effect of Nash's settlement with Twain on Benchley's right to recover contribution from Nash?

Here are the relevant provisions of the Uniform Act:

> 4. When a release or covenant not to sue or not to enforce judgment is given in good faith to one of two or more persons liable in tort for the same injury or the same wrongful death:
>
> (a) It does not discharge any of the other tortfeasors from liability for the injury or wrongful death unless its terms so provide; but it reduces the claim against the others to the extent of any amount stipulated by the release or the covenant, or in the amount of the consideration paid for it, whichever is the greater; and,
>
> (b) It discharges the tortfeasor to whom it is given from all liability for contribution to any other tortfeasor.

The first clause of §4(a) reverses the common law rule that releasing one tortfeasor released them all. Under §4(a), Twain may still sue Benchley even though he gave a release to Nash. However, if Benchley is found liable, he will get a credit against the judgment for the amount Nash paid in settlement. This basically codifies the equitable principle that the plaintiff is entitled to full satisfaction of her judgment, but no more. In this example, if Twain recovered a $20,000 judgment against Benchley, Benchley would only have to pay $18,000 after the credit for the $2,000 Nash paid in settlement.

However, §4(b) of the Uniform Act bars Benchley from recovering contribution from Nash, the settling tortfeasor. Thus, on these facts Benchley will pay $18,000 of Twain's damages, while Nash pays only $2,000. Naturally, this provision has little appeal for Benchley. If Nash had not settled, and both he and Benchley had been found liable, Benchley could still have been forced to pay $20,000 to Twain, but he would have had the right to recover $10,000 in contribution from Nash. Thus, he would only have been out $10,000. Why should he have to pay an extra $8,000 simply because Twain made a deal with Nash? Isn't this provision grossly unfair to the remaining defendant?

There are several arguments in favor of barring contribution from a settling tortfeasor. *First*, the purpose of settling a lawsuit is to buy one's

---

5. Some of the reasons for doing so are explored in Chapter 16, Example 1.

peace, to extinguish the liability, close the file and get on to other things. If Benchley is free to come back against Nash for contribution, Nash has gained little by settling. He is still exposed to $10,000 in liability (his pro rata share), and has simply paid $2,000 of it early. If contribution from the settling tortfeasor is not barred, there is little incentive to settlements, which are generally encouraged as a civilized, inexpensive alternative to litigation.

Second, Benchley is free to settle too. Indeed, the risk of paying an outsized share encourages him to do so. Thus, the settling tortfeasor's immunity promotes settlements. In many cases the plaintiff will settle with all tortfeasors rather than risk a loss at trial. In a sense, everyone wins in this scenario.

Third, it may turn out that Nash settled for *more* than his pro rata share. When Nash settles, he does not know how much a jury will award in damages. In our hypo, they awarded Twain $20,000 for his injuries, but damages are very difficult to predict; they might have given $50,000. To avoid that risk, Nash might pay $16,000 to settle the case instead of $2,000. If he did, and the jury later assessed the damages at $20,000 in Twain's suit against Benchley, Benchley would only have to pay Twain $4,000 after his credit for the settlement. Uniform Act, §4(a), second clause. As you can see, these possibilities make settlement an interesting business for all parties involved.

Fourth, the statute contains a good faith requirement. Uniform Act, §4. If the court is convinced that Twain and Nash colluded by settling for an insufficient amount, it need not bar contribution from Nash.

An alternative way to take account of a settlement with one tortfeasor is to give the remaining tortfeasor a pro rata credit for the settlement instead of a dollar credit. Under this approach, Twain would be viewed as selling half of his cause of action to Nash by settling with him. Thus, he can only recover from Benchley on the other half. Suppose, for example, that Nash settled for $2,000, and Twain later recovered a $20,000 judgment against Benchley. Under the pro rata credit approach, Twain would be viewed as having sold half of his claim for the $2,000. Obviously, if the jury determines later that his damages are $20,000, that half of the claim was worth $10,000, and Twain badly undersold it. Under the pro rata credit approach, he would be entitled to collect only one half of the judgment, or $10,000 from Benchley. He would receive only $12,000 in total.[6] By contrast, under the dollar

---

6. As a further example assume that there were three tortfeasors. In settling with one for $2,000, Twain would be viewed as selling one-third of the claim for that amount. He would be entitled to collect two-thirds of the judgment amount from the other two tortfeasors, or $13,334. He would collect a total of $15,334.

The pro rata method of accounting for settlements was adopted in §5 of the 1939 Uniform Contribution Among Tortfeasors Act. It has gained renewed popularity under comparative negligence, with the important modification that the pro rata shares are not equal, but proportional to the percentage of negligence ultimately ascribed to the settling tortfeasor. See Chapter 22, p.471.

credit approach he would get $18,000 (the judgment amount minus the dollar amount of the settlement) from Benchley and $20,000 altogether.

A Tactical Question

1.   Accounting for the settlement under this pro rata approach seems more fair. Twain gets what he bargained for from Nash, as well as Benchley's fair share of the damages from him. What is the disadvantage of this variation?

Can a Settling Tortfeasor Seek Contribution?

Now let's look at the other side of the equation. Suppose that Twain settles with Nash for $16,000, and gives Nash a release of his liability. Later, he is surprised to learn that the jury in the suit against Benchley assessed his total damages at $20,000. Benchley has lucked out: under §4(a) of the Uniform Act, which provides for a dollar credit, he will only have to pay Twain $4,000. Can Nash, the settling defendant, recover $6,000 in contribution from Benchley? The Uniform Act says no:

> 1(d) A tortfeasor who enters into a settlement with a claimant is not entitled to recover contribution from another tortfeasor whose liability for the injury or wrongful death is not extinguished by the settlement. . . .

Under §1(d) Nash has no right to seek contribution from Benchley, since Twain only released Nash, not both defendants. Since Nash made an unfavorable settlement (at least, unfavorable in retrospect), he ends up paying more than he would have if he had lost at trial and paid half the judgment. Even here, however, he may still "win" in some sense. He has saved the expense of trying the case, and he has avoided the risk — always difficult to assess — that the jury would assess much higher damages, say, $100,000. If they had done that, he would have paid at least $50,000, and perhaps $100,000 if Benchley were insolvent.

Some contribution statutes modeled on the Uniform Act have modified this section to allow a settling tortfeasor to seek contribution. See, e.g., Mass. Gen. L. ch. 231B §1(c) (1986), which leaves out the Uniform Act language barring a settling tortfeasor from seeking contribution. Under the Massachusetts version, Nash could obtain $6,000 in contribution from Benchley (the amount over his pro rata share) even if he only obtained a release of the claim against himself.

Since the adoption of comparative negligence, many states have modified the basic contribution principles of the Uniform Act. Some of the current permutations are explored in Chapter 22. However, it is important to master the basic principles of contribution, both because they remain applicable in some jurisdictions and because it is impossible to understand current approaches to contribution without appreciating the basic concepts from which they have evolved. In analyzing the following examples, assume that the Uniform Act applies unless otherwise stated. The relevant provisions of the Act are as follows:

Uniform Contribution Among Tortfeasors Act

(1) (a) Except as otherwise provided in this Act, where two or more persons become jointly or severally liable in tort for the same injury to person or property or for the same wrongful death, there is a right of contribution among them even though judgment has not been recovered against all or any of them.

(b) The right of contribution exists only in favor of a tortfeasor who has paid more than his pro rata share of the common liability, and his total recovery is limited to the amount paid by him in excess of his pro rata share. No tortfeasor is compelled to make contribution beyond his pro rata share of the entire liability. . . .

(c) There is no right of contribution in favor of any tortfeasor who has intentionally . . . caused or contributed to the injury or wrongful death.

(d) A tortfeasor who enters into a settlement with a claimant is not entitled to recover contribution from another tortfeasor whose liability for the injury or wrongful death is not extinguished by the settlement. . . .

(2) In determining the pro rata shares of tortfeasors in the entire liability (a) their relative degrees of fault shall not be considered; (b) if equity requires the collective liability of some as a group shall constitute a single share; and (c) principles of equity applicable to contribution generally shall apply.

(3)(a) Whether or not judgment has been entered in an action against two or more tortfeasors for the same injury or wrongful death, contribution may be enforced by separate action.

(b) Where judgment has been entered in an action against two or more tortfeasors for the same injury or wrongful death, contribution may be enforced in that action by judgment in favor of one against other judgment defendants by motion upon notice to all parties to the action.

(c) If there is a judgment for the injury or wrongful death against the tortfeasor seeking contribution, any separate action by him to enforce contribution must be commenced within one year after the judgment has become final by lapse of time for appeal or after appellate review.

(d) If there is no judgment for the injury or wrongful death against the tortfeasor seeking contribution, his right of contribution is barred unless he has either (1) discharged by payment the common liability within the statute of limitations period applicable to claimant's right of action against him and has commenced his action for contribution within one year after payment, or (2) agreed while action is pending against him to discharge the common liability and has within one year after the agreement paid the liability and commenced his action for contribution.

(e) The recovery of a judgment for an injury or wrongful death against one tortfeasor does not of itself discharge the other tortfeasors from liability for the injury or wrongful death unless the judgment is satisfied. The satisfaction of the judgment does not impair any right of contribution.

(f) The judgment of the court in determining the liability of the several defendants to the claimant for an injury or wrongful death shall be binding as among such defendants in determining their right to contribution.

(4) When a release or covenant not to sue or not to enforce judgment is given in good faith to one of two or more persons liable in tort for the same injury or the same wrongful death:

(a) It does not discharge any of the other tortfeasors from liability for the injury or wrongful death unless its terms so provide; but it reduces the claim against the others to the extent of any amount stipulated by the release or the covenant, or in the amount of the consideration paid for it, whichever is the greater; and,

(b) It discharges the tortfeasor to whom it is given from all liability for contribution to any other tortfeasor.

EXAMPLES

Burning Issues

2.   Rogers, owner of a small business, gives a Fourth of July barbecue for his employees behind the building. Impatient for the barbecued chicken, Dunne throws gasoline on the coals, and Thurber throws a lighted match into the grill. The resulting fire causes extensive damage to the building. Rogers brings a negligence suit against Dunne for the damage, and gets judgment for $42,000.

   a. Could Dunne obtain contribution from Thurber at common law? If so, how much?

   b. Could Dunne obtain contribution from Thurber under the Uniform Act? If so, how much?

3.   Dunne pays Rogers $21,000, and refuses to pay any more, arguing that Thurber is responsible for the other $21,000. Will the court order Dunne to pay him any more?

4.   Rogers gets a judgment against Dunne for $42,000, but Dunne does not pay. Could Rogers sue Thurber for the damage if the Uniform Act applied?

Fudd Fudges the Figures

5.   Rogers sues Dunne and Thurber, and gets a judgment against them both for $42,000. Dunne pays Rogers $34,000, all he is able to. He then makes a motion for contribution from Thurber and Judge Fudd orders Thurber to pay Dunne $17,000. What is wrong with Fudd's order?

Permutations

6.   Assume that Rogers sued both Dunne and Thurber, and the jury found Thurber liable, but not Dunne. After paying Rogers the $42,000 judgment, Thurber seeks contribution from Dunne. May he recover contribution, and, if so, how much?

7.   Assume that Rogers sued both Dunne and Thurber, and the jury found them both liable. After paying Rogers $42,000, Thurber seeks $21,000 contribution from Dunne. Dunne, however, argues that White, another guest at the picnic, was *also* negligent in starting the fire, because he placed the grill much too close to the building and left the trash sitting next to it. How much must Dunne pay in contribution?

8.   Rogers sues Dunne, Thurber, and White for their negligence in starting the fire. He recovers a judgment against all three for $42,000 and tries to collect it from White. Unfortunately, White has no money and pays nothing, so Rogers demands payment from Dunne, who pays the entire judgment. Dunne then seeks contribution from Thurber. How much will he get?

Some Unsettling Cases

9.   Rogers sues Dunne and Thurber for the fire damage. Dunne offers to settle with Rogers for $12,000. Rogers accepts, and releases Dunne from liability in exchange for payment of that amount. Rogers then recovers a judgment for $42,000 against Thurber. (In analyzing this example, assume that Dunne and Thurber are the only tortfeasors.)

    a. How much will Rogers collect from Thurber if the Uniform Act applies?

    b. After paying Rogers, Thurber seeks contribution from Dunne. How much will he recover if the Uniform Act applies?

    c. How much would Rogers collect from Thurber if the relevant contribution statute gave Thurber a pro rata credit for the settlement?

10. Assume that Rogers settled with Dunne for $35,000 and gave Dunne a release of his liability only. Subsequently, Rogers sues Thurber. The jury finds Thurber liable for the fire and assesses $42,000 in damages.

    a. Assuming that the Uniform Act applies, how much must Thurber pay Rogers?

    b. After the judgment is entered and Thurber satisfies it, Dunne sues Thurber for contribution. How much would he receive under the Uniform Act?

    c. How much would he receive under the Massachusetts version of the Act? (See the discussion at p.361).

    d. Assume that this settlement took place in a jurisdiction that gives the remaining defendant a pro rata credit for settlements by other tortfeasors. How much would Rogers collect altogether?

Confusion Worse Confounded

11. Assume that Rogers sues four tortfeasors, Dunne, Thurber, Mauldin and Burgess. Dunne settles for $15,000. Rogers recovers judgment against the others for $100,000.
    a. Assume that the Uniform Act applies. How much can Rogers collect from Thurber?
    b. How much can Thurber recover in contribution from Mauldin?
    c. After he recovers contribution from Mauldin, he sues Burgess for contribution. How much can he recover from Burgess?

12. After Dunne and Thurber negligently start the fire, Burgess, a guest at the picnic, unwisely tries to help by spraying water on the blaze. His aim is bad, and he mistakenly hoses down the main computer, which is not threatened by the blaze. In addition to the $42,000 damage from the fire, the computer has to be replaced, at a cost of $18,000.
    a. If Rogers sues Dunne, Thurber, and Burgess, how much will each be liable for?
    b. After judgment enters against the three, Thurber pays Rogers $60,000, the full amount of his damages. He then sues Burgess and Dunne for contribution. How much can he get from each?

Unlucky Number Thirteen

13. Rogers recovers a judgment for $42,000 against Thurber. Two years later he demands payment from Thurber, who pays the full judgment. Shortly thereafter, Thurber sues Dunne for contribution. How much must Dunne pay if the Uniform Act applies?

EXPLANATIONS

A Tactical Question

1.   Under the pro rata credit approach, plaintiffs have less incentive to settle than under the dollar credit approach. In a state that applies the dollar credit approach, Twain can still recover his full damages, even if he settles with Nash for less than Nash's full share: Benchley is still liable for the entire judgment, and will only get a credit for the amount Nash actually paid. For example, if Twain's damages are $20,000, he can settle with Nash for $5,000 and recover $15,000 from Benchley.

Ŝ   However, under the pro rata credit approach, Twain gives up 50 percent of his claim when he settles with Nash. If he settles for $5,000, and the jury assesses his damages at $20,000, he will end up with only $15,000, five from Nash and ten from Benchley (the $20,000 judgment minus Nash's pro rata share). Here is a comparison of the results under the two approaches:

	Settlement w/Nash	Jury Award at trial	Benchley pays	Plaintiff receives
Dollar credit approach:	$5,000	$20,000	$15,000	$20,000
Pro rata credit approach:	$5,000	$20,000	$10,000	$15,000

Thus, under the pro rata credit approach, a plaintiff is unlikely to sell half of his claim for much less than half its value.

Of course, the pro rata approach may still be more "fair," even if it discourages settlements. However, the tort system has to operate in the real world, including the unpleasant reality that the court system cannot possibly try all pending cases. While fairness is certainly a goal of the system, other goals, such as efficient use of resources, must also be considered. Thus, many states have opted for the dollar credit approach, which provides more incentive to the plaintiff to settle.

Burning Issues

2a. As the introduction indicates, there was no right at common law to demand contribution from a joint tortfeasor. If Dunne paid the judgment, he had no recourse against Thurber and was stuck with the entire liability, simply because Rogers chose to sue him instead of Thurber.

b. Dunne has no right to contribution under the Uniform Act. Surprised? Well, this answer is a little bit cute. The facts do not indicate that Dunne has paid anything to Rogers. The right to contribution arises in favor of a tortfeasor who has *paid* more than his pro rata share, not one who has been found liable. Uniform Act, §1(b). The difference between incurring a judgment for $42,000 and paying over $42,000 is dramatic; it is the difference between a bird in the hand and a bird in the bush.

Assuming that Dunne paid the $42,000 to Rogers, he would have a right to pro rata contribution from Thurber under the Uniform Act. He would be entitled to recover $21,000 from Thurber, *if* he proved that Thurber was also liable to Rogers for negligently causing the fire. Since Rogers only sued Dunne, Thurber has never been adjudged liable for the fire. Thus, Dunne would have to bring a contribution action against Thurber and prove Thurber's negligence in that suit before he could recover contribution.

3. The court will order Dunne to pay the entire judgment. The Uniform Act, like many contribution statutes, does not alter the fundamental premise that each tortfeasor is *fully liable* to the plaintiff. The plaintiff may still sue whichever tortfeasor he chooses, and collect the damages from whichever he chooses.

Contribution only deals with adjusting the payment of the damages among the defendants, after one has paid more than his share of the judgment.

Dunne may pay Rogers $42,000 and seek $21,000 from Thurber, but he cannot pay $21,000 and force Rogers to chase Dunne for the balance. That, in essence, would make the two tortfeasors "severally" liable for their pro rata shares, rather than "jointly and severally" liable for the plaintiff's full damages.[7] The very purpose of joint and several liability is to assure the plaintiff's right to collect fully from any one of the tortfeasors.

4.   At early common law, a judgment against one tortfeasor barred suit against others who might also be liable. The rationale was that a tort claim was a "single cause of action." Once sued upon, it was extinguished and replaced by the judgment. See Chapter 6, p.337. The courts later abandoned that approach, however, replacing it with the rule that a plaintiff could bring a second action against another party responsible for his injuries, so long as the prior judgment had not been fully satisfied. Section 3(e) of the Uniform Act codifies this later approach, which allows a plaintiff who has obtained a judgment against one tortfeasor to sue other tortfeasors until his claim is fully satisfied. Under §3(e), Rogers's judgment against Dunne does not bar him from suing Thurber, since the judgment has not been paid.

Fudd Fudges the Figures

5.   The Uniform Act allows a tortfeasor who has paid "more than his pro rata share" of the liability to recover contribution. Section 1(b). Dunne's pro rata share would be $21,000, one-half of the judgment. Since he has paid more than that, and Thurber has been held liable for the injury as well, Dunne is entitled to contribution. Fudd was right in awarding him contribution. His error was in determining the amount.

You can see the logic for Fudd's order; it makes Thurber absorb half of Dunne's payment. Another approach would be to require Thurber to pay Dunne his full pro rata share in contribution, or $21,000. The Uniform Act, however, provides otherwise. Under §1(b), Dunne can recover "the amount paid by him in excess of his pro rata share." Dunne's pro rata share is $21,000. Since he has paid $34,000, he can recover $13,000 from Thurber.

The logic of the Uniform Act provision is illustrated by considering what would happen if Fudd's order were upheld. Thurber would pay $17,000, but he would still be liable to Rogers for $8,000, the part of Rogers's judgment that he has not yet collected. If he paid $17,000 to Dunne and Rogers then demanded $8,000 more from him, he would end up paying $25,000, $4,000 more than his pro rata share, while Dunne paid $17,000, $4,000 less than his.[8]

---

7. Recently, some states have switched from joint and several liability to several liability, at least in limited classes of cases. Some examples are given in Chapter 22, pp.472-473.

8. I suppose he could then demand contribution from Dunne, but that seems like a circuitous means of redistributing the loss.

The Second Restatement of Torts takes the position that a tortfeasor cannot seek contribution at all until the plaintiff has been fully paid. See §886A(2) & cmt. f. Presumably, the logic for this position is that, if Thurber only has limited funds, Rogers should get first crack at them: Thurber should not pay contribution to Dunne and be left unable to satisfy the remainder of Rogers's judgment. However, §1(b) of the Uniform Act does not include a similar requirement.

Permutations

6.   Since Thurber is not liable to Rogers, he is not liable to Dunne for contribution. A tortfeasor may only recover contribution from someone who is liable to the plaintiff. See Uniform Act, §1(a) (authorizing contribution "where two or more persons become jointly or severally liable in tort"). He can hardly be liable for contribution as a joint tortfeasor if he isn't a tortfeasor at all, and that's what was decided by the jury in this case. See Uniform Act, §3(f) (providing that the findings as to the liability of the various defendants are binding in a subsequent contribution action).

7.   Under the Uniform Act, any person who "becomes jointly liable in tort for the same injury" is liable to contribute to the damages. Although White was not sued in the original action, he may still be a joint tortfeasor. Rogers might have decided not to sue him for myriad reasons; that decision does not necessarily mean that he is not "liable" for the injury. If his negligence contributed to the accident, he should be counted in calculating the pro rata shares of each tortfeasor. Thus, when Thurber seeks contribution, the court will have to determine whether White was also negligent in order to calculate Dunne's pro rata share. If it determines that White was also a tortfeasor, it will order Dunne to pay one-third of the judgment to Thurber ($14,000) instead of one-half.[9]

8.   Clearly, Dunne is entitled to contribution from Thurber. If White were solvent, he could recover $14,000 from Thurber and $14,000 from White. Since White cannot pay, shouldn't Thurber pay $21,000?

Section 1(b) of the Uniform Act suggests that Dunne would only recover $14,000, since it provides that "[n]o tortfeasor is compelled to make contribution beyond his pro rata share of the entire liability." Thurber's pro rata share is one-third, or $14,000; under §1(b), he can only be required to pay that to Dunne. If this is the answer, Dunne, having paid $42,000, will end up $28,000 out of pocket, because he cannot collect contribution from White. The burden of White's insolvency would fall on him.

---

9. Under some contribution schemes, Dunne may waive this argument by failing to implead White in the original suit. See, e.g., *Laue v. Leifheit*, 473 N.E.2d 939 (Ill. 1984). The Uniform Act does not require this, however. Uniform Act, §3(a).

Most courts that have adopted contribution have viewed it as an equitable doctrine; on facts like these they would likely have required Thurber to pay $21,000. See Restatement (Second) of Torts §886A, cmt. c. (when one tortfeasor insolvent, court may "do what is fair and equitable under the circumstances" in ordering contribution). This flexibility to account for the circumstances is preserved in §2(c) of the Uniform Act, which provides that, in determining the pro rata shares, "principles of equity applicable to contribution generally shall apply." Under this provision, the court would likely require Thurber to pay $21,000 in contribution to Dunne, despite the language of §1(b).

Some Unsettling Cases

9a. Thurber is still liable for the full judgment, but he receives a dollar credit for the amount of the settlement with Dunne. Uniform Act, §4(a). Thus, he will have to pay Rogers $30,000. As this example illustrates, once Dunne has settled, Thurber risks paying more than half of the damages unless he settles as well.

b. As the introduction indicates, §4(b) of the Uniform Act bars contribution from a settling tortfeasor. Thurber will not be able to force Dunne to pay anything above the $12,000 he paid to settle with Rogers. This gives defendants a strong incentive to settle cases. If Dunne can induce the plaintiff to settle for less than half of the likely damage amount, he will avoid paying his full "share" of the liability.

Thurber might argue that the settlement is so low that it is not "in good faith," that Rogers and Dunne have somehow conspired to force Thurber to bear the brunt of the damages by settling for an unreasonably low amount. However, many factors affect the parties' judgment about how much a claim is worth, and many of these factors are quite subjective, such as the risk that the settling defendant's negligence cannot be proved at trial, or the adverse effect of having a sympathetic defendant before the court. Due to such factors, it is doubtful that the court will find that the settlement was in bad faith simply because Dunne paid less than his pro rata share of the plaintiff's damages.

c. Under a pro rata credit approach, Rogers effectively sells half of his claim to Dunne by settling with him. He would be entitled to collect one-half of the damages awarded from Thurber. If the total damages found by the jury are $42,000, Rogers would collect $21,000 from Thurber, and $12,000 from Dunne, for a total of $33,000. Naturally, this approach makes plaintiffs cautious about settling with the first tortfeasor.

10a. Under joint and several liability, Thurber is liable for the full amount of Rogers's damages, but gets a dollar for dollar credit for the amount paid in settlement. He must pay Rogers $7,000 ($42,000 − $35,000).

b. Dunne is barred from seeking contribution from Thurber by §1(d), which provides that a settling tortfeasor cannot obtain contribution unless he has obtained a release of the other tortfeasor as well. The example indicates that Dunne received a release of *his* liability, but not Thurber's; thus, he cannot ask Thurber to contribute. Dunne cannot undo his bargain by seeking contribution if his settlement turns out to be higher than his share of the damages awarded. If Dunne had settled for *less* than half the damages assessed, he would not have had to pay contribution to Thurber. See Example 9b. Under the Uniform Act it works both ways, or, more accurately, neither way. If Dunne makes a good deal, he shifts more than half of the damages to Thurber. If he makes a bad deal, as he did here, he ends up paying more than half himself.

c. The Massachusetts contribution statute allows a settling tortfeasor to obtain contribution from another tortfeasor, even if he has not obtained a release of that other tortfeasor's liability. Under this type of statute, Dunne would recover contribution from Thurber in "the amount paid by him in excess of his pro rata share" or $14,000 ($35,000 − $21,000). This approach is more favorable to the settling tortfeasor. She can settle without fear of having to contribute to a judgment against another tortfeasor. But she also has a chance, if she pays too much, to recover contribution from that other tortfeasor.

d. In a pro rata jurisdiction, Rogers is viewed as having sold half of his claim to Dunne by settling with him. Thus, he may collect only the other half of the $42,000 judgment from Thurber, or $21,000. This amount, together with the $35,000 he obtained in settlement from Dunne, comes to $56,000 for a case in which the jury has determined the damages to be $42,000. Under the pro rata credit approach, the *plaintiff* gets the advantage of a favorable settlement; she collects more than her actual damages. Compare Example 10a, which illustrates that the *nonsettling defendant* gets the benefit from a high settlement in a dollar credit jurisdiction.

Confusion Worse Confounded

11a. Dunne can recover $85,000 from Thurber. The Uniform Act gives Thurber a dollar credit for Dunne's settlement, (§4(a)) but he remains jointly and severally liable for the remaining damages.

b. The outer limit on contribution from Mauldin is his pro rata share. Uniform Act, §1(b). The problem here is in determining Mauldin's pro rata share. Are there three shares or four?

Although Dunne has settled, he is apparently still "jointly or severally liable in tort for the same injury." Consequently, it appears that he would be counted in determining the pro rata shares. Thus there are four tortfeasors, the "common liability" is $100,000, and Mauldin's pro rata share is $25,000. Thurber can apparently recover only $25,000 in contribution from Mauldin.

c. Burgess's pro rata share is also $25,000. Apparently, this is all that Thurber can recover from him. If so, Thurber still ends up paying too much:

He gets $50,000 in contribution, and ends up paying $35,000 (the $85,000 he paid minus the $50,000 he obtained in contribution).

Wouldn't it seem fairer to view the "common liability" as the *remaining* common liability of Thurber, Mauldin, and Burgess, and divide this among the three of them? Under this approach Thurber would recover $28,333 from Mauldin and Burgess, and be out of pocket that amount as well. Although the language of §1(b) appears to support the first analysis, a court might reach the second result by invoking principles of equity. See Uniform Act §2(c) and the analysis of Example 8.

12a. Thurber and Dunne are liable for the entire damages, including the fire damage and the ruined computer. While it was Burgess who hosed down the computer, it is reasonably foreseeable that people will try to put out a fire, and that in doing so they may damage other property, even through negligence. Thus, Thurber and Dunne are likely liable for the additional damage caused by Burgess's negligence.

Burgess, on the other hand, is only liable for the $18,000 in damage to the computer. He had no part in causing the fire, and is not responsible for the other damage it caused.

b. The only problem with dreaming up these interesting variations is that you have to answer them. Here is my analysis:

Thurber is a joint tortfeasor with Dunne as to the fire damage. His pro rata share of these damages is thus $21,000, one-half the total. He is a joint tortfeasor with both Dunne and Burgess as to the ruined computer; his pro rata share of this loss is $6,000 (one-third of $18,000). He should end up paying $27,000 altogether after contribution from the other defendants; he has overpaid by $33,000 ($60,000 − $27,000).

Burgess should pay him $6,000, his pro rata share of the computer loss. Dunne should pay him $6,000 toward the computer loss (because he is one of three tortfeasors as to that claim) and $21,000 toward the fire loss, his pro rata share (one-half) of that loss. Fortunately, these three figures add up to $33,000. If Thurber is paid this amount in contribution, he ends up paying the proper amount, $27,000.

Unlucky Number Thirteen

13. Apparently, Dunne need not pay anything under the Uniform Act; he should move to dismiss the contribution action based on the statute of limitations in §3(c) of the Uniform Act. That section provides that an action for contribution must be brought within one year after the judgment in the original suit becomes final. Here, the plaintiff did not enforce the judgment, that is, collect the money, until more than a year had passed. Thus, the plaintiff's nonchalance about collecting from Thurber appears to defeat Thurber's right to contribution from Dunne.

What should a defendant in Thurber's position do in such circumstances? I suppose Thurber should do the honorable thing, that is, *pay* the judgment before the year goes by, so that he can sue Dunne for contribution within the one-year period. Indeed, the statute creates a very strong incentive for Thurber to do just that, in order to avoid losing his right to contribution.

18

Please Pass the Liability: Respondeat Superior and Nondelegable Duties

Introduction

The last two chapters have considered the allocation of liability in cases involving "joint tortfeasors." As those chapters indicate, where more than one party's negligence contributes to an injury, each negligent party is liable, but may be able to seek contribution from other tortfeasors. This chapter addresses the related situation in which one defendant incurs liability, not due to his own negligence, but due to the negligence of another. We will focus on two common examples of such "vicarious liability": liability of an employer for the torts of its employees, and liability of one who employs an independent contractor for torts committed by the independent contractor.

Rationales for Imposing Vicarious Liability on Employers

The common law has long accepted the premise that employers should be liable for the torts of their employees in the scope of employment. The premise is sufficiently entrenched to merit its own legal Latin, "respondeat superior," which is loosely translated, "let the master respond." While virtually all jurisdictions impose liability on employers for the torts of their employees, the rationales for the respondeat superior doctrine have varied.

It is sometimes said that the employer should pay because she can select and control her employees, and thereby prevent injuries due to negligence. It is doubtless true, as a general matter, that employers can reduce accidents by requiring their employees to exercise care, and that making employers liable for employees' torts gives them an incentive to enforce careful conduct. However, employers frequently have no realistic chance of preventing a particular negligent act by an employee, as where an employee drives alone to pick up a package or goes out alone to repair an elevator. Employers cannot hover over their employees from minute to minute, and, as an actuarial matter, even employees who are carefully selected and supervised will be negligent on occasion, despite the employer's most rigorous efforts to promote safety.[1] When they are, the employer is liable even if it took stringent measures to prevent accidents. This liability, in other words, is truly vicarious; it flows automatically from the employee's tort, regardless of the care the employer exercised in selecting or supervising him.

More skeptical observers have suggested that respondeat superior liability is simply a device to provide a "deep pocket" defendant able to pay the plaintiff's damages. Prosser & Keeton at 500. Certainly it serves this purpose in many cases, since employers are more likely to have the resources to pay judgments than their employees. Yet, if vicarious liability is imposed solely to assure a deep pocket, it might equally well be imposed on *any* party with substantial resources: We could make millionaires vicariously liable for torts, or any insurance company with a headquarters building over 25 stories, or — what the heck — how about the Government? Clearly, while assuring compensation is a factor, respondeat superior is intended to assure that such compensation comes from a party that is fairly made to pay it.

Another rationale increasingly cited for the doctrine is that employers are in a position to spread the costs of accidents by purchasing liability insurance and raising the price of their products to reflect the inherent accident costs of the enterprise. This argument, like economic analysis of tort law in general, looks at the issue not as a matter of individual fairness or blame, but rather as a question of the overall societal impact of placing the cost of accidents in one place or another. Respondeat superior encourages employers to insure; the cost of insurance gets incorporated into the price of the product, which consequently reflects more accurately the actual costs of producing it, including the accident costs. This argument makes sense, but, like the deep pocket argument, courts would probably not accept it if they did not view respondeat superior as inherently fair as well.

---

1. Vicarious liability may even *increase* the risk of negligence in many cases, since the employee, knowing that the employer will be liable, will have less incentive to exercise due care. Note, An Efficiency Analysis of Vicarious Liability Under the Law of Agency, 91 Yale L.J. 168, 172-173 (1981).

Perhaps the most basic rationale for the doctrine is that the employee acts for the master in the performance of the master's work. In the course of that work, he creates risks to further the master's goals, including the risk of injuries due to negligence. Where such risks are created for the master's benefit, it seems intuitively fair to ascribe the conduct to the party for whose benefit it was undertaken. As stated in an early English case, "the reason that I am liable is this, that by employing [an employee] I set the whole thing in motion; and what he does, being done for my benefit and under my direction, I am responsible for the consequences of doing it." *Duncan v. Findlater*, 7 Eng. Rep. 934, 940 (H.L. 1839). On the simplest level, if the master did not have the work done by another, he would have to do it himself, and would be liable for any torts committed in doing so. Under respondeat superior, the acts done at the master's bidding are treated, for liability purposes, as though he had performed them himself.

The Meaning of "Employee"

An employer is only liable for the torts of a worker if the worker is its employee and acts in the scope of his employment. In many cases it is unclear whether a party who acts for another is an employee or acts as an independent contractor. Suppose, for example, that Bogart hires Bacall to maintain his yard. Bacall could be an employee or an independent contractor, depending on the particular facts of the relationship. If Bogart provides all the tools, pays Bacall by the hour, determines when she will work and exactly what she will do, Bacall would likely be characterized as an employee. On the other hand, if Bacall works with her own truck and tools, comes whenever she chooses, is paid by the season, provides her own insurance, and decides for herself what needs to be done to make the yard sparkle, she would likely be characterized as an independent contractor.

It is often stated that a person is an employee (or, in common law parlance, a "servant") if the employer has the right of control over the person in the performance of the work.

> A servant is a person employed to perform services in the affairs of another and who with respect to the physical conduct in the performance of the services is subject to the other's control or right to control.

Restatement (Second) of Agency §220(1). However, this control test does not clearly resolve close cases, since even independent contractors are subject to some degree of control. Doubtless Bogart would have the authority to tell Bacall not to use chemical fertilizer, or to trim the rose bushes in the fall rather than the spring, even if Bacall's business was independent in most respects. Thus, courts have elaborated a number of factors that they consider in determining whether an actor is an employee. Section 220 of the Second Restatement of Agency, for example, lists the following factors:

- **The extent of control which the master is authorized to exercise over the details of the work.** Clearly, the more supervisory authority the employer has to specify how the work will proceed, the more likely it is that the worker will be viewed as an employee.

- **Whether the actor is engaged in a distinct occupation or business.** If Bogart employs a handy person to work around the house, she will more likely be viewed as an employee than if he calls in a computer repair person or an electrician.

- **Whether the type of work is customarily performed under the employer's supervision or by a specialist without supervision, and the extent of the skill required.** If the work involves a skilled task typically hired out to a specialized contractor, it will more likely be viewed as a contract situation. If Bogart hires Greenstreet to move his house, Greenstreet is more likely to be viewed as an independent contractor than if he is hired to wash it.

- **Who supplies the tools, other equipment and place of work.** If Bacall goes to Bogart's place of business every day to sew shirts and uses Bogart's sewing machines and material, she will probably be viewed as an employee. On the other hand, if she does piecework at home on her own machine, she may be an independent contractor.

- **The length of time for which the person is employed.** Frequently, persons hired for a single purpose and a brief period look more like independent contractors, since there is less of a relationship and a greater likelihood that she was called in to perform a specific task in her own manner. However, like the other factors, this one does not always help. If Bogart hires Bacall for a fall afternoon to rake leaves, she will likely be viewed as an employee. If he hires her for a season to maintain the grounds, she may well be a landscaping contractor.

- **Whether the person is paid on a time basis or by the job.** Workers hired by the hour or the week tend to be viewed as employees, since they are at the employer's "beck and call" on a regular basis. By contrast, contractors are typically hired to accomplish a given end result — such as building a house, or repairing a bridge — without detailed supervision during the process, and paid a flat sum to accomplish that result.

- **Whether the employer is in business, and whether the work is part of the employer's regular business.** If Bogart is a jeweler, and hires Bacall to cut diamonds, a court is likely to infer that she is an employee. On the other hand, if he hires her to renovate his jewelry store, the more likely inference is that she is an independent contractor hired on a one-time basis to accomplish a particular task.

- **The parties' belief as to the nature of the relation.** It is relevant, though not dispositive, that the parties view the relation as an employment relation, or otherwise. This belief may be reflected in various arrangements. For example, an employer is likely to pay employment and workers' compensation taxes, to insure its employees, and to comply with various other regulatory requirements regarding employees. The fact that the employer has treated the worker as an employee is suggestive that the master/servant relation actually exists.

This multi-factor test for determining employment status is widely accepted, not only in the context of tort liability, but in others as well. See, e.g., Rev. Ruling 87-41 (stating that common law test governs in determining employment status under the Internal Revenue Code, and listing factors similar to those discussed above). Like so many legal standards these days, this test is hardly cut and dried, and will often pose questions of fact for the jury. On the other hand, while ambiguous cases arise, in most cases it is pretty clear whether the individual is an employee or an independent contractor.

Acting in the Scope of Employment

Even if the court concludes that Bacall was Bogart's employee at the time that she negligently injured the plaintiff, Bogart will only be liable for her negligence if she acted in the scope of her employment. Bogart obviously is not liable for private acts of Bacall, but only those properly attributable to her employment.

Isn't the law tiresome in the way it finds interpretive problems around every corner? Perhaps so, but these interpretive problems arise from the necessary process of determining the outer limits of a principle. Unless we are to hold Bogart liable for everything Bacall does, we must define the limit of his responsibility. He should not be liable if Bacall gets in a motor vehicle accident over the weekend, because her driving is unrelated to her work for Bogart. Even if she gets in the accident on her lunch hour, Bogart should probably not be liable. This trip is for her own purposes, outside of Bogart's premises and control. On the other hand, Bogart clearly would be vicariously liable if Bacall hit a passing pedestrian with a ladder while working as a house painter for Bogart's painting company. Since this act took place in the course of and for the furtherance of the employer's work, it seems fair that it should pay.

The Restatement (Second) of Agency offers the following definition of "scope of employment":

> (1) Conduct of a servant is within the scope of employment if, but only if:
> (a) it is of the kind he is employed to perform;
> (b) it occurs substantially within the authorized time and space limits;
> (c) it is actuated, at least in part, by a purpose to serve the master, and
> (d) if force is intentionally used by the servant against another, the use of force is not unexpectable by the master

Restatement (Second) of Agency §228. This definition works well enough in the easy cases, but is less helpful in the close ones, such as acts that are incidental to the work experience but do not directly further the work. Suppose, for example, that Bacall starts a fire while smoking on the job or bumps into a visitor while on the way to the bathroom. These acts do not directly further the master's enterprise, but they are normal incidents of the work experience.

Although early cases limited "scope of employment" to acts intended to directly further the employer's business, the tendency in more recent cases is to hold incidental acts in the course of the work within the scope of employment. They take place at the employer's place of business, during working hours, and are related in a general way to the accomplishment of the work. If the rationale for vicarious liability is that the risks engendered by an enterprise should be absorbed and distributed by that enterprise, it seems supportable to hold the employer liable for such incidental risks. *George v. Bekins Van & Storage Co.*, 205 P.2d 1037, 1043 (Cal. 1949); see Restatement (Second) of Agency, §229 cmt. a (ultimate question is whether the loss should be considered one of the "normal risks" of the business).

Vicarious Liability for Intentional Torts

Another difficult problem is determining when employers will be held vicariously liable for intentional torts by employees. Intentional torts require, by definition, a deliberate decision by the actor to invade another's rights. In almost all cases, such deliberate invasions are unwanted, discouraged, and probably forbidden by the employer. There is some force, therefore, to the employer's argument that he should not be held liable for such acts in clear contravention of his wishes.

Most early cases held employers liable for intentional torts by their employees only if the employee acted at least in part to serve the employer's purposes. Prosser & Keeton at 505. Motivation to serve the master is not unusual in some recurring scenarios. For example, an employee of a repossession company who assaults an owner while repossessing his car is clearly trying to do her job. Similarly, a bouncer who uses excessive force in evicting a patron from a bar is motivated to serve his employer, albeit overzealously. He is probably not doing it the way the employer wants him to, but neither is an employee who is negligent. Once again, if the basis for respondeat superior is that the employer's business has created the risk, these cases appear to be good candidates for application of the doctrine.

Under this "motivation to serve" approach, employers were usually not held liable if the employment setting created the occasion for an employee's intentional tort, but the act had no relation to accomplishing the master's purposes. For example, if Bogart, a waiter in Bacall's nightclub, stole money from a patron's purse, he did not act to further the work of the master. This intentional tort is *related* to the employment, in the but-for sense that the job creates the opportunity for the theft, but the tort is not *motivated* by any work-related purpose. In these cases, courts traditionally denied recovery from the employer, and many still do. See, e.g., *Effort Enter., Inc. v. Crosta*, 391 S.E.2d 477 (Ga. App. 1990) (employer not liable where employees stole jewelry while moving other items into plaintiff's house).

Between these extremes lie many cases in which the intentional tort is not directly meant to serve the master's purpose, but arises from the performance of the work. A very common scenario involves brawls that arise in the course of the work. For example, Bacall, while delivering pizzas for Bogart, might get into a dispute with another driver at a traffic light and punch him, or two assembly line workers might argue about the proper way to do the job, causing one to hit the other with a wrench.

Again, the early courts tended to deny liability in these cases, on the ground that the assault did not further the master's work in any way. More recent cases, however, hold the employer liable for such disputes, on the theory that they are incidental risks engendered by the accomplishment of the work. See R. Brill, The Liability of an Employer for the Wilful Torts of his Servants, 45 Chi.-Kent L. Rev. 1, 11-14 (1968). However, liability is generally denied if the dispute arises from personal malice rather than the performance of the work. If Bacall is delivering pizza to Bergman's home, and assaults her because Bergman had slandered her the week before, most courts would hold the quarrel "purely personal" and refuse to impute liability to Bacall's employer.

While the cases are mixed, the trend is toward a broader definition of employer liability for intentional torts, parallel to the expansion of vicarious liability for negligence. For example, employers have been held liable for a sexual assault by a nursing assistant in a hospital (*Samuels v. Southern Baptist Hosp.*, 594 So. 2d 571 (La. App. 1992)), and by a delivery man enraged by a customer who disputed a bill. *Lyon v. Carey*, 533 F.2d 649 (D.C. Cir. 1976). But see *Taylor v. Doctors Hosp.*, 486 N.E.2d 1249 (Ohio App. 1985) (denying liability for rape of patient by hospital orderly). The acts in these cases clearly do not serve the master's purposes. Few courts would have imposed vicarious liability for them 50 years ago. Doubtless, the trend to hold employers liable in such cases is influenced by the view that economic enterprises should absorb and spread the costs of the risks they generate, even if those risks do not involve the direct accomplishment of the work.

Courts that have liberalized their approach to vicarious liability for intentional torts have substituted various more flexible tests for the traditional "motivation to serve" formula. In *Miller v. Federated Dept. Stores, Inc.*, 304 N.E.2d 573, 580 (Mass. 1973), for example, the court held that recovery would be allowed where an assault arose "in response to the plaintiff's conduct which was presently interfering with the employee's ability to successfully perform his duties." Other cases have suggested that the employer should respond where he had placed the employee in a position of authority that enhanced his opportunity to commit the tort. See, e.g., *White v. County of Orange*, 212 Cal. Rptr. 493, 495-496 (Cal. App. 1985) (county liable for rape and murder committed by a deputy sheriff whose position of authority enabled him to commit the crime).[2] Perhaps the broadest test found in the cases would simply require that the conduct be foreseeable or incidental to the work. *Martinez v. Hagopian*, 227 Cal. Rptr. 763, 766 (Cal. App. 1986); *Leafgreen American Family Mutual Ins. Co.*, 393 N.W.2d 275, 280 (S.D. 1986).

The Consequences of Independence

While employers are generally liable for the torts of their employees in the scope of employment, they generally are *not* liable for torts of an independent contractor, even though they arise from the contractor's work for the employer. Restatement (Second) of Torts, §409. (For the sake of clarity, I will call the party who hires an independent contractor the "owner," rather than the "employer" throughout this chapter.) This "rule of insulation" from tort liability (C. Morris and C. Morris Jr., Morris on Torts 256 (2d ed. 1980)) will obviously influence the way parties structure their business relationships. Owners may choose to hire independent contractors to perform work rather than using their own employees, simply to insulate themselves from tort liability. Of course, where the owner knows he is avoiding a potential liability, the contractor knows that he is assuming it. Consequently, the cost of insuring against tort liability will be considered in setting the price of the work.

Exceptions to the Rule: Nondelegable Duties

While hiring an independent contractor usually insulates an owner from liability for torts in the course of the work, it will not always do so. In some situations, courts have refused to allow owners to insulate themselves from liability, *even if* they use a contractor to do the work. In such situations, it is often said that the owner's duty of care is "nondelegable," so that the owner remains liable for tortious injury from the performance of the work, even though the tort was committed by an independent contractor.

The phrase *nondelegable duty* is something of a misnomer. The owner *has* delegated the work to an independent contractor in these cases; what the courts mean is that the owner may delegate the *work* but cannot delegate away the *liability* for tortious acts in the course of the work. Like the employer

---

2. But see *John R. v. Oakland Unified Sch. Dist.*, 769 P.2d 948 (Cal. 1989) (distinguishing *White* and refusing to impose liability on this rationale for off-campus sexual abuse of a student by a teacher).

under respondeat superior, the owner is liable in these cases *vicariously* for the torts of the independent contractor.

Several widely accepted categories of nondelegable duties illustrate the typical rationales for imposing vicarious liability for the acts of independent contractors. For example, courts often hold a duty nondelegable because the work involves inherent danger or requires special precautions. See Restatement (Second) of Torts §416 (owner liable for contractor's negligence if the work is "likely to create during its progress a peculiar risk of physical harm to others unless special precautions are taken"). The Restatement gives the example of an owner who hires a contractor to tear down a town house, knowing that special precautions must be taken to avoid injury to the party wall of the next building. Restatement (Second) of Torts §416, illus. 2. If the contractor's employees fail to take these precautions, and injury results from this "peculiar risk," the owner will be liable for that injury. The evident rationale for this exception is that, where the owner is aware that precautions are needed to avoid injury, it should assure that they are taken or incur the liability if they are not.

For similar reasons, §427 of the Second Restatement provides that the owner will be liable for the contractor's negligence in the performance of work "involving a special danger to others which the employer knows or has reason to know to be inherent in or normal to the work." This might apply, for example, to the repair of windows on a tall building in a city, which poses a risk that objects will fall on pedestrians. If an employee of the contractor fails to put up a sidewalk scaffold, and a pedestrian is injured by falling debris, the owner of the building will be liable vicariously for this negligent act.

Owners may also be held vicariously liable for their contractors' negligence in construction or repair of instrumentalities used in highly dangerous activities, such as transmission of high voltage electricity (see Restatement (Second) of Torts §423) and in the conduct of abnormally dangerous activities, such as blasting. See Restatement (Second) of Torts §427A. Here again, the unusual danger inherent in the work, which necessarily imposes a risk of injury and is done for the owner's benefit, supports holding the owner liable for the contractor's torts in the course of such activities.

Courts have also held owners vicariously liable for negligence of their contractors in the course of work done in a public place. Restatement (Second) of Torts §417. Under this exception an electric company would be liable, for example, if it hired an independent tree surgeon to trim trees along its power lines over the sidewalks, and the tree surgeon caused an accident by cutting a branch down in the path of the plaintiff's car. Similarly, owners are vicariously liable for torts of their independent contractors in maintaining highways and other public property (Restatement (Second) of Torts §418) and in maintaining premises open to the public for business purposes. Restatement (Second) of Torts §425. Vicarious liability in these cases is presumably based on the wide risk created by work done in public places, and the obvious need for particular care to protect the public from injury.

Another widespread category of nondelegable duties involves situations in which a statute evidences an intent to provide special protection to a particular class. For example, in *Celestine v. City of New York*, 446 N.Y.S.2d 131 (N.Y. App. Div. 1982), the court held that the duty under a New York statute to maintain safe working conditions for workers in the process of construction, excavation, and demolition is nondelegable. Even if the worker is injured due to negligence of the independent contractor, the owner may be held liable vicariously for the contractor's negligence. Similarly, courts have relied on statutes to find the duty to maintain rental premises for the benefit of residential tenants nondelegable. See, e.g, *Knickerbocker Bldg. Serv., Inc. v. Phillips*, 485 N.E.2d 260 (Ohio App. 1984). Other courts have held the duty to residential tenants nondelegable as a matter of common law. *Durkin v. Hansen*, 437 S.E.2d 550 (S.C. App. 1993).

It has been said repeatedly that "the rule [insulating the owner from liability] is now primarily important as a preamble to the catalog of its exceptions." *Pacific Fire Ins. Co. v. Kenny Boiler & Mfg. Co.*, 277 N.W. 226, 228 (Minn. 1937). However, this catchy phrase is a bit of an overstatement. In many garden variety cases independent contractors are solely liable for their torts. If Bogart hires Bacall to resurface his driveway, and she backs into the street causing an accident, most likely she alone will bear the liability. If he hires an electrical contractor to rewire his office, most likely the contractor alone will be liable if she negligently starts a fire in the course of the work.

It is not possible to catalog here all situations in which courts have applied the nondelegable duty doctrine. The central point of this discussion is to illustrate that the contractor's independence does not always absolve the owner of responsibility, since courts often refuse, for policy reasons, to allow owners to wash their hands of the matter by hiring out the work.

Liability for the Owner's Own Negligence

The nondelegable duty theory will frequently allow a plaintiff injured by a contractor's negligence to recover from the owner who hired the contractor, even though the owner has exercised due care. However, it is important to remember that owners can be negligent too; frequently, a plaintiff will have a claim against the owner based on his *own* negligence in connection with the contract work.

An owner may be negligent in various ways even though the work is delegated to an independent contractor. He may hire a contractor who is clearly incompetent to perform the type of work required. He may fail to properly supervise the contractor. He may fail to require the contractor to take necessary precautions, or specify that the work be done in an inappropriate manner. He may fail to inspect the work after it is done, or negligently perform work over which he retains control. See generally Restatement (Second) of Torts, §§410-415 (detailing bases of liability for owner's negligence in connection with contract work). In such cases, the owner is liable for his *own* negligence, not vicariously liable for negligence of the contractor.

Frequently, a plaintiff will assert claims against the owner based on both his own negligence and on vicarious liability theories, but it is important to distinguish these two bases for holding the owner liable: Even if there is no basis for holding the owner vicariously liable, he must still answer for his own conduct in connection with the work.

The examples below illustrate the nature and the limits of vicarious liability, both for the acts of employees and of independent contractors.

EXAMPLES

Respondeat Inferior

1. Grant, an employee of Metro Studios, is sued by Bergman, a passerby, for injuries arising from an accident in the course of making a movie. Grant answers the complaint, denying liability on the ground that he was acting in the scope of his employment for Metro at the time of the accident. Bergman moves to strike the defense as insufficient. Should the motion be granted?

2. Based on the accident, Bergman sues Grant and Metro (on a respondeat superior theory) for her injuries. Both are held liable for $50,000.
   a. Grant pays the judgment and seeks contribution from Metro. What result?
   b. Assume that Metro pays the judgment. How much should it be entitled to collect from Grant?

Expert Employment

3. Kildare, a physician with a general practice, is hired to conduct physical exams for Apex, a large manufacturing company. Apex specifies which employees will be examined, what the examinations will entail, what lab tests will be required, and how long Kildare has to submit his reports. The parties agree that Kildare will examine the patients at his office, will conduct a minimum of 20 exams per month, and that he will be paid a set amount for each exam. Kildare negligently injures Garbo during a physical, and she sues Apex. Is Apex liable on the ground that Kildare is its employee?

4. Freud, a psychiatrist, is hired by Columbia Hospital, a mental health facility, to conduct psychotherapy with in-patients at the hospital. Freud agrees to spend ten hours per week at the hospital, to treat patients designated by Columbia, and to accept one-fourth of a full time salary and associated benefits for her work. The parties agree that Freud shall have sole authority over the method of treatment of the patients she sees; however, she is subject to the general administrative regulations of the hospital concerning such

matters as treatment notes, guidelines for medicating patients, informed consent, and others. Jones, one of Freud's patients, commits suicide, and his estate sues Columbia for alleged negligence of Freud in failing to take steps to prevent the suicide. Should Freud be found to be an employee of Columbia for respondeat superior purposes?

Forewarned and Forearmed

5.   Rogers is a sales clerk for the Wild West Gun Shop, which sells firearms and ammunition. Evans, his boss, repeatedly reminds him that he is not to sell to minors. Garner, a 15 year-old, comes into the shop, and Rogers sells him a box of cartridges. Garner is injured using the cartridges and sues Wild West. Would respondeat superior apply?

The Master's Business?

6.   Larry, a house painter for Beta Construction Company, is painting an office with an electric paint sprayer when Curley, a fellow employee, happens by. Larry, in a spirit of horseplay, chases Curley around the room, aiming the sprayer at him and threatening to paint him blue. Unfortunately, he pulls the spray hose too far, knocking over the spray pump and spilling paint on the floor. The paint seeps through the ceiling and ruins office equipment in Moe's office below. Is Beta liable for the damage?

7.   Grimsley, a pitcher for the Baltimore Orioles, is harassed by fans while warming up in the bullpen. Thoroughly annoyed, he finally heaves the ball at the fans, injuring Flynn. Flynn sues the Baltimore Orioles Baseball Club. If you represented him, which of the tests discussed in the introduction concerning respondeat superior liability for intentional torts would you prefer to see the court apply?

8.   Hyde, a child care worker at Child Haven Day Care Center, secretly abuses three children who are cared for at the center. The children sue Child Haven for damages. Which of the various tests for holding the employer liable for this intentional tort would be most favorable to the plaintiffs?

9.   Frood, a psychologist employed by the Midwest Counseling Center, treats Jones, a college student. Frood convinces Jones that, as part of the transference essential to the therapeutic relationship, he must have sexual relations with her. Jones subsequently sues Midwest for malpractice by Frood. Should the Center be held liable?

Respondeat Judge Fudd

10. Charles Electronics tries to make employees feel appreciated. Often, on Friday afternoon, Loy, the assembly supervisor, would buy beer for the crew, and they would all tip a few before heading home for the weekend. One

Friday, Nick, one of the assembly workers, had four beers before leaving, and then headed downtown to meet his wife for dinner. On the way, he injured Nora in an accident. She sues Charles Electronics for her injuries.

At trial, Judge Fudd indicates that he will give the following instruction:

> If you find that, at the time of the accident, Nick was not in the course of his work for the defendant, was not on the premises of the defendant, and was not acting to further the purposes of the defendant, then you must find for the defendant.

What objection should Nora raise to the proposed instruction?

11. Colbert, an employee of Alpha Highway Construction Company, is ordered to keep watch over a large air compressor that powers several jack hammers used in making road cuts. At mid-morning, she slips off to place a bet with a bookie. While she is gone, the machine malfunctions, and the hose whips across the street injuring Gable. He sues Alpha for his injuries. Is Alpha liable for Colbert's conduct under respondeat superior?

Deja Vu

12. Tracy hires Hepburn Construction Company to rebuild the fire escapes on its apartment building, which immediately abuts Main Street. In the course of the work, a Hepburn employee negligently attaches a load of iron railings to a crane cable, and they fall, injuring Stewart, a passerby. Stewart sues Hepburn, the contractor, which denies liability on the ground that the duty of care was nondelegable because it involves a risk of injury unless special precautions are taken. Is this a good defense?

13. Stewart sues both Hepburn and Tracy, and both are found liable for Hepburn's negligence. Hepburn pays and seeks contribution from Tracy. What result?

Nondelegable Non-negligence

14. Assume, on the facts of the Hepburn example, that the load of iron railings was not negligently attached, but fell when the crane's hoisting cable snapped. Although the cable was new, subsequent metallurgical analysis revealed that it had an undetectable defect, which caused it to snap under a normal load. Is Tracy liable for Stewart's injury?

Delegable Duties

15. Tracy hires Hepburn Construction Company to build a garage for him. In the course of the work, Cagney, a Hepburn employee, is required to cut two-by-fours on a table saw. He fails to use the blade guard, and the force of the blade throws a piece of wood into the air, injuring Stewart's eye as he passes by on the street. Is Tracy liable?

16. Hometown hires Astaire Excavation Company to do the excavation for its new sewer system. The excavation must be done in one lane of a public street, with traffic routed around that lane. In the course of the work Rogers, a construction worker, drops a board on the foot of Colbert, a city inspector checking the job. Is Hometown liable for Colbert's injuries?

17. Assume in the fire escape case that Tracy includes a clause in the contract requiring Hepburn to take specific precautions against the risk of falling objects in performing the work. However, Hepburn does not take these precautions, performs the work and leaves. Tracy retakes possession of the apartment building but does not inspect the work. Three months later Colbert, a tenant, is injured coming down the fire escape when the ladder slips under her. Investigation reveals that the nuts that held the ladder were put on by hand, but never tightened with a lug wrench, and had gradually worked loose. Colbert sues Tracy.

    a. Would Tracy be liable to Colbert based on his own negligence?

    b. Would Tracy be vicariously liable for Colbert's injury because Hepburn failed to take special precautions in the course of the work?

EXPLANATIONS

Respondeat Inferior

1.   The judge should grant the motion. Grant is evidently under the impression (as many of my students are initially) that an employee is not personally liable for his torts in the scope of employment, since the employer is liable under respondeat superior. On the contrary, while respondeat superior provides *another*, potentially more solvent, target for the plaintiff, the doctrine does not bar suit against an employee for his own tortious conduct. Both may be sued, and frequently both will be.

2a.   Contribution statutes allow a tortfeasor who has paid a judgment to recover part of the judgment from other tortfeasors. It does not apply between Grant and Metro, however, because they are not joint tortfeasors. Metro is not a tortfeasor at all, but rather is vicariously liable for the tort of someone else. Although Metro is liable to Bergman under respondeat superior, it need not reimburse Grant, who caused the injury, if he pays the judgment. Respondeat superior exists to assure that the *plaintiff* can collect from Metro; it is not intended to insulate the actual tortfeasor from incurring the loss. If Grant pays, he will not recover any reimbursement from Metro.

b.   Most courts hold that an employer who pays the damages caused by his employee is entitled to indemnity — full reimbursement — from the employee, since the employee's negligence actually caused the injury and gave rise to the liability. Indemnity, unlike contribution, involves situations in which one party is liable with another, yet is able to seek reimbursement for the *entire* damages from the other. (Another common example of indemnity is a retail seller who is held liable without fault for selling a defective product, but has a right of indemnity from the manufacturer who actually produced the product. See Restatement (Second) of Torts §886B.)

Although employers held liable under respondeat superior have a right of indemnity from the negligent employee, it is seldom exercised. An action for indemnity would frequently be futile, since the employee is unable to pay. In addition, such losses are often paid by an insurance policy covering both the employer and employee. And, of course, such actions do not make for positive employee relations.

Expert Employment

3. Although Apex exercises some control over Dr. Kildare's work, the court will very likely conclude that he has acted as an independent contractor. Kildare is a practicing physician, a professional whose business is entirely distinct from that of Apex. He is hired to perform a task it requires, but which is not a normal part of its business. He works at his own office, using his own tools and equipment and is paid on a per capita basis. He doubtless schedules the exams according to his own availability and continues to see other patients as well.

It is true that Apex has specified in detail what it wants Kildare to do, but this is true in many contract situations. On a complex road construction job, for example, there will be hundreds of pages of specifications, yet it is clear that a contractor is being hired to perform the entire job for a fixed price. While Apex has specified particular aspects of the exams, it will clearly not hover over Kildare to control his detailed performance of the exams. Apex has contracted for a specified result; it has not hired Kildare to work for it on a day-to-day basis subject to detailed supervision.

4. Although Freud, like Kildare, is a physician, she will likely be held an employee of Columbia on these facts. Freud comes to Columbia to deliver services that are part of the hospital's basic function. She is paid as a salaried employee. True, she only works part time, but nothing in the test for employment suggests that part-time workers cannot be employees. Columbia assigns Freud her patients, provides her work space, and treats her like an employee for benefits purposes. She is also subject to Columbia's general administrative supervision while working there.

On the other hand, if the fundamental test for employment is the right to control the details of the work, Freud has an argument that she cannot be an employee: As a doctor, she is bound by the ethical code of the medical profession to exercise independent medical judgment in the treatment of patients. If Columbia cannot control her in the performance of her central task, the treatment of patients, how can she be an employee?

If this argument were accepted, virtually any professional or skilled worker would have to be viewed as independent. Accountants, lawyers, clergy, and psychologists, for example, frequently work for institutions, and look in virtu- ally all other respects like employees, yet are bound by codes of conduct. Similarly, architects and engineers, as well as pilots, plumbers, electricians, and myriad other skilled workers are subject to statutory codes that prevent their employers from exercising complete control over their work. Yet their employers do exercise broad control over the administrative aspects of their work life: when they work, where they work, how they are paid, their general conduct, their benefits, and many others. In such cases, courts have held professionals employees if the employer exercises control over these other aspects of their work. See Restatement (Second) of Agency §223 cmt. a (lawyers and physicians can be employees if the factors suggest an employ- ment relationship).

Forewarned and Forearmed

5.   The issue here is whether Rogers's act is in the scope of employment where Wild West expressly prohibited it, but Rogers sold to a minor anyway. Since one of the rationales for vicarious liability is that the employer can control negligence of its employees, you might think that where the employer exercised that control but the employee was negligent anyway, the employer would avoid respondeat superior liability.

The cases generally hold otherwise: The employer is liable despite its exercise of care to prevent negligence by its employees. See Restatement (Second) of Agency §230 & cmt. b. This result actually makes a good deal of sense. *First*, while it may seem unfair in the particular case, the across-the- board liability will provide an incentive for Wild West to continue to work to prevent injuries. Perhaps it will discipline Rogers or increase employee education efforts. *Second*, as a practical matter, allowing the employer to avoid liability by offering evidence of its care to prevent accidents would introduce a broad new issue — the employer's general quality control measures — into the suit. *Third*, inducing employers to minimize injuries is only one of the rationales for respondeat superior. Others, such as encouraging loss spreading, internalizing the costs of an enterprise, and placing the loss on the party for whose benefit the risk was created, still support application of the doctrine in this case.

The Master's Business?

6.   Although horseplay of this sort is common in the course of many jobs, it obviously does not further the purposes of the master; Beta hardly pays Larry to chase other workers with the spray gun. On the other hand, smoking does not further the master's purposes either. Like smoking, a certain amount of joking among co-workers is a foreseeable part of the ordinary course of the work experience, takes place in the workplace and during the course of the work, and serves to relieve the tedium of repetitive work.

Acts of horseplay have been held "in the course of employment" in worker's compensation cases, on the following rationale:

> Men do not discard their personal qualities when they go to work. Into the job they carry their intelligence, skill, habits of care and rectitude. Just as inevitably they take along also their tendencies to carelessness and camaraderie, as well as their emotional make-up. In bringing men together, work brings these qualities together, causes frictions between them, creates occasions for lapses into carelessness, and for fun-making and emotional flare-up . . . [t]hese expressions of human nature are incidents inseparable from working together.

Hartford Accident & Indem. Co. v. Cardillo, 112 F.2d 11, 15 (D.C. Cir. 1940). However, this rationale has not been generally accepted in respondeat superior cases involving horseplay. Most deny recovery against the employer for acts of horseplay, on the ground that they do not further the work in any way. See, e.g., *Bryant v. CSX Transp., Inc.*, 577 So. 2d 613, 615-616 (Fla. App. 1991); *Thomas v. Poole*, 262 S.E.2d 854, 857 (N.C. App. 1980).

In view of some of the intentional tort cases described in the introduction, this result seems open to question. Horseplay is more foreseeable and more related to the work experience than the rape of a patient by a hospital assistant or many of the assaults that arise from disagreements in the course of the work. It appears likely that courts that take a broader view of the risks engendered by an enterprise will increasingly impose vicarious liability for such common incidents of the work experience.

7. The Orioles would likely prevail under a more traditional test, such as whether the act was motivated in part by a desire to serve the master. Grimsley's act is motivated by annoyance, not any effort to prepare to enter the game. Nor would Grimsley be viewed as having a position of authority that facilitated this intentional tort. On the other hand, his act certainly does appear motivated by "present interference" with the ability to serve the master's purposes, since the heckling interfered with his concentration while warming up.[3] A fuzzy foreseeability test would also probably get Flynn to the jury, since this kind of harassment and retaliation is increasingly common in an age of declining manners.

8. Most of the tests for imposing respondeat superior liability for intentional torts would not support liability on these facts. Surely it does not further the master's purposes or stem from present interference with the accomplishment of the work. The most favorable test would be the "authority" test, which holds that, where the employer places an employee in a position to commit the tort, or confers authority on the employee that enhances her opportunity to do so, it can be liable for the tort. Here, the opportunity to commit the

---

3. In the case upon which this example is based, the court held that the Orioles could be liable under this test. See *Manning v. Grimsley*, 643 F.2d 20, 24-25 (1st Cir. 1981).

tort arises from Hyde's work with children, and his position of authority over them assists him in doing so. A pure foreseeability test might also support recovery.

If respondeat superior is meant to assure that enterprises internalize the costs of risks they create, liability on these facts may be warranted. Although child abuse is the last thing any day care center wants, its activity does create the risk of such abuse. However, many courts, swayed by the repugnant nature of the conduct, the purely personal motivation of the employee, and the obvious damage the conduct does to the employer's interests, would likely deny recovery. See, e.g., *Worcester Ins. Co. v. Fells Acres Day Sch., Inc.*, 558 N.E.2d 958, 967 (Mass. 1990).

9.   Whether the court applies respondeat superior in this case depends on how broadly it views the scope of employment. Several courts have found that sexual abuse of patients by therapists is outside the scope of employment, because it does not further the work of the employer and arises from purely personal motives. See, e.g., *Moses v. Diocese of Colorado*, 863 P.2d 310, 330 (Co. 1993); *Taylor v. Doctors Hosp.*, 486 N.E.2d 1249 (Ohio App. 1985).

Other cases, however, have taken a broader view. In *Doe v. Samaritan Counseling Ctr.*, 791 P.2d 344 (Alaska 1990), for example, the court rejected a "motivation to serve [the employer]" test and held that the defendant could be liable for sexual abuse by a pastoral counselor. The court emphasized the broad "risk" rationale that employers should be liable for and distribute all losses incident to carrying on an enterprise. 791 P.2d at 348-349.

It would enhance Jones's argument for vicarious liability here if she could show that Frood acted with intent to further Jones's therapy. If Frood believed that a sexual relationship was necessary to Jones's treatment, her acts would satisfy even the restrictive test that she act to accomplish the master's purposes. Granted, no one wanted her to do her work that way, but this is true in many respondeat superior cases. Repossession companies do not want their employees to assault car owners while retrieving cars; bar owners don't want their bouncers to maul unruly patrons, and so on.

Respondeat Judge Fudd

10.   Judge Fudd's mistake here is to focus on Nick's driving as the sole basis for imposing respondeat superior liability on Charles. Nora's counsel should hasten to point out to him that the negligent act of another employee — Loy — may also subject Charles to liability.

Even if Charles is not vicariously liable for Nick's driving, since the work day was over and Nick was on his way to dinner, it very likely *is* liable for the negligence of Loy in furnishing alcohol to Nick. Many courts would find that this act was in the scope of Loy's employment. Doubtless, such efforts to maintain employee morale, while peripheral to the physical production of the company's products, are intended to further the work of the employer in a general way, as do company picnics, the firm dinner dance, and similar happy occasions. Thus, if Loy was negligent in providing alcohol to Nick this will provide a separate basis for holding Charles liable. Nora should explain to Judge Fudd that his instruction is insufficient, because her claim against Charles is based not only on Nick's negligence, but also on Loy's.[4]

11. If you really thought about this one, it shouldn't have given you much of a problem. Certainly, placing bets is not in the scope of Colbert's employment, but Gable's claim is not based on Colbert's act of placing a bet; it is based on her negligent supervision of the compressor. There is no question that this is part of Colbert's assigned duties, that she has negligently performed that duty, and that Gable's claim arises out of this negligence. Even though the claim arises from an omission to act as the work required, rather than a negligent act, Alpha will be liable for it.

Deja Vu

12. It is entirely likely that the duty here is nondelegable, since lifting heavy objects with a crane above the sidewalk poses an obvious risk to the perambulating public unless special precautions are taken. Restatement (Second) of Torts §416. However, finding the duty nondelegable would not relieve Hepburn, the independent contractor, of liability. Just as respondeat superior does not bar suit against a negligent employee, the fact that an owner is vicariously liable in nondelegable duty situations does not bar the plaintiff from suing the contractor for its negligence. It simply means that the owner is liable for it as well. Thus, the fact that the duty is nondelegable is not a proper defense for Hepburn.

13. Here again, as in the analogous circumstances of Example 2, Tracy is not liable to the contractor for contribution. He is not a joint tortfeasor, or any other kind of tortfeasor; he is vicariously liable for damages caused by Hepburn's tort. Because his liability arises from Hepburn's negligence, he is entitled to indemnity from it, but it has no right to contribution or indemnity from him.

Indemnity is much more likely to be sought in this context than in the employer/employee situation, since the contractor is more likely to have adequate resources and insurance to cover the loss. Indeed, Tracy's lawyer should be careful to include a clause in the contract requiring evidence that Hepburn is fully insured, so that this right of indemnity would protect his client from absorbing losses caused by Hepburn's negligence.

---

4. Nora might also argue, though this is a closer question, that Nick's act of *consuming* the alcohol on the employer's premises was in the scope of employment, even if his later driving was not.

Nondelegable Non-negligence

14. This accident did not result from negligence by Hepburn's employees, since the defect was undetectable. If its employees were not negligent, Hepburn would not be liable for Stewart's injury. If so, Tracy would not be liable either. Declaring a duty "nondelegable" does not mean that the owner is strictly liable for *any* accident that occurs in the course of the work. It only means that he is vicariously liable for his contractor's *tortious* conduct. Tracy, as the owner, would be liable if Hepburn was negligent in failing to take necessary precautions, but if Stewart was injured without negligence, he has no claim against Hepburn, and therefore none against Tracy either.

Although Hepburn's employees were not negligent in causing the cable to snap, Stewart's counsel should consider whether they may have failed to take other appropriate precautions. It may be, for example, that if the worksite was properly cordoned off, Stewart would not have been within range of the railings. If such special precautions were necessary, and Hepburn failed to take them, Tracy could be held vicariously liable for that negligence.

Delegable Duties

15. Sawing two-by-fours may well be dangerous if the special precaution of putting the safety guard down is not taken. On the other hand, virtually *any* activity other than bookkeeping or watch repair involves some risk of injury if it is not done cautiously. If a duty is nondelegable whenever some appropriate precaution is omitted, the owner would be liable under the special precautions exception whenever its contractor is negligent. The exception would swallow the general rule that the contractor, not the owner, is usually liable for his torts.

Clearly, the special precautions exception is meant to apply to a narrower class of cases involving unusual risks.

> The situation is one in which a risk is created which is not a normal, routine matter of customary human activity, such as driving an automobile, but is rather a special danger to those in the vicinity, arising out of the particular situation created, and calling for special precautions.

Restatement (Second) of Torts §413 cmt. b. The examples offered by the Restatement, demolishing a building or digging an excavation, (see §413 cmt. c) clearly involve unusual dangers not encountered in sawing boards to build a garage.

16. The work in this example takes place in the public street. Many courts hold that the duty to exercise care for the safety of the public in conducting work in public places is nondelegable. See Restatement (Second) of Torts §417 (work done in a public place which poses risk to members of the public is nondelegable). The owner is made liable because of the evident danger to the public from such work and to give the owner an incentive to make sure that proper precautions are taken.

Here, however, Rogers's negligence does not involve the type of risk which induced courts to impose vicarious liability for work in a public place. Rogers's act did not involve special risk to the public, nor was a member of the public injured by it — Colbert was an inspector, and he was injured within the job site, not in the area open to the public. The owner's vicarious liability only applies to those unusual risks that led the courts to impose vicarious liability in the first place, not to "collateral negligence" unrelated to the special dangers of the work. Restatement (Second) of Torts §426. Vicarious liability is imposed in cases like this because of the risk to the traveling public in the vicinity of the work, not because of the risk of dropped boards within the work site, a risk that is common to all construction projects.

Similarly, in the fire escape example, if a worker left a railing on the ground and someone tripped on it, Tracy would not be vicariously liable. The fire escape work is nondelegable because of the risk of injuries from falling objects if special precautions are not taken, not because a worker might leave debris around the site. This is collateral negligence that could take place in any kind of construction.

17a. Colbert might consider several theories for holding Tracy liable for his *own* negligence. Tracy could be directly liable if he hired Hepburn to perform work that obviously required special precautions, but failed to require Hepburn to take such precautions. But here Tracy *did* require proper safety measures; while he had a duty to require Hepburn to take precautions, he fulfilled it.[5]

Tracy might also be negligent for failing to inspect the work after it was done. See Restatement (Second) of Torts §412 (owner liable for failure to make reasonable inspection after contract work is completed). However, Tracy would probably not have discovered this problem even if he had made an inspection. A reasonable owner would probably walk on the fire escapes to see if they feel tight, and examine them visually for any problems, but such an examination might well not reveal a problem of this sort. See generally Restatement (Second) of Torts §412 cmt. c (establishing a predictably slushy multifactor test for determining the extent of the owner's duty to inspect).

If a reasonable inspection would not have revealed the problem, Tracy's failure to make an inspection would not be an actual cause of the injury. See Chapter 7, pp.124-126 (discussing but-for test for causation). Thus, he would not be liable even if he was negligent for failing to do so.

---

5. An argument might be made that Tracy had a duty to see that the precautions were *actually taken*, not just to require them to be taken, that is, that he had to continuously supervise the work to make sure that Hepburn complied with the contract term requiring precautions. The Restatement does not go so far. See Restatement (Second) of Torts §413 (indicating that duty is fulfilled by requiring contractor to take needed precautions).

b.   If Colbert cannot find a basis for holding Tracy liable for his own negligence, she will look for some nondelegable duty theory for holding him vicariously liable. Clearly, hanging fire escapes with a crane involves unusual risks that require special precautions. See Restatement (Second) of Torts §416. Thus, Tracy could be vicariously liable for injuries resulting from Hepburn's failure to take special precautions to minimize those dangers.

However, the injury here does not result from the failure to take precautions against the peculiar risks associated with the *conduct* of the work — objects falling from the crane. It arises from simple negligence in tightening the bolts that hold the ladder on the fire escape. Here again, the owner is only vicariously liable for injuries which stem from the peculiar danger which makes the duty nondelegable. If a Hepburn crane operator dropped a railing on Colbert's head, Tracy would be vicariously liable, since the injury resulted from the nondelegable aspect of the work. But here the negligence was simply in failing to do the work properly, leading to a defective end result. Since this negligence does not involve the particular risk that makes the duty nondelegable, Tracy will not be vicariously liable for it.[6]

---

6. Tracy might be liable on the basis that it had a nondelegable duty to keep his rental premises in repair. Since this duty is based on the special protection the law accords to tenants, not on the risks created during the work itself, it would apply to any dangerous condition in the premises, not just to unusual risks in the course of the repair work.

PART EIGHT

The Effect of Plaintiff's Conduct

19

The Wave of the Past: Contributory Negligence

Introduction

It is true that we are teetering on the brink of the 21st century, that contributory negligence doctrine hails from the 19th, and that, throughout the intervening 20th, the doctrine has been slouching toward extinction at the usual glacial pace of the common law.

But let me defend the choice (made not only by me, but by most casebooks as well) to detain you momentarily with this wave of the past. *First*, it is still a wave of the present in some states, though not many. *Second*, as in so many areas of the law, understanding major historical trends such as contributory negligence is important to an understanding of current negligence principles. A negligence lawyer without a basic sense of the contributory negligence doctrine is like a student of our modern social welfare state without an understanding of the Great Depression. *Third*, contributory negligence and comparative negligence are in some ways the same concept: While the *effect* of the plaintiff's negligence differs under these two approaches, the nature of the conduct which constitutes negligence is the same under both. *Last*, contributory negligence figures in thousands of past cases which will be the tools of your trade for years. To use those cases effectively, you will have to understand them; to do that, you will have to understand contributory negligence.

With that apologia, let's get down to business. The concept of contributory negligence is simple enough: If the plaintiff's negligence contributed at all to causing an accident, the plaintiff cannot recover. The principle was announced in *Butterfield v. Forrester*, 103 Eng. Rep. 926 (1809), in which the defendant left a pole across the road, and the plaintiff was injured when, "riding violently," he crashed into it and was thrown from his horse. The trial court instructed the jury that the plaintiff could not recover if he was not using ordinary care, and the jury accordingly found for the defendant. On appeal, the judgment was upheld:

> One person being in fault will not dispense with another's using ordinary care for himself. Two things must concur to support this action, an obstruction in the road by the fault of the defendant, and no want of ordinary care to avoid it on the part of the plaintiff.

103 Eng. Rep. at 927. This passage states a conclusion, not a rationale. A lot of ink has been spilled since in search of a valid reason for the contributory negligence doctrine. Even more has gone to refuting the suggested rationales.

The Reasons for the Rule

One frequently cited rationale for the contributory negligence doctrine has its roots in a brief comment in *Butterfield*. Justice Bayley suggested that if plaintiff "had used ordinary care he must have seen the obstruction; so that the accident appeared to happen entirely from his own fault." Id. at 927. This implies that Butterfield alone was the cause of the accident, and that Forrester's negligence was irrelevant because it was not a cause of the resulting harm.

It is crucial to understand why this argument fails under current principles of causation. If anything is clear about causation, it is that an accident can have more than one. If the independent negligence of two parties leads to an accident, both are causes of that accident. This can happen where both are negligent at the same time (as in a motor vehicle collision where two drivers are inattentive) or where the parties are negligent at different times. See Chapter 7. *Butterfield* is an example of the latter type of multiple causation: The earlier negligence of the defendant, Forrester, in leaving the log in the road, and the later negligence of the plaintiff, Butterfield, in running into it, concurred to lead to the accident. Without Butterfield's negligence, there would have been no accident, and without Forrester's there wouldn't either. Both are therefore but-for causes. To say that only Butterfield caused the accident is to disregard this established principle of multiple causation.

Just to nail down the point, assume that Butterfield was negligently driving a coach with a sleeping passenger in it, ran into the obstruction left by Forrester, and his passenger was injured. Under basic principles of causation, both Forrester's and Butterfield's acts would be but-for causes of the passenger's injury, and both would be liable to the passenger. Restatement (Second) of Torts §479 cmt. a; Chapter 7 pp.124-126. If both Forrester and Butterfield are causes of that accident, it makes little sense to conclude that Forrester did not cause it if Butterfield's coach was empty and he alone was injured. Nor is this a case where Butterfield's negligence supersedes Forrester's. Only unforeseeable subsequent events supersede prior negligence; if you leave a pole across the road nothing could be more foreseeable than a coach driving into it.

Another problem with the sole cause rationale is that it completely fails to explain cases where the plaintiff's negligence *precedes* the defendant's. Suppose that Butterfield negligently fastens a wheel on his coach. The next day Forrester negligently drops a cricket bat in the road. An hour later, Butterfield is injured when the wheel falls off after hitting the bat. Here, the defendant's negligence comes after the plaintiff's. If contributory negligence bars recovery because the plaintiff is the last wrongdoer, it should not apply in such cases. But (apart from the last clear chance doctrine) it always has.

Another argument for the contributory negligence doctrine is that, where both the plaintiff and the defendant are at fault in causing the accident, neither should be able to shift the loss to the other. There is an interesting parallel between this argument and the common law refusal to allow contribution between joint tortfeasors. At common law, if Hull negligently caused injuries to Perkins, he was liable for her full damages; if she collected from him, he could not seek contribution from Stimson, even if Stimson's negligence also caused the harm. If Hull caused the injury, even in combination with Stimson, he was a wrongdoer and could be justly required to absorb the full damages. See Chapter 16 pp.338-339. Analogously, where the plaintiff was a partial cause of her own injuries, she was made to bear the entire loss, since the contributory negligence rule barred her from recovering against other negligent parties. As Dean Green reports, "19th century morality was a severe thing. It demanded absolutes. Either a defendant was responsible or he was not. Compromises were not to be endured." L. Green, Judge and Jury 122 (1930).

Nowadays, of course, morality, if not exactly in retreat, is viewed as a more complex matter, and contributory negligence as an overly simplistic solution.[1] Compromise is now the order of the day. Among defendants, distributing the plaintiff's judgment through principles of contribution has superseded the idea that any negligent tortfeasor should bear the whole loss. As between the negligent plaintiff and the defendants, dividing the damages under comparative negligence has largely superseded the contributory negligence doctrine.

In *Butterfield*, Lord Ellenborough suggested another rationale for contributory negligence. If the negligent plaintiff could recover, he noted, he could "cast himself upon an obstruction which has been made by the fault of another" and recover damages for it. Id. at 927. This reminds me of that

---

1. One major treatise condemns the doctrine as a "Draconian rule sired by a medieval concept of cause out of a heartless laissez-faire." Harper, James & Gray, §22.3, at 288 (footnote omitted).

moronic bumper sticker, "Go ahead and hit me; I need the money." Who in her right mind would deliberately incur personal injury in the vain hope that our ponderous, expensive, shot-in-the-dark litigation system would truly compensate her for either the injuries themselves or the endless aggravation that litigation provides for everyone but lawyers?[2] Perhaps the honorable justice was really suggesting that a plaintiff's *intentional* act in encountering danger should bar recovery. This result may follow in some cases under assumption of the risk doctrine or as a matter of superseding cause, but in such cases there is no need to base the result on contributory negligence. Certainly, this argument does not support a general principle that *negligent* conduct by a plaintiff should bar her recovery.

Another argument for contributory negligence is that negligent conduct should be discouraged: If plaintiffs are barred from recovery when their carelessness contributes to their injuries, they will be more likely to be careful. This argument assumes that people modify their conduct in light of the prevailing principles of tort law, a dubious proposition indeed. "If the prospect of losing life or limb does not make a plaintiff careful, little further inducement to care will be added by speculations as to the outcome of a lawsuit." Harper, James & Gray, §22.2, at 280; see also Schwartz, Contributory and Comparative Negligence: A Reappraisal, 87 Yale L.J. 697, 710-719 (1978) (questioning this assumption on numerous grounds). The argument also ignores the effect of the contributory negligence rule on the behavior of *defendants*. If the doctrine encourages plaintiffs to take care, it may discourage careful conduct by potential defendants, since they can avoid liability, even if they are negligent, by pleading contributory negligence.

Last, it has been suggested that the progenitors of the contributory negligence rule were not ignorant of its shortcomings, but simply couldn't think of any better way to deal with the negligent plaintiff. Judges of the *Butterfield* era were not prehistoric; they had thought of the idea of dividing the damages where both parties contributed to it. But the practical difficulties of apportioning fault among the parties seemed too great:

> This is an undertaking which not only is it perilous to entrust to the faculties of a jury, but which in most cases cannot be performed accurately by any human agency. . . . [I]t seems impossible to evolve any formulae which will produce even an approximately accurate apportionment in a large run of cases.

Lowndes, Contributory Negligence, 22 Geo. L.J. 674, 683-684 (1934).

As a purely intellectual matter, this argument has considerable force. How can a jury assign percentages in any rigorous way to the failure to signal a left turn compared to driving nine miles over the speed limit? As a practical matter, however, the law is "an instrument of governance, not a hymn to

---

2. Actually, it provides more than enough for them too.

intellectual beauty." *Newman-Green, Inc. v. Alfonso-Larrain R.*, 854 F.2d 916, 925 (7th Cir. 1988). Most states have found that juries *can* make a rough apportionment of the parties' fault in causing an accident, and that this is more equitable than barring recovery to the plaintiff, as contributory negligence does, no matter how minor her negligence may have been. Several decades of experience with comparative negligence have confirmed that this approach works tolerably well.

The Meaning of Plaintiff's Negligence

There is a good deal of law on what constitutes "negligence" on the part of defendants. See Chapter 4, which analyzes the concept of due care and "that odious character," the reasonable person. Is the negligence principle any different when it is the plaintiff's conduct that is in issue? It hardly seems that it should be: Reasonable care is reasonable care, no matter who ends up on which side in the ensuing lawsuit.

However, some authorities argue that there is a distinction between the negligence of plaintiffs and defendants. The negligent defendant, they suggest, is a person who has failed to exercise reasonable care for the safety of others. A negligent plaintiff, on the other hand, has simply failed to use the care that a reasonable person would use for his own safety. Prosser & Keeton 453; Morris on Torts at 206 (2d ed. 1980). The first involves a violation of a duty to others (the general duty to exercise due care for the protection of those placed at risk by the actor's conduct) while the second is arguably less culpable, since it only risks injury to the plaintiff herself.

It is doubtful that this distinction has made much difference in practice. The *standard* of careful conduct is essentially the same for both negligence and contributory negligence. Whether defendant or plaintiff, the actor is held to the standard of ordinary care:

> The plaintiff is required to conform to the same objective standard of conduct, that of the reasonable person of ordinary prudence under like circumstances. The unreasonableness of the risks which he incurs is judged by the same process of weighing the importance of the interest he is seeking to advance, and the burden of taking precautions, against the probability and probable gravity of the anticipated harm to himself.

Prosser & Keeton, 453-454 (footnotes omitted). This symmetry in the standard makes sense. In some situations the plaintiff may risk his own safety only, such as the dreaming pedestrian who wanders into a hole in the sidewalk. But conduct that risks injury to the plaintiff usually risks injury to others as well. If that same dreamer wanders into traffic, she may cause injuries to motorists trying to avoid her as well as to herself. Similarly, a driver who speeds or a homeowner who negligently installs an electric line imperils the safety of others as well as herself. Thus, an actor's conduct will often be assessed as both primary negligence and contributory negligence. For example, if Hull sues another driver, Perkins, for negligence, and Perkins counterclaims for her injuries, Hull will rely on the same acts to prove that Perkins was negligent (and therefore liable to him) and contributorily negligent (and therefore barred from recovering from him).

Because the standard of conduct is generally the same, the various corollaries of the reasonable person standard apply equally to a plaintiff's conduct. For example, the emergency doctrine, the special standard of care for children, the treatment of statutory standards of care, and the allowances made for physical disability will apply to the conduct of both plaintiffs and defendants.

Timber to Toothpicks: Avoiding the Contributory Negligence Defense

Contributory negligence is a harsh rule in many cases, since a minimally negligent plaintiff is barred from recovery even if she is seriously injured or the negligence of the defendant was greater. While the doctrine may have satisfied the severe morality of the 19th century and the economic necessities of an expanding industrial society, the 20th century has been less comfortable with its rigidity. Consequently, even courts that applied it in theory often tempered its harshness in practice:

> This tall timber in the legal jungle has been whittled down to toothpick size by the sympathetic sabotage of juries, whose inability to perceive contributory negligence in suits against certain defendants is notorious; by the emotional antagonism of judges who have placed constrictions upon the doctrine . . . ; by the popular prejudices of legislators who have pulled the teeth of the common-law dogma or damned it outright.

Lowndes, Contributory Negligence, 22 Geo. L. Rev. at 674.

As Lowndes suggests, several whittling devices eroded the impact of the doctrine. One was to leave the issue of the plaintiff's negligence to the jury, who often disregarded their instructions and found for the plaintiff even though she was negligent. This head-in-the-sand approach does little to project the grandeur of the law, but it was doubtless effective enough to achieve a more equitable result in many cases than the letter of the contributory negligence rule.[3]

Most courts also restricted the contributory negligence doctrine by refusing to apply it if the conduct of the defendant was reckless, wilful, or wanton. These terms embrace conduct that is not intentional, in the intentional tort

---

3. In other cases, it is fairly clear that the jury fashioned their own ad hoc comparative negligence rule by returning a "compromise" verdict: They would find for the plaintiff, but return a low verdict on damages to account for her negligence.

sense, but that disregards "a known or obvious risk that was so great as to make it highly probable that harm would follow." Prosser & Keeton at 213; see Restatement (Second) of Torts §500 (recklessness involves ignoring a risk of physical harm that is "substantially greater than that which is necessary to make his conduct negligent"). Clearly, this type of conduct is more aggravated, more "faulty" than mere negligence. Where the defendant's conduct showed such aggravated fault, the contributory negligence defense would not lie; the plaintiff recovered even if her negligence was a cause of the accident as well. *A fortiori*, (as we lawyers say) the defense was also inapplicable to intentional torts.

This exception for wilful, wanton, or reckless conduct represents a sort of comparative negligence rule in itself: Where the defendant's fault was disproportionate to the plaintiff's, the plaintiff recovered despite her negligence. However, this exception was unlike "true" comparative negligence in that the plaintiff recovered *fully* if the defendant's conduct was wilful, wanton, or reckless. No reduction was made for the plaintiff's negligence.

Last Clear Chance

The third common law device for avoiding contributory negligence was the notorious "last clear chance" doctrine. This doctrine arose out of another English case, *Davies v. Mann*, 152 Eng. Rep. 588 (1842). *Davies* is a classically simple common law case that spawned exquisitely convoluted corollaries (of which, more below). Davies negligently allowed his donkey to wander into the road and Mann's wagon ran it down. At the time, Mann's servant was walking some distance behind the wagon, and it was traveling too fast. Although Davies was negligent *earlier* for leaving the donkey in the road, the court concluded that this negligence did not bar recovery, since at the time of the accident, Davies was unable to avoid the accident, while the defendant, had he exercised due care, might have done so.

Davies makes a nice comparison with *Butterfield v. Forrester*. In *Butterfield*, the defendant was negligent first; his prior act of leaving the pole in the road combined with the plaintiff's later negligent riding to cause the accident. In *Davies*, the plaintiff was negligent first, by leaving the donkey in the road, and his prior act combined with the defendant's later negligent driving to cause the accident. In *Butterfield*, the plaintiff was barred from recovery by his failure to avoid the accident; in *Davies*, the defendant was made to pay because he failed to avoid the accident. In each case, the prior negligence was disregarded.

So, the cases are consistent in the sense that in each the last wrongdoer absorbed the entire loss. But that doesn't mean they are right. In *Davies*, as in *Butterfield*, there is a suggestion that the earlier negligence was not causal, but that is no more defensible in the one case than in the other. In each case, the earlier negligence was a but-for cause of the harm, and in each case the subsequent negligence was foreseeable. Why should the prior negligence be disregarded in either case?

No satisfactory explanation has been suggested for the result in *Davies*, other than a vague sense that the later negligence is more culpable because just prior to the accident the plaintiff was helpless to avoid the accident while the defendant might have. (Indeed, the doctrine may owe its nickname, "the jackass doctrine," as much to its logical force as to its origin.) Arguably, the doctrine placed the loss on the party viewed as more culpable, the party in the last position to avoid harm. But this assumes that the last negligent party is the more negligent party, and that is not necessarily true. The plaintiff who falls asleep on the tracks may well be more negligent than the engineer who fails to see him or negligently chooses to apply the brake before blowing the whistle to warn him.

There is an interesting human interest story in the Second Restatement's position on last clear chance. Dean Prosser, (he was a law school dean as well as the dean of Torts scholars) was the Reporter for the Restatement. The Restatement, as discussed earlier, is primarily meant to summarize the law, to "restate" it, rather than to change it. Thus, while Prosser roundly criticized the last clear chance doctrine in his treatise (see Prosser, Handbook of the Law of Torts 437-443 (3rd ed. 1964)), he included it in the Restatement. But his ambivalence toward the doctrine was reflected there as well. While §479 states the rule, the comment to that section emphatically rebuts the proximate cause rationale frequently offered for it. Restatement (Second) of Torts §479 cmt. a.

I promised you some exquisitely convoluted corollaries, so let's explore the four situations in which the last clear chance doctrine has been applied.

A. Convoluted Corollary #1

The first form of the doctrine was the "conscious last clear chance," called in some cases the doctrine of "discovered peril." In these cases, the plaintiff is placed in a perilous situation, due to her own negligence. However, once imperiled, she is helpless to avoid the risk created by the defendant's conduct. An example is a motorist who negligently gets her car caught on the track as the train approaches, or a drunk who passes out on the tracks.[4] After the plaintiff becomes helpless, the defendant actually discovers her peril, but acts negligently in attempting to avoid the accident.

The last clear chance doctrine has found the most support in this scenario. The plaintiff, while admittedly negligent, is unable to prevent the accident once she is trapped, while the defendant still can. In addition, the defendant

---

4. Virtually all the last clear chance cases involve collisions with trains, boats, street railways, or cars.

is aware of the plaintiff's situation in time to do something about it, but negligently fails to take proper steps to avoid the harm. Virtually all courts that accepted last clear chance at all allowed the plaintiff to recover in these cases, despite her negligence. The Restatement (Second) of Torts §479 also approves this form.

B. Convoluted Corollary #2

The second variant was the "unconscious last clear chance" doctrine. In these cases, the plaintiff had negligently placed herself in a helpless situation, but the defendant did not realize it. However, *had she exercised due care*, the defendant would have seen and appreciated the danger in time to avoid the accident. An example is the train engineer who is not keeping a proper lookout, and therefore bears down on the helpless plaintiff trapped on the track without seeing her. If the engineer had been careful, she would have seen the plaintiff in time to stop, but she wasn't, didn't, and a collision resulted.

The argument for placing the liability fully on the defendant (by ignoring the plaintiff's contributory negligence in getting into a helpless situation) is weaker here. Both parties are negligent. While the defendant has the later chance to avoid the accident, she is not aware of the need to do so. Presumably, one argument for applying the last clear chance doctrine in these cases is that the defendant should not be better off for failing to discover danger than she is when she discovers it but fails to respond adequately (corollary #1). Refusing to extend the doctrine to these cases would seem to reward the defendant for her failure keep a lookout.

However, the defendant's negligence here is mere inadvertence, the same kind of inadvertence that put the plaintiff in peril in the first place. (Remember, the plaintiff's negligence was irrelevant if the defendant's conduct was truly egregious; contributory negligence was not a defense if the defendant's conduct was wilful, wanton, or reckless.) The failure to realize the plaintiff's danger seems less culpable than the failure to avert a danger of which the defendant is aware. It appears that the courts that have applied the unconscious last clear chance doctrine rely simply on the fact that the defendant's negligence comes after the plaintiff's. While many courts have applied it in these circumstances, and §479 of the Second Restatement approves it, other courts that apply the conscious last clear chance doctrine reject this variant.

C. Convoluted Corollary #3

The third variant is the "inattentive plaintiff/conscious last clear chance." In these cases, the plaintiff is not helpless. Right up to the point of impact, she could avoid the accident but does not, since she is negligently unaware of her peril. An example is a pedestrian absorbed in a book who wanders into the path of an oncoming car. However, as in the discovered peril cases, the defendant *is* aware of the plaintiff's situation — including the fact that she is inattentive — in time to avoid the harm.

The Second Restatement (see §480) and many courts applied the last clear chance doctrine in these cases as well. However, disregarding the plaintiff's contributory negligence in these cases cannot be explained on the basis of the last opportunity to avoid harm, since both parties are equally able to do so up until the accident. The plaintiff is not only negligent in getting into a position of peril; she is *still negligent* at the time of the accident in failing to take heed and get out of the way. If there is a rationale here, it must rest on the fact that the defendant is *aware* of the risk, while the plaintiff merely should be. Arguably, the defendant is more negligent due to her actual appreciation of the danger, and her failure to react appropriately.

D. Convoluted Corollary #4

The fourth variation, in case you haven't guessed, is the situation in which the plaintiff is inattentive and the defendant would have realized it in the exercise of due care, but fails to do so through his own inattention. An example would be the plaintiff who wanders into the traveled part of the road and is hit by a motorist combing his hair in the rear view mirror. It is hard to discern any basis for preferring the plaintiff in this situation. Both plaintiff and defendant have an equal opportunity to avert the harm. Neither is conscious of the danger. They are both negligent up to the time of the accident. The Restatement and most of the cases refused to apply the last clear chance doctrine on such facts.

At bottom, the last clear chance doctrine appears to be a comparative negligence rule in proximate cause clothing. The doctrine allowed courts to act on their instinctive sense that the defendant was more culpable than the plaintiff, either because she was aware of the danger (corollaries #1 and #3) or because she had the later opportunity to avert it (corollaries #1 and #2) or both (corollary #1). The common law had no means of dividing the damages where one party was more negligent than the other, but last clear chance allowed courts to place the *whole* loss on the party it considered more blameworthy. The rule, though no hymn to intellectual beauty, supported results that courts found more satisfactory than unrestrained application of the contributory negligence bar.

The following examples should help you to sort out the application of the contributory negligence and last clear chance doctrines. In analyzing the examples assume that the contributory negligence doctrine applies.

EXAMPLES

Deductible Contributions

1.   Sullivan is driving down Pennsylvania Avenue at night. As he knows, his left headlight is burnt out, but he is only going a few blocks and decides to chance it. Roosevelt is driving in the other direction on bald tires. She hits a bump, the tire blows, and she loses control of the car, which swerves across the center line into Sullivan's line of travel. Sullivan sues Roosevelt for his resulting injuries, and Roosevelt pleads contributory negligence based on Sullivan's burnt out light. Does the defense bar recovery?

2.   Consider the example mentioned in the introduction, in which Butterfield negligently fastens the wheel on his coach, and the wheel falls off when it rolls over a cricket bat Forrester dropped an hour before the accident, injuring Butterfield. Is this a last clear chance case, and if so, which kind?

3.   Here is an excerpt from *Davies v. Mann*, describing the facts of the case:

> it appeared that the plaintiff, having fettered the fore feet of an ass belonging to him, turned it into a public highway, and at the time in question the ass was grazing on the off side of a road about eight yards wide, when the defendant's waggon, with a team of three horses, coming down a slight descent, at what the witness termed a smartish pace, ran against the ass, knocked it down, and the wheels passing over it, it died soon after. The ass was fettered at the time, and it was proved that the driver of the waggon was some little distance behind the horses.

152 Eng. Rep. 588, 588 (1842). Which version of the last clear chance doctrine, if any, applies on these facts?

Fudd's Last Chance

4.   Morgenthau is injured when his car is hit by a train at a railroad crossing. At trial, Morgenthau admits on cross-examination that he did not look for a train, because he lived in the area and knew from the train schedule that no train was due. A pedestrian also testifies that Morgenthau ventured onto the tracks without looking. Barkley, the engineer, testifies that he saw Morgenthau, blew the whistle and then tried to stop, but the pedestrian testifies that Barkley was not looking and that the train never slowed before hitting Morgenthau.

   a. If the last clear chance doctrine did not apply, would contributory negligence bar Morgenthau from recovering?
   b. Which convoluted corollary of the last clear chance doctrine applies here, if any?

> c. Assume that Barkley testified that he saw Morgenthau and tried to stop, but that the train's brakes failed due to poor maintenance. On this evidence, Judge Fudd instructs the jury as follows:

>> If you find that the plaintiff was negligent in failing to look both ways before crossing the tracks, but that the defendant, after realizing that the plaintiff was entering the tracks and unable to prevent a collision, failed to avoid the accident, then you should disregard the plaintiff's negligence in failing to keep a proper lookout.

What is wrong with Judge Fudd's instruction?

New York, New York

5.   Flanagan is driving a garbage truck down Second Avenue when a small hand suddenly starts banging on the window of the passenger's side of the cab. Flanagan, though bemused by this phenomenon, continues on for three blocks. As it turns out, Wallace, a 12 year-old boy, had hopped a ride on the running board of the truck, but tried to get Flanagan to stop when the road became bumpy and he became afraid he would fall off. In fact, he did fall off, slipped under the wheels of the truck and was injured.
   a. Was Wallace negligent?
   b. Which type of last clear chance is involved here?
   c. If last clear chance applies, *and* Wallace was negligent, could Wallace recover?

6.   LaGuardia is driving a New York City subway train through a darkened tunnel when the train suddenly brakes to a stop. The cars of the train are equipped with emergency devices that brake the train if any object is hit underneath the train. LaGuardia resets the brake and proceeds. It trips again. He resets it again. When it trips a third time, he gets out and investigates, and finds Sherwood lying dead under the fourth car. LaGuardia testifies (without contradiction) that he never saw Sherwood on the tracks. No evidence is found as to what Sherwood was doing in a New York City subway tunnel, but the medical evidence shows that he was heavily intoxicated, and quite likely unconscious at the time of the accident. Sherwood's estate brings suit against LaGuardia for negligence.
   a. Which type of last clear chance might apply on these facts?
   b. If the court concludes that last clear chance might apply (and therefore refuses to direct a verdict for LaGuardia based on Sherwood's contributory negligence) what will be the estate's major problem in proving its case?

7.   LaFollette negligently leaves his car sitting partly in the traveled way of a rural road after dark, while he makes a short excursion to the local bushes. Along comes Knox, driving home from town without his lights; he had just discovered that they had failed when he started home. He does not see

LaFollette's car until he is almost upon it, and plows into it. LaFollette sues him for damage to the car. Will LaFollette's negligence bar recovery?

Conditions Subsequent

8.   Baruch and Burns are working together clearing brush. Baruch sustains multiple lacerations when Burns negligently scrapes him with a chain saw. Baruch is hospitalized for a week while his wounds are treated, and misses a month of work. When he is discharged from the hospital, he is instructed to take an antibiotic for two more weeks, to prevent infection. Burns loses the prescription on the way home, and doesn't bother to get a copy and take the pills. Subsequently, he develops an infection, ends up back in the hospital for six more weeks, and is disabled for three months.

    a. Is Baruch contributorily negligent?

    b. Should he recover from Burns for the damages caused by the infection?

9.   Assume that Baruch was seriously cut by the saw, but simply tied the cut up with an ace bandage and continued to work, despite Burns's protestations that he should see a doctor. Subsequently, he develops an infection and is out of work for six weeks and disabled for three months as a result. He sues Burns for his injuries. At trial, Baruch's doctor testifies that he might have gotten the infection even with prompt treatment — or he might not. On cross-examination, however, he admits that the infection would almost certainly have been less severe if Baruch had sought treatment right away. Is Burns liable for the damages attributable to the infection?

10.   Assume that Baruch's cut leaves substantial scar tissue on his hand, impairing its function. Baruch seeks damages for the impairment. Burns claims that, with a new form of microscopic surgery, the function can be restored, and that Baruch refused to undergo the surgery, choosing instead to rely on physical therapy. How should the court decide whether to deny recovery for Baruch's impairment?

EXPLANATIONS

Deductible Contributions

1.   In this example Sullivan was negligent but his negligence is irrelevant, because it did not contribute to causing the accident. Roosevelt did not hit him because she didn't see him, but because she lost control of the car and swerved into the opposing traffic. She would have hit him if he had two functioning headlights. Sullivan's negligence is not a but-for cause of the accident.

    Just as the defendant is only liable for negligence that causes the harm, the plaintiff's negligence only bars recovery if it contributed to causing the accident. We are not testing Sullivan's general virtue, but whether his careless conduct is partly to blame for this accident. The same is true under comparative negligence; only *causal* negligence by the plaintiff affects her right to recover.

2.   Although Forrester was negligent in dropping the bat after Butterfield was in fastening the wheel, this is not a last clear chance case. The doctrine applies where the plaintiff is in peril, and the defendant knows it or should know it and has a chance to avert the harm but fails to exercise due care to do so. Here, Forrester presumably does not know that he dropped the bat, or that Butterfield is about to drive over it. Thus he is not in a position to prevent the accident just before it takes place. On these facts, Butterfield's contributory negligence would prevent recovery.

3.   While the last clear chance doctrine is said to have originated in *Davies*, it is not at all clear than *any* of the corollaries described in the introduction applies to the *Davies* facts. The driver was walking behind the wagon, which was moving at "a smartish pace." It seems unlikely that, after noticing the donkey, the driver could have run up to the wagon, jumped aboard, and stopped it before hitting the donkey.

Indeed, nothing in the court's discussion in *Davies* suggests that the judges thought that the driver could prevent the accident after seeing the donkey, or that the result depended on his having discovered the donkey's peril. The *Davies* court appeared to rely solely on the fact that the driver was negligent after Davies was. This is the same discredited rationale relied on in *Butterfield*, that the last cause is the only proximate cause of an accident.

Thus, *Davies* introduced an idea, but did not establish the elements of last clear chance. The more intricate requirements of our corollaries evolved later as courts attempted to find a more credible rationale for the doctrine than *Davies*'s discredited "last wrongdoer" analysis.

Fudd's Last Chance

4a.   There seems little doubt that Morgenthau was negligent in failing to check before crossing the tracks. Trains can be late, or unscheduled freights may come through. In Hand formula terms, the burden of taking a look is trivial compared to the grievous injury likely to result from a collision with a train. If the last clear chance doctrine does not apply, the court should direct a verdict for Barkley, since the uncontradicted evidence establishes Morgenthau's negligence, and contributory negligence, in any degree, bars recovery.

b. Whether any version of last clear chance applies here depends on what the jury finds the facts to be. Based on the pedestrian's testimony, they could conclude that neither Morgenthau nor Barkley was looking. If so, then this looks like corollary #4, in which both parties are inattentive, and in which most courts refused to apply the last clear chance doctrine.

On the other hand, if the jury credits Barkley's testimony, they could conclude that he was not negligent at all, since he did everything he could to avoid the accident after seeing Morgenthau. If that is true, the last clear chance doctrine is irrelevant; it only applies where a defendant negligently fails to take advantage of a "last clear chance" to avert an accident.

The jury might also conclude that Barkley saw the car approaching and realized the danger, but negligently failed to stop (perhaps unwisely relying on the whistle to warn Morgenthau). If Barkley saw the car, realized the danger, but negligently failed to avert the accident, the case would fall into the third last clear chance category, in which the plaintiff could avoid the accident but is inattentive up until the collision, while the defendant appreciates the risk in time to avoid it. Many courts applied the last clear chance doctrine in such cases.

Some scholars have suggested that the implicit rationale for contributory negligence was that it allowed judges to keep cases from "incurably plaintiff minded" juries, by granting directed verdicts. See W. Malone, The Formative Era of Contributory Negligence, 41 Ill. L. Rev. 151, 155-158 (1946). Where the facts established *any* causal negligence by the plaintiff, the judge could direct a verdict for the defendant, thus preventing the jury from finding for the plaintiff based on sympathy for the victim, the deep pocket of defendants, or resentment of large corporate enterprises. However, there must have been many cases like this one, in which the plaintiff was able to pose a jury question based on the last clear chance doctrine, even though it was clear that she was negligent. So long as the plaintiff made a plausible last clear chance argument, the judge would not be able to direct a verdict for the defendant, since the jury would have to decide whether, despite the plaintiff's negligence, she could recover anyway under the last clear chance doctrine.

c. Judge Fudd has once again missed his chance. Fudd's instruction tells the jury that they should find for Morgenthau if Barkley discovered his peril but failed to avoid the collision. However, the defendant is not automatically liable under the last clear chance doctrine if he becomes aware of plaintiff's peril and fails to avoid an accident. He is only liable if, after discovering her peril, he is negligent in his efforts to avoid it. Here, Barkley's uncontradicted testimony demonstrates that he made reasonable efforts to avoid the accident, once he discovered Morgenthau's peril, but was unable to do so due to the condition of the brakes. True, having bad brakes is negligent, but it is not negligent conduct of the engineer in avoiding the accident *after* discovering the plaintiff's peril.

Fudd should instruct the jury that if Barkley *was negligent* in failing to avoid the accident after discovering Morgenthau's peril, then Morgenthau's negligence should be disregarded. The following instruction would accurately explain to the jury the effects of last clear chance on the case:

> If you find that the plaintiff was negligent in failing to look both
> ways before he entered the intersection, but that the defendant, after

he saw the plaintiff in the intersection, failed to exercise reasonable care to avoid the accident, then the plaintiff's negligence will not bar him from recovery.

New York, New York

5a. Clearly an adult would be negligent if he or she were to hop a ride on the running board of a truck in traffic. The only argument that Wallace was not negligent is that he is too young to appreciate the risk. As the Introduction states, the negligence standard is basically the same for plaintiffs and defendants. Thus, Wallace's conduct will be assessed under the standard of care for children of like age, intelligence, and experience. Restatement (Second) of Torts §464(2).

Even making allowances for Wallace's youth, this is almost certainly negligence. A typical 12 year-old boy would realize the danger of riding on the outside of a fast moving vehicle. The fact that boys will be boys — that they do it anyway — doesn't make it careful conduct.

b. This is a discovered peril or conscious last clear chance case (corollary #1). Since Flanagan sees the hand, she must realize that there is a child attached to it, that any child riding on the truck is in a helpless position, is in danger of serious injury, and that only she can avert the harm by stopping the truck. On facts close to these the New York Court of Appeals concluded that a directed verdict should not have been granted for the defendant, since plaintiff might recover under the conscious last clear chance doctrine. *Chadwick v. City of New York*, 93 N.E.2d 625 (1950).

c. This is one of those deceptively simple questions I throw in once in a while to keep you on your toes. The answer to this is "absolutely." The very purpose of the last clear chance doctrine was to allow the jury to find for the plaintiff *despite* her contributory negligence. If the plaintiff was not negligent, the doctrine was irrelevant.

6a. This appears to be a corollary #2 case. We have a presumably helpless (though negligent) plaintiff passed out on the tracks. The evidence does not establish that LaGuardia was negligent in failing to see him before the train reached him — the tunnel was dark and Sherwood may well have been lying down. The tripping of the brake did not put LaGuardia on actual notice of Sherwood's peril, but it did suggest that there was an object on the track, that it could be a person, and that due care called for him to investigate rather than to simply reset the brake and proceed. Thus, the jury could find that LaGuardia was not, but should have been, aware of Sherwood's peril after the brake tripped the first time. If it so found, the unconscious last clear chance doctrine would apply, allowing Sherwood's estate to recover despite his negligence.

b. Even if the judge denies a directed verdict based on contributory negligence, the plaintiff will face a difficult problem in proving that LaGuardia's failure to use his last clear chance to avoid hitting Sherwood the second and third times was a cause of Sherwood's death. Remember that LaGuardia was only negligent after Sherwood was hit the first time, tripping the brake. If Sherwood was killed by that first impact, LaGuardia's later negligence in twice restarting the train would not be a cause of his death.

This example is also based (with changes) on a real case, *Kumkumian v. City of New York*, 111 N.E.2d 865 (N.Y. 1953). In *Kumkumian*, the court held that the medical evidence would support a finding that the later impacts caused the death, and that the case should have gone to the jury on a last clear chance theory.

7.   The last clear chance doctrine does not apply to this case. Knox did not discover the danger until it was too late to do anything about it, so it is not a discovered peril situation. Nor is it apparently a corollary #2 case, in which he *should* have discovered the peril in time to avoid the accident. His negligence is in the decision to drive without lights in the first place, not in his reaction just before the accident. See Example 4c; see also Restatement (Second) of Torts §479, illus. 4 (no liability on similar facts).

However, there should be no reason to worry about whether last clear chance applies here. As the introduction indicates, contributory negligence was not a defense to wilful, wanton, or reckless conduct. Driving at night without lights would very likely constitute such aggravated fault. Consequently, LaFollette's negligence in leaving the car partly on the road, though it constitutes contributory negligence, would still not bar recovery.

Conditions Subsequent

8a.   Strictly speaking, this is not a contributory negligence case. Contributory negligence refers to careless conduct of the plaintiff that is a cause of the accident that injures him. In this case, the accident was being scraped by a chain saw, and that was caused, as far as the example indicates, solely by the negligence of Burns. Baruch was negligent only *after* the accident, in failing to take reasonable steps to minimize the extent of the resulting injuries.

b. This example illustrates a common situation in which the plaintiff, after being injured by the defendant, fails to take reasonable steps to minimize her injuries. A plaintiff may fail to cover over a roof after the defendant negligently punctures it, causing much more extensive damage than necessary. She might drive a car after faulty repair, burning out the whole engine, or refuse physical therapy that would greatly reduce disability caused by an accident. There is a whole jurisprudence on such cases, often referred to as the "doctrine of avoidable consequences." See generally Harper, James & Gray, §25.4.

Even courts that apply the contributory negligence doctrine do not bar the plaintiff's recovery completely in cases like this. After all, Baruch did suffer some injury due solely to Burns's negligence. However, most courts deny recovery for the aggravated damages that she could have prevented through the exercise of reasonable care after the accident. See Minzer, Nates, ch. 16. Under the avoidable consequences doctrine, Baruch would recover for the pain and suffering, medical bills, and lost wages caused by his initial injury, but not for the additional period of disability or the extra medical bills caused by his unreasonable failure to follow the doctor's orders.

The common law was at least consistent in refusing recovery for these avoidable consequences. Baruch was, after all, negligent with regard to them, and a plaintiff's negligence generally barred her recovery. (The last clear chance doctrine is clearly inapplicable, since it is the plaintiff here who has the last, indeed, the only chance to avert the aggravation of the injury.) But again, note that the rule places a loss that was caused by two parties on only one. Burns's prior negligence is still a but-for cause of the extra damages as well as the cuts themselves: Baruch would not have failed to take proper care of the injury if it hadn't happened in the first place.

9.   Baruch was very likely negligent for failing to seek prompt medical attention for his cuts. However, it is unclear whether this negligence caused the resulting infection: The medical testimony is that it might (or might not) have occurred anyway.

The result here is likely to turn on where the court places the burden of proof. Most courts hold that if the defendant raises the avoidable consequence defense, it is up to her to prove that, more probably than not, the consequence would not have come to pass if the plaintiff had exercised reasonable care in seeking treatment. (Similarly, the burden to prove that the plaintiff was contributorily negligent was generally placed on the defendant.) Since the doctor's testimony here leaves it unclear whether the infection "probably" would have been avoided by prompt treatment, the court will likely hold that Burns has not proved that the consequence was "avoidable," and therefore allow Baruch to recover for it.

However, the doctor also testified that the infection would "almost certainly" have been less severe if Baruch had sought immediate treatment. This testimony proves that some part of Baruch's infection damages were avoidable, but does not give the jury much of a basis for estimating the difference between the damages he actually suffered and those he would have sustained with proper treatment. Again, the court is likely to place the burden of apportioning the damage on the defendant (who did, after all, cause the harm even if Baruch contributed to part of it as well). The jury will probably be instructed that, if a reasonable apportionment can be made between the harm suffered due to Baruch's failure to seek treatment and the harm that would have been suffered anyway, they should do so. Otherwise, they should find the defendant liable for the entire damages.

10. In the last example, the issue was how much of the plaintiff's damage was avoidable with proper treatment. Here the issue is when the court will

second-guess the plaintiff's choice about what type of treatment to choose in seeking to avoid damages. The issue can arise in many situations. The plaintiff might choose back surgery over chiropractic treatment, homeopathy over conventional drugs, or prayer over a blood transfusion. The plaintiff might elect chemotherapy over radical surgery for cancer, or accept treatment for physical injuries but refuse to enter psychotherapy to treat the emotional effects of the accident, and so on.

In such cases, most courts invoke a reasonableness test in determining whether the plaintiff has taken sufficient measures to mitigate damages from her injury. See Minzer, Nates, §16.31. However, courts recognize that there is a good deal of disagreement as to optimal approaches to many medical problems, and allow the plaintiff wide discretion in choosing among various arguably sensible courses of therapy. The plaintiff's autonomy in making choices about her person is clearly implicated here (see generally Chapter 1). Consequently, the fact that an alternative form of therapy is more generally accepted will not bar recovery, if plaintiff made a rational choice in selecting a method of treatment.

20

The Once and Future Defense: Assumption of the Risk

Introduction

The late 19th century was the formative era of the common law of negligence. It was a time of rugged individualism, particularly in the United States, which emphasized freedom of action, personal initiative and the right of self-determination. The ideal was the Horatio Alger type, the self-made man who grasped the myriad possibilities of an expanding nation through strong character and hard work. Doubtless, the reality of most people's lives had little to do with this ideal, but it still conditioned the thinking of the time, including legal thinking.

It is not surprising that judges steeped in such ideas should accept the principle that the individual is master of his own fate, with the right to choose a course of action and the responsibility to accept the consequences of the choice. The concept of contributory negligence, that a plaintiff whose careless acts contributed to his injuries should bear the consequences, is an example. Another example, also with roots in the 19th century, is the doctrine of assumption of the risk.

The basic premise of assumption of the risk is that a person who is aware of a risk, and knowingly decides to encounter it, accepts responsibility for the consequences of that decision, and may not hold a defendant who created the risk liable for resulting injury. The premise was articulated in 19th century terms by Professor Bohlen:

> The maxim *volenti non fit injuria* [that to which a person assents is not deemed in law an injury] is a terse expression of the individualis-

tic tendency of the common law, which, proceeding from the people and asserting their liberties, naturally regards the freedom of individual action as the keystone of the whole structure. Each individual is left free to work out his own destinies; he must not be interfered with from without, but in the absence of such interference he is held competent to protect himself . . . the common law does not assume to protect him from the effects of his own personality and from the consequences of his voluntary actions or of his careless misconduct.

Bohlen, Voluntary Assumption of the Risk, 20 Harv. L. Rev. 14 (1906). Based on this individualistic premise, assumption of the risk became an established shield to negligence liability, just as the analogous privilege of consent avoids liability for intentional torts.

Many of the early cases applying assumption of the risk arose in the context of injuries to workers on the job. A worker might accept employment in a factory with unguarded vats of molten metal, or requiring work on high scaffolds without railings. If he fell into the vat or off of the scaffold, the employer would argue that, by taking the job with knowledge of the working conditions, he had assumed the risk of injury from the known conditions of employment, and could not complain of the consequences of that choice.[1] Other cases arose in the context of injuries on land of another, where a guest or other licensee suffered injury due to an openly dangerous condition, such as an unfenced quarry or icy steps. As in the employee cases, the owner would argue that the plaintiff who chose to enter the premises with knowledge of open and obvious dangers accepted responsibility for possible injuries from those known risks.

In these and other contexts, courts accepted the argument that the plaintiff's knowing choice to encounter danger relieved the defendant of responsibility for resulting injury, even if the defendant *negligently created the risk* that caused it. Assumption of the risk became a companion defense along with contributory negligence. It differed, of course, in that assumption of the risk required a showing that the plaintiff actually knew of a danger and chose to proceed. If the plaintiff should have known of a risk, but did not, contributory negligence would apply but assumption of the risk would not.

An example may help to illustrate the relationship between assumption of risk and contributory negligence. Suppose that Newman lent his car to Knieval, and told him that the brakes didn't work. If Knieval shrugged and

---

1. "Assumption of risk . . . developed in response to the general impulse of common law courts at the beginning of this period [the industrial revolution] to insulate the employer as much as possible from bearing the human overhead which is an inevitable part of the cost — to someone — of the doing of industrialized business. The general purpose behind this development in the common law seems to have been to give maximum freedom to expanding industry." *Tiller v. Atl. Coast Line R.R.*, 318 U.S. 54, 58-59 (1943) (footnotes omitted).

said he would go slow and use the emergency brake, he assumed the risk of injury from the defective brakes. He might well be negligent in making such a conscious choice; if so, he both assumed the risk and was contributorily negligent. On the other hand, if Newman did not tell Knieval about the brakes, but Knieval noticed that the pedal felt loose before he started the car and didn't investigate before driving, he was probably contributorily negligent but did not assume the risk of the defective brakes. He was negligent because he should have checked the brakes when he noticed a problem. But he did not assume the risk of defective brakes, because he did not make a deliberate choice to drive without brakes with full knowledge of the risk.

The assumption of risk principle is confusing in practice because it has been applied in a variety of situations. Some of these overlap duty analysis, while others are confusingly similar to contributory negligence. In addition, courts have not been consistent in the way they classify assumption of risk cases. See Gaetanos, Essay — Assumption of Risk: Casuistry in the Law of Negligence, 83 W. Va. L. Rev. 471, 473 (1981) (noting five different classification schemes adopted by various torts scholars). Despite this confusion, it is important to come to grips with assumption of the risk, because, unlike contributory negligence, assumption of the risk is clearly *not* a wave of the past. In at least some of its incarnations, the doctrine is recognized today and will continue to be in the future.

This chapter is intended to give you an understanding of the basic situations in which courts have applied the concept of assumption of the risk, and of the areas in which it remains a "once and future defense."

Express Assumption of the Risk

Perhaps the clearest assumption of the risk cases are those in which the plaintiff expressly agrees that she will not hold the defendant liable for injury she suffers from a risk created by the defendant. Suppose, for example, that Knieval decides to try skydiving, and hires Newman to teach him the sport. Newman may agree only if Knieval consents in writing not to hold Newman liable for any resulting injuries. Or, Newman might agree to let Knieval use his land for motorcycle jumping practice, conditioned on a similar promise not to sue for any resulting injuries.

As a general matter, such express agreements to assume a risk, even a negligently created risk, are enforced by the courts. Restatement (Second) of Torts §496B; Restatement of Contracts (Second) §195(2) & cmt. a. The 19th century belief in individual initiative and freedom of choice persists, including the right to make silly choices, or even dangerous ones, and accept the consequences. Some people prefer that life should be interesting rather than safe, and such venturous souls may claim substantial accomplishments, such as discovering America and going to the moon. To a great extent, our culture continues to support such choices, even where there is little social value gained by accepting the risk.[2] Allowing participants to agree in advance to accept the risk of injury from high risk activities (that is, to agree *not* to sue if such injuries occur) promotes the availability of exciting and varied opportunities, by insulating providers from the high cost of injuries resulting from the activity.

While the principle of express assumption is generally accepted, it has been hedged around with some qualifications. *First*, it is essential that the consent to accept the risk is freely given: A consent extracted from a party with little bargaining power is inconsistent with the free choice principle underlying the doctrine, and will not be honored by the courts. For example, courts have struck down contractual "consents" to unsanitary living conditions in public housing or negligent treatment in local hospitals, on the theory that the plaintiff has no meaningful alternative, and therefore has not really consented at all. Similarly, courts have held that providers of quasi monopolistic public services, such as rail or electric service, cannot condition service on the passenger's acceptance of the risk of injury. Here again, the lack of choice makes the consumer's "consent" illusory. Interestingly, although assumption of the risk doctrine developed in the employment context, it is now generally held that the inequality of bargaining power inherent in the employment relationship bars express assumption of the risk by employees. Restatement (Second) of Torts §496B, cmt. f; Prosser & Keeton at 482.

A second qualification, which also follows from the rationale of assumption of the risk, is that the plaintiff must clearly consent to accept the particular risk that led to the injury. For example, some courts have held that a provision releasing the defendant from "all claims for personal injury" does not waive recovery for injury due to *negligence* of the defendant, since it does not sufficiently bring home to the plaintiff the extent of the risks she is accepting. See Harper, James & Gray, §21.6, at 251; but see *Boyce v. West*, 862 P.2d 592, 598 (Wash. Ct. App. 1993) (release held to encompass negligence though it did not specifically refer to negligence). Generally, contractual clauses assuming risk (also called waiver of liability or exculpatory clauses) are drafted by the party providing the risky activity — the skydiving school, the quarry owner that allows rock climbing for a fee, the horseback riding ranch. Such releases are construed against the drafter, and must be quite clear in stating the risks allocated to the participant.

Contractual assumptions of risk are also limited by general contractual principles concerning the understanding of the parties. Thus, an agreement to assume the risk of injuries will not extend to collateral risks beyond their contemplation. For example, if Ruth signs a general waiver of liability for

---

2. Witness the widespread resistance to mandatory seatbelt or helmet laws. For an interesting defense of the socially constructive role of risk-taking in self-actualization, see D. Judges, Of Rocks and Hard Places: The Value of Risk Choice, 42 Emory L.J. 1, 11-26 (1993).

injuries from playing in a baseball game, he would realize that he was assuming usual risks of playing baseball, such as being hit by the ball or another player. But he would not have in mind the risk of a sink hole in the base paths. If he fell into one, he would not be barred by express assumption of the risk, since the parties did not have this risk in mind at the time of contracting.[3]

Implied Assumption: Limited Duty Cases

A plaintiff may also accept risks simply by engaging in an activity with knowledge that it entails certain risks. Many activities involve a risk of injury even if conducted with due care. In such cases participants assume the risks of injuries from the inherent dangers of the activity. Here are a few examples:

- The plaintiff, after watching patrons at a fair try to maintain their balance on an inclined, moving belt called "The Flopper," buys a ticket, steps on the belt, and is thrown off, fracturing his knee cap.
- The plaintiff decides to take wilderness survival training in Minnesota in mid-winter. The plaintiff gets lost in a snowstorm and suffers serious frostbite.
- The plaintiff goes skating at the defendant's skating rink, is hit by a poor skater who loses control, and is injured when she hits the wall of the rink.
- The plaintiff takes rock climbing instruction and is injured when a seemingly solid rock is dislodged by a climber and falls on her.

In each of these cases, the defendant has offered an activity to the plaintiff, which he is under no duty to offer, and which the plaintiff is under no duty to attempt. That activity cannot be conducted without certain unavoidable risks of injury, even if conducted with due care, and the plaintiff has chosen to engage in the activity. As in the express assumption cases, the plaintiff considers the trade-off worthwhile, and accepts the possibility of injury because she enjoys the activity.

As in the express assumption cases, courts have honored the choice to encounter risk in implied assumption cases too. Plaintiffs who choose to engage in unavoidably risky activities assume the inherent risks of the activity, and have no claim for injuries resulting from those risks. Although this is often described as assumption of the risk of injury, the defendant has actually not breached the duty of due care in such cases. It is not negligent to organize

---

3. Express assumption may also be barred by public policy. For example, if a statute mandated certain safety standards for public stadiums (such as number of exits or a maximum number of patrons), a court would likely refuse to enforce a release on the plaintiff's ticket accepting risks of injury due to negligence covered by the statute. Stadium operators should not be allowed to avoid the statutory purpose by requiring the protected class to waive its protection in order to see the game. See generally A. Cava & D. Wiesner, Rationalizing a Decade of Judicial Responses to Exculpatory Clauses, 28 Santa Clara L. Rev. 611, 630-638 (1988).

a flag football league, to run a horseback riding ranch, or to offer hang gliding instruction, even though these activities involve some risk of injury. The plaintiff who knowingly engages in such sports impliedly accepts the inherent risks they entail, and cannot sue the defendant who offered it to her simply because those inherent risks lead to injury.

Because primary assumption of the risk is based on the fact that certain risks are inherent in the activity and unavoidable at a reasonable cost, primary assumption only applies where that is in fact the case. If Henne goes ice skating, she accepts the risk that she may be hit by other skaters. This is an obvious danger inherent in the sport. It does not result from negligence of the operator, and it cannot be eliminated at a reasonable cost. However, Henne would not assume the risk of a dangerous condition in the ice or a broken handrail along the edge. These risks are not inherent in the activity itself; they are dangers created by negligent operation of the rink. The plaintiff does not impliedly accept these risks by merely deciding to go skating.

Harper, James & Gray argue that the term "assumption of risk" should not apply to inherent risk situations at all; they are simply situations in which the defendant acted reasonably and the plaintiff suffered injury from a reasonable risk of the activity. Harper, James & Gray, §21.0. This makes good sense; the plaintiff in these cases cannot prove her prima facie case of negligence, because the defendant has not breached the duty of due care. It would be clearer to ask in these cases whether the defendant violated the duty of care than to use assumption of the risk terminology. However, the courts frequently analyze these as "primary assumption of the risk" or "primary implied assumption of the risk" cases. As a result, these situations (in which there is no negligence because the risk the defendant created was reasonable) are frequently confused with other cases (discussed immediately below) in which assumption of risk is properly viewed as a defense.

Secondary Implied Assumption: The Negligent Defendant and the Venturous Plaintiff

In the situations discussed above, the defendant created reasonable risks that plaintiffs chose to encounter. However, a plaintiff may also encounter risks created by a defendant's *unreasonable* conduct. Here are some examples:

- The defendant lends plaintiff his car. She notices that the car swerves sharply to the left while braking, but proceeds anyway, and is injured when she brakes for a light and swerves into an opposing car.
- The defendant is setting off fireworks in the public street. Plaintiff, anxious to see the show, stands next to him and is injured when a firecracker misfires.

- The defendant waxes part of the floor of his store while open for business. The plaintiff sees the wet floor, but anxious to get a box of Wheetabix for breakfast, walks on the wet floor and falls.
- The defendant riding stable provides the plaintiff an unruly horse. The plaintiff, after watching the horse start and buck, decides to try to ride it anyway.

In each of these cases, unlike the limited duty cases discussed above, the defendant breached the standard of due care by creating an unreasonable risk. If that negligence injured the plaintiff before she became aware of the risk, the defendant would be liable. For example, if the plaintiff who borrowed the car was injured the first time she applied the brake, she could sue, because it is negligent to lend someone a car without informing the person of known defects that may cause injury. Similarly, if the plaintiff in the fireworks example was an unsuspecting passerby, she could recover for her injury in the explosion, since it is negligent to explode firecrackers in the immediate vicinity of others.

However, in these cases the plaintiff, after becoming aware of the unreasonable risk created by the defendant, chooses to encounter it, and suffers injury as a result. This type of case is often called "secondary assumption of the risk" or "secondary implied assumption," presumably because the plaintiff's choice is secondary to (comes after) the negligence of the defendant. In secondary assumption situations the plaintiff has been injured due to the defendant's negligence, but the defendant argues that the plaintiff's free choice to encounter the negligently created risk should bar her recovery.

Arguably, the defendant should still be liable in these cases: He has created a risk through his negligence that injured the plaintiff. On the other hand, the plaintiff has freely chosen to encounter it for her own purposes, be it enjoyment of the fireworks display, immediate access to Wheetabix, or available but unsafe transportation. Just as the plaintiff's acceptance of deliberate invasions of her person prevents liability for an intentional tort (under the consent privilege), plaintiff's choice to encounter a negligently created risk should arguably avoid liability as well.

True to its individualistic assumptions, the common law held that the plaintiff, by knowingly encountering a danger created by the defendant's negligence, "assumed the risk" of resulting injury, and was barred from suing for that injury. Restatement (Second) of Torts §496C. Under secondary assumption of risk, the courts honored the plaintiff's willingness to confront negligently created risk, just as they honored her willingness to encounter inherent risk under the related doctrine of primary assumption of the risk. However, in secondary assumption cases, the doctrine really is an affirmative defense, since it bars the plaintiff from recovering even though she can establish a prima facie case of negligence.

Reasonable and Unreasonable Assumption

In secondary assumption cases, the plaintiff's decision to encounter the risk may be either reasonable or unreasonable. The decision to stand next to an adolescent playing with fireworks will virtually always be unreasonable. It might be reasonable to drive a car with bad brakes to get a heart attack victim to the hospital, but not to get to a poker game on time. A rescuer's decision to rescue a child from a fire is eminently reasonable, though it knowingly subjects the rescuer to a risk of injury.

Where the decision to encounter the risk was unreasonable, assumption of the risk overlapped with contributory negligence: By definition, the reasonable person does not unreasonably encounter unreasonable risks. At common law, both defenses could be pleaded, and in this set of cases (the unreasonable risk unreasonably encountered), either defense sufficed to bar plaintiff's recovery.

Where the plaintiff *reasonably* assumed a risk, contributory negligence would not bar recovery. *However*, assumption of the risk still did. The basis for the defense was individual choice, not fault. Even if the plaintiff chose to encounter the risk for good reason, the courts still "honored" the choice by denying recovery.

Nine Lives: Assumption of Risk in the Comparative Negligence Era

The advent of comparative negligence has sparked a lively controversy about the continued role of secondary implied assumption of the risk. Under comparative negligence, the plaintiff's negligence reduces her recovery, but does not usually bar it. Suppose, however, that the plaintiff's negligence consists of unreasonable but knowing assumption of the risk (secondary implied assumption); should it bar or reduce recovery? For example, assume that the defendant owns a warehouse without a fire alarm or sprinkler system. Gallo knows this, but decides to store her goods there because it is cheaper. This decision may well be negligent. It is also, however, a deliberate, knowing acceptance of the risk.

At common law, this case posed no problem: *Either* contributory negligence or assumption of the risk barred recovery entirely. In a comparative negligence state, however, if Gallo's conduct were treated as negligence, it would reduce her recovery rather than bar it entirely. On the other hand, if unreasonable assumption of the risk persists as a separate defense, *she would still be fully barred*. There is an argument for the latter result, since assumption of the risk is based on consent to encounter a risk, not on fault. If Gallo has accepted the risk with full knowledge, arguably the long standing assumption of risk rule denying recovery should continue to apply.

Despite this argument, most comparative negligence jurisdictions conclude that secondary *unreasonable* assumption of the risk should be treated as a form of negligence. Under this approach, the jury assigns a percentage of negligence to Gallo's unreasonable choice to accept the risk, and her recovery is reduced to reflect that negligence. Some comparative negligence statutes specifically require this result.[4] In other states, this same sensible result has been reached by judicial interpretation. See Schwartz, Comparative Negligence, §9.4(B).

It is fairly easy to conclude that comparative negligence displaces unreasonable secondary assumption of risk, because unreasonable assumption is by definition a form of negligence. It is more difficult to decide how *reasonable* secondary assumption should be meshed with comparative negligence. Suppose, for example, that the warehouse without a sprinkler was the only place within 75 miles of Gallo's home, and she was required to go away on business for three months. The decision to take the small risk of a fire loss might well be reasonable on such facts. If so, how should the decision affect her recovery under a comparative negligence statute?

Arguably her knowing choice to take the risk should not affect her recovery at all, since it was (by definition) a reasonable choice and recovery is only to be reduced for negligence. Some cases have taken this position. See *Rini v. Oaklawn Jockey Club*, 861 F.2d 502 (8th Cir. 1988) (a well reasoned case applying Arkansas law). However, others have argued that reasonable secondary assumption should completely bar recovery. Comparative negligence statutes only address the effect of the plaintiff's fault; the rationale for assumption of risk as a defense is knowing consent to take a risk, not fault. Arguably, the passage of a comparative negligence statute, which modifies the effect of plaintiff's *negligence*, should not affect the defense of reasonable assumption of risk.

The 1980s, the era of Ronald Reagan and the collapse of communism, witnessed a renewed emphasis on the 19th-century values of individual responsibility and freedom of choice. This megatrend has even found expression in obscure corners of tort law like assumption of risk. While it appeared that secondary assumption of the risk would fade away with the advent of comparative negligence, recent cases and articles have argued for retaining reasonable secondary assumption as a complete defense. See, e.g., *Ford v. Gouin*, 266 Cal. Rptr. 870 (Cal. Ct. App. 1st Dist. 1990), *aff'd by a divided court*, 834 P.2d 724 (Cal. 1992); Rosenlund & Killion, Once a Wicked Sister: The Continuing Role of Assumption of Risk Under Comparative Fault in California, 20 U.S.F.L. Rev. 225, 278-283 (1986); Spell, Stemming the Tide

---

4. The Washington comparative negligence statute, for example, defines "fault" to include "unreasonable assumption of risk." Wash. Rev. Code Ann. §4.22.015 (1988). The evident purpose of such a provision is to treat unreasonable assumption as a damage-reducing factor rather than a complete bar to recovery.

of Expanding Liability: The Coexistence of Comparative Negligence and Assumption of Risk, 8 Miss. Coll. L. Rev. 159 (1988).[5]

The major anomaly of this approach, of course, is that it totally bars recovery by a plaintiff who made a *reasonable* choice to assume a risk, while unreasonable assumption only reduces recovery under comparative negligence. Those who advocate a separate defense of reasonable assumption of risk argue that this is not inconsistent, since the defense is based on consent, not on fault. The logical corollary of that argument, it seems, is that *unreasonable* assumption should also be a complete defense. However, in many states this result is foreclosed by the comparative negligence statute itself, which expressly requires unreasonable assumption of the risk to be treated like plaintiff's negligence.

Thus, as the title of this chapter suggests, assumption of the risk is still very much with us. It has had nine lives in the secondary assumption cases just discussed. In addition, express and primary implied assumption of risk are alive and well, even in comparative negligence jurisdictions. Plaintiffs are still free to waive the right to sue by advance agreement. V. Schwartz, Comparative Negligence §9.2 (2d ed. 1986). And they still accept the inherent risks of activities which entail a certain amount of irreducible danger when conducted with due care. Schwartz, §9.4(C).

Assumption of the risk in all of its various incarnations is obviously complex. It is made even more puzzling in practice by the inconsistency of courts in discussing the various types of assumption of risk; in some cases, it is painfully clear that the judges themselves did not fully grasp the distinctions. Hopefully, the following examples will help you to understand the basic situations in which the assumption of risk issue arises, and the different ways each may be resolved.

EXAMPLES

False Assumptions

1.   Killey decides to ski the Big Mountain Ski Bowl. He arrives at the ski area, buys a small lift ticket that attaches to the lapel of his ski jacket, and

---

5. The following passage from the Spell article, for example, is reminiscent of the nineteenth century arguments for assumption of the risk:

> Notions of choice do not go so far as to afford the plaintiff, who once stood at the threshold of action armed with both knowledge of the risks ahead and the opportunity to avoid those risks, the ability to cast back upon the defendant the cost of his choice. The more equitable approach is to enforce the "fundamental principle" of assumption of risk that "where the plaintiff has voluntarily and intelligently consented to relieve the defendant of liability for certain known risks, the plaintiff's choice should be enforced."

8 Miss. Coll. L. Rev. at 171, (quoting from the Rosenlund and Killion article at 255).

starts to ski. While riding in the chair lift up to the expert trails, he is injured when the chair separates from the drive cable and falls to the ground. When he threatens to sue Big Mountain, its lawyer points out the following language printed on the back of the lift ticket: "The purchaser assumes all risks of injury from any source whatever, arising in the course of the activities authorized by this ticket, whether due to the negligence of the ski operator or third persons, or any other cause." Is Killey barred by express assumption of the risk?

2. Assume the same facts, except that before he began skiing, Killey was required to read and sign a form containing the following language: "The undersigned acknowledges that skiing is a hazardous sport; that bare spots, ice, changing snow, bumps, stumps, stones, trees, and other hazards exist in any ski area. By purchasing this ticket, the purchaser recognizes such dangers, whether marked or unmarked, accepts the hazards of the sport and the fact that injury may result therefrom, and agrees to assume all risk of such injuries." Is Killey barred from recovering for his injuries by express assumption?

3. Gavin decides to go skydiving and signs up for lessons with Freeflight Skydiving Inc. Freeflight requires him to sign a release acknowledging that skydiving is a dangerous sport and assuming the risk of any injury resulting from it. On his first dive, Gavin suffers a punctured ear drum as a result of the rapidly changing air pressure. Although he had realized that he might suffer broken bones, or even death from a failed parachute, Gavin never understood that there was a risk of injuries to his ears from skydiving. He sues for damages and Freeflight raises the release as a defense. Has Gavin assumed the risk?

Negative Implications

4. On the facts of Killey's ski lift accident, is he barred from suing Big Mountain by primary implied assumption of the risk?

5. Killey skis the expert slopes at Big Mountain. While coming down a particularly steep slope he is hit by another skier who had negligently failed to notice a turn in the trail and lost control. Killey's leg is broken. Is he barred from suing Big Mountain by primary implied assumption of the risk?

6. Since his leg is broken, Killey can't ski, so he goes to a baseball game for diversion. Killey is from France, and knows nothing of baseball. He sits behind third base, receives a concussion from a foul ball and sues for his injuries. The ball club pleads assumption of the risk. Killey argues that he could not have assumed the risk of being hit by a foul ball, since he knew nothing about this risk, and assumption of the risk requires subjective understanding of the risk and a conscious choice to accept the risk.

    a. What type of assumption of the risk, if any, is implicated in this case?

    b. Assuming that Killey did not understand the risk, is he barred?

Taking Negligence to Newcastle

7. Hermit, who lives on a little-traveled rural road, hitches a ride to town for supplies with a passing driver. It soon becomes apparent to Hermit that Driver has been drinking heavily. However, Hermit stays aboard, and is injured when Driver swerves into a ditch.

   a. What type of assumption of risk, if any, applies here?
   b. What would be the effect of Hermit's conduct in a jurisdiction that applies common law contributory negligence and assumption of risk doctrine?
   c. How would his conduct affect his right to recover in a comparative negligence jurisdiction?

8. Farmer, who also lives on a little-traveled rural road, suffers a serious leg injury while harvesting wheat. He hails a passing car and beseeches the driver, Hillary, to take him to the hospital. Hillary says, "Look, my brakes are acting up, but if you're willing to chance it, I'll take you." Farmer agrees and is injured when the brakes lock at a traffic light and the car is hit from behind. Which type of assumption of risk, if any, applies in this case?

9. Assume that Hillary said nothing about the brakes. However, Farmer watched Hillary apply the brakes several times during the ride, and observed that they locked abruptly as soon as applied. Anxious to get medical help, Farmer stays aboard.

   a. What type of assumption of the risk, if any, would this entail?
   b. Assume that, after Farmer realizes that the breaks are bad, they lock at the light and Farmer is injured. Would Farmer be barred from recovery in a jurisdiction that applies the common law contributory negligence and assumption of risk doctrines?
   c. On the same facts, would assumption of the risk bar recovery in a comparative negligence jurisdiction?

Judge Fudd Assumes the Risk

10. Dewey, a teacher in a West Dakota high school, agrees to participate in a "donkey basketball" game for the school scholarship fund. The game is what it says it is; the players play basketball while riding donkeys provided by the Buckeye Donkey Basketball Company. It is really very funny and a lot of students would gladly pay to see their teachers make such asses of themselves. Before the game, an employee of Buckeye explains to the teachers that the donkeys sometimes stop short and lower their heads, and there is a risk of falling off. In the middle of the game, Dewey's donkey executes such a maneuver, and Dewey is thrown, suffering a dislocated shoulder. He sues Buckeye for his injuries.

West Dakota has adopted a comparative negligence statute that provides for reducing plaintiff's damages to account for his fault. The statute also provides that "the defense of assumption of the risk is abolished." At trial, Buckeye's lawyer asks Judge Fudd to instruct the jury that they should find for the defendant if they conclude that Dewey assumed the risk of being thrown. Judge Fudd responds, "Counsel, I don't see how I can grant that instruction. It says right in the statute that assumption of the risk is abolished." Is Fudd right in rejecting the assumption of the risk argument?

A Little Knowledge of a Dangerous Thing

11. Pearson is driving down a little used country road behind Moses, a poky Sunday driver. Frustrated and hurried, he decides to pass. There is a curve in the road and Pearson can't see whether a car is coming the other way. Pearson attempts to pass but hits Henderson, who is driving in the opposite lane and speeding. Pearson sues for his injuries. Is he barred by assumption of the risk?

Legal Shape-Sorting

12. Try to fit the following examples into the categories discussed in the Introduction.

a. Mansfield rents a rustic cabin two hundred miles away, sight unseen, for his family's summer vacation in the North Woods. When they arrive, they discover that the cabin is not quite finished, and there is no railing on the stairs to the second floor. On the fifth day of their stay, Mansfield stumbles on the stairs and falls off due to the lack of a railing.

b. Bohlen borrows a table saw from Wade to use in putting a porch on his house. The saw had a kill switch on the side which, when engaged, would cause the blade to stop if the wood going through the saw was pushed too hard. This prevents the wood from kicking back and injuring the user. Wade usually left the switch in the "off" position because the blade tended to stop too often when the kill switch was used. Bohlen is not very familiar with table saws, does not know about the switch, does not switch it on, and is injured when a piece of wood is thrown back at him by the blade.

c. James, an experienced mason, is working on a scaffold three stories above the street, putting the brick facade on a new building. When he goes to break for lunch, he remembers that another worker borrowed the ladder that he had used to climb the scaffold, but has not returned it. Impatient to get to lunch, he starts to climb down the angled supports of the scaffolding, and is injured when he slips off.

d. Dobbs sees a small child playing obliviously in the path of a driver backing out of a driveway without looking. He rushes to rescue the child and is hit by the car.

EXPLANATIONS

False Assumptions

1.   As the Introduction states, parties can assume risks, including the risk of another's negligence, by an express agreement to do so. And the language in this release clause is certainly broad enough to cover the accident Killey suffered, since it specifically refers to injury "from any source whatever" and includes negligence of the operator. If Killey has accepted the release clause, he would be barred.

However, the gravamen of assumption of risk is the plaintiff's choice to assume the risks. Courts are wary of applying the doctrine of express assumption unless the party fully comprehended the risks that were being allocated to her. Killey will argue that he did not assume the risk of injury because he never knowingly agreed to the terms of the release. Since the terms were simply placed in fine print on the back of the lift ticket, where most people would not even read them, the court is likely to agree. See Restatement (Second) of Torts §496B cmt. c: "it must appear that the terms were in fact brought home to him and understood by him, before it can be found that he has accepted them."

2.   Clearly not. While he has assumed many of the risks of skiing itself by signing this form, it contains no language assuming the risk of negligent maintenance of the facility. The purchaser would not contemplate such negligence as one of the inherent hazards of skiing. In fact, by enumerating various natural risks, the form tends to confirm that other risks, such as negligent maintenance of the equipment, were not within the contemplation of the clause. Consequently, because the language does not clearly include this risk, Killey has not assumed it.

3.   This is an interesting problem. On the one hand, Gavin has expressly agreed to assume responsibility for injuries resulting from skydiving, and Free-flight provided the service with an understanding that this allocation of the risks would protect it from liability. On the other hand, if assumption of the risk turns on knowing acceptance of the risks, Gavin did not assume this risk, since he did not realize (whether he should have or not) that ear problems might result.

This case would likely turn on the basic contracts concept of the intent of the parties. If it is clear from the language of the release and the circumstances that Gavin understood that he was assuming the risk of *any* injury, anticipated or not, the release would probably be enforced. Express assumption usually honors the parties' choice in allocating the risk. If the parties clearly allocated this one to Gavin, he is likely to be barred by his express assumption of it, even though he did not know what the risk was. See Restatement (Second) of Torts §496D cmt. a (plaintiff may expressly assume unknown risk if agreement so intends); Prosser & Keeton at 489 (plaintiff may "consent to take his chances as to unknown conditions").

Perhaps, as a matter of good lawyering, Free-flight's counsel should draft the release to reveal as many potential risks as possible. A release that specifically refers to the risk of ear damage clearly demonstrates that this risk was within the parties' contemplation at the time of contracting. (A release that revealed all the risks involved might, of course, have a depressing effect on business.) The release should also specify that the plaintiff assumes the risks of the activity, even if he is not aware of them. This strengthens the argument that the plaintiff has chosen to accept all the risks, not just the ones she expected to encounter.

Negative Implications

4.   Primary assumption applies where the defendant has not breached a duty of due care, since the risk that injures the plaintiff is inseparable from the activity itself. The defendant is not liable in such cases, because it is not negligent, even though the activity it offered involves some risk. Primary assumption would bar Killey from suing if he were injured from the inherent risks of skiing, such as patches of icy snow, sharp drops in expert trails, trees along the side of the trail, bare spots, and others. But he does not assume the risk that the chair lift will fall off the cable. That is not an inherent risk of the sport if it is conducted with due care.

5.   The issue here is whether negligent acts of other skiers are an inherent risk of skiing that skiers assume by engaging in the sport. I would think so. Just as a quarterback can expect some overzealous hits, and a jockey some aggressive jockeying for position on the track, a skier should expect that there will be a few overconfident hot dogs on the expert slopes who will fail to keep a proper lookout or attempt maneuvers beyond their skills. It appears likely that, by choosing to ski the expert slopes, Killey assumes the risk of this accident. Stated another way, it is likely that Big Mountain is not negligent in conducting a ski operation, even though it entails this risk.

6a. Most courts conclude that foul balls are an inherent risk of America's favorite pastime, and that the reasonable ball club need not screen all the seats in the stadium. The risk of being injured by a foul ball is small and difficult to prevent without interfering with spectators' view of the game. Since it is not negligent to subject patrons to this risk, primary implied assumption of the risk applies. Patrons accept the risk because they enjoy watching baseball, can avoid most injuries by being watchful, and the risk is minimal.

b. The patron usually loses a "foul ball case" on the ground that she has assumed the risk, but this case is a little different. Killey really didn't *know* about foul balls. How can he assume a risk he knows nothing about? If the premise of the doctrine is the subjective choice to encounter a known risk, Killey never made such a choice.

The rationale for primary implied assumption of the risk is that the operator of the activity has conducted it with due care. If it has, it does not seem that Killey's ignorance of the non-negligent risks involved should make them liable. Otherwise the club's foul ball liability would depend on the state of mind of each patron. Kids at their first ball game could recover, but avid fans would have no cause of action for the same conduct. If the issue here is duty, it seems that the duty should be the same to all patrons — to conduct the game without imposing unreasonable risks on players or patrons. See, e.g., *Harrold v. Rolling "J" Ranch*, 23 Cal. Rptr. 2d 671, 676 (Cal. Ct. App. 1993) (emphasizing operator's duty to avoid risks of injury beyond those inherent in the activity).

This may well be the right answer, but the use of assumption of the risk analysis in cases like this raises some doubt. Many cases emphasize that the plaintiff must actually perceive and appreciate the risk in order to assume it. If Killey's case is analyzed in assumption of the risk terms, a court might hold that his ignorance bars the conclusion that he assumed this risk. Even a court that took this position, however, would probably only allow Killey to recover if he was hit on the first pitch of the game. Once he observes the nature of the game, the risk of being hit by the ball should become obvious to him. Where a danger is obvious, the court would be very unlikely to credit the plaintiff's plea that he did not actually understand it.

Taking Negligence to Newcastle

7a. Hermit has not expressly agreed in advance to assume the risk here. Nor is this implied primary assumption: Drunk driving is not an inherent risk of accepting a ride in a car. This is an example of secondary implied assumption of the risk. Hermit becomes aware of negligent conduct of Driver which poses a risk of injury to him, yet, fully appreciating the risk, chooses to encounter it. More specifically, this is *unreasonable* secondary assumption since Hermit need not get to town immediately and should have waited for a more suitable chauffeur.

b. At common law, assumption of a risk barred recovery entirely, even if the risk was negligently created by the defendant. The gist of the action, as reiterated before, was consent and free choice, and here Hermit made a misguided but informed choice to proceed despite the risk. The common law "honored" Hermit's right to choose by barring him from recovering from Driver.

Since Hermit's choice was unreasonable, it would constitute contributory negligence as well. At common law Hermit would have been barred from recovery by either defense.

c. Under most comparative negligence statutes, Hermit's unreasonable decision would be treated as negligent conduct, and would be compared to the negligence of the defendant in assessing liability. If, for example, the jury concluded that Hermit was 33 percent responsible for his injuries for riding with a drunk driver, they would reduce his damages by 33 percent. Thus, unreasonable secondary assumption reduces damages under most comparative negligence statutes, but no longer acts as a complete bar.

8.   Clearly, Hillary is negligent for driving with defective brakes; he would, for example, be liable to the driver of the other car in this case. But Farmer has *expressly* assumed the risk in this case. Hillary has no duty to take Farmer into town, but has offered to do so if Farmer is willing to accept the risk of injury due to the defective condition of the brakes. The principle of free choice says parties can make such arrangements to assume the risk. The assumption here may not constitute a contract, but Farmer has agreed in advance not to hold Hillary liable for the risks to which he is exposed. While express assumption is usually by contract, it need not be, and consideration is not essential to make the assumption binding. See Restatement (Second) of Torts §496B cmt. a.

It is true that this case looks a good deal like reasonable implied secondary assumption as well. Hillary is negligent for driving with defective brakes, and Farmer decides, for a compelling reason, to take the risk. However, since Farmer agrees in advance to relieve Hillary of a duty of care, it is best classified as express assumption. Note that the characterization makes a big difference in the outcome of the case: If it is express assumption, Farmer will be barred; if it is secondary implied assumption, he might not be in a comparative negligence jurisdiction. See Example 9c.

9a.   This is probably an example of reasonable implied secondary assumption of the risk. Secondary assumption arises when the defendant negligently subjects the plaintiff to a risk, and the plaintiff becomes aware of the risk yet chooses to encounter it anyway. Leaving aside any applicable guest statute, Hillary owes Farmer a duty of due care, and violates that duty by giving him a ride in a car with faulty brakes. However, when Farmer becomes aware of the risk posed by Hillary's negligence, he stays aboard because of the exigency caused by his injury. Although he signals no agreement to Hillary, he accepts the risk for his own sufficient reasons.

b. Assuming that Farmer's decision was reasonable under the circumstances, contributory negligence would not bar his recovery. However, in a jurisdiction that applied common law principles, he would still be barred by assumption of the risk, since he understood the risk and chose to encounter it. The basis for the defense was individual choice, whether reasonable or unreasonable. So long as the choice was made with full understanding of the risk, the defense applied. Note the symmetry under the common law approach between express assumption and reasonable secondary implied assumption. Whether the plaintiff agreed in advance to take on the risk, as in Example 8, or impliedly agreed by staying on board, as here, the result was to bar recovery despite the defendant's negligence.

The best argument for avoiding assumption of the risk in a case like this would be that Farmer did not fully comprehend the nature of the risk posed by the brakes. Because secondary assumption turns on appreciation of the specific risk that causes injury, the defense only applies if the risk is fully understood. Many courts have rescued plaintiffs from the assumption of risk defense by holding that they did not appreciate the *exact* risk that led to the injury. See, e.g., *Gault v. May*, 79 Cal. Rptr. 858 (1969) (although plaintiff was aware that roller skate pulled to left, she did not know of defective wheel, which caused injury). Here, Farmer might argue that, though he realized there was *something* wrong with the brakes, he did not realize that they would lock completely, and therefore did not assume the risk.

c. The result in a comparative negligence jurisdiction depends on the way the jurisdiction treats reasonable secondary assumption. As the introduction indicates, some states conclude that reasonable secondary assumption of the risk should not reduce or bar the plaintiff's claim. Other states, however, continue to treat reasonable secondary assumption as a complete defense. In these states, Hermit would recover substantial damages under comparative negligence (see Example 7) although he negligently chose to ride with Driver. Farmer, however, would be barred entirely, despite his reasonable decision to accept the ride to the hospital.

Although some courts take this approach, it seems extremely dubious when Farmer's and Hermit's cases are considered side by side. It seems anomalous that Hermit should recover substantial (albeit reduced) damages while Farmer takes nothing. In addition, if reasonable assumption of risk is a bar, Farmer's lawyer is placed in the bizarre position of trying to prove that he was negligent, but only a little: Since unreasonable assumption of risk is treated as damage-reducing conduct under the comparative negligence statute, a minimally negligent plaintiff will recover most of her damages. But if plaintiff argues that her conduct was completely reasonable, and the jury agrees, she recovers nothing![6]

---

6. A few courts have taken a quizzical intermediate approach to reasonable secondary assumption. They allow the jury to consider the plaintiff's choice to assume the risk as a damage reducing factor, even though that choice was reasonable. See Rosenlund and Killion, 20 U.S.F. L. Rev. at 269-271. Schwartz, §9.5 at 180.

Judge Fudd Assumes the Risk

10. Although the comparative negligence statute here appears to broadly eliminate assumption of risk, it must be read in light of the purposes of the comparative negligence statute and the various meanings of assumption of risk. This provision almost certainly was intended to make the plaintiff's choice to encounter a negligently created risk a damage-reducing factor rather than a complete bar to recovery. In other words, it calls for treating the *defense* of secondary implied assumption like negligence by the plaintiff.

However, it is unlikely that the legislature meant to affect in any way the longstanding limitations on duty represented by *primary* implied assumption of the risk. Buckeye should explain to His Honor that its argument is based on primary implied assumption, which is not a defense at all, but a limit on the defendant's duty of care. Dewey was fully informed of the risk of a bucking donkey, and chose to engage in the activity despite that inherent risk. If the risk was a reasonable one, and Dewey understood it, Buckeye has not breached its duty of care. Nothing in the statute suggests that *this* type of assumption of the risk is abolished. See *Arbegast v. Board of Educ.*, 490 N.Y.S. 2d 751, 753 (1985).

A number of comparative negligence statutes have language like that in the example. See, e.g., Mass. Gen. Laws Ann. ch. 231 §85 (1985). Only by fully understanding the different ways in which the phrase "assumption of the risk" has been used can you intelligently evaluate the effect — and the limits — of such language. Here, Buckeye's counsel might have been better advised to argue the entire issue on the basis of duty (an issue of law for the court), and avoid perplexing Judge Fudd with assumption of risk concepts at all.

A Little Knowledge of a Dangerous Thing

11. In a sense, Pearson assumes a risk by passing on the curve. He knows a car could be coming, and that if so a collision may result. But the risk here is general. If acting in the face of such generalized risk constitutes assumption of the risk, virtually any conscious negligent act would qualify. A carpenter who works too close to a bulldozer would assume the risk of being hit. A window washer who leans too far out would assume the risk of a fall. A driver who feels tired would assume the risk of an accident from falling asleep.

The cases suggest that the plaintiff must be aware of a more specific risk in order to assume it. Certainly, Pearson would assume the risk of a collision if he saw Henderson coming and could see that he was speeding. He probably would assume it even if he saw Henderson but didn't know that he was speeding. In either case, he perceives a very specific danger and decides to chance it. This is qualitatively different from realizing that the potential for danger exists and that it would be wiser to avoid it by being more cautious.

Legal Shape-Sorting

12a. The owner is negligent to rent out a cabin with dangerous stairs, so Mansfield can probably make a prima facie case for liability. However, the owner will assert as a defense that Mansfield assumed the risk by using the stairs anyway.

The reasonable person would probably not turn around and go home just because the stair lacked a railing; likely she would just be a bit more careful negotiating the stairs. Thus, this is probably reasonable secondary assumption by Mansfield. Whether Mansfield's decision bars recovery will depend on how the jurisdiction treats reasonable assumption of risk.

b. This is not assumption of risk at all. Bohlen did not knowingly decide to take the risk of leaving the switch off. He never knew it existed or appreciated the risk it was meant to prevent. He may well be contributorily negligent for failing to learn more about a dangerous power tool before using it, but he has not deliberately chosen to encounter the risk that caused his injury.

c. This is unreasonable secondary assumption of the risk. The other worker was negligent in failing to return the ladder, but James has deliberately encountered the resulting unreasonable risk. As an experienced mason, James is aware that it is dangerous to climb on these supports, but he decides to do so anyway rather than wait for someone to return with the ladder. This was an unreasonable choice, a negligent choice, but it was also knowing assumption of the risk. In most comparative negligence jurisdictions, it would be treated as a damage-reducing factor like other negligence by the plaintiff.

d. You may have already come across the "rescue doctrine" in Torts class. The doctrine holds that injury to a rescuer is foreseeable, and therefore the negligence of the person who made the rescue necessary is a proximate cause of resulting injury to the rescuer. See, e.g., *Wagner v. Intl. Ry. Co.*, 133 N.E. 437 (N.Y. 1921). But why aren't these cases resolved under assumption of risk doctrine instead? They appear to be the very paradigm of reasonable implied secondary assumption of the risk: The plaintiff becomes aware of a risk negligently created by the defendant, and makes an eminently reasonable choice to encounter it.

A few courts *have* barred recovery to a rescuer on the ground of assumption of the risk. See, e.g., *Siglow v. Smart*, 539 N.E.2d 636 (Ohio Ct. App. 1987). See also *Eckert v. Long Island R.R. Co.*, 43 N.Y. 502 (1871) (Allen, J. dissenting) (arguing that rescuer should be barred by assumption of the risk). The Second Restatement avoids this harsh result, however, by concluding that rescue is not "voluntary":

> The plaintiff's acceptance of a risk is not voluntary if the defendant's tortious conduct has left him no reasonable alternative course of conduct in order to . . . avert harm to himself or another.

Restatement (Second) of Torts §496E(2)(a). This is a laudable result, but it raises a fundamental question about the meaning of secondary assumption of the risk. If Dobbs's choice here is not voluntary, is a plaintiff's choice to confront a negligently created risk ever voluntary? In most cases, the plaintiff does not *prefer* to be confronted with the risk negligently created by the defendant: She would rather that the defendant had not been negligent in the first place. Here Dobbs would prefer not to have confronted the risk created by the driver's negligence. Similarly, in the vacation home example, the vacationer would have preferred that the stairs have a railing.

The plaintiff in these cases reluctantly goes forward to meet the danger, but in a sense her decision is not "voluntary," since she would prefer not to have been put to an unpalatable choice of alternatives in the first place. See K. Simons, Assumption of Risk and Consent in the Law of Torts: A Theory of Full Preference, 67 B.U. L. Rev. 213, 218-224 (1987), which argues that the doctrine should only apply where the plaintiff "fully prefers" to encounter the risk created by the defendant, rather than being placed in a position of having to choose between several unpalatable alternatives.

21

Casting the Second Stone: Comparative Negligence

Introduction

Somewhere in the Bible lies the telling maxim: "Let he who is without sin cast the first stone." A rich understanding of human experience lies behind this phrase, for it recognizes that human events are complex, that few of us are so pure that we can forswear responsibility for life's vicissitudes or piously condemn others without considering our own failings.

For many years, the common law refused to account for this basic truth in tort cases. The contributory negligence doctrine reflected the absolutist moral view that the plaintiff who was blameless was entitled to full vindication in a court of law, but that one who shared the taint of sin in any degree must be sent forth to languish in the wilderness. Today we are less pious and more pragmatic about accident causation. The more "modern" view is to recognize the complexity of causation in human affairs. This change in attitudes has led to widespread adoption of comparative negligence, which replaces the all-or-nothing approach of contributory negligence with a system that reduces a party's damages to account for her fault.

I hesitate to call this a "modern" view, because there is nothing new about it, really. Comparative negligence was apparently known to those most practical of lawmakers, the Romans, and has prevailed widely in civil law countries since the 19th century.[1] American admiralty practice also adopted

---

1. See E. Turk, Comparative Negligence on the March, 28 Chi.-Kent L. Rev. 189, 239-244 (1950).

a rough form of comparative negligence: Under the "equal division rule," if two ships were at fault in a collision, the court divided the damages equally, regardless of their relative degrees of fault. Suppose, for example, that the Queen Mary collided with the Queen Elizabeth, and sustained $200,000 in damage. If both ships were partly at fault in causing the collision, the owners of the Queen Mary would recover $100,000. This was true even if the Queen Mary's skipper was one percent at fault and the Queen Elizabeth's was 99 percent to blame. This may seem like a crude system, but it was a substantial retreat from contributory negligence: Under contributory negligence, the Queen Mary's owners would have recovered nothing at all.

Dissatisfaction with the all-or-nothing feature of contributory negligence also led several states to experiment with a *slight/gross* comparative negligence system. Under the Nebraska statute, for example, a plaintiff whose negligence was "slight" compared to that of the defendant was allowed to recover, but her recovery was reduced "in proportion to the amount of contributory negligence attributable to the plaintiff." Neb. Rev. Stat. §25-21,185. This provision, in force in Nebraska until recently, changes the result in those cases in which contributory negligence operated most harshly: where the plaintiff was only minimally negligent. However, even under the slight/gross system, if the jury finds that plaintiff's negligence was more than "slight," the traditional contributory negligence rule applies, and plaintiff loses entirely.

Such early systems showed that the contributory negligence rule was not immutable, but it was not until about 1965 that this trickle of reform turned into a flood. Since that date, more than 35 states have replaced contributory negligence with one form or another of comparative negligence. At this writing, only four or five states retain the contributory negligence doctrine. In some states the change has come from the courts — since contributory negligence is a judicial doctrine, some courts have been willing to abandon it by judicial decision. In many, however, comparative negligence has been introduced by statute.

Pure Comparative Negligence

Most states have adopted either *pure comparative negligence* or several common variations (called "modified comparative negligence"), which are described below. Under pure comparative negligence, advocated by most scholars, an injured party may recover, regardless of her degree of fault, but her recovery is reduced by her percentage of fault. For example, the Washington (state) statute provides in part:

> In an action based on fault seeking to recover damages for injury or death to person or harm to property, any contributory fault chargeable to the claimant diminishes proportionately the amount awarded as compensatory damages for an injury attributable to the claimant's contributory fault, but does not bar recovery.

Wash. Rev. Code Ann. §4.22.005 (1988). Assume that the Queen Mary's skipper was 40 percent at fault in causing the collision. Under a pure comparative negligence statute like Washington's, the owners of the Queen Mary would recover, but their damages would be reduced by 40 percent to reflect the Queen Mary's contribution to the accident. Thus, they would recover 60 percent of their damages, or $120,000. If the Queen Mary was only 1 percent at fault, they would recover 99 percent of their damages. If the Queen Elizabeth was 99 percent at fault and suffered a million dollars in damages, its owners would recover $10,000 (1 percent of $1,000,000).

While there is a pleasing symmetry about pure comparative negligence, it has had its critics too. It may not seem "fair" to pay damages to one who is the overwhelming cause of his own misfortune. If the Queen Elizabeth's skipper was 99 percent at fault, the Queen Mary's owners may be understandably reluctant to pay its owners a penny, much less $10,000, which is one million pennies.

Modified Comparative Negligence

Many states have compromised between the extremes of contributory negligence on the one hand and pure comparative negligence on the other. The slight/gross system was an early example, but it proved hard to apply, due to the difficulty in defining "slight" negligence and controlling jury verdicts based on such an amorphous standard. A more popular approach, particularly in states that have switched to comparative negligence by statute rather than judicial decision, has been *modified* comparative negligence. Modified comparative negligence systems, like the slight/gross system, bar the claimant from any recovery if her negligence reaches a certain level, but they set the level at the point where the plaintiff's negligence either equals or exceeds that of the defendant.

The Kansas comparative negligence statute, for example, provides that a party's negligence will not bar her recovery

> if such party's negligence was less than the causal negligence of the party or parties against whom claim for recovery is made, but the award of damages to any party in such action shall be diminished in proportion to the amount of negligence attributed to such party.

Kan. Stat. Ann. §60-258a(a) (1983 & Supp. 1993). This statute is typical of the *not-as-great-as* form of modified comparative negligence. Under this approach, the plaintiff recovers her damages, reduced by her percentage of fault, so long as her fault was not as great as that of the defendant or defendants. A plaintiff who was 45 percent at fault would recover 55 percent of her damages under this type of statute, but a plaintiff who was 70 percent negligent would recover nothing. In the frequent scenario in which the jury concludes that the parties were equally at fault, the plaintiff loses, since her fault is as great as that of the defendant.

The other common system of modified comparative negligence allows the plaintiff to recover reduced damages so long as her negligence was not greater than that of the defendant:

> Contributory negligence shall not bar recovery in an action by any person or his legal representative to recover damages for negligence . . . if such negligence was not greater than the negligence of the person against whom recovery is sought or was not greater than the combined negligence of the persons against whom recovery is sought. Any damages sustained shall be diminished by the percentage sustained of negligence attributable to the person recovering.

N.J. Stat. Ann. §2A:15-5.1 (1987). This approach is the same as the not-as-great-as system in every case except where the plaintiff's and defendant's negligence is equal. While the plaintiff loses in the 50/50 case in a not-as-great-as state, she recovers 50 percent of her damages in a not-greater-than state like New Jersey. Since juries frequently conclude that the parties are equally at fault, this can change the result in quite a few cases.

Modified comparative negligence is perhaps less logically defensible than pure comparative negligence. Suppose that Hobbes is 51 percent at fault in causing an accident and suffers $100,000 in damages. Suppose also that Mill, the other driver, is 49 percent at fault, suffers $100,000 in damages and counterclaims for his injuries. In a modified comparative negligence jurisdiction, Hobbes recovers nothing; he will absorb all of his own loss, and pay Mill $51,000 as well (since Mill is only 49 percent at fault and thus entitled to recover his damages reduced by 49 percent). This disparity in recovery hardly seems justified on the basis of a two percent difference in the negligence of the parties. By contrast, under pure comparative negligence, Hobbes would recover $49,000 from Mill, and Mill would recover $51,000 from Hobbes.[2]

Despite examples like this, most states that have adopted comparative negligence by statute have chosen one of the modified forms. Perhaps the best explanation, other than pure political compromise between contributory and comparative negligence, is that of a sponsor of the New Hampshire statute, whose "sandlot instinct" rebelled against allowing recovery to a party who is primarily to blame for her own injury. Nixon, The Actual "Legislative Intent" Behind New Hampshire's Comparative Negligence Statute, 12 N.H.B.J. 17, 24-25 (1969).

Under both pure and modified systems, the seeming precision of the calculations is obviously illusory. It is people — usually 12 ordinary people — who apply the comparative negligence rules to actual cases. Affixing exact percentages of negligence in complex accidents at a trial four or five years after the fact is a dubious business. However, as Dean Prosser persuasively notes, any system of assigning damages in negligence cases is inherently imprecise:

---

2. See R. Keeton, Comment on *Maki v. Frelk*, 21 Vand. L. Rev. 906, 911 (1968).

[A] division of the plaintiff's damages [on the basis of comparative fault] is at least more accurate than one based on the arbitrary conclusion that 100 percent of the responsibility rests with the plaintiff and none whatever with the defendant, or, if the last clear chance is applicable, 100 percent with the defendant and none with the plaintiff — both of which are demonstrably wrong. Nor is such an estimate in itself any more foolish, or more difficult, than the one which assigns $2,000 as fair value and compensation for the pain of a broken leg, or the humiliation of a disfigured nose, to say nothing of estimates based on a prognosis of speed of recovery, future earnings or permanent disability.

W. Prosser, Comparative Negligence, 51 Mich. L. Rev. 465, 475 (1953).

Who is Compared?

Some practical problems arise in applying comparative negligence to specific cases, especially under modified comparative negligence. A basic question is who gets compared to whom. For example, assume that Rousseau's car collides with Locke's and Rousseau suffers $100,000 in damages. He sues Locke for negligent driving and the city for leaving a pothole in the road, which contributed to causing the accident. At trial, the jury concludes that Rousseau was 45 percent at fault, Locke 15 percent, and the city 40 percent. In a modified comparative negligence jurisdiction (of either type) Rousseau will lose if his fault is compared to that of each defendant *individually*, since his is greater than either of theirs. However, if his fault is compared to the *total negligence* of the defendants together, he can still recover 55 percent of his damages, since 45 percent is less than their combined total of 55 percent.

Some states take the harder line on this issue, comparing the plaintiff's negligence to that of each defendant individually. These states bar the plaintiff from recovering from any defendant who is less negligent, though he may recover from others who are more negligent. Most modified comparative negligence states, however, compare the plaintiff's negligence to the combined negligence of the defendants.

There are cogent arguments for both approaches. Comparing Rousseau's negligence to all defendants combined seems unfair since Locke will be held liable to Rousseau for $55,000 (55 percent of $100,000), even though he was only 15 percent to blame and Rousseau's fault was three times greater. That result looks like pure comparative negligence, since a party more at fault recovers from one less at fault. On the other hand, comparing the plaintiff's negligence to each defendant's individually places a plaintiff at a disadvantage if there are multiple parties: She may lose even if her negligence is substantially less than 50 percent. It also leaves defendants who are found more negligent than the plaintiff holding the bag for others who contributed to the accident but were less negligent than the plaintiff. For example, if Rousseau were 35 percent at fault, the city 40 percent, and Locke 25 percent, the city would be liable for 65 percent of Rousseau's damages (since it is more negligent than him), while Locke would not be liable at all.

What is Compared?

Another basic issue in applying comparative negligence is what is compared among the parties: is it the *negligence* of each party, or the degree to which each party's negligence *caused* the plaintiff's injury? This problem is conceptually difficult: How do you distinguish causation from the extent of negligence? It is hard to think about degrees of causation: Either the negligence contributed to the accident or it didn't. Suppose, for example, that Montesquieu makes a left turn without putting on his turn indicator, and is hit head on by Milton, who is doing 75 M.P.H. in a 35 M.P.H. zone. Most jurors would find Milton more to blame, but that both acts equally "caused" the harm. If the goal of comparative negligence is to place the greater burden on the more culpable party, it seems that Milton should be found substantially more responsible than Montesquieu.

Changing the example a bit, assume that Montesquieu was driving while severely intoxicated and made the same left turn without looking, leading to the same accident with the speeding Milton. On these facts, as in the first example, both parties contributed to causing the accident, but the relative culpability of the parties is much more nearly equal, and most juries would ascribe a higher percentage of fault to Montesquieu than in the first example.

Dean Prosser is emphatically of the view that it is the degrees of negligence of the parties that is compared. See W. Prosser, Comparative Negligence, 51 Mich. L. Rev. 465, 481-482 (1953). Most statutes appear to take this position, since they require the jury to consider the comparative "fault" or "negligence" of the parties. However, some cases hold that both negligence and causation are to be considered (see Harper, James & Gray, §22.16, at 397-398) and the Uniform Comparative Fault Act explicitly requires the jury to consider both:

> In determining the percentages of fault, the trier of fact shall consider both the nature of the conduct of each party at fault and the extent of the causal relation between the conduct and the damages claimed.[3]

As a practical matter, it probably doesn't matter in most cases which approach is taken. Assessing fault is not a scientific process; the jury makes an instinctive judgment about the culpability of each party without focusing on the technical

---

3. Uniform Comparative Fault Act, §2(b), 12 U.L.A. 45 (Supp. 1994). The Uniform Comparative Fault Act is a model act, written by the National Conference of Commissioners on Uniform State Laws, to encourage development of uniform state legislation on issues of general applicability.

distinction between negligence and causation. However, one thing can be said with certainty: If the plaintiff's negligence was not an actual cause of the injury the jury should not consider it. If the plaintiff is hit from behind while stopped at a light, irrelevant negligence in failing to get her brakes checked should not reduce her recovery.

Caveat: A Fundamental Fundamental of Comparative Negligence

A final, fundamental point should be made here, and it is one that is easily missed. Comparative negligence regimes allow a plaintiff who is partly at fault to recover reduced damages, and provide a formula for calculating those reduced damages. But the adoption of comparative negligence, by itself, does *not* change the basic rule of joint and several liability, under which each defendant is liable for the entire judgment awarded to the plaintiff. Nor does adoption of comparative negligence, of itself, change the basic contribution rules governing the redistribution of damages among the defendants.

For example, if Rousseau recovers from Locke and the city in the example given earlier, he will be entitled to 55 percent of his damages, or $55,000. Under traditional joint and several liability principles, both Locke and the city would be liable to Rousseau for $55,000. Put another way, the adoption of comparative negligence does *not* mean that the plaintiff's judgment will be apportioned to the defendants in proportion to their negligence. In the Rousseau case, the city will not be ordered to pay $40,000 of the judgment, and Locke only $15,000. Judgment will enter against each for $55,000, because, under joint and several liability, each defendant who is liable to the plaintiff is liable for the entire judgment. Rousseau will be entitled to collect $55,000 from either Locke or the city. If Locke pays he can seek contribution from the city, or vice versa, under applicable principles of contribution. See Chapter 17.

Since the adoption of comparative negligence, many states have also changed the traditional principles of joint and several liability and contribution. Chapter 22 explores some of the changes to contribution principles and joint and several liability that have been prompted by the adoption of comparative negligence. But it is important to understand that the adoption of comparative negligence does not in itself change these principles, and some states that have adopted comparative negligence still apply fairly traditional approaches to both contribution and joint and several liability.

The following examples illustrate the application of the various types of comparative negligence to actual cases. Assume in analyzing them that joint and several liability applies. After the examples and explanations, there is a short additional discussion of special verdicts, with several examples to illustrate how comparative negligence issues are usually submitted to the jury.

EXAMPLES

Comparing Comparative Negligence

1. Paine is injured when his hand is caught in a printing press operated by Burke. He sues Burke for negligence. The jury finds that Paine has suffered $60,000 in damages, and that each party was 50 percent at fault.
    a. How much would Paine recover in a jurisdiction that applies a not-as-great-as form of comparative negligence?
    b. How much would Paine recover in a not-greater-than jurisdiction?
    c. How much would Paine recover under a pure comparative negligence approach?
    d. How much would Paine recover in a jurisdiction that retains contributory negligence?

2. Assume that Paine sued both Burke and Calkins, who had recently repaired the press. The jury finds that Paine was 65 percent negligent in causing his own injuries, that Burke was 15 percent negligent and that Calkins was 20 percent negligent. Paine's damages are again $60,000.
    a. Would Burke or Calkins be liable to Paine if the suit were brought under pure comparative negligence?
    b. How much would Burke or Calkins be liable for, if anything?
    c. Assume that the accident takes place in a state that applies the not-as-great-as approach? Who would be liable to Paine?
    d. Who would be liable under the not-greater-than approach?

3. Assume that the jury found Paine 33 1/3 percent negligent, Calkins 33 1/3 percent negligent, and Burke 33 1/3 percent negligent. Paine's damages are again $60,000.
    a. How much would Paine recover from each defendant under pure comparative negligence?
    b. How much would he recover under the not-as-great-as version of modified comparative negligence?
    c. How much would he recover under the not-greater-than approach?

Judgments, More or Less

4. Descartes sues Mill, Calkins, and Newton for injuries arising from a boating accident. The jury concludes that Descartes was 25 percent at fault, Mill was 10 percent at fault, Calkins was 25 percent at fault, and Newton was 40 percent at fault. They assess Descartes's damages at $100,000. Assume that the suit is brought in a not-as-great-as jurisdiction which compares the negligence of the plaintiff to that of each defendant individually.
    a. Who may Descartes recover from?
    b. Will Descartes recover $75,000, $62,838, or $40,000?
    c. How much would Descartes recover from Mill and Calkins if the statute measured the plaintiff's negligence against the aggregate negligence of all defendants?

5.   Suppose, on the same facts, that Descartes had only sued Calkins. How much, if anything, would he recover from her?

Judge Fudd Redux

6.   Pascal sues Hume for negligently dropping a board on him from a ladder. Hume claims that Pascal was also negligent, for philosophizing under the ladder during construction. The case is tried before the indomitable Fudd, who instructs the jury as follows:

> If you find that the plaintiff was negligent, then you must reduce the damages awarded in the proportion that the plaintiff's negligence bears to the defendant's.

The jury finds that Pascal suffered $60,000 in damages, that he was 20 percent at fault and that Hume was 80 percent at fault.

    a. How much should the jury award to Pascal under Judge Fudd's instruction?

    b. What is wrong with the instruction and how much did the error cost Pascal?

    c. What should the instruction be?

7.   Assume, on the facts of Example 6, that Pascal claims that Hume had the last clear chance to avoid the injury by warning him that the board was falling. In a contributory negligence jurisdiction, this, if proved, would require the jury to disregard Pascal's negligence. See Chapter 19, p.406. Should the judge instruct the jury to disregard Pascal's negligence if they find that Hume had the last clear chance to avoid the accident?

8.   Assume that Hume was also injured in the foregoing fiasco, when Pascal jumped back, knocking over the ladder. He counterclaims against Pascal in the suit, and the jury assesses his damages at $200,000. They assign the same percentages of negligence to Pascal (20 percent) and to Hume (80 percent).

    a. What judgments would result in a contributory negligence jurisdiction?

    b. What judgments would result in a pure comparative negligence jurisdiction?

Credit Where Credit is Due

9.   Assume that Pascal, on the facts of the ladder example, also sued Hamilton, who settled with Pascal for $15,000 before trial. The case is tried in a jurisdiction which requires the jury to apportion the negligence among all negligent parties, not just those who are defending at trial. The jury finds that Pascal was 20 percent at fault, Hume 60 percent at fault, and Hamilton 20 percent at fault, and that Pascal's damages are $60,000. How much will Pascal be able to recover from Hume for his injuries in the accident? Assume that the Uniform Contribution Among Joint Tortfeasors statute, discussed in Chapter 17, applies. (See especially §4a, quoted at p.363.)

EXPLANATIONS

Comparing Comparative Negligence

1a. Paine will not recover at all in a not-as-great-as jurisdiction, since his negligence was as great as that of Burke. This form of comparative negligence bars a plaintiff from recovery if her fault equals (or exceeds) the defendant's.

b. In a not-greater-than jurisdiction, Paine would recover $30,000. He is not barred from recovery, because his fault was not greater than Burke's. However, his damages will be reduced by his percentage of negligence (.50 × $60,000).

c. The result in a pure comparative negligence jurisdiction is the same as in the last example. Paine may recover but his fault reduces his recovery proportionally, to $30,000.

d. Obviously, Paine will recover nothing in a contributory negligence jurisdiction, since his negligence contributed in part to causing the accident.

2a. Both Burke and Calkins are liable to Paine under pure comparative negligence, since both were negligent. The fact that Paine was *more* negligent than either of them does not bar him from recovering under a pure comparative negligence statute. It will, however, reduce the amount he recovers proportionally.

b. In a pure comparative negligence jurisdiction, Paine's judgment will be reduced by 65 percent to reflect his negligence. He will therefore recover $21,000 ($60,000 − (.65 × 60,000)). As the introduction indicates, in many jurisdictions Burke and Calkins will both be liable to Paine for this amount, since they are jointly and severally liable for the damages their negligence contributed to causing. Even though each was considerably less at fault than Paine, each is liable to Paine for $21,000.

c. Neither defendant is liable to Paine under the not-as-great-as form of comparative negligence, since Paine's negligence was greater than 50 percent. This case, in which the plaintiff is more than half at fault, demonstrates the most marked difference between pure and modified comparative negligence systems. Under pure comparative negligence, plaintiff recovers, with a reduction for her percentage of negligence. Under modified comparative negligence, she loses entirely.

d. Paine loses under the not-greater-than approach too, since her negligence was greater than that of the defendants. Both forms of modified comparative negligence bar the plaintiff from recovery if she is more than 50 percent at fault.

3a. In a pure comparative negligence jurisdiction, Paine would recover his full damages, $60,000, reduced by his own percentage of fault, or $40,000 ($60,000 − (.333 × 60,000)). Each defendant would be liable for the $40,000 judgment under joint and several liability.

b. The answer here depends on whether the jurisdiction compares Paine's negligence to that of Burke and Calkins individually, or to the total negligence of all defendants. Most comparative negligence statutes provide for comparison to the combined negligence of all defendants. Under this approach, Paine's negligence would be compared to the combined negligence of Burke and Calkins. Paine would recover, since his negligence (33 1/3 percent) is less than that of Burke and Calkins combined (66 2/3 percent). His recovery would be reduced by 33 1/3 percent, to $40,000, to account for his negligence.

If the traditional rules of joint and several liability apply, Paine will get a judgment for $40,000 against each defendant. Note again, as in Example 1, that pure and modified comparative negligence systems reduce Paine's damages in the same manner. The difference is that under modified comparative negligence, Paine loses entirely if his fault reaches a certain percentage.

If this case were tried in a state which applies the not-as-great-as approach, but compares the plaintiff's negligence to each defendant individually, Paine would lose entirely, since his fault is as great as that of each of the other defendants.

c. Under the not-greater-than approach Paine would recover even if his negligence were compared to Locke's and Calkins's individually. Because his negligence is not greater than that of either defendant, he would recover a judgment for $40,000 against each defendant, assuming joint and several liability applies.[4]

Judgments, More or Less

4a. Since the case arises in a state that compares the plaintiff's negligence to each of the defendant's individually, Descartes may recover against Newton, because his negligence was not as great as Newton's. But he cannot recover from Calkins, since his negligence equals Calkins's. And, *a fortiori*, he cannot recover from Mill, who was less at fault.

b. Descartes will recover $75,000 from Newton, his total damages reduced by his own percentage of negligence. This may seem unfair to Newton, since it makes Newton bear the full damages, even though two other parties who contributed to it are not liable at all. Wouldn't it be fairer to ignore the negligence of the other defendants, and compare Descartes's negligence (25 percent) to the combined total of his and Newton's, (25 percent + 40 percent, or 65 percent), the only liable defendant? That's how I got the $61,838 figure, which reduces Descartes's damages by 25/65ths of $100,000. Alternatively, it may seem appropriate to make the one liable defendant pay only his percentage of negligence. This approach would yield the $40,000 figure.

---

4. Of course, he could only collect a total of $40,000, as explained in Chapter 16, p.337.

Maybe that would be fairer, but many comparative negligence statutes do not change the basic principle that those defendants who are liable are liable for the full amount of the plaintiff's judgment. They do *not* limit a defendant's liability to her own percentage of negligence. If the rule seems unfair, remember that under the common law approach, every defendant who was found negligent at all was *fully* liable to the plaintiff, even if other tortfeasors also contributed to the injury. In one sense, a defendant like Newton in this case is better off under comparative negligence, since the damages he must pay are at least reduced to account for Descartes's negligence. But he is worse off in the sense that less negligent defendants, like Mill and Calkins in this case, are not liable at all, leaving Newton liable for the entire judgment without benefit of contribution from the others. (This assumes that joint and several liability still applies; see Chapter 22, pp.472-473, 476-478, for current variations in jurisdictions that have changed this doctrine.)

c. If the statute called for comparison of the plaintiff's negligence to that of all defendants together, Descartes would get a judgment against all three defendants, since his negligence (25 percent) is less than the aggregate negligence of all defendants (75 percent). Descartes would obtain a judgment for $75,000, his full loss reduced by his percentage of negligence, against each defendant. Consequently Calkins, who was only 25 percent to blame, would be liable for 75 percent of Descartes's damages. Mill, who was only 10 percent to blame, would also be liable for $75,000. Of course, if Mill paid the $75,000, he could seek contribution from the other defendants, assuming they are able to pay.

Under this version of modified comparative negligence, more plaintiffs will recover, since their negligence is less likely to exceed that of all defendants together. More defendants will end up splitting the damages, since they will be liable even if they were less negligent than the plaintiff. The judgment will likely then be spread among them through contribution, so defendants in Newton's position will not end up with the whole bill, as he did in Example 4b.

5. This example introduces a perplexing problem. In assessing percentages of negligence, should the jury only consider the parties to the lawsuit, or should they consider all persons who may have contributed to causing the accident? If they only consider Descartes and Calkins, they might assess 50 percent of the negligence to each, but they might also assess the negligence somewhat differently than they did in the last example, in which all parties were sued. They might find Calkins 60 percent at fault compared solely to Descartes's 40 percent, in which case he would recover 60 percent of his damages from her, (compared to zero in Example 4b).

If only the parties before the court are considered, Descartes will have greater control over the process, since he chooses which defendants to sue. By suing Calkins alone, he may increase his chances of recovering from her, as the previous paragraph suggests. If this seems unfavorable to Calkins, she may be able to ensure that other tortfeasors are considered by bringing them into the suit as third-party defendants.

It seems highly artificial to assess the negligence of some of the contributing parties while ignoring others who may have played a major role in causing the accident. Yet, if absent tortfeasors are considered without being made parties, the parties before the court will have to prove the negligence of absentees who do not participate in the process. In a state that compares the plaintiff's negligence to each defendant's individually, Calkins might benefit by shifting blame to the absent tortfeasors: Perhaps she could convince the jury to assign a higher percentage to their negligence and get her own down below that of Descartes.

There is no single "right" approach to this problem. Some statutes expressly provide that the plaintiff's negligence should be compared to that of the defendants in the suit. See Or. Rev. Stat. §18.470 (1993) (plaintiff's negligence must be not greater than "the combined fault of the person or persons against whom recovery is sought"). Others, however, require consideration of all possibly negligent parties in determining the percentages assigned to the parties. See generally Schwartz, Comparative Negligence §16.5.

An interesting related issue is how to compare the parties' negligence in a multi-*plaintiff* case. Is the negligence of each plaintiff compared to the negligence of the defendants, or is the negligence of all the parties, plaintiffs and defendants, calculated to add up to 100 percent? In *Churchill v. F/V Fjord*, 892 F.2d 763, 772 (9th Cir. 1989), for example, the following percentages of negligence were assigned at trial: P1, 20 percent; P2, 20 percent; D1, 35 percent; D2, 25 percent; D3, zero percent. The appellate court reversed, holding that the negligence of each plaintiff must be compared *separately* against the negligence of the defendants. Thus, in calculating each plaintiff's negligence, the jury must ignore the negligence of the other plaintiff, just as they ignore the negligence of absent tortfeasors in a state that considers only the negligence of parties before the court.[5]

---

5. The jury would have to produce two separate sets of calculations, each adding up to 100 percent, and each ignoring the other plaintiff, even though she was negligent. Hypothetically, the calculations might look like this:

P1 compared to defendants:
P1 15 percent; D1 25 percent; D2 60 percent (Total 100 percent)
P2 compared to defendants:
P2 25 percent; D1 20 percent; D2 55 percent (Total 100 percent)

Note that the defendants' percentages differ in the two calculations, since the jury has found one plaintiff more negligent than the other.

Judge Fudd Redux

6a. Under Judge Fudd's instruction, the jury should reduce Pascal's award by 20/80, or 25 percent, "the proportion that his negligence bears to the defendant's." He would recover $45,000.

b. The judge's error has cost Pascal $3,000. The problem with the instruction is that it asks the jury to relate the plaintiff's negligence to the defendant's, rather than to the total negligence of all parties. The proper method would be to reduce Pascal's award by 20/100, to $48,000.

c. Jury instructions frequently require the jury to "reduce the total amount of plaintiff's damages by the proportion or percentage of negligence attributable to the plaintiff." See, e.g., Illinois Pattern Jury Instructions, A45.05 (1968). It would be even clearer to instruct as follows:

> If you find that the plaintiff was negligent, then you must reduce the damages awarded to the plaintiff by the proportion which her negligence bears to the total negligence of all parties.

This instruction makes it clear to the jury that the plaintiff's negligence is to be compared to that of all parties, not just to that of the defendant.

7.   The issue posed here is whether the last clear chance doctrine applies in a jurisdiction that has changed over to comparative negligence. The last clear chance doctrine provided a means of avoiding the harshest applications of contributory negligence. The court would find for the plaintiff, despite her negligence, if the defendant had the last chance to avoid the accident (and hence was at least arguably the more negligent party). Here, Pascal argues that, since Hume had the last clear chance to avoid the accident, his (Pascal's) negligence should be ignored entirely, as it was before the adoption of comparative negligence.

Once comparative negligence is adopted there is no need for a doctrine that ignores the plaintiff's negligence simply because the defendant was (arguably) more negligent. If the defendant is more negligent, she can be assigned a higher percentage of negligence, but the plaintiff's negligence can still be taken into account. On this rationale, most courts have concluded that the last clear chance doctrine does not apply under comparative negligence. See Schwartz at 130-134 (discussing both positions). If the court adopts the majority position, Pascal would still be assigned a percentage of negligence, which would reduce his damages, even though Hume had the last chance to avoid the accident.

As Chapter 20 explains, (see pp.424-426) many jurisdictions have similarly concluded that secondary unreasonable implied assumption of the risk should not be a complete bar to recovery once comparative negligence is adopted. Instead, the plaintiff's unreasonable decision to encounter a risk should be considered a form of "fault" that the jury uses in assessing her percentage of negligence.

One vestige of the common law approach, however, has not been changed. A plaintiff's recovery will not be reduced under comparative negligence if the defendant's conduct was *intentional.* These are, after all, comparative *negligence* statutes; where the defendant's conduct is intentional she will still be made to bear the entire loss, even though the plaintiff's negligence contributed to the injury.

8a.   In a contributory negligence state, neither party would recover, since each was partially at fault. The court would enter a judgment dismissing each party's claim against the other.

b. There is nothing to prevent an injured defendant from recovering from a plaintiff under comparative negligence. After all, if Hume had gone to court first, he would have been the plaintiff; he shouldn't be prejudiced by merely losing the race to the courthouse. Thus, if both parties are injured, but both negligent, each may be entitled to some recovery in a pure comparative negligence jurisdiction. Here, Pascal would recover $48,000 from Hume ($60,000 reduced by 20 percent) and Hume would recover $40,000 from Pascal ($200,000 reduced by 80 percent).

Credit Where Credit is Due

9.   Pascal will get a judgment against Hume for $48,000, his full damages reduced by his 20 percent responsibility for causing the accident. However, Pascal has already been paid $15,000 by Hamilton. As Chapter 17 explains, Hume gets a credit against the judgment for this settlement amount. Thus, he will only have to pay $33,000.

One of the most common mistakes students make is taking the credit for the settlement before reducing the plaintiff's recovery for his negligence. That is, they subtract $15,000 from $60,000, reduce the remaining $45,000 by 20 percent to account for the plaintiff's negligence, and conclude that Hume must pay $36,000. Most states take the position that the credit for Hamilton's settlement is a credit against the *judgment*, not against the raw damages figure before adjustment for the plaintiff's negligence. Thus, the credit should be calculated by determining how much Hume is liable for ($48,000), and *then* applying the credit for Hamilton's prior settlement.

Special Verdicts: Guiding the Jury in Applying Comparative Negligence

While comparative negligence may be fairer than the all-or-nothing contributory negligence rule, it is more complicated for a jury to apply. Under contributory negligence, the jury's role was clear. If it found that the plaintiff was negligent, it rendered a verdict for the defendant, since any negligence barred the plaintiff from recovery. If it found that the plaintiff was not negligent, but that the defendant was, it decided how much the plaintiff should be awarded in damages to compensate her for her injuries, and came back with a verdict for the plaintiff for that amount.

Under comparative negligence, by contrast, the jury must decide the percentage of negligence of each party, including the plaintiff, and perhaps of absent tortfeasors as well. It must then determine the value of the plaintiff's damages, and apply the comparative negligence statute to reduce those damages and render a verdict for the reduced damages against the appropriate defendants. Since the jurors presumably know little about comparative negligence, they must be fully instructed as to how to compare the negligence of the parties, the effect of the plaintiff's negligence, and how the damages are to be reduced.

These instructions will be complicated. If the jury simply renders a general verdict ("verdict for plaintiff for $50,000" or "verdict for the defendant"), it will be impossible to know whether they understood and followed the instructions. Many states address this problem by authorizing or requiring the use of special verdicts, which ask the jury to make factual determinations about the negligence of each party and damages, and leave it to the court to apply the comparative negligence statute to fashion a proper judgment. For example, if the Rousseau case (see p.443) were tried in a pure comparative negligence jurisdiction, the court might use a special verdict form like that in Figure 21-1[6] (see p.459).

A special verdict form like Figure 21-1 allows the court to insure that the more complex comparative negligence rules are properly applied. The jury is simply instructed to make the necessary factual findings concerning the negligence of each party and the plaintiff's resulting damages. It then fills in these findings on the special verdict form. After the jury renders the special verdict, the court applies the comparative negligence statute to its findings by reducing the plaintiff's damages to account for her negligence and entering judgment against the defendants who are liable under the statute, or if the statute requires, entering a judgment for the defendant. The special verdict procedure simplifies the jury instructions, since the court does not have to explain to the jury how to compare the negligence of the various parties in fashioning a final judgment.

For example, if the Rousseau case were tried under pure comparative negligence doctrine, and the jury rendered the special verdict in Figure 21-1, the judge would enter judgment for Rousseau against Locke for $18,000 (45 percent of $40,000), but dismiss the claim against the city, since the jury did not find it negligent. If the case had been tried in a modified comparative negligence state, the judge would enter judgment for both defendants, since the plaintiff was more than 50 percent negligent.

---

6. Adapted, with modifications, from an earlier California form, B.A.J.I. 14.94 (1977).

Here are several examples of special verdicts. Consider what judgment the judge should render based upon each of them.

EXAMPLES

Verdicts and Judgments

10. Assume that the jury returned the special verdict shown in Figure 21-2 (see p.461), in a not-greater-than state that compares the plaintiff's negligence to the aggregate negligence of the defendants. What judgment should the judge render? What if the jurisdiction compared plaintiff's negligence to each defendant individually?

11. Assume that the state applies pure comparative negligence. The jury fills out the form as shown in Figure 21-3 below at p.460. What should the judge do?

12. One of the advantages of the special verdict is that the jury need not be given complicated instructions on the effect of their factual findings. For example, they do not need to know that the plaintiff will lose if she is more negligent than the defendant in a modified comparative negligence state. All they need do is find the actual percentages, since the judge fashions the verdict based on their findings. However, some states require the judge to inform the jury of the effect of finding the plaintiff more negligent than the defendant, even though logically it is unnecessary — or perhaps even an impediment to rational decision making — for them to know. See, e.g., Iowa Code Ann. §668.3(5) (1987). Under such a statute, the judge would give an instruction like this in a state which applies the 50 percent bar rule:

> If the plaintiff's negligence is as great as or greater than the negligence of the defendant, she may not recover. If the plaintiff's negligence is less than that of the defendant, she may recover her damages, reduced in proportion to her negligence in causing the accident.

Who wants the jury to be given this instruction, the defendant or the plaintiff?

Unlucky Number Thirteen

13. While special verdicts are very useful in clarifying issues, they can be difficult to draft. All issues must be covered, in order to obtain a set of jury findings that fully resolve the case. To illustrate how difficult this can be, consider again Example 8 from Chapter 19. In that example, Baruch was injured when Burns cut him with a chain saw, was hospitalized for a week and missed a month of work. On his release, he was instructed to take an antibiotic to prevent infection, but lost the prescription and didn't take the pills. He then developed a serious infection, was hospitalized for six weeks and disabled for three more months. Under the avoidable consequences doctrine, he would be barred from recovery for these additional damages if he was negligent in failing to prevent them.

Assume that Baruch brings suit against Burns for his injuries, and that Baruch alleges that Burns's negligence in reaching in front of the saw contributed to the accident. The case goes to trial, and evidence is offered of both parties' conduct and the damages from both the cut and the infection.

    a. Draft a special verdict form for the jury to use in determining the issues before it.

    b. Look at the special verdict form in Figure 21-4 (see p.465). Based on the findings the jury has made, what judgment should the judge enter? Assume that pure comparative negligence applies.

EXPLANATIONS

Verdicts and Judgments

10. The judge should enter judgment for Rousseau for $55,000 against both Locke and the city. Rousseau is entitled to recover since his negligence is not greater than that of all defendants combined. If joint and several liability applies, both defendants are liable for the resulting judgment of $55,000, despite the disparity in their degrees of negligence.

    If the jurisdiction compared the plaintiff's negligence to each defendant's individually, the judge would enter a judgment for Rousseau against Locke for $55,000, and a judgment dismissing Rousseau's claim against the city, since Rousseau's negligence is greater than its.

11. The special verdict here indicates that the jury has failed to follow its instructions. If the city's negligence was not a proximate cause of the accident, as the answer to the second question indicates, the jury should not have considered it in assigning the percentages of negligence at the end. The jury may have concluded that, as long as *some* defendant's negligence caused the accident, both could be liable. Or, perhaps the jury misunderstood proximate cause (now really, how could it?) to mean the most important cause, and answered "no," since it found Locke much more negligent. For whatever reason, the jury's factual findings are inconsistent; it has assigned negligence percentages to all parties despite its finding that the city's negligence was not a proximate cause of Rousseau's injuries.

    If the jury comes back with this verdict, the judge can reinstruct it on proximate cause and send it back to clarify its verdict. This may well "save the trial" if it comes back with a consistent verdict after the supplemental instruction.

    Consider what would have happened if the jury had simply been asked to render a general verdict in this case. If it mistakenly considered the city's negligence, even though it did not cause the injuries, it probably would have come back with a verdict against each defendant for $90,000 (Rousseau's damages reduced by his 10 percent negligence). This would look on the surface like a perfectly permissible verdict, even though in fact it was based on a misunderstanding of the law. The general verdict often hides such mistakes. That is its virtue or its vice, depending on how you look at it.

Interestingly, although the special verdict appears to make so much sense in comparative negligence cases, not all states favor them. Some require the court to use a special verdict; others permit them, and one or two, remarkably, *bar* them entirely, despite their obvious utility in revealing the jury's reasoning process. See, e.g., Vt. Stat. Ann. tit. 12 §1036 (1973 & supp. 1993) (requiring use of general verdict).

12. Naturally, the plaintiff will seek this instruction, since it alerts the jury to the fact that, if they find the plaintiff as faulty as the defendant (or more at fault), she will lose entirely. Realistically, this is likely to influence a jury in a close case to find the plaintiff 49 percent negligent instead of 50 percent (or 55 percent, or 60 percent for that matter). Statutes that require an instruction like this recognize the practical reality that juries often structure their findings to help plaintiffs in close cases, and that in a practical torts world there is nothing particularly shocking about that.

Unlucky Number Thirteen

13a. Drafting this special verdict form requires some thought. Figure 21-4 (p.465)is my effort to draft a form that sets forth all the findings the jury must make in order to apply both comparative negligence and the doctrine of avoidable consequences to the case.

Under the doctrine of avoidable consequences, the defendant is not liable for aggravated damages that the plaintiff could have avoided with reasonable care. Restatement (Second) of Torts §918. Therefore, the special verdict form requires the jury to make separate findings as to whether Burns caused the cut (Issue #2) and the infection (Issue #3). It also requires the jury to determine whether the infection resulted from the cut; just because Baruch got an infection after the cut does not necessarily mean the one caused the other. This separate finding on causation assures that Burns will not be held liable if the infection would have developed even if Baruch had not been injured. And, of course, the verdict form must ask the jury to determine whether Baruch was negligent (Issue #4), whether his negligence caused his initial injury (Issue #5) and to determine the relative degrees of negligence of the parties in causing that injury (Issue #6). The form also requires the jury to make separate findings on the total damages Baruch has suffered and on the separate damages due to the infection (Issues #7 and #10).

Last, the form requires the jury to determine whether Baruch acted unreasonably in failing to take precautions to prevent the infection (Issue #8), and whether that negligence caused the infection (Issue #9). This allows the judge to decide whether the infection damages will be denied under the doctrine of avoidable consequences.[7] Note that the jury is only asked to make a finding on the amount of damages from the infection (Issue #10) if it finds that Baruch was negligent in failing to take the medication, and that his negligence contributed to these damages. If it finds that his negligence led to the infection, he is not entitled to recover for it.

b. The jury has found that both parties were negligent, that their negligence contributed to the accident and that Baruch could have avoided the infection by reasonable care. Because Baruch could have avoided the infection damages, Burns is not liable for them, even though his negligence was a proximate cause of them. Thus, in calculating Baruch's damages, the judge should subtract the $25,000 for the infection from the total damages. Then she should reduce the remaining $20,000 by 30 percent to account for Baruch's negligence in causing the initial injury. Judgment should enter for Baruch for $14,000.

It seems odd that Baruch should be barred from recovering for his infection damages. True, his negligence in failing to get the antibiotic was partly responsible, but so was Burns's in causing the initial injury (see answer to Issue #3, which finds that Burns's negligence was a proximate cause of the infection). If the subsequent negligence had been a doctor's, in failing to prescribe the antibiotic, Burns would have been liable for all resulting injuries, including the infection. See Prosser & Keeton at 309 (medical malpractice foreseeable intervening cause for which original defendant may be held liable). Why should the result differ if the subsequent negligence is the plaintiff's?

The Restatement explains the refusal to give Burns even partial recovery for the aggravated injury as follows: "[P]ublic policy requires that persons should be discouraged from wasting their resources, both physical or economic." Restatement (Second) of Torts §918, cmt. a. Sounds a bit stodgy, but there you are.

---

7. The verdict form does not take into account one further possibility, that the jury may be unable to separate the damages from the cut and the infection. In a case where the damages are too intertwined to separate, the defendant may be held liable for them all. But this seems like a case in which a reasonable apportionment can be made.

STATE OF WEST DAKOTA

SUTTER COUNTY   SUPERIOR COURT
                            NO. 94-3217

JOHN J. ROUSSEAU,

    Plaintiff,

    v.   SPECIAL VERDICT

JOHN LOCKE,
CITY OF PARIS

    Defendants

    We, the jury in the above entitled case, find
the following special verdict on the issues submitted to us:

    Issue #1: Were the defendants, or either of
               them, negligent? (Answer ''yes'' or
               ''no'')

    Answer: Defendant John Locke   **YES**
               Defendant City of Paris   **NO**

               [If you answered ''yes'' as to ei-
               ther defendant, then answer the next
               issue]

    Issue #2: Was the negligence of the defendant,
               or either of them, a proximate cause
               of the injury to the plaintiff?
               (Answer ''yes'' or ''no'')

    Answer: Defendant John Locke   **YES**
               Defendant City of Paris   **—**

               [If you answered ''yes'' to Issue #2
               as to either defendant, please answer
               Issue #3]

Figure 21-1

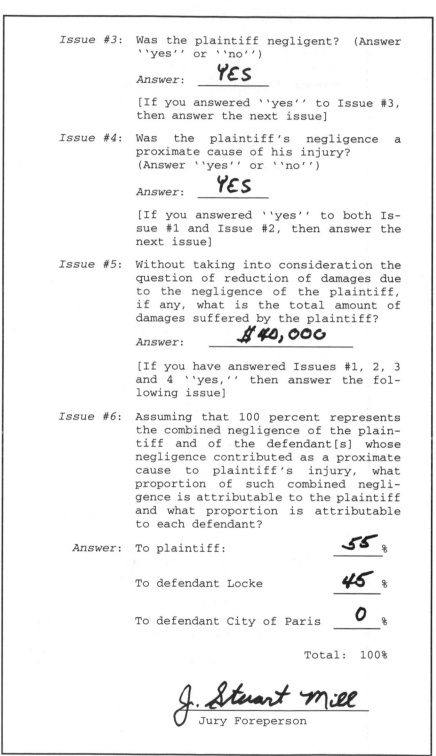

Issue #3: Was the plaintiff negligent? (Answer ``yes'' or ``no'')

Answer: ____YES____

[If you answered ``yes'' to Issue #3, then answer the next issue]

Issue #4: Was the plaintiff's negligence a proximate cause of his injury? (Answer ``yes'' or ``no'')

Answer: ____YES____

[If you answered ``yes'' to both Issue #1 and Issue #2, then answer the next issue]

Issue #5: Without taking into consideration the question of reduction of damages due to the negligence of the plaintiff, if any, what is the total amount of damages suffered by the plaintiff?

Answer: ____$40,000____

[If you have answered Issues #1, 2, 3 and 4 ``yes,'' then answer the following issue]

Issue #6: Assuming that 100 percent represents the combined negligence of the plaintiff and of the defendant[s] whose negligence contributed as a proximate cause to plaintiff's injury, what proportion of such combined negligence is attributable to the plaintiff and what proportion is attributable to each defendant?

Answer: To plaintiff: ____55____%

To defendant Locke ____45____%

To defendant City of Paris ____0____%

Total: 100%

J. Stuart Mill
Jury Foreperson

Figure 21–1 (*continued*)

```
                        STATE OF WEST DAKOTA


    SUTTER COUNTY                      SUPERIOR COURT
                                       NO. 94-3217


    JOHN J. ROUSSEAU,            |
                                 |
         Plaintiff,              |
                                 |
         v.                      |
                                 |    SPECIAL VERDICT
    JOHN LOCKE,                  |
    CITY OF PARIS                |
                                 |
         Defendants             |

    -----------------------|
```

    We, the jury in the above entitled case, find
the following special verdict on the issues submitted to us:

     Issue #1: Were the defendants, or either of
           them, negligent? (Answer ''yes'' or
           ''no'')

     Answer: Defendant John Locke   **YES**

           Defendant City of Paris   **YES**

     [If you answered ''yes'' as to either
     defendant, then answer the next
     issue]

     Issue #2: Was the negligence of the defendants,
           or either of them, a proximate cause
           of the injury to the plaintiff?
           (Answer ''yes'' or ''no'')

     Answer: Defendant John Locke   **YES**

           Defendant City of Paris   **YES**

     [If you answered ''yes'' to Issue #2
     as to either defendant, please answer
     Issue #3]

Figure 21-2

Issue #3: Was the plaintiff negligent? (Answer ''yes'' or ''no'')

Answer: ___YES___

[If you answered ''yes'' to Issue #3, then answer the next issue]

Issue #4: Was the plaintiff's negligence a proximate cause of his injury? (Answer ''yes'' or ''no'')

Answer: ___YES___

[If you answered ''yes'' to both Issue #1 and Issue #2, then answer the next issue]

Issue #5: Without taking into consideration the question of reduction of damages due to the negligence of the plaintiff, if any, what is the total amount of damages suffered by the plaintiff?

Answer: ___$100,000___

[If you have answered Issues #1, 2, 3 and 4 ''yes,'' then answer the following issue]

Issue #6: Assuming that 100 percent represents the combined negligence of the plaintiff and of the defendant[s] whose negligence contributed as a proximate cause to plaintiff's injury, what proportion of such combined negligence is attributable to the plaintiff and what proportion is attributable to each defendant?

Answer: To plaintiff: __45__ %

To defendant Locke   __50__ %

To defendant City of Paris __5__ %

Total: 100%

J. Stuart Mill
_____
Jury Foreperson

Figure 21–2 (*continued*)

STATE OF WEST DAKOTA

SUTTER COUNTY
SUPERIOR COURT
NO. 94-3217

JOHN J. ROUSSEAU,

    Plaintiff,

    v.

JOHN LOCKE,
CITY OF PARIS

    Defendants

SPECIAL VERDICT

We, the jury in the above entitled case, find the following special verdict on the issues submitted to us:

Issue #1: Were the defendants, or either of them, negligent? (Answer ''yes'' or ''no'')

Answer: Defendant John Locke   **YES**
Defendant City of Paris   **YES**

[If you answered ''yes'' as to either defendant, then answer the next issue]

Issue #2: Was the negligence of the defendant, or either of them, a proximate cause of the injury to the plaintiff? (Answer ''yes'' or ''no'')

Answer: Defendant John Locke   **YES**
Defendant City of Paris   **NO**

[If you answered ''yes'' to Issue #2 as to either defendant, please answer Issue #3]

Figure 21-3

Issue #3: Was the plaintiff negligent? (Answer
``yes'' or ``no'')

Answer: __YES__

[If you answered ``yes'' to Issue #3,
then answer the next issue]

Issue #4: Was the plaintiff's negligence a
proximate cause of his injury?
(Answer ``yes'' or ``no'')

Answer: __YES__

[If you answered ``yes'' to both Issue #1 and Issue #2, then answer the
next issue]

Issue #5: Without taking into consideration the
question of reduction of damages due
to the negligence of the plaintiff,
if any, what is the total amount of
damages suffered by the plaintiff?

Answer: __$100,000__

[If you have answered Issues #1, 2, 3
and 4 ``yes,'' then answer the following issue]

Issue #6: Assuming that 100% represents the
combined negligence of the plaintiff
and of the defendant[s] whose negligence contributed as a proximate
cause to plaintiff's injury, what
proportion of such combined negligence is attributable to the plaintiff and what proportion is
attributable to each defendant?

Answer: To plaintiff: __10__ %

To defendant Locke __25__ %

To defendant City of Paris __15__ %

Total: 100%

J. Stuart Mill
_____
Jury Foreperson

Figure 21–3 (*continued*)

STATE OF WEST DAKOTA

BRIDGER COUNTY   SUPERIOR COURT
                                 NO. 95-8107

BERNHARDT BARUCH,

     Plaintiff,

     v.   SPECIAL VERDICT

JAMIE BURNS,

     Defendant

We, the jury in the above entitled case, find the following special verdict on the issues submitted to us:

Issue #1: Was the defendant negligent in his use of the chain saw while working with the plaintiff on January 5, 1994? (Answer ''yes'' or ''no'')

Answer: __YES__

[If you answered ''yes'' to the preceding issue, then answer the next two issues]

Issue #2: Was the defendant's negligence a proximate cause of the cut sustained by the plaintiff on January 5, 1994? (Answer ''yes'' or ''no'')

Answer: __YES__

Issue #3: Was the defendant's negligence a proximate cause of the infection and resulting damages suffered by the plaintiff after his release from the hospital on January 12, 1994? (Answer ''yes'' or ''no'')

Answer: __YES__

Figure 21–4

[If you answered ''yes'' to Issue #1 and Issue #2 (or to Issues #1, 2, and 3), please answer the following issue]

Issue #4:   Was the plaintiff negligent while working with the defendant on January 5, 1994? (Answer ''yes'' or ''no'')

Answer: **YES**

[If you answered ''yes'' to Issue #4, please answer the following two issues]

Issue #5:   Was the plaintiff's negligence while working with the defendant a proximate cause of the cut sustained by the plaintiff on January 5, 1994? (Answer ''yes'' or ''no'')

Answer: **$ 45,000**

[If you have answered ''yes'' to Issues #1, #2, #4 and #5, please answer the following issues]

Issue #6:   Assuming that 100% represents the combined negligence of the plaintiff and the defendant in causing the plaintiff's initial injury on January 5, 1994, what proportion of such combined negligence is attributable to the plaintiff and to the defendant?

Answer: To plaintiff: **30** %

            To defendant   **70** %

                  Total: 100%

Issue #7:   Without taking into account the question of reduction of damages due to the negligence of the plaintiff, what is the total amount of damages suffered by the plaintiff as a result of the cut, his initial hospitalization and related damages, and damages resulting from the subsequent infection.

Answer: **$ 45,000**

Figure 21–4 (*continued*)

[If you answered ``yes'' to Issue #3, please answer the following issues]

Issue #8:   Do you find that the plaintiff failed to take those precautions which a reasonable person would take to avoid the infection which developed after his release from the hospital on January 12, 1994? (Answer ``yes'' or ``no'')

Answer: **YES**

[If you answered ``yes'' to Issue #8, please answer the following issue]

Issue #9:   Do you find that the plaintiff's failure to take proper precautions to avoid infection was a proximate cause of the infection which developed after his release from the hospital on January 12, 1994? (Answer ``yes'' or ``no'')

Answer: **YES**

[If you answered ``yes'' to Issues #8 and #9, please answer the following issue]

Issue #10:   What is the amount of damages suffered by the plaintiff as a result of the infection which developed after his release from the hospital on January 12, 1994?

Answer: **$25,000**

Jeremy Bentham
_____
Jury Foreperson

Figure 21–4 (*continued*)

22

The Fracturing of the Common Law: Loss Allocation in the Comparative Negligence Era

Introduction

Until recently, negligence doctrine developed largely through the evolutionary process of case law. Successive court opinions refined basic principles such as duty, breach, and causation, and affirmative defenses such as assumption of the risk and contributory negligence. Throughout this formative era, there was never any doubt that legislatures had the power to change such common law principles. Indeed, dramatic changes were made by statute in certain areas, such as workers' compensation and wrongful death. But these were exceptions; for the most part, negligence law was common law.

In the last few decades, however, legislatures have gotten heavily into the business of restructuring the common law of torts. The prime example, of course, is comparative negligence, which has been adopted by statute in many jurisdictions. Many states have also enacted statutes placing caps on noneconomic damages, creating screening panels for medical malpractice cases and limiting the scope of the collateral source rule.

Legislatures have been especially tempted to tinker with two traditional doctrines governing the allocation of negligence damages: joint and several liability and contribution. Recent statutes have fractured these fairly straight-forward doctrines into a profusion of idiosyncratic approaches, many applicable only in a single state. These legislative changes to the principles allocating damages among tortfeasors illustrate a movement, found in many areas of the law, from broad general principles that may operate unfairly in particular instances to more precise, detailed rules that may be more "fair" but also introduce administrative complexities.

This chapter illustrates some of the changes legislatures have made to basic doctrines governing liability of multiple tortfeasors. It is not intended to make you an expert in the details of any state's doctrine, but rather as a case study of the extent to which legislatures have fractured previously monolithic common law doctrine in the search for greater equity.

Comparative Negligence: The Catalyst for Change

As earlier chapters explain, before comparative negligence the defendants' responsibility for damages was determined by principles of joint and several liability and contribution. Each tortfeasor was fully liable for the plaintiff's damages. A tortfeasor who paid the plaintiff was entitled to collect "pro rata" contribution from the other tortfeasors. That is, the tortfeasors shared the damages equally; if there were two tortfeasors, the one who paid would recover half, if there were six, each paid a sixth, and so forth.

In most states, these principles were well established before the advent of comparative negligence. While the adoption of comparative negligence did not automatically change them, it provided new information about the relative fault of the parties which suggested that the classic principles were too blunt.

Suppose, for example, that Nell sued Fagan and Twist for negligence, and the jury found Nell 20 percent at fault, Fagan 70 percent at fault and Twist a mere 10 percent at fault. If Nell's damages were $100,000, she would be entitled to recover $80,000, her full damages reduced by her percentage of negligence. Under joint and several liability, both Fagan and Twist would each be liable for the $80,000, the plaintiff's damages adjusted to account for her negligence. Under basic contribution doctrine, whichever defendant paid that amount would recover a pro rata share, or $40,000, from the other (assuming the contributing tortfeasor was able to pay).

However, in light of the parties' percentages of negligence, these results appear inequitable. Twist, who was found only 10 percent at fault, will argue that he should not be liable to Nell (who was twice as faulty) for $80,000, as he would be under joint and several liability. Similarly, he will argue that if Fagan paid the judgment, he should not get half of it back from Twist (as he would under pro rata contribution), since Twist was one-seventh as faulty as Fagan.

Logical Implications: Proportional Contribution

Perhaps the most obvious implication of comparative negligence is that contribution among tortfeasors should be in proportion to their degrees of fault. Under this approach Fagan would contribute seven-eighths of the judgment ($70,000) and Twist would contribute one-eighth ($10,000). Because the defendant's relative degrees of fault are determined in comparative negligence cases, this appears both simple and fair: The proportions can be calculated from the jury's verdict, and tortfeasors who are more "faulty" will pay more than those who are less so. If each defendant is able to pay, each will end up contributing to the judgment in proportion to the fault assigned by the jury.[1]

Some tinker-prone legislatures have adopted proportional contribution. The Minnesota statute, for example, provides: "When two or more persons are jointly liable, contributions to awards shall be in proportion to the percentage of fault attributable to each, except that each is jointly and severally liable for the whole award." Minn. Stat. Ann. §604.02, subd. 1.

While proportional contribution distributes the loss in proportion to the fault of the parties, calculating the defendants' shares is more complex under proportional contribution than it is under pro rata contribution. Instead of simply dividing by the number of tortfeasors, judges and juries have to deal with fractions. In the example, Twist should bear 10/80ths of the judgment ($10,000) and Fagan 70/80ths ($70,000). (The proportions can be calculated by adding the defendants' percentages of negligence together to form the denominator of the fraction; each individual tortfeasor's percentage will form the numerator for that tortfeasor.) If Fagan paid Nell her $80,000 (remember that he is liable for the whole judgment under joint and several liability), he would receive 10/80ths ($10,000) from Twist, and absorb 70/80ths ($70,000) of the judgment himself.

These fractions don't seem so bad; this amount of increased complexity is clearly worth it for the gain in fairness. As the following examples illustrate, however, applying proportional contribution not only requires judges to dust off their math skills, but also raises administrative problems. In considering these examples, don't get bogged down in the math; the concept of proportional contribution, and the complexities it can raise, are the main point. (The explanations begin on p.478.)

---

1. In fact, so does the plaintiff, in a sense, since 20 percent of her damages are deducted from her recovery to account for her negligence.

EXAMPLES

Out of Proportion

1.   Flite sues Micawber, Heap, and Murdstone for negligence. The jury finds Flite 20 percent at fault, Micawber 50 percent, Heap 20 percent, and Murdstone 10 percent. They find Flite's damages to be $60,000.

    a. Assume that the case takes place in a modified comparative negligence jurisdiction which compares the plaintiff's negligence to that of all defendants combined. Assume further that the Minnesota proportional contribution statute applies. How much would Flite be entitled to collect from Heap?

    b. If Heap paid the judgment, how much would he recover in contribution from Murdstone?

    c. Assume that the case takes place in a modified comparative negligence jurisdiction that compares the plaintiff's negligence to that of each defendant individually, and allows her to recover from any defendant as long as she was not more negligent than that defendant. If Heap paid the judgment, and proportional contribution applied, how much would he recover from Micawber in contribution?

2.   Suppose that Heap pays the judgment and seeks contribution from Turveydrop, who allegedly was *also* negligent in causing the accident, but wasn't sued by Flite. How should Turveydrop's liability for contribution be determined?

More Logical Implications: Several Liability

The adoption of proportional contribution does not change the principle of joint and several liability. It only changes the rules for *reallocating* the loss once one of the tortfeasors has paid the judgment amount to the plaintiff. Thus, proportional contribution still requires a two-step process: a suit by the plaintiff that establishes her right to recover damages, followed by a second action for contribution by the tortfeasor who pays those damages.

Logically, wouldn't it be simpler to make the defendants separately liable to the plaintiff for their *respective percentage shares of the judgment*? In Nell's action, for example, Fagan would be liable to Nell for 70/80ths of her adjusted damages ($70,000) and Twist would liable for 10/80ths ($10,000). Nell would recover $80,000 (her raw damages reduced by her percentage of negligence) just as she did under joint and several liability, but each defendant would only be "severally" liable for the portion of the damages he "caused."

Obviously, one great advantage of this approach is that it eliminates the need for contribution entirely: None of the defendants need seek contribution, since none pays in excess of his "share" of the damages. However, several liability has a great *disadvantage* from the plaintiff's point of view: It casts the burden of the insolvent tortfeasor on her. If Fagan cannot pay, Nell will only recover $10,000 under several liability, because Twist is not liable for Fagan's share. Under joint and several liability, by contrast, both tortfeasors would be liable to Nell for the entire judgment. If Fagan were insolvent, Nell could collect his share from Twist. Of course, this advantage of joint and several liability to the plaintiff carries a corresponding *disadvantage* to defendants: Under joint and several liability, Twist could end up paying the entire judgment if Fagan is insolvent, even though he was only 10 percent at fault.

An increasing number of states have adopted several liability, either for all cases or for some situations. Utah's comparative negligence statute, for example, provides

> No defendant is liable to any person seeking recovery for any amount in excess of the proportion of fault attributable to that defendant under Section 78-27-39. Utah Code Ann. §78-27-38(3) (1992 & Supp. 1994).

Similarly, Vermont's statute provides that

> [E]ach defendant shall be liable for that proportion of the total dollar amount awarded as damages in the ratio of the amount of his causal negligence to the amount of causal negligence attributed to all defendants against whom recovery is allowed. Vt. Stat. Ann. tit. 12, §1036 (1973 & Supp. 1993).

The following examples illustrate how Flite's case might come out under several liability. (Assume in each example that several liability applies.) Again, the examples illustrate that the attempt to make the rules more equitable carries its own problems of administration.

Several Examples

3. Assume the same facts as in Example 1: Flite sues Micawber, Heap, and Murdstone for negligence. The jury finds Flite 20 percent at fault, Micawber 50 percent, Heap 20 percent, and Murdstone 10 percent. They find Flite's damages to be $60,000.
   a. If all defendants are solvent, how much will Flite recover from each defendant under several liability?
   b. If Micawber pays the judgment against him, how much can he get in contribution from Murdstone?
4. Assume that Flite's case was litigated in a state that requires the jury to assign percentages to all tortfeasors, including tortfeasors who are not before the court at trial. Assume that Flite settled with Micawber for $9,000 before trial. The jury assigns 20 percent to Flite, 50 percent to Micawber, 20 percent to Heap, and 10 percent to Murdstone. The damages are again assessed at $60,000. How much should Heap and Murdstone pay to Flite?

One Among Several

5.   Suppose that Flite sued Micawber only, that under the applicable statute the negligence is apportioned only to the parties at trial, and the jury determined that Flite was 25 percent at fault and Micawber was 75 percent at fault.

   a. Assuming again that the damages are $60,000, how much would Micawber be liable for?

   b. Could Micawber implead Heap and Murdstone in the action, to assure that their negligence is considered in allocating percentages?

6.   Suppose that Flite sued Micawber and Murdstone only, that under applicable law only the negligence of parties before the court at trial is considered, and that the jury apportions the negligence 25 percent to Flite, 45 percent to Micawber, and 30 percent to Murdstone.

   a. Assuming again that the damages are $60,000, how much would Micawber and Murdstone be liable for?

   b. Suppose that, after getting the judgment against Micawber and Murdstone and collecting from Micawber, Flite learns that Murdstone is insolvent. Since he has not been fully compensated, he sues Heap, another tortfeasor he left out of his first action. How should Heap's liability be determined?

7.   It is sometimes said that several liability makes more sense, because it allocates the loss according to the amount of damage caused by each tortfeasor. What would a classic old common law judge like Judge Fudd think about this reasoning?

8.   Assuming that it appears that Murdstone's negligence was a relatively minor factor in causing the accident, how would you expect the switch to several liability to affect the dynamics of settlement negotiations between him and Flite?

More Legislative Tinkering: Reallocating the Uncollectible Share

Once tempted to tinker, states have become even more finicky about fine-tuning loss allocation principles among tortfeasors. An example is the enactment of statutes that redistribute the shares of insolvent tortfeasors.

Consider the example of Nell, who was found 20 percent at fault, versus Fagan (70 percent) and Twist (10 percent). If Fagan was unable to pay, Twist, as a joint tortfeasor, had to pay the full judgment, with no hope of contribution. The common law had little sympathy for a defendant who ended up paying the entire judgment because other tortfeasors were insolvent. A tortfeasor was a tortfeasor, and was expected to take his medicine without complaint.

This result is arguably unfair, since the risk of Fagan's insolvency falls entirely on Twist. If, on the other hand, the jurisdiction switches to several liability, *it falls entirely on Nell instead*, who would collect nothing from Fagan and could not collect his share from Twist.

Some states have fine tuned their allocation schemes to address this apparent unfairness — but again only at the expense of increased complexity. Under Minnesota law, for example, tortfeasors remain jointly and severally liable to the plaintiff, and contribution is "in proportion to the percentage of fault attributable to each." Minn. Stat. Ann. §604.02(1) (West 1988 & Supp. 1994). The statute further requires that the other negligent parties absorb the share of a tortfeasor who is unable to pay:

> Upon motion made not later than one year after judgment is entered, the court shall determine whether all or part of a party's equitable share of the obligation is uncollectible from that party and shall reallocate any uncollectible amount among the other parties, including a claimant at fault, according to their respective percentages of fault. A party whose liability is reallocated is nonetheless subject to contribution and to any continuing liability to the claimant on the judgment.

Minn. Stat. Ann. §604.02(2) (West 1988 & Supp. 1994). Under this statute, Fagan's share, which is $70,000 (70/80ths of $80,000) would be redistributed between Twist and Nell. They would absorb it in proportion to their fault. Nell would absorb 20/30ths[2] of Fagan's share ($46,666.66) — that is, she would be barred from recovering this amount as her "share" of Fagan's liability. Twist is jointly and severally liable to Nell for the judgment amount ($80,000), but he does not have to pay Nell's reallocated portion of Fagan's liability. Thus, Nell could only collect $33,333.33 from Twist.[3]

Interestingly, under the Minnesota version, a negligent plaintiff also absorbs a part. Some states reallocate the uncollectible share among the other tortfeasors only. See, e.g., Ariz. Rev. Stat. Ann. §12-2508 (1994).

To get a general understanding of such reallocation provisions, consider the following example.

Spreading the Risk

9. Assume again that the jury finds Flite 20 percent at fault, Micawber 50 percent, Heap 20 percent and Murdstone 10 percent. They find Flite's damages to be $60,000. Assume that Micawber pays the judgment and seeks contribution, but that Heap is insolvent.

---

2. Once again, the denominator is determined by adding the percentages of the parties who absorb the uncollectible share. Here that is Nell (20 percent) and Twist (10 percent) so the denominator is 30.

3. If Twist had already paid her the full amount of her judgment ($80,000), as he is required to do under joint and several liability, he would be entitled to recover her portion of the uncollectible share back from her. She would owe him $46,666.66 once it became clear that Fagan was insolvent.

a. Who would bear the risk of Heap's uncollectible share if the jurisdiction retained joint and several liability and applied proportional contribution, but had no provision for reallocating the uncollectible share?

b. If the case took place in Minnesota, and Micawber paid the judgment, how much could he get in contribution from Murdstone, including adjustment for Heap's uncollectible share?

c. How much would Micawber obtain in contribution if proportional contribution applied, and the governing statute called for reallocating the uncollectible share proportionally among the tortfeasors only?

Warning! Stop Here! Absurdly Fine Distinctions Ahead

All of this makes the classic rules look like pretty blunt instruments, though perhaps blissfully so. But recent statutes have created many elegant variations on the basic allocation rules. Legislatures, which so often seem unable to grapple with the big issues, have truly fractured this allocation issue to smithereens. Here, for example, are four statutes that take different approaches to the issue of joint and several liability.

The Iowa comparative negligence statute retains joint and several liability only for defendants found more than 50 percent at fault. Below that level, liability is several:

> In actions brought under this chapter, the rule of joint and several liability shall not apply to defendants who are found to bear less than fifty percent of the total fault assigned to all parties.

Iowa Code Ann. §668.4 (West 1987). Nevada provides that any defendant less negligent than the plaintiff is only severally liable:

> Where recovery is allowed against more than one defendant in such an action, the defendants are jointly and severally liable to the plaintiff, except that a defendant whose negligence is less than that of the plaintiff or his decedent is not jointly liable and is severally liable to the plaintiff only for that portion of the judgment which represents the percentage of negligence attributable to him.

Nevada Rev. Stat. §41.141(3) (1986). New Jersey distinguishes economic damages from noneconomic damages. It makes some defendants jointly and severally liable for both types, some severally liable for noneconomic damages, and others severally liable for all damages:

> Except as provided in subsection d of this section, the party so recovering may recover as follows:

a. The full amount of the damages from any party determined by the trier of fact to be 60% or more responsible for the total damages.

b. The full amount of economic damages plus the percentage of noneconomic damages directly attributable to that party's negligence from any party determined by the trier of fact to be more than 20% but less than 60% responsible for the total damages.

c. Only that percentage of the damages directly attributable to that party's negligence from any party determined by the trier of fact to be 20% or less responsible for the total damages.

New Jersey Stat Ann. §2A:15-5.3 (West Supp. 1994). Last, under the Oregon statute the nature of the defendant's liability depends on both the nature of the damages and the proportion of negligence in relation to the plaintiff:

(2) In any civil action arising out of bodily injury, death or property damage, including claims for emotional injury or distress, loss of care, comfort, companionship and society, and loss of consortium, the liability of each defendant for noneconomic damages awarded to plaintiff shall be several only and shall not be joint.

(3) The liability of a defendant who is found to be less than 15 percent at fault for the economic damages awarded the plaintiff shall be several only.

(4) The liability of a defendant who is found to be at least 15 percent at fault for the economic damages awarded the plaintiff shall be joint and several, except that a defendant whose percentage of fault is less than that allocated to the plaintiff is liable to the plaintiff only for that percentage of the recoverable economic damages.

Or. Rev. Stat. §18.485 (1993).

These statutes certainly illustrate that the monolithic common law approach to allocating liability has yielded to a good many experiments in the "laboratory"[4] of the states. Such statutes represent legislative attempts to make the punishment fit the crime, if you will, but obviously are more complex for courts and parties to apply. For a quick test of these further complexities, consider the following examples based on these fractured approaches to negligence liability.

Compound Fractures

10. Jingle sues Weller, Snubbin and Buzfuz for negligence. After trial, the jury finds Jingle 20 percent at fault, Weller 60 percent, Snubbin 15 percent, and Buzfuz 5 percent. The jury further finds, by special verdict,

---

4. *New State Ice Co. v. Liebmann*, 285 U.S. 262, 311 (1932) (Brandeis, J. dissenting).

that Jingle's economic damages are $80,000, and his noneconomic damages are $120,000. How much would Jingle recover from Weller under each of the four statutes?

11. How much would he recover from Snubbin under each?

12. How much would Jingle recover from Snubbin under each statute if Jingle's percentage were switched to 10 percent and Snubbin's raised to 25 percent?

EXPLANATIONS

Out of Proportion

1a. Because Flite's negligence is less than the total negligence attributed to the defendants, she would recover a judgment of $48,000, her raw damages reduced by 20 percent. Under joint and several liability, each defendant would be liable for that amount. Proportional contribution does *not* change the principle of joint and several liability to the plaintiff; it simply changes the rules for reallocating the judgment after one of the tortfeasors pays it. The Minnesota statute quoted at p.471 makes this clear.[5]

b. To determine Murdstone's liability for contribution, it is necessary to calculate his proportion of the judgment. As the introduction indicates, Murdstone's proportion can be calculated easily by taking the total of the negligence percentages of all defendants as the denominator (here 80) and Murdstone's percentage (10) as the numerator. Multiply that fraction times the judgment amount, which is $48,000. If Heap paid $48,000 to Flite, he should recover 10/80ths of it from Murdstone, or $6,000. He'll get 50/80ths ($30,000) from Micawber, and absorb 20/80ths ($12,000) himself.

c. The problem here is in determining the proportional shares. Since the jurisdiction compares the negligence of the plaintiff to that of each defendant individually, Flite cannot recover from Murdstone, who was less negligent. She can recover from Heap, whose negligence was equal to hers. If joint and several liability applies, Heap and Micawber are still liable to Flite for $48,000, 80 percent of her damages. Heap pays the $48,000, and now seeks proportional contribution from Micawber.

Since Murdstone is not liable to Flite, he is also presumably not required to contribute to the judgment: It doesn't seem logical that a defendant should recover contribution from Murdstone when the plaintiff can't recover anything from him. Contribution statutes typically provide

---

5. Some states have abandoned joint and several liability in favor of several liability, as Examples 3 to 8 of this chapter illustrate. In such a jurisdiction, there is no need for contribution, since each defendant only pays his proportional share of the plaintiff's damages.

for contribution among parties "jointly liable in tort," or "liable for the same injury." Since Murdstone is not liable, he presumably cannot be forced to contribute.[6]

So, Heap and Micawber should contribute proportionally to the $48,000 judgment. Between them, they account for 70 percent of the fault. Presumably Heap should pay 20/70ths and Micawber should pay 50/70ths. Thus, Heap will recover 50/70ths of 48,000 ($34,286) in contribution from Micawber. He ends up paying $13,714, which is 20/70ths of $48,000.

2. Our theme is simplicity versus fairness. It is probably more equitable to make contribution proportional, but this example illustrates the price that must be paid in terms of increased complexity of administration. If all tortfeasors are parties to the first action, proportional contribution is fairly simple to administer: The jury's findings can be applied to redistribute the judgment according to the defendants' percentages of negligence. But the plaintiff need not sue every tortfeasor. Here, for example, Flite did not sue Turveydrop, and no negligence percentage was assigned to him. Heap, who paid the judgment, should be entitled to contribution from Turveydrop, but it is not clear how to calculate the proportion of the judgment Turveydrop should pay.

Some courts require the jury in comparative negligence actions to assess percentages of negligence for *all* tortfeasors, even if the plaintiff has not made a claim against them and they are not before the court. (Others restrict the jury to assessing percentages for the parties before the court at trial.) However, even if Turveydrop were assigned a percentage in Flite's initial suit, it would not bind him, since he has not had the opportunity to litigate his proportion of negligence. See Glannon, Civil Procedure: Examples and Explanations 398 (2d ed.), Example 1 (explaining leniency of surly myrmidons toward parties who have not litigated issue in prior action). Alternatively, some comparative negligence statutes require the defendant to implead other tortfeasors in the original suit to obtain contribution from them. However, this has problems too, since there may not be personal jurisdiction over all tortfeasors in the plaintiff's initial action.

Since Turveydrop was not a party to the first action, it appears that the court in the contribution action would have to make a new finding of the relative percentages of negligence of all the parties, including Turveydrop.[7]

---

6. Most cases have so held. See, e.g., *Horton by Horton v. Orbeth, Inc.*, 342 N.W.2d 112 (Minn. 1984) (refusing contribution on similar facts since there was no "common liability"). But see *Otis Elevator Co. v. F.W. Cunningham & Sons*, 454 A.2d 335 (Me. 1983) (despite plaintiff's inability to recover, considerations of fairness support contribution from the less negligent tortfeasor).

7. See Uniform Comparative Fault Act of 1977, 12 U.L.A. 44 (Supp. 1994), Section 5, comment, which indicates in somewhat analogous circumstances that a new comparison of the negligence of the tortfeasors would be determined in the contribution action.

Turveydrop would be liable for the percentage allocated to him in the contribution action, but presumably the other tortfeasors would pay according to the percentages assessed against them in the original action. This is awkward — somehow, the accounting is not going to work out right — and imposes an additional burden on the court in the contribution action. On the other hand, a somewhat similar burden arises under pro rata contribution: A tortfeasor who seeks contribution from a person who was not a party to the plaintiff's suit must always prove that person's liability in the contribution action in order to recover contribution.

Several Examples

3a. Flite should recover a total of $48,000 if all defendants pay their several shares. Micawber is liable for 50/80ths of the damages after adjustment for Flite's negligence, or $30,000. Heap pays 20/80ths of the adjusted judgment, or $12,000. And Murdstone owes 10/80 of $48,000, or $6,000. Their three several shares together total $48,000.

Thus, Flite recovers the same amount as she would under joint and several liability, as long as everyone is solvent. The difference is that each defendant pays according to his proportion of negligence, instead of being liable for the full judgment. And, of course, Flite must *do the collecting* from each defendant; she cannot collect the full judgment from one and leave him to seek contribution from the other defendants. Since collecting judgments can be an arduous and expensive process in itself, this is a significant shift in the burden on the parties.

b. Micawber recovers nothing in contribution from Murdstone. The judgment against Micawber will be for his share ($30,000) but no more, since he is only liable to Flite for his share. Thus, he has no right of contribution from any other tortfeasor. Nor does anyone have a right of contribution from him. This is an obvious advantage of several liability.

4.   Under several liability, a tortfeasor who settles simply extinguishes liability for his share. There is no need to give anyone else a credit for the payment, because they are only separately liable for their own shares. If Micawber had not settled, his share would have been $30,000, but Flite settled this share for $9,000. The remaining tortfeasors are only liable for their shares. Heap would pay 20/80ths of $48,000, or $12,000, and Murdstone would pay 10/80ths, or $6,000.

Thus, Flite would recover $27,000 altogether ($9,000 from Micawber, $12,000 from Heap and $6,000 from Murdstone). She would collect less than her full judgment because she sold Micawber's share ("worth" $30,000 (50/80ths of $48,000)) for $9,000. Of course, when she settled with Micawber, she did not know how the jury would allocate fault, so her choice was at best a guess.[8]

One Among Several

5a. Here is another example that illustrates that several liability, while arguably more equitable, is also more complicated than it first appears. While several liability is meant to confine each defendant's liability to his share, the plaintiff has a good deal of control over what that share will be, since a tortfeasor's share depends on whose fault is considered. Here, since Micawber is the only defendant, he will be liable for 75 percent of the damages, or $45,000. Yet it appears that in a several liability jurisdiction he will have no right to contribution, since, in theory, he is only paying his share. Had Flite sued Heap and Murdstone as well, Micawber's percentage would presumably have been considerably smaller, since they were also partially at fault.

One way to address this problem is to require the jury to assign shares to all tortfeasors, whether or not they are made parties to the action. Under this approach, Micawber could reduce his share by proving that Heap and Murdstone were also negligent, even though they are not defendants.

b. Since the jurisdiction only allows the jury to consider the negligence of the parties to the suit, Micawber would clearly like to bring the other tortfeasors in as third-party defendants and prove that they were negligent. However, many impleader rules only allow a defendant to bring in other parties who may be liable to *him*, that is, to the defendant, not to the plaintiff. See, e.g., Fed. R. Civ. P. 14(a). Typically, other tortfeasors are brought in for contribution, but in a jurisdiction that applies several liability, there is no contribution. See Example 3b.

---

8. Want to try a more perplexing variation? Suppose that Micawber settled with Flite for $9,000 in a state which only assigns negligence percentages to the parties who are before the court at trial (not a tortfeasor like Micawber who has settled). The jury assigns 15 percent to Flite, 60 percent to Heap, and 25 percent to Murdstone. The damages are again assessed at $60,000. How much should Heap and Murdstone pay to Flite?

Here is my a priori analysis of this problem (I have not found a case on point). In this type of jurisdiction Heap and Murdstone should get some kind of credit for Micawber's settlement payment. Otherwise Flite will be overcompensated. I would reduce Flite's $60,000 in damages to $51,000 to reflect her negligence, and then reduce it $9,000 more for the settlement. Heap and Murdstone, between them, should pay the remaining $42,000 in proportion to their negligence. Heap would be liable for 60/85ths of $42,000, and Murdstone for 25/85ths of $42,000. My calculator yields $29,647.06 for Heap and $12,352.94 for Murdstone. (Note that under this approach, Flite gets her full damages, despite her low settlement with Micawber.)

This analysis may be right or wrong; either way it illustrates the basic point that the legislative "fine tuning" of damage allocation has created some problems of its own.

Some comparative negligence statutes authorize a defendant to prove negligence of other tortfeasors even though they are not made parties. See, e.g., Ind. Code Ann. §34-4-33-10 (West Supp. 1994). Where such a "non-party defense" is pleaded, the negligence of the nonparty tortfeasor will be considered in assigning percentages of fault. Yet this approach can also be awkward, since the nonparties are not represented. Presumably, the plaintiff will try to establish that their fault was minimal, while the defendant will try to shift as much fault as possible to them, thereby reducing his several share. Whatever the result, it will not bind the nonparty tortfeasor if the plaintiff later seeks damages from him.

6a. Flite's damages should be reduced by 25 percent to account for her negligence. This brings them down to $45,000. Under several liability, Murd-stone would be liable for 30/75ths, or $18,000. Micawber would be liable for 45/75ths, or $27,000.

b. This is another imponderable. Percentages have already been assigned to Micawber and Murdstone, but no room has been left to add Heap! If Flite now sues Heap, presumably percentages would only be assigned to Flite and him in the second trial. Thus Heap (like Micawber in Example 5) may be assigned a fairly high percentage of fault because he is the only tortfeasor before the court. If he were found 60 percent at fault and Flite 40 percent, and the damages are $60,000, what would he pay? Is his "several share" $36,000 (60 percent of $60,000)? If so, Flite collects $63,000 ($27,000 plus $36,000), which is much too high.

I don't know the answer to this problem, but it does illustrate that while several liability appears to be a simple means of distributing the damages, it entails some thorny administrative problems. Had all these been anticipated, some states might have resisted the urge to tinker, and stuck with the rough and ready older rules instead.

7.   Judge Fudd would think this was arrant nonsense. Under traditional causation analysis any person whose act is a but-for cause of the harm has caused *all* the harm, not a part of it. That is still true under comparative negligence: the jury still must find that each defendant's negligence caused indivisible harm to the plaintiff before that defendant is liable. (If they caused divisible harm, they would be separately liable for that harm only. See Chapter 16, p.335)

Thus, the jury does not assign a party a 15 percent share of the negligence because she only caused 15 percent of the plaintiff's damages. When juries assign percentages of negligence, they are making findings as to how *faulty* each defendant was in causing the single, indivisible harm the plaintiff suffered. In finding one defendant 15 percent at fault and another 85 percent, they are saying that the one was considerably less negligent than the other, even though each was a but-for cause of *all* of the plaintiff's resulting damages.

8.   Under several liability, Murdstone's potential damage exposure is much less than it is under joint and several liability, because he is only liable for his

percentage share of the total damages. He will therefore take a harder line in settlement negotiations than he could under joint and several liability, which exposed him to liability for the plaintiff's full damages. Under joint and several liability, plaintiff could argue, "Look, as long as the jury finds you negligent at all — even one percent — you are liable to me for the entire judgment." This is a forceful argument in many cases because, even though a plaintiff like Murdstone has a theoretical right of contribution from more negligent tortfeasors, they are often unable to pay.

Under several liability, this sword of Damocles is removed; Murdstone is only at risk for the share of fault that the jury assesses to him. If this is likely to be small, defendants like Murdstone are likely to be a good deal more stingy in considering settlement.

Spreading the Risk

9a. Micawber would be the loser. He has paid the judgment, but only recovers Murdstone's proportionate share (10/80ths of $48,000, or $6000) from him. Thus, he would absorb Heap's share, since he was required to pay it to Flite — under joint and several liability — but could not get it back from Heap.[9]

b. Under the Minnesota statute, Heap's uncollectible share, $12,000, would be reallocated among Flite, Micawber, and Murdstone. Flite should absorb 20/80ths of it ($3,000); Micawber 50/80ths ($7,500), and Murdstone 10/80ths ($1,500).[10] Thus, Murdstone should pay Micawber his own share ($6,000) plus his reallocated portion of Heap's share ($1,500), for a total of $7,500.

The example indicates that Micawber has already paid the judgment before seeking contribution. Thus, he has overpaid Flite and should get $3,000 *back* from her. Let's hope she hasn't gone on a spending spree.

c. Under this type of reallocation statute, Heap's $12,000 share should be reallocated between Micawber and Murdstone in proportion to their degrees of fault. Micawber should absorb 50/60ths of Heap's $12,000 ($10,000) himself. He would get 10/60ths of Heap's share ($2,000) from Murdstone, together with Murdstone's own share of $6,000. His total contribution from Murdstone would be $8,000. Micawber should end up out-of-pocket his own share ($30,000) plus the $10,000 reallocated to him, for a

9. Some courts, as a matter of equity, might disregard Heap in determining the proportions for Micawber and Murdstone. If the court did this, it would allow Micawber to recover 10/50ths of the judgment from Murdstone, which would automatically reallocate Heap's share between the two defendants. See Chapter 17, Example 8.

10. Note again that the fractions are constructed by adding the negligence percentages of the parties involved (Flite, Micawber, and Murdstone) and using that as the denominator. The numerators are the negligence percentages of each party.

total of $40,000. Since he paid Flite $48,000, and gets $8,000 back from Murdstone, this works out right.

Note that under this approach, Flite still recovers fully, since she does not have to absorb part of the uncollectible share.

Presumably, provisions like these for reallocating uncollectible shares can be applied under several liability as well as joint and several liability. The separate liability of each solvent tortfeasor would simply be increased to reflect his portion of the insolvent tortfeasor's share.

Compound Fractures

10. *Iowa*: The limitation in the Iowa statute doesn't apply, since Weller is more than 50 percent negligent. Thus, Weller is liable for the entire judgment. That judgment will be $200,000, the total damages, reduced by 20 percent for Jingle's negligence. Weller is liable for $160,000.

Nevada: Since Weller is more negligent than Jingle, he is jointly and severally liable under the Nevada statute for Jingle's damages, after reduction for his negligence. He is liable for $160,000.

New Jersey: Weller's negligence is at least 60 percent, so his liability is governed by subsection (a) of the New Jersey statute. That subsection provides that the defendant is liable for the full amount of "the damages." Although it is not entirely clear from the sections quoted, this means the "raw" damages ($200,000) reduced by the plaintiff's percentage of negligence. See N.J. Stat. Ann. §2A:15-5.1 (1987) (requiring reduction of damages to account for plaintiff's negligence). Thus "the damages" here are $160,000. Weller is again liable for that amount.

Oregon: This one makes up for the last three easy ones. Subsection 2 provides that the defendants are severally liable for the noneconomic damages. Thus Weller is liable for 60/80ths of the noneconomic damages. This presumably refers to the noneconomic damages after reduction for Jingle's negligence, not the raw damage figure. Thus, the $120,000 figure should first be reduced 20 percent to account for Jingle's negligence. This brings it down to $96,000. Weller is liable for 60/80ths of these noneconomic damages, or $72,000. He is fully liable for the economic damages (also adjusted for Jingle's negligence) since he does not come within the limitation in subsection (3) or (4). This is $64,000 ($80,000 minus Jingle's 20 percent). Thus, he is liable for $136,000.

Statutes that distinguish between economic and noneconomic damages represent a compromise between the goal of assuring compensation to the plaintiff and the goal of limiting liability of defendants who are only partly at fault. By retaining joint and several liability for economic damages in most cases, they assure that plaintiffs recover their out-of-pocket losses. By making recovery for noneconomic losses several, they protect defendants from paying more than their share of the intangible damages.

11. *Iowa*: The limitation in the Iowa statute applies, so Snubbin is only severally liable for his proportion of the damages. The total damages are $200,000. These are reduced to $160,000 to account for Jingle's negligence. Snubbin's share is 15/80ths of that, or $30,000 only.

Nevada: Snubbin's liability is also several under the Nevada statute, since he is less negligent than Jingle. He is liable for $30,000.

New Jersey: Snubbin's liability is governed by subsection (c), since he is less than 20 percent at fault. Once again, he is only severally liable for his share of the damages, economic and noneconomic.

Oregon: First, under subsection (2) of the Oregon statute, Snubbin is severally liable for his proportion of the adjusted noneconomic damages. This is 15/80ths of $96,000, or $18,000. Next, under subsection (4) he is only severally liable for his share of the economic damages as well, since he is less negligent than Jingle. This is $12,000. Here again, he is severally liable for $30,000.

12. *Iowa*: Since Snubbin is less than 50 percent at fault, he is severally liable for his proportion of all the adjusted damages, or 25/90ths of $180,000. My calculator grudgingly concludes that this comes to $50,000.

Nevada: Snubbin is jointly and severally liable for the entire adjusted damages of $180,000, since the limitation in the Nevada statute does not apply.

New Jersey: Subsection (b) of the New Jersey statute would apply. Snubbin would be jointly liable for the adjusted economic damages ($72,000), and severally liable for his share of the adjusted noneconomic damages. The second figure would be 25/90ths of the adjusted noneconomic damages ($108,000), which comes to $30,000. His total liability is $102,000.

Oregon: Snubbin is severally liable for his proportion of the adjusted noneconomic damages (subsection (2)) and jointly liable for all the adjusted economic damages under subsection (4). Thus, here again, he is liable for $30,000 of the noneconomic damages and $72,000 (all of the economic damages) for a total of $102,000.

Now, was that fun or what?

Index